The Woman Question

Mary Evans has been lecturer in sociology at the University of Kent at Canterbury since 1971. Her other books are *Work on Women* (with David Morgan; 1979) and *Lucien Goldmann: an Introduction* (1981).

The Woman Question

Readings on the subordination of women

Edited by Mary Evans

Fontana Paperbacks

First published by Fontana Paperbacks 1982

Copyright © in the selection and introductions,
Mary Evans 1982

Details of copyright in the readings are on pages 531-2

Set in 9½ point Linotron Times
Printed in Great Britain at the
University Press, Oxford

For some women of Kent

Contents

Acknowledgments   11

Introduction: **What Is to be Done?**   13

Section One: **Feminism**   25

Lawrence Stone   Early Feminist Movements   29
Mary Wollstonecraft   Observations on the State of
   Degradation to which Woman Is Reduced by
   Various Causes   33
John Stuart Mill   The Subjection of Women   36
Sheila Rowbotham   Middle-class Women Begin to
   Organise   38
Simone de Beauvoir   Woman's Life Today   43
Jill Johnston   The Myth of the Myth of the Vaginal
   Orgasm   50
Gail Chester   I Call Myself a Radical Feminist   58
Leeds Revolutionary Feminist Group   Political
   Lesbianism: the Case against Heterosexuality   63
Sheila Rowbotham   The Trouble with 'Patriarchy'   73
Sally Alexander and Barbara Taylor   In Defence of
   'Patriarchy'   80
Sheila Rowbotham, Lynne Segal and Hilary Wainwright
   The Insights of Feminism   84

Section Two: **Women and Men**   87

Ann Oakley   The Politics of 'Sex Differences' Research   91
Jean Baker Miller   Ties to Others   95
Jessie Bernard   The Wife's Marriage   107

Section Three: **Female Sexuality**   121

Beatrix Campbell   A Feminist Sexual Politics:
   Now You See It, Now You Don't   125
Simone de Beauvoir   Sexual Initiation   146
Stevi Jackson   Constructing Female Sexuality   154
Adrienne Rich   Alienated Labor   164

Section Four: **Domestic Life and Labour**   167

Charlotte Perkins Gilman   House Service as a
  Livelihood   171
Margery Spring Rice   The Day's Work   176
Mirra Komarovsky   The Quality of Domestic Life   187
Margaret Benston   The Political Economy of Women's
  Liberation   192
Richard Scase and *Robert Goffee*   Home Life in a
  Small Business   203

Section Five: **Women and Paid Work**   213

Eric Richards   Women in the British Economy since
  about 1700: an Interpretation   220
Veronica Beechey   Some Notes on Female Wage
  Labour in Capitalist Production   246
Irene Bruegel   Women as a Reserve Army of Labour:
  a Note on Recent British Experience   273
Hilary Land   The Family Wage   289

Section Six: **Women and the State**   297

Mary McIntosh   The State and the Oppression of
  Women   303
Marcia Millman   Images of Deviant Men and
  Women   334
Katherine O'Donovan   The Male Appendage: Legal
  Definitions of Women   344
Jenny Shaw   Finishing School: Some Implications
  of Sex-segregated Education   363

Section Seven: **Culture and Ideology**   381

Cora Kaplan   Radical Feminism and Literature:
  Rethinking Millett's *Sexual Politics*   386
Barbara Bellow Watson   On Power and the Literary
  Text   401
Janice Winship   Sexuality for Sale   410
Wendy Martyna   Beyond the 'He/Man' Approach:
  the Case for Nonsexist Language   420
Tillie Olsen   Silences: When Writers Don't Write   433

Section Eight: **Cross-cultural Studies** 447

Kate Young and *Olivia Harris* The Subordination of
  Women in Cross-cultural Perspective 453
Sally Slocum Woman the Gatherer: Male Bias in
  Anthropology 473
Sherry B. Ortner Is Female to Male as Nature
  Is to Culture? 485
Ernestine Friedl The Position of Women: Appearance
  and Reality 508
Frederick Engels Private Property and the World
  Historic Defeat of the Female Sex 519

Bibliography 525
Copyright Acknowledgments 531
Index 533

Acknowledgments

While I was preparing this reader I was teaching on the initial two years of the M.A. in Women's Studies at the University of Kent at Canterbury. I should like to acknowledge here the help of those students and teachers who created a rewarding and stimulating intellectual and social environment. My thanks, therefore, to Jane Attala, Roisin Battel, Kythe Beaumont, Jane Boston, Steve Box, Sybil Carter, Jill Chadwick, Jane Cholmeley, Linda Edwards, Marie France, Stella Furlong, Maree Gladwin, Christine Hammerton, Valerie Hey, Michiko Kato, Renate Duelli-Klein, Helly Langley, Melanie Lewin, Joy Lyon, Pat Macpherson, Joanne Mason, Kate McLuskie, Janet Montefiore, Shamila Mukherjee, Jayne Nelson, Katherine O'Donovan, Nanneke Redclift, Pat Reed, Kim Rice, Helen Richardson, Jan Robinson, Joan Russell, Joan Ryan, Janet Sayers, Ann Seller, Christine Shannon, Thea Sinclair, Safie Singhateh, Gillian Squirrell, Jenny Stephens, Erica Syszczak, Jill Thompson, Joyce Ulrich, Clare Ungerson, Caroline Waller, Jenny Walton and Jeffrey Weeks. I would also like to thank Helen Fraser of Fontana for her assistance, Yvonne Latham for invaluable secretarial services, and David Morgan for his many forms of support and encouragement.

INTRODUCTION:

What Is to be Done?

In 1955 an eminent male sociologist wrote of feminism, 'It is not
a subject on which men and women easily find their ways to
rational views', and, he continued, '... a formidable obstacle [to
the study of women] is the vast, repellent literature raised by the
hagiographers of the women's movement.'[1] This collection contains, with no apology, some of that 'repellent literature' which
has, for at least four hundred years, documented and analysed the
subordination of women. Many of the extracts suggest that the
conditions of their lives which women most abhor have not
changed for centuries: women were always, and are still, given
automatic and often exclusive responsibilities for childcare and for
the maintenance of the household, and these duties in the home
prevent them from playing as full a part as men in the wider social
and political world. It is, of course, true that the general rise in
living standards in the last one hundred years has benefited women
as much as men, and that women's entry into paid employment has
given them greater financial independence and autonomy, but it is
still the case that in terms of social power and control women
remain less privileged than men. Moreover, it remains a truth
generally acknowledged that women's social role is primarily that
of a wife and mother – a view economically expressed when Patrick
Jenkin, then Secretary of State for Social Services, remarked, 'If
God had meant women to go out to work, he would not have
created two sexes.' Despite the somewhat inflammatory nature of
this statement, it is nevertheless interesting since it contains two
assumptions which have long been attacked by feminists. The first
is that women's 'natural' place is in the home, and the second is
the suggestion that 'work' only takes place outside the household.
As some of the authors included in this volume point out, women
(and men) are most adaptable social beings and can be persuaded
into a variety of social roles to suit the constraints of particular
situations. It is inevitably true that women, rather than men, bear
children, but the elaboration of a female identity based on this
physical difference would appear to be a largely social, rather than
natural, process.

1. O. R. McGregor, 'The Social Position of Women in England, 1850-1914: a Bibliography', *British Journal of Sociology*, vol. 6, 1955, pp. 48-9.

Yet the assumption of women's natural association with childrearing underlies both the general social stereotype of women in our own society and a number of institutional practices. It has now been demonstrated at some length that all societies have rigid, if very different, stereotypes about appropriate male and female behaviour. Women are generally assumed to be gentler, more passive, less independent and less intellectually able than men, beliefs which are then integrated into various social structures. For example, the belief that women have a relatively feeble intellect can lead to the limited encouragement which many girls receive from the educational system, while the view that girls are naturally better behaved and less unruly than boys makes it impossible for many of those professionally concerned with deviance or crime to entertain the possibility of female criminality. But this latter instance also provides an example of the way in which women's supposed passivity and helplessness can act to their advantage: in some situations they are provided with special protection and understanding, albeit of an inherently paternalistic kind. Yet this exclusion from the full moral responsibilities of citizenship, or what might be seen as latent chivalry or archaic protectiveness towards women, is itself part of a wider social ideology about women – that an essential condition of their existence is a natural and inevitable dependence on men.

However, as the articles and essays in this collection demonstrate, a long tradition of feminist writing has challenged this assumption, not the least of the arguments being that the enforced dependence of women impoverishes all human relationship, since women are reduced to little more than chattels of their husbands or fathers. As John Stuart Mill pointed out in the middle of the nineteenth century, there are many instances where women are treated kindly by their husbands and live with them on terms of affection and mutual concern, yet while this situation depends upon individual good nature, there is no true equality between the sexes. The changes which Mill advocated – a more equitable form of marriage contract, improved rights for women to education and divorce – have to a large extent been achieved in the West, yet the liberation of women remains as seemingly distant as at the time when Mill was writing.

Many feminists would not see the reasons for the continued subordination of women as varied or complex. They would argue that women remain subordinate because women are still assigned domestic roles and responsibilities, and that men gain, both materially and psychologically, from this sexual division of labour. Thus each and every improvement which women wish to make in their situation has to be fought for in a long and bitter battle, in which men do everything that they can to maintain the *status quo*. Yet this account of the position of women and of the history of women's emancipation obscures a number of issues in the development of feminism both as an ideology and a social movement.

The women's movement that has emerged in the West in the last twenty years shares many of the concerns which dominated nineteenth-century feminism: the limited access of women to economic, social and political power, the nature of the sexual division of labour and those social expectations about the behaviour of women which limit and inhibit their achievements. As many contemporary feminists have pointed out, women have been given, in the majority of industrial societies, formal legal equality with men, and yet have still not achieved equality in any wider sense. The extention of bourgeois civil liberties to women has, it is often argued, made little impact on the relatively powerless and underprivileged status of women. Inevitably, many contemporary feminists have turned to analyses and programmes which do not see the achievement of sexual equality as coming about through the statute book, since the material that has now been collected about the universal subordination of women suggests that it is a phenomenon which is unlikely to be altered by changes in legal and administrative practices.

The problem is thus raised of exactly how equality between the sexes is to be achieved – or, to put the issue in more specifically feminist terms, how the subordination of women is to be ended. From the evidence of the past one hundred years it would not appear that feminist energies are most usefully devoted to campaigns for changes in the law. Moreover, many campaigns fought by feminists to improve the lot of women can contain assumptions and arguments that are often reactionary in practice. For example, in the nineteenth century many valiant women fought for the amelioration of the situation of the wife – demanding that married women should have a share in matrimonial property, that women, in heterosexual relationships, should be able to control their own fertility and that women, because of their childbearing capacity, should be afforded protection both by individual men and the law. All these demands undeniably resulted in improvements in the condition of women. Yet these very demands, radical as they were at the time, took for granted the value of family life and did not question the fundamental organising principles of the Western family of heterosexuality and monogamy. Thus radicals, liberals, reactionaries and feminists all united in the common cause of wishing to maintain the structure of family life: what was to be altered, at least according to more liberal and progressive views, was a form of sexual relations in which women were materially and socially subservient and subordinate to men. For many Victorian liberals, such as Mill, the answer to the subordination of women lay in more formal education for women; indeed, the extension of educational opportunities for women constitutes, from Wollstonecraft to Mill and Friedan, a major 'liberal' solution for female subordination. On the other hand, materialists such as Engels argued that the subordination of women would only end if all women participated in wage labour and became economically independent of men. Again, this view forms part of a tradition which today fights for the disaggregation of family income.

But what has now become manifestly clear is that no single solution exists that can end the inequality of women. In most industrial societies formal barriers to the education of women have disappeared and life long wage labour is the normal experience of the majority of women, yet still women occupy a social position that is generally inferior in terms of formal social power, material rewards and personal autonomy to that of men. Contemporary feminists, in identifying and documenting this inferiority, have also shown the complexity, and the intractability to social engineering, of the causes of the subordinate status of women.

It is, however, a notable feature of contemporary feminism that it has identified a primary (if not the prime) cause of women's subordination as the sexual division of labour in the home. Hence it is no longer supposed that alterations in the world external to the household will, in themselves, liberate or emancipate women. The women's movement slogan 'the personal is the political' has focused attention on those areas of social life previously regarded as too trivial or too private to be of concern. But at the same time as it is important to emphasise the contribution that contemporary feminism has made to the analysis of the position of women in its emphasis on the private world of the household, it would be wrong to suppose that it was not until the latter part of the twentieth century that the examination of moral, emotional and material relations between men and women became a subject both of debate and struggle. As the long tradition of the English novel testifies, the issue of how men and women can live together in fulfilling and non-exploitative relationships has a long history, and novelists from Samuel Richardson onwards have taken as their basic theme the miseries and misunderstandings that can arise when men and women are expected to live together in life-long unions, while socialised and educated in ways that often exaggerate rather than minimise the differences between the sexes. Nor, as many Victorian novelists realised, was the problem merely one of differences between two categories of socially equal beings. Rather, what is explored by the Brontës, Mrs Gaskell and George Eliot is a situation in which women are socially and materially less powerful than men. In Eliot's *Daniel Deronda* and Mrs Gaskell's *Ruth* the blatant use of male economic power as a basis for the control of women is demonstrated with vivid clarity.

Nevertheless, the material inequalities between men and women did not lead, in the nineteenth century any more than in the twentieth, to relationships between the sexes which corresponded, or correspond, to a simple model of domination or oppression. What becomes apparent, in an examination of the history of sexual relations in the nineteenth century, was that women struggled, often very successfully, against the imposition by men of patri-archal attitudes and legislation. For example, in mid-Victorian Britain women rejected the institutionalisation, in the Contagious Diseases Act, of the sexual double standard and asserted that the behaviour of men and women should be judged by the same moral standards.[2] Equally, campaigns were fought – and won – for female suffrage, the rights of women to control their own property and to enter higher education and the professions. Yet all these advances foundered on the expectation that women's biological capacity to bear children carried with it an exclusive obligation to rear children and to provide domestic services for men and dependent relatives. The formal emancipation of women had been accomplished, yet the majority of women remained relatively ill-educated and confined to a life of domestic work and economic dependence. Even if society was prepared to allow them (or, in the case of Britain, to compel them) to enter the labour force in times of war and national emergency, the end of hostilities was always accompanied by the end of the brief entry of women into the labour market.

The situation of women in the West in the years after the Second World War was thus largely domestic – women were 'naturally' associated with the domestic hearth, and the majority of women spent the greater part of their lives around it. In the early 1960s, however, this normality was challenged by a number of books, of which the most influential was Betty Friedan's *The Feminine Mystique*, which advanced the view that women's place was not

2. This issue is discussed in Judith Walkowitz, *Prostitution and Victorian Society: Women, Class and the State*, Cambridge: CUP, 1980; see also Barbara Taylor's review in the *New Statesman*, 23 January 1981.

'naturally' in the home and that life lived exclusively within a domestic world was harmful to women's psychological and physical health. It began to be suggested, albeit tentatively, that the life of the suburban dream was something of a nightmare for women. Confined to an isolated suburb, constantly at the beck and call of others, and committed to a life of unending domesticity, women were trapped in a prison of family life. (However, in her latest book, *The Second Stage*, it is interesting to note that Betty Friedan sees the commitment of either sex exclusively to paid work as psychologically and emotionally harmful.)

The work of Friedan and others very rapidly evoked a sympathetic response in a large number of readers. By the beginning of the 1970s a systematic study of the social role and position of women had begun, which developed the general arguments of earlier feminists within a number of contexts. The term 'sexism' was introduced and used to describe any practice which was found to be dismissive or derogatory about women. Demands for new laws were made, for positive discrimination in favour of women, and women were encouraged and exhorted to think positively about themselves. Consciousness-raising became a feature of many women's groups, and an articulate women's movement catalogued and distributed evidence about the widespread prejudice and discrimination against women.

But as the 1970s wore on and some of the demands of the women's movement were implemented, many of the problems which had beset earlier feminists began to reappear. Laws could be changed and women could be encouraged to enter traditionally male spheres of activity, yet these changes were of little value to women as long as they continued to want to bear children and were then held exclusively responsibile for their care. As numerous feminists pointed out, women in paid employment who lived with men did 'double time' – as well as paid work, they also performed unpaid domestic labour. If women wished to bear children, it remained, and remains, generally assumed that those children will be cared for by women who will be kept by men. This last assumption is institutionalised in both Britain and North America by state laws about welfare provisions: men are supposed to provide economic support for their wives and dependent children. In return for this support, women are expected to housekeep for men and care for children and, at least in Britain, it is impossible for women to claim any assistance which would enable them to provide alternative care for their children. A quite unambiguous policy towards women and children is thus enshrined in British welfare policies – men may beget children, whom they have a duty to maintain financially, but the day-to-day care of those children is the responsibility of women. Since the demands of children are largely incompatible with those of full-time paid employment, for most women with dependent children employment outside the home becomes a part-time and often haphazard activity, fitted in to accommodate the needs of others. Such a pattern is particularly unsuitable to professional employment, since all career structures are based on the assumption that all employees are male and do not interrupt their careers to bear children.

Given the nature of the organisation of the present social and economic structure of the West, and its failure to meet many of the needs of women, it is scarcely surprising that contemporary feminism, very much more than its nineteenth-century predecessor, sees little scope for piecemeal changes and improvements. However, while a consensus can be detected within British feminism that women will not be fully emancipated through the legal system and reform of the *status quo*, it does not also imply that a generally accepted view exists of the causes of women's subordination or that all feminists agree on the essential issues which they should confront. While the universal subordination of women is not in doubt, analyses of this subordination differ in their identification of its causes. Although it is generally agreed that women are discriminated against in a large number of institutional contexts, and relatively less able to control their destiny than men, agreement on how this situation might be changed is less evident.

Two problems are particularly important in any discussion of this issue. The first is that of whether or not men and women can ever be equals, if individual heterosexual relationships are maintained. That is, the question must be posed as to whether or not in a relationship between a man and a woman some degree of female subordination, or at least dependence, is not inevitable, and particularly so if the woman bears children. It is perhaps paradoxical that Freudian accounts of the relations between the sexes and those of some contemporary radical feminists who are otherwise bitterly opposed to Freud should both suggest that the anatomical differences between the sexes give rise to two sexes which are psychologically and emotionally distinct. Any attempt to reconcile those differences is doomed to failure since the differences between the sexes are greater than the similarities. However, this view raises a second problem: that of whether or not there are circumstances in which the similarities between people of both sexes are not greater than the differences. In particular, it must be asked if class differences between people are not often more significant than sexual differences; for example, whether or not a working-class woman does not have more in common with a working-class man than she would have with a middle-class woman. The political consequences of the answer to this question are extremely important for feminists, since if it is decided that all women share a common class position and that sex is the most important form of social stratification, then all women, regardless of race or class, can organise together and share political aims. If, on the other hand, it is assumed that the class differences between women are more important than the similarities created by their sex, then women are – like men – divided by class interests and loyalties which will remain paramount.

Both the problems identified above suggest that a major issue which confronts anyone interested in the social roles and identities of women and men is that of the extent to which female and male behaviour is a social or a natural construct. It is interesting to note that many contemporary feminists are now adopting an argument about sexual identity which is largely a-historical, and certainly a-social. That is, they are arguing with some fervour that women constitute a distinct kind of human personality – a personality which has to be rediscovered since it has been abused and distorted by centuries of male dominance. This position, which stresses the value of exclusively female activities such as childbirth and childcare, seeks to alter the domination of the social world by an ideology which is perceived as 'male' by elevating the strengths and interests of a specifically female condition. This argument has been described as the 'politics of health and childbirth' by some Marxist and socialist feminists, who argue that feminist politics must be about the transformation of class, just as much as sexual, relations. Yet it is clear that few radical feminists support a class society any more than do Marxist feminists; the debate is perhaps more concerned with emphasis than with essential disagreement. Nevertheless, it is possible to detect in the emphasis of radical feminists on the value and importance of specifically female activities some of the same problems that led to the more reactionary elements of Victorian feminism and in particular to the development of a cult, not of domesticity, but of femininity.

But a genuine difficulty exists for all feminists as far as the problem of identifying the 'real' nature of women and men is concerned, and feminism has, in the course of its history, taken up a number of contradictory positions on the issue. Some feminists have stressed the inherently different natures of the two sexes, others have argued that little separates the sexes except the differences that are produced by socialisation. The first position tends to lead to separating the activities of men and women, the second to assuming that men and women can perform exactly the same tasks. The second argument is particularly well supported by two kinds of evidence. In the first place, it has been demonstrated by a number of social psychologists that very few inherent differences exist between the intelligences and the personalities of the two sexes. In the fullest and most comprehensive review of the literature on sex differences Maccoby and Jacklin argue that in terms of intelligence, aptitude and personality structure men and women are very much more alike than dissimilar. They allow that there are some differences between some men and some women but on the whole the two sexes are indistinguishable in ability and aptitude. As they point out, most of the differences that develop between the sexes are a result of social habits and pressures.[3]

However, not all societies encourage the development of distinctions and differences between the sexes and a second kind of evidence – that of the experience of societies other than those of the industrial West – suggests that the sexual division of labour which is accepted as normal in the West is largely a product of particular social and economic circumstances. A cursory glance at the sexual division of labour in both the Third World and some state socialist societies indicates that the definition of what is male work and what is female work is far from being a constant in all societies. But, and most significantly as far as feminists are concerned, a general distinction can be seen in all societies between male and female work. It is that whatever kind of work women do, and however essential that work is to the continuation of social life, it receives a lower social status than the work done by men. Moreover, in those societies where all women are expected to take part in paid employment, women still retain primary responsibility for the care of children and the maintenance of the household. As numerous feminists have now pointed out, it is no doubt laudable to socialise production and to attempt to emancipate women from an exclusively domestic life, but hardly praiseworthy if this form of emancipation is not accompanied by the recognition, in both ideological and material terms, that women do bear children and do need certain kinds of special consideration. Unfortunately, no society has yet evolved a system of allowing women particular protection without at the same time interpreting women's special needs as evidence of inferiority and dependence.

The manifest failure of almost all societies both to offer women

3. E. Maccoby and C. Jacklin, *The Psychology of Sex Differences*, Stanford: Stanford University Press, 1974.

specific forms of help and assistance and to allow them an equal role in social life lends a certain amount of weight to those arguments which suggest that the only way that women will achieve real emancipation and liberation is through complete independence and separation from men. It is pointed out that even in those societies where equality between sexes was, or is, a stated aim of the government, the meaning of this equality for many women is simply a double work-load: work outside the home coupled with exclusive responsibility for household chores. The most notorious example of this form of 'emancipation' is that of Soviet Russia where all women, married or single, childless or not, have to participate in paid labour and maintain the fabric of domestic life. However, before critics of the Soviet Union leap happily upon yet another instance of Soviet barbarity, let it also be said that for increasing numbers of married women in the West there is a much diminishing amount of choice about the decision of whether or not to work outside the home. Many working-class women have always had to seek paid work (particularly when unmarried) but inevitably, as Western economies sink further into recession and male unemployment rises, they are forced to seek employment in order to maintain or augment the family income. The factors forcing women into the labour market are not those of formal or legal constraint, but the need for income is nevertheless a real and powerful force.

Since neither industrial capitalist nor state socialist societies provide the conditions in which women can play as full a part as men in social life, feminists must confront a third question, that of deciding how the subordination of women is to be ended. Given the example of most socialist societies, the answer would not appear to lie simply in the transformation of industrial capitalism into socialism. Equally, it is clear that industrial capitalism, with its inherent need to maintain profitability, has little concern with the situation of those who cannot contribute directly to the accumulation of capital. That is not to say that women's unpaid domestic labour is not of value to the capitalist economy, but simply that capitalism as an economic system has no particular interest in improving, let alone changing, the nature and conditions of domestic work. As long as wage labourers are provided with domestic services, and the next generation of the labour force is socialised, capitalism has no reason to alter a sexual division of labour which is very much to its advantage. Indeed, as long as women perform unpaid, privatised domestic labour, capitalism (and state socialism) is assured of a highly efficient and economical means of maintaining and reproducing social life and social order.

However, it is now becoming increasingly obvious that large numbers of women in both capitalist and state socialist societies are refusing to continue to fulfil traditional expectations about the female social role. Discontent with a traditional female role is hardly a novel phenomenon, but what is different about contemporary dissatisfaction among women is that it is now much more possible for women to make, or consider, non-traditional choices. Two particular developments have taken place which have created the conditions of the further emancipation of women. The first is that effective contraception has made possible the limitation of family size. This improvement in the technology of contraception has been accompanied by a reduction in the demand for labour in almost all societies, industrial or otherwise. Few societies now need to compel women to bear children, indeed the majority of societies are anxious to limit the rate of growth of their population and women's reproductive role. Second, as increasing numbers of women participate in the labour force for longer periods of their lives, the experiences and social worlds of men and women begin to coincide. The separation of the home and the work-place, and the identification of women with the former and men with the latter, thus become things of the past. The consequences of this change are twofold: women's expectations and aspirations are altered and raised and they begin to acquire the economic ability to fulfil them. Financial independence decreases the need to maintain an unsatisfactory marriage, or to embark on married life. Why be a wife becomes a question that is relevant to increasing numbers of women.

But as yet all these changes remain only possibilities for the majority of women, even if for some highly educated and financially independent women they have already become realities. That changes in the social position of all women are long overdue is the premise on which this volume is based. Its function, however, is not to prescribe how these changes should occur, but to enable readers to identify and draw their own conclusions about the causes of the subordination of women. The question then arises of what is to be done, but it is a question for each and every reader to answer for themselves.

Feminism

Any collection of extracts from feminist writing must confront critically the problem of defining the nature of feminism. It is possible to identify feminist writing as any statement made by a woman about her situation, thus implying that if the subject-matter is woman, or the writer female, the writing must be feminist. The pitfall of this assumption is that women may well be 'falsely conscious', in the sense that their understanding of their situation is limited and far from critical. For example, not all novels that are written by women are, as Rosalind Coward has pointed out, necessarily feminist novels.[1] Equally, it would be hard to detect the feminist content in Doris Day's singing that she 'enjoyed being a girl', since much of the song is a celebration of that dependence and passivity in women so disliked by feminism. Feminism must be assumed, therefore, to be a critical examination of the present, or past, situation of women: a challenge to the majority of values that are presented to women about themselves.

Since most societies have assumed that woman's primary social role is domestic, and her talents rather less than those of men, it is hardly surprising that the history of feminism is long and consistent. The major complaint of feminists has always been that women are regarded as inferior to men and treated with a mixture of contempt and occasional reverence. Individual women may have been able to assert their own views and maintain a degree of independence from patriarchal values and practices, but this has generally been a matter of accident and a particular set of circumstances. The feminist argument is, and always has been, that all women should be able to enjoy the same freedoms and possibilities for self-fulfilment as all men.

The relationship between the development of feminism and specific social and economic conditions has not, to date, been very fully explored. However, it would appear that some connection does exist between the development of individualism in Western Europe in the fifteenth and sixteenth centuries and the emergence of an identifiable feminist tradition. It is impossible to measure the relative intensity of feminist thought before the fifteenth century

1. Rosalind Coward, 'Are Women's Novels Feminist Novels?', *Feminist Review*, no. 5, 1980, pp. 53-64.

since, in a largely illiterate society in which access to the means of communication was largely restricted to a small, male elite, few instances of radical thought, feminist or otherwise, were recorded. We know that Chaucer's Wife of Bath was more than able to manipulate the social world in her own interests, but have almost no recorded instances of women arguing for improvements in the lot of their sex as a whole until the middle of the sixteenth century. Even then, examples of feminist thought are very few in number and it is not until the middle of the seventeenth century, when Protestantism, with its emphasis on the equality of all human souls, was well established in Britain, that women begin to assert that equality, both moral and social and in this world quite as much as in the next, should be extended to female as well as male human beings. The most famous instance of seventeenth-century feminist activity in Britain was the petition by four hundred women to the House of Commons in January 1642, which is described in Lawrence Stone's *The Family, Sex and Marriage in England 1500-1800*. The women demanded the same rights to religious freedom as men and protested against the generally accepted subordination of women within the family. Marriage should not involve, the women argued, freedom for men and slavery for women. As Stone points out, the demands of 1642 were far from being an isolated example of discontent; on the contrary, they mark the beginning of feminism as a social movement.

As feminism has matured, however, its demands have become rather more complex. By the nineteenth century, women are no longer protesting just against the conditions of domestic life, they are concerned with asking more radical and complex questions about the basis and nature of relations between the sexes, the kind of relationship with men that women want and how far the differences between the sexes can be reconciled. These questions were asked in a world of rapidly changing standards and conventions; however repressive and narrow we consider the dominant ideology of sexuality in Victorian Britain, it was increasingly challenged by a number of radical and deviant views about the proper conduct of sexual relationships between men and women. For example, the trial of Oscar Wilde brought to public attention the possibility that for some members of both sexes, sexual relations were most satisfactory when conducted between partners of the same sex. Heterosexuality is necessary if the species is to survive, but there is, it was suggested, no necessary justification for elaborating an entire system of sexual morality and behaviour on isolated acts of procreation.

The view that heterosexuality inevitably involves procreation began to disappear as the technology of contraception became more reliable and sophisticated. Yet, as sexual relations between men and women lost the implicit assumption and risk of reproduction and conception, it became even more important for feminists to confront the issue of why men and women should enter into any form of sexual relationship. Sexual pleasure and gratification, and emotional stability and support, are demonstrably as likely, or unlikely, in homosexual as in heterosexual relationships. Given the material amassed by feminism about the subordination of women in heterosexual relationships, the reasons for women to embark on, and maintain, sexual relationships with men become less clear. Elements in contemporary feminism have, therefore, begun to argue that the proper activity for feminists should not be to attempt to improve institutionalised heterosexual relationships, but to establish a social order in which women and men occupy different, and distinct, social spheres. As the extract from Jill Johnston's work suggests, some contemporary feminists see no justification for continuing relationships which they see as leading inevitably to the oppression of women.

Thus by 1970 feminism had come a long way from many of its earlier demands. The hopes entertained for improvements in women's relationship to men, a more equal form of marriage contract and for institutional changes that allow women some of the same educational and professional opportunities as men have either been achieved or declared to be irrelevant. While the marriage agreement of John Stuart Mill and Harriet Taylor was, in the context of nineteenth-century Britain, a radical and innovative document, many contemporary feminists would argue that such a contract, whatever its progressive or liberal intentions, merely institutionalises certain expectations and assumptions about the behaviour of men and women, and in particular the view that monogamous heterosexual marriage constitutes the ideal form of sexual relationship. So long as it is taken for granted that children must be afforded the protection of a father's name, women are bound to marriage. Mill took for granted, as have many feminists, the need for children to be born legitimate. Later feminists have challenged this view: most radically, Simone de Beauvoir has suggested that women should only exceptionally bear children, since, she argues, it is childbirth and childcare that force women into dependence, both material and emotional. Yet, as many feminists have now pointed out, it is not childbirth and childcare *per se* that create dependence, but the conditions in which they take place, conditions in which women's control over their situation is limited. The first step towards women's independence of men might therefore be, as Shulamith Firestone has suggested, a form of human reproduction in which heterosexual intercourse is excluded.[2]

The call for an end to a world in which women's reproductive capacity inevitably involves social dependence and inferiority provides a common theme in the history of feminism: more than any other demand, it is perhaps this which constitutes the essential feminist demand. Yet while this issue unites all feminists, others divide us. The most critical problem is that of the kind of society that feminists should work for. Some feminists argue that feminism and socialism are fundamentally linked and that the transformation of sexual relationships must involve the transformation of all social relationships. Others assert that there is no necessary connection between feminism and socialism. Many feminists describe themselves as socialists, others – pointing out the subordinate status of women in state socialist societies – argue that the socialisation of production does not inevitably bring with it any improvement in the situation of women. Given fundamental differences of opinion on this issue, it is little wonder that feminism has yet to develop a single strategy or programme. As the extracts from Gail Chester, Hilary Wainwright and others in this collection suggest, priorities for feminists do differ, as does the definition of feminism's main enemy. Hence while it is agreed among feminists that women are universally subordinated to men, many feminists would stress – as does Sheila Rowbotham in the essay reproduced here – that assuming a fixed, and rigid, model of male oppression of women ignores much of the consensus, and even co-operation, that can exist between the sexes. The reply to Rowbotham by Barbara Taylor and Sally Alexander questions this assumption. Yet despite the differences between the authors on this issue, it should be emphasised that they share a common commitment – a defining characteristic of feminists – that women's subordination must be questioned and changed.

2. Shulamith Firestone, *The Dialectic of Sex*, New York: Morrow, 1970.

Lawrence Stone

Early Feminist Movements

From Lawrence Stone, *The Family, Sex and Marriage in England 1500-1800*, Harmondsworth: Penguin Books, 1979, pp. 225-8

During the Civil War of the 1640s, women played a very prominent role in the host of radical sects which based themselves on the extreme interpretation of the doctrine of Grace. In these independent churches, women were at last allowed to debate, to vote, to prophesy when moved by the Spirit, and even to preach. Many left the former family church without the consent of their husbands, and some even abandoned their unregenerate spouses and chose new mates who shared their new-found faith. Their opponents saw these developments as a threat to family subordination, claiming that they were demanding sexual equality of rights:

> We will not be wives
> And tie up our lives
> To villanous slavery.

What is more remarkable, however, is the way the breakdown of royal government in 1640, the prolonged political crisis between King and Parliament of 1640-2, the Civil Wars of 1642-8, and the emergence of many extremist independent sects and of a genuinely radical political party, stimulated the women of London and elsewhere to unprecedented political activity. On 31 January and 1 and 4 February 1642, women, operating without help from fathers, husbands or other males, took independent political action on the national level as women, for the first time in English history: they petitioned the Houses of Lords and Commons for a change of public policy. They numbered some four hundred or more, and were apparently composed of working women, artisans, shop-girls and labourers, who were suffering severe financial hardship as a result of the decay of trade. When the outraged Duke of Richmond cried 'Away with these women, we were best have a Parliament of women', the petitioners attacked him physically and broke his staff of office.

Another crisis came in April and May 1649 when very severe

economic hardship coincided with a political showdown between the army and Parliament and the London-based lower-middle-class radical movement of the Levellers. Once again masses of women assembled at Westminster, complaining of the economic crisis and demanding the release of the Leveller leaders who had been imprisoned. This time the House responded with disdain, telling the women that they were petitioning about matters above their heads, that Parliament had given an answer to their husbands, who legally represented them, and that they should 'go home and look after your own business and meddle with your housewifery'.

By now, however, the women were not satisfied with these patronizing replies and were making statements which revealed the development of a wholly new level of feminine consciousness. 'The lusty lasses of the Levelling party' were now claiming equal participation with men in the political process, and were backing up their claims with petitions signed, so they said, by up to ten thousand women. In 1642 the petitioners had humbly emphasized that women were not 'seeking to equal ourselves with men, either in authority or wisdom', but merely 'following the example of the men which have gone ... before us'; moreover, they frankly admitted that their intervention 'may be thought strange and unbeseeming our sex'. By 1649, however, they were rejecting the idea that they were represented by their husbands: 'we are no whit satisfied with the answer you gave unto our husbands'. They coolly faced a barrage of criticism that they were claiming to 'wear the breeches', and that 'it can never be a good world when women meddle in state's matters ... their husbands are to blame, that they have no fitter employment for them'. In reply the women quoted the example of Esther from the Bible and even rewrote history to argue that 'by the British women the land was delivered from the tyranny of the Danes ... and the overthrow of episcopal tyranny in Scotland was first begun by the women of that nation'. They claimed an equal share with men in the right ordering of the Church 'because in the free enjoying of Christ in his own laws, and a flourishing estate in the Church ... consisteth the happiness of women as well as men'. This principle they then extended to the state: 'we have an equal share and interest with men in the Commonwealth', a claim which logically led to a demand for female voting rights. But 1649 was the apogee of this movement towards women's political liberation, and it is very noticeable that even the Leveller leaders always excluded women from their proposals for a greatly enlarged suffrage. This feminine agitation at a time of temporary breakdown of law and order should, therefore, best be seen as a symptom rather than as a cause. The episode is significant as the first emergence on a mass level of feminist ideas among an artisan urban population, but it was a movement without a future.

New claims concerning the status and rights of women were set in motion by the repudiation of monarchical patriarchy in the state in 1688, and were publicized by a handful of zealous feminists at the end of the seventeenth century. Most notable among them were Hannah Woolley, Aphra Behn, Mary Astell and Lady Chudleigh.

Few were as savage as the last, in her poem of 1703 addressed 'To the Ladies':

> Wife and servant are the same,
> But only differ in the name
>
> When she the word 'obey' has said,
> And man by law supreme has made,
>
> Fierce as an Eastern Prince he grows
> And all his innate rigor shows.
>
> Then shun, oh shun that wretched state
> And all the fawning flatterers hate.
> Value yourselves and men despise:
> You must be proud if you'll be wise.

The rise of the blue-stockings a century later as leaders of salons which included the most distinguished intellects and wits of London is proof of how at any rate some women were now forcing themselves upon male society and holding their own there. At the same time, inspired first by the American and then by the French Revolution, there emerged a new wave of feminists far more radical in their demands, their personal behaviour and their religious attitudes than their predecessors had been a century earlier. The most prominent among them was Mary Wollstone-craft, who probably did the cause of women's rights positive harm, for her passionate claim to sexual equality, together with her sympathy for the French Revolution and her irregular personal life, merely alienated the support of all but the most tolerant of men. It was this combination of radicalism in both national and sexual politics that drove Horace Walpole to describe her as 'that hyena in petticoats'.

It is hard to see that any of these feminist movements of the seventeenth and late eighteenth centuries had much effect in changing attitudes towards relations between the sexes. Consciousness of the problem of sexual equality was certainly aroused by them, but the fears engendered in men by these indignant women may have inhibited change rather than speeded it up.

Mary Wollstonecraft

Observations on the State of Degradation to which Woman Is Reduced by Various Causes

From Mary Wollstonecraft, *A Vindication of the Rights of Women*, London: Dent, 1970, pp. 67-9 (first published in 1792)

... women, in general, as well as the rich of both sexes, have acquired all the follies and vices of civilisation, and missed the useful fruit. It is not necessary for me always to premise, that I speak of the condition of the whole sex, leaving exceptions out of the question. Their senses are inflamed, and their understandings neglected, consequently they become the prey of their senses, delicately termed sensibility, and are blown about by every momentary gust of feeling. Civilised women are, therefore, so weakened by false refinement, that, respecting morals, their condition is much below what it would be were they left in a state nearer to nature. Ever restless and anxious, their over-exercised sensibility not only renders them uncomfortable themselves, but troublesome, to use a soft phrase, to others. All their thoughts turn on things calculated to excite emotion and feeling, when they should reason, their conduct is unstable, and their opinions are wavering – not the wavering produced by deliberation or progressive views, but by contradictory emotions. By fits and starts they are warm in many pursuits; yet this warmth, never concentrated into perseverance, soon exhausts itself; exhaled by its own heat, or meeting with some other fleeting passion, to which reason has never given any specific gravity, neutrality ensues. Miserable, indeed, must be that being whose cultivation of mind has only tended to inflame its passions! A distinction should be made between inflaming and strengthening them. The passions thus pampered, whilst the judgment is left unformed, what can be expected to ensue? Undoubtedly, a mixture of madness and folly!

This observation should not be confined to the *fair* sex; however, at present, I only mean to apply it to them.

Novels, music, poetry, and gallantry, all tend to make women the creatures of sensation, and their character is thus formed in the mould of folly during the time they are acquiring accomplishments, the only improvement they are excited, by their station in society, to acquire. This overstretched sensibility naturally relaxes the other powers of the mind, and prevents intellect from attaining that sovereignty which it ought to attain to render a rational creature useful to others, and content with its own station; for the exercise of the understanding, as life advances, is the only method pointed out by nature to calm the passions.

Satiety has a very different effect, and I have often been forcibly struck by an emphatical description of damnation; when the spirit is represented as continually hovering with abortive eagerness round the defiled body, unable to enjoy anything without the organs of sense. Yet, to their senses, are women made slaves, because it is by their sensibility that they obtain present power.

And will moralists pretend to assert that this is the condition in which one-half of the human race should be encouraged to remain with listless inactivity and stupid acquiescence? Kind instructors! what were we created for? To remain, it may be said, innocent; they mean in a state of childhood. We might as well never have been born, unless it were necessary that we should be created to enable man to acquire the noble privilege of reason, the power of discerning good from evil, whilst we lie down in the dust from whence we were taken, never to rise again.

It would be an endless task to trace the variety of meannesses, cares, and sorrows, into which women are plunged by the prevailing opinion, that they were created rather to feel than reason, and that all the power they obtain must be obtained by their charms and weakness:

Fine by defect, and amiably weak!

And, made by this amiable weakness entirely dependent, excepting what they gain by illicit sway, on man, not only for protection, but advice, is it surprising that, neglecting the duties that reason alone points out, and shrinking from trials calculated to strengthen their minds, they only exert themselves to give their defects a graceful covering, which may serve to heighten their charms in the eye of the voluptuary, though it sink them below the scale of moral excellence.

Fragile in every sense of the word, they are obliged to look up to man for every comfort. In the most trifling danger they cling to their support, with parasitical tenacity, piteously demanding succour; and their *natural* protector extends his arm, or lifts up his voice, to guard the lovely trembler – from what? Perhaps the frown of an old cow, or the jump of a mouse; a rat would be a serious danger. In the name of reason, and even common sense, what can save such beings from contempt; even though they be soft and fair.

These fears, when not affected, may produce some pretty attitudes; but they show a degree of imbecility which degrades a rational creature in a way women are not aware of – for love and esteem are very distinct things.

I am fully persuaded that we should hear none of these infantine airs, if girls were allowed to take sufficient exercise, and not confined in close rooms till their muscles are relaxed, and their powers of digestion destroyed. To carry the remark still further, if fear in girls, instead of being cherished, perhaps, created, were treated in the same manner as cowardice in boys, we should quickly see women with more dignified aspects. It is true, they could not then with equal propriety be termed the sweet flowers that smile in the walk of man; but they would be more respectable members of society, and discharge the important duties of life by the light of their own reason. 'Educate women like men,' says Rousseau, 'and the more they resemble our sex the less power will they have over us.' This is the very point I aim at. I do not wish them to have power over men; but over themselves.

In the same strain have I heard men argue against instructing the poor; for many are the forms that aristocracy assumes. 'Teach them to read and write,' say they, 'and you take them out of the station assigned them by nature.' An eloquent Frenchman has answered them, I will borrow his sentiments. 'But they know not, when they make man a brute, that they may expect every instant to see him transformed into a ferocious beast. Without knowledge there can be no morality.'

Ignorance is a frail base for virtue! Yet, that it is the condition for which woman was organised, has been insisted upon by the writers who have most vehemently argued in favour of the superiority of man; a superiority not in degree, but offence; though, to soften the argument, they have laboured to prove, with chivalrous generosity, that the sexes ought not to be compared; man was made to reason, woman to feel: and that together, flesh and spirit, they make the most perfect whole, by blending happily reason and sensibility into one character.

John Stuart Mill

The Subjection of Women

From John Stuart Mill, *On the Subjection of Women*, London: Dent, 1970, pp. 244-5 (first published in 1869)

The general opinion of men is supposed to be, that the natural vocation of a woman is that of a wife and mother. I say, is supposed to be, because, judging from acts – from the whole of the present constitution of society – one might infer that their opinion was the direct contrary. They might be supposed to think that the alleged natural vocation of women was of all things the most repugnant to their nature; insomuch that if they are free to do anything else – if any other means of living or occupation of their time and faculties, is open, which has any chance of appearing desirable to them – there will not be enough of them who will be willing to accept the condition said to be natural to them. If this is the real opinion of men in general, it would be well that it should be spoken out. I should like to hear somebody openly enunciating the doctrine (it is already implied in much that is written on the subject) – 'It is necessary to society that women should marry and produce children. They will not do so unless they are compelled. Therefore it is necessary to compel them.' The merits of the case would then be clearly defined. It would be exactly that of the slave-holders of South Carolina and Louisiana. 'It is necessary that cotton and sugar should be grown. White men cannot produce them. Negroes will not, for any wages which we choose to give. *Ergo* they must be compelled.' An illustration still closer to the point is that of impressment. Sailors must absolutely be had to defend the country. It often happens that they will not voluntarily enlist. Therefore there must be the power of forcing them. How often has this logic been used! and, but for one flaw in it, without doubt it would have been successful up to this day. But it is open to the retort – First pay the sailors the honest value of their labour. When you have made it as well worth their while to serve you, as to work for other employers, you will have no more difficulty than others have in obtaining their services. To this there is no logical answer except 'I will not': and as people are now not only ashamed, but are not desirous, to rob the labourer of his hire, impressment is no longer advocated. Those who attempt to force women into marriage by closing all other doors against them, lay themselves open to a similar retort. If they mean what they say, their opinion must evidently be, that men do not render the married condition so desirable to women, as to induce them to accept it for its own recommendations. It is not a sign of one's thinking the boon one offers very attractive, when one allows only Hobson's choice, 'that or none'. And here, I believe, is the clue to the feelings of those men, who have a real antipathy to the equal freedom of women. I believe they are afraid, not lest women should be unwilling to marry, for I do not think that anyone in reality has that apprehension; but lest they should insist that marriage should be on equal conditions; lest all women of spirit and capacity should prefer doing almost anything else, not in their own eyes degrading, rather than marry, when marrying is giving themselves a master, and a master too of all their earthly possessions. And truly, if this consequence were necessarily incident to marriage, I think that the apprehension would be very well founded. I agree in thinking it probable that few women, capable of anything else, would, unless under an irresistible *entraînement*, rendering them for the time insensible to anything but itself, choose such a lot, when any other means were open to them of filling a conventionally honourable place in life: and if men are determined that the law of marriage shall be a law of despotism, they are quite right, in point of mere policy, in leaving to women only Hobson's choice. But, in that case, all that has been done in the modern world to relax the chain on the minds of women, has been a mistake. They never should have been allowed to receive a literary education. Women who read, much more women who write, are, in the existing constitution of things, a contradiction and a disturbing element: and it was wrong to bring women up with any acquirements but those of an odalisque, or of a domestic servant.

Sheila Rowbotham

Middle-class Women Begin to Organise

From Sheila Rowbotham, *Hidden from History*,
London: Pluto Press, 1974, pp. 47-50

Feminism came, like socialism, out of the tangled, confused response of men and women to capitalism. Feminism protested against the continuation of man's property in woman. It contained an essential ambiguity, however, for the feminist attack on man's continued possession of woman did not necessarily imply a rejection of the private ownership of capital or of the wage-system. On the contrary, women could well ask for admission into that system on terms of equality, but this would mean that men of all classes faced competition from women. It would also shatter the middle-class image of woman and the family as a retreat from the hostile competition of the world outside. The model of the free market and freely competing economic atoms required sentiment to give it cohesion, as long as this emotion was kept in its proper place. Otherwise bourgeois man was left with a Hobbesian world which dissolved under its own rationality.

The Victorian middle classes found their sentiment in their womenfolk encased in their crinolines. The Victorian wife was quite literally insulated from the sources of her man's prosperity. As the century progressed not only women's clothes but also the household became larger and more upholstered. It was the visible sign of the wealth and security of the middle-class man. The number of servants multiplied and by the 1870s there were complaints that women were no longer involved in even supervising them. Although the circumstances of middle-class women improved with the growing power in society of their men, their relationship was one of increasing economic dependence. In this sense patriarchy was strengthened. The women were part of the man's belongings, their leisure the sign of his conspicuous consumption.

This situation had no sooner started to develop, however, when some women came to regard it as intolerable. Even in the 1830s and 1840s women had come to question their relationship to men and their position in society not because they wanted to transform all forms of domination but because they wanted particular improvements which were apparently consistent with capitalism. An ex-governess, Anna Jameson, observed that it was absurd to educate girls to be 'roses' and then send them to pass their life in an arctic zone.[1] It was evident that women's situation was an incongruity. A few years later Anne Lamb criticised the idea of spheres of influence for women and the way women were treated as children, angels, or playthings to be discarded when they ceased to amuse.

A new ideal of the relationship between men and women, reminiscent of the puritans, and of Defoe's notion of wives as companions appeared very clearly by the middle of the century. In Tennyson's 'The Princess' the old man asserts the traditional notion of patriarchy. Women, once promised, were property to be taken by force if they resisted. But the young man wants to possess the proud, independent woman in a different way. He wants to possess her through her feelings and subdues her with a kiss. The Victorian bourgeois hero thus played 'the slave to gain the tyranny'.[2]

As the idea of marriage as a companionship developed, direct patriarchal power became unacceptable to many middle-class women at a time when their actual economic dependence on men was increasing.

The similarities between the slave as property and the woman as property were brought out by the anti-slavery agitation. In 1840 an anti-slavery conference was held in London, and although Lucretia Mott and Elizabeth Stanton were delegates from the US a vote taken at the conference excluded women from the discussion. This decision provoked antagonism. The general connection between the English anti-slavery movement and subsequent feminist organisation remains unexplored. In America it was very close. Though less important than in the US it has probably been greatly underestimated.

As the reports on women's conditions in industry, especially the 1842 report on the mines, appeared, the idea of feminine incapacity and delicacy was made to look increasingly absurd. In *Shirley* by Charlotte Brontë, the heroine longed for a trade – even if it made her coarse and masculine – instead of the vacant, weary, lonely life of a woman of her class. Out of this despair over uselessness came the energy of middle-class women, bustling about doing charity

1. John Kilham, *Tennyson and The Princess; Reflections of an Age*, London, 1958, pp. 113-14, 134-5.
2. Tennyson, 'The Princess', quoted in *ibid.*, p. 135.

work. At worst they were interfering intruders, at best they found
a kind of peace through activity and learned to respect the workers
they sought to reform. But they remained aliens. The gulf between
them is hard to imagine now. The cultural values and lifestyle of
the middle class in the nineteenth century was as remote from the
working class as it was from the African tribes which this same
middle class was conquering and 'converting'. Indeed they saw
themselves as colonisers winning the workers for civilisation –
their civilisation of thrift, abstinence and hard work. In the
mid-nineteenth century most middle-class people involved in
charity still believed the unequal distribution of wealth was
justified by the personal failings of the poor and by economic law.
Poverty was intimately connected to sin. However, within the
limitations of this framework they were beginning to search for a
'scientific' approach to charity. Cautiously women began to argue
in the meetings of the National Association for the Promotion of
Social Science that women should be educated for charity work.

'It has now become the fashion to advocate the industrial
training of girls of the lower classes. The need of it is nearly as great
amongst the upper,' declared Mrs Austin at a Conference of the
Association in Birmingham in October 1857. She argued that
educated women should be appointed to administer the female
workhouses and that committees of visiting ladies – there was
already one in West London – should be set up. She believed that
this would not only improve the conditions of women and young
girls in the workhouses but would also provide an outlet for the
'longing for practical work' that 'comes to us all'. She noted that
it was not only ladies who were idle and useless but the wives and
daughters of trades people as well:

> 'Young women of this class do not now, as formerly, occupy
> themselves exclusively with household drudgery, as it is called,
> and no longer follow the good old paths of their grandmother in
> the care of the house and family.'[3]

The notion that social service was a secular and scientific task that
required its own investigations and its own training, rather than a
religious duty based on spiritual purity, began to undermine some
of the assumptions of earlier charitable endeavour. The Con-
gresses of the National Association for the Promotion of Social
Science provided an intellectual outlet for the women who

3. 'Workhouses and Women's Work', reprinted from the Church of England *Monthly
Review* ..., London, 1858.

participated and were early testing grounds for the talents of several who were later to become active feminists.

Women started to campaign for particular reforms in the nineteenth century not because they saw themselves as feminists but because circumstances in their own life forced them to protest. An aristocratic woman, for example, Caroline Norton, struggled tirelessly to limit the legal control of husbands over wives. Her alcoholic husband whom she had left prevented her from seeing her dying child. In 1839 children were declared in Parliament not to be the property of their fathers in certain cases. Another Act in 1858 allowed a woman who left her husband to retain anything she inherited or owned after separation. The married woman was still not affected by this legislation. However, they were eventually allowed to keep their own earnings, and in 1882 finally came into independent ownership of their own property.

But while some of the legal power of patriarchy was whittled away, the control of men over women in society was evident in education, work and politics. The long struggle of women for entrance into schools and colleges was heartbreakingly slow.

The vote seemed to be the key. If women could vote they could change man-made laws. The working-class agitation for the franchise raised the hope that women might be included. When J. S. Mill, the author of *The Subjection of Women*, became an MP he introduced an amendment to the 1867 Reform Act by substituting the word 'person' for the word 'man'. When this was defeated, supporters of women's suffrage started a legal case to establish that words of the masculine gender legally included women. In Manchester the Suffrage Society began a great campaign to get women to register, but the judges decided that only in cases of punishment and obligations were women included under the term 'man'. Patriarchy remained supreme. Another bill was introduced but blocked by Gladstone. The women had to wait until 1884 for the issue to be raised in Parliament again when a new bill to widen the franchise was introduced. Gladstone threatened to drop the whole bill if the women's amendment was not taken out. At the end of the 1880s there was another bill, but again the women were disappointed. Women were not to be included in the franchise in the wake of the working-class man. The militant feminist movement was to come out of these constitutional setbacks.

For in 1889, exasperated by the apologetic caution of the leaders of the suffrage movement, a new group, The Women's Franchise League, was formed. Among its council members was Mrs Emmeline Pankhurst, encouraged by her husband Richard Pankhurst, but still afraid of public speaking. The Franchise League took up the rights of married women. The feminists had tended to seek reforms for the unmarried – the failures – even excluding married women from their demand for the vote. The League campaigned for complete equality of women in divorce, inheritance and custody of children. The politics of the League were radical-liberal, although the Pankhursts had already had some contact with the socialist movement and were soon to join the Independent Labour Party.

Simone de Beauvoir

Woman's Life Today

From Simone de Beauvoir, *The Second Sex*, tr. H. M. Parshley, New York: Bantam, 1964, pp. 677-83 (first published in France, 1949)

We have seen why men enslaved women in the first place; the devaluation of femininity has been a necessary step in human evolution, but it might have led to collaboration between the two sexes; oppression is to be explained by the tendency of the existent to flee from himself by means of identification with the other, whom he oppresses to that end. In each individual man that tendency exists today; and the vast majority yield to it. The husband wants to find himself in his wife, the lover in his mistress, in the form of a stone image; he is seeking in her the myth of his virility, of his sovereignty, of his immediate reality. 'My husband never goes to the movies,' says his wife, and the dubious masculine opinion is graved in the marble of eternity. But he is himself the slave of his double: what an effort to build up an image in which he is always in danger! In spite of everything his success in this depends upon the capricious freedom of women: he must constantly try to keep this propitious to him. Man is concerned with the effort to appear male, important, superior; he pretends so as to get pretense in return; he, too, is aggressive, uneasy; he feels hostility for women because he is afraid of them, he is afraid of them because he is afraid of the personage, the image, with which he identifies himself. What time and strength he squanders in liquidating, sublimating, transferring complexes, in talking about women, in seducing them, in fearing them! He would be liberated himself in their liberation. But this is precisely what he dreads. And so he obstinately persists in the mystifications intended to keep woman in her chains.

That she is being tricked, many men have realized. 'What a misfortune to be a woman! And yet the misfortune, when one is a woman, is at bottom not to comprehend that it is one,' says

Kierkegaard.[1] For a long time there have been efforts to disguise this misfortune. For example, guardianship has been done away with: women have been given 'protectors', and if they are invested with the rights of the oldtime guardians, it is in woman's own interest. To forbid her working, to keep her at home, is to defend her against herself and to assure her happiness. We have seen what poetic veils are thrown over her monotonous burdens of house-keeping and maternity: in exchange for her liberty she has received the false treasures of her 'femininity'. Balzac illustrates this maneuver very well in counseling man to treat her as a slave while persuading her that she is a queen. Less cynical, many men try to convince themselves that she is really privileged. There are American sociologists who seriously teach today the theory of 'low-class gain'. In France, also, it has often been proclaimed – although in a less scientific manner – that the workers are very fortunate in not being obliged to 'keep up appearances' and still more so the bums who can dress in rags and sleep on the sidewalks, pleasures forbidden to the Count de Beaumont and the Wendels. Like the carefree wretches gaily scratching at their vermin, like the merry Negroes laughing under the lash and those joyous Tunisian Arabs burying their starved children with a smile, woman enjoys that incomparable privilege: irresponsibility. Free from trouble-some burdens and cares, she obviously has 'the better part'. But it is disturbing that with an obstinate perversity – connected no doubt with original sin – down through the centuries and in all countries, the people who have the better part are always crying to their benefactors: 'It is too much! I will be satisfied with yours!' But the munificent capitalists, the generous colonists, the superb males, stick to their guns: 'Keep the better part, hold on to it!'

It must be admitted that the males find in woman more complicity than the oppressor usually finds in the oppressed. And in bad faith they take authorization from this to declare that she has *desired* the destiny they have imposed on her. We have seen that all the main features of her training combine to bar her from the roads of revolt and adventure. Society in general – beginning with her respected parents – lies to her by praising the lofty values

1. *In Vino Veritas*. He says further: 'Politeness is pleasing – essentially – to woman, and the fact that she accepts it without hesitation is explained by nature's care for the weaker, for the unfavored being, and for one to whom an illusion means more than a material compensation. But this illusion, precisely, is fatal to her.... To feel oneself freed from distress thanks to something imaginary, to be the dupe of something imaginary, is that not a still deeper mockery?... Woman is very far from being *verwahrlan* (neglected), but in another sense she is, since she can never free herself from the illusion that nature has used to console her.'

of love, devotion, the gift of herself, and then concealing from her the fact that neither lover nor husband nor yet her children will be inclined to accept the burdensome charge of all that. She cheerfully believes these lies because they invite her to follow the easy slope: in this others commit their worst crime against her; throughout her life from childhood on, they damage and corrupt her by designating as her true vocation this submission, which is the temptation of every existent in the anxiety of liberty. If a child is taught idleness by being amused all day long and never being led to study, or shown its usefulness, it will hardly be said, when he grows up, that he chose to be incapable and ignorant; yet this is how woman is brought up, without ever being impressed with the necessity of taking charge of her own existence. So she readily lets herself come to count on the protection, love, assistance, and supervision of others, she lets herself be fascinated with the hope of self-realization without *doing* anything. She does wrong in yielding to the temptation; but man is in no position to blame her, since he has led her into the temptation. When conflict arises between them, each will hold the other responsible for the situation; she will reproach him with having made her what she is: 'No one taught me to reason or to earn my own living'; he will reproach her with having accepted the consequences: 'You don't know anything, you are an incompetent,' and so on. Each sex thinks it can justify itself by taking the offensive; but the wrongs done by one do not make the other innocent.

The innumerable conflicts that set men and women against one another come from the fact that neither is prepared to assume all the consequences of this situation which the one has offered and the other accepted. The doubtful concept of 'equality is inequality', which the one uses to mask his despotism and the other to mask her cowardice, does not stand the test of experience; in their exchanges, woman appeals to the theoretical equality she has been guaranteed, and man the concrete inequality that exists. The result is that in every association an endless debate goes on concerning the ambiguous meaning of the words *give* and *take*: she complains of giving her all, he protests that she takes his all. Woman has to learn that exchanges – it is a fundamental law of political economy – are based on the value the merchandise offered has for the buyer, and not for the seller: she has been deceived in being persuaded that her worth is priceless. The truth is that for man she is an amusement, a pleasure, company, an inessential boon; he is for her the meaning, the justification of her existence. The exchange, therefore, is not of two items of equal value.

This inequality will be especially brought out in the fact that the time they spend together – which fallaciously seems to be the same time – does not have the same value for both partners. During the evening the lover spends with his mistress he could be doing something of advantage to his career, seeing friends, cultivating business relationships, seeking recreation; for a man normally integrated in society, time is a positive value: money, reputation, pleasure. For the idle, bored woman, on the contrary, it is a burden she wishes to get rid of; when she succeeds in killing time, it is a benefit to her: the man's presence is pure profit. In a liaison what most clearly interests the man, in many cases, is the sexual benefit he gets from it: if need be, he can be content to spend no more time with his mistress than is required for the sexual act; but – with exceptions – what she, on her part, wants is to kill all the excess time she has on her hands; and – like the storekeeper who will not sell potatoes unless the customer will take turnips also – she will not yield her body unless her lover will take hours of conversation and 'going out' into the bargain. A balance is reached if, on the whole, the cost does not seem too high to the man, and this depends, of course, on the strength of his desire and the importance he gives to what is to be sacrificed. But if the woman demands – offers – too much time, she becomes wholly intrusive, like the river overflowing its banks, and the man will prefer to have nothing rather than too much. Then she reduces her demands; but very often the balance is reached at the cost of a double tension: she feels that the man has 'had' her at a bargain, and he thinks her price is too high. This analysis, of course, is put in somewhat humorous terms; but – except for those affairs of jealous and exclusive passion in which the man wants total possession of the woman – this conflict constantly appears in cases of affection, desire, and even love. He always has 'other things to do' with his time; whereas she has time to burn; and he considers much of the time she gives him not as a gift but as a burden.

As a rule he consents to assume the burden because he knows very well that he is on the privileged side, he has a bad conscience; and if he is of reasonable good will he tries to compensate for the inequality by being generous. He prides himself on his compassion, however, and at the first clash he treats the woman as ungrateful and thinks, with some irritation: 'I'm too good to her.' She feels she is behaving like a beggar when she is convinced of the high value of her gifts, and that humiliates her.

Here we find the explanation of the cruelty that woman often shows she is capable of practicing; she has a good conscience because she is on the unprivileged side; she feels she is under no obligation to deal gently with the favored· caste, and her only thought is to defend herself. She will even be very happy if she has occasion to show her resentment to a lover who has not been able to satisfy all her demands: since he does not give her enough, she takes savage delight in taking back everything from him. At this point the wounded lover suddenly discovers the value *in toto* of a liaison each moment of which he held more or less in contempt: he is ready to promise her everything, even though he will feel exploited again when he has to make good. He accuses his mistress of blackmailing him: she calls him stingy; both feel wronged.

Once again it is useless to apportion blame and excuses: justice can never be done in the midst of injustice. A colonial administrator has no possibility of acting rightly toward the natives, nor a general toward his soldiers; the only solution is to be neither colonist nor military chief; but a man could not prevent himself from being a man. So there he is, culpable in spite of himself and laboring under the effects of a fault he did not himself commit; and here she is, victim and shrew in spite of herself. Sometimes he rebels and becomes cruel, but then he makes himself an accomplice of the injustice, and the fault becomes really his. Sometimes he lets himself be annihilated, devoured, by his demanding victim; but in that case he feels duped. Often he stops at a compromise that at once belittles him and leaves him ill at ease. A well-disposed man will be more tortured by the situation than the woman herself: in a sense it is always better to be on the side of the vanquished; but if she is well-disposed also, incapable of self-sufficiency, reluctant to crush the man with the weight of her destiny, she struggles in hopeless confusion.

In daily life we meet with an abundance of these cases which are incapable of satisfactory solution because they are determined by unsatisfactory conditions. A man who is compelled to go on materially and morally supporting a woman whom he no longer loves feels he is victimized; but if he abandons without resources the woman who has pledged her whole life to him, she will be quite as unjustly victimized. The evil originates not in the perversity of individuals – and bad faith first appears when each blames the other – it originates rather in a situation against which all individual action is powerless. Women are 'clinging', they are a dead weight, and they suffer for it; the point is that their situation is like that of a parasite sucking out the living strength of another organism. Let them be provided with living strength of their own, let them have the means to attack the world and wrest from it their own subsistence, and their dependence will be abolished – that of man also. There is no doubt that both men and women will profit greatly from the new situation.

A world where men and women would be equal is easy to visualize, for that precisely is what the Soviet Revolution *promised*: women raised and trained exactly like men were to work under the same conditions[2] and for the same wages. Erotic liberty was to be recognized by custom, but the sexual act was not to be considered a 'service' to be paid for; woman was to be *obliged* to provide herself with other ways of earning a living; marriage was to be based on a free agreement that the spouses could break at will; maternity was to be voluntary, which meant that contraception and abortion were to be authorized and that, on the other hand, all mothers and their children were to have exactly the same rights, in or out of marriage; pregnancy leaves were to be paid for by the State, which would assume charge of the children, signifying not that they would be *taken away* from their parents, but that they would not be *abandoned* to them.

But is it enough to change laws, institutions, customs, public opinion, and the whole social context, for men and women to become truly equal? 'Women will always be women,' say the skeptics. Other seers prophesy that in casting off their femininity they will not succeed in changing themselves into men and they will become monsters. This would be to admit that the woman of today is a creation of nature; it must be repeated once more that in human society nothing is natural and that woman, like much else, is a product elaborated by civilization. The intervention of others in her destiny is fundamental: if this action took a different direction, it would produce quite a different result. Woman is determined not by her hormones or by mysterious instincts, but by the manner in which her body and her relation to the world are modified through the action of others than herself. The abyss that separates the adolescent boy and girl has been deliberately opened out between them since earliest childhood; later on, woman could not be other than what she *was made*, and that past was bound to shadow her for life. If we appreciate its influence, we see clearly that her destiny is not predetermined for all eternity.

We must not believe, certainly, that a change in woman's economic condition alone is enough to transform her, though this factor has been and remains the basic factor in her evolution; but until it has brought about the moral, social, cultural, and other consequences that it promises and requires, the new woman cannot

2. That certain too laborious occupations were to be closed to women is not in contradiction to this project. Even among men there is an increasing effort to obtain adaptation to profession; their varying physical and mental capacities limit their possibilities of choice; what is asked is that, in any case, no line of sex or caste be drawn.

appear. At this moment they have been realized nowhere, in Russia no more than in France or the United States; and this explains why the woman of today is torn between the past and the future. She appears most often as a 'true woman' disguised as a man, and she feels herself as ill at ease in her flesh as in her masculine garb. She must shed her old skin and cut her own new clothes. This she could do only through a social evolution. No single educator could fashion a *female human being* today who would be the exact homologue of the *male human being*; if she is raised like a boy, the young girl feels she is an oddity and thereby she is given a new kind of sex specification. Stendhal understood this when he said: 'The forest must be planted all at once.' But if we imagine, on the contrary, a society in which the equality of the sexes would be concretely realized, this equality would find new expression in each individual.

Jill Johnston

The Myth of the Myth
of the Vaginal Orgasm

From Jill Johnston, *Lesbian Nation: the Feminist Solution*, New York: Simon and Schuster, 1974, pp. 164-74

Should the hypothesis be true that one of the requisite çornerstones upon which all modern civilizations were founded were coercive suppression of women's inordinate sexuality, one looks back over the long history of women and their relationship to men, children and society since the Neolithic revolution with a deeper, almost awesome, sense of the ironic tragedy in the triumph of the human condition. [Mary Jane Sherfey, MD]

The process of physical and psychic self-affirmation requires full relation with those like oneself, namely women. [*Ecstasy*, a paper written by a gay revolutionary party]

Many of the new theories and descriptions of woman's basic equipment and orgasm may sound right to a lot of women. They don't sound bad to me, but they're almost exclusively written in relation to the man with the implicit instruction that the man had better shape up and recognize this 'inordinate' sexuality of women and learn the more effective means of stimulating and satisfying his partner. Although many women can satisfy themselves in relation to the man it's not well known at all that the woman can satisfy herself just as well if not better in relation to herself or to other women. The sexual satisfaction of the woman independently of the man is the *sine qua non* of the feminist revolution. This is why Gay/Feminism expresses the proper sexual-political stance for the revolutionary woman. Sexual dependence on the man is inextricably entangled in the interdependence of man and woman at all levels of the social structures by which the woman is oppressed. It is in any case difficult to conceive of an 'equal' sexual relationship between two people in which one member is the 'biological aggressor'. Although a hole also moves forward to enclose a sword it is the sword in all known personal-political forms of life throughout history which has assumed initiative to invade and conquer. The man retains the prime organ of invasion. Sexual congress between man and woman is an invasion of the woman, the woman doesn't get anything up to participate in this congress, and although a woman may be conditioned to believe that she enjoys this invasion and may in fact grow to like it if her male partner makes rare sacrifices of consideration in technical know-how, she remains the passive receptive hopeful half of a situation that was unequal from the start. The fate that woman has to resign herself to is the *knowledge* of this biological inequity. A fate that was not originally the occasion for the *social* inequities elaborated out of the biological situation. From this knowledge the woman can now alter her destiny or at least reclaim certain ancient historical solutions, namely the self-sufficient tribes of amazons, to a physical problem in relation to men. Some Marxist-Socialist thinkers envision the solution in our technological advancement whereby the test-tube baby will relieve the woman of her reproductive function and release her to the wideranging sexual pleasures traditionally arrogated by the man. But *no* technological solution will be the answer to the spiritual needs of the woman deprived of herself in relation to the man. Feminism at heart is a massive complaint. Lesbianism is the solution. Which is another way of putting what Ti-Grace Atkinson once described as Feminism being a theory and lesbianism the practice. When theory and practice come together we'll have the revolution. Until all women are lesbians there will be no true political revolution. No feminist per se has advanced a solution outside of accommodation to the man. The complaints are substantial and articulate and historically sound and they contain by implication their own answers but the feminists refuse to acknowledge what's implicit in their own complaint or analysis. To wit: that the object of their attack is not going to make anything better than a *material* adjustment to the demands of their enslaved sex. There's no conceivable equality between two species in a relation in which one of the two has been considerably weakened in all aspects of her being over so long a period of historical time. The blacks in America were the first to understand that an oppressed group must withdraw into itself to establish its own identity and rebuild its strength through mutual support and recognition. The first unpublicized action of many feminists *was* in fact to withdraw from the man sexually. Feminists who still sleep with the man are delivering their most vital energies to the oppressor. Most feminists understood this immediately but were confounded in their realization by the taboo against the obvious solution of sex with another woman. Not only is the psychic-emotional potential for satisfaction with another woman far greater than that with a man, insomuch as every woman like every man was originally most profoundly attached to herself as her mother, but there is more likelihood of sexual fulfillment with another woman as well since all organisms best understand the basic equipment of another organism which most closely resembles themselves. The erotic potential between like organisms consists in the enhancement of self through narcissistic identification. Narcissism is the ideal appreciation of self. Women who love their own sex love the sameness in the other. They become both subject and object to each other. That makes two subjects and two objects. Narcissism is the totality of subject-object unity within the self extended to another. 'When a heterosexual woman loves a man she is confronted with otherness, and so is a man who loves a woman. Otherness implies something completely different from oneself, something one has to learn to understand and live with ... At one time or another, the "normal" (heterosexual) woman will always be put back into the place of being an object.' (Charlotte Wolff, *Love Between Women*, p. 70.) Normalcy for women is the adaptation to their own oppression. Or to the male standard for perpetuating his privilege in unequal relationships. Normalcy is the fucked up condition of woman. Normalcy is the unsuccessful attempt to overcome the obstacle of otherness by resigning oneself to one's own deprivation of self. Normalcy is an appeal to numbers in the form of majorities to justify coercion in plans to cooperate for the benefit of 'mankind'. Normalcy is the disease of maladjusted coupling by different or hetero or otherness species. Normalcy is achieved by puritan ethical appeals to the moral correctness of doing things that are worthwhile by their difficulty and hard labor through delayed gratification of real instincts, or uniting with self. True normalcy would mean the return of all women to themselves. Majority behavior, which defines civilized schizophrenia, is pseudo-normalcy. The first order of business for a woman is the redefinition of herself through assertion of her sexuality in relation to herself or her own equal, in other words, independently of the man. Early feminist writings project the suggestion of lesbianism as an alternative to the widespread sexual dissatisfaction of women in relation to men. There was, in these early manifestos, both fortunately and not so fortunately, a concentration on that aspect of the basic equipment in which orgastic satisfaction originates. I thought everybody knew the clitoris was the doorway to orgasm, the way a certain type of jill-in-the-box might pop open after sufficient rhythmic friction against its trap door. Apparently this glorification of the clitoris was a revelation to women who remained frigid in intercourse through neglect of prior stimulation of the external or clitoral part of the organ. Or who remained frigid in intercourse regardless of said prior stimulation, this actually being the true situation, according to early pronouncement, based on the total absence of feeling or orgastic potential within the vagina itself. I have a record entry 18 June 1970: 'find out what they mean by the myth of the vaginal orgasm.' Subsequently I asked a few 'feminists'. They informed me, in effect, that I don't experience what I say I feel or feel what I say I experience or any combined way of being a liar. And their chief authority was Masters & Johnson. Studying the feminist literature I decided that the feminists had found the perfect rationale for their frustration and excuse for not being required to fuck with the man any more. They didn't actually say this. They were mainly contesting the 'myth of the liberated woman and her vaginal orgasm'. The refutation of Freud's thesis of sexual maturity in the woman consisting of her transference to the father as proper love object developing parallel to the shifting of orgasmic location in the clitoris to the 'mature' vagina. Wherever these feminists obtained their 'evidence' for an insensitive vagina, if not in themselves, it seemed not to matter either about the source or the (in)sensitivity if the issue constituted a rebellion against being defined sexually in terms of what pleases the man. It seems actually amazing that what they were asserting was a stubborn refusal to submit to conventional intercourse on grounds of an insensitive vagina. *Equating* intercourse with vaginal orgasm as it were. (No mention of hands or bananas or dildoes.) Really as though one was unthinkable without the other. As though the case for an insensitive vagina provided women with their first legal brief for the indictment of phallic imperialism. This rather misguided attempt of women to dissociate themselves from the suppression of their pleasure in 'reproductive sexuality' was nonetheless a crucial rudimentary step in establishing sexual independence from the man and leading to the fuller dimension of womanhood in Gay/Feminism. In fact within two years or so after the appearance of these papers the feminist line includes more overt accommodation to and recognition of lesbians, as well as lesbianism itself within the ranks. I said 'misguided' because the feminist equation along the old standard of 'reproductive sexuality' or penis-in-vagina as proper model or primal scene, and their 'discovering' of the insensitive female half of the bargain, important as it was, left them with only one operable part of the basic equipment – the clitoris – and the ignorance of a solution involving all the equipment with their sisters. I always agreed with one half of Freud's equation. That a woman moves from clitoral to vaginal orgasm. And that the latter *is* more mature in the sense that the activation of the inner walls brings about a more profound intensification of orgasm. I would add that this shift occurs in two kinds of time – over a period of months or years as a 'discovery' of the orgastic potential of the internal walls, and as a transition in every sexual encounter, moving from initial stimulation of clitoris (as the seat of sensation, the *origin* of satisfaction) to full orgasm experienced in the total organ which includes the 'deep' vaginal wall. I take issue like the feminists with Freud's postulation of 'heterosexual maturity'. Since a woman can achieve a vaginal orgasm herself or with another woman clearly his case for maturity was in the interests of the continuation of phallic imperialism. The rights of the father to the mother. The Gay/Feminist revolution involves the rights of the mother to the mother. Women's thighs are the gateways to infinity for women as well as for men. For women give birth to themselves as well as to boys. I was struck particularly by these remarks in the Masters & Johnson book on female orgasm: 'During the first stage of subjective progression in orgasm, the sensation of intense clitoral-pelvic awareness has been described by a number of women as occurring concomitantly with a sense of bearing down or expelling. This last sensation was reported only by parous study subjects, a small number of whom expressed some concept of having an actual fluid emission or of expending in some concrete fashion.' And: 'Twelve women, all of whom have delivered babies on at least one occasion without anesthesia or analgesia, reported that during the second stage of labor they experienced a grossly intensified version of the sensations identified with this first stage of subjective progression through orgasm.' These reports seemed to confirm my long suspicion that orgasm itself originated in the parthenogenetic birth of our unicellular beginnings. The daughter cells. The immaculate conception is the female fantasy of her own birth without the aid of the male. I can personally testify to the aboriginal reality of this state of being through having experienced a 'psychic parthenogenesis' in certain hallucinatory symptoms of childbirth – psychosomatic labor pains – attending the birth of myself during a critical period of cosmic consciousness more commonly called insanity. Women of course do the same for each other in any intense relationship. I should also remark that my 'rebirth' was accompanied by a great expansion of sexuality in the realms of both sensual awareness and orgastic potential. During this time for instance I began to experience the intensification or deepening of orgasm that I could only describe as 'inner' or 'internal'. The feminists claimed Masters & Johnson as an authority in their case for an insensitive vagina. Yet Masters & Johnson say, 'The physiologic onset of orgasm is signaled by contractions of the target organs, starting with the *orgasmic platform in the outer third of the vagina*. This platform, created involuntarily by localized vasocongestion and myotonia, contracts with recordable rhythmicity as the tension increment is released' (italics mine). And the 'Vaginal spasm and penile grasping reactions have been described many times in the clinical and non-professional literature.' And 'Regularly recurring orgasmic-platform contractions were appreciated subjectively as pulsating or throbbing sensations of the vagina.' And 'Finally, as the third stage of subjective progression, a feeling of involuntary contraction with a specific focus in the vagina or lower pelvis was mentioned consistently.' The Masters & Johnson team remain loyal to the standard of heterosexual coupling but they've presented the most impressive physiological findings to date of the extensive orgasmic response of the woman. I really think the feminists basically were making a common complaint in the new terminological context of feminism. That the man was no good in bed. That he was insensitive to the essential clitoris. That he just didn't know how to do it. And as an added fillip the new challenge that a woman or feminist anyway would henceforth refuse to accept responsibility for a frigidity that wasn't her own fault. The solution has still not been posed within feminist theory. It can't be because feminism is not a solution. It's the complaint that got the movement going. When the feminists have a solution they'll be Gay/Feminists. Until then, they've got the best problem around and that's the man. Feminism is a struggle terminology. Concerning women at odds with the man. Since women have always been at odds with the man feminism is the collectivized articulated expression of women's demeaned status. Feminism will no longer need itself when women cease to think of themselves as the 'other' in relation to the 'other' and unite with their own kind or species. Being male and female is, above all, defined in terms of the other. Feminists could begin by realizing that not only do they not need a penis to achieve their supreme satisfaction but they could easily do better without one since the timing involving the essential stimulation of the outer tissues prior to and/or concomitant with penetration requires a penis that can be erect for entry at a more or less precise moment in the progress toward climax. Some women and men work this thing out, or in, but most women, as the feminists observed, consistently receive a penis into a dead or dying chamber from which the penis eventually emerges as the savior in the form of a child. In any case the question many people are asking now is if 'reproductive sexuality' is no longer the standard for sexual approach – for men it never was completely – what is keeping women from their total pleasure with other women. We know why. 'Women far more than men are trapped in a social view that suggests that their ultimate worth is derived from a suitable heterosexual attachment and the result of this is that they come to despise both themselves and other women.' (Altman, p. 79.) In order for a girl to achieve an adequate motherhood, she must to some degree relinquish her libidinal attachment to her own mother. The acculturation of women to believe most exclusively in 'reproductive sexuality' remains pervasive and powerful. Altman (p. 60) again: 'As a consequence of the utilitarian view of sex there is an extremely strong negative attitude toward all sexual urges other than those that are genital and heterosexual.' Or: 'Sex has been firmly linked, and nowhere more clearly than in Christian theology, with the institution of the family and with child bearing. Sex is thus legitimized for its utilitarian principles, rather than as an end in itself ... even where sexual pleasure is accepted as a complementary goal, the connection between marriage and sex still remains.' As a complementary goal women have no need to stay in relation to the aggravation caused by the 'biological aggressor'. If the male fears absorption and the female penetration, and both fears represent the disturbance of a static equilibrium – in which nothing is either gained or lost – (Slater, p. 103) it seems clear that the various global disturbances now accelerated by technological expansion are material visible extensions of the primal antagonism between men and women in some evolutionary distortion of destiny. (Not that there is such a thing as an evolutionary distortion.) Marcuse commented on Norman O. Brown: 'If I understand his mysticism correctly it includes abolition of the distinction between male and female and creation of an androgynous person. He seems to see the distinction between male and female as the product of repression. I do not. It is the last difference I want to see abolished.' Speaking of sexism in high places! If I understand Marcuse correctly. Since I too would not like to see the distinction abolished, but not I think for the same reasons. Agreeing with Brown, I'm not sure that he would envision the solution in the withdrawal of women from participation in that repression by which the distinction was created and sustained. Or even that he would define it that way. The fall was from some primeval division into two sexes. I think any bio-analytically oriented person knows we were originally one sex. The fall is a constant reoccurrence through birth or separation. 'The sin is not between the lover and the beloved, but in parentage.' The project in our cycle toward species extinction should be clear enough. The present revolution of women is a clamorous reminder of that destiny and the proper organic means of achieving it. Many male intellects hope to see the abortion of this destiny. Not necessarily specifically identifying the agent of that abortion in the potential technological disasters of the male power problem. The key to survival in the interests of a natural death is the gradual extinction of the reproductive function as it is now still known and practiced. For it is by this function that the woman is so desperately deprived of herself. Lesbian or woman prime is *the* factor in advance of every projected solution for our embattled world. In her realization of herself both sensually polymorphously and genitally orgasmically she experiences her original self-reproductive or parthenogenetic recreation of herself apart from the intruding and disturbing and subjugating male. Genitalorgasmic sex between women is absolutely consistent with our total sensual and emotional mutually reflecting relations with each other. The lesbian woman is not properly equipped to oppress her own kind. But she *is* equipped to give herself pleasure, and she doesn't need any artificial substitute for the instrument of oppression to give herself that pleasure.

References

Altman, Dennis, *Homosexual Oppression and Liberation*, New York: Outerbridge and Dienstfrey, 1971.
Slater, Philip, *The Glory of Hera*, Boston: The Beacon Press, 1968.

Gail Chester

I Call Myself a Radical Feminist

In *Feminist Practice, Notes from the Tenth Year*,
London: In Theory Press, 1979, pp. 12-15

'I call myself a Radical Feminist.' What does that mean? In the beginning, you said you were in Women's Liberation, you called yourself a feminist, the two terms were synonymous. Then modern feminists began to investigate our history, we discovered that we were the second wave of feminists. The first wave had begun with the Seneca Falls Convention of 1848 and had remained radical in intent until its energy was entirely spent on concentration on the single issue of winning the vote. Even after the vote was won, a few feminists remained active, fighting for such women's issues as contraceptive rights, abortion law reform, the admission of women to certain professions, right up to the emergence of the Women's Liberation Movement. As Women's Liberation developed, it became clear that it was necessary to distinguish ourselves from the reformist/emancipationist/liberal strands of feminism (historical and contemporary) which called themselves 'feminists' too – as they were perfectly entitled to do. Women's Liberationists did this by starting to call ourselves *radical* feminists, to stress our revolutionary perspective, to maintain that emancipation was not enough.

As time went on, with organisations which allowed men to participate, such as the Working Women's Charter and the National Abortion Campaign, claiming the right to be included under the broader affiliating banner of the 'women's movement', the need became more pressing to emphasise that radical feminism was something different from feminism. To be feminist now can be defined as to be generally concerned about the position of women in society, but it says nothing about one's opinions about how that position is to be changed, and it does not signify active fighting for our liberation. Taking the 'Liberation' out of the Women's Movement was a way of liberalising our struggle, of making it more socially acceptable to men, who could then legitimately also claim to be feminists.

Today, to be a feminist is no longer synonymous with being in the Women's Liberation Movement. In order to define myself as being active in, and believing in the need for, a strong, autonomous, revolutionary movement for the liberation of women, I continue to call myself a radical feminist. In doing so, I am affirming my historical link with the earliest phases of the second wave of feminism – the rise of the Women's Liberation Movement. I am not implying that I do not believe the concept of feminism itself to be inherently radical, almost the reverse. To call myself a socialist feminist or a revolutionary feminist would be to imply that (radical) feminism is not socialist, or is not revolutionary. To me, radical feminism, as expressed through the Women's Liberation Movement, is both. But it is more, too. It is a recognition that no single element of our society has evolved free from male definition, so that to practise radical feminism means to question every single aspect of our lives that we have previously accepted as normal/given/standard/acceptable and to find new ways of doing things where necessary – which is most places. Thus, language is male-defined. This does not mean that some women have not become very good at using it, but that the language as presently constructed is based on male-dominated values, since patriarchy was in control long before Saxon times. I am not arguing against being articulate in male language – at present it's the best we've got – nor am I suggesting that patriarchy and male-definition are constant, immutable, biological factors. All I am suggesting is that until radical feminism told many women that there were important concepts missing from our thought patterns/language, and that this was yet another weapon in the armoury of male oppression, many women thought/felt that they were stupid, inarticulate, inferior for not having the words to describe the conditions of their being.

Others of us have looked at other areas of our previously taken-for-granted existence, such as believing that some people know more about some things, and therefore we call them experts and pay them higher wages and don't answer back when they tell us things about ourselves that we know are wrong. Remember that most of these experts have been men. Radical feminism told us it was possible to take on the man, especially if we do it collectively, and win. We also discovered that a lot of the information of these so-called experts that was valuable to us could be learned fairly easily, once we gained confidence in our ability to do it. Concepts such as 'knowledge', 'science', 'rationality' are being constantly reassessed.

Likewise revolutionary strategy. No more is it possible to accept the male definition of what is revolutionary, neither in terms of what we want, nor how we get there. Marx said a lot of very important things, but, like us all, he was a product of his milieu –

a nineteenth-century, urban, Western European, Jewish, intellectual man. All these things, and more, led him to make assertions incorrect for achieving a twentieth-century and/or rural and/or non-European and/or feminist revolution. Treating *Das Kapital* like the Bible or Marx as an Expert are male-defined attitudes. But perhaps the most pernicious and male-defined aspect of treating Marx in this way is the attitude it gives us towards evolving a revolutionary theory. If we absorb Marxism as the model, at least as it is latterly practised, we accept that there is such a thing as revolutionary theory separable from revolutionary practice, which can moreover tell us what practice to follow, and we can be led to believe that the development of theory alone is a sufficient revolutionary practice.

This is not to suggest that there cannot or should not be such a thing as radical feminist theory – indeed the mistake of those who are trapped in patriarchal thinking is to believe that there has not been a radical feminist theory since early in Women's Liberation. Radical feminist theory is that theory follows from practice and is impossible to develop in the absence of practice, because our theory is that practising our practice is our theory. If this sounds like semantic hoop-jumping I am sorry, and would invite you to read the previous sentence again, while I try to think of a concrete example. The point is that for radical feminists, theory and practice are not separate things done by different groups of people, but a constant refinement of our practice as we discover with experience what was wrong with the last action we took. The reason radical feminist theory has not been recognised by some women is that it has not been written down much, which can be seen as our failing to some extent, but it should also be appreciated that if your theory is embodied in your practice, then the way you act politically has as much right to be taken as a serious statement of your theoretical position as writing it down in a book which hardly anybody will read anyhow. Whilst we remain tied to patriarchal notions of what constitutes existence, the non-existence of radical feminism is confirmed by our relative absence from writings on feminism, and while we are not present to explain ourselves, we are meanwhile available to be misinterpreted by others, our contribution to revolutionary theory can be written out, and has been.

The small group is a good example of radical feminist theory/-practice – although the practice was borrowed, then modified from alternative therapy techniques, the notion of consciousness-raising (CR) as a revolutionary tool was developed by radical feminists. When the WLM started, we did not at first automatically break up into small groups for consciousness-raising – some of us can remember the excitement and dynamics being generated in large meetings of seventy women, week after week, a feeling that would sometimes be good to recapture. The organisational form of small groups – not all solely consciousness-raising, some were primarily task-oriented – meeting separately from the large group was a good way of keeping in touch with other women at various levels, and changing our consciousnesses at the same time. Somewhere along the line, form and content became confused, so that now meeting in a small group seems to have become the trade mark of Women's Liberation, whilst what happens within it is not rigorously questioned, nor, too often, is a practical connection made between one small group and another. Without understanding why it is politically important to meet in small groups, the perpetuation of this form of organisation can lead simply to an ossified practice which is no longer any help to us.

It has remained an important part of our theory/practice that all members of Women's Liberation should be in initial CR group and should continue to do it whilst they continue to identify with the Women's Liberation Movement. But there are now many women who have never been in a CR group, or feel that they have grown beyond it – a position I strongly disagree with. However, it is a healthy test of our theory/practice if we can examine the current practices of those women who do not agree with consciousness-raising, and compare them with our own, and thus see whether we should re-examine the consciousness-raising process, and modify it if necessary. There might then need to be a change in our theory/practice – it will be achieved by a collective decision that it is an important aspect of the way we conduct our activities which we all need to look at afresh.

Because radical feminists do not recognise a split between our theory and our practice, we are able to say that the revolution can begin now, by us taking positive actions to change our lives. Although this is not to suggest that any action a woman takes to change her life is necessarily revolutionary, it is a much more optimistic and human vision of change than the male-defined notion of the building towards a revolution at some point in the distant future, once all the preparations have been made. How can you judge whether you are making the right preparations for something whose shape and form you have no way of envisaging, or identifying with? To bring revolutionary change within the realm of the possible is one of the most important attitudes I have learned from radical feminism – even though all the changes are unlikely to happen in my lifetime, the small advances I have contributed to will have made life better for some people, and most importantly, myself.

The most fundamental political lesson I have learnt as a radical feminist is that I am an important part of the revolution. Insofar as I am oppressed, I can struggle to change my life in the company of other women, I am significant. I am not in the Women's Liberation Movement because I am self-sacrificing, or loving and giving as women were always supposed to be, but because I believe that my life must be changed and so must the lives of all women.

That is the only point.

Leeds Revolutionary Feminist Group

Political Lesbianism: the Case against Heterosexuality

In *Love Your Enemy? The Debate between Heterosexual Feminism and Political Lesbianism*, London: Onlywomen Press, 1981, pp. 5-10, 66-8 ('Political Lesbianism' was written for a conference in 1979 and first published in *Wires*; the 'Afterword' has been revised for this book)

We know that the question of whether all feminists should be lesbians is not new. We have had to work out our ideas on the subject because often when we talk about our politics and what it means to say men are the enemy, with other women, we are asked whether we are saying that all feminists should be lesbians.

We realise that the topic is explosive. It is something we are supposed to talk about at home and in close and trusted groups of friends and not make political statements about in the movement, lest our heterosexual sisters accuse us of woman-hating. Is it true that we must conceal our strong political beliefs on the subject when talking with other feminists? We would like to raise the whole issue for discussion in a workshop; not just whether all feminists should be lesbians, but precisely why we think they should be and whether and how we may begin to talk about it more openly.

We do think that all feminists can and should be political lesbians. Our definition of a political lesbian is a woman-identified woman who does not fuck men. It does not mean compulsory sexual activity with women. The paper is divided into two parts. The first covers the reasons why we think serious feminists have no choice but to abandon heterosexuality. The second is arranged in the form of questions raised and comments made to us about the subject of political lesbianism and the way we think they should be answered.

(1) WHAT HETEROSEXUALITY IS ABOUT AND WHY IT MUST BE ABANDONED

Sexuality

What part does sexuality play in the oppression of women? Only in the system of oppression that is male supremacy does the oppressor actually invade and colonise the interior of the body of the oppressed. Attached to all forms of sexual behaviour are meanings of dominance and submission, power and powerlessness, conquest and humiliation. There is very special importance attached to sexuality under male supremacy when every sexual reference, every sexual joke, every sexual image serves to remind a woman of her invaded centre and a man of his power. Why all this fuss in our culture about sex? Because it is specifically through sexuality that the fundamental oppression, that of men over women, is maintained. (This should be a book, can't really be gone into now.)

The heterosexual couple

The heterosexual couple is the basic unit of the political structure of male supremacy. In it each individual woman comes under the control of an individual man. It is more efficient by far than keeping women in ghettoes, camps or even sheds at the bottom of the garden. In the couple, love and sex are used to obscure the realities of oppression, to prevent women identifying with each other in order to revolt, and from identifying 'their' man as part of the enemy. Any woman who takes part in a heterosexual couple helps to shore up male supremacy by making its foundations stronger.

Penetration

Penetration (wherever we refer to penetration, we mean penetration by the penis) is not necessary to the sexual pleasure of women or even of men. Its performance leads to reproduction or tedious/dangerous forms of contraception. Why then does it lie at the heart of the sexualised culture of this particular stage of male supremacy? Why are more and more women, at younger and younger ages, encouraged by psychiatrists, doctors, marriage guidance counsellors, the porn industry, the growth movement, lefties and Masters and Johnson to get fucked more and more often? Because the form of the oppression of women under male supremacy is changing. As more women are able to earn a little more money and the pressures of reproduction are relieved, so the hold of individual men and men as a class over women is being strengthened through sexual control.

The function of penetration

Penetration is an act of great symbolic significance by which the oppressor enters the body of the oppressed. But it is more than a symbol, its function and effect is the punishment and control of women. It is not just rape which serves this function but every act of penetration, even that which is euphemistically described as 'making love'. We have all heard men say about an uppity woman, 'What she needs is a good fuck.' This is no idle remark. Every man knows that a fucked woman is a woman under the control of men, whose body is open to men, a woman who is tamed and broken in. Before the sexual revolution there was no mistake about penetration being for the benefit of men. The sexual revolution is a con trick. It serves to disguise the oppressive nature of male sexuality and we are told that penetration is for our benefit as well.

Every act of penetration for a woman is an invasion which undermines her confidence and saps her strength. For a man it is an act of power and mastery which makes him stronger, not just over one woman but over all women. So every woman who engages in penetration bolsters the oppressor and reinforces the class power of men.

(2) QUESTIONS AND COMMENTS

(a) But it sounds like you are saying that heterosexual women are the enemy!

No. Men are the enemy. Heterosexual women are collaborators with the enemy. All the good work that our heterosexual feminist sisters do for women is undermined by the counter-revolutionary activity they engage in with men. Being a heterosexual feminist is like being in the resistance in Nazi-occupied Europe where in the daytime you blow up a bridge, in the evening you rush to repair it. Take Women's Aid for example: women who live with men cannot tell battered women that survival without men is possible since they are not doing it themselves. Every woman who lives with or fucks a man helps to maintain the oppression of her sisters and hinders our struggle.

(b) But we don't do penetration, my boyfriend and me

If you engage in any form of sexual activity with a man you are reinforcing his class power. You may escape the most extreme form of ritual humiliation but because of the emotional accretions to any form of heterosexual behaviour, men gain great advantages and women lose. There is no such thing as 'pure' sexual pleasure.

Such 'pleasure' is created by fantasy, memory and experience. Sexual 'pleasure' cannot be separated from the emotions that accompany the exercise of power and the experience of powerlessness.

(If you don't do penetration, why not take a woman lover? If you strip a man of his unique ability to humiliate, you are left with a creature who is merely worse at every sort of sensual activity than a woman is.)

(c) But my boyfriend does not penetrate me, I enclose him

A rose is a rose by any other name and so is penetration. Or possibly, 'You can't make a silk purse out of a boar's ear' is a more apt expression. The kindest interpretation is to say that believing in enclosure is wishful thinking. It would be more realistic to say that it is a cop-out and a rationalisation for continuing the activity. Enclosure, where an active vagina (helped by strengthening exercises) sucks in a penis could only take place where a woman and a man were born fully formed, totally innocent, on to an uninhabited desert island (where they might well never discover fucking anyway). No act of penetration takes place in isolation. Each takes place in a system of relationships that is male supremacy. As no individual woman can be 'liberated' under male supremacy, so no act of penetration can escape its function and its symbolic power.

(d) But I like fucking

Giving up fucking for a feminist is about taking your politics seriously. Women who are socialists are prepared to give up many things which they might enjoy because they see how these things tie into and support the whole system of economic class oppression which they are fighting. They will resist buying Cape apples because the profits go to South Africa. Obviously it is more difficult for some feminists to give up penetration which is so fundamental to the system of oppression which we are fighting.

(e) It is much easier for you in the lesbian ghetto than for me. I have to live out the contradictions of my politics which is a hard, relentless, day-by-day struggle with the man I live with

That's simply not true. Living without heterosexual privilege is difficult and dangerous. Try going into pubs with groups of women or living in a women's house where youths in the street lay siege with stones and catcalls.

Heterosexual privileges are male approval, more safety from physical attack, greater ease in dealing with the authorities, getting repairs done, safety from a besieging obscene phone-caller, being able to refer to a man in the bus queue or at work which brings smiles of approval from women and men, let alone the financial advantages of being attached to a member of the male ruling class who has greater earning power.

Because we choose to live without these privileges we resent being used by heterosexual feminists as fuelling stations when they are worn down by their struggles with their men. Women's liberation groups and women's households should be a refuge and support for heterosexual sisters in resolving their contradictions by getting out but should not be used to prop up heterosexual relationships and thereby shore up the structure of male supremacy.

(f) But lesbian relationships are also fucked up by power struggles

That is sometimes true, but the power of one woman is never backed up by a superior sex-class position. Struggles between women do not directly strengthen the oppression of all women or build up the strength of men. Personal perfection in relationships is not a realistic goal under male supremacy. Lesbianism is a necessary political choice, part of the tactics of our struggle, not a passport to paradise.

(g) I won't give up what I've got unless what you offer me is better

We never promised you a rose garden. We do not say that all feminists should be lesbians because it is wonderful. The lesbian dream of woman-loving, bare-breasted, guitar-playing softballers, gambolling on sun-soaked hillsides is more suited to California, supposing it bears any resemblance to reality, than to Hackney.

But yes, it is better to be a lesbian. The advantages include the pleasure of knowing that you are not directly servicing men, living without the strain of a glaring contradiction in your personal life, uniting the personal and the political, loving and putting your energies into those you are fighting alongside rather than those you are fighting against, and the possibility of greater trust, honesty and directness in your communication with women.

Communication with heterosexual women is fraught with difficulties, with static which comes from their relationships with men. Men distort such communication. A heterosexual woman will have a different perception and reaction to things you say; she may be defensive and is likely to be thinking 'What about Nigel?' When you talk of women's interests and the future and survival of women, her imagination may be blocked by concern for her man and his brothers. You feel under pressure to say nice things which will not threaten her.

(h) You are guilt-tripping us

No. Guilt-tripping is used to prevent women from telling the truth as they see it and from talking about hard political realities. It is you, heterosexual sisters, who are guilt-tripping us. It is possible to stop collaborating and asking you to do that is not a guilt-trip.

(i) Are all lesbian feminists political lesbians?

No. Some women who are lesbians and feminists work closely with men on the male left (either in their groups or in women's caucuses within them), or provide mouthpieces within the women's liberation movement for men's ideas even when non-aligned. It may well be that these women find it more difficult to see that men are the enemy because they are treated as substitute but inferior men by left males and are able to feel superior to the straight women who are still struggling against sexual oppression in their beds. They are not woman-identified and gain privileges through associating with men and putting forward ideas which are only mildly unacceptable to male left ideology.

(j) But you don't understand how difficult it is to give up men

Most of us know from personal experience how practically difficult and painful it is to decide not to fuck again and get out from the man we live with and/or love. It is usually only done with the love, support and strength of other women who have made that break and whose criticism and straight-talking spurred us on. We know that for some women, e.g. those with children, those with no easy access to the movement, and those without the experience of living on their own, the break is more difficult than for others and they need more time and *practical* support. We know how difficult it is to find a women's house to move into and what it is like to feel like a 'new girl' at the women's disco. But part of the support must be in explaining as clearly as possible the political reasons for our own choice and talking honestly about all the difficulties with the women who are making it.

Afterword

For some time before this paper was written those of us who had been invited to Women's Liberation groups to talk about our politics felt very dishonest and uneasy when women asked whether we thought all feminists should give up sexual relationships with men. We thought yes, but did not say so because we feared women would be alienated from all the rest of what we had to say. The paper was written partly to resolve our unease and dishonesty.

'Political Lesbianism' was written very quickly in a high-energy brain-storming session one evening, for discussion at a Revolutionary and Radical Feminist Conference in September 1979. It reflected some discussions our group had had, but in a very condensed form. This was because we knew that we would be able to expand and unpack these ideas in workshops at the conference. It went down quite well at the time and there were four workshops on the subject.

We were asked to put the paper in *Wires* (the Women's Liberation newsletter) because it had sparked off discussion, and women at the conference wanted other women to join in with the original paper available to them. If it had sunk like a stone it wouldn't have received any wider distribution.

The paper provoked many letters in *Wires* and other Women's Liberation newsletters, agreeing, disagreeing, and making new points. A selection of these, together with the original paper, was published in April 1981 by Onlywomen Press under the title *Love Your Enemy?* It included this 'Afterword' which we have slightly altered here.

Because it appeared in *Wires*, it was seen as a finished product, which was never intended. We were moving towards an analysis of how heterosexuality is central to women's oppression. The debate that followed made us look back at the paper again and again, and our own discussions benefited from the feedback. We found some of our comments flip, offensive and inconsistent, such as 'Why not take a woman lover?' We now think that 'collaborators' is the wrong word to describe women who sleep with men, since this implies a conscious act of betrayal. Even if applied solely to heterosexual feminists, rather than to heterosexual women in general, it is inaccurate: most feminists do not see men as the enemy, or heterosexuality as crucial to male supremacy. And there are many women at present unable to leave their men for reasons such as threat of deportation or fear of death – for example, the experience of Linda Marciano ('Lovelace'), described in her book *Ordeal*. Again, our list of heterosexual privileges is incorrect, and does not answer the question we raised. We realise that this is a very important and complex issue and needs fuller discussion.

Some lesbians and some heterosexual feminists saw the paper as an attack on heterosexual women: in fact, we were criticising heterosexuality as the accepted form of sexuality under male supremacy, and saying that it is used to oppress us. This is not clear when we make statements like 'Attached to all forms of sexual behaviour are meanings of dominance/submission. . . .' By 'sexuality' we mean *male* sexuality, as it is *male* sexuality that determines the form that heterosexuality takes. Penny Cloutte, one of the contributors to *Love Your Enemy?*, points out that we don't explain *how* heterosexuality shores up male supremacy – this omission also came out in discussions at the conference. The discussion which followed has forced us to return to this and clarify it for ourselves.

The paper does not explain how we personally arrived at these ideas. Personal experience is important, as it is through this that we become feminists, but we couldn't go into our individual backgrounds as there were several women in the group, so the paper would have ended up being far too long; besides, we wanted to point conference discussion towards political strategies, and thought that our personal experiences could be talked about in the workshop if relevant. We tried to be accountable by listing our names at the front of the conference papers.

Some women have seen the paper as suggesting that withdrawal of sexual services from men is the sum total of our political strategy. We completely disagree with the idea that living as separately as possible from men is by itself sufficient to overthrow male supremacy; and we said so in a paper we wrote on tactical separatism for the same conference. It would have been clearer if we had put this paper in *Wires* alongside 'Political Lesbianism'.

THE TITLE

Some women have been puzzled about why a paper called 'Political Lesbianism' concentrates on heterosexuality. In retrospect, the sub-title we added in the *Wires* version, 'The Case against Heterosexuality', is more accurate; but we also recognise that many women were glad to have the term 'political lesbian' brought to their attention. We certainly didn't invent it, but not every woman has read 'Redstockings' and other American feminist writing from the early 1970s where it was first used. Also, some women were confused as the term has been used since then to mean lots of quite different things, such as lesbians with a socialist awareness, non-lesbians accepting the lesbian label as a gesture of solidarity with lesbians, lesbians who were members of the Gay Liberation Front, etc., etc.

THE DEFINITION

We defined a Political Lesbian as a woman-identified woman who did not fuck men. We now think it's rubbish to say that women fuck men; what happens is that men fuck women, or women get fucked by men.

Woman-identified woman has been used so much that it is hard to think about what it really means. When we re-examined the phrase, we realised that we took it to mean: women who, by withdrawing their energy and support from men, have put women first. In doing so, they have found that it is incompatible with sleeping with men. This had been the experience of some of us in the group. One woman in the group had not given up men for consciously feminist reasons. We realise that many lesbians have never slept with men at all. We were trying to describe the process by which some feminists become lesbians, and to say that it was possible for women to stop sleeping with men for political reasons without necessarily sleeping with women. The value of calling yourself a political lesbian is to state that you are not sexually available to men; to repeat what we said in the paper, it is not about compulsory sexual activity with women.

THE QUESTIONS

A lot of women presumed we made them up. In fact, they were questions we'd either asked ourselves, or had been asked by friends, or had come up at conference or meetings.

THE AFTERMATH

The furore that resulted after the paper was published in *Wires* led some of us to believe that there was no room in the Women's Liberation Movement for real honesty about something as controversial as sexual politics. We don't think that now, as a fully fledged discussion around sexuality is taking place, as this pamphlet shows.

Sometimes we found it difficult to recognise ourselves in some of the caricatures that emerged from the debate as cadres, an elite, authoritarian. The paper was written by a small group of women who really were in no position to impose anything, except a paper for discussion, upon the Movement. We really thought, when writing the paper, that we were merely expressing commonly held views which were just not usually written down. To some extent we were scapegoated for writing them down.

We were distressed to be accused of being anti-heterosexual women, when one of the major aims of the paper was to start an honest dialogue about what sexual orientation had to do with our politics. We see heterosexuality as an institution of male domination, not a free expression of personal preference. Heterosexuality is forced upon us from babyhood, it is extremely difficult to break away from; but this fact is often dismissed. Believing the personal is political means we cannot separate sexuality off from male supremacy as a politics-free zone.

Lal Covency, Tina Crockett, Al Garthwaite, Sheila Jeffreys, Valerie Sinclair.

Sheila Rowbotham

The Trouble with 'Patriarchy'

In R. Samuel, ed., *People's History and Socialist Theory*, London: Routledge and Kegan Paul, 1981, pp. 364-9 (first published in *New Statesman*, December 1979)

When contemporary feminists began to examine the world from a new perspective, bringing their own experience to bear on their understanding of history and modern society, they found it was necessary to distinguish women's subordination as a sex from class oppression. Inequality between men and women was not just a creation of capitalism: it was a feature of all societies for which we had reliable evidence. It was a separate phenomenon, which needed to be observed in connection with, rather than simply as a response to, changes that occurred in the organisation and control of production. So the term 'patriarchy' was pressed into service – as an analytical tool which might help to describe this vital distinction.

The term has been used in a great variety of ways. 'Patriarchy' has been discussed as an ideology which arose out of men's power to exchange women between kinship groups; as a symbolic male principle; and as the power of the father (its literal meaning). It has been used to express men's control over women's sexuality and fertility; and to describe the institutional structure of male domination. Recently the phrase 'capitalist patriarchy' has suggested a form peculiar to capitalism. Zilla Eisenstein, who has edited an anthology of writings under that heading, defines patriarchy as providing 'the sexual hierarchical ordering of society for political control'.[1]

There was felt to be a need (not confined to feminists) for a wider

---

1. For critical accounts of how the word 'patriarchy' has been used, see: Paul Atkinson, 'The Problem with Patriarchy', *Achilles' Heel*, 2, 1979; Zilla Eisenstein and Heidi Hartmann, *Capitalist Patriarchy and the Case for Socialist Feminism*, London, 1978; Linda Gordon and Allen Hunter, 'Sexual Politics and the New Right', *Radical America*, Nov. 1977 and Feb. 1978; Olivia Harris and Kate Young, 'The Subordination of Women in Cross-cultural Perspective', *Patriarchy Papers*, London, 1976; Roisin McDonough and Rachel Harrison, 'Patriarchy and Relations of Production', in *Feminism and Materialism*, ed. A. Kuhn and A. M. Wolpe, London, 1978; Gayle Rubin, 'The Traffic in Women', in *Towards an Anthropology of Women*, ed. Rayna Reiter, London, 1975; Veronica Beechey, 'On Patriarchy', *Feminist Review*, 3, 1979.

understanding of power relationships and hierarchy than was offered by current Marxist ideas. And with that came the realisation that we needed to resist not only the outer folds of power structures but their inner coils. For their hold over our lives through symbol, myth and archetype would not dissolve automatically with the other bondages, even in the fierce heat of revolution. There had to be an inner psychological and spiritual contest, along with the confrontation and transformation of external power.

However, the word 'patriarchy' presents problems of its own. It implies a universal and historical form of oppression which returns us to biology – and thus it obscures the need to recognise not only biological differences, but also the multiplicity of ways in which societies have defined gender. By focusing upon the bearing and rearing of children ('patriarchy' = the power of the father) it suggests there is a single determining cause of women's subordination. This either produces a kind of feminist base-superstructure model to contend with the more blinkered versions of Marxism, or it rushes us off on the misty quest for the original moment of male supremacy. Moreover, the word leaves us with two separate systems in which a new male/female split is implied. We have patriarchy oppressing women and capitalism oppressing male workers. We have biological reproduction on the one hand and work on the other. We have the ideology of 'patriarchy' opposed to the mode of production, which is seen as a purely economic matter.

'Patriarchy' implies a structure which is fixed, rather than the kaleidoscope of forms within which women and men have encountered one another. It does not carry any notion of how women might act to transform their situation as a sex. Nor does it even convey a sense of how women have resolutely manoeuvred for a better position within the general context of subordination – by shifting for themselves, turning the tables, ruling the roost, wearing the trousers, hen-pecking, gossiping, hustling, or (in the words of a woman I once overheard) just 'going drip, drip at him'. 'Patriarchy' suggests a fatalistic submission which allows no space for the complexities of women's defiance.

It is worth remembering every time we use words like 'class' and 'gender' that they are only being labelled as structures for our convenience, because human relationships move with such complexity and speed that our descriptions freeze them at the point of understanding. Nancy Hartstock[2] recalls Marx's insistence that we

2. See Eisenstein and Hartmann, *op. cit.*

should regard 'every historically developed social form as in fluid movement'; thus we must take into account its 'transient nature not less than its momentary existence'. Within Marxism there is at least a possibility of a dialectical unity of transience and moment. But it seems to me that the concept of 'patriarchy' offers no such prospect. We have stretched its meaning in umpteen different ways, but there is no transience in it at all. It simply refuses to budge.

A word which fails to convey movement is not much help when it comes to examining the differences between the subordination of women, and class. The capitalist is defined by his or her ownership of capital. This is not the same kettle of fish at all as a biological male person. Despite the protestations of employers, their activities could be organised quite differently and, in this sense, the working class carries the possibility of doing without the capitalist and thus of abolishing the hierarchies of class. But a biological male person is a more delicate matter altogether and is not to be abolished (by socialist feminists at least).

It is not sexual difference which is the problem, but the social inequalities of gender – the different kinds of power societies have given to sexual differences, and the hierarchical forms these have imposed on human relationships. Some aspects of male-female relationships are evidently not simply oppressive, but include varying degrees of mutual aid. The concept of 'patriarchy' has no room for such subtleties, however.

Unless we have a sense of these reciprocities and the ways they have changed among different classes, along with the inequalities between men and women, we cannot explain why women have perceived different aspects of their relationship to men to be oppressive at different times. We cannot explain why genuine feelings of love and friendship are possible between men and women, and boys and girls, or why people have acted together in popular movements. In times of revolution (such as the Paris Commune, the early days of Russian communism, or more recent liberation struggles in developing countries), women's public political action has often challenged not only the ruling class, the invader or the coloniser, but also the men's idea of women's role. Less dramatically in everyday life, men's dependence on women in the family, in the community and at work, is as evident as women's subordination – and the two often seem to be inextricably bound together. Some feminists regard this as an elaborate trick, but I think it is precisely within these shifting interstices that women have manoeuvred and resisted. We thus need an approach which can encompass both the conflict and the complementary association between the sexes.

If we could develop an historical concept of sex-gender relationships, this would encompass changing patterns of male control and its congruence or incongruence with various aspects of women's power. It would enable us to delineate the specific shapes of sex-gender relationships within different social relationships, without submerging the experiences of women in those of men, or vice versa. If we stopped viewing patriarchy and capitalism as two separate interlocking systems, and looked instead at how sex-gender as well as class and race relations have developed historically, we could avoid a simple category 'woman' – who must either be a matriarchal stereotype or a hopelessly downtrodden victim, and whose fortunes rise and fall at the same time as all her sisters. We could begin to see women and men born into relationships within families which are not of their making. We could see how their ideas of themselves and other people, their work, habits and sexuality, their participation in organisation, their responses to authority, religion and the state, and the expression of their creativity in art and culture – how all these things are affected by relations in the family as well as by class and race. But sex-gender relationships are clearly not confined to the family (we are not just sex-beings in the family and class-beings in the community, the state and at work): like class relations, they permeate all aspects of life.

Equally, we inherit the historical actions and experience of people in the past through institutions and culture – and the balance of sex-gender relations is as much part of this inheritance as is class. The changes which men and women make within these prevailing limitations need not be regarded simply as a response to the reorganisation of production, not even as a reflection of class struggle. Indeed, we could see these shifts in sex-gender relationships as *contributing* historically towards the creation of suitable conditions for people to make things differently and perceive the world in new ways.

Rosalind Petchesky has argued that

> if we understand that patriarchal kinship relations are not static, but like class relations, are characterised by antagonism and struggle, then we begin to speculate that women's consciousness

and their periodic attempts to resist or change the dominant kinship structures will themselves affect class relations.[3]

Relations between men and women are also characterised by certain reciprocities, so we cannot assume the antagonism is a constant factor. There are times when class or race solidarity are much stronger than sex-gender conflict and times when relations within the family are a source of mutual resistance to class power. Nonetheless, the approach suggested by Petchesky opens up an exciting way of thinking about women's and men's position in the past, through which we can locate sex-gender relations in the family and see how they are present within all other relationships between men and women in society.

However, we need to be cautious about the assumptions we bring to the past. For instance, women have seen the defining features of oppression very differently at different times. Large numbers of children, for example, could be regarded as a sign of value and status, whereas most Western women now would insist on their right to restrict the numbers of children they have, or to remain childless. Feminist anthropologists are particularly aware of the dangers of imposing the values of Western capitalism on women of other cultures. But we can colonise women in the past, too, by imposing modern values.

We also need to be clear about which groups we are comparing in any given society, and to search for a sense of movement within each period. For instance, the possibilities for women among the richer peasantry in the Middle Ages were clearly quite different from those of poor peasants without land. And presumably these were not the same before and after the Black Death. Change – whether for better or worse – does not necessarily go all one way between the classes, nor even between their various sub-strata, and the same is true of changes which varying modes of production have brought to sex-gender relationships. The growth of domestic industry, for example, is usually associated with the control of the father over the family. But it could also alter the domestic division of labour, because women's particular work skills were vital to the family economy at certain times in the production process. This might have made it easier for women in domestic industry to question sexual hierarchy than for peasant women.

Similarly, nineteenth-century capitalism exploited poor women's labour in the factories, isolated middle-class women in

3. See *ibid.*

the home, and forced a growing body of impecunious gentlewomen on to the labour market. Yet at the same time it brought working-class women into large-scale popular movements at work and in the community, in the course of which some of them demanded their rights as a sex while resisting class oppression. Out of domestic isolation, the extreme control of middle-class men over their wives and daughters, and the impoverished dependence of unmarried women, came the first movement of feminists.

An historical approach to sex-gender relations could help us to understand why women, radicalised by contemporary feminism, have found the present division of domestic labour and men's continued hold over women's bodies and minds to be particularly oppressive. These were not really the emphases of nineteenth-century feminism. What then are the specific antagonisms we have encountered within sex-gender relationships? And what possibilities do they imply for change?

It has often been said that as women we have come to know that the personal is 'political' because we have been isolated in the personal sphere. I think this is only half the story. We *were* isolated in the personal sphere, but some of us were hurtled dramatically out of it by the expansion of education and the growth of administrative and welfare work, while some (working-class and black women) were never so luxuriously confined. What is more, modern capitalism has created new forms of political control and social care, and has produced new technologies and methods of mass communication, which have disturbed and shifted the early nineteenth-century division of private and public spheres. As a result, the direct and immediate forms through which men have controlled women have been *both* reinforced *and* undermined. Kinship relations have increasingly become the province of the state (we have to obey certain rules about the way we arrange our private lives in order to qualify for welfare benefits, for example). Contraceptive technology has enabled women to separate sexual pleasure from procreation. And the scope for sexual objectification has grown apace with the development of the visual media. Men are being sold more strenuously than ever the fantasy of controlling the ultimate feminine, just as their hold over real women is being resisted. Women are meanwhile being delivered from the possibility of acting out male-defined fantasy of ultimate femininity in order to compete with other women for men. All the oppressive features of male culture have been thrown into relief and have served to radicalise women: who does the housework, unequal pay and access to jobs, violence in the home, rape, the denial of abortion rights, prostitution, lack of nursery provision, and male-dominated and exclusively heterosexual attitudes towards sex and love.

This convoluted state of affairs has created a new kind of political consciousness in socialist feminism. In tussling with the specifics of sex-gender relations in modern capitalism, feminists have challenged the way we see our identities and experience our bodies, the way we organise work and childcare, and the way we express love and develop thoughts. In other words, they have challenged the basic components of hierarchy to create a vision of society in which sexual difference does not imply subordination and oppression.

Just as the abolition of class power would release people outside the working class, and thus requires their support and involvement, so the movement against hierarchy which is carried in feminism goes beyond the liberation of sex. It contains the possibility of equal relations not only between women and men, but also between men and men, and women and women, and even between adults and children.

Sally Alexander and Barbara Taylor
In Defence of 'Patriarchy'

In R. Samuel, ed., *People's History and Socialist Theory*, London: Routledge and Kegan Paul, 1981, pp. 370-3 (first published in *New Statesman*, December 1979)

The major problem with the theory of patriarchy, Sheila Rowbotham claims, is that it ascribes women's subordination and men's domination to their respective biological roles – a politically dangerous position which can only lead to a call for the abolition of all 'biological male persons'. Feminists must realise, she says, that 'it is not sexual difference which is the problem, but the social inequalities of gender': it is not men we want to eliminate, but male power.

Like Sheila, we are socialist feminists. But we believe that sexual difference *is* the problem, or at least a fundamental part of it. Does that mean that we are busy training for a final day of sexual Armageddon, when all 'biological male persons' will receive their just deserts (castration or annihilation, as we choose at the time)? No doubt every woman has had moments when such a vision seemed attractive, but what we have in mind is (to use Sheila's words) 'a more delicate matter altogether'.

Throughout her article Sheila assumes that sexual difference is a biological given, linked to reproduction. Clearly if it is defined in this way, it is hard to see how it can be changed. However, one of the most important breakthroughs in feminist theory occurred when women began to question this commonsense definition of sex, pushing past all the old assumptions about 'natural' womanhood and manhood to examine how deep the roots of women's oppression really lay. What was needed then, was a theory of gender itself, a new way of thinking about reproduction and sexuality. The search drew some of us towards structural anthropology and psychoanalysis. From a feminist reading of anthropology we learned that the social meaning of maleness and femaleness is constructed through kinship rules which prescribe patterns of sexual dominance and subordination. From psychoanalysis we learned how these kinship rules become inscribed on

Thanks to Rosalind Delmar for her excellent advice on the first draft; and to Gareth Stedman-Jones, Maureen Mackintosh, Carole Furnivall and Jane Caplan.

the unconscious psyche of the female child via the traumatic re-orientation of sexual desire within the Oedipal phase away from the mother and towards the father ('the law of the father'). The two arguments combined, as in Juliet Mitchell's highly influential *Psychoanalysis and Feminism*, provide a powerful account of the 'generation of a patriarchal system that must by definition oppress women'.

This account remains controversial within the women's movement, but it has greatly expanded our theoretical and political horizons. For if the mechanisms by which women's subordination are reproduced are also those which reproduce family structure and gendered individuals, then a revolution to eliminate such subordination would have to extend very widely indeed. It would need to be, as Juliet says, a 'cultural revolution' which not only eliminated social inequalities based on sexual difference, but transformed the meaning of sexuality itself. We would need to learn new ways of being women and men. It is this project, not the annihilation of 'biological male persons', which the theory of patriarchy points towards.

Constructing a theory of patriarchal relations is hazardous, not least because it analyses gender in terms wholly different from those of class. But without a theory of gender relations, any attempt to 'marry' the concepts of sex and class will simply do for theories of sex what marriage usually does for women: dissolve them into the stronger side of the partnership. It was precisely because a Marxist theory of class conflict, however elaborated, could not answer all our questions about sexual conflict that we tried to develop an alternative. If we need to keep the two areas of analysis apart for a time, so be it. Theories are not made all at once.

However, Sheila's own anxiety about this theoretical dualism conceals a greater anxiety about the whole attempt to construct a theory of sexual antagonism. She seems to view any such theory as an iron grid of abstractions placed over the flow of direct experience; and, as an alternative, she appeals to history to answer questions about female subordination which the 'fixed' and 'rigid' categories of theory cannot answer.

As feminist historians, we share Sheila's desire for more research into women's lives and experience. But this is no substitute for a theory of women's oppression. History only answers questions which are put to it: without a framework for these questions we shall founder in a welter of dissociated and contradictory 'facts'. Nor can women's own testimony about their relations with men be taken as unproblematic. Women have dwelt within their oppression at all times, but it is only occasionally that some have become sharply aware of it. Our analysis of women's consciousness must (as Sheila says) explain the periods of quiescence, as well as the times of anger. Simply recording how women behaved or what they said cannot give us this analysis, any more than recording what workers do gives us a theory of class: it is the underlying reality which must be examined.

Finally, Sheila is unhappy with the concept of patriarchy because it seems to discount all the good things which happen between men and women. She reminds us that women love men, that men need women, and that both sexes often find real support in each other, especially in moments of class confrontation – all true (at least of heterosexual women). But does all this loving and needing and solidarising prove there is no general structure of sexual antagonism, only bad times and good times? Does it mean that loving men is unproblematic for women, something to be gratefully accepted rather than critically investigated? Surely not. Learning to love men sexually is a social process, not a natural one, and in a patriarchal society it involves at least as much pain as joy, as much struggle as mutual support. Again, it is the analysis of kinship rules and unconscious mental life – not the study of biology – which helps us to understand how this channelling of desire towards reproductive heterosexuality occurs, and also what some of its costs have been: not only in terms of the systematic repression of homosexual love and lovers in most cultures, but also in terms of 'normal' feminine sexuality. Did not Freud help us to understand that in learning to love men we learn also to subordinate ourselves to them? The ropes which bind women are the hardest to cut, because they are woven with so many of our own desires.

The concept of patriarchy points to a strategy which will eliminate not men, but masculinity, and transform the whole web of psycho-social relations in which masculinity and femininity are formed. It is a position from which we can begin to reclaim for political change precisely those areas of life which are usually deemed biological or natural. It allows us to confront not only the day-to-day social practices through which men exercise power over women, but also mechanisms through which patterns of authority and submission become part of the sexed personality itself – 'the father in our heads', so to speak. It has helped us to think about sexual division – which cannot be understood simply as a by-product of economic class relations or of biology, but which has an independent dynamic that will only be overcome by an independent feminist politics. Finally, it has allowed us to look past our immediate experiences as women to the processes underlying and shaping that experience. For like class, sexual antagonism is not something which can be understood simply by living it: it needs to be analysed with concepts forged for that purpose. The theories which have developed around 'patriarchy' have been the first systematic attempts to provide them.

Further Reading

As our text indicates, we regard Juliet Mitchell's *Psychoanalysis and Feminism*, Harmondsworth, 1975 – a feminist reading of Freud – as a fundamental contribution to the issue of this debate. *Patriarchy Papers*, London, 1976, contains some of the most accessible British contributions to the discussion. We would also refer readers to 'The Unhappy Marriage of Marxism and Feminism: Towards a More Progressive Union', by Heidi I. Hartmann, *Capital and Class*, Summer 1979. As well as the articles cited by Sheila we would recommend – though they are not written from our position – Kate Millett, *Sexual Politics*, London, 1980; and Shulamith Firestone, *The Dialectics of Sex*, London, 1979. Firestone gives a biological reading of social-sexual relations without resorting to a theory of patriarchy.

Sheila Rowbotham, Lynne Segal and Hilary Wainwright

The Insights of Feminism

From Sheila Rowbotham, Lynne Segal and Hilary Wainwright, *Beyond the Fragments*, London: The Merlin Press, 1979, pp. 12-14

The women's movement, arising as it does to resist an oppression which comes from inequalities of power and confidence in interpersonal relations, and from a hierarchical division of labour, has been intensely sensitive and self-conscious about inequality and hierarchy in the creating of its organizational forms. In this process the women's movement has made important insights which are directly relevant to how we organize as socialists. Moreover, again because of the form of oppression which it confronts, the women's movement has radically extended the scope of politics and, with this, has changed who is involved in politics and how. Much of the oppression of women takes place 'in private', in areas of life considered 'personal'. The causes of that oppression are social and economic, but these causes could only be revealed and confronted when women challenged the assumptions of their personal life, of who does the housework, of the way children are brought up, the quality of our friendships, even the way we make love and with whom. These were not normally the subject of politics. Yet these are the problems of everyday life, the problems about which women talk most to other women (and about which many men would talk more if they could). When the women's movement made these issues part of socialist politics, it began to break down the barriers which have kept so many people, especially women, out of politics. Before the women's movement, socialist politics, like all other sorts of politics, seemed something separate from everyday life, something unconnected with looking after children, worrying about the meals and the housework, finding ways of enjoying yourself with your friends, and so on. It was something professional, for men and among men, for the shop steward or the party activist. The activities of the women's movement have begun to change that as far as women are concerned. But it's meant a different way of organizing, a way of organizing which does not restrict political activity to 'the professional'.

The insights of the women's movement then do not simply concern the issue of 'sexism' in a socialist organization. They could contribute in general ways to creating a more democratic, more truly popular and more effective socialist movement than was possible before.

SECTION TWO:

Women and Men

In Billy Wilder's film *Some Like it Hot*, Tony Curtis, dressed as a woman, staggers along a station platform in a tight skirt and high heels. 'How', he says, 'do they walk in these things? They must be a whole different sex.' Exactly how, and why, women differ from men (or men from women) is explored both here and in the following section on female sexuality. Within this context, however, what concerns us is the nature of, and the reasons for, the psychological differences between the sexes. While not conceding that innate psychological differences between men and women exist, it has to be acknowledged that in our culture, as indeed in all others, society has distinct expectations of how men and women will behave, and the aptitudes and abilities which each sex possesses.

The crucial question about male and female behaviour is the extent to which it is determined by biology. Freud's famous article 'Some Psychical Consequences of the Anatomical Distinction between the Sexes'[1] was among the first coherent attempts to establish a relationship between male and female biology and the psychological characteristics of the sexes. Most particularly, as far as women were concerned, Freud argued that their lack of a penis leads them to feel themselves 'unfairly treated' and to re-orientate their sexuality from mother to father, from women to men. Inevitably, such an account of female psycho-sexual development has not been widely accepted by feminists, who argue that Freud incorrectly assumes that socially created differences between the sexes that are present in patriarchal society must be a feature of male/female relationships in all cultures and historical epochs. Despite Juliet Mitchell's attempt, in *Psychoanalysis and Feminism*,[2] to rescue Freud from his feminist critics, the consensus among feminists is that although Freud's work represents a significant advance in the study of human psycho-sexual development he consistently confuses biological sex differences and socially constructed gender.[3]

1. In *On Sexuality*, vol. 7, Pelican Freud Library, Harmondsworth: Penguin, 1977.
2. Juliet Mitchell, *Psychoanalysis and Feminism*, Harmondsworth: Penguin, 1975.
3. An excellent account of Freud, Mitchell and feminist debates on psychoanalysis is given in Michèle Barrett's *Women's Oppression Today*, London: Verso, 1980, pp. 42-83.

But if Freud did this, he was neither the first, nor the last, since the problem of studying the behaviour of men and women (or girls and boys) and distinguishing between their innate and learned behaviour consistently confronts any researcher. The nature/nurture debate raises its head yet again, with some feminists arguing an essentialist position (that women *are* different from men) while others assert that all differences between the sexes are the result of socialisation. The only fixed point in these debates is, as Janet Sayers points out, that physical differences do exist between men and women and that these differences *may* create different psychological characteristics in the two sexes.[4] Some authors – perhaps most notoriously Corinne Hutt in *Males and Females*[5] – argue that marked innate psychological differences exist between the sexes: that almost from birth boys are more aggressive, combative and competent at abstract thought than girls, who are generally the talkative and nurturant sex. Hutt's picture of sexual differences immediately conjures up a vision of the sexes as predestined to play out the childish game of doctors (played by boys) and nurses (played by girls) for the rest of their lives.

Accounts such as Hutt's, which suggest marked differences in aptitudes and abilities between the sexes, have been sharply criticised by numerous psychologists. Among the many important contributions to this debate, that by Maccoby and Jacklin in their *The Psychology of Sex Differences* is perhaps the most comprehensive.[6] Maccoby and Jacklin argue that marked psychological differences between the sexes are few: the great majority of men and women are very similar in terms of their intelligence, spatial and verbal aptitude and aggression. A small number of each sex has markedly pronounced psychological characteristics of the stereotypical kind, but these Janes and Tarzans are few in number.

What emerges, therefore, from studies such as that by Maccoby and Jacklin is that the sexes are very similar in terms of their innate characteristics. Yet men and women are socially subject to different kinds of expectations, although both sexes are expected to direct their sexual desires towards members of the opposite sex. As numerous feminists have pointed out, men and women are socialised in different ways, brought up in distinct worlds, and then expected, in early adult life, to direct their emotional attentions, loyalties and commitments towards a member of that amazing

4. Janet Sayers, 'Anatomy is Destiny: Variations on a Theme', *Women's Studies International Quarterly*, vol. 2, 1979, pp. 19-32.
5. Corinne Hutt, *Males and Females*, Harmondsworth: Penguin, 1972.
6. E. Maccoby and C. Jacklin, *The Psychology of Sex Differences*, Stanford: Stanford University Press, 1974.

'whole different sex'. Inevitably, tensions and difficulties result from the isolation in monogamy and the nuclear family of two adults whose acquaintance and knowledge of the opposite sex may be very limited – and perhaps confined exclusively to their own relationships with parents or siblings. The problems that can develop from this casting aside on the desert island of monogamy and the nuclear family are suggested in the extract from Mirra Komarovsky's *Blue-collar Marriage* in the section on Domestic Life and Labour. Suffice to say here that intimacy and understanding between husband and wife are – hardly surprisingly – far from automatic or common in our culture. Moreover, the lack of familiarity with other patterns of adult sexual relationships produces a situation in which men and women easily fall into familiar patterns: husbands become surrogate fathers, whose duty is to maintain and exercise authority, while wives become the providers of all those services once provided by the mother.

Within marriage, and what passes, in our culture, for 'normal' heterosexuality, it is easy to see the reproduction from one generation to the next of expectations about men and women which stress women's supposed innate capacity to nurture. In her influential work *The Reproduction of Mothering*, Nancy Chodorow has argued:

> Women, as mothers, produce daughters with mothering capacities and the desire to mother. The capacities and needs are built into and grow out of the mother-daughter relationship itself. By contrast, women as mothers (and men as not-mothers) produce sons whose nurturant capacities and needs have been systematically curtailed and repressed. This prepares men for their less affective later family role, and for primary participation in the impersonal extra-familial world of work and public life. The sexual and familial division of labor in which women mother and are more involved in interpersonal, affective relationships than men produces in daughters and sons a division of psychological capacities which leads them to reproduce this sexual and familial division of labor.[7]

Chodorow's very powerful argument is that little will change, let alone improve, in heterosexual relationships, until men learn to nurture and care for children in the same way as women. Chodorow therefore stresses, as many feminists have done, the

7. Nancy Chodorow, *The Reproduction of Mothering*, Berkeley: University of California Press, 1978, p. 7.

positive psychological characteristics of women's biological role: that is, that caring for children is a good thing, and an activity too long devalued (or not valued at all) by male society. If men learned to acquire more expressive and nurturant characteristics, then:

> This would reduce men's needs to guard their masculinity and their control of social and cultural spheres which treat and define women as secondary and powerless, and would help women to develop the autonomy which too much embeddedness in relationship has often taken from them.[8]

Whether or not this change alone would radically improve the understanding between the sexes is a moot point, since it presupposes an ideal of mothering that is always committed and nurturant and a view of men which over-emphasises their supposed aggressive and assertive characteristics.[9] Nevertheless, there can be little doubt that any diminution in our present cultural stereotypes of masculinity and femininity would contribute to greater mutual understanding by men and women.

8. *Ibid*, p. 218.
9. A full discussion of *The Reproduction of Mothering* can be found in *Signs*, vol. 6, no. 3, Spring 1981, pp. 482-514.

Ann Oakley

The Politics of 'Sex Differences' Research

From Ann Oakley, *Subject Women*, London: Fontana
Paperbacks, 1982, pp. 60-2

A curious relationship between the size of people's feet, their
sex, and whether they are left- or right-handed has been
discovered by American researchers. After measuring the foot
sizes of 150 individuals, they were able to show that there was
a strong association between right-handedness and a right foot
bigger than the left – and vice versa – in men. In women, the
reverse is true: right-handed women tend to have bigger left feet,
and vice versa. [*Sunday Times*, 25 June 1978]

Unless this research were prompted by some charitable intention
on the part of shoe-manufacturers and retailers to sell different-
sized shoes to accommodate people's different-sized left and right
feet, it is difficult to see what relevance it could have to any aspect
of social or personal life. Like most of the 'scientific' research on
sex and gender differences on which this chapter has had to draw,
it is based on the assumption that sex differences matter – and that
they matter more than sex similarities. In this way scientific work
starts from and reinforces the status quo of everyday beliefs about
the roles of men and women. In the closing section of this chapter
I add some important caveats to the 'evidence' summarized in the
preceding pages.

Firstly, the search for sex differences inevitably serves to
magnify them and 'obscures the fact that they may be the
conveniently stereotyped extremes of broadly overlapping poten-
tialities and functions' (Star, 1979, p. 63; see also Lloyd, 1976).
Even in the case of biological sex polarity, around half a per cent
of the population is markedly intersexual (Overzier, 1963). The
large overlap between the sexes on all characteristics of personality and behaviour is veiled by the common strategy of investigating
some trait (e.g. cyclical mood variation) in single groups. Where
dual sex groups of subjects are taken, some 'sex differences' are
bound to occur for statistical reasons. In one longitudinal study in
which 35 categories of behaviour were rated yearly for 57 females

and 58 males, 7 per cent of 442 female-male differences achieved the 5 per cent level of significance. This is hardly greater than the number of 'findings' that would have been expected to occur by chance (Tresemer, 1975).

Secondly, socialization processes are quite sufficient to account for most of the observed and 'documented' sex differences. The socialization effect cannot be dismissed even from research on neonates, one of the two fields to which sex differences researchers have most hopefully looked for 'pure' data (the other field is the cross-cultural one). One striking omission is that much of this research does not control for the impact of circumcision, which is an injury inflicted on 80-90 per cent of North American male babies with relevant identifiable behavioural consequences in the direction of altered arousal levels, more wakefulness and more irritability (Richards et al., 1976).

Thirdly, much sex differences research is conducted on the assumption that conclusions about human behaviour may be drawn from studies of animal behaviour. Such extrapolations ignore (a) the importance of learning in humans, (b) the much greater complexity of humans' verbal communication, and (c) the tremendous extent to which humans are able to manipulate their environment.

Fourthly, biology is not a 'given', a cultural constant. The biological body and its 'natural' divisions are not perceived in the same way in all cultures, or by different social groups within the same culture (S. Ardener, 1978; see also E. Ardener, 1971, 1977; Williams, 1975). One reason why the nature versus nurture debate is outmoded, in other words, is because nurture affects nature.

Last, but by no means least, the status quo that much scientific research on sex differences claims to discover is one that legitimizes the social inferiority of women. Jessie Bernard asks:

How does it happen that so much is made of the fact that the blood of males has more androgen than that of females, but nothing is made of the fact that it also has more uric acid? And how does it happen that the net effect of the vast corpus of research leads to the conclusion that men are superior to women on all the variables that are highly valued in our society, namely: muscular or kinetic strength, competitiveness, power, need for achievement, and autonomy? In brief, the components of the archetypal macho variable, offensive aggressiveness? These are the variables that interest men. These are the variables they judge one another by. These are the variables that are rewarded in our society. [Bernard, 1975, p. 10][1]

Among the stimuli within the scientific community that led the debate about sex differences to assume the form it did in the late 1970s were: (1) the counting of chromosomes first made possible by the work of Tjio and Levan in 1956; (2) the development of the radio-immunoassay method of measuring body hormones in the late 1960s; (3) the demonstration of cellular uptake of radioactively labelled oestrogen in individual brain cells in the early 1960s (Michael and Glascock, 1963), which paved the way for speculations about the hormonal basis of adult gender differences. These can hardly be considered to be completely accidental discoveries. They occurred in the political context of a sexist medical-scientific community with a shared ambience and shared standards of rewarded achievement (Kuhn, 1962), and were publicized in a society in which the position of women had come, once more, to be regarded as something of a riddle.[2] In the nineteenth century, a nascent feminist uneasiness produced scientific theories of great biological simplicity. In the 1900s, the era of the suffragettes, a concern with the relative intelligences of men and women flourished. Today, the issue is one of the origin of the present gender role system. From the emphasis on cultural factors evident in the 1950s and 1960s, we have moved through the middle ground of an interactionist line back towards outright biological determinism as the assertiveness of women shows no sign of abating. For, as Crook (1970) has pointed out, in situations of social change, biological explanations may assume the role of an ethical code akin in their moral persuasiveness to religion. They provide powerful, easily understood arguments about the undesirability of change by fuelling a retreatist emphasis on the immutability of the natural world.

1. Those who make this observation tend to be female. Lehrke (1973) notes that, of those researchers accepting the hypothesis of greater male variability in intelligence, all have been males, whereas all who have rejected it have been females. The issue is not one of bias, but one of the contrasting perspectives that 'opposite' sexes are bound to bring to the same question.
2. The same is true of research on ethnic differences (Lynn, 1973).

References

Ardener, E. (1971), *Social Anthropology and Language*, London: Tavistock.

Ardener, E. (1977), 'The Anthropologist as Translator of Culture', paper delivered to the Wenner Gren Symposium on *Focus on Linguistics*, Burg Wartenstein, Austria.

Ardener, S., ed. (1975), *Perceiving Women*, London: Malaby Press.

Ardener, S. (1978), 'Introduction: the Nature of Women in Society', in Ardener, ed.

Ardener, S., ed. (1978), *Defining Females*, London: Croom Helm.

Bernard, J. (1975), *Women, Wives, Mothers*, Chicago: Aldine.

Crook, J. H. (1970), 'Introduction – Social Behaviour and Ethology', in J. H. Crook, ed., *Social Behaviour in Birds and Mammals*, London: Academic Press.

Hubbard, R., Henifin, M. S. and Fried, B. (1979), *Women Looking at Biology Looking at Women*, Boston, Mass.: G. K. Hall and Co.

Kuhn, T. (1962), *The Structure of Scientific Revolutions*, Chicago: University Press.

Lehrke, R. G. (1973), 'Sex Linkage: a Biological Basis for Greater Male Variability in Intelligence', in Osborne *et al.*, eds.

Lloyd, B. (1976), 'Social Responsibility and Research on Sex Differences', in Lloyd and Archer, eds.

Lloyd, B. and Archer, J., eds. (1976), *Exploring Sex Differences*, London: Academic Press.

Lynn, R. (1973), 'Ethnic and Racial Differences in Intelligence: International Comparisons', in Osborne *et al.*, eds.

Michael, R. P. and Glascock, R. F. (1963), 'The Distribution of C^{14}- and H^3-labelled Oestrogens in the Brain', *Proceedings of the Fifth (1961) International Congress of Biochemistry*, 9, p. 1137.

Millman, M. and Kanter, R. M., eds. (1975), *Another Voice: Feminist Perspectives on Social Life and Social Science*, New York: Anchor Books.

Osborne, R. T., Noble, C. E. and Wehl, N., eds. (1973), *Human Variation: The Biopsychology of Age, Race and Sex*, London: Academic Press.

Overzier, C. (1963), *Intersexuality*, London: Academic Press.

Richards, M. P. M., Bernal, J. F. and Brackbill, Y. (1976), 'Early Behavioural Differences: Gender or Circumcision?', *Developmental Psychobiology*, 9, no. 1, pp. 89-95.

Star, S. L. (1979), 'The Politics of Right and Left: Sex Differences in Hemispheric Brain Asymmetry', in Hubbard *et al.*, eds.

Tjio, J. H. and Levan, A. (1956), 'The Chromosome Number of Man', *Hereditas*, 42, pp. 1-6.

Tresemer, D. (1975), 'Assumptions Made about Gender Roles', in Millman and Kanter, eds.

Williams, D. (1975), 'Brides of Christ', in Ardener, ed.

Jean Baker Miller

Ties to Others

From Jean Baker Miller, *Toward a New Psychology of Women*, Harmondsworth: Penguin Books, 1979, chapter 8 (first published in 1976)

Male society, by depriving women of the right to its major 'bounty' – that is, development according to the male model – overlooks the fact that women's development *is* proceeding, but on another basis. One central feature is that women stay with, build on, and develop in a context of attachment and affiliation with others. Indeed, women's sense of self becomes very much organized around being able to make and then to maintain affiliations and relationships. Eventually, for many women the threat of disruption of an affiliation is perceived not as just a loss of a relationship but as something closer to a total loss of self.

Such psychic structuring can lay the groundwork for many problems. Depression, for example, which is related to one's sense of the loss of affiliation with another(s), is much more common in women, although it certainly occurs in men.

What has not been recognized is that this psychic starting point contains the possibilities for an entirely different (and more advanced) approach to living and functioning – very different, that is, from the approach fostered by the dominant culture. In it, affiliation is valued as highly as, or more highly than, self-enhancement. Moreover, it allows for the emergence of the truth; that for everyone – men as well as women – individual development proceeds *only* by means of affiliation. At the present time, men are not as prepared to *know* this. This proposition requires further explanation. Let us start with some common observations and examples and then return to unravel this complex, but basic, issue.

Paula, a married woman with children ... had been raised to make a relationship with a man 'who would make her happy', and she had organized her life around serving his needs. Most of her sense of identity and almost all of her sense of value rested on doing so. She believed that Bill 'made her valuable', even though, in fact, few could surpass her ability to run a big household and respond to everyone's needs. As time went on, she felt some diminution in her central importance to Bill. As this feeling increased, she doubled her efforts to respond to and serve him and his interests, seeking to bind him to her more deeply. The actual things she did were not in themselves important to her. (In fact, she accomplished what she set out to do with great ease and efficiency.) They counted only as they produced an inner sense that Bill would be attached to her intensely and permanently, and that this, in turn, would make her worthwhile. Thus, her successful life activity did not bring satisfaction in itself; it brought satisfaction only insofar as it brought Bill's interest and concern.

When Paula's efforts did not produce the result she was after, she became depressed, although she did not know why. She was filled with feelings that she was 'no good', that she 'didn't matter', that 'nothing mattered'. She felt Bill did not care enough, but she could not document convincing evidence for this feeling. He was fulfilling his role as a husband and father according to the usual standards; in fact he was 'a better husband than most', said Paula. This factor, of course, made her feel even more 'crazy'. She *knew* Bill cared, but she could not *feel* that he did somehow. She became persuaded then that there must be something terribly wrong with *her*. At the same time, none of the worthwhile things she did, provided her with any satisfaction at all.

It is important to note here that Paula was not 'dependent', at least in the meaning usually implied by that term. In fact, she 'took care' of Bill and their children in many ways. It is rather that Paula's whole existence 'depended on' Bill's word that she existed or that her existence mattered.

Paula, like many depressed patients, was a very active, effective person. But underlying her activity was an inner goal: that the significant other person – in this case Bill – must affirm and confirm her. Without his affirmation, she became immobilized, she felt like no one at all. What did it matter how she thought of herself? Such words had no meaning.

Even women who are very accomplished 'in the real world' carry with them a similar sort of underlying structure. One woman, Barbara, holds a high academic appointment. In discussion she is a rigorous and independent thinker. Yet she struggles with an inner feeling that all of her accomplishment is not worthwhile unless there is another person there to make it so. For her, that other person must be a man.

Beatrice, a very successful business woman who could 'sell' and persuade shrewd bargainers who intimidated many men, used to ask, 'But what does it all mean if there isn't a man who cares about me?' Indeed, when there was, she found her activities alive and stimulating. When there was not, she became depressed. All of her successes became meaningless, devoid of interest. She was still the same person doing the same things but she could not 'feel them' in the same way. She felt empty and worthless.

Kate, a woman who was actively working for women's development, was sophisticated in her understanding of women's situation. At certain times she would become acutely aware of her need for others and condemn herself for it. 'See, I'm not so advanced at all. I'm as bad as I always was. Just like a woman.'

While Barbara and Kate did not become depressed, they felt the same underlying factor operating. Depression is used here only as an illustration of one end result of this factor. There are many other negative consequences.

HOW AFFILIATION WORKS

All of the women cited offer hints of the role that affiliations with other people play for women. We see the kinds of problems that can result when all affiliations, as we have so far known them, grow out of the basic domination-subordination model.

According to psychological theory, the women discussed above might be described as 'dependent' (needing others 'too much') or immature in several ways (not developed past a certain early stage of separation and individuation or not having attained autonomy). I would suggest instead that while these women do face a problem, one that troubles them greatly, the problem arises from the dominant role that affiliations have been made to play in women's lives. Women are, in fact, being 'punished' for making affiliations central in their lives.

We all begin life deeply attached to the people around us. Men, or boys, are encouraged to move out of this state of existence – in which they and their fate are intimately intertwined in the lives and fate of other people. Women are encouraged to remain in this state but, as they grow, to transfer their attachment to a male figure.

Boys are rewarded for developing other aspects of themselves. These other factors – power or skills – gradually begin to displace some of the importance of affiliations and eventually to supersede them. There is no question that women develop and change too. In an inner way, however, the development does not displace the value accorded attachments to others. The suggestion here is that the parameters of the female's development are not the same as the male's and that the same terms do not apply. Women can be highly developed and still give great weight to affiliations.

Here again, women are geared all their lives to be the 'carriers' of the basic necessity for human communion. Men can go a long distance away from fully recognizing this need because women are so groomed to 'fill it in' for them. But there is another side: women are also more thoroughly prepared to move toward more advanced, more affiliative ways of living – and less wedded to the dangerous ways of the present. For example, aggression will get you somewhere in this society if you are a man; it may get you quite far indeed if you are one of the few lucky people. But if you continue to be directly aggressive, let us say in pursuit of what seem to be your rights or needs as a man, you will at some time find that it will get you into trouble too. (Other inequalities such as class and race play an important part in this picture.) However, you will probably find this out somewhat later, *after* you have already built up a belief in the efficacy of aggression; you already believe it is important to your sense of self. By then it is hard to give up the push toward aggression and the belief in its necessity. Moreover, it is still rewarded in some measure: you can find places to get some small satisfaction and applause for it, even if it is only from friends in the local bar, by identifying with the Sunday football players, or by pushing women around. To give it up altogether can seem like the final degradation and loss – loss especially of manhood, sexual identification. In fact, if events do not go your way you may be inclined to increase the aggression in the hope that you can force situations. This attempt can and often does enlarge aggression into violence, either individual or group. It is even the underlying basis of national policy, extending to the threat of war and war itself.

Instead, one can, and ultimately must, place one's faith in others, in the context of being a social being, related to other human beings, in their hands as well as one's own. Women learn very young that they must rest primarily on this faith. They cannot depend on their own individual development, achievement, or power. If they try, they are doomed to failure; they find this out early.

Men's only hope lies in affiliation, too, *but* for them it can *seem* an impediment, a loss, a danger, or at least second best. By contrast, affiliations, relationships, make women feel deeply satisfied, fulfilled, 'successful', free to go on to other things.

It is not that men are not concerned about relationships, or that men do not have deep yearnings for affiliation. Indeed, this is exactly what people in the field of psychodynamics are constantly finding – evidence of these needs in men as well as in women, deep *under the surface* of social appearance. This has been said in many different ways. One common formulation states, for example, that men search all their lives for their mothers. I do not think that it is a mother *per se* that they seek. I do think men are longing for an affiliative mode of living – one that would not have to mean going back to mother if one could find a way to go on to greater human communion. Men have deprived themselves of this mode, left it with women. Most important, they have made themselves really unable to *believe* in it. It is true that the time with their mothers was the time when they could really believe in and rely on affiliation. As soon as they start to grow in the male mold, they are supposed to give up this belief and even this desire. Men are led to cast out this faith, even to condemn it in themselves, and build their their lives on something else. *And they are rewarded for doing so.*

Practically everyone now bemoans Western man's sense of alienation, lack of community, and inability to find ways of organizing society for human ends. We have reached the end of the road that is built on the set of traits held out for male identity – advance at any cost, pay any price, drive out all competitors, and kill them if necessary. The opportunity for the full exercise of such manly virtues was always available only to the very few, but they were held out as goals and guidelines for all men. As men strove to define themselves by these ideas, they built their psychic organizations around this striving.

It may be that we had to arrive at a certain stage of 'mastery' over the physical environment or a certain level of technology, to see not only the limits but the absolute danger of this kind of social organization. On the other hand, it may be that we need never have come this long route in the first place; perhaps it has been a vast, unnecessary detour. It now seems clear we have arrived at a point from which we must return to a basis of faith in affiliation – and not only faith but recognition that it is a requirement for the existence of human beings. The basis for what seem the absolutely essential next steps in Western history if we are to survive is already available.

A most basic social advance can emerge through women's outlook, through women putting forward women's concerns. Women have already begun to do so. Here, again, it is not a question of innate biological characteristics. It is a question of the kind of psychological structuring that is encompassed differentially by each sex at this time in our development as a society of human beings – and a question of who can offer the motivation and direction for moving on from here.

The central point here is that women's great desire for affiliation is both a fundamental strength, essential for social advance and at the same time the inevitable source of many of women's current problems. That is, while women have reached for and already found a psychic basis for a more advanced social existence, they are not able to act fully and directly on this valuable basis in a way that would allow it to flourish. Accordingly, they have not been able to cherish or even recognize this valuable strength. On the contrary, when women act on the basis of this underlying psychological motive, they are usually led into subservience. That is, the only forms of affiliation that have been available to women are subservient affiliations. In many instances, the search for affiliation can lead women to a situation that creates serious emotional problems. Many of these are then labeled neuroses and other such names.

But what is most important is to see that even so-called neuroses can, and most often do, contain within them the starting points, the searching for a more advanced form of existence. The problem has been that women have been seeking affiliations that are impossible to attain under the present arrangements, but in order to conduct the search women have been willing to sacrifice whole parts of themselves. And so women have concluded, as we so readily do, that we must be wrong or, in modern parlance, 'sick'.

THE SEARCH FOR ATTACHMENT – 'NEUROSES'

We have raised two related topics: one is social and political, the other more psychological. One is the question of how women can evolve forms of affiliation which will advance women's development and help women to build on this strength to effect real change in the real world. Secondly, until we accomplish this task – and along the way – can we understand more about the psychological events of our lives? Can we better understand why we suffer? At the very least, we may be able to stop undermining ourselves by condemning our strengths.

In the attempt to understand the situation further we can return to some of the women mentioned at the beginning of this chapter. They all expressed a common theme: the lack of ability really to value and credit their own thoughts, feelings, and actions. It is as if they have lost a full sense of satisfaction in the use of themselves and all of their own resources – or rather, never had the full right to do so in the first place. As Beatrice put it, there is the sense 'that there has to be that other person there'. Alone, her being and her doing do not have their full meaning; she becomes dry, empty, devoid of good feeling. It is not that Beatrice needs someone else to reflect herself back to her. (She knew she was, in fact, an excellent and accurate judge herself.) Her need seems even more basic than that. Unless there is another person present, the entire event – the thought, the feeling, the accomplishment, or whatever it may be – lacks pleasure and significance. It is not simply that she feels like half a person, lacking total satisfaction and wanting another person, but still able to take some satisfaction from her own half. It is like being no person at all – at least no person that matters. As soon as she can believe she is using herself *with* someone else and *for* someone else, her own self moves into action and seems satisfying and worthwhile.

The women referred to in this chapter are not so-called 'symbiotic' or other immature types of personalities. (Such terms, incidentally, may well require re-examination in relation to women.) In fact, they are very highly developed and able people who could not possibly be categorized in such a way. Nor, on a more superficial level, do phrases like 'seeking approval' or 'being afraid of disapproval', really cover the situation, although these factors play a part.

Their shared belief that one needs another person in a very particular way manifests itself in different ways for different people. In one form it leads readily into depression. The experiences of the women described here may thus provide some further clues to depression, may help us understand some aspects of it. While Paula and Beatrice did suffer depression, for other women there are different manifestations.

Everyone in the various psychological fields would probably readily admit that we do not fully understand depression (or fully understand anything else for that matter). Depression, in general, seems to relate to feeling blocked, unable to do or get what one wants. The question is: what is it that one really wants? Here we find difficult and complicated questions that do not seem to 'make sense'. On the surface it may even seem that a person has what she wants. It often turns out, however, that, instead, she has what she had been led to believe she should want. (For many young middle-class women it was the house in the suburbs, a nice husband, and children.) How then to discover what one is really after? And why does one feel so useless and hopeless?

Beatrice's experience may offer some understanding on this point. She eventually said that she sought to bind the important other person to her absolutely, and she wanted a guarantee of that bond. She was anything but a passive, dependent, or helpless woman; but all of her activity was directed to this goal, which she believed she needed to attain. While she did not really need *that* kind of relationship, she was not convinced of it internally. (Often her activity in search of this goal took on a very forceful and manipulative character. Although the goal was usually pursued covertly and obscured from herself, it was felt very distinctly by those around her.)

Beatrice had developed the inner belief that everything she does feels right *only* if she does it for that other person, not for herself. Above all, she had lost the sense that the fulfillment of her needs or desires could *ever* bring her satisfaction. It is almost as if she had lost the inner 'system' that registers events and tells her whether they make *her* happy or satisfied. The 'registering' of what feels like satisfaction has shifted; it now comes only through her sense that she can make the other person remain in a particular kind of relationship to her. Only then can she feel strong and good. (In more complex depressions, like Beatrice's, it may not be the other person *per se* that one desires to bind but the image of the *kind* of relationship one believes one needs. For example, women whose children have grown up may not want to retain the individual children but they feel they must have the mother-child kind of relationship. In fact, one may not really need such a relationship; but the belief is strong, and a person who has spent a long time organizing her psyche on that basis will not easily relinquish the idea. Further, she has long since lost the belief that she can really have any other kind of relationship.)

Another facet of Beatrice's problem was the large amount of anger generated. To compound the problem, like many other women, she had great difficulty in allowing herself to recognize her own wrath, much less express it. Even so, she was likely to become furious if the other person did anything that seemed to threaten to alter the bond. It seems clear that being in such a position is very conducive to rage. How could she not get angry at that other person to whom she had given so much control over her life? But Beatrice would become even more depressed because of the anger. In spite of her deep unhappiness, she could not really believe that there was any other possible way to live.

Like Beatrice, people liable to depression are often very active, very forceful; but the activity must be conceived of as benefiting others. Furthermore, it is organized around a single pursuit – seeking affiliation is the only form that seems possible: 'I will do anything if only you will let me stay in this kind of relationship to you.'

Some other aspects of depression may help to explain these points. It has long been recognized that there are so-called paradoxical depressions, which are most often observed in men. They occur after a man who has been competent receives a promotion or other advance that presumably should make him happy and even more effective. Such depressions may reflect the fact that the individual is forced to admit to increased self-determination and to admit that he, himself, is responsible for what happens. He is not doing it for someone else or under the direction of someone else. Women do not get promotion depressions so commonly because they do not get many promotions. Nonetheless, in Beatrice, who could accomplish prodigious feats as long as she had at least one person in a position superior to her, a very similar dynamic was at work. She would absolutely never let herself have the top job, although several had been offered to her.

A similar process may be at work in a phenomenon seen in psychoanalysis. It has long been recognized that people sometimes have what are called 'negative therapeutic reactions'. This means that they make a major gain and then seem to get worse after it. Bonime has suggested that many of these reactions are in fact depressions and that they occur when a person has made a major step toward taking on responsibility and direction in her/his own life.[1] The person has seen that she/he can move out of a position of inability and can exert effective action in her/his own behalf, but then becomes frightened of the implications of that new vision; for example, it would mean the person really doesn't need the old dependent relationships. She/he then pulls back and refuses to follow through on the new course. Such retreats occur in men as well as women, but for women this situation is an old story, very similar to what goes on in life.

The significance for women of these two examples may be this: 'If I can bring myself to admit that I can take on the determination and direction of my own life rather than give it over to others, can I exist with safety? With satisfaction? And who will ever love me, or even tolerate me, if I do that?' Only after these questions are confronted, at least to some degree, can one begin to ask the even more basic question: what do I really want? And this question, too, will not always be answered easily. Most women have been led too far from thinking in those terms. It often takes strenuous exploration, but usually it turns out that there are deeply felt needs that are not being met at all. Only then can one begin to evaluate these desires and to see the possibility of acting to bring about their attainment; *and* only then does one realize that there can be satisfaction in such a course. Moreover, it then becomes apparent

1. Walter Bonime, 'The Psychodynamics of Neurotic Depression', in Silvano Asieti, ed., *American Handbook of Psychiatry*, vol. 3, New York: Basic Books, 1966.

that one does not need or want the kind of binding one believed was so essential.[2] Since the process described in this paragraph is so often thwarted, it seems obvious why women are set up for depression.

Many complications come in to compound the situation for women, as they did for Beatrice. If one believes that safety and satisfaction lie in relationships structured in particular kinds of bonds, then one keeps trying to push people and situations into these forms. Thus, Beatrice was constantly working very actively at getting a man into this kind of relationship. She had a program for action, the only one she was able to construct, but the program created her own bondage. This is why psychological troubles are the worst kind of slavery – one becomes enlisted in creating one's own enslavement – one uses so much of one's own energies to create one's own defeat.

All forms of oppression encourage people to enlist in their own enslavement. For women, especially, this enlistment inevitably takes psychological forms and often ends in being called neuroses and other such things. (Men, too, suffer psychological troubles, as we all know; and the dynamic for them is related, but it *does* take a different path.)

In this sense, psychological problems are not so much caused by the unconscious as by deprivations of full consciousness. If we had paths to more valid consciousness all along through life, if we had more accurate terms in which to conceptualize (at each age level) what was happening, if we had more access to the emotions produced, and if we had ways of knowing our own true options – if we had all these things, we could make better programs for action. Lacking full consciousness, we create out of what is available. For women only distorted conceptions about what is happening and what a person can and should be have been provided. (The conceptions available for men may be judged as even more distorted. The possible programs for action and the subsequent dynamic are, however, different.)

Even the very words, the terms in which we conceptualize, reflect the prevailing consciousness – not necessarily the truth about what is happening. This is true in the culture at large and in psychological theory too. We need a terminology that is not based on inappropriate carryovers from men's situation. Even a word like *autonomy*, which many of us have used and liked, may need

2. Jean B. Miller and Stephen M. Sonnenberg, 'Depression Following Psychotic Episodes: a Response to the Challenge of Change?', *Journal of the American Academy of Psychoanalysis*, 1 (1973), pp. 253-70.

revamping for women. It carries the implication – and for woman therefore the threat – that one should be able to pay the price of giving up affiliations in order to become a separate and self-directed individual. In reality, when women have struggled through to develop themselves as strong, independent individuals they did, and do, threaten many relationships, relationships in which the other person will not tolerate a self-directed woman. But, when men are autonomous, there is no reason to think that their relationships will be threatened. On the contrary, there is reason to believe that self-development will win them relationships. Others – usually women – will rally to them and support them in their efforts, and other men will respect and admire them. Since women have to face very different consequences, the word *autonomy* seems possibly dangerous; it is a word derived from men's development, not women's.

There is a further sense in which the automatic transfer of a concept like autonomy as a goal for women can cause problems. Women are quite validly seeking something more complete than autonomy as it is defined for men, a fuller not a lesser ability to encompass relationships to others, simultaneous with the fullest development of oneself. Thus, many of our terms need re-examination.

Many women have now moved on to determine the nature of their affiliation, and to decide for themselves with whom they will affiliate. As soon as they attempt this step, they find the societal forms standing in opposition. In fact, they are already outside the old social forms looking for new ones. But, they do not feel like misfits, wrong again, but like seekers. To be in this unfamiliar position is not always comfortable, but it is not wholly uncomfortable either – and indeed it begins to bring its own *new* and different rewards. Here, even on the most immediate level, women now find a community of other seekers, others who are engaged in this pursuit. No one can undertake this formidable task alone. (Therapy, even if we knew how to do it in some near perfect way – which we do not – is not enough.)

It is extremely important to recognize that the pull toward affiliation that women feel in themselves is not wrong or backward; women need not add to the condemnation of themselves. On the contrary, we can recognize this pull as the basic strength it is. We can also begin to choose relationships that foster mutual growth. . . .

Other questions are equally hard. How do we conceive of a society organized so that it permits both the development and the mutuality of all people? And how do we get there? How do women move from a powerless and devalued position to fully valued effectiveness? How do we get the power to do this, even if we do not want or need power to control or submerge others? It would be difficult enough if we started from zero, but we do not. We start from a position in which others have power and do not hesitate to use it. Even if they do not consciously use it against women, all they have to do is remain in the position of dominance, keep doing what they are doing, and nothing will change. The women's qualities that I believe are ultimately, and at all times, valuable and essential are not the ones that make for power in the world as it is now. How then can we use these strengths to enhance our effectiveness rather than let them divert us from action?

One part of the answer seems clear already. Women will not advance except by joining together in cooperative action. What has not been as clear is that no other group, so far, has had the benefit of women's leadership, the advantage of women's deep and special strengths. Most of these strengths have been hidden in this culture, and hidden from women themselves. I have been emphasizing one of these strengths – *the* very strength that is most important for concerted group action. Unlike other groups, women do not *need* to set affiliation and strength in opposition one against the other. We can readily integrate the two, search for more and better ways to use affiliation to enhance strength – and strength to enhance affiliation.

For women to derive strength from relationships, then, clearly requires a transformation and restructuring of the nature of relationships. The first essential new ingredients in this process are self-determination and the power to make the self-determination a reality. But even before getting to this major issue, there are questions facing many women: 'If I want self-determination, what is it I really want to determine? What do I want? Who am I anyhow?' The difficulty of answering these questions has sometimes served to discourage women. The discouragement occurs even in women who are convinced that there is something deeply wrong with the old way. Given the history that women's lives have been so totally focused on others, it is easy to see that such questions bear a special cogency and come from a particularly hidden place in women. . . .

It is important here to note that this discussion of the importance of affiliations for women is by no means exhaustive. Nor is it a full discussion of any of the related, complicated problems, such as depression. Rather, it is an attempt to unravel a topic that requires much new examination. I hope that it will give rise to further discussion.

Jessie Bernard

The Wife's Marriage

From Jessie Bernard, *The Future of Marriage*, Harmondsworth: Penguin, 1976, pp. 56-68 (first published in 1972)

FEMALE INTO NEUTER

Some of the changes brought about by marriage are extremely subtle. In sexuality, for example. Women at marriage move from the status of female to that of neuter being. In the East European shtetl this important change was recognized and marked by a rite of passage, the cutting off of a woman's hair; she must not be attractive to other men. Much of the alleged decline in sexual attractiveness of women which is attributed to age is really attributable to the prescriptions for the role of wife. Women who remain active in nonmarital roles often retain their attractiveness far into middle age and even beyond, for modern women are potentially 'sexier' than women were in the past. They mature as sexual beings earlier and reach menopause later than in the past, and Kinsey and his associates noted that early sexual maturation was associated with great sexual activity and longer duration of sexual interest.

In the 1890s, as Henry Seidel Canby remembered it, 'women past their twenties, or married, suffered dumbly from an imagination that made them sexless, because they did not know what was wrong and would not have admitted the truth if it had been told to them'. Married women were 'cinders – agreeable, yes, admirable often, interesting often, yet cinders, ... long emptied of fire – and like cinders they responded'. Nor, according to Philip Slater, has the situation changed much since then. Stylistically, he tells us, 'it is only young unmarried girls who are allowed to be entirely female ... As soon as they are married they are expected to mute their sexuality somewhat, and when they become mothers this neutral-ization is carried even further.' Some women in desperation to validate their own sexuality engage in flirtation or even serious affairs to prove to themselves that they are still sexual beings.

All of these changes brought about by marriage can contribute something to the explanation that we are seeking for the sad picture of the mental health of married women. But there is still another change which may outweigh them. It has to do with the position of the housewife.

MARRIAGE AND LIFE STYLE

We are going to have a great deal to say later about households and life styles. They are inextricably bound up with marriage. Marriage has to do with the commitment of husbands and wives to one another; life styles have to do, obviously, with the way they live. And the way in which most husbands and wives live today is alone, or with their young children, in a separate isolated household, the care of which is the wife's almost exclusive responsibility. This life style, Philippe Ariès has taught us, is not very old – a few centuries – and, if trends now incipient continue, may not have a very long future ahead of it in its present form. But for the present and at least the immediate future, the individual, separate, isolated, privatized household will be the stage on which most marriages will play themselves out. And it will be the wife's responsibility to take care of it.

OCCUPATIONAL CHANGE IN MARRIAGE

One of the basic differences in the wife's and the husband's marriages result from this life style – namely, the almost complete change in work that marriage brings in her life but not in his. Until yesterday, and for most women even today, every wife becomes a *house*wife. And this is not always a congenial role. Militant feminists have argued that this occupational change amounts to the same thing as requiring all men upon marriage to give up their jobs and become janitors, whether they like janitor work or not. Regardless of whether this analogy is fair or not, it is true that interest in and aptitude for housework are not as equally distributed among the female population as is the occupation of housework, wherefore a large number of vocational misfits is almost inevitable. For, as it happens, not all women have an interest in or aptitude for the job of housewife – just as, no doubt, there are many men who do and would prefer it to what they are doing.

Thus, for example, despite the powerful engines of socialization which almost from infancy begin to prepare girls for domesticity, only about a third of the girls among high school graduates showed interest in the domestic arts a generation ago, and even fewer – less than a fifth – among college women. The figures would doubtless be less today. These data, taken at their face value, indicate that a fairly large number of women are drawn into housework as an occupation by marriage, in spite of an absence of positive interest in the domestic arts. Coming to terms with domesticity is not the least of the housewife's trauma, however much the sheer drudgery has been alleviated. Housekeeping remains an uncongenial occupation to many women.

'The housewife is a nobody,' says Philip Slater, and almost everyone agrees. Her work is menial labour. Even more status-degrading is the unpaid nature of her job. Few deny the economic as well as the sociological importance of housework and home-making. Housework is part of the great infrastructure on which, as David Riesman has reminded us, the entire superstructure of the economy and the government rests. If women did not supply the services of taking care of the living arrangements of workers, industry would have to do so, as in the case of lumber camps, ships, and the military. But housewives are not in the labour force. They are not paid for the services that they perform.

The low status of the wife's work has ramifications all through her marriage. Since her husband's work is not only higher in status but usually competitive, as hers is not, and he has to meet certain clothing and grooming standards or lose his job, his needs have to be catered to. If there has to be a choice, his new suit is more important than hers. This, quite apart from whatever personal or institutional prestige his work confers, tends to put him in a position of status superiority to the wife.[1]

Housework is a dead-end job; there is no chance of promotion. One cannot grow in it. There is a saying that passes as wit to the effect that Washington is full of talented men and the women they married when they were young. The couple who began their marriage at the same stages of their development find themselves far apart in later years. 'Persons who took the initiative in seeking divorce,' Nelson Foote has noted, 'in explaining their experience, and likewise observers of broken marriages, speak frequently of a mate's having outgrown the other. It is the husband who usually outgrows the wife.' Not only does the wife not grow, but the

1. Even if a wife is working, a disparity in occupational status between her job and her husband's may make a difference to her. If her occupation is lower in status than her husband's, she is more likely to show symptoms of anxiety (Lawrence J. Sharp and F. Ivan Nye, 'Maternal Mental Health', in F. Ivan Nye and Lois Wladis Hoffman, eds., *The Employed Mother in America*, Rand McNally, Chicago, Ill., 1963, pp. 309-19). When both are on the same occupational level, as among blue-collar and unskilled workers, the status differential does not exist and the anxiety symptoms do not show up.

nonspecialized and detailed nature of housework may actually have a deteriorating effect on her mind, as Mary Roberts Coolidge observed long ago, rendering her incapable of prolonged concentration on any single task. No wonder that after hours of passive, often solitary, absorption in television and radio soap operas, she comes to seem dumb as well as dull.

Nelson Foote assesses to the husband some of the responsibility for the deterioration of housewives in his developmental theory of marriage. He points out that

one's direction of growth as well as the rate of learning is powerfully affected by the responses of those particular others upon whom he inescapably depends for evaluations of his behavior ... Husbands are hardly prepared by cultural history [to perform the role of] the most beneficent other in the development of wives for whom the performance of household duties no longer seems to challenge their capacities ... The commonest picture in American marriages is that in which the husband has no concept whatever of contributing by his manner of speaking and listening to the elaboration of his wife's career, particularly when she has no ostensible professional career. While her constructive achievements with home and children may be honored, her ventures in other directions appear more often to be subject to insensitive disparagement than to insightful and competent facilitation.

Sympathetic encouragement instead of indifference or positive belittling from husbands would doubtless lessen the alienating effect of housework as an occupation on the marriage, but in and of itself could not overcome it, for the sympathy would be, in effect, patronizing.

The difference in the work of wives and husbands has other alienating effects on the relationship also. It is quite hard even for men in occupations that differ widely to maintain close friendships. They do not share the same kinds of problems. For example, imagine a case like this:

'Jim and I were great friends at college; we belonged to the same fraternity. We enjoyed one another's company and had lots of good times together. After graduation I took a management trainee job in a large establishment and he opened up a small neighbourhood grocery shop. We maintained contacts for a while but we soon drifted apart. Our interests began to diverge. He couldn't appreciate the kinds of problems I had to face in a large bureaucracy and his own absorption in the piddling problems of running his little operation seemed uninteresting to me.'

The same kind of alienation can occur in marriage. Change Jim's name to Jane, the grocery shop to a household, a graduation to marriage, and the story would not have to be changed very much. The occupational split that occurs at marriage can have the same kind of alienating effect on married partners as on friends of the same sex.

The occupation of the housewife has other than intellectual effects that can be damaging. As life is now organized in small, private living units, housework is isolating. 'The idea of imprisoning each woman alone in a small, self-contained, and architecturally isolating dwelling is a modern invention,' Philip Slater reminds us, 'dependent upon an advanced technology. In Muslim societies, for example, the wife may be a prisoner, but she is at least not in solitary confinement. In our society the housewife may move about freely, but since she has nowhere in particular to go and is not a part of anything her prison needs no walls. This is in striking contrast to her premarital life, especially if she is a college graduate. In college she was typically embedded in an active group life with constant emotional and intellectual stimulation. College life is in this sense an urban life. Marriage typically eliminates much of this way of life to her, and children deliver the *coup de grace*. Her only significant relationships tend to be with her husband who, however, is absent most of the day. Most of her social and emotional needs must be satisfied by her children, who are hardly adequate to the task.'

Isolation has negative psychological effects on people. It encourages brooding; it leads to erratic judgements, untempered by the leavening effect of contact with others. It renders one more susceptible to psychoses. Melvin Seeman has found that it also heightens one's sense of powerlessness. Anything, therefore, that increases isolation constitutes a hazard, even something as seemingly trivial as the increase in isolation contributed by which storey of a building you live on. A study by D. M. Fanning of the families of servicemen in Germany, published in 1967, found, for example, that women living in apartment buildings were more susceptible to psychoneurotic disorders than women who lived in houses, and the higher the apartment the greater the susceptibility. 'The incidence of psychoneurotic disorders was nearly three times as high among women living in flats as [it was among] those living in houses, and this [incidence] increased as the height of homes increased ... For mothers with preschool children, the confinement within flats provided an added irritant to the monotony and boredom of their lives.'

THE HOUSEWIFE SYNDROME

That it is being relegated to the role of housewife rather than marriage itself which contributes heavily to the poor mental and emotional health of married women can be demonstrated by comparing housewives, all of whom may be presumed to be married, with working women, three fifths of whom are also married. Marriage *per se* is thus at least partially ruled out as an explanation of differences between them. The comparison shows that wives who are rescued from the isolation of the household by outside employment show up very well. They may be neurotic, but, as Sharp and Nye have shown, they are less likely than women who are exclusively housewives to be psychotic. And even the allegation of neuroticism can be challenged. For Sheila Feld tells us that 'working mothers are less likely than housewives to complain of pains and ailments in different parts of their body and of not feeling healthy enough to carry out things they would like to do'.[2]

But the truly spectacular evidence for the destructive effects of the occupation of housewife on the mental and emotional health of married women is provided by the relative incidence of the symptoms of psychological distress among housewives and working women. In all except one of twelve such symptoms – having felt an impending nervous breakdown – the working women were overwhelmingly better off than the housewives. Far fewer than expected of the working women and more than expected of the housewives, for example, had actually had a nervous breakdown. Fewer than expected of the working women and more than expected of the housewives suffered from nervousness, inertia, insomnia, trembling hands, nightmares, perspiring hands, fainting, headaches, dizziness, and heart palpitations. The housewife syndrome is far from a figment of anyone's imagination.

If this chapter were a musical composition, table 1 would be accompanied by a loud clash of symbols. And a long silence would ensue to give a chance for its emotional impact to be fully

2. Actually, in the earlier age brackets, twenty-five to forty-four, working women averaged more days of restricted activity or bed disability than housekeeping women, though in the later age brackets the reverse was true. (Data from an unpublished table by the National Center for Health Statistics.)

experienced. For table 1 provides one of the most cogent critiques yet made of marriage as it is structured today.

Dismissing the housewife syndrome, as some unsympathetic observers do, is like telling a man dying of malnutrition that he's lucky he isn't dying of cancer. Perhaps he is. But this is no reason to dismiss malnutrition because it is slower and less dramatic. The conditions producing both are worthy of attack as epidemiological challenges. In terms of the number of people involved, the housewife syndrome might well be viewed as Public Health Problem Number One.

TABLE 1   Selected Symptoms of Psychological Distress among White Housewives and Working Women

Symptom	Housewives	Working Women
Nervous breakdown	+1·16	−2·02
Felt impending nervous breakdown	−0·12	+0·81
Nervousness	+1·74	−2·29
Inertia	+2·35	−3·15
Insomnia	+1·27	−2·00
Trembling hands	+0·74	−1·25
Nightmares	+0·68	−1·18
Perspiring hands	+1·28	−2·55
Fainting	+0·82	−2·69
Headaches	+0·84	−0·87
Dizziness	+1·41	−1·85
Héart palpitations	+1·38	−1·56

SOURCE: National Center for Health Statistics, *Selected Symptoms of Psychological Distress*, US Department of Health, Education and Welfare, 1970, Table 17, pp. 30-1.

COMMENT

I pause here a moment to say that I consider this chapter to be the most important one in the book. And I have been so tediously careful to document the mental and emotional state of health of wives and the possible reason for it – especially the status denigration that marriage brings – because I believe it important to put the evidence beyond cavil or frivolous disparagement or ridicule. For the woman suffering from the housewife syndrome is not likely to elicit much sympathy; she's sitting pretty, and has no cause for complaint. She annoys us if she even mentions any symptoms of psychological distress. They are not worthy of anyone's attention. Who but advertisers could take the housewife seriously? And even to the advertisers she seems to be only a laughable idiot.[3]

In 1970, Margaret Mead was quoted by Robert Williams as warning women in the Women's Liberation Movement that they might literally be driving men insane. The reverse seems more likely. It is wives who are driven mad, not by men but by the anachronistic way in which marriage is structured today – or, rather, the life style which accompanies marriage today and which demands that all wives be housewives. In truth, being a housewife makes women sick.

If we were, in fact, epidemiologists and saw bright, promising young people enter a certain occupation and little by little begin to droop and finally succumb, we would be alerted at once and bend all our research efforts to locate the hazards and remove them. But we are complacent when we see what happens to women in marriage. We have, in fact, almost boxed women into a corner. Or, to change the figure of speech, we have primed young fillies to run fast and then put impossible hurdles in their way. We tell young women that they are free to embark on careers, and then make it almost impossible for them to succeed in them. We tell them they may have access to all the privileges and prerogatives of professionals, and then punish them if they accept the challenge. More important still, we put an enormous premium on their getting married, but make them pay an unconscionable price for falling in with our expectations. We then blame them no matter what they do – refuse to run, kick over the traces, run wild, or become inert.

3. The members of the National Capital Area chapter of the National Organization for Women (NOW) monitored television programmes, including advertisements, during the month of April 1971. Viewed through the eyes of these stern, no-nonsense monitors, the enormous pathos of the housewife comes through with a heart-sinking thud: young housewives who have to fortify themselves with pills to get through their day; housewives in a tizzy for fear that neighbours will catch them with their furniture unpolished; housewives cattily comparing the relative whiteness of their laundry; housewives being patronized by smug husbands . . . Are *these* really the young women we saw in high school and college? Is *this* what they have been reduced to? Mrs Millamant's 'dwindling' was nothing compared to this. It might be mentioned in passing that advertising agencies were not pleased with NOW monitoring.

HAPPINESS IS...?

If the wife's marriage is really so pathogenic, why do women marry at all? They marry for a wide variety of reasons. They want emancipation from the parental home, and marriage is one way to achieve it. They want babies, and marriage is the only sanctioned way – as yet – to get babies in our society. In addition, there is the pressure of social expectations, what some radical young women call an 'idolatry' of marriage. There are, in fact, few if any better alternatives to marriage for young women in their late teens and early twenties. Most of the alternatives are – or, to date, have seemed to be – too awful. If marriage helps young women to achieve any of these goals and to avoid worse alternatives, their stampede into marriage is understandable.

The problem is not why do young women marry, but why, in the face of all the evidence, do more married than unmarried women report themselves as happy? As, in fact, they do. For it is strange to find wives, such a large proportion of whom are filled with fears and anxieties, so many of whom are depressed, reporting themselves as happy. More of the young than of the old, more of the college-educated than of the less well-educated, and among the college-educated, more of them even than of their husbands.

There are several ways to look at the seeming anomaly involved here. One is that happiness is interpreted in terms of conformity. Wives may, in effect, be judging themselves happy by definition. They are conforming to expectations and are therefore less vulnerable to the strains accompanying nonconformity. The pressures to conform are so great that few young women can resist them. Better, as the radical women put it, dead than unwed. Those who do not marry are made to feel inferior, failures. What's a nice girl like you doing unmarried? The situation may not be as bad as it was in colonial times when sanctions were actually brought against the unmarried, but the opprobrium still remains. Rozanne Brooks, a sociologist, studying the stereotypes of the unmarried, asked her students to describe unmarried women. They did, and the conventional image of a frustrated, repressed, pursed-lipped, unnatural being came through. When asked to describe some specific unmarried women they knew well, a quite different image came through, one more conformable to the statistical picture drawn above. Escape from being 'an old maid' is one definition of happiness.

Such conformity to the norm of marriage does not have to be imposed from the outside. Women have internalized the norms prescribing marriage so completely that the role of wife seems the only acceptable one. And since marriage is set up as the *summum bonum* of life for women, they interpret their achievement of marriage as happiness, no matter how unhappy the marriage itself may be. They have been told that their happiness depends on marriage, so, even if they are miserable, they *are* married, aren't they? They *must* therefore be happy.

Another way to explain the anomaly of depressed, phobic, and psychologically distressed women reporting themselves as happy may be that they are interpreting happiness in terms of adjustment. Even researchers have confused happiness and adjustment. In their measures of success in marriage, 'happiness', 'satisfaction', and 'adjustment' have received different weights; in all but one, adjustment has received far greater weight than either happiness or satisfaction. If the researchers define success in marriage in terms of adjustment, it is understandable why wives do too. The married woman has adjusted to the demands of marriage; she is reconciled to them. She interprets her reconciliation as happiness, no matter how much she is paying for it in terms of psychological distress.

Orden and Bradburn offer corroboration of such a 'calculus'. They found that marital happiness, like individual psychological well-being, was a matter of 'affect balance'. There were both pluses and minuses in the marital relationship, one positive (relating to companionship and sociability) and one negative (relating to tension). The positive contribution made to wives' happiness by companionship and sociability – small as it may be – was apparently great enough to overcome the negative effect of tension. It was not, therefore, anomalous when wives reported more marital stress than husbands but at the same time more overall marital satisfaction also. It was just that they had to pay more than husbands for companionship and sociability.

THE HIDDEN DEFORMITIES OF WOMEN

Another way to solve the paradox of depressed wives reporting their marriages as happy is to view the socialization process as one which 'deforms' them in order to fit them for marriage as now structured. We cut the motivational wings of young women or bind their intellectual feet, all the time reassuring them that it is all for their own good. Otherwise, no one would love them or marry them or take care of them. Or, if anyone did, they would be unhappy and feel caged if they had wings and could not fly, or unbound feet and could not run.

There may have been a time when this made sense. It might well be asked if it still does. But whether it makes sense or not, we are quite remarkably successful. We do not clip wings or bind feet, but we do make girls sick. For to be happy in a relationship which imposes so many impediments on her, as traditional marriage does, a woman must be slightly ill mentally. Women accustomed to expressing themselves freely could not be happy in such a relationship; it would be too confining and too punitive. We therefore 'deform' the minds of girls, as traditional Chinese used to deform their feet, in order to shape them for happiness in marriage. It may therefore be that married women say they are happy because they are sick rather than sick because they are married.

There are some researchers who believe that this is indeed the case. They note that our standards of mental health for men are quite different from those for women, that if we judged women by the standards which we apply to men they would show up as far from well. A generation ago, Terman could judge women who were conformist, conservative, docile, unaggressive, lacking in decisiveness, cautious, nontolerant to be emotionally stable and well balanced. They were the women who had achieved an adjustment standard of mental health. They fitted the situation they were trained from infancy to fit. They enjoyed conformity to it. They were his 'happily' married women.

But modern clinicians see them in a different light. Inge K. Broverman and her associates, for example, ask whether a constellation of traits which includes 'being more submissive, less independent, less adventurous, more easily influenced, less aggressive, less competitive, more excitable in minor crises, having their feelings more easily hurt, being more emotional, more conceited about their appearance, less objective' – a constellation of traits which a set of clinicians attributed to mature adult women – isn't a strange way of 'describing any mature, healthy individual'. These researchers conclude that we have a double standard of mental health, one for men and one for women. We incorporate into our standards of mental health for women the defects necessary for successful adjustment in marriage.

We do our socializing of girls so well, in fact, that many wives, perhaps most, not only feel that they are fulfilled by marriage but even hotly resent anyone who raises questions about their marital happiness. They have been so completely shaped for their dependency and passivity that the very threat of changes that would force them to greater independence frightens them. They have successfully come to terms with the conditions of their lives.

They do not know any other. They do not know that other patterns of living might yield greater satisfactions, or want to know. Their cage can be open. They will stay put.

SOLUTION TO THE PARADOX

'But what about love? Isn't that what marriage is all about?' the young bride cries. 'None of what you say has even included the word!' True, love has been what marriage has been partially if not all about at least since the seventeenth century. Love is, in fact, so important to women that they are willing to pay an exorbitant price for it – even all the costs that marriage exacts.

Women need and want the love and companionship and the mere presence of men in some kind of close relationship. They demonstrate this need by clinging to marriage regardless of the cost. They are willing to pay dearly for it. This fact assures its future.

But the basic question is, does the satisfaction of these needs for love and companionship have to extort such excessive costs? Should young women have to pay so much for them? Should we not try to reduce the costs of marriage to them? Shouldn't it be possible to devise a structure that permits them to eat some of the cake and still have a little left over?

References

Ariès, Philippe, *Centuries of Childhood, A Social History of Family Life*, Jonathan Cape, 1962.

Broverman, Inge K. *et al.*, 'Sex-Role Stereotypes and Clinical Judgments of Mental Health', *Journal of Counseling and Clinical Psychology*, 34, February 1970, pp. 6-7.

Canby, Henry Seidel, *The Age of Confidence*, Constable, 1935.

Coolidge, Mary Roberts, *Why Women Are So*, Holt, New York, 1912, chapter 4.

Feld, Sheila, *see* Gurin, Gerald.

Feld, Sheila, *see* Veroff, Joseph.

Foote, Nelson, 'Matching of Husband and Wife in Phases of Development', *Transactions of the Third World Congress of Sociology*, 4, 1956.

Gurin, Gerald, Veroff, Joseph, and Feld, Sheila, *Americans View Their Mental Health*, Basic Books, New York, 1960, pp. 42, 72, 110, 190, 234-5.

Nye, F. Ivan, 'Marital Interaction', in F. Ivan Nye and Lois Wladis Hoffman (eds.), *The Employed Mother in America*, Rand McNally, Chicago, Ill., 1963, pp. 263-81.

Orden, Susan R. and Bradburn, Norman, 'Dimensions of Marriage Happiness', *American Journal of Sociology*, 73, May 1968, p. 717.

Riesman, David, introduction to Jessie Bernard, *Academic Women*, The Pennsylvania State University Press, Philadelphia, Pa., 1964, p. xxiv.

Seeman, Melvin and Evans, John W., 'Alienation and Learning in a Hospital Setting', *American Sociological Review*, 27 December 1962, pp. 772-82.

Sharp, Lawrence J. and Nye, F. Ivan, 'Maternal Mental Health', in F. Ivan Nye and Lois Wladis Hoffman (eds.), *The Employed Mother in America*, Rand McNally, Chicago, Ill., 1963, pp. 309-19.

Slater, Philip, 'What Hath Spock Wrought?', *Washington Post*, 1, March 1970.

Terman, Lewis M. and Wallin, Paul, 'Marriage Prediction and Marital-Adjustment Tests', *American Sociological Review*, 14, August 1949, p. 502.

Tharp, Roland G., 'Psychological Patterning in Marriage', *Psychological Review*, 60, March 1963, p. 144.

Veroff, Joseph and Feld, Sheila, *Marriage and Work in America*, Van Nostrand-Reinhold, 1971.

Williams, Robert, 'Book Power to the Fore', *Washington Post*, 16, May 1970.

Female Sexuality

When Simone de Beauvoir wrote that 'Women are made, not born', she suggested that femininity, and female emotional and social behaviour, are entirely a result of socialisation, and have nothing whatsoever to do with any innate characteristics that women might possess. It is a view which is diametrically opposed to all psychoanalytic theory and to most taken-for-granted Western assumptions about the behaviour of the sexes. But whether or not the full implications of de Beauvoir's remark are accepted, it does point to the wide variations that exist throughout the world in the way in which the 'feminine' is socially constructed, and suggests that the behaviour of women deemed acceptable in the contemporary West is not the only, or definitive, version of how women should behave.

Of all the aspects of social life in which women are engaged, the most problematic – particularly for feminists – is that of sexuality, and sexual relationships with men. For feminists, sexuality presents a crucial dilemma, since if women are to engage in heterosexual relationships and wish to bear children they must associate with men, and thereby institute those social relationships which are often oppressive to women. It is only very recently, and largely in the industrial West, that women have been able to separate both sexuality from reproduction, and childbearing from institutionalised marriage. Sex, children and some form of socially recognised marriage are, in the majority of societies, locked together in an undissolvable trinity. Moreover, the expression of female sexuality outside marriage, or some other form of socially sanctioned relationship is, unlike that of men, generally regarded as unacceptable. Western, Christian societies have always placed a high value on female premarital chastity, but in this they are merely conforming to a pattern which is to be found in numerous societies throughout the world: brides are expected to be virgins and wives faithful, while women who are too generous with their sexual favours are socially outlawed or stigmatised. Men, on the other hand, are allowed more freedom of sexual expression: the only social problem being that 'unofficial' male sexuality has to be contained, so that social order is not threatened by the compromise of large numbers of women. There are, of course, certain well-known exceptions to the general expectation of aggressive male, and passive female, sexuality. For example, in her study of the Arapesh Margaret Mead pointed out that in that society men fear rape by women as much as women fear rape by men elsewhere.

The assumption underlying most social conventions associated with sexuality is that men have far greater sexual appetites than women, and that these desires are perfectly socially acceptable. Indeed, an implicit assumption of a great deal of existing literature on prostitution is that without regular sexual intercourse men will become ill or in some way deranged. It is, of course, a view which has been utterly rejected by a long tradition of feminists: from Josephine Butler to the present-day feminists have pointed out that the supposed high level of male sexual desire is a social construct and one which depends upon the exploitation of a minority of women for its satisfaction, since in order to maintain the purity of wives and daughters those women who satisfy the supposedly natural sexual desires of men are labelled whores and prostitutes. Yet at the same time as it is believed that men are sexually aggressive and virtually sexually insatiable, so it is frequently supposed, and particularly so in Western cultures, that women experience little or no sexual desire *per se*. Women's need for sexual intercourse is frequently interpreted as a desire for impregnation; heterosexuality is tolerable, but only if it has a strong association with the likelihood of maternity. The mature woman, as Freud supposed, is one who recognises that her sexuality is essentially about reproduction. Sexual pleasure may be a fortunate side-effect of acts of procreation but for women it is not recognised as an end in itself.

The confusions and contradictions that now surround female sexuality as a result of centuries of commonsense, taken-for-granted assumptions about the character of female sexual response are now legion. On the one hand, a long tradition still associates female sexuality primarily with maternity; on the other, a new, liberal and permissive ideology about sexual relationships asserts that women have as much right to, and capacity for, sexual pleasure as men. Indeed, as a now well-established school of contemporary sexology asserts, women's sexual response is both more varied and more sustained than that of men. A huge publishing industry has now developed which is largely concerned with instructing men in the appropriate sexual techniques for pleasing women. Far from expecting women to suffer and merely tolerate the sexual activities of men, women are now taught that men have a duty to comprehend and appreciate specifically female sexual response. Sexual intercourse is not, in the pages of the modern manuals of copulation, associated with pregnancy, marriage, sexual fidelity or even a great deal of human association. An individual is exhorted to develop her or his sexual technique so that any random sexual partner can immediately be brought to a peak of feverish sexual pleasure.

The social world in which sophisticated sexual expertise can be demonstrated randomly is, however, as yet far from typical of human experience. Most sexual activity, in most societies, takes place within marriage or recognised sexual relationships and is far more limited, in both its physical and social form, than some fictional accounts of the social world would suggest. For most women, heterosexual intercourse would still appear to be largely unsatisfactory, but a necessary part of a bargaining process in which sexual intercourse is exchanged either for the promise of marriage or the expectation of pregnancy. Since sexual relationships between members of the same sex are still, in most parts of the world, stigmatised and socially unacceptable, heterosexuality remains the only sexual option for the majority of human beings. Furthermore, it is the only form of sexual activity which also has a recognised social form: that of marriage and the establishment of a household and family. Since homosexuality cannot offer the procreation of children or social legitimacy, it remains, for most people, an unacceptable social option.[1]

For some feminists however, homosexuality is, whatever its social costs, the only acceptable form of sexual relationship, since, *ipso facto*, it is the only form of sexual relationship in which women are not vulnerable to male exploitation. The cost of lesbianism – apart from its social stigma – is the exclusion of the possibility of reproduction. Hence, while women might be oppressed within heterosexual relationships, within homosexual partnerships they are denied the possibility of a crucial element of female sexuality, that of maternity. Thus although lesbianism might offer a partial solution to the dilemmas of sexuality, it does not offer a complete ideological or pragmatic solution any more than contemporary feminism itself does. Although feminism shares with Western culture an ideological veneration of maternity, its views on female sexuality in general are less coherent. The central problem both for feminists and for others would appear to be that of reconciling

1. The bias towards heterosexuality of Western culture is bitterly attacked in Adrienne Rich's polemical article, 'Compulsory Heterosexuality and Lesbian Experience', *Signs*, vol. 5, no. 4, Summer 1980, pp. 631-60; and the ideology of male sexual needs in Mary McIntosh, 'Who Needs Prostitutes?' in C. and B. Smart, eds., *Women, Sexuality and Social Control*, London: Routledge and Kegan Paul, 1978.

woman's capacity for sexual pleasure with her capacity for reproduction. The issue is particularly problematic for feminists, since they must ask whether heterosexual relationships can offer women emotional and sexual fulfilment, or if the relationship is primarily of value to men.

The contradictory attitudes to women's sexuality that exist in the West are nowhere better expressed than in the different views of women to be found in pornography and in the institutionalised practices of medicine. In pornography, women are portrayed as the means to male sexual pleasure; even in pornography which depicts lesbianism, the depiction is designed to gratify men.[2] In medical practice, women are seen primarily as mothers: the practice of gynaecology and obstetrics is thus largely about safeguarding women's reproductive, rather than sexual, capacity.[3] The possibility that the two are linked, both emotionally and physically, is scorned by practices, which, like those of pornography, are seemingly incapable of seeing sexuality and reproduction as constituent elements of a complex system of response. However, male-dominated institutions (of which Western medicine is no exception) find it easiest to confront women's sexuality if the sexual can be completely divorced from the reproductive. Athough industrial societies do not attempt to limit female sexual response through the vicious practice of clitoridectomy, they – like many other societies – make little attempt to understand the totality of female sexual experience.

2. For full discussions of feminist attacks on pornography see Laura Lederer, ed., *Take Back the Night*, New York: Morrow, 1980. Two important articles are Irene Diamond, 'Pornography and Repression: a Reconsideration', *Signs*, vol. 5, no. 4, Summer 1980, pp. 686-701, and Beverley Brown, 'A Feminist Interest in Pornography – Some Modest Proposals', *M/F*, nos. 5 and 6, 1981, pp. 5-18.
3. The feminist literature on women and medicine (and particularly the masculine control of medicine) is now vast. For a general introduction see Joyce Leeson and Judith Gray, *Women and Medicine*, London: Tavistock, 1979, and Ann Oakley, 'Wisewoman and Medicine Man', in A. Oakley and J. Mitchell, eds., *The Rights and Wrongs of Women*, Harmondsworth: Penguin, 1977. Other important works, from different points of view, include Mary Daly's *Gyn/Ecology*, Boston: Beacon Press, 1978; *Our Bodies, Ourselves*, New York: Simon and Schuster, 1976; and Barbara Ehrenreich and Deidre English, *Witches, Midwives and Nurses: a History of Women Healers*, London: Writers and Readers Publishing Co-operative, 1973; and, by the same authors, *For Her Own Good: 150 Years of Expert's Advice to Women*, London: Pluto, 1979.

Beatrix Campbell

A Feminist Sexual Politics:
Now You See It, Now You Don't

In Feminist Review, no. 5, London, 1980, pp. 1-18

There was a time when feminism was caricatured as being obsessed with orgasm and life's private parts. It couldn't and probably wouldn't be now, not least perhaps because of the demise of a *feminist sexual politics* as an optimistic feature of the women's liberation movement. The time is ripe to review our sexual politics, and I get the feeling anyway that there are the rumblings of an uprising in the mainstream of the movement. There is dissatisfaction among lesbian, celibate and heterosexual women certainly, but the greatest sense of grievance is among heterosexual feminists who've felt outcast – they're the Fifth Form Remove, the bad girls who smoke in the changing room and go with men.

Heterosexuality has to feature in our politics as more than a guilty secret; indeed, in order that women mobilize any political combativity around it, it must be restored as a legitimate part of feminism's concern. It is, after all, the primary sexual practice of most women. It also needs to be present to help clarify lesbianism's place within feminism. Lesbianism is a specific sexual practice between women, with its own history and culture; it is not *the same as* sexual expression between women, political rejection of men, or a historically specific sexual liberation movement.

It's a commonplace to say that feminism in part grew out of the sexual and student revolutions of the 1960s. What's less clear is why and how. Any account of that period is doomed to be selective and subjective. So, after owning up to both, I'd say that there were two important themes in women's response – an ambiguity about sexual freedom at the expense of sexual protection (actually it's probably doubtful whether the men ever thought that their sexual freedom meant we could have it too) and an incipient critique of patriarchal heterosexuality.

The sixties evoke a little less than nostalgia. It is not so much a remembered resistance to men's clamour for sex, but that it was more of a rather antique variety. No doubt there was, too, a certain lack of sympathy with an ideology of freedom that did not acknowledge the non-equivalence of men's and women's social and sexual position. For many women historically men's sexual freedom was associated with the loss of women's protection, albeit a protection associated with dependence. Having said that, the permissive era had some pay-off for women in so far as it opened up political-sexual space. It permitted sex for women too. What it did not do was defend women against the differential effects of permissiveness on men and women. It was a sexual revolution that implied the separation of sex from reproduction, but that remained implicit and besides, then as now, there was no *absolute* guarantee against the risk of pregnancy. But anyway, it was primarily a revolt of young *men*. It was about the affirmation of young men's masculinity and promiscuity; it was indiscriminate, and their sexual object was indeterminate (so long as she was a woman). The very affirmation of sexuality was a celebration of *masculine* sexuality.

By the onset of the women's liberation movement, women's critique of the sexual revolution was about the quality of the act. Having bounded into sex with considerable gusto, we were faced with rapid and relentless disillusion. Women were acknowledged to be sexual – the Kinsey Report and Masters and Johnson had shown that already. Men's duty was to satisfy women. That's what the books told us. They just had to be patient in the knowledge that we might be slow in coming, but with the right knack and a strong wrist come we would. It was a waiting game for us and a fitness test for them, where the climax deserved a Duke of Edinburgh award for heroic acts of endurance in deep and dark places. There was no disgrace worse than battle fatigue.

Women's nostalgia for pre-fucking sex rather than that unmemorable first fuck seems to be for the rampant sensuality of those adolescent fumblings and gropings. When the agonized decision about whether to go the 'whole way' or not was resolved into 'doing it' the fun seemed to stop. It was down to a quick prelude, known in those days as 'foreplay' (which all the books said was very important to women) and then bang. The books seemed to pre-empt women's disappointment with 'it' when they counselled patience in the face of failure and frigidity. Frigidity, we knew, was a female condition, but having embraced sex nothing could be worse than having to own up to yourself being part of that female condition. In my school, whenever someone did actually 'do it' the collective curiosity about 'what is it like' was never met with celebration. At best it was 'all right'. I don't think that low-profile response, nor the fond memories of endless snogging at parties and bop speaks of women's preference for the sensual rather than the sexual, but rather expressed a dumb critique of normative patriarchal fucking. The trouble was, it wasn't even a tentative critique that could be informed by a culture of masturbation equivalent to men's adolescent masturbatory culture, which at least might have given clues. Instead we lurched rather unselfconsciously into feminism either with a mysterious sense of sexual disappointment, or with a strong, yet untheorized sense of the mismatch between the natural order of heterosexual practice and the nature of women's desire.

Initially the women's liberation movement detonated the whole problematic, not least because through the medium of small, consciousness-raising groups women were beginning to organize their ideas about sexual practice together, without men. And this provided women with a political instrument with which to reorganize their sexual relation to men. But despite the affirmation of autonomy, that is, of women's right to organize separately from men, the politics of autonomy remained untheorized, and ultimately fell prey to paralysing confusion as the emergent radical-feminist tendency in the movement equated autonomy with separatism. In effect two quite separate things were conflated – political separation for definite means and ends, and lived separation.

Separation as political autonomy has a political function, which is to provide a context in which women prepare their intervention in society, in social relations with both men and women, and in politics. It is a means of organizing that intervention. It is not sanctuary from society. By 1973 the confrontation between socialist-feminists and radical-feminists had become chronic, and resulted in the hegemony of radical-feminist rhetoric. The guilt and difficulty associated with heterosexual struggles were damned by a rhetoric which castigated it as 'sleeping with the enemy'. No doubt many heterosexual women talked to one another about what they were doing, but there was, and still is, no culture within the women's liberation movement that represented or legitimated their struggles. This had the effect of denying what had been precariously achieved. Heterosexuality as a political problematic was dismissed by radical-feminism's dismissal of men. Problem solved.

It is from this perspective that the following notes consider the sexual reform movements that pre-dated contemporary feminism, and review the development of sexual politics within women's liberation.

SEXUAL REFORM IN THE TWENTIETH CENTURY

A dominant feature of sexual reform movements in the twentieth century, apart from control of fertility, has been the recruitment of women into *active* participation in heterosexuality, in contrast to the fetishistic reticence which demobilized the sexuality of the feminine women in nineteenth century ideology.

Woman as conundrum is the object of sexual discourse in the twentieth century. Woman is object, a problem for men and a problem for heterosexuality. Until the women's liberation movement, when women became the subject of sexual politics, the quest of sexual reform was, in a sense, to release the dumb insolence and resentful, thwarted immobility of many women's sexual relation to men.

Having constituted the feminine as sexless, the imperative became to reconstruct her, albeit modestly, as (in Simone de Beauvoir's phrase) man's sexual counterpart. The object was to mobilize women's active engagement in sex by disinterring her entombed organicity and restoring bits and pieces of her biology (generally the wrong bits, as it happened) to their 'natural' place and purpose.

Clearly the debates of the sexual reform movements should not be treated as reflecting reality. Their importance for us lies rather in the extent to which they were reference points for contemporary feminist sexual politics. The main preoccupations of these debates were virginity and extra-marital sex; reproduction, sex and political repression; and frigidity and the nature of orgasm.

FRIGIDITY AND ORGASM – NOW YOU SEE IT NOW YOU DON'T

The problems of frigidity and fertility control were the key questions preoccupying the sex reform movements of the early twentieth century. Frigidity was held to be symptomatic of something approaching mass neurosis among women. Frigidity, you will remember, was the diagnosis offered by men to the women they'd failed to 'satisfy' – or rather women who'd failed to be satisfied. Feminine participation, it seemed, could not be guaranteed by spontaneous combustion; since femininity was constitutionally passive, woman had to be wooed and won, patiently. Woman wasn't only passive, however, she was enigmatic. Her engagement demanded virtuosity and depended on man's organizational flair. His failure was her frigidity. Thus feminine sexuality was rendered dependent upon masculine resourcefulness, indeed the masculine sexual project seemed to involve a delicate war against a tendentially frigid femininity.

R. L. Dickinson and L. Beam (Dickinson and Beam, 1932) in the first major medical analysis of marriage, revealed dreadful pain and maladjustment. Of the 1,000 cases they studied only 363 were 'adjusted' and without complaint. Some writers suggested – tentatively – that frigidity could be seen as covert rebellion. One survey of about 150 women said that some described the pain of sex not as frigidity 'but lack of consent'. 'It takes two persons to make one frigid woman', said the sympathetic Dickinson, a gynaecologist who had worked with women for forty years. 'Frigidity is best understood as a positive quality and cannot be translated into absence of sexual desire.' British sex reformers such as Dora Russell, Stella Browne and Marie Stopes, strenuously affirmed women as sexual beings. They saw this as being confirmed by the evidence offered by women's freer lives during the First World War, the twenties and the thirties; and they rejected oft-repeated allegations of women's sexual apathy or anaesthesia. There is a tone in some of their work of resistance to, or impatience with, feminist antecedents who had advocated sexual restraint, and cold, sex-denying women. Stella Browne deplored this (Browne, 1915): 'Cold women', she declared, have 'a perfect mania for prohibition as a solution for all ills.'

Dr Magnus Hirschfeld, founder of the World League for Sexual Reform, which attracted participation from individuals such as Dora and Bertrand Russell, Bernard Shaw and Vera Brittain as well as from marriage and birth control counsellors operating in working-class districts, warned of the devastating effect on men of women's frigidity, and produced graphs to show the unfortunate effect of the different *pace* of arousal in men and in women. He attributed the problem to the (Hirschfeld, 1935): 'divergence between the curve of sensual pleasure in the male and the female: the man has passed the peak point of sexual excitement while the woman is still getting there'. Failure to reach orgasm, recorded explicitly or suggested implicitly, operated for anywhere between one third and two thirds of women in most of the case studies carried out in the first half of the twentieth century. Problems of pregnancy and the question of orgasm were the fundamental issues which emerged in the work of East London counsellor Janet Chance, who reported on her work with the Bow Marriage Education Centre to the 1929 Sexual Reform Congress; while according to Hannah and Abraham Stone, failure to reach orgasm

(Stone and Stone, 1952): 'is perhaps the most frequent sexual complaint among women who are otherwise entirely normal'.

But despite the good intentions of sexual reformers, their movement suffered from fatal flaws which derived from its location of woman as *the* problem for heterosexuality. This meant that although birth control was advocated alongside the positive affirmation of women's sexuality, there was no critique of 'normal' heterosexuality and its essentially (for women) procreative mode. Thus its form always put women at risk of pregnancy. Secondly, there was (and is) an assumption of necessary complementarity between men's and women's sexual (as against procreative) faculties, which meant that the clitoris was necessarily subsumed to the vagina as the throne of the women's sensuality.

Thus the radical implications of what Simone de Beauvoir later referred to as the independence of the clitoris for women's non-procreative pleasure were dissolved, which allowed the concept of the Sex Act to depend both on procreation and the penis. Dora Russell's views illustrate this difficulty and some of the social implications of women's independence. She welcomed disruption of enforced chastity and compulsive monogamy and encouraged a light-hearted treatment of sex-play, not least amongst the children in her school – she commented that the children still made jokes about sex. That was okay, she said (Russell, 1927): ('the sexual process is, after all, rather odd'), but she reprimanded those flighty feminists who were busy earning their own living and being sexually independent, since they were at the same time thwarting parenthood. For women, she insisted, the sexual moment was but (Russell, 1927): 'the merest incident in the satisfaction of the older impulse to gain power and abundant and eternal life by multiplying her own body'. For her, sexual freedom was not to be achieved at the expense of maternity – a dilemma many contemporary feminists share. And there were few in her time (but a few there were) who were not prepared to celebrate maternity.

A later sexual reformer, Dr Eustace Chesser, who wrote numerous sex handbooks and became momentarily notorious in Britain in the fifties on account of some of his views, adopted a similar position in opposing 'free love'. He polemicized against the work of individuals such as the American radical judge, Ben E. Lindsay, who became the object of a Ku Klux Klan witchhunt because he advocated 'companionate love', a variant on the trial marriage theme. Chesser alerted his many readers to the fate worse than death that awaited the 'free woman', who, he claimed, envied married women, since the sex act for women was only a prelude to satisfaction of the maternal instinct 'and finding joy in the life of the family'.

Even those sexual reformers who were feminist usually represented the subject of sexuality as male, which had the effect of blurring the distinction between women's reproductive and sexual faculties. It would be too simple to argue that in this schema the clitoris was banished. It was always there, sort of. Havelock Ellis (Ellis, 1928) claimed that its importance had only been recognized in the latter half of the nineteenth century. So little had been known about it that in 1593 a man by the name of Columbus first claimed to have 'discovered' this organ, although it was later shown that other anatomists had discovered it before. Presumably its discovery was as much a surprise to its owners as the discovery of America was to its indigenous occupants.

It is not so much denial of the clitoris that is striking as its appearance and disappearance in theories of female sexuality and, where it is acknowledged, its displacement in favour of the mythologized vagina, in defence of the penis as the organizing principle of the sexual act. This displacement allows the idealization of the simultaneous orgasm and a plethora of neurotic symptoms, notably premature ejaculation and frigidity. It has been common for frigidity to be blamed on premature ejaculation. Marie Stopes emphasized that 'mutual orgasm is extremely important'. Sadly, too often the man 'comes so swiftly that the woman's reactions are not really ready, and she is left without it'. She condemned *coitus interruptus*: 'while it may have saved the woman the anguish of bearing unwanted children yet it is very harmful to her, and is to be deprecated. It tends to leave the woman in "mid air" as it were; to leave her stimulated and unsatisfied.'

The Dutch gynaecologist Thomas Van de Velde typified the progressive view. He recognized the clitoris as (Van de Velde, 1928): 'an organ of voluptuous sensation exclusively' and acknowledged women's multi-orgasmic capacity, but still shifted that sensibility to the vagina by insisting that the final climax was realized on the signal either of the contractions of a man's penis during his orgasm, or by the impact on the vaginal walls of his ejaculation (Van de Velde, 1928): 'It forms a fit and perfect line in the wonderful chain of love process.' The procedures envisaged bestowed the favours of loveplay on the clitoris until the lady was suitably aroused and the pair reached a 'crescendo of emotion' at which the penis penetrated and it all happened.

Following Havelock Ellis, Van de Velde asserted that in the sexual act man and woman exult in male dominance; the act expresses the 'essential force of maleness' for male eroticism 'belongs to the moment of coitus and not to its preliminaries. If the force fails to ignite the organ of voluptuous sensation then the man should manipulate her to "concert pitch" and if that, too, fails then the objections are far from trivial.' Our man on sex, Chesser, followed this patriarchal model, though with rather less bravado; because women are slower than men they have to be stimulated by loveplay until 'union' is desired and (hopefully) mutual orgasm takes place.

The Stones in their classic and much-reprinted *Marriage Manual* described the clitoris as: 'perhaps the main seat of the woman's sensuous feelings'. Its stimulation is the prelude to the big moment. It induces a state of: 'readiness for entry and mutual orgasm'. However, they point out that many women never reach orgasm. This high rate of failure seemed inexplicable. Perhaps it was anatomical, they suggested. They acknowledged, too, that: 'in many cases the sexual response can only be evoked by direct stimulation of the clitoris' and then slipped into a prescription for normative fucking which was supported by the commonly held faith that while the clitoris remained the erotic place par excellence, the vagina, if worked on, might become sensitized and even have primary erotic sensation transferred to it. The success rate was expressed in Chesser's calculation, based on American and European studies, that seventy per cent of women never achieved satisfaction.

Up to this point only a particular genre of sexual reform has been considered, which does not incorporate the impact of psychoanalysis. Without offering an account of this, it is important to note the consensus – within which sexual reform and psychoanalysis co-existed – about the subsidiary role, or immaturity of clitoral orgasm. However, a crucial divergence erupted over precisely the role of the clitoris, and took a particularly acrimonious form in the fifties after the publication of the Kinsey Report in 1953.

Within the genre of sex counselling a poignant confrontation with the contradictions lurching around all this stuff is to be found in the work of Dr Helena Wright in Britain. Her book *The Sex Factor in Marriage* is a model: the sole purpose of the clitoris is pleasure, man has the joy of arousing woman and 'creating in her an ardour equal to his own' ... at the moment of sufficient excitement the woman is ready to receive the male, the mutual climax consummating the act is completed: 'thought is abandoned, a curious freeing of the spirit, very difficult to describe ... a pleasure of the soul ...' In this account, which typifies contemporary sentimentality, there are caveats, however, which are significant in her later revisions of this scheme. First she insists on two essential conditions for success: constant contact with the clitoris and free hip movement. Clitoral sensation seems natural in every woman, she observes. Vaginal excitement is more difficult. Although: 'theoretically it might be said the ideal type of feminine sensation is concerned with the vagina alone . . . that ideal is seldom realized'. In a classically suggestive phrase she declares: 'nearly all women find vaginal sensation through, as it were, the gateway of clitoris sensation . . .'

More than twenty-five years later she criticized the naive view that the main problem of the day was ignorance, largely it seems because she had to face her readers' complaints that they'd rigorously followed her blueprint but it didn't work: 'Try as we may my wife can attain no orgasm from intercourse', complained a reader, one among many. Wright's attention was thus dramatically drawn back to the site of woman's pleasure, and she isolated three major misunderstandings. Firstly; there was a failure to grasp the difference between general sexual response and orgasm; there was a lack of understanding as to the unique role of the clitoris; and lastly there were preconceptions about women's feelings during intercourse, based on the male pattern. This last produced the belief that during penetration (Wright, 1947):

> women will have an answering orgasm felt in the vagina induced by the movement of the penis . . . so strongly held and widespread is this expectation that it can be said to amount to a penis-vagina fixation.

Her autocritique, which pre-empted the findings of the 1953 Kinsey Report, reflected upon: 'being confronted for many years by the complaints of patients'. In vain they had followed her advice and still failed to achieve vaginal orgasm. Thus (Wright, 1947):

> I began to criticize this universal demand . . . as soon as I began to shake myself free of the current ideal and expectations, and to doubt the efficacy of the penis-vagina combination for producing an orgasm for a woman, the path was cleared and progress began to be made.

Having snuffed out the vagina she then confronted the nature of orgasm. Here, too, confusion was rampant among readers and patients; it was clear that many had no idea what an orgasm was like. So she told them. Firstly, anyone who only *thinks* they've had one hasn't. Secondly it isn't a general sensation, but very specific; like a sneeze it is preceded by tension, there's a short explosion, then relief, and it happens in one place only – in the relevant organ.

However, the nub of Wright's self-criticism was bitterly contested in sex literature. What is fascinating from our point of view is that what the women's liberation movement may have thought it invented, in Anne Koedt's essay 'The Myth of the Vaginal Orgasm', had a long pre-feminist history.

Among the influential analysts, clinicians and counsellors, there had long been little doubt as to the erotic significance of the clitoris. During and after the Second World War empirical research confirmed Wright's conclusions and there is evidence among some sexologists of growing confidence in challenging what Dickinson called 'phallic fantasies'. However, their work was still treated as more or less scandalous. Furthermore, the absence of a substantial feminist movement after the First and still more after the Second World War meant that the implications of such work could not readily be pursued or generalized. It seems to have fallen on deaf ears. It is worth noting that the very influential Chesser continued in the wake of Wright's *mea culpa* to write mushy manuals which replicated the very mystifications which Wright had tried to disentangle. Perhaps it is an index of the political mood in Britain after 1945 that Chesser's own sex report, modelled on Kinsey's and which provoked something of a scandal, aroused this response less because of its sexual than because of its moral implications. Chesser later had an essay in a British Medical Association handbook banned. Despite his rather devastating findings on the lack of 'satisfaction' among women, Chesser went down as the man who got banned for saying chastity was outmoded.

At the heart of the conundrum, which Wright was to spot and later sexologists were to confront, too, was the problem of the absence of any necessary correspondence between the reproductive act and the orgasmic moment for women. A number of other myths came under attack in the Kinsey Report (Kinsey, 1953). Kinsey made the outrageous proposal that there was no essential difference between the infant and the adult orgasm – which was to prove one of its major points of contention for Freudian opponents. The Report also suggested a much more widespread engagement in the erotic than the moralists thought proper. Thirty per cent of those questioned by Kinsey recalled pre-adolescent heterosexual fun and games, and thirty-three per cent recalled homosexual practices, the latter being very important in teaching women how to masturbate successfully, indeed it seems to have been a more relevant pedagogical resource than heterosexual hanky-panky. Sixty-four per cent of married women had experienced orgasm before marriage, mostly through masturbation, half had had pre-marital coitus, and seventy-one per cent achieved orgasm in 'marital coitus'.

The Kinsey Report was a sociological survey which had enormous impact, both because of the scale of its sample (although this was predominantly middle class) and because of its committed findings which tended to challenge the penis-vagina fixation as well as myths about women's chastity. It became a major issue of public concern. Among Kinsey's most virulent antagonists were Freudian fundamentalists who not only challenged the basis of the study (which did not calculate for *unconscious* response) but also the criteria for frigidity. Edmund Bergler (Bergler, 1954), who fiercely contested the Kinsey findings, insisted that: 'under frigidity we understand the incapacity to have a vaginal orgasm during intercourse . . . the sole criteria of frigidity is the absence of vaginal orgasm'. Not surprisingly he claimed a frigidity rate of between eighty and ninety per cent. This kind of claim was to founder on the clinical evidence produced a decade later by William H. Masters and Virginia Johnson (Masters and Johnson, 1966). But even before this, Albert Ellis was to make an intervention in the Kinsey debate which anticipated modern feminism. He rejected the Freudian notion that clitoral orgasm was immature and confirmed that in most women it was the occasion of greatest intensity. It was (Ellis, 1953): 'clinically certain' that some women 'who experience the most intense kinds of orgasm imaginable, experience it only or mainly as a result of clitoral (or other non-coital) stimulation'. There was no evidence, he said, that what was known as the vaginal orgasm came from that place, nor any that the clitoral orgasm didn't have a more general pelvic effect. Later he was to infer from the Kinsey Report a more general critique of the sex manuals' 'emphasis on coital techniques' and suggested attention to the labia and clitoris 'rather than concentration on coital positions'.

Masters and Johnson were to consummate this decades-long project. 'Phallic fantasy' had fostered the way that (Masters and Johnson, 1966): 'clinical error has dominated the assignment of the clitoral function . . . The primary focus for sexual response in the human female's pelvis is the clitoral body.' Marriage manuals concentrated on clitoral stimulation 'as the basis of adequate coital foreplay' when the 'infinitely more important question' was how to address the clitoris in its own right. Men didn't appreciate this, and vainly went for 'the deepest possible vaginal thrust' followed by 'spastic deep vaginal entrenchment' during ejaculation. Wrong! said Masters and Johnson. But despite these devastating insights they still baulked at the full separation of penetration from the independent interests of the clitoris, because, they argued, vaginal thrusting stimulated the clitoris by 'traction exerted on the wings of the minor labial hood' which enables them in turn to locate the vagina as the 'primary physical means for heterosexual expression for the human female'. Vaginal and clitoral orgasm, for them, became the same thing. (A quaint reminder of the heterosexist equation of penetration with the sex act came in the trial of Jeremy Thorpe, ex-leader of the British Liberal Party, who was accused of having had a homosexual relationship with Norman Scott and of having subsequently conspired to murder him when Scott threatened to make their relationship public, and did begin to make it public. During the trial, Thorpe's alleged involvement with Scott was not represented as 'buggery' but rather as 'the sexual act' or its synonym – penetration, proof that 'real sex' had taken place.) Kinsey and these other writers fuelled the moral angst which surrounded the sexual debates of the fifties and sixties, and which particularly focused in Britain on homosexual law reform and pre-marital sex. Whatever the crisis in the moral climate, it was clear that people were 'doing it' and on a rather large scale, aided and abetted by an anti-censorship, anti-obscenity-law lobby which if it didn't fully embrace any amount of any kind of sex as a good thing, affirmed it as possibly fun, as a sacrament and – when it was written about – as art. The political significance of sexual difference between men and women was increasingly blurred as the sexual revolution took sway, with women's resistance being represented as conservative diffidence. Lesbianism may have had more space to develop, simply as a function of liberalism, but the Permissive Era in the end consolidated the heterosexual imperative. Elizabeth Wilson (Campbell, 1979) has commented that lesbianism was equated with celibacy. The Permissive Era's object was consonant with the twentieth century theme described earlier; to recruit women into an active engagement in heterosexuality. The chastity lobby didn't give in, of course, but there were certain facts which reinforced the liberationists, from Kinsey and in Britain from the Registrar General himself: in 1950 one quarter of mothers conceived their first child before their wedding day (Wimperis, 1960). But underneath the chastity debate, there remained the core theme – the mystery of women's sexuality, and the implications of women's sexual self-assertion, exemplified in a grumpy satire by Malcolm Muggeridge (before he became totally ridiculous) in which he lamented the substitution of sexual revolution for social revolution. He growled that (Muggeridge, 1965): 'to the self-evident rights in the Declaration of Independence must be added another – the right to orgasm'. Writing of the Masters and Johnson study he wondered what could be more gross than the investigation of the female orgasm in a laboratory (Muggeridge, 1965): 'this surely is the apogee of the sexual revolution, the ultimate expression of the cult of the orgasm'. What he *didn't* own up to was that the problem wasn't just any old orgasm, but *women's*. This dotty volley from Muggeridge is interesting nevertheless for its hostility to the central concern of sexual reform movements in this century – women's sexuality – even though that preoccupation was not necessarily disclosed in the rhetoric of the sexual revolution.

I've gone through all this to indicate some of the ideological conditions out of which a feminist sexual politics emerged, in particular to illustrate the instabilities inherent in the sexual reform movement's approach to heterosexuality. Firstly, it is clear that there was a relative decline of the vagina to a subsidiary role in the representation of women's physical sexuality. Secondly, however, there was still a continuing dependence on the vagina in concepts of heterosexuality. Even though the centre of gravity shifted to the clitoris, the quintessential moment of heterosexuality remained penetration, the Sexual Act. A feminist heterosexuality has not yet been fully and confidently elaborated that, by making woman subject, marginalizes penetration for women, and in so doing dissolves the notion of the Sex Act. The necessity of penetration for men had hitherto constructed the moment of penetration as *the* sexual moment. And while feminist heterosexual practice may not exclude penetration, it would seem that it renders it subsidiary for women. I suspect that while this may be the case in practice, indeed surely is the case, feminism's dissolution of the notion of penetration as the Sexual Act has not been fully brought to the movement's sense of a feminist sexual politics.

THE WOMEN'S LIBERATION MOVEMENT

The subsequent notes are intended to be a polemical review of contemporary British feminism's development of sexual politics.

The first thing that can be said is that feminism more fully politicized sexuality than the advocates of the Permissive Era ever did, both by establishing women as the subject of feminist sexual politics, and by proposing a politics of personal life. Women's Liberation was initially concerned to make heterosexuality problematic. And secondly it established orgasm and women's pleasure as a stake in sexual struggle. This shifted the centre of gravity of permissive sexual politics in which women were simply objects of pleasure. Even though it may have been influenced by the permissive radicalism of left sexual politics of the sixties, it readily criticized the Marcusian or Reichian approach for failing to specify the contradiction between men and women and failing to address the patriarchal character of normative heterosexuality. Implicit, too, in the development of feminist sexual politics was a critique of the essentialism inherent in the Marcusian repression thesis, which envisaged liberation of erotic sensuality as a socio-political detonator (Marcuse, 1970). It is a critique that goes much further than latterday libertarian cynicism about the sexual revolution, which has simply expressed a weary disappointment at the ways in which capital, no longer needing compulsive monogamous marriage, has corralled and appropriated the supposedly disruptive impact of sexual liberation (Dahmer, 1978). Feminism was, then, initially concerned to scrutinize heterosexuality as a practice in which femininity itself was constructed. In that sense it went beyond the sixties pleasure programme, even though it may not yet have had available to it a vocabulary that enabled the theorization of sexuality as a site in which femininity is constructed, and is thus a site of combat. A theoretical idiom for this only began to emerge in the seventies, with the application of Althusserian Marxism and psychoanalysis. The typical preoccupations of feminist sexual politics (exemplified by say Whiting, 1971) were with women's active sexual engagement and an opposition to subordination/passivity, together with an insistence on the separation of sex from reproduction.

The political instrument by which sexuality was politicized was consciousness-raising in which other women provided the means for collective self-recognition. It provided an alternative to the dispersal of women in male-dominated politics, by means of separation, distance, autonomous political space. It is worth recalling that all this was happening in the context of the dominance of heterosexuality as a practice. Most feminists were *in* heterosexuality, and through women's liberation were beginning to be able to *organize* their engagement in heterosexuality. At the very least it encouraged a culture in which a critique of heterosexuality was feasible – and I will argue later that, sadly, this process was thwarted by other political problems within feminism. The effect was to block the growth of confident feminist mobilization around heterosexuality, except in so far as autonomy was a condition of mobilizing *any* feminist critique of heterosexuality. Consciousness-raising was also a provisional means of constructing alternative representations of women, because within that process women were able to make problematic the category 'woman'. Consciousness-raising was a means of opposing habitual ways of being feminine. It also served as a place of resource (one of the functions outlined by the Italian Marxist Gramsci [1971] for the political forms of subordinate social classes or groups [Campbell, 1978]). However, the full political potential suggested by this development was not realized – largely because of divisions within the movement from about 1973. But a feminist sexual politics was also thwarted by feminism's approach to sex itself. It would seem that an essential component of feminist sexual politics should be a feminist erotica. But with a few exceptions there's been little enough of that. There has been little space for a feminist erotica which could represent heterosexuality as both erotic and as an arena of contradiction and contestation. There's some contemporary lesbian erotica, though much of it, in my view, tends to be maudlin, complacent or didactic rather than erotic. It still seems difficult to produce an erotica that isn't easily happy or halcyon.

The struggle is not helped, no doubt, by men. Few seem worth wooing. And just as women's relationship to femininity remains problematic, so does our response to masculinity. A simple inversion won't do – the feminization of masculinity, the enervation of men and a celebration of passivity and lack of energy in men, rendering soft sex the 'sound' mode. Then there are those men who assume that feminism produces a simple transition in women from passivity to activity – their dream come true, access to the pyrotechnical lady lover. And of course feminism can be used to beat her over the head if she remains passive.

CRISIS OF SISTERHOOD

Apart from the conflict between socialist-feminism and radical-feminism within women's liberation, confidence in the autonomy of the movement cracked also because of the experience of the limits of consciousness-raising on the one hand, and the sense of marginality in relation to political forces outside the movement on the other hand. Furthermore, the movement's internal practice celebrated a form of sisterhood, again through the medium of consciousness-raising, which depended on common identification as the source of collective self-knowledge and the condition of collaboration – it didn't easily accommodate difference. Sisterhood became transposed in some variants of feminism into a cult of woman. It took many forms, from resurrection of the matriarchy, through Earth-Motherhood to bovver-girl with a bottle of Newcastle Brown. What was common to all these modes was a sentimentalization of femaleness and an essentialism based on a cult of women-are-wonderful, or rather women-without-men-are-wonderful, in their natural state, free of men's rude interruptions. Through sisterhood some women searched for authenticity, a female essence, which could be achieved by a voluntaristic choice – to become woman through being with women. The woman cult depoliticized women's sexuality, firstly by romanticizing it and secondly by abstracting it from gendered social relations and practices. This produced a new femininity – it didn't matter that it mirrored entrenched stereotypes, what mattered more was that these modes fetishized women-togetherness. And all this coincided with the increasingly antagonistic contradiction between radical-feminism and socialist-feminism. A feminist sexual politics was defeated indirectly by the hegemony of radical-feminism. That's not to say that only socialist-feminism could have produced a feminist sexual politics. Socialists in the movement were probably still too tentative about the status of personal life at that time. But rather, it is to say that the conditions for its construction were wiped out by the bust-up between the two major tendencies. Heterosexuality was banished to the swamp. Those women unfortunate enough to remain unreconstructed, languishing in the het. jungle were, in effect, accused of not only allowing themselves to be cosseted and corrupted by men – cowards who chose to sink with the men rather than swim with the ladies – but also of failing politically to prioritize women.

That the political sectarianism was armed by radical-feminist appropriation of lesbianism, and now by 'political lesbianism', which tuned in less to erotic affirmation of women (which, if nothing else, lesbianism historically has been about) than to a polemical inquisition against women who fuck men. So in that sense it's more about men than about women.

Lesbianism first emerged as a hot issue at the national conference of the women's liberation movement at Skegness in 1971, when a couple of small but powerful Maoist groups fell in round one in their attempts to isolate lesbianism as a bourgeois deviation. That was not only a specific campaign against lesbianism, but also against *any* sexual politics, and reflected their belief that the capital-labour contradiction was sufficient to account for the sexual antagonism. Lesbianism became an issue in its own right, just about, at the movement's national conference in Edinburgh in 1974 with the adoption of the Sixth Demand, which coupled an end to discrimination against lesbians with a general demand for women's right to be sexually self-determining (an unhelpful coupling which still needs to be parted). But it was during

1974-5 that the combat between the two major tendencies assumed a particularly destructive force, over arguments about the nature of the Women's Liberation Workshop in London, and over the presence of men on the International Women's Day marches. The effect was to dismember the Workshop as a centre for the whole movement in London, and to disperse the many groups previously associated with it. Many women in the movement retreated in hurt confusion, and there's a feeling of alienation that still prevails today among many activists – they feel it doesn't belong to them. What was left took on all the characteristics of an exclusive and marginal culture. This was compounded in the autumn of 1974 by the approving serialization over ten issues of the Women's Liberation Workshop Newsletter of a toxic diatribe which had first appeared in the New York radical-feminist publication, *Off Our Backs* ('The Clit Statement', 1974): 'straight women think, talk, cross their legs, dress, come on like male transvestite "femme" drag queens. Bisexuality maintains the patriarchy. Lesbianism understood is a revolt against the patriarchy ... Everybody knows from the first minute the Women's Liberation Movement hit that feminism means lesbianism ...' Half a dozen issues on, the next instalment declared: 'The danger of straight women is their disguise, they look like women ... they are men in disguise.' There we had it. Heterosexual women were dangerous. They weren't even women. There were rather timorous complaints in the Newsletter, but the diatribe went on and on. And just when it seemed to wane there would be a new wave. Radical-feminism re-grouped, appropriated and inverted Marxist theory and ultimately came up with a novel but strategically inept formulation, '"workers" control of reproduction', the novelty wore off, things quietened down only to erupt at the 1978 Women's Liberation Movement national conference in Birmingham, and then towards the end of last year we were gonged into the next round with the emergence of 'political lesbianism' in a debate in the national Newsletter, *Wires.*

To some extent this culture was armed with the vocabulary of the movement's tentative explorations of sexuality, which drew on a perfectly honourable tradition, not least *The Second Sex* by Simone de Beauvoir (1953), which represented penetration as trespass and invasion, and as the moment of women's subordination. Of course it had a certain strength as a critique of patriarchal fucking. It was supported by the argument that penetration was fairly insignificant to women except insofar as it brought pleasure to men, and only incidental pleasure to women; and also that penetration was a practice involving risk to women insofar as it was coupled with ejaculation, leaving women with the penalty of pregnancy and total responsibility for contraception. However, the representation of penetration by feminists as *the* moment of heterosexuality's subordination ignored its place as an arena of struggle between men and women, both to transform its meaning for both sexes, and to displace it as The Sexual Act. Radical-feminism drew on a vocabulary of visceral colonialism – we had a plethora of phallic imperialisms, penile tyrannies and so on enumerated in the Newsletter, for example, which in effect rendered the act of penetration and the possession of a penis as, of themselves, constituting domination. And it still goes on. 'Only in the system that is male supremacy does the oppressor actually invade and colonize the interior of the oppressed', writes Leeds Revolutionary Feminist Group in *Wires* Number 81, December 1979. All this rhetoric flourished in the absence of a feminist erotica and despite the development of theoretical work on ideological practices. The effect was to reduce the mainstream of the movement to dumb insubordination in the sex war, leaving heterosexual struggle to the individual initiatives of women more or less on their own. The representation of penetration as necessarily colonialistic foreclosed any programme of struggle in heterosexual practice.

In the end feminist sexual politics has become an analogue of lesbian politics. This has been primarily expressed in two ways. Firstly it emerges in the slogan 'Any woman can (be a lesbian)'. While no doubt, in a certain sense, true, this denies the specific autonomy of lesbianism within feminism, and it also denies the specific sexual circumstances of most women. Secondly there has been the equation of lesbianism with prioritization of women and not wasting time on men. Strategically this approach offers only flight from heterosexuality which is represented as sex collaboration equivalent to class collaboration – fraternizing with the enemy. Far from proposing lesbianism as a *possible* practice, with all its important implications of non-dependence on men, within a pluralism of practices in feminism including heterosexuality and celibacy, lesbianism is represented as the *only* possible practice. The new 'political lesbianism' confounds the development of a *sexual* politics by suggesting that a political lesbian 'is a woman-identified woman who does not fuck men. It does not mean compulsory sexual activity with women.' So it isn't even about sex.

These approaches have to be rejected not only because they are undemocratic, but also because they deny any political practice within heterosexuality and they don't safeguard specifically lesbian culture and sex. They *prohibit* the formulation of a feminist sexual politics. What would the conditions for the latter be?

First, pluralism in the movement; second, heterosexuality would have to be legitimated as a field for feminist presence and recognition of feminism's impact on sexual relations with men. Feminist intervention in heterosexuality proposes its reorganization. Radical-feminist-lesbianism has to deny the possibility of any change in heterosexuality, of course, and its prophecy has been self-fulfilling – we've little idea how women have been able to intervene in heterosexuality; but it also has to deny possible change because its advocacy of lesbianism depends on a failure of heterosexuality – and that, to me as a lesbian, smacks of the failure slur that lesbians only do it with women because they can't get it together with men. Thirdly, rather than proposing lesbianism as the only possible feminist sexual practice, it seems to me that the autonomy of a lesbian presence as such has to be defended in the Women's Liberation Movement.

Fourthly, it is clear that feminism has enabled both the beginnings of a transformation of heterosexuality and the possibility of a politically supported sexual practice which engages both men and women, and which is neither categorically heterosexual or lesbian; furthermore this can't be represented as the closet gayness which could have been asserted politically by Gay Liberation. Part of the problem here is that on the one hand gayness can't be denied its cultural concomitants, which I think is an effect of so-called political lesbianism, but equally while bisexual practice in the context of feminist politics can't be tarred with the closet brush, it doesn't yet have a political agreement, for which (contrary to how things might seem) common ground exists – it is a shared critique of sexist heterosexuality. But that needs to be armed by a political alliance engaged in diverse and shifting practices.

An essential condition for this must be an organizational form within which the politics of personal life can be developed. That we lack at the moment because of the demise of consciousness-raising, but without suggesting a nostalgic and uncritical rehabilitation of the movement's early forms it does seem that we need to review that experience with a view to constructing a new political space for personal life.

For their time and talk, thanks to Susan Todd, Peter Horne and the Red Rag Collective; and thanks to Jean Radford, Jean McCrindle and Maria Duggan, and the Feminist Education Group and Feminist Review for comments and criticisms.

References

Bergler, Edmund and Kroger, William (1954), *Kinsey's Myth of Female Sexuality*, New York: Grune and Stratton.

Browne, Stella (1915), 'Sexual Variety and Variability Among Women', *British Journal for the Study of Sex Psychology*.

Campbell, Beatrix (1978), 'Sweets From a Stranger', *Red Rag*, no. 13.

Campbell, Beatrix and Deer, Brian (1979), 'The Pride and the Passion', *Time Out*, no. 479.

Chesser, Eustace (1946), *Marriage and Freedom*, London: Rich and Cowan.

Chesser, Eustace (1956), *The Sexual, Marital and Family Relationships of the English Woman*, London: Hutchinson.

Chesser, Eustace (1961), *Is Chastity Outmoded?*, London: Heinemann.

Chesser, Eustace (1966), *Love Without Fear*, London: Arrow.

Clit (1974), 'The Second Statement', *Off Our Backs*, reprinted in the Women's Liberation Newsletter.

Dahmer, Helmut (1978), 'Sexual Economy Today', *Telos*, 36.

de Beauvoir, Simone (1953), *The Second Sex*, London: Jonathan Cape.

Dickinson, Robert and Beam, Lura (1932), *A Thousand Marriages*, London: Balliere, Tindall and Cox.

Ellis, Albert (1953), 'Is the Vaginal Orgasm a Myth?', *International Journal of Sexology*.

Ellis, Havelock (1918), 'Erotic Rights of Women', *British Journal for the Study of Psychology*.

Ellis, Havelock (1928), *Studies in the Psychology of Sex*, Philadelphia: F. A. Davis and Co.

Gramsci, Antonio (1971), *The Prison Notebooks*, London: Lawrence and Wishart.

Hirschfeld, Magnus (1935), *Sex in Human Relations*, London: John Lane.

Kinsey, Alfred (1953), *Sexual Behavior in the Human Female*.

Koedt, Anne (1970), 'The Myth of the Vaginal Orgasm', *Notes from the Second Year*.

Lindsey, Ben (1928), *The Companionate Marriage*, London: Brentano's.

Marcuse, Herbert (1970), *Eros and Civilization*, London: Sphere.

Masters, William and Johnson, Virginia (1966), *Human Sexual Response*, London: Churchill.

Muggeridge, Malcolm (1965), 'The Sexual Revolution', *New Statesman*, 2 April.

Russell, Dora (1927), *The Right to be Happy*, London: Routledge and Kegan Paul.

Stone, Hannah and Stone, Abraham (1952), *A Marriage Manual*, London: Gollancz.

Van de Velde, Thomas (1928), *Ideal Marriage*, London: Heinemann.

Wandor, Michelene (1972), ed., *The Body Politic*, London: Stage 1.
Whiting, Pat (1971), 'Female Sexuality: Its Political Implications', in Wandor (1972).
Wimperis, Virginia (1960), *The Unmarried Mother and Her Child*, London: George Allen and Co.
Wright, Helena (1947), *More About the Sex Factor in Marriage*, London: Williams and Northgate.

Simone de Beauvoir

Sexual Initiation

From Simone de Beauvoir, *The Second Sex*, tr. H. M. Parshley, New York: Bantam, 1964, pp. 371-8 (first published in France, 1949)

It is certainly true that woman's sex pleasure is quite different from man's. I have already noted that it is uncertain whether vaginal feeling ever rises to a definite orgasm: statements by women on the matter are rare, and they remain extremely vague even when precision is attempted; it would appear that the reactions are widely variable in different individuals. But there is no doubt that for man coition has a definite biological conclusion: ejaculation. And certainly many other quite complex intentions are involved in aiming at this goal; but once attained, it seems a definite result, and if not the full satisfaction of desire, at least its termination for the time being. In woman, on the contrary, the goal is uncertain from the start, and more psychological in nature than physiological; she desires sex excitement and pleasure in general, but her body promises no precise conclusion to the act of love; and that is why coition is never quite terminated for her: it admits of no end. Male sex feeling rises like an arrow; when it reaches a certain height or threshold, it is fulfilled and dies abruptly in the orgasm; the pattern of the sexual act is finite and discontinuous. Feminine sex enjoyment radiates throughout the whole body; it is not always centered in the genital organs; even when it is, the vaginal contractions constitute, rather than a true orgasm, a system of waves that rhythmically arise, disappear, and re-form, attain from time to time a paroxysmal condition, become vague, and sink down without ever quite dying out. Because no definite term is set, woman's sex feeling extends toward infinity; it is often nervous or cardiac fatigue or psychic satiety that limits woman's erotic possibilities, rather than a specific gratification; even when overwhelmed, exhausted, she may never find full deliverance: *lassata nondum satiata*, as Juvenal put it.

A man is very wrong in undertaking to impose his own rhythm or timing upon his partner and in working furiously to give her an orgasm: he would often succeed only in shattering the form of eroticism she was on the way to experiencing in her special manner.[1] It is a form sufficiently plastic to set its own term: certain spasms localized in the vagina or in the sexual system as a whole, or involving the entire body, can constitute a resolution; in some women they are strong enough and are produced with sufficient regularity to be regarded as orgasms; but a woman in love can also find in the man's orgasm a conclusion that brings appeasement and satisfaction. And it is also possible for the erotic state to be quietly resolved in a gradual manner, without abrupt climax. Success does not require a mathematical synchronization of feeling, as in the oversimplified belief of many meticulous men, but the establishment of a complex erotic pattern. Many suppose that to 'make' a woman feel pleasure is a matter of time and technique, indeed of violent action; they do not realize to what a degree woman's sexuality is conditioned by the total situation.

Sex pleasure in woman, as I have said, is a kind of magic spell; it demands complete abandon; if words or movements oppose the magic of caresses, the spell is broken. This is one of the reasons why the woman closes her eyes; physiologically, this is a reflex compensating for the dilation of the pupils; but she lowers her eyelids even in the dark. She would abolish all surroundings, abolish the singularity of the moment, of herself, and of her lover, she would fain be lost in a carnal night as shadowy as the maternal womb. And more especially she longs to do away with the separateness that exists between her and the male; she longs to melt with him into one. As we have seen, she wants to remain subject while she is made object. Being more profoundly beside herself than is man because her whole body is moved by desire and excitement, she retains her subjectivity only through union with her partner; giving and receiving must be combined for both. If the man confines himself to taking without giving or if he bestows pleasure without receiving, the woman feels that she is being maneuvered, used; once she realizes herself as the Other, she becomes the inessential other, and then she is bound to deny her alterity.

This accounts for the fact that the moment when the two bodies separate is almost always distressing for the woman. After coition the man always disowns the flesh, regardless of whether he feels happy or depressed, the dupe of nature or the conqueror of woman; he becomes once more an honest body, he wants to sleep, take a bath, smoke a cigarette, go out for a breath of fresh air. The woman

---

1. Lawrence saw clearly the contrast between these two forms of sex feeling. But his statement that women *should* not experience the orgasm is arbitrary. It is a mistake to try to induce it at any cost; it is also wrong to withhold it at all times as does Don Cipriano in *The Plumed Serpent*.

wants to prolong the carnal contact until the spell that made her flesh is completely dissipated; to separate is for her a painful uprooting like being weaned all over again; she feels resentful toward a lover who moves away from her too abruptly. But she is hurt even more by words that run counter to the amalgamation in which for a moment she has firmly believed. Madeleine Bour-douxhe tells of a woman who recoiled when her husband asked if she had enjoyed herself, putting her hand over his mouth; the expression horrifies many women because it reduces erotic pleasure to an immanent and separately felt sensation. 'Was it enough? You want more? Was it good?' – the very fact of asking such questions emphasizes the separation, changes the act of love into a mechanical operation directed by the male. And that is, indeed, why he asks them. He really seeks domination much more than fusion and reciprocity; when the unity of the pair is broken, he is once more sole subject: to renounce this privileged position requires a great deal of love or of generosity. He likes to have the woman feel humiliated, possessed, in spite of herself; he always wants to take her a little more than she gives herself. Woman would be spared many difficulties if man did not carry in his train the many complexes that make him regard the act of love as a battle; then she could cease to view the bed as an arena.

And yet one does observe in the young girl a desire to be dominated, along with her narcissism and her pride. Masochism, according to some psychoanalysts, is one of woman's characteristics, and it is this tendency that enables her to adapt herself to her erotic destiny. But the concept of masochism is most confused, and we must take a close look at it.

Following Freud, psychoanalysts distinguish three types of masochism: one consists in the alliance of pain and sex pleasure, another would be feminine acceptance of erotic dependency, the third would rest upon a mechanism of self-punishment. In this view woman would be masochistic because pleasure and pain, for her, are allied through defloration and childbirth, and because she accepts her passive role.

We must note first of all that attributing an erotic value to pain does not at all imply behavior marked by passive submission. Frequently pain serves to raise muscle tonus, to reawaken sensitivity blunted by the very violence of sex excitement and pleasure; it is a sharp beam of light flashing in the night of the flesh, it raises the lover from the limbo where he swoons so that he may be hurled down again. Pain is normally a part of the erotic frenzy; bodies that delight to be bodies for the joy they give each other, seek to find each other, to unite, to confront each other in every possible manner. There is in erotic love a tearing away from the self, transport, ecstasy; suffering also tears through the limits of the ego, it is transcendence, a paroxysm; pain has always played a great part in orgies; and it is well known that the exquisite and the painful intermesh: a caress can become torture, torment can give pleasure. The embrace leads easily to biting, pinching, scratching; such behavior is not ordinarily sadistic; it shows a desire to blend, not to destroy; and the individual who suffers it is not seeking rejection and humiliation, but union; besides, it is not specifically masculine behavior – far from it. Pain, in fact, is of masochistic significance only when it is accepted and wanted as proof of servitude. As for the pain of defloration, it is not closely correlated with pleasure; and as for the sufferings of childbirth, all women fear them and are glad that modern obstetrical methods are doing away with them. Pain has no greater and no less a place in woman's sexuality than in man's.

Feminine docility, furthermore, is a very equivocal concept. We have seen that usually the young girl accepts *in imagination* the domination of a demigod, a hero, a male; but this is still no more than a narcissistic game. It in no way disposes her to submit in reality to the carnal exercise of such authority. Often, on the contrary, she rejects the man she admires and respects and gives herself to a man of no distinction. It is a mistake to seek in fantasies the key to concrete behavior; for fantasies are created and cherished as fantasies. The little girl who dreams of violation with mingled horror and acquiescence does not really *wish* to be violated, and if such a thing should happen it would be a hateful calamity. We have already noted a typical example of this dissociation in Marie le Hardouin's *La Voile noire*, and she confesses further that 'there is not a stealthy infamy that I have not committed in my dreams'. And we may quote Marie Bashkirtsev again: 'All my life I have sought to subject myself to some *illusory domination*, but all the men I tried were so commonplace in comparison to myself that I only felt disgust.'

Still, it is true that the sexual role of woman is largely passive; but the actual performance of that passive part is no more masochistic than the normal aggressive behavior of the male is sadistic; woman can transcend caresses, excitement, and penetration, toward the attainment of her own pleasure, thus upholding her subjectivity; she can also seek union with her lover and give herself to him, which represents transcendence of self and not abdication. Masochism exists when the individual chooses to be made purely a thing under the conscious will of others, to see herself as a thing, to play at being a thing. 'Masochism is an attempt not to fascinate the other by my objectivity, but to be myself fascinated by my objectivity in the eyes of the other.'[2] Sade's Juliette and the young virgin in his *Philosophie dans le boudoir*, who give themselves to the male in every possible way but always for their own pleasure, are in no way masochistic. Neither are Lady Chatterley and Kate, in spite of their abandon. Masochism exists only when the *ego* is set up as separate and when this estranged self, or double, is regarded as dependent upon the will of others.

In this sense, indeed, a true masochism is to be observed in certain women. The young girl is inclined toward it, since she is often narcissistic and since narcissism consists in the setting up of the ego as a double, a stranger. If she feels from the beginning of her erotic initiation a high degree of excitation and desire, she will genuinely *live* her experiences inwardly and will cease to project them upon this ideal pole she calls 'myself'; but if she is frigid, this outer 'myself' will continue to be asserted, and then to be a man's thing seems a transgression. Now, 'masochism, like sadism, is the assumption of guilt. I am guilty, in fact, simply because I am object.' This idea of Sartre's is in line with the Freudian conception of self-punishment. The young girl considers herself to blame for submitting her ego to others, and she punishes herself for it by voluntarily redoubling her humiliation and slavishness; as we have seen, virgins feel defiant toward their lovers-to-be and punish themselves for their coming submissiveness by various kinds of self-torment; when the lover is finally real and present, they persist in this attitude. Frigidity, indeed, as we have seen, would appear to be a punishment that woman imposes as much upon herself as upon her partner: wounded in her vanity, she feels resentment against him and against herself, and she denies herself pleasure. In her masochism she will desperately enslave herself to the male, she will utter words of adoration, she will want to be humiliated, beaten; she will alienate her ego more and more profoundly for rage at having permitted the alienation to start. Such is rather clearly the behavior of Mathilde de la Môle, for example; she is vexed at having yielded to Julien; this is why, at times, she falls at his feet, willingly bends to his every caprice, sacrifices her hair to him; but at the same time she is revolted as much against him as against herself; we readily divine her cold as ice in his arms.

The sham abandon of the masochistic woman creates new barriers between her and enjoyment; and at the same time she is taking vengeance upon herself by means of this inability to know enjoyment. The vicious circle involving frigidity and masochism

2. J.-P. Sartre: *L'Être et le néant*.

can be set up permanently, and may then induce sadistic behavior by way of compensation. Her erotic maturation, in some cases, may deliver a woman from her frigidity, her narcissism, and, accepting her passive sexuality, she may experience it in actuality instead of continuing her play-acting. For it is the paradox of masochism that the subject constantly asserts herself in the very effort to abdicate; it is in the unpremeditated giving of oneself, the spontaneous reaching out toward the other, that one attains forgetfulness of self. It is true, then, that woman is more liable than man to the masochistic temptation; her erotic position as passive object leads her to play at passivity; this game is the self-punishment to which she is invited by her narcissistic revolts and her resulting frigidity. The fact is that many women and in particular many young girls are masochists. Colette, referring to her first amorous experiences in *Mes apprentissages*, confides in us as follows:

> With the connivance of youth and ignorance, I had indeed begun in a state of exaltation, a culpable exaltation, a hideous and impure adolescent surge. Many are the young girls, hardly of marriageable age as yet, who dream of being the private spectacle, the plaything, the licentious masterpiece of a mature man. It is an ugly longing that they atone for by satisfying it, a longing of a piece with the neuroses of puberty, the habit of gnawing chalk and charcoal, drinking mouthwash, reading indecent books, and sticking pins in one's palm.

The fact could not be better expressed that masochism belongs among the juvenile perversions, that it is no true solution of the conflict created by woman's sexual destiny, but a mode of escaping from it by wallowing in it. Masochism by no means represents the normal and happy flowering of feminine eroticism.

Such full development requires that – in love, affection, sensuality – woman succeed in overcoming her passivity and in establishing a relation of reciprocity with her partner. The dissimilarity that exists between the eroticism of the male and that of the female creates insoluble problems as long as there is a 'battle of the sexes'; they can easily be solved when woman finds in the male both desire and respect; if he lusts after her flesh while recognizing her freedom, she feels herself to be the essential, her integrity remains unimpaired the while she makes herself object; she remains free in the submission to which she consents. Under such conditions the lovers can enjoy a common pleasure, in the fashion suitable for each, the partners each feeling the pleasure as being his or her own but as having its source in the other. The verbs *to give* and *to receive* exchange meanings; joy is gratitude, pleasure is affection. Under a concrete and carnal form there is mutual recognition of the ego and of the other in the keenest awareness of the other and of the ego. Some women say that they feel the masculine sex organ in them as a part of their own bodies; some men feel that they *are* the women they penetrate. These are evidently inexact expressions, for the dimension, the relation of the *other* still exists; but the fact is that alterity has no longer a hostile implication, and indeed this sense of the union of really separate bodies is what gives its emotional character to the sexual act; and it is the more overwhelming as the two beings, who together in passion deny and assert their boundaries, are similar and yet unlike. This unlikeness, which too often isolates them, becomes the source of their enchantment when they do unite. The woman sees in man's virile impetuosity the reverse aspect of the passive fever that burns within her; the man's potency reflects the power she exercises upon him; this life-engorged organ belongs to her as her smile belongs to the man who floods her with pleasure. All the treasures of virility, of femininity, reflect each other, and thus they form an ever shifting and ecstatic unity. What is required for such harmony is not refinement in technique, but rather, on the foundation of the moment's erotic charm, a mutual generosity of body and soul.

This generosity is often inhibited in man by his vanity, in woman by her timidity. So long as her inhibitions persist, this generosity cannot prevail, which explains why full sexual flowering in woman is generally more or less delayed: she attains her erotic zenith toward the age of thirty-five. Unfortunately, if she is married, her husband is by that time too accustomed to her relative frigidity; she is still able to charm new lovers, but she begins to lose the bloom of youth: her days are numbered. It is precisely at the moment when they cease to be desirable that many women finally make up their minds to become frankly desirous.

The conditions under which woman's sexual life unfolds depend not only upon these matters but also upon her social and economic situation as a whole. It would be unrealistic to undertake further study apart from this context. But several conclusions of general value already emerge from our investigation. The erotic experience is one that most poignantly discloses to human beings the ambiguity of their condition; in it they are aware of themselves as flesh and as spirit, as the other and as subject. This conflict has a more dramatic shape for woman because at first she feels herself to be object and does not at once realize a sure independence in sex enjoyment; she must regain her dignity as transcendent and free subject while assuming her carnal condition – an enterprise fraught with difficulty and danger, and one that often fails. But the very difficulty of her position protects her against the traps into which the male readily falls; he is an easy dupe of the deceptive privileges accorded him by his aggressive role and by the lonely satisfaction of the orgasm; he hesitates to see himself fully as flesh. Woman lives her love in more genuine fashion.

Whether she adjusts herself more or less exactly to her passive role, woman is always frustrated as an active individual. It is not the possessive organ she envies the male: it is his prey.

It is an old paradox that the male inhabits a sensual world of sweetness, affection, gentleness, a feminine world, whereas woman moves in the male universe, which is hard and rough; her hands still long for contact with soft, smooth flesh; the adolescent boy, a woman, flowers, fur, the child; a whole region within her remains unoccupied and longs to possess a treasure like that which she gives the male. This explains the fact that in many women there subsists a tendency toward homosexuality more or less marked. There is a type of woman in whom, for a variety of complex reasons, this tendency manifests itself with unusual strength. Not all women are able and willing to solve their sexual problems in the standard fashion, the only manner approved by society.

Stevi Jackson

Constructing Female Sexuality

From Stevi Jackson, *On the Social Construction of Female Sexuality*, London: Women's Research and Resources Centre, 1978, pp. 8–18

THE CULTURAL SHAPING OF THE SEXUAL: REPRESSIVE OR CONSTRUCTIVE?

How, then, does culture create the sexual? The processes whereby an individual is socialised into particular modes of sexuality may be conceptualised in two essentially oppositional ways. We might begin by positing the existence of some form of innate sexual drive which is then moulded, modified, or repressed by the operation of social forces: i.e. that learning involves the curbing of instinctual urges. In terms of this model it could be argued that a particularly severe repression of libido undergone by women accounts for the form female sexuality takes. Alternatively we might postulate a process of learning through social interaction whereby the sexual is assimilated to the individual's self-concept. According to this view, psycho-sexual development is not contingent upon biological determinants, but on the milieu and content of social learning. The feminine mode of sexual expression would then be explained as the outcome of a particular form of learning rather than the repression of some quantifiable sexual energy.

The former premise is the basis on which Freudian theory was founded. Later work in this area, even when repudiating Freudianism, has tended to adopt the concept of libido or at least the assumption that some basic sexual drive exists. This has tended to favour a rather over-determined view of sexuality as an innate force emanating from the individual. The alternative approach, as outlined by Gagnon and Simon, attempts to counteract these tendencies (Simon and Gagnon, 1969).

The latter approach has several advantages. In the first place, by disallowing the primacy of biological drives, it permits a more positive conception of the socio-cultural influences involved, providing a sense of the social construction of sexuality rather than viewing the learning process as a negative tampering with innate biological mechanisms – even supposing that it is possible to identify an inborn, unsocialised drive. Secondly, this approach lends itself to a more sophisticated handling of the concept of socialisation. To view this as the repression of innate drives is to present the individual as the passive product of a struggle between biological and social forces. Even if the latter are declared the victors of the battle, there is a danger of replacing biological determinism with an equally rigid and over-simplified sociologistic explanation. Although such dangers are by no means absent from theories of social learning, Gagnon and Simon provide an interactionist framework within which the subject may be seen as active in her or his socialisation: in the construction of the sexual self.

Finally, and perhaps most importantly, this perspective avoids the difficulties posed by the heritage of Freudian phallocentricity. It has been argued that

> ... the fact is that the male sex is not only considered relatively superior to the female, but it is taken as the universal human norm. [Georg Simmel, quoted in Klein, 1946, p. 82]

This assumption is an integral part of Freudian theory – the libido is seen as an active, masculine force. If female sexuality is assumed to be the product of a repressed libido, there is a danger of perceiving it as either a distorted version of the masculine (and of therefore evaluating male sexuality as 'better') or as a functional complement to it. Most of the theorising in this area has been done by men who have indeed conceptualised female sexuality in these terms. Gagnon and Simon's model enables us to see masculine and feminine forms of sexuality as the results of differing learning experiences rather than as the outcome of differential repression. Hence the problem of treating the feminine as merely the negation of the masculine is avoided.

Although Freud's theory may be rejected on these grounds, it cannot easily be dismissed as not worth discussing, for his massive contribution to theories of sexuality should not be ignored. His work represents the first comprehensive theory of psycho-sexual development and is a most impressive attempt to come to terms with the complexities of the problem, to understand the interrelationship between biological, psychological and environmental influences and to relate sexuality to the rest of personality. Freud's theory assumes further importance by virtue of the great impact it has had upon everyday thinking about the sexual. Not only did it provide a starting point for the development of later theories, but it has filtered into the folk-knowledge of our society and helped to shape common-sense conceptions of sexuality. An examination of

Freud's ideas and of the criticisms Gagnon and Simon offer will illuminate some of the problems involved in discussing the emergence and development of sexuality.

TALES OF TRAUMA AND TRANSFERENCE: FREUD ON FEMININITY AND SEXUALITY

I do not wish to question Freud's observations of the forms of female sexuality he encountered, for these were often quite insightful. It is in the attribution of causality that I consider him to have been at fault; in particular in his concept of the libido and the role played by social factors.

Freud traces the development of the libido, an inborn sexual energy, through various stages which condition the final form of adult sexuality. But the significance of this development is not only sexual: for him the whole of human personality is determined by a series of crises assailing the libido. He hopes to find the key to the 'mystery' of femininity and female sexuality in such phenomena as penis envy, the Oedipal situation, and the clitoral-vaginal transference. Of these it is the 'genital trauma' which is apparently the major influence upon the female psyche.

When a little girl of three or four years of age first sets eyes upon the male organ, Freud informs us, she is immediately overcome by an intense envy from which she will never fully recover. On the basis of her own experience of clitoral activity she will make a correct judgment of the sexual, or at least masturbatory function of this organ and will 'realise' that her own is inadequate for the purpose. She will see herself as castrated. This traumatic discovery, Freud argues, is responsible for the greater degree of envy in the mental life of women and for their 'extraordinary vanity', the latter being a compensation for their anatomical 'deficiency'. Babies, too, are compensation; a male baby is particularly desired since he brings with him the 'longed-for penis' (Freud, 1925, 1931 and 1933).

Yet why should a little girl covet the boy's penis in the first place? At this age children positively evaluate the like-self (Kohlberg, 1967) and it is therefore more likely that she will regard the male genitals as an ugly protuberance than as something desirable. Her own body she sees as whole and complete. Again, why should she then decide that her own organ is inferior for masturbatory purposes? It is unlikely that she will see her clitoris as a truncated penis, even if she is aware of its existence, which she need not be to engage in infantile styles of masturbation. In all likelihood she will come to the conclusion that the penis is simply a urinary organ, and in respect of this function it is true she may feel some envy. Simone de Beauvoir argues that, since at this age children are fascinated by their excretory functions, the girl may envy the boy's practical advantage in this matter. There is nothing to suggest, however, that this envy assumes the obsessive proportions Freud attributes to it. Moreover, this feeling would evaporate once the child outgrew her interest in such things, were it not that the penis becomes a symbol of the greater power and freedom enjoyed by the male (de Beauvoir, 1969). It is interesting to note, in this context, that children form a stable concept of the anatomical basis for the distinction between the sexes when they are between the ages of five and seven, a time when they also begin to perceive that men are the power-holders in our society (Kohlberg, 1967). It is possible that this anatomical difference comes to be symbolic of male prestige. So perhaps in this sense the penis may become an object of envy – not for what it is, but for what it has come to represent.

Freud makes much of the idea that in the course of her psychic development a girl has to change both her object choice – from her mother to her father, and her leading erotic zone – from the clitoris to the vagina. The energy absorbed in this process is supposed to lead to an arrest of psychic development, and hence to a psychic rigidity and a lack of creativity. Furthermore, because the girl, lacking a penis to begin with, has no castration fears, she remains in the Oedipal situation indefinitely. In not being forced to abandon it, she fails to develop the strong super-ego characteristic of the male and her mental life therefore remains closer to the instinctual level: she is somehow less civilised than the male.

Her situation is the reverse of his: whereas the male's castration complex drives him away from the Oedipal situation, the girl's genital trauma prepares her for it. It is her envy of the penis that enables the girl to transfer her object choice from her mother to her father. She blames her mother for her lack of a penis and therefore feels hostility towards her. She realises, too, that her mother shares her 'inferiority' since castration is a fate common to all women, and so she comes to devalue all that is feminine, including her mother. No explanation is given as to why the child should blame her mother for this cruel fate. Nor is it by any means obvious that she will see that her mother's body is like her own. It is, after all, as unlike hers as that of her father if presence or absence of a penis is not taken to be the sole criterion by which such comparisons are made.

Penis envy, Freud argues, also prepares the way for the

clitoral-vaginal transference which is supposedly consummated at puberty and which is crucial in the development of 'normal' femininity and mature, passive, narcissistic and masochistic sexuality. It is now known that physiologically such a transference is a myth and that orgasms are not vaginally, but clitorally centred (Masters and Johnson, 1966). Juliet Mitchell suggests that we interpret this transference as being a change in mental attitude. In this sense the idea retains some validity (Mitchell, 1972). Women in Western societies are expected to be sexually passive, to think of sexuality as synonymous with coitus, and to associate coitus with reproduction. Hence they must abandon the active pursuit of sexual pleasure associated with the clitoris, and prepare for the passive, receptive, reproductive role consistent with vaginal penetration. If it is viewed in this way, however, this transference cannot be considered to be 'constitutionally prescribed' or as determining (in the sense that Freud used this term) the final form of sexuality. Rather, the transference itself depends upon expectations concerning the form that adult female sexuality ought to take.

In making these pronouncements on femininity, Freud never looked beyond the fixed concepts and categories he imposed upon his observations. His obvious prejudices, made clear in his use of language, distort his analysis. The female is a mutilated male; that which is masculine is normal and unmysterious, while things feminine are seen as aberrations, as enigmas. Underlying all this, however, are more basic problems concerning the nature of sexual drives, the idea of infantile sexuality, and a lack of appreciation of the influence of social factors on the moulding of human personality.

In formulating his theories on sexuality, Freud interprets a wide range of infant and childhood behaviour as being inherently sexual, as prototypical of adult sexuality, and as determining its character. Though social factors are assumed to play some part, it is doubtful whether Freud would concede their primacy, for he seems to regard 'inhibitions' as being as much constitutionally determined as culturally imposed. He conceptualises these as 'dams ... restricting the flow ... of sexual development':

One gets the impression from civilised children that the construction of these dams is the product of education, and no doubt education has much to do with it. But in reality this development is organically determined and fixed by heredity ... Education [is] following the lines already laid down organically and ... impressing them somewhat more clearly and deeply. [Freud, 1905, pp. 177-8]

So education (or socialisation) plays only a secondary part in the process: that of furthering 'nature's' ends.

Freud's use of the term 'repression' is also ambiguous. He states, for instance, that puberty leads to an accession of libido in boys, but is 'marked in girls by a fresh wave of repression' (Freud, 1905, p. 220). His words seem carefully chosen, here and elsewhere, to leave us in ignorance of the source of this repression. Is it to be viewed as originating from within the individual or from without, as innate or acquired, as constitutional or imposed? Since this repression provides the impetus for the clitoral-vaginal transference which Freud perceives as essential to the development of normal femininity, it must be assumed that he considers it to be an integral part of psychic development. If women's sexuality is repressed, it is not the result of social pressures, but of some internal psychological mechanism. He seems, in effect, to be assuming that organic factors take precedence over socio-cultural ones.

It is with Freud's conception of these innate sexual drives that Gagnon and Simon take issue. They argue that he has mistakenly imposed the language of adult sexual experience on the behaviour of children and has imputed sexual motives to them solely on the basis of the meaning their behaviour would have if performed by an adult actor. No act, in their terms, is sexual in itself, but only if it is defined as such. A child's behaviour cannot be construed as sexual since it does not, as yet, carry such meaning for the child. If this is accepted then there is little basis for assuming that sexual drives exist.

Sexual behavior is socially scripted behavior and not the ... expression of some primordial drive. [Simon and Gagnon, 1969, p. 736]

It is not until the onset of puberty in our society that these socio-sexual scripts are learnt, for it is not until then that the subject comes to be defined as a potential sexual actor and to accept herself or himself as such. An emphasis on continuity with childhood is, from this perspective, misleading. Obviously sexual learning does not happen all at once with no reference to previous experience, but the aspect of pre-adolescent development that has greatest relevance for sexuality is the learning of gender roles. It is the feminine or masculine self-identity acquired through this process which provides the framework within which the learning of sexual scripts occurs.

> ... the crucial period of childhood has significance not because what happens is of a sexual nature, but because of the non-sexual development that will condition subsequent encounters with sexuality. [Simon and Gagnon, 1969, p. 741]

Gagnon and Simon are, in effect, reversing Freud's conception of the interrelationships between sexuality and sex role behaviour. Whereas Freud sees the sexual as determining all other areas of personality development, they view the emergence of sexuality as contingent upon the development of other, non-sexual, aspects of gender identity. For Freud the feminine character is created by the pattern of female sexual development, while for Gagnon and Simon female sexuality is itself built upon an earlier foundation of gender role learning.

The latter theory stresses the importance of adolescence as the crucial turning point in the development of the sexual self. The onset of this period is heralded by the physical changes of puberty, but it is not these changes in themselves which determine the development of sexuality, but the meaning which is attached to them. They serve, in effect, as signals to others, indicating that the child may be defined as a potential sexual actor, and will be expected to learn the scripts which govern adult sexual behaviour. In the course of this new phase of learning the individual assimilates the sexual into her or his self-identity and comes to see herself or himself as capable of playing sexual roles. Previous to these developments, before learning the scripts of socio-sexual dramas and casting themselves in them, an individual's behaviour cannot be said to be sexual.

> It is in the process of converting external labels into internal capacities for naming that activities become more precisely defined and linked to a structure of socio-cultural expectations and needs that define what is sexual. [Simon and Gagnon, 1969, p. 734]

PERCEPTIONS OF CHILDHOOD EROTICISM:
PLEASURE AND THE SEXUAL

These theoretical frameworks raise two interrelated and interdependent questions concerning the process of sexual learning. First, to what extent can the development of sexuality in adolescence be seen as continuous or discontinuous with childhood experiences which might be perceived as having implications for the emergence of sexuality?

I would argue, with Gagnon and Simon, that in terms of sexual learning in our society adolescent experiences do involve a significant break with the past. It is in this period of life that the individual becomes fully aware of the sexual meanings attached to certain aspects of her or his social environment, comes to be defined as a sexual actor, and begins to build an image of herself or himself as such. It is the time when conscious sexual learning begins, when new discoveries are made and novel experiences undergone that are not always easy to relate to childhood experience.

This is not to say that all this occurs totally independently of any former influences. Some continuity must exist, for in childhood the basis of the individual's self-identity, to which the sexual is assimilated, is established. Also, certain childhood experiences may, when combined with the new knowledge gained in adolescence, contribute to the individual's understanding of sexuality. There is an implicit distinction here between two categories of learning which have implications for later psycho-sexual development. The first involves the creation of a larger framework of self-identity of which gender identity is an essential component, and in terms of which sexual scripts are learnt and interpreted. The second arises out of behaviour which, though not intrinsically sexual, is likely to be labelled as such and which might therefore be retrospectively interpreted as sexually relevant in the light of later experience and therefore provide a more direct link between childhood and adolescence. By positing the possible existence of such a link I do not wish to attribute some sort of causal precedence to this variety of childhood experiences. Their importance lies not in determining later sexual development, but in providing the adolescent with data that she or he may be able to build into her or his emerging conception of the erotic or which may provide moral categories for sexual activities.

This in no sense, then, implies an acceptance of Freud's interpretations of children's sexuality. Whether based on observations of children or psychoanalytical case studies, his conclusions are somewhat suspect. In the former case he tends to arrive at somewhat absurd conclusions, not simply because he apprehends the behaviour of young children with the vocabulary of adult sexual experience, but because, in so doing, he imputes specifically sexual motives to them. He does not simply note the affinities between infant behaviour and adult sexual acts, but regards them as being manifestations of the same primordial drive, as satisfying the same need. So, for example, he holds that the child's flushed cheek and contented sleep after being fed is analogous to the adult post-orgasmic state (Freud, 1905). That these two varieties of contentment may have something in common is no grounds for arguing, as Freud does, that the one is an early expression of the other, a manifestation of infantile sexuality.

The other source of 'evidence', involving retrospective inter-pretations of childhood experiences, may also be distorting. As Simon and Gagnon argue:

> ... rather than the past determining the present it is possible that the present significantly reshapes the past, as we reconstruct our autobiographies in an effort to bring them into greater con-gruence with our present identities, roles and available vocabu-laries. [Simon and Gagnon, 1969, p. 734]

It is such biographical reconstruction, attempting to explain the present by reference to the past, that forms the basis of the psychoanalytical method. Freud, reasoning from the premised existence of the libido as a powerful sexual drive determining human personality, may then interpret adult behaviour in terms of inferred childhood sexual experiences. In this process the child's behaviour, responses and affections are infused with sexual meaning. It is in the nature of psychoanalysis that it imposes preconceived categories on to behavioural phenomena and then purports to have explained them.

Freud, having stated (correctly) that we must not confuse the sexual with the genital, proceeds to interpret a wide range of behaviour and responses as sexual, as satisfying some drive. He argues that the child *needs* to have such sensations repeated, rather than that she or he finds them simply pleasurable and therefore enjoys their repetition. He notes the rhythmical nature of such activities as thumbsucking and regards that as proof of their sexual nature. This is a prime example of the mis-labelling of childhood experiences: could it not be that the child simply finds this activity pleasurable? That sexual acts may also incorporate this charac-teristic may only mean that rhythmical stimuli in general are found to be pleasurable, rather than that such sensations are inherently sexual. It is, says Freud, the quality of stimuli that determines whether or not they are sexual, but apart from offering the example of rhythmical sensations he declines to elaborate further. Apparently the ineffable wisdom of psychoanalysis can uncover sexual motives underlying such apparently innocent childish activities and desires as playing on swings or wanting to be an engine driver!

By such arguments as these, Freud contrives to label as sexual almost anything a child apprehends as pleasurable. It might be argued against this that anything we might perceive as sexual in children's behaviour is, for them, merely pleasurable experience. If sexuality lies not in the quality of an act but in the meaning given to it, then a child's behaviour or responses cannot be interpreted as being sexual when the child has not yet learnt the vocabulary of motives through which sexual activity is mediated.

References

de Beauvoir, Simone (1969), *The Second Sex*, New York: Bantam Books.

Freud, S. (1905), 'Three Essays on Sexuality', in *The Standard Edition of the Complete Works of Sigmund Freud*, London: The Hogarth Press, 1953, vol. VII.

Freud, S. (1925), 'Some Psychical Consequences of the Anatomical Distinction between the Sexes', *The Standard Edition of the Complete Works of Sigmund Freud*, vol. XIX.

Freud, S. (1931), 'Female Sexuality', *The Standard Edition of the Complete Works of Sigmund Freud*, vol. XXI.

Freud, S. (1933), 'Femininity', *The Standard Edition of the Complete Works of Sigmund Freud*, vol. XXII.

Klein, V. (1946), *The Feminine Character*, London: Routledge and Kegan Paul.

Kohlberg, L. (1967), 'A Cognitive Developmental Analysis of Children's Sex Role Concepts and Attitudes', in E. Maccoby, ed., *The Development of Sex Differences*, London: Tavistock.

Masters, W. and Johnson, V. (1966), *Human Sexual Response*, Boston: Little, Brown and Co.

Mitchell, J. (1972), *Female Sexuality*, Marie Stopes Memorial Lecture, University of York.

Simon, W. and Gagnon, J. (1969), 'On Psychosexual Development', in Goslin, ed., *Handbook of Socialisation Theory and Research*, Chicago: Rand McNally.

Adrienne Rich

Alienated Labor

From Adrienne Rich, *Of Woman Born: Motherhood as Experience and Institution*, London: Virago Press, 1977, pp. 182-5

Childbirth is (or may be) one aspect of the entire process of a woman's life, beginning with her own expulsion from her mother's body, her own sensual suckling or being held by a woman, through her earliest sensations of clitoral eroticism and of the vulva as a source of pleasure, her growing sense of her own body and its strengths, her masturbation, her menses, her physical relationship to nature and to other human beings, her first and subsequent orgasmic experiences with another's body, her conception, pregnancy, to the moment of first holding her child. But that moment is still only a point in the process if we conceive it not according to patriarchal ideas of childbirth as a kind of production, but as part of female experience.

Beyond birth comes nursing and physical relationship with an infant, and these are enmeshed with sexuality, with the ebb and flow of ovulation and menses, of sexual desire. During pregnancy the entire pelvic area increases in its vascularity (the production of arteries and veins) thus increasing the capacity for sexual tension and greatly increasing the frequency and intensity of the orgasm.[1] During pregnancy, the system is flooded with hormones which not only induce the growth of new blood vessels but increase clitoral responsiveness and strengthen the muscles effective in orgasm. A woman who has given birth has a biologically increased capacity for genital pleasure, unless her pelvic organs have been damaged obstetrically, as frequently happens. Many women experience orgasm for the first time after childbirth, or become erotically aroused while nursing. Frieda Fromm-Reichmann, Niles Newton, Masters and Johnson, and others have documented the erotic sensations experienced by women in actually giving birth. Since there are strong cultural forces which desexualize women as mothers, the orgasmic sensations felt in childbirth or while suckling infants have probably until recently been denied even by the women feeling them, or have evoked feelings of guilt. Yet, as

1. Mary Jane Sherfey, *The Nature and Evolution of Female Sexuality*, New York: Vintage, 1973, pp. 100-1.

Newton reminds us, 'Women ... have a more varied heritage of sexual enjoyment than men';[2] and the sociologist Alice Rossi observes,

> I suspect that the more male dominance characterizes a Western society, the greater is the dissociation between sexuality and maternalism. It is to men's sexual advantage to restrict women's sexual gratification to heterosexual coitus, though the price for the woman and a child may be a less psychologically and physically rewarding relationship.[3]

The divisions of labor and allocations of power in patriarchy demand not merely a suffering Mother, but one divested of sexuality: the Virgin Mary, *virgo intacta*, perfectly chaste. Women are permitted to be sexual only at a certain time of life, and the sensuality of mature – and certainly of aging – women has been perceived as grotesque, threatening, and inappropriate.

If motherhood and sexuality were not wedged resolutely apart by male culture, if we could *choose* both the forms of our sexuality and the terms of our motherhood or nonmotherhood freely, women might achieve genuine sexual autonomy (as opposed to 'sexual liberation'). The mother should be able to choose the means of conception (biological, artificial, or parthenogenetic), the place of birth, her own style of giving birth, and her birth-attendants: midwife or doctor as she wishes, a man she loves and trusts, women and men friends or kin, her other children. There is no reason why it should not be an 'Amazon expedition' if she so desires, in which she is supported by women only, the midwife with whom she has worked throughout pregnancy, and women who simply love her. (At present, the father is the only nonmedical person legally admitted to the labor and delivery room in American hospitals, and even the biological father can be legally excluded over the mother's decision to have him there.)[4]

But taking birth out of the hospital does not mean simply shifting it into the home or into maternity clinics. Birth is not an isolated event. If there were local centers to which all women could go for

2. Niles Newton, 'The Trebly Sensuous Woman', *Psychology Today*, issue on 'The Female Experience', 1973.
3. Alice Rossi, 'Maternalism, Sexuality and the New Feminism', in *Contemporary Sexual Behavior: Critical Issues in the 1970's*, ed. J. Zubin and J. Money, Baltimore: Johns Hopkins University Press, 1973, pp. 145-71.
4. Kathy Linck, 'Legalizing a Woman's Right to Choose', in *Proceedings of the First International Childbirth Conference*, 1973, New Moon Communications, Box 3488, Ridgeway Station, Stamford, Conn. 06905.

contraceptive and abortion counseling, pregnancy testing, prenatal care, labor classes, films about pregnancy and birth, routine gynecological examinations, therapeutic and counseling groups through and after pregnancy, including a well-baby clinic, women could begin to think, read about, and discuss the entire process of conceiving, gestating, bearing, nursing their children, about the alternatives to motherhood, and about the wholeness of their lives. Birth might then become one event in the unfolding of our diverse and polymorphous sexuality: not a necessary consequence of sex, but one experience of liberating ourselves from fear, passivity, and alienation from our bodies.

I am a woman giving birth to myself. In that psychic process, too, there is a 'transistion period' when energy flags, the effort seems endless, and we feel spiritually and even physically 'nauseous and chilled to the bone'. In such periods, turning to doctors for help and support, thousands of women have been made into consumers of pain-numbing medication, which may quell anxiety or desperation at the price of cutting the woman off from her own necessary process. Unfortunately, there are too few trained, experienced psychic midwives for this kind of parturition; and the psycho-obstetricians, the pill-pushers, those who would keep us in a psychological lithotomy position, still dominate the psychotherapeutic profession.

There is a difference between crying out for help and asking to be 'put under'; and women – both in psychic and physical labor – need to understand the extremity and the meaning of the 'transition stage', to learn to demand active care and support, not 'Twilight Sleep' or numbing. As long as birth – metaphorically or literally – remains an experience of passively handing over our minds and our bodies to male authority and technology, other kinds of social change can only minimally change our relationship to ourselves, to power, and to the world outside our bodies.

Domestic Life and Labour

Until recently, the nature and conditions of domestic life in Western industrial societies remained one of the least investigated areas of social life, largely because the domestic world was regarded as 'private' and outside the proper sphere of social investigators. The separation between the world of male paid labour and female unpaid labour which had occurred as a result of the Industrial Revolution was reflected uncritically by social scientists: men's paid work deserved study, women's unpaid work in the household did not. The dismissal of women's paid work as socially insignificant was justified, on the rare occasions that it was attacked, on the grounds that few women were employed in production, particularly industrial production, and therefore contributed little to the accumulation of social wealth.

This argument has now been extensively criticised by a large quantity of feminist work which has both documented the amount of domestic work which women perform and questioned previously held distinctions between 'productive' and 'unproductive' work. Although feminists have always pointed out the harshness of the conditions endured by some women in domestic life (for example, Margery Spring Rice in her study *Working-class Wives*), it was not until the 1960s that the nature of domestic life, and women's unpaid labour, received systematic attention.

The first development that took place in the study of the 'private' world of the household was the documentation of the amount of work involved in the maintenance of the household and the servicing of men and children. Hannah Gavron's *The Captive Wife* and Ann Oakley's *Housewife* and *The Sociology of Housework* all argued that without the unpaid work of women in the home, children would not be socialised and male wage labourers would need to use the expensive services of restaurants and laundries. But as these and earlier studies such as Mirra Komarovsky's *Blue-collar Marriage* also showed, however much women contributed to the household, they received little social recognition, worked in conditions of considerable psychological isolation and were often powerless in domestic bargaining. In industrial society, in which the majority of work has been collectivised, routinised and mechanised, housework remains an outstanding example of uneven social development.

The demonstration by feminist social scientists that domestic labour was immensely time-consuming, labour-intensive and socially vital led to the theoretical reconsideration of the nature of housework and its part in the social structure. Two debates have been particularly significant here. The first is the dispute about whether or not housework is, in the strict Marxist sense, productive or unproductive work. For example, Secombe argues that since domestic labour does not relate directly either to the process of production or the process of market exchange, the housewife does not produce surplus value and is not exploited in the same way as the wage labourer. Opponents of this view, most notably Jean Gardiner and Dalla Costa and James, argue that housework is productive work because it is only through domestic work that labour power is both reproduced and maintained. The somewhat talmudic nature of this debate should not be allowed to obscure the fact that all the protagonists agree that female unpaid domestic work makes a contribution of fundamental importance to industrial capitalism.[1]

But, as has also been pointed out, the unpaid domestic work of women contributes to the material existence and reproduction of all societies and is not merely a feature of capitalism. Thus a second debate has developed concerning the relative importance of different material and social conditions in the subordination of women and the exploitation of women's unpaid domestic work. The essential question at issue in the debate is that of whether or not all women (of any social group and in any society) occupy the same social class, by virtue of the fact that all women are expected to perform domestic labour, of various kinds, for all men. Those who argue, as, for example, does Christine Delphy, that all women do occupy the same social class, do so on the basis of the assertion that the unpaid labour of women is expected of them by men. Women's labour power is thus expropriated by their husbands and male relatives and contributes, not to female economic wealth, but to that of men. Delphy writes: 'The appropriation of their labour

1. See W. Secombe, 'The Housewife and her Labour under Capitalism', New Left Review, no. 83, 1973; Jean Gardiner, 'Women's Domestic Labour', New Left Review, no. 89, 1975; M. Dalla Costa and S. James, The Power of Women and the Subversion of the Community, Bristol: The Falling Wall Press, 1972. Many of the arguments of these articles, and others, are summarised in Maxine Molyneux, 'Beyond the Domestic Labour Debate', New Left Review, no. 116, 1980.

within marriage constitutes the oppression common to all women.'[2] Certainly, in the article by Richard Scase and Robert Goffee which is reproduced here, it would appear that in the process of capital accumulation typified by the small business, wives work for their husbands rather than as equal partners in the enterprise.

Delphy's thesis has now been widely discussed, most particularly in an article by Michèle Barrett and Mary McIntosh.[3] They point out that in the majority of societies there is a system of class, as well as sexual, stratification and that while all women may occupy a common position in the status structure of a society (in which all men are ranked higher than all women) this does not also imply that they occupy the same class position. Although both McIntosh and Barrett and Delphy are largely concerned with industrial societies (and generally industrial capitalist societies) the observation must also be made that the social processes and practices of most societies suggest that distinctions are constantly being made between women and that it is only in ideological terms that women are seen as a single category.

However, the existence of an ideology which sees women as a collectivity can, on occasions, have a very powerful social effect. One example of this is the Western, Christian ideology which states that all women should be '. . . subject to their husbands as to the Lord, for the husband is the head of the wife, as Christ is the head of the Church'. The statement makes no distinctions between women: all are to accept the authority of their husband, however illiberal and oppressive that authority might be. Thus if the Church's teaching is accepted, women are constrained to accept domination. Yet the ideology can only be truly effective if women are materially dependent upon their husbands; the economic independence of women does not guarantee their emancipation from male oppression but it does constitute an essential condition. For this reason female economic emancipation has always been a major concern of feminists, for women can never be assured of independence and autonomy until they are also assured of freedom from financial dependence. Hence feminists are inevitably concerned with ending any form of social organisation which creates dependent and impoverished beings out of those who perform socially necessary domestic labour.

The issue of the allocation of economic resources within the household has recently become an area of major concern to

2. Christine Delphy, *The Main Enemy: a Materialist Analysis of Women's Oppression*, London: Women's Research and Resources Centre, 1977, p. 16.
3. Michèle Barrett and Mary McIntosh, 'Christine Delphy: Towards a Materialist Feminism?', *Feminist Review*, no. 1, 1979.

feminists. The 'de-privatisation' of the family has resulted, therefore, not just in the study of who does what within the household, but of how decisions are taken about the distribution of resources. The ideal is, of course, that husbands and wives share economic resources and discuss sensibly and rationally how money is to be spent. The reality, as a number of studies have pointed out, is that negotiations about money are frequently acrimonious, secretive (the husband not declaring his income) and divisive.[4] Husbands and wives argue, it has become clear, far more about money than anything else, and as a source of domestic tension it is unparalleled. In a study of women living in a refuge for battered wives, Jan Pahl found that for many women dependence on state benefits was infinitely preferable to dependence on a husband or lover.[5] The state, however parsimonious, did reliably pay up. Similarly, recent attempts by the state to alter the system of the payment of child benefits have demonstrated the intense feeling that it is women's right to receive these benefits directly and not through the unreliable channels of a husband's pay packet.

For those women living in refuges for battered women domestic life had obviously reached the point of absolute breakdown, where all negotiation and consensus had disappeared. Yet the question that is raised for many feminists is that of how typical these apparently aberrant women are of their sex as a whole: that is, that in marriage or other heterosexual relationships, the conditions of existence of women are little short of servitude. That the conditions of servitude differ is seen by any study of housework or housewives, but what is perhaps consistent is that within those households where women are dependent on men lie the conditions for the development of real and often violently expressed antagonism between the sexes.

4. See, for example, Colin Bell and Howard Newby, 'Husbands and Wives: the Dynamic of the Deferential Dialectic', in D. Barker and S. Allen, eds., *Dependence and Exploitation in Work and Marriage*, Harlow: Longman, 1976; and Jan Pahl, 'Patterns of Money Management in Marriage', *Journal of Social Policy*, vol. 9, no. 3, 1980.
5. Jan Pahl, *A Refuge for Battered Women*, London: HMSO, 1978.

Charlotte Perkins Gilman
House Service as a Livelihood

From Charlotte Perkins Gilman, *Women and Economics*, New York: Harper and Row, 1966, pp. 12-22 (first published in 1898)

If the wife is not, then, truly a business partner, in what way does she earn from her husband the food, clothing, and shelter she receives at his hands? By house service, it will be instantly replied. This is the general misty idea upon the subject, – that women earn all they get, and more, by house service. Here we come to a very practical and definite economic ground. Although not producers of wealth, women serve in the final processes of preparation and distribution. Their labor in the household has a genuine economic value.

For a certain percentage of persons to serve other persons, in order that the ones so served may produce more, is a contribution not to be overlooked. The labor of women in the house, certainly, enables men to produce more wealth than they otherwise could; and in this way women are economic factors in society. But so are horses. The labor of horses enables men to produce more wealth than they otherwise could. The horse is an economic factor in society. But the horse is not economically independent, nor is the woman. If a man plus a valet can perform more useful service than he could minus a valet, then the valet is performing useful service. But, if the valet is the property of the man, is obliged to perform this service, and is not paid for it, he is not economically independent.

The labor which the wife performs in the household is given as part of her functional duty, not as employment. The wife of the poor man, who works hard in a small house, doing all the work for the family, or the wife of the rich man, who wisely and gracefully manages a large house and administers its functions, each is entitled to fair pay for services rendered.

To take this ground and hold it honestly, wives, as earners through domestic service, are entitled to the wages of cooks, housemaids, nursemaids, seamstresses, or housekeepers, and to no more. This would of course reduce the spending money of the wives of the rich, and put it out of the power of the poor man to 'support' a wife at all, unless, indeed, the poor man faced the situation fully, paid his wife her wages as house servant, and then she and he combined their funds in the support of their children. He would be keeping a servant: she would be helping keep the family. But nowhere on earth would there be 'a rich woman' by these means. Even the highest class of private housekeeper, useful as her services are, does not accumulate a fortune. She does not buy diamonds and sables and keep a carriage. Things like these are not earned by house service.

But the salient fact in this discussion is that, whatever the economic value of the domestic industry of women is, they do not get it. The women who do the most work get the least money, and the women who have the most money do the least work. Their labor is neither given nor taken as a factor in economic exchange. It is held to be their duty as women to do this work; and their economic status bears no relation to their domestic labors, unless an inverse one. Moreover, if they were thus fairly paid, – given what they earned, and no more, – all women working in this way would be reduced to the economic status of the house servant. Few women – or men either – care to face this condition. The ground that women earn their living by domestic labor is instantly forsaken, and we are told that they obtain their livelihood as mothers. This is a peculiar position. We speak of it commonly enough, and often with deep feeling, but without due analysis.

In treating of an economic exchange, asking what return in goods or labor women make for the goods and labor given them, – either to the race collectively or to their husbands individually, – what payment women make for their clothes and shoes and furniture and food and shelter, we are told that the duties and services of the mother entitle her to support.

If this is so, if motherhood is an exchangeable commodity given by women in payment for clothes and food, then we must of course find some relation between the quantity or quality of the motherhood and the quantity and quality of the pay. This being true, then the women who are not mothers have no economic status at all; and the economic status of those who are must be shown to be relative to their motherhood. This is obviously absurd. The childless wife has as much money as the mother of many, – more; for the children of the latter consume what would otherwise be hers; and the inefficient mother is no less provided for than the efficient one. Visibly, and upon the face of it, women are not maintained in economic prosperity proportioned to their motherhood. Motherhood bears no relation to their economic status. Among primitive races, it is true, – in the patriarchal period, for instance, – there was some truth in this position. Women being of no value whatever save as bearers of children, their favor and indulgence did bear direct relation to maternity; and they had reason to exult on more grounds than one when they could boast a son. To-day, however, the maintenance of the woman is not conditioned upon this. A man is not allowed to discard his wife because she is barren. The claim of motherhood as a factor in economic exchange is false to-day. But suppose it were true. Are we willing to hold this ground, even in theory? Are we willing to consider motherhood as a business, a form of commercial exchange? Are the cares and duties of the mother, her travail and her love, commodities to be exchanged for bread?

It is revolting so to consider them; and, if we dare face our own thoughts, and force them to their logical conclusion, we shall see that nothing could be more repugnant to human feeling, or more socially and individually injurious, than to make motherhood a trade. Driven off these alleged grounds of women's economic independence; shown that women, as a class, neither produce nor distribute wealth; that women, as individuals, labor mainly as house servants, are not paid as such, and would not be satisfied with such an economic status if they were so paid; that wives are not business partners or co-producers of wealth with their husbands, unless they actually practise the same profession; that they are not salaried as mothers, and that it would be unspeakably degrading if they were, – what remains to those who deny that women are supported by men? This (and a most amusing position it is), – that the function of maternity unfits a woman for economic production, and, therefore, it is right that she should be supported by her husband.

The ground is taken that the human female is not economically independent, that she is fed by the male of her species. In denial of this, it is first alleged that she is economically independent, – that she does support herself by her own industry in the house. It being shown that there is no relation between the economic status of woman and the labor she performs in the home, it is then alleged that not as house servant, but as mother, does woman earn her living. It being shown that the economic status of woman bears no relation to her motherhood, either in quantity or quality, it is then alleged that motherhood renders a woman unfit for economic production, and that, therefore, it is right that she be supported by her husband. Before going farther, let us seize upon this admission, – that she *is* supported by her husband.

Without going into either the ethics or the necessities of the case, we have reached so much common ground: the female of genus homo is supported by the male. Whereas, in other species of animals, male and female alike graze and browse, hunt and kill, climb, swim, dig, run, and fly for their livings, in our species the female does not seek her own living in the specific activities of our race, but is fed by the male.

Now as to the alleged necessity. Because of her maternal duties, the human female is said to be unable to get her own living. As the maternal duties of other females do not unfit them for getting their own living and also the livings of their young, it would seem that the human maternal duties require the segregation of the entire energies of the mother to the service of the child during her entire adult life, or so large a proportion of them that not enough remains to devote to the individual interests of the mother.

Such a condition, did it exist, would of course excuse and justify the pitiful dependence of the human female, and her support by the male. As the queen bee, modified entirely to maternity, is supported, not by the male, to be sure, but by her co-workers, the 'old maids', the barren working bees, who labor so patiently and lovingly in their branch of the maternal duties of the hive, so would the human female, modified entirely to maternity, become unfit for any other exertion, and a helpless dependant.

Is this the condition of human motherhood? Does the human mother, by her motherhood, thereby lose control of brain and body, lose power and skill and desire for any other work? Do we see before us the human race, with all its females segregated entirely to the uses of motherhood, consecrated, set apart, specially developed, spending every power of their nature on the service of their children?

We do not. We see the human mother worked far harder than a mare, laboring her life long in the service, not of her children only, but of men; husbands, brothers, fathers, whatever male relatives she has; for mother and sister also; for the church a little, if she is allowed; for society, if she is able; for charity and education and reform, – working in many ways that are not the ways of motherhood.

It is not motherhood that keeps the housewife on her feet from dawn till dusk; it is house service, not child service. Women work longer and harder than most men, and not solely in maternal duties. The savage mother carries the burdens, and does all menial service for the tribe. The peasant mother toils in the fields, and the workingman's wife in the home. Many mothers, even now, are wage-earners for the family, as well as bearers and rearers of it. And the women who are not so occupied, the women who belong to rich men, – here perhaps is the exhaustive devotion to maternity which is supposed to justify an admitted economic dependence.

But we do not find it even among these. Women of ease and wealth provide for their children better care than the poor woman can; but they do not spend more time upon it themselves, nor more care and effort. They have other occupation.

In spite of her supposed segregation to maternal duties, the human female, the world over, works at extra-maternal duties for hours enough to provide her with an independent living, and then is denied independence on the ground that motherhood prevents her working!

If this ground were tenable, we should find a world full of women who never lifted a finger save in the service of their children, and of men who did *all* the work besides, and waited on the women whom motherhood prevented from waiting on themselves. The ground is not tenable. A human female, healthy, sound, has twenty-five years of life before she is a mother, and should have twenty-five years more after the period of such maternal service as is expected of her has been given. The duties of grandmother-hood are surely not alleged as preventing economic indepen-dence.

The working power of the mother has always been a prominent factor in human life. She is the worker *par excellence*, but her work is not such as to affect her economic status. Her living, all that she gets, – food, clothing, ornaments, amusements, luxuries, – these bear no relation to her power to produce wealth, to her services in the house, or to her motherhood. These things bear relation only to the man she marries, the man she depends on, – to how much he has and how much he is willing to give her. The women whose splendid extravagance dazzles the world, whose economic goods are the greatest, are often neither houseworkers nor mothers, but simply the women who hold most power over the men who have the most money. The female of genus homo is economically dependent on the male. He is her food supply.

Margery Spring Rice

The Day's Work

From Margery Spring Rice, *Working-class Wives*,
London: Virago Press, 1981, pp. 94-108 (first published
in 1939)

'I believe myself that one of the biggest difficulties our mothers
have is our husbands do not realise we ever need any leisure time.
My life for many years consisted of being penned in a kitchen 9 feet
square, every fourteen months a baby, as I had five babies in five
years at first, until what with the struggle to live and no leisure I
used to feel I was just a machine, until I had my first breakdown,
and as dark as it was and as hard as it was it gave me the freedom
and privilege of having an hour's fresh air. And so I truly know this
is the lot of many a poor mother. I know my third baby had rickets,
but what could I do, I was expecting another little one and already
had a baby three years of age and one two years. So many of our
men think we should not go out until the children are grown up. We
do not want to be neglecting the home but we do feel we like to have
a little look around the shops, or if we go to the Clinic we can just
have a few minutes. . . . It isn't the men are unkind. It is the old idea
we should always be at home.'

Not many of the women go into such detail as this about the trials
of their lives, but the record given of hours spent at work, the size
of the family, the inability to pay for any help outside, the
inconvenience of the house, the lack of adequate utensils and of
decent clothes – let alone any small household or personal luxury
– yields a picture in which monotony, loneliness, discouragement
and sordid hard work are the main features, – a picture of almost
unredeemed drabness. It is not that all of the women are unhappy
as the writer of the above letter manifestly is. Taken as a whole,
their vitality must be prodigious, for, in spite of every possible
embarrassment, life goes on undiminished in bulk, even if with a
lessening vigour and enjoyment. Happiness, like health, can suffer
an almost unperceived lowering of standard, which results in a
pathetic gratitude for what might be called negative mercies, the
respite for an hour a day, for instance, from the laboriousness of
the other eleven, twelve or thirteen; the help that a kind husband
will 'occasionally give on washing days, when he comes home from
work', the relief when a major disaster which threatened one of the

children (in the case of a woman in Leeds whose eldest son lost one eye in an accident and was threatened with the loss of the other) was 'miraculously overcome'.

It is little comfort that these women have learnt to accept their lot with so little complaint, often with such cheeriness and apparent satisfaction. For they are the mothers of the new generation and their outlook must to a certain extent be passed on to their daughters who will harbour no more than a vague hope that somehow, and through no direct action of their own, matters will have improved by the time they embark on the business of wife and mother. But that they do not raise the banner outside their own homes is neither surprising nor discreditable. Throughout their lives they have been faced with the tradition that the crown of a woman's life is to be a wife and mother. Their primary ambition is therefore satisfied. Everyone is pleased when they get married, most of all the great public, who see therein the working of Nature's divine and immutable laws. If for the woman herself the crown turns out to be one of thorns, that again must be Nature's inexorable way. It would be presumptuous on her part to think that she could or should do anything to change it. It is little short of a miracle that some women, even some of the most hard-worked, find time and mental energy to belong to such organisations as the Women's Co-operative Guild, the Salvation Army or a branch of their political party where they can hear and talk about the wider aspects of their own or other people's problems. It is, however, very rare to find amongst the active members of these organisations, the women whose poverty and consequent hard work demand the greatest measure of consideration and carefully planned reform. The poorest women *have no time* to spare for such immediately irrelevant considerations as the establishment of a different system, a better education, a more comprehensive medical service, or some sort of organised co-operation. They are not themselves going to be given the second chance, whatever reforms may be introduced, and meantime they have their twelve or thirteen or fourteen hours' work to do every day and their own day-to-day life to lead. It cannot stop, it cannot be interrupted; no one else can do any of their jobs; and even if there is anyone else, like an adolescent daughter or a kind husband, this would mean losing time at any rate for a little while the pupil was learning; it might mean one meal at least being spoilt, one saucepan allowed to boil over, and there is no margin whatever for such waste, such loss of time; it requires less thought, even less physical energy to do the job oneself.

This is not a question of health. Whatever the condition of

fitness, the mother who does the work for a whole family of husband and three or more children has a titanic job under present conditions. If she is fortunate enough to be abnormally strong, she will manage to keep up with it, as long as her daily routine is not checked by some unusual misfortune. But if the ordinary round is harder than her body is strong her health must surely suffer with the result that she will find the course more and more difficult to hold; the less able she is to get through her task, the harder it will become ... a circle of peculiar and tragic viciousness.

For the majority of the 1,250 women under review the ordinary routine seems to be as follows. Most of them get up at 6.30. If their husband and/or sons are miners, or bakers, or on any nightshift, they may have to get up at 4 (possibly earlier), make breakfast for those members of the family, and then, if they feel disposed to further sleep, go back to bed for another hour's rest. The same woman who does this has probably got a young child or even a baby, who wakes up early, and sleeping in the same room will in no case give his mother much peace after 6 a.m. If there is a suckling baby as well (and it must be remembered that the woman who has had seven or eight children before the age of 35 has never been without a tiny baby or a very young child), she will have had to nurse him at least as late as 10 the night before. There are many complaints of children who for some reason or other disturb the night's rest. Her bed is shared not only by her husband but, in all probability, by one *at least* of her young family. Sleeplessness is not often spoken of in this investigation, because it is not considered an ailment, but it is quite clear that a good night's rest in a well-aired, quiet room and in a comfortable, well-covered bed, is practically unknown to the majority of these mothers. A woman can become accustomed to very little sleep just as she can to very little food.

When once she is up there is no rest at all till after dinner. She is on her legs the whole time. She has to get her husband off to work, the children washed, dressed and fed and sent to school. If she has a large family, even if she has only the average family of this whole group, four or five children, she is probably very poor and therefore lives in a very bad house, or a house extremely inadequately fitted for her needs. Her washing up will not only therefore be heavy, but it may have to be done under the worst conditions. She may have to go down (or up) two or three flights of stairs to get her water, and again to empty it away. She may have to heat it on the open fire, and she may have to be looking after the baby and the toddler at the same time. When this is done, she must clean the house. If she has the average family, the rooms are very 'full of beds', and this will make her cleaning much more difficult than if she had twice the number of rooms with half the amount of furniture in each. She lacks the utensils too; and lacking any means to get hot water except by the kettle on the fire, she will be as careful as possible not to waste a drop. The schoolchildren will be back for their dinner soon after 12, so she must begin her cooking in good time. Great difficulties confront her there. She has not got more than one or two saucepans and a frying pan, and so even if she is fortunate in having some proper sort of cooking stove, it is impossible to cook a dinner as it should be cooked, slowly and with the vegetables separately; hence the ubiquitous stew, with or without the remains of the Sunday meat according to the day of the week. She has nowhere to store food, or if there is cupboard room, it is inevitably in the only living room and probably next to the fireplace. Conditions may be so bad in this respect that she must go out in the middle of her morning's work to buy for dinner. This has the advantage of giving her and the baby a breath of fresh air during the morning; otherwise, unless there is a garden or a yard, the baby, like herself is penned up in the 9 ft. square kitchen during the whole morning.

Dinner may last from 12 till 3. Her husband or a child at work may have quite different hours from the schoolchildren, and it is quite usual to hear this comment. Very often she does not sit down herself to meals. The serving of five to six other people demands so much jumping up and down that she finds it easier to take her meals standing. If she is nursing a baby, she will sit down for that, and in this way 'gets more rest'. She does this after the children have returned to school. Sometimes the heat and stuffiness of the kitchen in which she has spent all or most of her morning takes her off her food, and she does not feel inclined to eat at all, or only a bite when the others have all finished and gone away. Then comes the same process of washing up, only a little more difficult because dinner is a greasier meal than breakfast. After that, with luck at 2 or 2.30 but sometimes much later, if dinner for any reason has had to go on longer, she can tidy herself up and REST, or GO OUT, or SIT DOWN.

Leisure is a comparative term. Anything which is slightly less arduous or gives a change of scene or occupation from the active hard work of the eight hours for which she has already been up is leisure. Sometimes, perhaps once a week, perhaps only once a month, the change will be a real one. She may go to the Welfare Centre with baby, or to the recreation ground with the two small children, or to see her sister or friend in the next street, but most times the children don't give her the opportunity for this sort of leisure, for there is sewing and mending and knitting to be done for them; and besides there is always the shopping to be done, and if she possibly can, she does like to rest her legs a bit and sit down. So unless there is some necessity to go out, she would rather on most days stay indoors. And she may not have any clothes to go out in, in which case the schoolchildren will do the shopping after school hours. (Clothes are a great difficulty, 'practically an impossibility'.)

Then comes tea, first the children's and then her husband's, when he comes home from work; and by the time that is all over and washed up it is time the children began to go to bed. If she is a good manager she will get them all into bed by 8, perhaps even earlier, and then at last, at last, 'a little peace and quietude!' She sits down again, after having been twelve or fourteen hours at work, mostly on her feet (and this means *standing* about, not *walking*,) and perhaps she then has a 'quiet talk with hubby', or listens to the wireless, 'our one luxury'. Perhaps her husband reads the paper to her. She has got a lot of sewing to do, so she doesn't read much to herself, and she doesn't go out because she can't leave the children unless her husband undertakes to keep house for one evening a week, while she goes to the pictures or for a walk. There is no money to spare anyhow for the pictures, or very seldom. She may or may not have a bite of supper with her husband, cocoa and bread and butter, or possibly a bit of fried fish. And so to her share of the bed, mostly at about 10.30 or 11.

This is the way that she spends six days out of seven, Sundays included, although Sunday may bring a slightly different arrangement of her problems because the shops are shut, the children and husband are at home. If she has been able to train her family well, and has got a good husband, they will relieve her of a little of the Sunday work, but it must be remembered that her husband is the breadwinner and must have his rest – and the children are young and will have their play. With luck, however, the mother will get 'a nice quiet read on Sundays' – or a pleasant walk, or a visit to or from a friend; sometimes, if she is disposed that way, a quiet hour in church or chapel. But for her the seventh day is washing day, the day of extra labour, of extra discomfort and strain. At all times and in all circumstances it is arduous, but if she is living in the conditions in which thousands of mothers live, having to fetch water from the bottom floor of a four-storied house or from 100-200 yards or even a quarter of a mile along the village street; if she has nowhere to dry the clothes (and these include such bedclothes as there may be) except in the kitchen in which she is cooking and the family is eating, the added tension together with the extra physical exertion, the discomfort of the house as well as the aching back, make it the really dark day of the week. There is no avoidance of it. Even if she could raise the money to send the washing out – she hasn't got the second set of clothes or bed coverings which this necessitates. The bedclothes have to be used again, possibly on the same day as washing.

There is also no avoidance of the other great labour which is superimposed on the ordinary round, the labour of child-bearing. The work will have to be done in the same way for those nine months before the baby comes and for the two or three months after she is about again but still not feeling 'quite herself'. The baby will probably be born in the bed which has already been described, the bed shared by other members of the family, and in the room of the use of which, even if she can get the bed to herself for a week, she cannot possibly deprive the family for more than a few hours. It is out of the question, she thinks, to go to hospital, and leave her husband and children either to fend for themselves – or to the care of a stranger, or of an already overworked but friendly neighbour. Even if she is in bed, she is at least in her own home; and can direct operations, even perhaps doing some of the 'smaller' jobs herself – like drying crockery, ironing,[1] and of course the eternal mending. How is it possible that she could stay in bed for long enough to regain her full physical strength, the strength that has been taxed not only in the actual labour of child-birth, but in six or seven of the preceding months, when every household duty has been more difficult to accomplish and has involved a far greater strain than it does when she is in her 'normal' health? If she is sensible, she will have got help from the Clinic, extra milk if she is very poor, and tonics and, perhaps, if she is fortunate enough to live in an enlightened municipality, a good meal once a day for herself. But her scene and her work will not have changed, and unless she goes into hospital for the confinement, it cannot bring that rest and comfort which she needs and deserves, but only extra difficulties for everyone in the family and very often serious ill-health for herself.

So the days, the weeks, the months, the years go on. There may be a break for an hour or two in the month when she attends some Guild or Women's Institute meeting. Once a year there may be a day's outing; but a holiday in the sense of going away from home, eating food she has not herself cooked, sleeping in another bed,

1. The writer found one woman sitting up in bed three days after the birth of her sixth baby ironing on a tray across her knees; the iron was handed to her by a neighbour who was washing up the dinner.

living in a different scene, meeting other people and doing the things she can never do at home, – this has been unheard of since the family arrived. She cannot go without the family, and there can be no question of taking them too. Possibly the children are somehow or other got into the country for a few days in the summer, if they live in the town; but it is without mother, unless she will go hop-picking, taking the small children with her. But it is only a very, very few who get the chance of even this 'holiday'. There is – again for the very few – another possibility of a holiday – convalescence. If the mother has been 'really ill' she may be sent away by the hospital or under some insurance scheme, or by the Salvation Army or by one of the agencies whose merciful function it is to procure this kind of intermission for the woman whose strength has at last given way. She is sent away . . . away from her home, away from the smell of inferior and inadequately prepared food, away from the noise and worry of her family, away to the sea, for a fortnight or even three weeks. It may be that she is too ill to get much active enjoyment out of it, but oh, the blessedness of the rest, the good food, the comfortable bed, the difference of scene for her eyes, the glorious feeling of having nothing to do. 'As dark as it was and as hard as it was, it gave me the privilege of having an hour's fresh air.'

But if illness has been so severe as to merit this magnificent atonement, it has meant months probably of crippling indisposition which has added enormously to the burden of work, and robbed it of all that potential satisfaction that can be found in the fulfilment of her task. She has had to let things slide, and she has slipped back so far that it will take months and months to catch up again even to her old standard of order and efficiency. This, in her eyes, is probably the worst disaster that can happen – her own illness. Other disasters are bound to come in the ordinary course of family life; the sickness of a child – the unemployment of her husband – the care of an old and perhaps tiresome grandparent. But if she can keep fit, she will meet the extra burden. She may even voluntarily adopt another child, whose parents are dead; or she will augment the family income by going out to work herself, somehow or other squeezing her own housework into shorter hours. It may be a little less efficient, but the compensation is that she has a little more money for food, and can get better cooking utensils. At whatever cost of labour and effort a little more money is what she really wants; that is the magic which unties the Gordian knot. But there is little opportunity for this, and the poorer she is, the more difficult it is to arrange things in her own home so as to make it possible to leave it for even a couple of hours a day. Where it *must* be done, as in the case of a widow, or a woman with an invalid husband, the strain is nearly always almost insupportable.

Naturally there are some who seem to get more out of life than others; but almost without exception it is those women who have very few children, one, two or at the most three, and who for this or some other reason are in much better financial circumstances, who are able to get more real rest and change of scene and to employ their leisure in some way which suggests an interest in outside things. But there are not more than half a dozen who speak of politics, literary interests, study of any sort or music. The cinema is very rarely mentioned, and many women say that they have *never* been to the pictures. A few who live in the country speak of walking and gardening; others of going to chapel or church on Sundays. An overwhelming proportion say that they spend their 'leisure' in sewing and doing other household jobs, slightly different from the ordinary work of cooking and house-cleaning.

The subject of husbands could form a thesis by itself. They are not very often specifically mentioned in the answers to this interrogatory, except in regard to their occupation and the money with which they provide their wives for housekeeping. But when a man adds to the embarrassments of life by bad temper or drunkenness, or is exasperatingly impatient with the wife's ill-health or unsympathetic with her difficulties, he generally appears in the list of her grievances directly or by implication. It is more often the visitor than the wife who makes special note of him. Equally, great solicitude for or sympathy with his wife is specially commended in a husband. Many instances are given of the husband carrying heavy tubs or coals for his wife – keeping watch over the children one evening a week, so that she can go out – reading aloud to her – or – if she is really ill – looking after her with great care, as far as his occupation allows. But the impression given in general of the attitude of the husbands in this enquiry is that of the quotation at the head of this chapter:– 'our husbands do not realise that we ever need any leisure'. With the best will in the world, it is difficult for a man to visualise his wife's day – the loneliness, the embarrassments of her work, the struggle to spend every penny of his money to the best advantage. In most cases he can count upon her devoted service to himself and to their children, – and he feels instinctively that her affection gives a pleasant flavour to her work which is absent from his own – and that she is fortunate in not being under the orders of an employer, and subject to regulations of time and speed of work etc. etc. If he is unemployed and therefore spends more time at home, the additional worry for both of them will take precedence of all other difficulties, and if he then notices the harassing conditions of her life, he will attribute them largely to this cause. Besides, the unemployed man can and does generally give his wife some help in the housework, which does much to lighten her physical burden, although it is little compensation for the additional mental worry.

Note is sometimes made in the women's accounts of the help given to them by the older of their schoolchildren. It is very usual to find mention of a child being kept back from school to do some of the work that the mother is too ill to do. Only a few mothers speak of training their children to help in the house as part of a regular routine – but this is probably less rare than it appears to be. It must be realised, however, that any help that a child under twelve can give costs so much in supervision and probably worry for a careful mother, that she feels it is easier to send the child out of the way and get on with the job herself. This may be a short-sighted policy, but it is easily forgiven in the woman who has no time to organise or plan.

It may be said that, even granting that there is no exaggeration in the above account of the working-class mother's life, there is no ground for giving special consideration to her case as apart from that of the father and the children; that their lot is just as hard as hers, and that the want from which she suffers is equally severe for them. That in many respects this is so, cannot be denied; but it is abundantly clear from the accounts given by the women themselves in this investigation that they are subject to many hardships from which circumstance or they themselves protect their families. To begin with, the working mother is almost entirely cut off from contact with the world outside her house. She eats, sleeps, 'rests', on the scene of her labour, and her labour is entirely solitary. However arduous or unpleasant the man's work has been, the hours of it are limited and he then leaves not only the work itself but the place of it behind for fourteen or sixteen hours out of every twenty-four. Even if he cannot *rest* in this time, he changes his occupation and his surroundings. If he is blessed with a capable hard-working wife, his home will represent to him a place of ease and quiet after an eight or ten hour day spent in hard, perhaps dangerous toil. He will have had ample opportunity for talking with his fellows, of hearing about the greater world, of widening his horizon. The children have equally either been out at work or at school, where for many hours of the day they have lived in airy well-lighted rooms, with ample space for movement and for play. They too have met and talked with their fellows, and whatever the deprivations of their home, they go there to find that someone else has prepared their food, mended their clothes, and generally put things in order. Naturally they suffer, as the father does too, from the poverty of the home, the lack of sufficient food and clothes and warmth and comfort, but it is undoubtedly true that even in these respects the mother will be the first to go without. Her husband *must* be fed, as upon him depends the first of all necessities, money. The children must or will be fed, and the school will if necessary supplement. Equally husband and children must be clothed, not only fairly warmly but for school or work fairly decently. She need not be; she need not even go out, so it is not *absolutely* necessary for her to have an outdoor coat. And lastly, whatever the emotional compensations, whatever her devotion, her family creates her labour, and tightens the bonds that tie her to the lonely and narrow sphere of 'home'. The happiness that she often finds in her relationship of wife and mother is as miraculous as it is compensatory.

   Much might be done even without dealing with the basic evil of poverty and without disintegrating the sacred edifice of the home, to introduce some ease into the lives of these women and so to lighten their work that they would have time to rest, to make contacts with the outer world, and to enjoy some at least of those cultural and recreative pursuits which would release them spiritually as well as physically from their present slavery. First of all, domestic and household training. As the Essex woman, quoted at the head of the preceding chapter, writes further on in her description of her life 'Never having been trained to housework, I find it very difficult to run my home efficiently – very small allowance prevents purchase of many labour-saving devices.' If this is said of housework, how much oftener can it be said of more skilled work such as cooking and household management. Very few of these women know how to make *the best* of their slender resources by the wise expenditure either of money or of time. Better housing with equipment designed *to the very special needs of the woman who does all her own work* and every opportunity, if not compulsion to learn her trade would immediately release her from much of her present bondage. As to the lack of labour-saving devices, she might with gentle persuasion be induced to make use of certain communal amenities where these are too expensive to install in her individual house. Communal wash-houses, bake-houses, sewing rooms with good machines, should all be within easy reach of her home, for her use for a minute charge which would be less than she spends in individual firing at home; they would mean an immense saving of time and therefore indirectly of money expended in the attempt to do an expert job without the proper tools. This would also serve the very desirable purpose of bringing her in the course of her daily work into contact with other women doing the same job, and she would no longer have to find out for herself the better ways of doing things. And she should have also not too far from her home a club to which at any time in the week she can go to seek rest and companionship, cultural and recreative occupation and a blessed change of scene. If her work has been eased in the ways suggested above, she will find time for this, just as somehow now, she sometimes finds time for the weekly visit to the Welfare Centre with her babies. Here she could read, educate herself, talk to other women, listen, if she wanted to, to lectures, and get advice and help on any problem that worried her. Here too she should be able to bring her husband or friends for games or 'socials'; but it should be *her* club, designed above all to meet *her* needs and to bring her enjoyment in whatever form she sought it. And lastly she should have a holiday 'with pay' once a year. She should be able for a week or a fortnight completely to stop work. Someone else must cook and clean and mend and bend not only for her husband and children but for herself. There is absolutely nothing revolutionary in any of these suggestions. It is as clear as day that even in the difficult question of finance they will save so much in sickness, hospital expenses and all the bolstering activities for which at present the nation is so heavily taxed, that they would very soon become self-supporting and be entirely free from that flavour of charity which is rightly so distasteful to the millions whose first wish is to be independent and to be enabled of themselves to lead the lives of human beings.

Mirra Komarovsky

The Quality of Domestic Life

From Mirra Komarovsky, *Blue-collar Marriage*, New
York: Vintage, 1967, pp. 155-9

THE IMPOVERISHMENT OF LIFE

Writers concerned with the meagerness of marital communication
sometimes imply that it would flow abundantly were we only able
to open the floodgates. However, the impoverishment of the
quality of life not only narrows the overlapping of interests and
consequent sharing of experiences, but also stunts personal
development. There may be little or nothing to communicate.
Speaking of television, for example, typical comments by the
respondents were: 'We both see it, why talk about it,' and 'What's
there to talk about other than to say it's good or bad.' In more
general terms, one woman put it this way: 'We tell each other
things, but I don't know as how we talk about them. He'll tell me
or I'll tell him something has happened, but there ain't nothing
much to say.' In contrast, one father reported that he and his wife
'go on and on' discussing the different reactions of their children
to discipline. Another man and his wife spoke of their frequent
debates about whether good character or success in life is the more
important goal of child rearing. Such topics require a psychological
sophistication lacking in many of the families. 'We don't have any
back-and-forth on it,' explained one woman when asked whether
she and her husband ever talked about their child's reaction to
discipline.

If external life is restricted for these families, so is their inner
world. For example, the meagerness of joint social life deprives the
couples of conversation about mutual friends, gossip, planning of
social affairs and 'party post-mortems'. Over one-third of these
couples either never visit with another couple apart from relatives
or do so only very infrequently, a few times a year on some special
occasion of an anniversary or a New Year's celebration. Low level
of interest in reading, in current events and in cultural subjects has
a similar impoverishing effect.

Couples who are exposed to the middle-class values of companionship, but whose mode of life does not stimulate common
interests, are sometimes acutely aware of this discrepancy. They

know that husbands and wives are supposed to talk with one another, but they do not have anything to say. Characteristically, one young husband, a high school graduate, said: 'I wish we had more things to talk about, but when I try to think of something I don't know anything to talk to her about. I wish we could get out and see the shows or something like that.' And another man expressed a similar dissatisfaction: 'If my wife and I had a little more education maybe we'd have what you call it – more interests? Maybe we could come together better, maybe life would be more interesting for us.'

The barriers to communication described so far derive from the meager content of common interests. Deficient skills of communication, especially on the part of the less-educated husbands, also hinder the sharing of experiences.

THE TRAINED INCAPACITY TO SHARE

The phrase 'trained incapacity to share' aims to convey a certain view about the men's inarticulateness. The ideal of masculinity into which they were socialized inhibits expressiveness both directly, with its emphasis on reserve, and indirectly, by identifying personal interchange with the feminine role. Childhood and adolescence, spent in an environment in which feelings were not named, discussed or explained, strengthened these inhibitions. In adulthood they extend beyond culturally demanded reticence – the inhibitions are now experienced not only as 'I shouldn't', but as 'I cannot'. In explaining instances of reserve in marriage many more husbands than wives say: 'It is hard to talk about such things.'

'I used to try to ask him when we were first married,' said a twenty-six-year-old woman about her husband, 'why he gets into those real flippy moods, but he used to say nothing was wrong, and asking seemed to make him worse. The more I tried, the worse he'd get. So I found out that if you just don't bother him, it wears off.' Another young woman described her husband: 'Sometimes he could get real black and quiet and you'd just better keep out of his way and not say anything.'

The wives endorse the therapeutic value of talk more frequently than the husbands. Thus a thirty-year-old woman:

> Lots of people say it's not good to go around shooting off your lips about what's eating them, but I think the good thing is to talk it out and get it out of your system. But I have to leave him alone because if I try to get him to talk he'll get really sore, or he'll go

off the deep end and walk out of here. Or maybe he'd tell me something else, lying like, just so I wouldn't get at the thing that makes him sore. He is strictly hands-off if something hurts him.... It makes it rough ... not knowing what's eating him hurts you worse than it hurts him.

The foregoing remarks were made by less-educated women, but a thirty-nine-year-old high school graduate, married to a man with ten years of schooling, told a similar story:

He can clam up and not talk for a long time. Sometimes I ask him what are you so clammy for, spit it out and you'll feel much better but he'll answer me coarsely or just say, 'Oh yeah.' Sometimes I can worm it out of him but I believe in leaving him alone. When he begins to work it out then I'll say 'something is the matter with you' and then he'll say, 'Oh – that foreman.' Maybe he'll tell me or maybe he'll just get over it. I watch other people and they have the same thing. Sometimes they ask me what to do and I tell them, 'leave the man alone.'

These comments are not exceptional. Twenty-six per cent of the wives, but only 9 per cent of the husbands, in answer to questions about dissatisfactions with communication, complain that their mate 'does not reveal worries'.... Of twenty-three qualities of a good husband, the women ranked 'speaks his mind when something is worrying him' as the second most important quality. These rankings reflect current deprivations – not merely ideals. The wives value the trait of speaking out precisely because they miss it in their husbands.

The ideal of masculinity accepted by the men is certainly one factor in the meager disclosure of stressful feelings. To gripe about the job carries the connotation of weakness. A strong man bears his troubles in silence and does not 'dump his load on the family'; he does not ask for solace and reassurance. Indeed, an adult male does not even experience hurt, much less admit it. 'When I don't feel good,' said one husband, 'I light out and don't dump my load on them.' Speaking of his wife, a forty-year-old carpenter (with eight years of school) described the masculine norm quite explicitly: 'Sure she gets hurt. Men are supposed to be braver than women, but women is bound to get hurt, it's in their nature, ain't it?'

The strength of such norms is demonstrated in the section of the interview dealing with feelings of hurt and anger. When asked for sources of hurt feelings, almost twice as many men as women expressed disapproval of the very experience of hurt in an adult: 'After a man gets on his feet, he shouldn't be hurt deeply about anything'; 'You ought to outgrow it.' More men than women say, 'Nothing can hurt me anymore,' or 'Don't know what could reach me anymore.' They generally add that at some earlier time – in childhood, 'before the army', 'before marriage', their feelings were hurt. Among the less-educated, 30 per cent of the men, but only 15 per cent of the women, denied completely that they experienced hurt at present. The sexes, however, report the experience of anger with nearly identical frequency: only 5 per cent of the women and 8 per cent of the men maintain that they are never angry.

It may be argued that the men experience hurt feelings less frequently (thus not merely concealing such feelings) than the allegedly more sensitive females. But the testimony of the high school graduates weakens this argument because the difference by sex in the reporting of hurt feelings narrows: 12 per cent of women and 17 per cent of the men in this educational category deny feelings of hurt. The high school men may have a less rigid norm of masculinity and be more willing to admit being hurt than the less-educated men. Consistent with this idea is the similarity between the two groups of men in their admission of anger: only 8 per cent of the less-educated and only 6 per cent of the high school graduates denied the experience of anger. Unlike the experience of hurt, anger does not carry the connotation of weakness to the less-educated men.

Socialized to identify the expression of certain emotions with a lack of masculinity, the men inhibit self-disclosure. Lack of education plays an independent role in limiting the capacity to identify, interpret and express feelings.... Of the four subgroups (high school and less-educated husbands and wives) the less-educated husbands are consistently the most withdrawn. They reveal less of themselves to their wives, are less inclined to find relief by openly expressing emotion, and tend to react to marriage conflict by withdrawal. Of all the aids in overcoming emotional stress listed by the uneducated husbands, only 28 per cent involved interaction with others, as against 42 per cent of such aids for the less-educated wives. These men seek relief in action rather than in talk.

The reticence of the less-educated husbands is also apparent in the relative scantiness of their replies to the section of the interview on self, personality and psychological relationships. The questions called for sources of feelings of hurt, happiness, worry, self-satis-faction and guilt, and for assessments of one's strong points and shortcomings. The less-educated husband lists fewer items per person than any of the other respondents. For example, in describing his strong and weak traits, he lists 5.4 fewer traits than does the less-educated woman. But among the high school graduates the sex difference is narrowed to only 2.1 items in favor of women. The inhibitions of the less-educated men are further revealed by the fact that, of all the four subgroups, the less-educated husbands are the only ones who list fewer items about their own personality than about the personality of their mates.

Margaret Benston

The Political Economy of Women's Liberation

In *Monthly Review*, New York,
September 1969, pp. 13-27.

The position of women rests, as everything in our complex society, on an economic base. [Eleanor Marx and Edward Aveling]

The 'woman question' is generally ignored in analyses of the class structure of society. This is so because, on the one hand, classes are generally defined by their relation to the means of production and, on the other hand, women are not supposed to have any unique relation to the means of production. The category seems instead to cut across all classes; one speak of working-class women, middle-class women, etc. The status of women is clearly inferior to that of men,[1] but analysis of this condition usually falls into discussing socialization, psychology, interpersonal relations, or the role of marriage as a social institution.[2] Are these, however, the primary factors? In arguing that the roots of the secondary status of women are in fact economic, it can be shown that women as a group do indeed have a definite relation to the means of production and that this is different from that of men. The personal and psychological factors then follow from this special relation to production, and a change in the latter will be a necessary (but not sufficient) condition for changing the former.[3] If this special relation of women to production is accepted, the analysis of the situation of women fits naturally into a class analysis of society.

The starting point for discussion of classes in a capitalist society is the distinction between those who own the means of production

1. Marlene Dixon, 'Secondary Social Status of Women'. (Available from US Voice of Women's Liberation Movement, 1940 Bissell, Chicago, Illinois 60614.)
2. The biological argument is, of course, the first one used, but it is not usually taken seriously by socialist writers. Margaret Mead's *Sex and Temperament* is an early statement of the importance of culture instead of biology.
3. This applies to the group or category as a whole. Women as individuals can and do free themselves from their socialization to a great degree (and they can even come to terms with the economic situation in favorable cases), but the majority of women have no chance to do so.

and those who sell their labor power for a wage. As Ernest Mandel says:

> The proletarian condition is, in a nutshell, the lack of access to the means of production or means of subsistence which, in a society of generalized commodity production, force the proletarian to sell his labor power. In exchange for this labor power, he receives a wage which then enables him to acquire the means of consumption necessary for satisfying his own needs and those of his family.
>
> This is the structural definition of wage earner, the proletarian. From it necessarily flows a certain relationship to his work, to the products of his work, and to his overall situation in society, which can be summarized by the catchword alienation. But there does not follow from this structural definition any necessary conclusions as to the level of his consumption . . . the extent of his needs, or the degree to which he can satisfy them.[4]

We lack a corresponding structural definition of women. What is needed first is not a complete examination of the symptoms of the secondary status of women, but instead a statement of the material conditions in capitalist (and other) societies which define the group 'women'. Upon these conditions are built the specific superstructures which we know. An interesting passage from Mandel points the way to such a definition:

> The commodity . . . is a product created to be exchanged on the market, as opposed to one which has been made for direct consumption. *Every commodity must have both a use-value and an exchange-value.* It must have a use-value or else nobody would buy it . . . A commodity without a use-value to anyone would consequently be unsalable, would constitute useless production, would have no exchange-value precisely because it had no use-value.
>
> On the other hand, every product which has use-value does not necessarily have exchange-value. It has an exchange-value only to the extent that the society itself, in which the commodity is produced, is founded on exchange, is a society where exchange is a common practice . . .

4. Ernest Mandel, 'Workers Under Neocapitalism', paper delivered at Simon Fraser University. (Available through the Department of Political Science, Sociology and Anthropology, Simon Fraser University, Burnaby, BC, Canada.)

In capitalist society, commodity production, the production of exchange-values, has reached its greatest development. It is the first society in human history where the major part of production consists of commodities. It is not true, however, that all production under capitalism is commodity production. Two classes of products still remain use-value.

The first group consists of all things produced by the peasantry for its own consumption, everything directly consumed on the farms where it is produced...

The second group of products in capitalist society which are not commodities but remain simple use-value consists of all things produced in the home. Despite the fact that considerable human labor goes into this type of household production, it still remains a production of use-values and not of commodities. Every time a soup is made or a button sewn on a garment, it constitutes production, but it is not production for the market.

The appearance of commodity production and its subsequent regularization and generalization have radically transformed the way men labor and how they organize society.[5]

What Mandel may not have noticed is that his last paragraph is precisely correct. The appearance of commodity production has indeed transformed the way that *men* labor. As he points out, most household labor in capitalist society (and in the existing socialist societies, for that matter) remains in the pre-market stage. This is the work which is reserved for women and it is in this fact that we can find the basis for a definition of women.

In sheer quantity, household labor, including childcare, constitutes a huge amount of socially necessary production. Nevertheless, in a society based on commodity production, it is not usually considered 'real work' since it is outside of trade and the market place.

It is pre-capitalist in a very real sense. This assignment of household work as the function of a special category 'women' means that this group does stand in a different relation to production than the group 'men'. We will tentatively define women, then, as that group of people who are responsible for the production of simple use-values in those activities associated with the home and family.

Since men carry no responsibility for such production, the difference between the two groups lies here. Notice that women

5. Ernest Mandel, *An Introduction to Marxist Economic Theory*, New York: Merit Publishers, 1967, pp. 10-11.

are not excluded from commodity production. Their participation in wage labor occurs but, as a group, they have no structural responsibility in this area and such participation is ordinarily regarded as transient. Men, on the other hand, are responsible for commodity production; they are not, in principle, given any role in household labor. For example, when they do participate in household production, it is regarded as more than simply exceptional; it is demoralizing, emasculating, even harmful to health. (A story on the front page of the *Vancouver Sun* in January 1969 reported that men in Britain were having their health endangered because they had to do too much housework!)

The material basis for the inferior status of women is to be found in just this definition of women. In a society in which money determines value, women are a group who work outside the money economy. Their work is not worth money, is therefore valueless, is therefore not even real work. And women themselves, who do this valueless work, can hardly be expected to be worth as much as men, who work for money. In structural terms, the closest thing to the condition of women is the condition of others who are or were also outside of commodity production, i.e., serfs and peasants.

In her recent paper on women, Juliet Mitchell introduced the subject as follows: 'In advanced industrial society, women's work is only marginal to the total economy. Yet it is through work that man changes natural conditions and thereby produces society. Until there is a revolution in production, the labor situation will prescribe women's situation within the world of men.'[6] The statement of the marginality of women's work is an unanalyzed recognition that the work women do is *different* from the work that men do. Such work is not marginal, however; it is just not wage labor and so is not counted. She even says later in the same article, 'Domestic labor, even today, is enormous if quantified in terms of productive labor.' She gives some figures to illustrate: in Sweden, 2340 million hours a year are spent by women in housework compared with 1290 million hours spent by women in industry. And the Chase Manhattan Bank estimates a woman's overall work week at 99.6 hours.

However, Mitchell gives little emphasis to the basic economic factors (in fact she condemns most Marxists for being 'overly economist') and moves on hastily to superstructural factors, because she notices that 'the advent of industrialization has not so

6. Juliet Mitchell, 'Women: the Longest Revolution', *New Left Review*, December 1966.

far freed women'. What she fails to see is that no society has thus far industrialized housework. Engels points out that the 'first premise for the emancipation of women is the reintroduction of the entire female sex into public industry ... And this has become possible not only as a result of modern large-scale industry, which not only permits the participation of women in production in large numbers, but actually calls for it and, moreover, strives to convert private domestic work also into a public industry.'[7] And later in the same passage: 'Here we see already that the emancipation of women and their equality with men are impossible and must remain so as long as women are excluded from socially productive work and restricted to housework, which is private.' What Mitchell has not taken into account is that the problem is not simply one of getting women into *existing* industrial production but the more complex one of converting private production of household work into public production.

For most North Americans, domestic work as 'public production' brings immediate images of Brave New World or of a vast institution – a cross between a home for orphans and an army barracks – where we would all be forced to live. For this reason, it is probably just as well to outline here, schematically and simplistically, the nature of industrialization.

A pre-industrial production unit is one in which production is small-scale and reduplicative; i.e., there are a great number of little units, each complete and just like all the others. Ordinarily such production units are in some way kin-based and they are multi-purpose, fulfilling religious, recreational, educational, and sexual functions along with the economic function. In such a situation, desirable attributes of an individual, those which give prestige, are judged by more than purely economic criteria: for example, among approved character traits are proper behavior to kin or readiness to fulfill obligations.

Such production is originally not for exchange. But if exchange of commodities becomes important enough, then increased efficiency of production becomes necessary. Such efficiency is provided by the transition to industrialized production which involves the elimination of the kin-based production unit. A

7. Frederick Engels, *Origin of the Family, Private Property and the State*, Moscow: Progress Publishers, 1968, chapter IX, p. 158. The anthropological evidence known to Engels indicated primitive woman's dominance over man. Modern anthropology disputes this dominance but provides evidence for a more nearly equal position of women in the matrilineal societies used by Engels as examples. The arguments in this work of Engels do not require the former dominance of women but merely their former equality, and so the conclusions remain unchanged.

large-scale, non-reduplicative production unit is substituted which has only one function, the economic one, and where prestige or status is attained by economic skills. Production is rationalized, made vastly more efficient, and becomes more and more public – part of an integrated social network. An enormous expansion of man's productive potential takes place. Under capitalism such social productive forces are utilized almost exclusively for private profit. These can be thought of as *capitalized* forms of production.

If we apply the above to housework and childrearing, it is evident that each family, each household, constitutes an individual production unit, a pre-industrial entity, in the same way that peasant farmers or cottage weavers constitute pre-industrial production units. The main features are clear, with the reduplicative, kin-based, private nature of the work being the most important. (It is interesting to notice the other features: the multi-purpose functions of the family, the fact that desirable attributes for women do not center on economic prowess, etc.) The rationalization of production effected by a transition to large-scale production has not taken place in this area.

Industrialization is, in itself, a great force for human good; exploitation and dehumanization go with capitalism and not necessarily with industrialization. To advocate the conversion of private domestic labor into a public industry under capitalism is quite a different thing from advocating such conversion in a socialist society. In the latter case the forces of production would operate for human welfare, not private profit, and the result should be liberation, not dehumanization. In this case we can speak of *socialized* forms of production.

These definitions are not meant to be technical but rather to differentiate between two important aspects of industrialization. Thus the fear of the barracks-like result of introducing housekeeping into the public economy is most realistic under capitalism. With socialized production and the removal of the profit motive and its attendant alienated labor, there is no reason why, *in an industrialized society*, industrialization of housework should not result in better production, i.e., better food, more comfortable surroundings, more intelligent and loving childcare, etc., than in the present nuclear family.

The argument is often advanced that, under neocapitalism, the work in the home has been much reduced. Even if this is true, it is not structurally relevant. Except for the very rich, who can hire someone to do it, there is for most women, an irreducible minimum of necessary labor involved in caring for home, husband and children. For a married woman without children this irreducible minimum of work probably takes fifteen to twenty hours a week; for a woman with small children the minimum is probably seventy or eighty hours a week.[8] (There is some resistance to regarding childrearing as a job. That labor is involved, i.e., the production of use-value, can be clearly seen when exchange-value is also involved – when the work is done by baby-sitters, nurses, childcare centers, or teachers. An economist has already pointed out the paradox that if a man marries his housekeeper, he reduces the national income, since the money he gives her is no longer counted as wages.) The reduction of housework to the minimums given is also expensive; for low-income families more labor is required. In any case, household work remains structurally the same – a matter of private production.

One function of the family, the one taught to us in school and the one which is popularly accepted, is the satisfaction of emotional needs: the needs for closeness, community, and warm secure relationships. This society provides few other ways of satisfying such needs; for example work relationships or friendships are not expected to be nearly as important as a man-woman-with-children relationship. Even other ties of kinship are increasingly secondary. This function of the family is important in stabilizing it so that it can fulfill the second, purely economic, function discussed above. The wage-earner, the husband-father, whose earnings support himself, also 'pays for' the labor done by the mother-wife and supports the children. The wages of a man buy the labor of two people. The crucial importance of this second function of the family can be seen when the family unit breaks down in divorce. The continuation of the economic function is the major concern where children are involved; the man must continue to pay for the labor of the woman. His wage is very often insufficient to enable him to support a second family. In this case his emotional needs are sacrificed to the necessity to support his ex-wife and children. That is, when there is a conflict the economic function of the family very often takes precedence over the emotional one. And this in a society which teaches that the major function of the family is the satisfaction of emotional needs.[9]

8. Such figures can easily be estimated. For example, a married woman without children is expected each week to cook and wash up (10 hours), clean house (4 hours), do laundry (1 hour), and shop for food (1 hour). The figures are *minimum* times required each week for such work. The total, 16 hours, is probably unrealistically low; even so, it is close to half of a regular work week. A mother with young children must spend at least six or seven days a week working close to 12 hours.

9. For evidence of such teaching, see any high school text on the family.

As an economic unit, the nuclear family is a valuable stabilizing force in capitalist society. Since the production which is done in the home is paid for by the husband-father's earnings, his ability to withhold his labor from the market is much reduced. Even his flexibility in changing jobs is limited. The woman, denied an active place in the market, has little control over the conditions that govern her life. Her economic dependence is reflected in emotional dependence, passivity, and other 'typical' female personality traits. She is conservative, fearful, supportive of the status quo.

Furthermore, the structure of this family is such that it is an ideal consumption unit. But this fact, which is widely noted in Women's Liberation literature, should not be taken to mean that this is its primary function. If the above analysis is correct, the family should be seen primarily as a production unit for housework and childrearing. *Everyone* in capitalist society is a consumer; the structure of the family simply means that it is particularly well suited to encourage consumption. Women in particular *are* good consumers; this follows naturally from their responsibility for matters in the home. Also, the inferior status of women, their general lack of a strong sense of worth and identity, makes them more exploitable than men and hence better consumers.

The history of women in the industrialized sector of the economy has depended simply on the labor needs of that sector. Women function as a massive reserve army of labor. When labor is scarce (early industrialization, the two world wars, etc.) then women form an important part of the labor force. When there is less demand for labor (as now under neocapitalism) women become a surplus labor force – but one for which their husbands and not society are economically responsible. The 'cult of the home' makes its reappearance during times of labor surplus and is used to channel women out of the market economy. This is relatively easy since the pervading ideology ensures that no one, man or woman, takes women's participation in the labor force very seriously. Women's real work, we are taught, is in the home; this holds whether or not they are married, single, or the heads of households.

At all times household work is the responsibility of women. When they are working outside the home they must somehow manage to get both outside job and housework done (or they supervise a substitute for the housework). Women, particularly married women with children, who work outside the home simply do two jobs; their participation in the labor force is only allowed if they continue to fulfill their first responsibility in the home. This is particularly evident in countries like Russia and those in Eastern Europe where expanded opportunities for women in the labor force have not brought about a corresponding expansion in their liberty. Equal access to jobs outside the home, while one of the preconditions for women's liberation, will not in itself be sufficient to give equality for women; as long as work in the home remains a matter of private production and is the responsibility of women, they will simply carry a double work-load.

A second prerequisite for women's liberation which follows from the above analysis is the conversion of the work now done in the home as private production into work to be done in the public economy.[10] To be more specific, this means that childrearing should no longer be the responsibility solely of the parents. Society must begin to take responsibility for children; the economic dependence of women and children on the husband-father must be ended. The other work that goes on in the home must also be changed – communal eating places and laundries for example. When such work is moved into the public sector, then the material basis for discrimination against women will be gone.

These are only preconditions. The idea of the inferior status of women is deeply rooted in the society and will take a great deal of effort to eradicate. But once the structures which produce and support that idea are changed then, and only then, can we hope to make progress. It is possible, for example, that a change to communal eating places would simply mean that women are moved from a home kitchen to a communal one. This *would* be an advance, to be sure, particularly in a socialist society where work would not have the inherently exploitative nature it does now. Once women are freed from private production in the home, it will probably be very difficult to maintain for any long period of time a rigid definition of jobs by sex. This illustrates the interrelation between the two preconditions given above: true equality in job opportunity is probably impossible without freedom from housework, and the industrialization of housework is unlikely unless women are leaving the home for jobs.

The changes in production necessary to get women out of the home might seem to be, in theory, possible under capitalism. One of the sources of women's liberation movements may be the fact that alternative capitalized forms of home production now exist. Day care is available, even if inadequate and perhaps expensive; convenience foods, home delivery of meals, and take-out meals are widespread; laundries and cleaners offer bulk rates. However, cost usually prohibits a complete dependence on such facilities, and they are not available everywhere, even in North America. These

10. This is stated clearly by early Marxist writers besides Engels.

should probably be regarded as embryonic forms rather than completed structures. However, they clearly stand as alternatives to the present system of getting such work done. Particularly in North America, where the growth of 'service industries' is important in maintaining the growth of the economy, the contradictions between these alternatives and the need to keep women in the home will grow.

The need to keep women in the home arises from two major aspects of the present system. First, the amount of unpaid labor performed by women is very large and very profitable to those who own the means of production. To pay women for their work, even at minimum wage scales, would imply a massive redistribution of wealth. At present, the support of a family is a hidden tax on the wage earner – his wage buys the labor power of two people. And second, there is the problem of whether the economy can expand enough to put all women to work as a part of the normally employed labor force. The war economy has been adequate to draw women partially into the economy but not adequate to establish a need for all or most of them. If it is argued that the jobs created by the industrialization of housework will create this need, then one can counter by pointing to (1) the strong economic forces operating for the status quo and against capitalization discussed above, and (2) the fact that the present service industries, which somewhat counter these forces, have not been able to keep up with the growth of the labor force as presently constituted. The present trends in the service industries simply create 'underemployment' in the home; they do not create new jobs for women. So long as this situation exists, women remain a very convenient and elastic part of the industrial reserve army. Their incorporation into the labor force on terms of equality – which would create pressure for capitalization of housework – is possible only with an economic expansion so far achieved by neocapitalism only under conditions of full-scale war mobilization.

In addition, such structural changes imply the complete breakdown of the present nuclear family. The stabilizing consuming functions of the family, plus the ability of the cult of the home to keep women out of the labor market, serve neocapitalism too well to be easily dispensed with. And, on a less fundamental level, even if these necessary changes in the nature of household production were achieved under capitalism it would have the unpleasant consequence of including *all* human relations in the cash nexus. The atomization and isolation of people in Western society is already sufficiently advanced to make it doubtful if such complete psychic isolation could be tolerated. It is likely in fact that one of the major negative emotional responses to women's liberation movements may be exactly such a fear. If this is the case, then possible alternatives – cooperatives, the kibbutz, etc. – can be cited to show that psychic needs for community and warmth can in fact be better satisfied if other structures are substituted for the nuclear family.

At best the change to capitalization of housework would only give women the same limited freedom given most men in capitalist society. This does not mean, however, that women should wait to demand freedom from discrimination. There *is* a material basis for women's status; we are not merely discriminated against, we are exploited. At present, our unpaid labor in the home is necessary if the entire system is to function. Pressure created by women who challenge their role will reduce the effectiveness of this exploitation. In addition, such challenges will impede the functioning of the family and may make the channeling of women out of the labor force less effective. All of these will hopefully make quicker the transition to a society in which the necessary structural changes in production can actually be made. That such a transition will require a revolution I have no doubt; our task is to make sure that revolutionary changes in the society do in fact end women's oppression.

Richard Scase and Robert Goffee

Home Life in a Small Business

In *New Society*, London, 30 October 1980, pp. 220-2

The families of business proprietors have rarely attracted the attention of social scientists. This is a pity, since they function quite differently from other kinds of families. Generally, the 'typical' family consumes income. Wages and salaries are earned through employment and then largely spent, within the family, on day-to-day living, recreation and leisure. But for business families, there is a constant process of making decisions: how much income should they consume privately, and how much should they reinvest in the business? There is a direct trade-off, therefore, between living standards and business growth.

We found other differences in our study of eighty-seven family-owned businesses, selected from the personal services' sector of the economy last year.

One important difference lies in the way both the family and domestic property are used to support the business. Many shops, restaurants and hotels are only profitable because the overheads are subsidised by the unpaid services of family members, and domestic facilities are used for business purposes. It is hard, therefore, to distinguish clearly between domestic and business life.

In fact, the fate of one is highly dependent on the fortunes of the other. While a divorce can destroy a business, a successful relationship between wife and husband can be a vital base for business growth. Though most businesses are formally 'run' by men, married women will often determine to a large degree whether their husbands will initially become self-employed and how far private savings, domestic amenities and family labour will be available to the business. For example, when initially setting up a small business, a part of the home is sometimes surrendered to the business. Many of the people we interviewed had started their businesses at home, using the garage as a small workshop and a bedroom for an office.

If domestic amenities are frequently sacrificed for the good of the business, so, too, is time. In a newly established business with little or no labour, the husband's working day often extends from eight in the morning until six in the evening, with two or three additional hours after the evening meal. Typically, 'physical work' is undertaken during the day and paperwork is completed in the evenings and often at weekends as well. As a small employer with eight workers told us:

> My working day starts at 7.30 am until six. I come home and some evenings I might work from about nine till 10.30 'booking-up' and also nearly all day Sunday – from about eleven in the morning round till perhaps ten at night, except for the odd walks with the dogs in between. I used to work more than this – most evenings it was from seven till 10.30 – but I don't do quite so much now that I'm getting older.

For this small employer, then, there is little time for pleasure. His business is his pleasure. We found this to be typical of small employers. They undertake a normal, productive working week, which is supplemented by evening and weekend work when all the non-productive administrative activities are undertaken. This sort of life puts an enormous strain on family relationships, but it is often an essential 'investment' in the business. Without such unpaid extra work, many small businesses would collapse.

If the 'cost' of this is borne by family relationships, there is always hope that things will improve as the business grows. In the meantime, the whole family, and especially the spouse, may have to accept the constraints and, in effect, subsidise the business. All these problems were aptly summed up by one proprietor:

> This job involves some bloody hours – probably eighty-five hours a week. You never know when to stop working. It's never away from your mind. The phone never stops ringing and the aggravation you get from stupid, irate, bloody customers. I've got so much work and not enough time. We want to take the kids to Disneyland. We want to do lots of things. We want to *start living*. I want to see my children – they're growing up around my ears and I don't even know it. Sometimes when I leave in the morning they're still asleep and when I get home they're in bed. I don't see them – it's no way to have a family. In fact, it's been no life for the last ten years. We've been nowhere.

However, as the business expands and the male proprietor withdraws from physical or manual work to concentrate on administration, a clearer distinction between 'family' and 'business', 'work' and 'leisure', and 'home' and 'office' emerges. Business premises, separate from the home, are acquired and the extent of unpaid labour by the family falls. But typically, dedication to the business continues and the owners often *choose* to work long hours and take on heavy commitments though they have the option of an easier life.

As the role of male business owners changes with the growth of the enterprise, so does that of their spouses. Wives not only make substantial domestic sacrifices, but they also take on unpaid much of the secretarial work and book-keeping, which has to be done in addition to household activities. In effect, they often have two unpaid jobs – housewife and administrator. Their contribution can be crucial to the success of the business. As one of the small employers emphasised:

> My wife does all the wages on a Thursday night and the end of the month accounts. She looks at the mail in the morning and shoves the invoices in the envelopes. She also answers the phone and keeps people away from me, if you know what I mean. If I didn't have her, I would have to employ somebody who would cost me at least £3500. This is one of the perks of the business in that I can show my wife as earning so much money on the books but, in fact, she doesn't draw any – it's still kept in the business.

Another small employer said:

> I would not be able to carry on the business without my wife. She deals with *all* the financial side of it. I would have to employ somebody to do what my wife does. But then, obviously, it's in both our interests so we're both pulling for the same thing. I don't know whether you would get the same commitment from an employee.

As this statement suggests, the wife is often much more than the office manager. She becomes, in fact, the real financial decision-maker. Many of the married women we met had some relevant experience as ledger clerks, book-keepers and, sometimes, as assistants in firms of accountants. As one small employer explained:

> This can be very useful. I do detest paperwork, although my wife does all the books side of it. I may scribble out an account but she will take over from there. She was an accounts manageress – although I didn't marry her for that! I think a lot of our success is due to her. She earns most of the money. For example, she'll

phone around to get the right quotations for materials. If you don't buy at the right price, you can't be competitive and sell it and make a profit.

Wives, then, are indispensable to the survival of their husbands' small businesses. But it is clear that their role in the business makes it almost impossible for them to pursue independent careers. Hardly any of the married women we met have either part-time or full-time jobs outside the business. Furthermore, husband-wife relationships within the family are 'traditional', and characterised by a rigid division of labour. Because of the time devoted to the business by the husband, the wife undertakes almost all of the domestic tasks. She looks after the children and runs the household budget largely on her own.

Occasionally a wife without dependent children is able to pursue her own career, but this is usually *within* the family business – as part and parcel of a process of small-scale diversification. One example of this was Mrs Sims. Her husband, a small employer, told us:

My wife's shop is far more successful than our original business because of the effort she's put into it. It was a new venture for her – and having been company secretary and having dealt with customers before, she has the right outlook. Her turnover has already trebled this year. She is prepared to work and make something of it. She loves it.

However, the normal pattern is for married women to withdraw from the business as it expands. With the growth of the enterprise, the business owner concentrates solely upon administration and hires people to do the work previously done by his wife. But though these wives are less involved in working for the business, there is a tendency for them to represent the family and the company symbolically, through a wide range of activities: entertaining potential customers, the maintenance of company 'morale', participation in a number of locally based associations.

An owner of one of the larger businesses we studied said:

I think it's right that any business should have an involvement in the local community. I feel that quite strongly. My wife, for example, is fairly heavily involved in the community. So, to a fair extent, she's involved in the business. I don't regard that as part of our private life. I regard it as part of our business life.

The fact that it spills over till ten o'clock at night a couple of evenings a week is immaterial.

Clearly, then, even though married women may no longer fulfil a productive role in the larger companies, their involvement remains important. For the businessman, family and business relationships are always closely interrelated.

This is vividly reflected in the process of passing on ownership of the business and bringing the children in. To ensure that the business stays in the family, competent children have to be produced – and at the right time. Their absence can often reduce the owner's commitment to his enterprise. As one of them told us:

> I've always had a good income – a good living from the firm. But having got plenty of money and not having a family, I've never let business be my boss. I've always taken a leisurely attitude towards business. If I had two or three children, there would be something to work for. But the wife can't have any children, and so it really boils down to the fact that we've nothing to work for – nothing to pass on.

But bringing children into the business when they are either inexperienced or incompetent can cause serious problems. As the senior manager of a family-owned business said:

> If you've got the right person from the family in the right position, it's a good situation to be in. If you've got the wrong person, then life can be troublesome. Previously, this happened with other members of the family. They were brought into the business in places of responsibility just because they happened to be part of the family. This is where the family business falls flat on its face – it's a recipe for disaster.

However, by no means all business owners are determined to pass their businesses on to their children. Many of the owners make every effort to enable their children to acquire capital which can then be used for a variety of entrepreneurial activities. Fathers tend to be keen for their children to continue the tradition of 'entrepreneurship' and to extend the family's assets in preference to the pursuit of careers within large-scale bureaucratic organisations. A small employer, for example, claimed:

> I don't think I would want my son to come in with me – not in

this particular business. I don't know what he will do. He's trying to get an interest in the business, but I'm doing my best to keep him out of it. But I would like both my son and daughter to run their own businesses. Then they can choose their own way of life.... When you work for yourself, you have more self-respect.

The concern to pass on assets within the entrepreneurial family can be jeopardised, however, by quarrels and disputes. If, for example, husband and wife are the major shareholders, a divorce can threaten the future of a company. So can a dispute among shareholding brothers. In this sort of case, difficulties can sometimes be resolved by the creation of 'separate' businesses, operating under the general umbrella of the family holding company, within which family members can pursue their interests independently.

In other cases, however, such conflicts may encourage a son or a brother to realise his assets and 'start again'. Some of these problems were illustrated for us by Paul Ewing:

The company split right through the middle about three years ago. It was due, basically, to family differences. It's difficult to identify one particular reason but one side of the family didn't think too much of the capabilities of the other. That puts it in a nutshell. We, from our side, said it wasn't going to work in the future and so the best thing we could do was to split – so we could go our own ways and have no axes to grind.

The proprietors of family-owned businesses tend to live rather modestly, primarily because they give priority to the business. The level of salary they pay themselves is clearly linked to the size of the business and to personal taxation. Almost all of them supplement their income with a wide range of fringe benefits, like private health insurance, expense accounts and company cars which are taxed, insured and fuelled by their businesses. Consequently, they are able to enjoy a material standard of living that is concealed behind a low, formal income but which is considerably above that of employees on a comparable level of earnings. Nevertheless, an ascetic attitude prevails which seems to be partly a function of their business experience. As George Arthur told us:

You create the sort of environment in your working hours in which you think of ways of making money and saving money.

Particularly, saving money. It's a bit like acolander. If you're going to be successful you've got to stop up the holes and stop the water pouring out everywhere in order to make it profitable. And if you're doing that all day, it flows over into your personal life.

At the early stage of business growth it is necessary to invest rather than spend. But at a later phase, it is important to 'be seen to spend' to advertise the success of the company. However, it is often difficult for many business owners to change their behaviour. As a result of their business activities, they are investors rather than consumers.

Most of the proprietors we talked to felt quite unable to compare their living standards with other people. They often see themselves outside any clearly defined class structure or status system. As one of them stated:

I don't think I've even compared myself to other groups. That sort of thing doesn't worry me. Over the years I've come to feel that I'm not in a class at all. I'm just myself and that's it. I know that a lot of people do concern themselves with these comparisons but it doesn't worry me.

Another small business owner told us:

I've never made comparisons because I'm not interested in how anybody else goes on. We don't bother with what other people have got. We're quite happy in our own way, thank you. We don't ask for too much – we feel that just living here is Shangri-La compared with where we used to live. So, compared with the past, no one can deny we are much better off. I was pretty ambitious when I was younger. I used to be worried about whether the business was going wrong and how it could be improved. I'm not going to say that ambition has been thrown out of the window but I'm contented with my lot.

The absence of any comparative groups for the purposes of assessing notions of personal well-being is reinforced by the existence of a private, family-centred way of life. The owner of a large company stated quite typically:

I've been invited to join various clubs and societies – Round Table and Rotary and what have you. I've never done so because I've always felt that the business has got to come first. If I'm fully involved with the business, I haven't got time for these other things. I've also got a family and I want to spend as much time as I can with them.

Business owners, then, tend to lead very private lives. Because they devote so much of their lives to business they have scarcely any time for anything else. As a result, they seem to lose the skill to cultivate extended social relationships. Furthermore, a majority of the owners we interviewed came from relatively poor working-class backgrounds and they had few educational qualifications. But with the growth of their enterprises, they had become 'middle class' in their material standard of living. Consequently, they now saw themselves as 'outside' the class structure – too affluent to be working class, but lacking in the cultural skills of the middle class.

This ambiguity, and its implications for personal lifestyle, was summed up by Harold Doyle:

> I'm still working-class in a sense – perhaps a little bit up from the bottom. But then there's speech, there's accent, and then there's other things that always give the game away to people who know. You often wonder, no matter how much money you had, whether you'd ever be quite so 'nice' as what they are. This is the difference. But it's never bothered me. I've never had time for 'social life'. When I go home, I want to go home to a fire, an armchair and a paper or a good book, that's all I want. I don't want to go out for drinks or to parties.

But the consequences can be more far-reaching. Take the experience of Eddie Lawrence:

> Money creates materialistic things, but the more materialistic things you get the less valuable they are. . . . If I find something I want I get it. I don't particularly want it but I've got it. You mentioned the swimming pool. You haven't got one. You'd love to have one. But if you've got one it doesn't mean that much. . . .
>
> I really don't know whether I'm satisfied or not. My basic ambition was to earn a lot of money quickly and retire. But during the time you're earning the money, you're so involved that you don't develop any hobbies to speak of. Then, when you arrive at the level you thought you wanted to stop at, you suddenly realise, 'Well, what do I do now?'

There are, then, heavy social and personal costs. Married women, in particular, and the family in general, provide a 'hidden' investment during the early stages of the business. Family life is often severely restricted as the business grows because family and business are intricately interconnected, the entrepreneurial family's relationships can affect the long-term prospects of the business enterprise. For most people, by contrast, work and family relationships are kept quite separate.

Are the costs worthwhile? This is something which only the individuals themselves can decide. Certainly, some of the proprietors we interviewed made conscious decisions to stop at various stages of business growth, if only because the costs for personal satisfaction, lifestyle and social relationships were too much. Others achieve considerable business 'success', only to be subject to severe self-doubts about their personal competence and the meaning of their lives. Nevertheless, society regards such families as highly successful.

Women and Paid Work

Women in all societies work. They do not, however, all work for money, and thus do not constitute part of what economists traditionally describe as the labour market. Hence the paid work of women has received almost as little attention as their unpaid work, the former being regarded as a highly deviant form of activity that occasionally intrudes on the proper domestic concerns of women. Until the late 1960s, married women who worked outside the home were considered to do so for two reasons: eccentric commitment to a career or a desire for 'pin money'. No right-minded woman with a husband in full-time employment undertook paid work. The policies of the state and organised labour endorsed the assumption that married men would support a wife who did not work outside the home.

As with all generalisations, the idea that women did not work outside the home was full of problems and contradictions. The first was the empirical fact that many women, both married and single, were in employment, had always been employed and – in the case of married women – were employed in increasingly large numbers throughout the 1960s and 1970s. To suppose that married women did not undertake paid work, and that women were only employed for relatively short periods of their lives was, by 1980, a quite anachronistic assumption. Second, contrary to the taken-for-granted view that women's earnings are used for the purchase of what are described as 'luxuries', it has become clear that for many families women's earnings are essential for the material survival of the household, since in many instances either the male income is insufficient to support a wife and family or the woman is the sole breadwinner.

The history of women's participation in the labour force of industrial capitalism has been one of the gradual incorporation of more and more women into paid work. The early years of the Industrial Revolution, as both Scott and Tilly and Richards suggest, had seen the recruitment of large numbers of single women into factory work, most notably the cotton industry.[1] But throughout the nineteenth and early twentieth centuries, the majority (although, emphatically, far from all) of married women of all social classes did not work outside the home. Indeed, it was widely regarded as a sign of social progress that women should not have to work other than at home, where they would be supported by a 'family wage' earned by men.[2] Of those women who were employed, the majority worked in domestic service, or industries (such as textiles) which had some association with traditional female skills. Industrial production, management and labour relations were all dominated by men. In the case of the latter, the consequences of the exclusion of women from the trade union movement were, as Sally Alexander points out, to institutionalise the weak industrial bargaining power of women and strengthen patriarchal authority:

> ... women workers remained almost entirely outside the trade union movement throughout the nineteenth century, and into the twentieth. Their position as home workers, slop-workers, sweated workers and cheap labour both made them difficult to organise, and reinforced the ideology which prohibited their organisation. By excluding women from trade societies, men preserved their patriarchal authority at the expense of their industrial strength.[3]

But as the structure of the economy began to change, and particularly as a service sector began to develop, opportunities for female employment were created, which were first taken by single women and, in the 1950s and 1960s, by married women. The development in all Western industrial societies of a welfare state which needed large numbers of trained personnel to run it provided a further impetus to the employment of women. Yet these new jobs might not have been filled by women had not two further

1. See Eric Richards (article reproduced here), Joan Scott and Louise Tilly, 'Women's Work and the Family in Nineteenth-century Europe', in *Comparative Studies in Society and History*, January 1975, and Ivy Pinchbeck, *Women Workers and the Industrial Revolution*, London: Cass, 1977.
2. See the article by Hilary Land reproduced here and, by the same author, 'The Family Wage', in *Feminist Review*, no. 6, 1980.
3. Sally Alexander, 'Women's Work in Nineteenth-century London', in Ann Oakley and Juliet Mitchell, eds., *The Rights and Wrongs of Women*, Harmondsworth: Penguin, 1976, p. 83. The attempts by men to exclude women from trade unions are discussed in Barbara Taylor's 'The Men are as Bad as their Masters: Socialism, Feminism and Sexual Antagonism in the London Tailoring Trade in the early 1830s', *Feminist Studies*, vol. 5, no. 1, 1979.

developments taken place at the same time: the first being the decline in the birth rate, which allowed women a longer proportion of their adult lives free from the demands of childcare, and the second being the inexorable decline in real terms of male wages as inflation became a constant feature of late twentieth-century capitalism.

By 1980 it had become apparent, at least in Britain, that industrial capitalism could no longer guarantee full male employment and a constantly rising standard of living. In these economic conditions women, whether married or not, have little option except to enter, and remain in, the labour force. Whatever choice some women might once have had about entering the work force is rapidly disappearing as male unemployment rises and a general decline in industrial profitability forces employers (both private and public) to enforce rigid wage restraint. But as it becomes essential for increasing numbers of women, regardless of their marital status, to become and remain wage labourers, so it becomes important for feminists both to examine the conditions on which women enter the labour market and the possible consequences of the large-scale integration of women into the labour force and to question those analyses of women's paid work which do not include a discussion of other aspects of sexual relations and the sexual division of labour.

The prevailing orthodoxy among bourgeois economists concerning women's position in the labour market contains two assumptions that feminists would now question.[4] The first is the unspoken view that the world of paid employment can be examined in isolation from domestic life and the general pattern of social relations between the sexes. Bourgeois economists may, therefore, point out that the majority of women paid workers are concentrated in badly rewarded, low-status occupations and offer no further explanation other than referring to the 'low human capital' of women. The reasons why women acquire relatively fewer marketable skills than men is thus ignored, as is any discussion of those demands on the time and energy of women (particularly married women) which prevent them both from working to improve their individual position in paid work (through promotion or further training) or the conditions of their fellow workers (through trade union activity). The manifest shortcomings of traditional analyses of the position of women in the labour

4. A full account of traditional theories of the 'dual labour market' is given by R. Barron and G. Norris, 'Sexual Divisions and the Dual Labour Market', in D. Barker and S. Allen, eds., *Dependence and Exploitation in Work and Marriage*, Harlow: Longman, 1976.

market have now been examined by feminist economists, who have pointed out that paid labour is only part of the labour process as a whole and that theoretical relationships have to be established between the worlds of the household and the work-place. What has been extensively illustrated and documented by feminist economists is that because of their domestic responsibilities women are easily exploited in paid work: they have to take part-time work, or work which can be reconciled with domestic demands. Moreover, it is only exceptionally that girls are educated to consider the nature of their future paid work. A vicious circle develops in which girls are socialised into seeing marriage and motherhood as their major adult experience, receive little vocational or professional training, become wives and mothers and are then forced to take ill-rewarded jobs because of the domestic responsibilities which automatically become theirs.[5]

A second feature of orthodox discussions of women's paid labour which has also now been questioned by feminists is the view that the jobs taken by women demand little skill. Conventional wisdom has it that women take 'unskilled' jobs and that some objective criteria of 'skill' operates which is independent of the sex of the person in the particular occupation. Yet as Anne Phillips and Barbara Taylor have argued:

Skill definitions are saturated with sexual bias. The work of women is often deemed inferior simply because it is women who do it. Women workers carry into the workplace their status as subordinate individuals, and this status comes to define the value of the work they do. Far from being an objective economic fact, skill is often an ideological category imposed on certain types of work by virtue of the sex and power of the workers who perform it.[6]

What this suggests is that in examining the question of women and paid work it is impossible to regard the occupational structure as a fixed, immutable and sex-blind structure. On the contrary, it has to be considered that our very categories of 'work' and 'skill' are, at least in part, ideological constructs. Male socialists have always questioned the reward structure of capitalism, in which some skills

5. This issue is discussed by Jenny Shaw in the paper reproduced in this volume. See also Dale Spender, *Invisible Women*, London: The Women's Press, 1982; and Ann Marie Wolpe, 'Education and the Sexual Division of Labour', in A. Kuhn and A. Wolpe, eds., *Feminism and Materialism*, London: Routledge and Kegan Paul, 1978.
6. Anne Phillips and Barbara Taylor, 'Sex and Skill: Notes Towards a Feminist Economics', *Feminist Review*, no. 6, 1980, p. 79.

(usually, and typically, white-collar, managerial skills) are rewarded more highly than those associated with manual labour. Equally, feminists have to challenge the double implications of this entrenched belief: that both female white-collar and manual labour are less valuable than their male equivalents.

In questioning both patriarchal values – that women's rightful place is in the home – and the values of the Western occupational structure – that the rewards of work should be related to factors other than those of the social value of a particular job – feminists are challenging two structures of not inconsiderable strength: patriarchy and capitalism. The relationship between these two structures has been explored by Michèle Barrett, Heidi Hartmann, Al Szymanski and many others,[7] but in this context it is perhaps most useful to mention three issues about this vexed and complex relationship. The first issue is that of whether or not women constitute a 'reserve army of labour' in capitalism: a work force which can be employed, or not, as the needs of capital dictate. In the article reproduced here, Irene Bruegel argues that women are a 'reserve army' and this view is endorsed by the work of Jane Humphries and Ruth Milkman.[8] The essential problem with the 'reserve army' thesis is, as Michèle Barrett points out, the extent to which the sexual segregation of the work force makes it possible to dispense with women workers quite as easily as the 'reserve army' argument suggests. As she points out, '... if all typists and cleaners are female (which is virtually the case), it is implausible to suggest that they can all be dispensed with.'[9]

The second issue which must be raised in any discussion of the relationship of patriarchy and wage labour is that of the way in which the interests of patriarchy conflict with the maximisation of economic interests, be they those of capital or an individual male worker. On some occasions it may be in the interests of men – as either employers or members of a household – to encourage the economic activity of women, on other occasions the reverse may be the case. But what is apparent is that even in those situations when the maximisation of economic interests might be served by employing women (or encouraging individual women to enter

7. See Michèle Barrett, *Women's Oppression Today*, London: Virago, 1980; Heidi Hartmann, 'The Unhappy Marriage of Marxism and Feminism', in Lydia Sargent, ed., *The Unhappy Marriage of Marxism and Feminism*, London: Pluto, 1981; and Al Szymanski, 'The Socialisation of Women's Oppression: a Marxist Theory of the Changing Position of Women in Advanced Capitalist Society', *Insurgent Sociologist*, vol. VI, no. 2, 1976.
8. Jane Humphries, 'Women: Scapegoats and Safety Valves in the Great Depression', *Review of Radical Political Economics*, vol. 8, no. 1, 1976; and Ruth Milkman, 'Women's Work and Economic Crisis', in the same journal.
9. Michèle Barrett, *Women's Oppression Today*, p. 161.

employment) patriarchal ideology is so deeply entrenched and internalised that it works against possible increases in material rewards.

But the very conditions which are now making it essential that more women undertake the dual responsibilities of both paid and unpaid work may, paradoxically, be conditions which further the eventual emancipation of women. This raises a third issue about the relationship of patriarchy and capitalism: the question of whether or not entry into paid labour will lead to equality between the sexes. Since the number of households which can survive on one income is decreasing each year, so it becomes inevitable that women's experience of employment becomes more similar to that of men. As this occurs, so the relationship between men and women, husbands and wives, may change, since it is no longer a relationship in which the consistent economic dependence of the wife on the husband can either be assumed or expected. It may well be the case that for short periods of their lives (the years of childbearing and pre-school childcaring) women remain financially dependent on men, but this interruption has become significantly shorter as family sizes has decreased.

Given the factors that now encourage women to enter, and remain in, paid employment, it may now be the case that the conditions now exist for the end of that separation of the sexes into male wage labourers and female dependants which the Industrial Revolution created. This, in turn, suggests a possible end to those conditions which lead to the domination of men over women within the family and personal relations. As Engels suggested in *The Origin of the Family, Private Property and the State*:

> ... similarly, the peculiar character of man's domination over woman in the modern family, and the necessity as well as the manner of establishing real social equality between the two, will be brought out into full relief only when both are completely equal before the law. It will then become evident that the first premise for the emancipation of women is the reintroduction of the entire female sex into public industry; and that this again demands that the quality possessed by the individual family of being the economic unit of society be abolished.[10]

Thus as women enter public production and wage labour it is

10. F. Engels, *The Origin of the Family, Private Property and the State*, in F. Engels and K. Marx, *Selected Works*, vol. 2, Moscow: Foreign Languages Publishing House, 1955, p. 232.

supposed that two changes may occur: the balance of power within the family shifts, to become more equally divided between husband and wife, and women become more fully social beings, in the sense that their relationship to the public, social, world is no longer mediated through men.

However, two very important qualifications must be made to this blueprint for the emancipation of women. The first is that it cannot be automatically assumed that women will have the opportunity to enter paid employment or that capitalism will continue to need a supply of female labour. The second qualification is that in the light of the experience of those socialist societies which have integrated women into the labour force in large numbers, it is impossible to assume, with quite the same confidence as Engels, that women's entry into employment will necessarily and inevitably liberate women.[11] For these reasons it is one of the most urgent tasks of feminism to raise the consciousness of women about paid work and their relationship to it.[12] Although feminism itself cannot guarantee the availability of employment for women it can, perhaps, do something to ensure that women do not maintain those traditionally female attitudes towards paid work which ensure their continued exploitation.[13]

11. See Alena Heitlinger, *Women and State Socialism: Sex Inequality in the Soviet Union and Czechoslovakia*, London: Macmillan, 1979; and Hilda Scott, 'Eastern European Women in Theory and Practice', in *Women's Studies International Quarterly*, vol. 1, no. 2, 1978.
12. One of the issues now raised by feminists about women and paid work is the problem of sexual harassment at work. See Mackinnon, *Sexual Harassment of Working Women*, New Haven: Yale University Press, 1979; and J. Root, 'Sexual Harassment at Work', *Leveller*, 17 April 1981.
13. Although the material on women and paid work included here relates to Western society, the impact of industrialisation on the sexual division of labour and gender divisions in the Third World should not be ignored. For an introductory discussion of this issue see Barbara Rogers, *The Domestication of Women*, London: Tavistock, 1981.

Eric Richards

Women in the British Economy since about 1700: an Interpretation

In *History*, vol. 59, no. 197, London,
October 1974, pp.337-57

In early Victorian Britain only about one woman in five was recorded as part of the work force. Why was female labour, as a factor of production, employed so sparingly by the first great industrial economy? Had women lost their economic utility during the Industrial Revolution? This paper is a speculative exploration of the hypothesis that, in the long perspective of modern British history, there was a substantial diminution of the economic role of women during the nineteenth century.[1] It argues that industrialization, far from 'emancipating' women, led to a contradiction of some of their traditional functions in the economy – to a degree from which they have yet fully to recover. While the argument is addressed essentially to the problem of women in the history of the labour supply, the theme carries wider implications for interdisciplinary discussion.

Development economists, observing the recent experience of industrialization in the third world, have identified surprising trends in the rates of participation of women in economic life. The highest activity rates for women are found in the least developed countries; during the initial phases of development the rates decline, and it is only in the long run that women regain their previous high degree of participation. Studies of Indian and international data have concluded that economic development tends to induce a decline in the subsistence sector at a faster rate than the growth of the modern sector, so that the participation rate, especially of women, falls. In Puerto Rico, for instance, 'the total effect of these changes is that participation may follow a U-shaped

1. This paper began life as a talk to a course entitled 'Women's Studies' at The Flinders University of South Australia in March 1973. I wish to thank the following for their comments: Paul Bourke, David Close, Monica Clough, Mel Davies, Brian Dickey, Joan Hancock, Grant Kirkpatrick, David Mosler, Helen Pearce, Graeme Snooks, Ron Witton and Cathy Yates.

curve as the society is transformed'.[2] In historical terms, there is considerable evidence that the role of women in Britain during the last 250 years bears a striking resemblance to the pattern suggested by the twentieth-century experience in these developing countries. The British case, indeed, may well fit the U-shaped curve – though the time scale must be a good deal more extended.

With the honourable exception of Ivy Pinchbeck's *Women in the Industrial Revolution*,[3] economic historians have not felt justified in discussing the work of women as an analytically significant element in the process of economic growth in Britain. Yet women are potentially a very substantial part of the labour force: on some assumptions (such as a society with a very low birth rate and a very high retirement age) the proportion could approach 50 per cent.[4] It is plain that such factors as family size, age at marriage, and the availability of employment, have influenced the participation of women in the economy. So also have changing social *mores* relating to the accepted place of the woman in domestic and social life. In numerical terms, most women most of the time during the last two centuries have been either peasants or proletarians. But, in the transition from the pre-industrial economy to the world of the mid-twentieth century, women have been an inconstant proportion, a markedly variable component within the total labour force. This proposition, of course, relates to the labour force as conventionally defined – that is, the income-earning part of the population. It is clear that, in both pre- and post-industrial economies, a considerable amount of activity is not directly rewarded in a financial sense. A great deal (but a fluctuating proportion) of female labour enters the category of 'non-market household labour'.[5]

Since about 1700 the pool of female labour has been drawn upon in significantly different degrees during the evolution of the British economy. It is the tentative thesis of this paper that the participation of women in the economy has been subject to three distinct trends. In general it is suggested that before the Industrial

2. Robert H. Weller, 'A Historical Analysis of Female Labour Force Participation in Puerto Rico', *Social and Economic Studies*, vol. 17 (1963), p. 60. See also J. N. Sinha, 'Dynamics of Female Participation in Economic Activity in a Developing Economy', in United Nations, *World Population Conference 1965*, vol. IV (New York, 1967), and Andrew Collver and Eleanor Langlois, 'The Female Labour Force in Metropolitan Areas: an International Comparison', *Economic Development and Cultural Change*, X (1962).
3. First published in 1930.
4. Cf. Glen G. Cain, *Married Women in the Labor Force* (Chicago, 1966), p. 14.
5. On definitional problems see C. E. V. Leser, 'Trends in Women's Work Participation', *Population Studies*, XII (1958-9), pp. 102 and 107, and D. Turnham and I. Jaeger, *The Employment Problem in Less Developed Countries* (Paris, 1971).

Revolution (as conventionally dated) the utilization of women in the economy was close to a notional maximum. During the nineteenth century participation rates fell in the new industrial economy. Only in the middle decades of the twentieth century has the trend produced a level of involvement reminiscent of the pre-industrial economy two centuries earlier.[6] It is a curious thing that the unfettered capitalist economy – in the full flood of industrialism in the mid-nineteenth century – should have utilized a principal supply of labour in so modest a fashion.

I

The pre-industrial economy was not, of course, homogeneous in its economic and social structure. There was a pronounced degree of regional diversity as well as change over time. Consequently there are difficulties in the way of general statements concerning the nature of female labour before the Industrial Revolution; the more so as one approaches the transitional phases between the pre-industrial, proto-industrial and industrialized worlds. Nevertheless high participation rates for women (and indeed for children) in virtually all aspects of the economy may be specified as one of the general characteristics of the underdeveloped, labour-intensive, agriculture-dominated economy of Britain before about 1750.[7] There are very many descriptions that indicate that female labour was universal and that it was normal for women to share in the heaviest manual work.[8] It could hardly have been otherwise in

6. At various points in this paper the argument rests upon a number of heroic assumptions, is supported by impressionistic evidence of a fragile nature, and is openly speculative by intent. It deals mainly in aggregates in a subject where even local studies are sparse. The main methodological difficulty concerns the comparative approach, over time, between a peasant economy and its industrialized successor, where statistical evidence is available for only the latter. Questions of 'work-definition' are prominent, and serve to highlight the qualitative changes in economic and social relationships that came with industrialization.

7. In his list of 'Characteristics of Underdeveloped Areas', Harvey Leibenstein includes 'Inferiority of women's status and position', but does not specifically relate this 'cultural and political' characteristic to the woman's role in the underdeveloped economy. *Economic Backwardness and Economic Growth* (New York, 1963), pp. 40-1. D. C. Coleman has remarked that 'It is to economies of this sort that we should look in order to see the reflections of many, though obviously not all, of the economic features of seventeenth-century England'; 'Labour in the English Economy of the Seventeenth Century', in E. M. Carus-Wilson (ed.), *Essays in Economic History*, II (1962), pp. 285-6. This then raises the important but difficult question of precisely how backward was the pre-industrial English economy.

8. The best source is Pinchbeck, *op. cit., passim*. See also Fitzherbert quoted in Harriet Martineau, 'Female Industry', *Edinburgh Review*, vol. CLXXII (1859), p. 295, and Peter Laslett, *The World We Have Lost* (1965), p. 12.

an economy where in Stuart England between a quarter and a half of the active population were chronically below what contemporaries regarded as the official poverty line.[9] The age-structure of the population, especially the high proportion of children, created an unusually high level of dependency in the society, and these circumstances necessarily entailed a generally low participation rate in the labour force.[10] One corollary was that women had little alternative but to work. Low productivity tended to create a pressure in the same direction, for this was an economy – even in the late seventeenth century – still largely unspecialized in character.

The birth rate was probably high – though there is no certainty about this[11] – which may have reduced further the potential supply of female labour. As Laslett remarks, 'the labourer ... would be liable to fall into want directly his wife began to have children and he lost the earnings of his companion.'[12] Hence women without children were at a high premium in the work force. Moreover labour was the most important factor of production and the utility of female labour – in relation to its position in modern economies – was so much the greater. Above all, 'low productivity, static techniques and labour as the main factor of production meant long hours of arduous toil to produce a small amount.' Such circumstances rendered both child and female labour normal. Where there was small chance of incorporating labour-saving innovations, any expansion in economic activity necessarily required an increase in the labour input. But the age-structure and life expectancy of the

9. Coleman, op. cit., p. 295.
10. Coleman, op. cit., p. 298-9.
11. Some economic historians have argued the opposite case: that there were special demographic circumstances operating in Western Europe, and particularly in England, in the pre-industrial world, which entailed an exceptionally late average age of marriage. It is contended that a high age of marriage, together with general obstacles to high nuptiality, may well have provided 'a longer period during which couples would save and make provision for marriage', thereby raising a demand for non-agricultural products, and creating 'the groundwork for a competitive and acquisitive society in which the ratio of resources to population was thereby kept in favourable balance'. This important interpretation of the relationship carries also an important corollary – it implies that the level of participation in the economy was high. J. D. Chambers, Population, Economy and Society in Pre-Industrial England (1972), pp. 34, 50. See also J. Hajnal, 'European Marriage Patterns in Perspective', Population Studies, VII, 1953. Evidence on family size is summarized in Chambers, op. cit., chapters 2 and 3.
12. Laslett, op. cit., p. 15. There is a well-known remark of the 1750s that 'none but a fool will take a wife whose bread must be earned solely by his labour and who will contribute nothing towards it herself' – J. D. Chambers and S. D. Chapman, The Beginnings of Industrial Britain (1970), p. 10. A similar thought occurred to a large landowner in South Australia in 1843 when advising his immigrating bachelor brother: 'A wife, if a good one, is a cheap stock and maybe a great saving where a man has all to manage.' Quoted in D. Pike, Paradise of Dissent, South Australia, 1829-1857 (1967), p. 497.

population set sharp limits on the size and elasticity of the labour supply. These conditions created a pressure on wages, persuaded authorities to consider very closely policies of wage restraint, and enhanced the role of female labour.[13]

The proposition concerning high female participation rates in this type of economy is not irreconcilable with another generalized feature in the late-Stuart/early-Hanoverian economy, namely the 'persistent tendency towards chronic underemployment'. The latter may be related to the scarcity of consistent employment and the problem of seasonality in agriculture and the rural-based industries. Domestic industry was also essentially erratic in its use of labour.[14] Coleman adds to these points the phenomenon of quasi-voluntary underemployment: 'The regularity, consistency and intensity of work, which the latter [i.e. the modern industrialized community] demands were quite alien to the worker of the seventeenth century and indeed of Tudor England.' This necessarily exacerbated the problem of the general labour supply in the pre-industrial economy.[15]

Notwithstanding such general circumstances of the pre-industrial economy as high dependency levels and the allegedly backward-sloping supply curve of labour, the participation rates of women in the full range of employment were probably very high. It is however exceedingly difficult to give a quantitative dimension to the question: 'pre-industrial' can almost invariably be equated with 'pre-statistical'. But few would disagree with Witt Bowden's statement of the position: 'The system preceding the modern industrial regime based the family economy by the sternest necessity upon the labour of the mother and of the children of tender age as well as upon the labour of the man.'[16]

Ivy Pinchbeck, of all the writers on the subject, is emphatic that

13. Coleman, op. cit., pp. 298-300. See also Joan Thirsk, 'Industry in the Countryside', in F. J. Fisher (ed.), Essays in the Economic and Social History of Tudor and Stuart England (1961).

14. On the specific determinants of the general and local levels of economic activity in the pre-industrial economy, see T. S. Ashton, Economic Fluctuations in England, 1700-1800 (1959).

15. Coleman, op. cit., p. 303. These points may go some way towards explaining the apparent co-existence of population pressure and labour deficiencies at various times in the pre-1700 economy. Participation rates for women probably varied from region to region, though I would suspect that they were generally high by nineteenth-century standards. See Dorothy George's England in Transition (1953), pp. 23-6 and E. W. Gilboy, Wages in Eighteenth Century England (1934), esp. pp. 54, 86, 151, 196.

16. Witt Bowden, Industrial Society in England towards the End of the Eighteenth Century (1925), p. 229. See also R. M. Garnier, Annals of the British Peasantry (1908), pp. 308-10, and M. D. George, London Life in the XVIIIth Century (1925), especially chap. iv and appendix vi.

pre-industrial women were involved in the worst conditions of the economy – that they were a substratum of the labour force receiving no apprenticeship, less education and the lowest wages – 'their labour was subsidiary, it was cheap'. In the family economy women assisted and supplemented: it was a role which was dependent, immobile and characterized by drudgery and monotony.[17] According to Arthur Young, a female spinner in the mid-eighteenth century obtained 4d to 6d a day – which represented about one third of the male day labourer's wage.[18] Pinchbeck makes no bones about the social consequences of the economic half-status that was woman's lot – as expressed in high suicide and mortality rates, and prostitution in London.

But the typical woman's work was the ageless toil on the land – that of the peasant woman. Those regions of Britain which preserved (almost as in amber) pre-industrial conditions into the nineteenth century provide vivid evidence of the economic functions of women. One such region was the Highlands of Scotland which, in parts, remained resolutely peasant-based throughout the age of British industrialism. In July 1823 Hugh Miller, the Scottish geologist, journalist and religious leader, described the work of a Highland community:

There is neither horse nor plough in the village – a long, crook-handled kind of spade, termed a cass-chrom, and the hoe, supplying the place of the latter – the Highlander himself, and more particularly his wife, that of the former – for here (shall I venture the expression?) as in all semi-barbarous countries, the woman seems to be regarded rather as the drudge than the companion of the man. It is the part of the husband to turn up the land and sow it; the wife conveys the manure to it in a square creel with a slip bottom, tends the corn, reaps it, hoes the potatoes, digs them up, and carries the whole home on her back. When bearing the creel she is also engaged in spinning with the distaff and spindle. I wish you but saw with what patience these

17. *Op. cit.*, pp. 1-5.
18. P. Mantoux, *The Industrial Revolution in the Eighteenth Century* (1961), p. 70. Clara Collet, *Women in Industry* (no date), p. 10, quotes Sir William Petty's *Political Arithmetick* (1690), to the effect 'that all women and girls over seven years of age are to labour except among the upper tenth', i.e. female labour was a universal assumption in the pre-industrial world. For a particular industry in the eighteenth century – iron wares in the Midlands – see W. H. B. Court, *The Rise of Midland Industries, 1600-1838* (1939), pp. 209-11. On domestic spinning, see E. Lipson, *The Economic History of England*, ii (1948), pp. 50-1. More generally see E. P. Thompson, 'Time, Work-discipline and Industrial Capitalism', *Past and Present*, no. 38 (1967), p. 79, and his criticisms of the use of the category 'pre-industrial', p. 80.

poor females continue thus dumbly employed, for the greater
part of a long summer's day.[19]

Miller wrote that 'I scarce saw a Gairloch woman of the humbler
class turned of thirty, who was not thin, sallow, and prematurely
old.'[20]

Highland conditions were particularly 'backward', but it would
not be difficult to find similar descriptions for other parts of
agrarian Britain early in the nineteenth century. When a large
number of Irish girls arrived as assisted immigrants in Adelaide,
South Australia, in 1855, their prospective employers had to be
told, expressly, that these girls should be treated as men because
they were used to doing all the tasks of a male agricultural
labourer.[21] We do not need to assume that such cases as these are
perfect time-capsules of a pre-industrial economy to observe a
significant parallel with descriptions from other parts of Britain in
the late seventeeth-century. The pre-industrial economy, needless
to say, accommodated a range of conditions for both men and
women, region and region, class and class. Yet overall there is a
powerful impression that for women, it was a life of labour – either
in child-bearing or in work, either paid or *en famille*.[22]

Several social historians have taken pains to emphasize that the
employment of married and single women long pre-dated the
Industrial Revolution, and there is general concurrence that there
is 'little reason to believe in any decline and fall of women from
a golden age in which they did only work which was "suitable" and
that in the bosoms of their families'.[23] Indeed, surveying the

19. Peter Bayne (ed.), *The Life and Letters of Hugh Miller* (2 vols. 1871), i, p. 115.
20. Hugh Miller, *My Schools and Schoolmasters* (no date), p. 287. See also Valerie
Morgan, 'Agricultural Wage Rates in Late Eighteenth Century Scotland', *Economic
History Review*, xxiv, no. 2 (1971), pp. 193-7.
21. State Library of South Australia. Archives Department. GRG 24/6 (1855), Immigration
Officer, Port Adelaide to Colonial Secretary, 18 October 1855. 'Anyone accustomed to
visit the rural districts of either Scotland or Ireland must know well that females there are
employed in outdoor farm work in a way not customary in England. The female peasantry
of both these countries think it no degradation either to make hay or reap the cornfields,
to milk cows or manage the details of the farm yard.' For an English parallel see the
fascinating analysis by N. L. Tranter, 'The Social Structure of a Bedfordshire Parish in
the Mid-Nineteenth Century', *International Review of Social History*, xviii (1973), pp.
90-106.
22. See the considerable literary evidence presented in Alice Clark, *Working Life of
Women in the Seventeenth Century* (1919), esp. pp. 234 ff.
23. Margaret Hewitt, *Wives and Mothers in Victorian Industry* (1958), quoting Barbara
Hutchins. For a recent description of labour allocation in the domestic system of the early
eighteenth century, see Chambers and Chapman, *op. cit., passim*, and Frances Collier, *The
Family Economy of the Working Class in the Cotton Industry 1784-1833* (1964).

fragments of evidence of the peasant woman's work in pre-industrial Britain, it may be feasible to invert the 'golden-age' thesis. For instance it was only a later age, that of the factory girl and the Victorian social conscience, that was able to express comprehensive outrage against female labour in coalmines – yet this was, in many ways, an anachronistic remnant of pre-industrial systems of labour. And so Victorian Britain prohibited this particular employment opportunity for women. Further than this, however, there is a generally accepted assumption that there was a uniform progression of women's work in recent centuries: in effect, that the scope and extent of female labour had increased continuously in pre-industrialized times, and then proceeded to accelerate in the Industrial Revolution. On the contrary, it is the contention here that the participation of women in the economy (though not necessarily as wage-labour *per se*) was substantially *greater* before the Industrial Revolution than during that process itself.

II

The general process known as the Industrial Revolution is widely interpreted as vital in the history of women in British social and economic life. R. M. Hartwell has observed that 'there is little doubt that the industrial revolution commences the social revolution in the status of women', and, in another place, he writes, 'It was during the industrial revolution . . . and largely because of the economic opportunities it afforded to working-class women, that there was the beginning of that most important and most beneficial of all the social revolutions of the last two centuries, the emancipation of women.'[24] Quite different, but no less sanguine, is the view of Rhodes Boyson that 'The Industrial Revolution brought a real advance for wives and families because it introduced the idea that men's wages should be sufficient to maintain a wife and family and that women should make their contribution by looking after the home. For the first time the wives of the industrial classes could concentrate on the business of home making and the care of their children, who stood to benefit by the changed home conditions.'[25] The optimistic view derives in some measure from Ivy Pinchbeck whose treatment is generally favourable – even

24. R. M. Hartwell, *The Industrial Revolution and Economic growth* (1971), pp. 96, 343.
25. Rhodes Boyson, 'Industrialization and the Life of the Lancashire Factory Worker', in *The Long Debate on Poverty* (The Institute of Economic Affairs, 1972), p. 78.

though she gives considerably more emphasis to the transitional difficulties that impeded the emergence of emancipated women.[26]

The more pessimistic school of historians has argued that women, in common with the rest of the population, suffered a decline, or at least a stagnation, in their living standards. Competition from cheap female labour in factories is said to have reduced the power of resistance of the working class, and 'was used both to beat down wages and to extend the hours of labour to an inhuman length'.[27] For Engels the social consequences were patent: 'when women work in factories the most important result is the dissolution of family ties', the destruction of family cohesion.[28] Yet it was Marx who recognized, with striking clarity, that 'large-scale industry ... is building the new economic foundation for a higher form of family and the relations between the sexes'.[29] In both pessimist and optimist camps the discussion is grounded, implicitly, on suppositions concerning the rates of participation of women in the economy during the process of industrialization.

It is plain that there were a great many circumstances which affected the opportunities of women to contribute to activity in the labour force, e.g., the birth rate, infantile mortality rates, the balance of the sexes in the population, the age at marriage,[30] life expectation, levels of *per capita* income, government policy, levels of education, the mobility of the labour force, changing social conventions, the composition of employment, overall employment levels, and the general rate of economic expansion. Nevertheless it may be possible to pick out three critical and general variables which influenced the rate of participation by women in the British economy during the process of industrialization, say during the

26. Pinchbeck, *op. cit.*, p. 4. Even more roseate is the recent view of Dorothy Marshall in *Industrial England 1776-1851* (1973), pp. 100, 190.

27. G. D. H. Cole, *Short History of the British Working Class Movement* (1948), p. 20.

28. Quoted in Harold Perkin, *The Origins of Modern English Society* (1969), p.149.

29. Quoted in Boyson, *op. cit.*, p. 79. For a modern Soviet echo of Marx's doctrine see K. G. Illyina, 'The Participation of Women in the Economic Activities of the Soviet Union', United Nations, *World Population Conference 1965*, vol. IV, p. 301. Another Marxist interpretation may be found in Grace Hutchins, *Women Who Work* (no date), who quotes Marx to the effect that, as a result of industrial capital, 'In order that the family may live, four persons [i.e. the family] must now not merely work, but supply labour for capital' (p. 13).

30. It is possible that a lowering of the average age at marriage in the late eighteenth century in England may have caused a decline in the supply of the female labour force. See Chambers, *op. cit.*, p. 58. But the number of women in the age group 20-40 is estimated to have increased from 1,149,000 in 1781 to 2,553,000 in 1841. See T. H. Marshall, 'The Population Problem during the Industrial Revolution', in E. M. Carus Wilson (ed.), *Essays in Economic History*, I (1954), p. 323.

century after 1780. First was the general growth of population which, among many other consequences, eventually increased the potential supply of female labour at working age. Second was the expansion in the number of employment opportunities in the new growth sectors of the industrial economy – notably in factory textiles, but also in other sectors. Third were those substantial changes in employment in the traditional sectors of the economy – some of which declined rapidly in the early phases of the Industrial Revolution, others which expanded at unprecedented rates until perhaps 1830 and then withered away, and others which carried on much as they had been in the previous century. The second and third of these variables were together part of the multiple structural transformation of the economy which can be identified with the Industrial Revolution. The changes were simultaneous and overlapping and the results, for women, were complex. Sadly it is not until late in the nineteenth century that the statistical evidence begins to provide an unambiguous picture of the consequences for female participation in the economy. In the absence of better evidence, the historian has to deal in fragments of statistical and literary data.

The accelerated growth of the British economy in the last decades of the eighteenth century generated employment opportunities in both old and new sectors – for instance, in handloom weaving[31] and in cotton spinning factories, in road construction as well as in canal building. It was a growth of activity of a highly volatile character, and upon it were superimposed the demands of the war economy between 1793 and 1815. In all, these expanding requirements were related to a labour market already in the process of natural increase from the upsurge in population growth dating from, perhaps, the 1750s. At certain times, and in certain localities, the pressure on the labour supply seems to have been intense. Moreover, in the most spectacular growth sector, cotton, there was a disproportionate expansion in jobs which were to become almost specific to women.

The early cotton mills, set in the countryside – particularly in Derbyshire, Lancashire and Lanarkshire – provide the classic example. The problems of labour recruitment were acute and the cotton masters appear to have turned to women as the main component of their labour supply. The time-discipline required, the rural setting, the confusion in the public mind between the

---

31. The evidence given in D. Bythell, *The Handloom Weavers* (1969), p. 63, is consistent with a temporary expansion in the number of female handloom weavers to about 1830.

cotton mill and the poorhouse, and the nature of the work, all created a reluctance among the work force to enter the factories. The consequence was that the lower elements in the economy were drawn upon – the 'transient, marginal and deviant'[32] – but particular resort was made to the labour of women and children. In Scotland there was a quite disproportionate expansion in the number of jobs for the last group: the new lines of work in the factories did not require muscular strength, but did require a degree of docility best supplied by women.[33] W. A. Armstrong remarks plainly that 'as machinery lightened the burden of manual effort it was found convenient and cheaper to use the labour of women and children'.[34] These developments in the cotton industry mark the dramatic, prefatory phase in the long slow migration of many functions and trades from the homes of the workers to the factories, from the countryside to the towns. For many decades some of the domestic trades expanded *pari passu* with the mechanized factory branches of the industries concerned, for example, the weaving trades, nail-making,[35] kelp-making and brewing. As E. J. Hobsbawm remarked, 'the *obvious* way of industrial expansion in the eighteenth century was not to construct factories, but to extend the so-called domestic system.'[36] Many of these older forms of activity were characterized by relatively high female participation rates – as indeed was agricultural labour, which underwent a similar expansion until the middle decades of the nineteenth century. However it was over this long period that gradually and painfully the hand trades succumbed to the productive superiority of the factory sections of their respective industries. One by one the old gave way to the new. For women in particular the loss of employment in the traditional lines was probably greater than the creation of new opportunities: in hypothetical terms, the level of

32. S. Pollard, *The Genesis of Modern Management* (1968), p. 190. See also Mantoux, *op. cit.*, p. 410. Of the very early, mid-century mills, Dorothy George has remarked 'since no one had yet dreamed that the employment of women and children was other than highly beneficial to society, no one had complained that few of the factory hands were men'. *Op. cit.*, p. 103.
33. See T. C. Smout, *A History of the Scottish People, 1530-1830* (1969), pp. 406-7.
34. W. A. Armstrong, 'The Use of Information about Occupation', in E. A. Wrigley (ed.), *Nineteenth-Century Society: Essays in the use of quantitative methods for the study of social data* (Cambridge, 1972), p. 199. See also S. D. Chapman, *The Early Factory Masters* (Newton Abbot, 1967), pp. 150 ff.
35. J. H. Clapham's evidence of 50,000 nailers in the Black Country in 1830 – men, women and children employed in a domestic industry, and 'half-naked girls turning out 1000 nails a day'. *An Economic History of Modern Britain*, vol. 1 (1939), pp. 72-3.
36. E. J. Hobsbawm, *The Age of Revolution 1789-1848* (1964), p. 55.

technological/structural unemployment, for women, rose.[37] And one might guess that the sharply competitive years after 1815 were especially critical in the general evolution.

It is argued, therefore, that 'the rise of the factory girl' was an exceptional and atypical development in the industrializing economy. The new cotton industry rapidly generated tens of thousands of jobs for women. But it was regionally concentrated in its impact, and other industries created few employment opportunities. Even within textiles (wool, linen and cotton), if the gains are balanced against the losses of work for women in all branches, including bleaching and spinning, the net consequence may have been a reduced female participation.[38] More definitely one can see a clear shrinkage of opportunities in many of the metal trades and in agriculture after 1815. And the great leading sectors of the economy – iron and steel, railways, chemicals, building – offered derisory employment benefits for women.

Hence the impressionistic evidence that is available suggests the bare possibility that, during the early transitional decades, say until 1820, the number of jobs for women rose, even in proportion to the rising female population as a whole. But thereafter it is very likely that the female participation rates declined. The increasing diversification of the industrial economy appears to have benefited women very little – and, possibly for that reason, gave rise to the mid-Victorian social problem of the underemployed female.[39] The greatest difficulty is that of giving a quantitative foundation to this hypothesis: as J. H. Clapham remarked, 'mostly the work of women did not enter the statistical collections.'[40] Moreover the statistical problem remains until the virtual demise of domestic

37. Pinchbeck remarks, 'women's opportunities for productive work at home were gradually lessened as the agrarian revolution proceeded, while at the same time industrial changes deprived them of employment in the older domestic industries. In other directions also, women's activities ... were gradually diminishing in the latter half of the eighteenth century.' *Op. cit.*, pp. 306, 375.

38. G. H. Wood's estimates indicate that between 1830 and 1851 the number of handloom weavers fell by 200,000, while factory workers in cotton increased by only 154,000. The longer period, 1820-62, shows 237,000 fewer weavers, but 326,000 more cotton operatives. Derived from B. R. Mitchell, *An Abstract of British Historical Statistics* (1962), p. 187. Note that the proportion of men and women in factory work was greater in the early nineteenth century than in say 1911. Moreover Pinchbeck, *op. cit.*, p. 196, remarks 'the proportion of men was remarkably higher in the days of machine industry' than had been the case in domestic industry. Wood's estimates are criticized in Bythell, *op. cit.*, pp. 8-9.

39. See below. A similar process seems to have occurred in nineteenth-century Scandinavia. See Harriet Holter, 'Women's Occupational Situation in Scandinavia', *International Labour Review*, 93 (1966), p. 385.

40. Clapham, *op. cit.*, pp. 72-3.

employment. The point is made paradoxically by E. J. Hobsbawm when, of the later nineteenth century, he writes:

> The rise of woman labour is statistically masked by its decline in some industries: while the percentage of occupied women did not increase significantly between 1851 and 1881, no less than 122,000 disappeared from such occupations as ribbon, lace, straw hats, shirt and glove manufacture and sewing.[41]

The number of women working in textile factories is one area of reasonable certainty. In 1833 there were 65,000 women as compared with 60,000 men in the cotton factories – still, of course, a tiny fraction of the national work force. More than half of the numbers of both sexes were under the age of fourteen, and no more than one sixth of the women were married. Leonard Horner, in 1847, found that only 27 per cent of women in factories were married. Moreover it is probable that the textile trades employed a larger proportion of married women than any other sector of the economy. The evidence tends to sustain the view of John Bright that 'most women left the factory on marriage'. The typical factory girl was unmarried, and in the age group 16-21.[42] So far as the social consequences of factory work are concerned, Harold Perkin is able to emphasize the gradualness of the transition from 'the integration of work, leisure, homemaking and childrearing in the domestic worker's household to the segregation of these activities within the factory operative's family, and between his home and the family, the school, friendly society, clubs and so on'.[43] The cotton industry, however, was not typical of nineteenth-century industrial Britain. In many respects the differentiation of functions in the family which is observable in the cotton industry in about 1850 was not generalized in the economy at large until the middle decades of the twentieth century. The cotton industry (by creating jobs for women) was a precursor of these later trends, but for many decades remained essentially atypical in its labour requirements.

41. E. J. Hobsbawm, *Labouring Men* (1968), p. 281. See also the work on Preston by Michael Anderson which shows the variability of female labour, and the statistical problems involved in their tabulation. 'Well over a third of all working wives in Preston in 1851 were employed in non-factory occupations, but were not recorded.' Michael Anderson, *Family Structure in Nineteenth-Century Lancashire* (1971), p. 71.
42. Hewitt, *op. cit.*, pp. 10 ff.
43. Perkin, *op. cit.*, p. 155.

Between 1851 and 1881 adult women comprised something close to one third of the entire population. Yet only one fifth of this vast potential reservoir of labour was actually in recorded employment.[44] The rest were dependants of one sort or another, but mainly housewives. In their authoritative book on the long-run experience of British economic growth, Deane and Cole identify 'what seems to have been an important characteristic of the process of industrialisation, the tendency for economic opportunities for child and female employment to increase'. It is a surprising conclusion, and the more so if the ancillary problem concerning the co-existence of domestic female employment is kept in mind. Extrapolating backwards from the female participation rate of about 30 per cent in 1851 must produce a remarkable and very low rate for the pre-industrial labour force. By restricting their purview to the category of 'full-time employment', and by concentrating attention on the factory cotton industry, Deane and Cole produce the verdict that the Industrial Revolution yielded a widening range of economic activity for the most unskilled sections of the growing labour force, notably women and children: 'These were the groups which would have found it difficult to obtain regular employment outside domestic service in the pre-industrial era.'[45] Contrariwise it may be argued that, in the pre-industrial framework, women were absorbed in a broad range of activity which was subsequently narrowed by the structural changes associated with the Industrial Revolution. For example, the employment of women in agriculture declined in proportional terms in the nineteenth century.[46] The hand trades experienced a withering of employment opportunities as they lost their contests with modern substitutes. This process affected women differentially – but in most industries the labour force was increasingly male-dominated. The cotton textile industry appears to be an exception to the rule. It is by no means clear that the creation of new jobs in the economy in general counterbalanced the loss of old jobs – and it is several degrees less certain that the new employment opportunities for women kept pace with the

44. See S. G. Checkland, *The Rise of Industrial Society in England, 1815-1885* (1964), p. 216.
45. P. Deane and W. A. Cole, *British Economic Growth* (1962), pp. 139-40, 294.
46. Ivy Pinchbeck, perhaps somewhat contentiously, suggested that enclosure had reduced employment opportunities for women. When the land was divorced from the family 'it mattered little how willing and anxious she was to work; she could no longer assist in the support of her family nor maintain her own independence', *op. cit.*, p. 44. On the survival of certain forms of female labour in British agriculture into the mid-nineteenth century see chap. IV of William Howitt's *The Rural Life of England* (1844).

growth of their total numbers.[47] The upshot was that, by the mid-nineteenth century, the range of opportunities for these women was tragically restricted. There emerged a surplus army of employable women in the labour market which was to be a very considerable social problem of the Victorian age. The origin of this phenomenon must represent a genuine historical question, unless it is assumed that the surplus of women had always existed.

III

It was a striking feature of the capitalist economy of Victorian Britain that something like one third of the potential labour was not normally employed.[48] Karl Marx and R. M. Hartwell may well be correct in saying that the Industrial Revolution created the possibilities for the emancipation and independence of women, that is, by way of employment divorced from the family context yielding a separate income to the woman, if employed. But for the overwhelming majority of women this particular benefit of industrialization did not accrue until the middle of the twentieth century.[49] New employment opportunities for women did not emerge in a significant degree during the transitional period. There was a delay until the structure of the British economy underwent radical diversification in the second quarter of the twentieth

47. This is not to deny that there was an absolute rise in the number of jobs for women through the period. E. P. Thompson has suggested that 'Some economic historians appear to be unwilling (perhaps because of concealed "progressivism" which equates human progress with economic growth) to face the evident fact that technological innovation during the Industrial Revolution, until the railway age, did displace (except in the metal industries) adult skilled labour.' *The Making of the English Working Class* (1963), p. 312. It is the view of this paper that this proposition applies more especially to women than to men, with the exception of the textile industries. See also Pinchbeck, *op. cit.*, p. 315.

48. The first reliable figures, for 1851, show that, of all females over ten, 2,832,000 were 'occupied' and 5,294,000 were 'unoccupied'. Mitchell, *op. cit.*, p. 60. On the problems of interpreting census data see E. Bridge, 'Women's Employment: Problems of Research', *Society for the Study of Labour History*, Bulletin No. 26 (Spring 1973), pp. 5-7. The question of female underemployment is of course related to the wider, very important, but equally unresearched problem of the general level of unemployment that was 'normal' in the nineteenth-century economy.

49. If one takes the argument over sufficiently long a period most things, good or bad, can be traced to the Industrial Revolution – and this may have the effect of drawing attention away from 'transitional problems' which may, in their turn, have operated for the best part of a century. Improvements in the working-class environment are often written about in this vein, e.g., H. Perkin: 'In the long run better homes and housewifery were the product of higher living standards and education, and so directly and indirectly of industrialism', *op. cit.*, p. 154. Similarly Hartwell makes the claim that the Industrial Revolution can be credited with 'the increasing social and economic independence of women', *op. cit.*, p. 355.

century – which was partly associated with the emergence of a full-scale tertiary sector together with new consumer industries. Like many other benefits commonly ascribed to the Industrial Revolution, those for female emancipation did not reach recognizable fruition until the middle of the present century. Hence, for the majority of Victorian women, the employment problem was severe.

The most widespread opportunity for female employment was domestic service. This was the largest single occupational category in the Victorian economy,[50] and operated partly as a substitute employment for women who, in an earlier age, would have found a niche in the domestic economy. Indeed, it may be argued that the domestic service sector of the Victorian economy was, in part, a form of disguised underemployment. In 1881 there were 1.8 million domestic servants, most of whom were women. Most women who worked were skivvies. Moreover this occupation was a rising percentage of total female employment – in 1851 domestic servants represented 13 per cent of the total labour force, but in 1891 the figure was 16 per cent. In absolute numbers there was a continuous rise until 1911. While male employment in this sector fell, the number of women rose thus:

Female domestic servants (England and Wales)
1851	971,000
1861	1,214,000
1871	1,486,000
1881	1,545,000

These figures represent between 10.6 per cent and 12.8 per cent of the female population. Domestic service was clearly the prime resort of unmarried women over the entire period.[51] Apart from domestic service, textiles, stitching and washing, there was little else open to women of any class in England before the final decades of the century. Concurrently there was a diminution in 'the coarser kinds of manual labour' for women: the decline in female labour in agriculture was very substantial (from 144,000 in 1851 to 50,000 in 1881, in England and Wales). In domestic textiles there

50. It is extraordinary that the greatest industry of Victorian Britain has no economic history. Note that Pinchbeck claims that 'domestic service had always been the chief employment for women', *op. cit.*, p. 3.
51. See Mitchell, *op. cit.*, p. 60; Geoffrey Best, *Mid-Victorian Britain, 1851-1875* (1971), p. 103. For an important contrast with present-day problems of developing countries see E. Boserup, *Women's Role in Economic Development* (1970), p. 5.

was a comparable transfer so that, by the 1880s, more than three quarters of all textile labour was located in factories.[52]

The putative decline in female participation rates in the British economy seems to have reached its social nadir in the third quarter of the nineteenth century. As Best observes, 'The basic fact is, that work-necessitous women throughout the mid-Victorian years remained a reservoir of cheap labour, wanted for a limited variety of employments ... and absolutely without organisation or bargaining power.'[53] Partly, the problem of 'superfluous women' (as one contemporary author described them) was a reflection of demographic and differential emigration considerations. There were more women than men, more spinsters than bachelors, and in more than the usual degree. The 1851 census indicated that 42 per cent of women in the age group 20-40 were spinsters.[54] Men emigrated more than women. In all it seems very likely that the potential supply of women overstretched demand in many trades – which suggests that the low aggregate participation rate was primarily involuntary in character. But there were other influences operating in the same direction. The size of the Victorian family is a point to be reckoned with. In a pre-contraceptive age, the level of infantile death-rate was the main determinant of family size. The mid-nineteenth century probably experienced the highest average size of family in British history. The tyranny of repeated pregnancy *and* continuous child-rearing was at a peak, and this may have helped to reduce the female participation rates.

It is a commonplace that the problem of the underemployed Victorian woman was exacerbated by prevailing attitudes; in effect, the low participation rates were reinforced by Victorian social conventions. The bourgeois ideal of the ornamental female with 'no function besides inspiring admiration and bearing children',[55] of genteel uselessness, exerted a pervasive influence beyond the middle classes. Aspirations, and opportunities for financial independence, were constricted not only by the framework of employment, but also by notions of social approval. Hence

52. Nevertheless some of the older types of female work lingered on. For the survival of 'Outwork' in the domestic environment into twentieth-century Birmingham, see the account in chap. iv of Edward Cadbury, M. C. Matheson and George Shann, *Women's Work and Wages* (1906). Their discussion uses the interesting category 'Extended Domestic Occupations'. On female labour in the Sheffield cutlery trades in 1900, see R. W. Breach and R. M. Hartwell, *British Economy and Society 1879-1970* (1972), p. 110.
53. Best, *op. cit.*, p. 103.
54. Hobsbawm, in *Labouring Men*, p. 293, reckons that, for the age group 15-49 in the period 1851 to 1911, there was an average 108 women to every 100 men, and that this helped to create 'a very large surplus of the lowest paid type of labour'.
55. Perkin, *op. cit.*, p. 159.

McGregor is able to write of the 'wretched condition of the increasing number of women for whom almost the only socially approved occupation was a marriage denied by demographic trends.'[56] But professional employment grew very slowly. Women employed in commerce, public administration, medicine and education increased from 95,000 in 1851 to 138,400 in 1871.[57] Women in Victorian Britain were in comparable position to those in urban areas of developing countries in the mid-twentieth century – for example, in Egypt, Iran, Pakistan, the Caribbean and Latin America – where there are low female work participation rates, and of those in work a very high proportion is in domestic service.[58] Indeed, the plight of the Victorian woman in the absence of the absorptive sponge of domestic service would be hard to imagine.

The narrow limits of acceptable and accessible female employment in the mid-century provoked from some women – almost entirely middle-class in origin – a response which generated fuel for the feminist developments of the age. A surge of sympathetic writing also helped – titles such as Jessie Boucherett's *How to Provide for Superfluous Ladies* (1869), Mrs Hugo Reid's *A Plea for Women* (1843), A Philanthropist's *Domestic Tyranny* (1841) and Josephine Elizabeth Buller's *Women's Work and Women's Culture* (1869), reflected both the underlying problem and the response of the fractional minority building the foundations of feminism. Quite typical were the remarks of W. R. Greg in his essay 'Why Are Women Redundant?' where he wrote feelingly of:

> beautiful lay nuns, involuntary takers of the veil – who pine for work, who beg for occupation, who pant for interest in life, as the hart panteth after water-brooks, and dig for it more earnestly than for hid treasures.[59]

Social attitudes changed very slowly and probably owed as much or more to the changing realities of the economy than to the stirring propaganda of the vocal female minority. By the final decade of the century there appears to have been a switch in the central point of the problem – employment opportunities had widened (notably for single middle-class women whose numbers were relatively

56. O. R. McGregor, 'The Social Position of Women in England, 1850-1914: a Bibliography', *The British Journal of Sociology*, 6 (1955), p. 51. See also Constance Rover, *Women's Suffrage and Party Politics in Britain, 1866-1914* (1967), *passim.*

57. J. A. and Olive Banks, *Feminism and Family Planning in Victorian England* (1964), p. 37. See also Mitchell, *op. cit.*, p. 60.

58. Collver and Langlois, *op. cit.*, p. 367.

59. W. R. Greg, *Literary and Social Judgements* (1869), pp. 282-3.

insignificant), and the social question began to shift to the specific position of the married woman, to a degree greater than before – and, indeed, this was to become the preoccupation of twentieth-century feminists.

Prior to these changes there existed for most women only a narrow range of employment opportunities, almost totally dominated by domestic service. The latter was a curious feature of the Victorian economy. It represented the growth of a non-industrial sector of the economy, a growth which was only indirectly related to the changes in economic structure which we associate with the Industrial Revolution. One may hypothesize on the origins of the growth of domestic service *vis-à-vis* two complementary changes. One was the rise of income for the servant-employing classes during the middle fifty years of the century. As the Bankses report, 'Between 1850 and 1870 the growing prosperity of the middle- and upper-middle classes expressed itself not only in a more luxurious style of life but in a drive for social esteem. This took the form of displaying all the paraphernalia of gentility – large and expensive houses, numerous domestic servants employed outdoors as well as in.'[60] Second was the relative decline of other types of employment opportunities for women during the classic period of industrialization. The somewhat paradoxical development of domestic service is mainly explicable in terms of the relative decline in other types of female employment.[61] Domestic service was a kind of giantism of the new industrial economy, the origins of which may be sought in the aggregate trends in the structure of employment.

IV

The real origins of the 'emancipation of women' (in the modern sense of economic opportunity and independence) must be sought in the shifting balance of the occupational framework which began to emerge in the last quarter of the nineteenth century. The process

60. *Op. cit.*, p. 12. See also S. Pollard and D. W. Crossley, *The Wealth of Britain* (1968), pp. 212-13, and J. F. C. Harrison, *The Early Victorians, 1832-1851* (1971), p. 46. In 1886 Charles Booth made a related and significant point: 'With regard to Domestic Service it is noteworthy that the increase lies mainly in the women and girls, the indoor men servants having decreased from 74,000 in 1851 to 56,000 in 1881, while the population had risen from 18 to 26 millions – a fact which would seem to indicate a greater diffusion of expenditure among the very rich.' Charles Booth, 'Occupations of the People of the United Kingdom, 1801-1881', *Journal of the Royal Statistical Society*, xlix (1886), p. 321.

61. See the passages from the *Handloom Weavers Report* of 1840 quoted in Pike, *op. cit.*, p. 230, which indicates the special position of the cotton areas, and also Daniel J. Boorstin, *The Americans*, II (1969), p. 189.

of change, however, was extremely gradual. The gains in some trades continued to be offset by losses in others. In effect there was a further long transitional period for women. In the latter half of the nineteenth century there was a considerable decline in the proportion of wives and widows engaged in service and industry. Clara Collet, at the turn of the century, concluded a survey of female labour by remarking that 'In the past half century there has been no real invasion of industry generally by women, but rather a withdrawal from it.'[62] Industrial occupations continued to migrate from the domestic workshop to the factories. Moreover there had occurred a widening institutionalization of activities, which, in 1850, had been performed 'in service' – that is, in the home. By the end of the century most teachers were engaged in schools and few remained in families. Similarly washing, child-minding, clothes-making and nursing had mainly departed from the upper-middle-class family home. Female labour in agriculture and in the domestic textile trades also declined. Collet was able to identify a further consequence of the cumulative differentiation of employment in the economy: 'Even the declining industries employ a smaller proportion of women because the plain needlewoman casually employed has to a great extent been replaced by a smaller proportion of full-time workers in clothing factories and work-shops.' In 1901, 32 per cent of girls and women over the age of ten were occupied outside the home – 14 per cent were in family, institutional or personal service, 18 per cent were in industry, and of these almost two thirds were engaged in the clothing and textile trades.[63]

Nevertheless it is clear that before the First World War widening opportunities were developing for female employment at a time when the stigma of married work was beginning to diminish. Partly it was consequent upon the broadening base of secondary industry, itself contingent upon the rise of *per capita* incomes for the majority of the population. Industries such as those related to food processing – geared to rising consumption levels – were emerging in an industrialized form[64] and generating employment, especially

62. Clara C. Collet, *Women in Industry* (pamphlet, no date, circa 1900), p. 9. See also Booth, *op. cit.*, p. 322.
63. Collet, *op. cit.*, p. 9. The general trends detected by Collet are confirmed by W. Ashworth, *An Economic History of England, 1870-1939* (1960), p. 192 n., but the latter considers that supply determinants were more important and that rising real incomes persuaded more married women to stay at home.
64. See Charles Wilson, 'Economy and Society in Late Victorian Britain', *Economic History Review*, xviii (1965).

for women. The growth of the tertiary sector – notably in education, clerical work and retailing, as well as nursing – created a broadening range of occupations regarded as increasingly suitable for women. Institutional changes helped. The Women's Property Act of 1882 at last gave recognition to a basic requirement of 'emancipation' – an acceptance that the family might contain two recipients of income, and two owners of property. The provision of compulsory education was another fundamental alteration in the circumstances of married women: it helped to reduce her child-minding responsibilities while also providing the possibility for greater equality of opportunity for girls in the future. Such changes were only in the making before the turn of the century. The most significant developments had occurred in the great growth of the nursing and teaching professions which absorbed large numbers of women – releasing them from 'the prison of domesticity'.[65] The tide had turned, but this success was hardly attributable to feminist propaganda even though it undoubtedly had an impact on public attitudes. The widening spectrum of female employment by 1900 was fundamentally a function of the autonomous diversification of the industrial economy.[66]

The First World War consolidated and accelerated the trends. 'Shifts in employment produced a revolutionary advance in the economic position of women, whose new-found economic independence was rewarded with a vote after the war with virtually no opposition,' writes Sidney Pollard.[67] The war placed unprecedented pressure on the labour supply which created a need to draw upon the underutilized pool of female workers – and their participation rate rose dramatically. Total female employment rose from 3.28 million in July 1914 to 4.95 million in November 1918. Half a million women entered clerical work in private offices. But, in addition, women were taking up 'unfeminine', twentieth-century type jobs – such as conducting on trams and buses – while

65. See Checkland, *op. cit.*, p. 400.

66. Cf. McGregor, *op. cit.*, p. 50, and see Barbara Drake, *Women in the Engineering Trades* (1918), p. 13, where she lists 'the electrical and other new and progressive branches' of industry which had witnessed 'a female invasion' before 1914. The fear of the trades unions was 'the determination of the employer to exploit for profit a new and unlimited supply of cheap and docile labour'.

67. S. Pollard, *The Development of the British Economy 1914-1967* (1968), p. 77.

900,000 women entered engineering shops.[68] The complement of these decisive changes was the sudden decline in the Victorian stand-by of the underemployed woman, domestic service; there were 400,000 fewer women employed in domestic service in 1918 than in 1914. The war was a considerable psychological moment for women, and once again institutional recognition followed, in the shape of the Sex Disqualification Act of 1919.

In quantitative terms the advance of women was far from revolutionary in the sense of a permanent development. War conditions commonly stimulate freak growths in the economy which promptly wither away in peace-time circumstances. Three-quarters of a million women left paid employment at the time of demobilization – 'with hardly a trace'.[69] Moreover the rate of progress of women into professional occupations was not maintained. A. J. P. Taylor writes that, 'In practice, most women remained dependants, particularly in the working class. Wives were lucky to be given a housekeeping allowance. In almost every occupation women were paid less than men for doing the same work.'[70] Hence the full realization of equality of income and opportunity (or anything like it) remained emphatically a distant aspiration of women, and this continued to be reflected in the participation rates. Indeed the level for 1921 was marginally lower than 1911, and the figure for 1951 was lower than 1931.[71] The interwar years brought extreme problems of unemployment across the entire economy during a period when the occupational structure was undergoing very considerable readjustment.[72] But these structural changes (partly anticipated by the movements in the late Victorian economy) generally, and again with a noticeably delayed impact, favoured women in terms of new employment opportunities. The hesitant, but demonstrable, rise of new industries tended to generate a disproportionate increase in the number

68. Already in 1908 a trade union witness before the Poor Law Commission had declared that 'The women are ousting the men in most trades, including the iron trades. Many women are doing the light kind of drilling etc. which used to be done by men. We have hundreds of them in Manchester now doing work that was formerly done by men on drilling machines. Women in the iron works were unknown a few years ago, but there are hundreds of thousands of them now.' Quoted in Drake, *op. cit.*, p. 8. Drake notes a parallel decline in female labour in the traditional employments, including domestic service (p. 41). See also R. S. Sayers, *A History of Economic Change in England, 1880-1939* (1967), pp. 128, 159-60.
69. Pollard, *op. cit.*, p. 88. See also Alan S. Milward, *The Economic Effects of the World Wars on Britain* (1970), pp. 31-2.
70. A. J. P . Taylor, *English History, 1914-1945* (1970), p. 220.
71. See below.
72. See, for instance, the account in D. H. Aldcroft, *The Inter-War Economy* (1970), chap. 6.

of jobs which became available for women. Industries – especially in the spectacular new science-based areas (producing, for example, artificial fibres, plastics and electrical/automative products) – were specific in their labour requirements. As Pollard observes, 'In place of skilled or brawny male labour, most of the new industries required adaptable but essentially unskilled labour, much of it female.'[73]

In 1931 a little more than 34 per cent of women over fifteen years of age were employed.[74] This figure, which is close to the pre-war level, indicates that the decline in employment in domestic service and textiles had been fully offset by the expansion of the newer sectors. But the *net* effect for women was still not yet positive,[75] though the trends had been established. The Second World War, of course, reinforced these trends once again. Female conscription, employment in the civil service and ordnance factories and in private industry, further emphasized the trends in the deployment of female labour in the mid-twentieth-century British economy. In 1945 34 per cent of the labour force in engineering was female.[76] The continued decline in older industries – notably in textiles – operated to counterbalance many of the gains for the participation of women in the newer sectors of the economy. In 1911 women occupied 6 per cent of jobs in the higher professions, and 8 per cent in 1951. Nursing and library work have increased faster than teaching for women. But the greatest increase has been in clerical work which absorbed 179,000 women in 1911 and 1,414,000 in 1951. Concurrent declines in domestic service, textiles, engineering and printing have, in part, offset the rises of employment in, for instance, the retail trade.[77] But, in aggregate, the balance has been in favour of the extension of women's employment to an increasing degree in the post-war years.[78]

73. Pollard, *op. cit.*, p. 130.
74. Guy Routh, *Occupation and Pay in Great Britain, 1906-1960* (1965), p. 45.
75. Most women did not work: cf. the portrait of the working-class mother in Richard Hoggart's *Uses of Literacy* (1958), pp. 27-37, in which there is little reference to any employment in 'out-side work'.
76. The war has exploded the old idea that a married woman is a mere 'adult dependant' wrote the *Picture Post*, 6 March 1943.
77. Routh, *op. cit.*, pp. 4-5.
78. The upward trend was not ambiguous until the 1950s. The participation rates for women over 15 calculated by Routh are 1911: 35.3%; 1921: 33.7%; 1931: 34.2%; 1951: 34% and 1961: 39.7%; *op. cit.*, p. 45. Much of the growth is represented by the larger number of women over 30 in employment; *op. cit.*, p. 46. In 1966 there were 8,863,000 women in a total work force of 24,857,000. See *British Labour Statistics: Historical Abstract, 1886-1968*, Department of Employment and Productivity (HMSO, 1971), p. 198. See also Leser, *op. cit.*, p. 104. In September 1972 women constituted 9,143,000 of a total work force of 25,056,000. *Department of Employment Gazette*, June 1973, p. 595.

The trends in female employment in the mid-twentieth century have particularly benefited married women, though the general participation rate has also been rising. Richard Titmuss was able to record that 'In 1961 more than one half of all the women in paid employment in the United Kingdom were married. The proportion had been rising steadily for over a decade. It is now higher than the figure reached during the peak years of employment during the Second World War, the highest, indeed, in Britain's industrial history, and probably the highest in the Western World.'[79] It is more problematical, however, that this was the highest level of participation in the long period since 1700.

Of the general forces permitting the rise of employment for women in the twentieth century, three or four may be given special emphasis. The spread of birth control, and the revolt against continuous pregnancy, has had a profound effect. In addition the extended length of life of women has increased their years of potential work. Pollard states the point pithily: 'The typical Victorian family had five children living at home while the typical modern family had two only. As the span of life lengthened at the same time, the proportion of the lifetime spent with the children living at home was falling also, and the average family household size was falling even faster than the birth figures would indicate.'[80] Universal education helped to equalize training opportunities to a greater degree – as well as releasing mothers from much of their child-minding function. The return of older married women to the work force was especially significant and accounted for most of the numerical increase. Most important of all has been the ongoing, though uneven, change in the composition of economic activity in Britain – changes associated with the phase of development inadequately labelled 'the age of high mass consumption', which has radically altered the composition of labour demand in industry. Furthermore, detailed statistical analyses of current labour activity rates have demonstrated the importance of the growth of active female labour. John Bowers recently came to the conclusion that 'variations in female activity can justly be regarded as labour reserves in that they seem to originate from variations *on the side of demand rather than supply.*'[81]

Guy Routh has provided an admirable evaluation of the

79. Foreword to Pearl Jephcott, *Married Women Working* (1968).
80. Pollard, *Development, op. cit.*, p. 286.
81. John Bowers, *The Anatomy of Regional Activity Rates* (National Institute of Economic and Social Research, Regional Paper, no. 1, 1970), p. 52, emphasis added. See also Leser, *op. cit.*, p. 97. Cf. the discussion of 'the inertia of social custom' in John D. Durand, *The Labor Force in the United States, 1890-1960* (New York, 1968), pp. 122-36.

significance of the question for contemporary British economic welfare. He writes:

> Women are contributing more than men both to the expansion and enrichment of the work force. Full employment, wider occupational choice, improved educational opportunity, increased demand for professional skills, higher productivity and real incomes, shorter hours, earlier marriage, mechanisation of housekeeping, have interacted to bring about a social change since 1951 that may be of outstanding importance for the future: that is the return of married women to the work force.... But the unused potential is still very great.[82]

V

The purpose of this paper has been to consider the manner in which the process of industrialization in Britain may be related to the role of women, with especial regard to their levels of participation in the economy. It has attempted to establish a perspective on the long-run tendencies. Not surprisingly the conclusion has been that the relationship was complex and, in historical terms, not easy to pin down – partly for definitional reasons, and partly also because of evidential problems.

To say that 'The emancipation of women was in fact one of the most important and characteristic consequences of industrialization'[83] is only half the truth and therefore misleading. To chide Mary Wollstonecraft for complaining bitterly that there were so few occupations for a woman in 1792 when opportunities were 'widening'[84] is very likely a misinterpretation. As this paper has contended, the availability of employment for women in relative terms (that is, as indicated by participation rates) may have diminished seriously during the period normally specified as the Industrial Revolution. Looking at modern British economic history in perspective it seems most likely that pre-industrial levels of female participation were markedly higher than in the Victorian economy. The climb of women into the work force in the middle decades of the twentieth century represents a return to levels of activity reminiscent of the pre-industrial economy. It has been a monumentally 'lagged effect' of industrialization.

82. Routh, *op. cit.*, p. 49.
83. Perkin, *op. cit.*, p. 157.
84. Pike, *op. cit.*, p. 219.

The benefits that women derived from industrialization were yielded only in the extremely long run. The historical experience of British women may lend weight to the words of Ester Boserup in relation to contemporary development problems. She observes that economic development entails the disintegration of the traditional work patterns of the village. 'The obvious danger', she warns, 'is ... that in the course of this transition women will be deprived of their productive functions, and the whole process of growth will thereby be retarded.'[85] The putative decline of female participation rates in the Industrial Revolution and the plight of women in mid-Victorian England suggests a very substantial 'deprivation of productive functions'. Nevertheless, in the very long perspective, it is plain that the rise of the industrial economy has altered radically the relationship of employment to the various members of the family. For women the differentiation of work tasks is still a process in train.

The transformations in the functions of women in the economy since 1700 have resulted primarily from general trends in the framework of occupations, rather than, for instance, the impact of government policy or feminist agitation (though neither has been negligible). It is from the quasi-autonomous changes in the structure of the economy, rather than from politically initiated developments, that the past determinants of women's economic roles are to be sought. Nevertheless social *mores* have powerfully reinforced trends in the economy during long stretches of the story. Economists have recognized that the behaviour of the female labour market is complex, and warrants special modes of analysis.[86] The economic history of women is a neglected field and it will be obvious that much more research is indispensable before the hypotheses of this paper can be accepted or rejected. But there is a *prima facie* case for saying that women have performed a significantly variable role in the British economy during the transition from the pre-industrial world to modern times. These variations of participation are not only symptomatic of underlying changes in the economy; they also present a set of questions about the operation of the modern economy, and about the subtle and elusive relationship between social roles and economic change.

85. Boserup, *op. cit.*, p. 5.
86. See Cain, *op. cit.*, Introduction, and especially the discussion in Leser, *op. cit.*, pp. 105-6.

Veronica Beechey

Some Notes on Female Wage Labour in Capitalist Production

In *Capital and Class*, no. 3, London, 1977, pp. 45-66

The object of this brief paper is to raise some of the problems which are involved in analysing the position of female wage labour in the capitalist mode of production.[1] This is essentially an introductory and exploratory paper which is intended to contribute both to the Marxist Feminist discussion of the subordination of women in capitalist society,[2] and to the growing Marxist discussions on the labour process and the foundations of divisions within the working class.[3] My main concern is with the form of female wage labour which is known in popular discourse as 'women's work', i.e., low paid, unskilled and semi-skilled work which is concentrated in particular centres of modern industry and is usually performed by married women.[4]

1. This paper is restricted to an analysis at the level of political economy, which is broadened to include the family-production relationship. It is not directly concerned with the important questions of the role of the State in reproducing a particular form of family and role for women, and the ideology of domesticity.
2. I am utilising the term Marxist Feminist, which is now common parlance within the Women's Liberation Movement, since in my view a correct analysis of the subordination of women cannot be provided by Marxists unless Marxism is itself transformed. The term Marxist Feminist implies a commitment to, and attempt to move towards, such a transformation.
3. It is unfortunate that many Marxist discussions of the labour process and divisions within the working class (including recent contributions) fail to consider the sexual division of labour as significant. See e.g. the paper written by the Brighton Labour Process Group, 'The Capitalist Labour Process'; Christian Palloix, 'The Labour Process: From Fordism to Neo-Fordism'; and A. Sivanandan, *Race, Class and the State*. A notable exception to this is Harry Braverman, *Labor and Monopoly Capital*.
4. This paper is only concerned with the applicability of Marx's analysis to female wage labour. Further work is required to consider how far this framework can be utilised to analyse the position of women in service industries and occupations, and to develop a Marxist Feminist analysis of the position of women who are employed by the State (e.g., in the health service, education system, social services).

ENGELS: THE ORIGIN OF THE FAMILY, PRIVATE PROPERTY AND THE STATE

Most Marxist writings on the subordination of women comprise a debate with Engels who, in *The Origin of the Family, Private Property and the State*, laid the foundations for the analysis of the position of women in class society. For Engels the determining factors in history are twofold: the production of the means of subsistence, on the one hand, and the reproduction of human beings, on the other hand.[5] Engels argues that the social institutions under which people live are conditioned by both the stage of development of labour (which produces the means of subsistence) and the stage of development of the family (which reproduces human beings). Thus, the material conditions of production are related to the family form, and the development of the mode of production and the form of family are constituted as a problem of history. Engels analyses a number of stages in the development of the mode of production and the family form in pre-capitalist and capitalist societies. Although the major focus of his analysis is upon social formations which could be described as 'primitive communist', it is Engels' brief account of the transition to modern industry which is relevant to this paper.

Engels follows Marx in presuming that the development of modern industry makes possible the entry of women into social production. The position of the woman in social production is, however, in contradiction with her position in the family, since:

> when she fulfils her duties in the private service of her family, she remains excluded from public production and cannot earn anything; and when she wishes to take part in public industry and earn her living independently, she is not in a position to fulfil her family duties. [Engels, pp. 509-10]

The preconditions for the resolution of this contradiction between the position of the woman in production and her position in the family arise, according to Engels, with the development of modern industry, since this gives rise to a new form of family within the working class:

> the first premise for the emancipation of women is the reintroduction of the entire female sex into public industry ...

5. Engels succinctly outlines his theory in his 'Preface to the First Edition' of *The Origin of the Family, Private Property and the State*, written in 1884. See Engels, pp. 454-6.

> [which] demands that the quality possessed by the individual family of being the economic unit of society be abolished. [Engels, p. 510]

The embryo of this new form of family can be found, in Engels' characterisation, in the proletarian family as modern industry draws women into social production.

> since large-scale industry has transferred the woman from the house to the labour market and the factory, and makes her, often enough, the breadwinner of the family, the last remnants of male domination in the proletarian homes have lost all foundation – except, perhaps, for some of that brutality towards women which became firmly rooted with the establishment of monogamy. [Engels, p. 508]

Engels offers three reasons for the disappearance of male domination in the epoch of modern industry:[6] first, the proletarian family lacks private property which is the foundation of the monogamous family; second, the woman, herself a wage labourer, is no longer the property of her husband and has economic independence from him; third, the proletarian family lacks the means for securing male domination in bourgeois law. Thus, as Rosalind Delmar points out, Engels defines women's oppression in terms of the role ascribed to women in production, and their emancipation in terms of the absence of private property:

> Engels ... locates women's oppression at the level of participation in production, links the conflict between the sexes to the appearance of private ownership of wealth, and posits the reconciliation of the sexes as possible only when private property has been abolished. The fortunes of women and of oppressed classes are intimately connected: neither can be free until economic foundations based on private property have been abolished. [Delmar, p. 275]

Engels is correct in postulating the centrality of production and the family in determining the position of women and in constituting the form of family as an historical question. His analysis is, however, deficient in a number of respects, as contemporary Marxist

6. Cf. Rosalind Delmar, 'Looking Again at Engels' *Origin of the Family, Private Property and the State*', which develops these arguments.

Feminist critics have emphasised.[7] Among the criticisms which can be levelled against Engels' analysis are the following:[8]

(i) that he fails to recognise the role of the woman's domestic labour in reproducing labour power within the family;

(ii) that he does not regard the sexual division of labour as problematic, and therefore requiring explanation;

(iii) that he does not analyse the role of the State in reproducing the position of women within the family, and in circumscribing the forms of employment available to women;

(iv) that he fails to analyse the ideology of domesticity which is involved in reproducing a particular form of family and the relations of male domination and female subordination;

(v) that he uncritically presumes that the monogamous family would disappear among the working class as women were drawn into social production.

Furthermore, a number of changes which have occurred in the epoch of monopoly capitalism require modification of Engels' analysis to take account of:

a) the extension of forms of property to the working class family (e.g., home ownership, ownership of consumer durables, etc.) which, while different from the forms of property in the means of production which Engels discusses, nevertheless involve female dependence upon the male head of household;

b) the extension of the law as a mechanism regulating the working class family;

c) the involvement of the welfare state in the reproduction of labour power, and maintenance of a particular form of family and role for the woman within it.

These criticisms and modifications can be summarised by the argument that Engels fails to recognise what feminists have consistently argued, that the patriarchal family has remained

7. There is a considerable critical literature on Engels' 'Origins'. While some of it, e.g., Kathleen Gough, *The Origin of the Family*, is concerned with Engels' analysis of primitive communist societies, others discuss the relevance of Engels' analysis more generally. See, e.g., Kate Young and Olivia Harris, 'The Subordination of Women in Cross-cultural Perspective'; Karen Sacks, 'Engels Revisited; Women, the Organisation of Production and Private Property'; Irene Brennan, *Engels' Origin of the Family, Private Property and the State*; Chris Middleton, 'Sexual Inequality and Stratification Theory', and Rosalind Delmar, *op. cit.*, who provides an extremely useful critique which my discussion draws from.

8. Cf. Rosalind Delmar, *op. cit.*

within capitalist society, and that its persistence is not merely a 'hangover' from a pre-industrial stage of capitalism or from pre-capitalist society,[9] nor even of sexist attitudes and prejudices which can be purged through argument and education,[10] but is of fundamental economic, political, and ideological importance to the capitalist mode of production. In this paper I shall indirectly consider the implication of Engels' arguments from another perspective, that of the organisation of wage labour within capitalist society, and shall suggest that the inadequacies of Engels' account of the implications of the development of modern industry for the position of women stem not only from his failure to analyse the patriarchal family, but also from his failure to analyse the ways in which the changing capitalist labour process structures the organisation of wage labour, creating divisions within the working class.[11] My starting point in analysing the specificity of the position of female wage labour is Marx's analysis of the labour process in *Capital*. I shall argue that Marx's analysis of the general tendencies within capitalism must provide the foundation of the analysis of female wage labour, but that his specific, and extremely fragmentary, allusions to the position of women are unsatisfactory because he, like Engels, does not adequately analyse the relationship between the family and the organisation of capitalist production.

THE FAMILY AND THE CAPITALIST MODE OF PRODUCTION

The background against which the position of women in capitalist production must be understood is the separation of the family from

9. Juliet Mitchell, among others, appears to suggest this in the following quotation: 'Part of the function of the ideology of the family under capitalism is to preserve . . . [the] unity [of the family] in the face of its essential breakup', *Woman's Estate*, p. 157.
10. Clearly the ideological subjection of women, which is reproduced at the individual level through sexist attitudes and prejudices, is an important component of women's subordination. I am arguing, however, that the tendency to regard the family as primarily an agency of ideological reproduction is to provide a one-sided picture. An example of this tendency is Judith and Alan Hunt's statement that: 'The economic and material base for women's oppression *need* no longer exist in society; its continued re-creation is a measure of the strength of traditional ideas and prejudice', 'Marxism and the Family'.
11. Cf. the statement in 'Women, the Family and Industrialisation in Britain' that 'Engels obviously does not view the sexual differentiation of the labour process in factory production as itself forming a new barrier to female emancipation. But this is not surprising, since Engels does not see male domination functioning through the sexual division of labour, but through property relations and specifically women as transmitters of property', p. 4.

the means of production, which occurs in the course of capital accumulation. Historically this occurred through the 'putting out' system, in which capital engages the entire family in wage labour, usually under the domination of the male head of the household, and work takes place within the household. As capitalist production develops, however (through the stages of co-operation, manufacture and modern industry), the production of commodities for exchange takes place within the workshop or factory, while the woman as a domestic labourer in the family continues to produce use values for family consumption, whether or not she is also engaged in wage labour in the factory, workshop or home.[12]

Although with the development of the capitalist labour process (in particular the emergence of modern industry, when capitalist domination of the labour process becomes direct) the family *appears* to have become separated from the capitalist mode of production, it is in reality divorced only from the labour process (the site of production), and continues to play a vitally important role in the system of capitalist production as a whole.[13] This suggests that it is essential to penetrate beneath the apparent separation of the family from production, and to analyse the relationship between the family and the organisation of production as capital accumulation develops.[14] It is important, however, to transcend the mechanistic form of explanation provided by Engels, whereby the family form is presumed to change as a mechanical result of changes in the organisation of production, and to make the family-production relationship the object of analysis. In this

12. Sally Alexander points out, in 'Women's Work in Nineteenth-century London: Study of the Years 1820-1850', that much women's work tended to be concentrated in manufacturing workshops or took place in the home, and that the entry of women into modern industry was therefore limited in London in this period. This excellent essay emphasises the point which Marx makes in *Capital*, vol. 1, chapter XV, that modern industry gives rise to new forms of domestic industry, and that these are an important source of employment for women and children.

13. One implication of this paper is that in order to comprehend the subordination of particular groups (e.g. women, immigrant and migrant workers) within the capitalist mode of production, this must be analysed in its totality. This suggests that the attempt to abstract the analysis of the labour process from the organisation of production as a whole provides a limited analysis.

14. To postulate the centrality of the family-production relationship and that this changes historically, differentiates Marxist Feminism from structural functionalist sociology, from Radical Feminism, and from the ahistorical structuralist approach of some of the recent contributions to the theory of patriarchy. One problem with my analysis in this paper is that it does not provide a satisfactory analysis of this changing relationship. In particular, it suggests that the family must be presupposed if the specificity of the position of female wage labour is to be comprehended, instead of seeing that the family is itself constituted in a particular form and transformed in the process of producing and reproducing labour power.

paper I attempt to analyse one aspect of this relationship, and specifically to argue that the existence of the family must be presupposed if Marx's implicit arguments about the advantage of female wage labour are to constitute a satisfactory explanation.

FEMALE WAGE LABOUR AND THE CAPITALIST LABOUR PROCESS

Marx's analysis of the capitalist labour process must be located in his theory of capital accumulation and the contradictions to which the process of accumulation gives rise. According to Marx the object of capitalist production is the extraction of surplus value by capital through the employment of labour power in the capitalist labour process. In the surplus-value producing process, the wage labourer sells her/his labour power to the capitalist in exchange for a wage. The wage, however, does not represent payment for the entire time worked, but rather corresponds to what Marx calls the value of labour power. This is equivalent to the costs involved in the production and reproduction of labour power as a commodity which, in Marx's view, corresponds to the costs of reproducing the worker. A number of writers on domestic labour have pointed out[15] that Marx had little concern for the ways in which the reproduction of labour power was transformed by the advent of capitalism, or of how it takes place in the epoch of modern industry, merely stating that:

> The maintenance and reproduction of the working-class is, and must ever be, a necessary condition to the reproduction of capital. But the capitalist may safely leave its fulfilment to the labourer's instincts of self-preservation and of propagation. All the capitalist cares for, is to reduce the labourer's individual consumption as far as possible to what is strictly necessary. [Marx, *Capital*, 1, p. 572]

The analysis of domestic labour has shown how the woman, labouring in the home without remuneration, and outside the direct domination of capital, produces use values for the reproduction and maintenance of the male labourer and his family. The recognition of the role of domestic labour in the reproduction and

15. See, e.g., Jean Gardiner, 'Women's Domestic Labour', the paper written by the Political Economy of Women Group, 'Women's Domestic Labour', and the RCG paper, 'Women's Oppression under Capitalism'.

maintenance of labour power has required a modification of Marx's definition of the value of labour power, as the following argument suggests:

> The value of labour power is therefore defined as the value of commodities necessary for the reproduction and maintenance of the worker and his family. This implies that the value of labour power is not synonymous with the labour-time embodied in the reproduction and maintenance of labour power once one takes account of domestic labour (and the state). [CSE Pamphlet no. 2, pp. 10-11]

because domestic labour is itself involved in the reproduction of labour power as a commodity.

Marx discusses two main forms of extraction of surplus value. These are:

1. Absolute Surplus Value which takes the main form of the extension of the working day; and
2. ˈthe production of Relative Surplus Value, which consists in increasing the intensity of labour.

Essential to Marx's theory is the analysis of contradictions. Each of these methods of extracting Surplus Value gives rise to contradictory tendencies:

1. The attempt to increase Absolute Surplus Value founders on the physical conditions of the population (high sickness and mortality rates, high infant mortality and morbidity rates) and on State restrictions on the length of the working day which the working class has won in the process of class struggle.
2. The attempt to increase Relative Surplus Value founders on the tendency for the rate of profit to fall through the changing organic composition of capital.

Historically, the development of modern industry made possible an increase in both Absolute and Relative Surplus Value, although as limits were placed upon the hours which could be worked in any given day capital has concentrated in the metropolitan countries upon the production of Relative Surplus Value. In a situation of declining profitability a major offensive of capital thus involves attempting to keep down, or lower, the value of labour power, in order to counteract the tendency for the rate of profit to fall as a result of the changing organic composition of capital.

Modern industry, according to Marx, arises at a stage of capital accumulation at which machines are created which can make machinery. The instruments of labour, or workman's tools, are converted into machines, and there emerges a new form of division of labour in which the worker becomes an appendage of the machine:

> Along with the tool, the skill of the workman in handling it passes over to the machine. The capabilities of the tool are emancipated from the restraints that are inseparable from human labour-power. Thereby the technical foundation on which is based the division of labour in Manufacture, is swept away. Hence, in the place of the hierarchy of specialised workmen that characterises manufacture, there steps, in the automatic factory, a tendency to equalise and reduce to one and the same level every kind of work that has to be done by the minders of the machines; in the place of the artificially produced differentiations of the detail workmen, step the natural differences of age and sex. [Marx, *Capital*, 1. p. 420]

This tendency for capital to equalise the forms of labour through deskilling forms the basis of Braverman's analysis of the labour process in the epoch of monopoly capitalism in *Labor and Monopoly Capital*.

Marx suggests that there is a tendency in modern industry for unskilled labour to be substituted for skilled, female labour to be substituted for male labour, and mature labour to be replaced by young labour. He ascribes this tendency to the fact that machinery dispenses with the need for muscular strength, his argument relying upon the naturalistic assumption that the physical strength of women is less than that of men and that this determines the demand for sexually differentiated labour powers.

> In so far as machinery dispenses with muscular power, it becomes a means of employing labourers of slight muscular strength, and those whose bodily development is incomplete, but whose limbs are all the more supple. The labour of women and children was, therefore, the first thing sought for by capitalists who used machinery. That mighty substitute for labour and labourers was forthwith changed into a means for increasing the number of wage-labourers by enrolling, under the direct sway of capital, every member of the workman's family, without distinction of age or sex. [Marx, *Capital*, 1, p. 394]

The resort by Marx to a naturalistic form of explanation is, I suggest, clearly inadequate, especially in view of the historical fact that women have been involved in heavily physical work both in pre-capitalist society and in the early stages of capitalism (e.g. in mining). Marx's analysis can, however, be reconstituted on a more properly materialist basis, as I hope to demonstrate in the following section.

FEMALE WAGE LABOUR AND THE VALUE OF LABOUR POWER

How, then, would one explain the demand for female labour in modern industry? I want to suggest in the first place, the theoretical possibility that the employment of married women who are dependent upon the family for part of the costs of producing and reproducing their labour power can be advantageous to capital in three ways:

(i)   in reducing the value of labour power overall. The tendency of capital to reduce or force down the value of labour power arises as a countertendency to the tendency for the rate of profit to fall.

(ii) because female labour power has a lower value than male labour power.

(iii) because women can be paid wages at a price which is beneath the value of labour power.

While (ii) and (iii) do not refer to a general tendency, individual capitals will always seek to employ forms of labour power which have lower average values, and to pay wages which are below the value of labour power, in order to increase their share of surplus value. I shall now examine each of these possibilities in turn.

(i) Marx assumes that the value of labour power is a societal average value, which is culturally and historically determined. He suggests that the value of labour power is determined by the labour-time which is necessary to maintain the individual male labourer, and by that which is necessary to reproduce his family. Marx is not clear how this cultural and historical determination of the costs of reproducing the male labourer and his family is reached. This presumably is a question of the historically determined definitions of subsistence and minimum wage, and the historical assumption that the male wage constitutes a family wage – determinations which are, in the last analysis, an outgrowth of class struggle. Marx suggests that there is a tendency, in the epoch of modern industry, for the value of labour power to be lowered when all the members of the workman's family enter into employment:

> The value of labour-power was determined not only by the labour-time necessary to maintain the individual adult labourer, but also by that necessary to maintain his family. Machinery, by throwing every member of that family on to the labour-market, spreads the value of the man's labour-power over his whole family. It thus depreciates his labour-power. To purchase the labour-power of a family of four workers may, perhaps, cost more than it formerly did to purchase the labour-power of the head of the family, but, in return, four days' labour takes the place of one, and their price falls in proportion to the excess of the surplus-labour of four over the surplus-labour of one. In order that the family may live, four people must now, not only labour, but expend surplus-labour for the capitalist. Thus we see, that machinery, while augmenting the human material that forms the principal object of capital's exploiting power, at the same time raises the degree of exploitation. [Marx, *Capital*, 1, p. 395]

The value of labour power is lowered when all the members of the workman's family enter into employment, since the costs of the production and reproduction of labour power are spread over all the working population. Thus the portion of the working day in which the labourer works for himself is lowered, and more surplus value can be extracted. This is a general tendency which Marx generalises from the historical experience of the textiles industry in which men, women and children were extensively employed in the early stages of modern industry.

(ii) Marx also states at various points in *Capital* that while the value of labour power is theoretically assumed to be averaged for a given society, in practice labour powers may have different values. He cites as determinants of these concrete differences in the value of labour power a number of factors, including the expenses involved in training, natural diversity and the part played by the labour of women and children. Marxists have argued that the uneven development which characterises imperialism can be expressed through different average values of labour power, and also that different regions within one society may have labour powers of differing average values, as a result of regional development and underdevelopment.[16] Marx's general argument, as well as the specific analyses of Marxists who have studied imperialism and regional development and underdevelopment, makes it possible to raise the question of whether female labour power can have a lower value than male labour power. I am not clear whether it would be correct to argue that the sexual division of labour within a given society could give rise to labour powers with different average values, but this is a theoretical possibility. These different values could exist for two reasons. First, that women have less training, and therefore the costs of reproducing their labour power are lower; and second that, by virtue of the existence of the family, and their dependence on their husbands for part of the costs of production and reproduction of labour power, married women do not bear the total costs of reproducing their labour power themselves, and their labour power has a lower value than male labour power.

(iii) Although the value of labour power is assumed theoretically to be averaged for a given society, in practice individual capitals will attempt to purchase labour powers at prices which are below the average social value. Marx states that the

> forcible reduction of wages below this value plays . . . in practice too important a part, for us not to pause upon it for a moment. It, in fact, transforms, within certain limits, the labourer's necessary consumption-fund into a fund for the accumulation of capital. [Marx, *Capital*, 1, p. 599]

Marxists have usually discussed the practice of individual capitals of paying wages below the value of labour power with reference to semi-proletarianised workers on the agricultural periphery of capitalist production.[17] In this case, capital pays wages which are lower than the costs of production and reproduction, since part of the costs of reproduction are met within the subsistence economy. Thus, in the typical case of the male semi-proletarianised worker who becomes part of the industrial reserve army, capital can pay wages below the value of labour power when his wife is engaged in subsistence production through which she can contribute to the reproduction of herself, her children and her husband when he is unemployed. This occurs in many underdeveloped countries, the male semi-proletarianised worker being drawn either into wage

16. Cf. Ernest Mandel, *Late Capitalism*, chapter 3.
17. Cf. *ibid.*, chapter 5.

labour in the metropolitan society as a migrant worker, or into the capitalist sector of the dependent society. A similar argument has been advanced with respect to black workers on the South African Bantustans, the worker's family remaining on the Bantustan where the costs of reproduction of his wife and children are also met through the subsistence economy, in which the costs of his day-to-day reproduction can be met when he is unemployed.[18] In each of these cases it is important to note that the sexual division of labour, in which the woman remains in subsistence agricultural production while the male worker moves away to become part of the industrial reserve army, lies at the foundation of capital's ability to pay the man low wages[19] (or, rather, to the ability of the man and his family to survive physically on wages which are below the value of labour power).[20] One consequence of this form of organisation of labour is that the State does not have to pay unemployment benefits and poor relief (in societies in which these exist) to the male wage labourer since the costs of his day-to-day reproduction can then be met in the subsistence economy on the periphery.

I want to argue that married women workers are like semi-proletarianised workers so far as capital is concerned, since they too can be paid wages at a price which is below the value of labour power. In the case of married women, it is their dependence upon male wages within the family for part of the costs of production and reproduction of labour power which accounts for the possibility of individual capitals paying wages which are below the value

18. For specific arguments concerning black workers in the South African economy see Harold Wolpe, 'Capitalism and Cheap Labour Power: from Segregation to Apartheid'; and Martin Legassick, 'The Analysis of Racism: the Case of the Mining Economy'.

19. Carmen Deere points out in 'Rural Women's Subsistence Production in the Capitalist Periphery' that it is 'women's contribution toward the maintenance and reproduction of labor power within the rural labor reserve [which] permits the non-capitalist mode of production to absorb the costs of production and reproduction of labor power [and that it is] . . . the division of labor by sex, based on the articulation between modes of production [which] serves to lower the value of labor power for capital, enhancing the relative rate of surplus value for peripheral capital accumulation', p. 9. The fact that the sexual division of labour lies at the foundation of the position of the male semi-proletarianised worker within the capitalist economy is overlooked, so far as I can see, in most of the literature on semi-proletarianised and marginalised workers.

20. It could be argued that capital is not concerned with the conditions for the reproduction of labour power, and that whether or not the male semi-proletarianised worker or the married woman worker has means of subsistence other than the wage is of no interest to capital. While this is true at an abstract level, an historical analysis of the development of modern industry in Britain reveals that the individual capitals have been concerned about the conditions of reproduction of labour power, and that capital in general has, through the State, introduced legislation (through, e.g., the Factory Acts) to restrict women's work, and to constitute a particular form of family.

of labour power. The married woman does not, therefore, have to pay for the entire costs of reproducing her labour power, nor for that of her children who will become the next generation of wage labourers and domestic labourers. This argument, if correct, can explain why women's wages are significantly lower than men's.

The foregoing arguments suggest the theoretical possibility that the employment of women who are dependent upon the family for part of the costs of producing and reproducing labour power can be advantageous to capital in three ways:

(i)   in reducing the value of labour power overall;
(ii) because female labour power has a lower average value than male labour power;
(iii) because married woman can be paid wages at a price which is below the value of labour power.

If correct, these arguments suggest that it is *married* women's labour which is particularly advantageous to capital, since it is *married* women who do not, by virtue of the existence of the family, have to bear the total costs of production and reproduction out of their own wages.

What, then, becomes of the position of single women? Does the employment of single women require a distinctive form of analysis? Tentatively I would suggest that the position of single women wage labourers might be analysed along the following lines:

a.   In the case of young single working class women their family of origin bears some of the costs of day-to-day reproduction (provision of housing, cleaning and feeding, for example – Mum's domestic labour) and generational reproduction is not a problem. Here the economic position of young single women is similar to that of young single male workers (for whom Mum no doubt performs even more domestic labour).

b.   Since the wages of single women are paid on the assumption that they do not have to bear the costs of reproduction, those categories of women who do not have husbands whose wages can contribute to the costs of reproduction, and who do not have families of origin to meet at least part of the costs of reproduction, are depressed into poverty. If they also have children, and thus have to meet the costs of reproducing the next generation of labour power and domestic labourers from their wages, then single and widowed mothers are frequently depressed into severe poverty.[21]

DESKILLING AND THE INTRODUCTION OF FEMALE WAGE LABOUR

I have suggested (pp.254-5) that modern industry tends, in Marx's words, 'to equalise and reduce to one and the same level every kind of work that has to be done by the minders of the machines' (Marx, *Capital*, 1, p. 420), that is, it gives rise to the tendency of deskilling. Discussing this tendency, Marx suggests that while the hierarchy of concrete labours is no longer inherent in the labour process in the epoch of modern industry as it was in manufacture, because of the tendency of deskilling, the division of labour nevertheless hangs on through what he calls traditional habit, and becomes in modern industry a way of intensifying exploitation through fostering competition. There thus emerges a contradiction between the possibilities which are unleashed by the development of modern industry and the social character which is inherent in its capitalist form – a fact which Engels loses sight of in his optimistic assertion that the entry of women into modern industry is a precondition for their emancipation. This social character is formed and transformed in the process of class struggle.

Marx points, in his discussion, to a very important characteristic of modern industry – to the fact that, although there exists a tendency towards deskilling, in practice the extent to which this occurs may be limited. The limitations on the possibilities for capital to transform the labour process through deskilling which are imposed by working class resistance are crucial in determining the concrete development of the labour process – a fact which Braverman fails to appreciate in his analysis of the degradation of work in the epoch of monopoly capitalism in which the development of the labour process is portrayed as an outgrowth of capitalist strategies, rather than of class struggle. The analysis of the tendency towards deskilling on the one hand, and of the organised working class resistance to it on the other hand can also be important in determining the conditions of entry of female labourers into industry, as well as the position which they occupy within the labour process.

21. For evidence on this see the *Finer Report on One-parent Families*, vol. 1, para 4.86 and fig. 5.1.

I suggest, therefore, that Marx points to an important characteristic of modern industry, but that his analysis in terms of traditional habit is unsatisfactory. It is not habit, but the organised power of the working class which has struggled to resist deskilling, and this organised power has, historically, been overwhelmingly representative of male, white, skilled workers. While capital can in principle introduce any workers as agencies of deskilling, Marx suggests that in concrete situations it has introduced women and children in order to break down the resistance to changes in the organisation of the labour process which skilled workers have shown, e.g. in the manufacturing period:

By the excessive addition of women and children to the ranks of the workers, machinery at last breaks down the resistance which the male operatives in the manufacturing period continued to oppose to the despotism of capital. [Marx, *Capital*, 1, p. 402]

One implication of this is that while the introduction of women and children may be advantageous to capital, both because they can be paid lower wages and because their introduction may be used to foster competition, the employment of women is frequently opposed by male workers who are attempting to resist deskilling. One consequence of the coincidence of the struggle against the process of deskilling with the struggle against the introduction of female wage labour is that, so far as women are concerned, they have been denied the opportunity to enter into skilled jobs, and the hierarchy of concrete labours within the labour process has come increasingly to coincide with the sexual division of labour.

A good example of capital's using female labour in this way can be seen in employment practices in the munitions and engineering industries during the First World War.[22] This was a period in which

22. This example comes directly out of the work on women in the First World War which the Women and Labour Process Group has undertaken. The most useful introductory references on the position of women in the labour process in this period are: G. D. H. Cole, *Trade Unionism and Munitions*; Barbara Drake, *Women in the Engineering Trades*; Irene Andrews and Margaret Hobbs, *Economic Effects of the War upon Women and Children in Great Britain*.

Arthur Marwick's *Women at War*, while containing some beautiful photographs, fails to analyse the ways in which the subordination of women was structured within the labour process as they entered into employment and projects a simple-minded view of the war as a march towards progress in female emancipation. Unfortunately James Hinton's book on *The First Shop Stewards Movement* is insufficiently aware of the relationship between the process of dilution and the subordinate position of women, and of the ways in which trade union organisation, as well as capital's strategies in this period, reinforced the subordination of women.

large numbers of women, both single and married, entered into paid employment in the centres of modern industry, since female labour as part of the industrial reserve army of labour was pressed into service during the wartime labour shortage. Female labour was also used as a means of deskilling. The employment of women was strongly resisted by the engineers (organised in the ASE) who eventually reached a series of agreements with the employers and the Government that women should only be allowed to enter industry as unskilled and semi-skilled workers, and stated that where women had to be employed on skilled jobs because there were no available men, they should leave these at the end of the war, since these were men's jobs. The organised engineers' resistance to deskilling became displaced on to the women workers who were separately unionised (in the National Federation of Women Workers), *de facto* denied equal pay, and forced to leave employment in the engineering industry at the end of the war. The restructuring of the labour process which occurred in the war economy is an excellent example of the ways in which the introduction of female labour can be utilised by capital as an agency of deskilling, thereby fostering competition among the workforce, with the consequence that the hierarchical divisions within the labour process come to resemble the sexual division of labour.

It would be incorrect to generalise from the experience of women in munitions and engineering in the First World War, or to use this example as a prototype. Clearly the extent to which female labour has been utilised as an agency of deskilling and as a condition of competition can only be discerned through the concrete investigation of particular industries and trades. In such an investigation it would be important to consider:

(i)   to what extent there has been struggle around the substitution of female wage labour for male wage labourers, and how this struggle has been resolved;
(ii) to what extent the introduction of female labourers has functioned to depress wage levels.

A NOTE ON WOMEN, THE FAMILY AND THE
INDUSTRIAL RESERVE ARMY

The introduction of female wage labour into the capitalist labour process cannot be separated from the question of which categories of labour comprise the industrial reserve army.[23]

Marx argues that capital needs an industrial reserve army as a lever of capital accumulation. This is:

(i) a population which acts as a reserve of labour which can be brought into particular branches of production as the market expands or new branches of production are established, and dispensed with as changes in the organisation of the labour process require a different kind of labour force, or smaller labour force. Marx's discussion suggests that the industrial reserve army must be a flexible population which can easily be introduced into production, and disposed of again when the conditions of production change.

23. There is a growing literature on the question of the industrial reserve army. Other than *Capital*, vol. 1, chap. 25, the most useful works which utilise this concept are those by Harry Braverman (1974) and Ernest Mandel (1975). Braverman's analysis is subject to a number of criticisms, however, e.g. (i) that it does not consider the attempt to constitute and reconstitute the industrial reserve army in relation to the operation of the law of value; (ii) that it tends towards technological determinism, (iii) that although in chapter 13 Braverman discusses the ways in which capital seizes upon the family, bringing women under its direct domination, he does not link this to the analysis of the industrial reserve army, as I have tried to do in this paper. In *Late Capitalism*, chapter 5, Mandel argues that the attempt to reconstitute the industrial reserve army has been a major tendency of capital since the end of the nineteenth century, in its attempt to counteract the falling rate of profit. Unlike Braverman, however, Mandel has scant regard for the role of women workers within the industrial reserve army. This criticism could also be extended to the Brighton Labour Process Group's paper, 'The Capitalist Labour Process' (second part, unpublished), and to A. Sivanandan, 1976. Ruth Milkman, in 'Women's Work and the Economic Crisis: Some Lessons of the Great Depression'; and Jean Gardiner, 'Women and Unemployment', argue that the concept of the industrial reserve army is inapplicable to women's work, because the sexual segregation of occupations creates an inflexibility in the labour market which prevents the expulsion of women from employment in times of crisis (Jean Gardiner argues that the expulsion of women from manufacturing employment has been absorbed by the services sector). In arguing this, both Milkman and Gardiner point to an important aspect of women's work, that it is sexually segregated. Their analyses in my view involve a partial interpretation of Marx's conception however. It is not inherent in Marx's use of the concept of the industrial reserve army that labour should be expelled from production altogether. Marx utilises the concept of the industrial reserve army both as an abstract law of accumulation and as a description of particular sources of labour (in his discussion of the floating, latent and stagnant forms). The problem is to analyse the mediations between the abstract law and the concrete instances, and to specify what these forms are at particular levels of capital accumulation. Martin Legassick and Harold Wolpe, in 'The Bantustans and Capital Accumulation in South Africa' attempt to do this in their critique of Anibal Quijano Obregon, 'The Marginal Pole of the Economy and the Marginalised Labour Force', centring their analysis on the distinctions between the absolute and relative surplus populations, and the latent and floating forms. I am not aware of any satisfactory attempts to utilise the concept with regard to female wage labour, and to analyse the specific form which this takes as a relative surplus population. This is in my view an important task.

(ii) a population which acts as a competitive force, through a) depressing wage levels, or b) forcing workers to submit to increases in the rate of exploitation, thus increasing the level of surplus value extraction. In this way the industrial reserve army functions to increase surplus value, and as a countertendency to the tendency for the rate of profit to fall.

It is difficult to say how one could precisely define who is and who is not in any given situation a part of the industrial reserve army – this is an important question which requires further analysis. Clearly such an analysis would have to examine the role of the State in constituting and reconstituting the industrial reserve army (through immigration legislation, race relations legislation, and the provision of work permits, so far as immigrant and migrant workers are concerned[24] and through regulations governing women's work – e.g. on shiftwork – as well as Equal Pay, Sex Discrimination and Employment Protection legislation, so far as women workers are concerned).[25] It would also have to examine the practices of particular capitals in labour recruitment, and organised labour's resistance to the employment of particular categories of labour.

I want to suggest, somewhat tentatively, that a possible criterion of the preferred sources of the industrial reserve army, from the viewpoint of capitalism, is those categories of labour which are partially dependent upon the sources of income other than the wage to meet some of the costs of the reproduction of labour power. The advantages of such labour are:

a. they can be paid wages which are below the value of labour power, for reasons which I have already suggested;
b. they provide a flexible working population which can be brought into production and dispensed with as the conditions of production change.

Clearly, since the State has assumed responsibility for some of the costs of reproduction (through education, council housing, the health service, unemployment benefits and poor relief, family allowances, etc.) no section of the working class is entirely

24. A. Sivanandan, 1976, has begun to do this so far as immigrant and migrant workers are concerned.
25. I am not aware of any work which analyses the ways in which the recent State legislation, the Equal Pay Act, the Sex Discrimination Act, and the Employment Protection Act have functioned to constitute women as a particular form of industrial reserve army. This is an extremely important question.

dependent for the costs of reproduction upon the wage.[26] Neverthe-less it is possible to make two sets of distinctions which may prove fruitful in differentiating sections of the working class from one another:

1. between those sections of the working population which are predominantly dependent upon the wage to meet the costs of reproduction of labour power and those which are not;
2. between those sections of the working population which are dependent upon sources other than the State for some of the costs of reproduction (e.g. married women's dependence upon the family, semi-proletarianised workers' dependence upon the subsistence economy) and those which are primarily dependent upon the State (e.g. to provide unemployment benefits when unemployed, and poor relief when underemployed or low paid). The position of married women could then be defined, in terms of these distinctions, as follows:
   (i) married women comprise a section of the working class which is not predominantly dependent upon its own wage for the costs of production and reproduction of labour power;
   (ii) married women are a section of the working class which is not heavily dependent upon the welfare state, which refuses to recognise married women as individuals in their own right (e.g. denying them social security benefits if married or cohabiting).

I have in this section pointed to some similarities between the position of married women and semi-proletarianised workers from the point of view of capital. It is important, however, in suggesting such similarities, not to underestimate the differences between different categories of labour. One important difference is that married women have a world of their very own, the family, into which they can disappear when discarded from production, without being eligible for State benefits, and without appearing in unemployment statistics (unless they sign on). The existence of the family, and of the fact that the married woman also performs domestic labour within it, differentiates the position of the married woman within the metropolitan society from that of the semi-proletarianised worker who enters into the metropolitan society on a temporary basis.

26. Norman Ginsburg, in 'Poor Relief: the Development of State Policy in the Context of Class Struggle and the Struggle for Accumulation' begins to analyse the role of the State in constituting particular forms of the industrial reserve army through the provision of poor relief.

A further point of difference between the married woman and the semi-proletarianised worker becomes apparent if one analyses the role of the wage labourer and the family in the circulation process. Marx argues that capital attempts to penetrate all areas of the world with capitalist relations of exchange in order to create an expanding market for its commodities. Furthermore, since in order to be a consumer of commodities which are capitalistically produced the worker must be in receipt of a wage which s/he can exchange for commodities, capital attempts to create a large class of wage labourers. Marx points out that this is the site of a contradiction within capitalism, between the interests of an individual capital which attempts to force down the wages of its own workers in order to increase its share of surplus value, and the interests of all other capitals producing consumable commodities (what Marx calls Department II) which attempt to create a class of wage labourers in receipt of high wages which can become elements of the circulation process.[27] These contradictory tendencies operate both on a world scale and nationally. One reason why one might expect capital in general to tend towards employing married women in preference to semi-proletarianised workers is that when the married woman enters into wage labour the family is entirely dependent upon the wage – indeed, upon two wages in the case of the typical nuclear household. It is therefore dependent almost entirely upon the consumption of capitalistically produced commodities for its survival. The family of the semi-proletarianised worker, in contrast, is still located partly within the subsistence economy. It is therefore less dependent upon capitalistically produced commodities. Thus capital in general will tend to penetrate all areas of the world with capitalist relations of exchange. It will also tend to bring married women under the direct domination of capital, both within the metropolitan working class, and also within the subsistence economy.

The question of who constitutes the preferred sources of the industrial reserve army in any given historical situation must be concretely investigated. It cannot be derived from the logic of capitalism, but is determined by class struggle – by the strategies employed in individual capitals, by trade union practices, and by State policies which are themselves a product of class struggle. I have advanced various reasons why in theory married women might have become a preferred source of the industrial reserve army – reasons which could account for the empirical evidence on the growth of female employment which Braverman produces in

27. Cf. Marx, *The Grundrisse*, pp. 419-20.

analysing the structure of the working class in the United States in the epoch of monopoly capitalism. In Britain, which has not employed migrant workers (other than the Irish) on a large scale (unlike West Germany, for example), it is possible that married women have become a preferred source of the industrial reserve army in the period since the Second World War. Since Commonwealth immigrants and Irish and European migrant workers are also important groups which comprise the industrial reserve army in the same period, it is important to examine the historical demand for different kinds of labour in different branches of production.

A CONCLUDING NOTE ON CONTRADICTIONS

Coulson, Magas and Wainwright have argued that:

> the central feature of women's position under capitalism is not their role simply as domestic workers, but rather the fact that they are *both* domestic and wage labourers. It is this dual and contradictory role that imparts a specific dynamic to their situation. [Coulson, Magas and Wainwright, p. 60]

In conclusion I want to emphasise that it is essential to analyse the contradictory tendencies within capitalism to which women are subject, and to avoid falling into functionalist forms of explanation as some analyses of domestic labour and wage labour have done.[28] I have emphasised in this paper the tendencies within capitalism towards bringing married women under the direct domination of capital as wage labourers and as consumers.[29] These tendencies have been accompanied by some moves on the part of the State to

28. The RCG paper 'Women's Oppression under Capitalism' has a particularly functionalist approach to the position of women within the capitalist mode of production. It fails to analyse the contradictory tendencies which capitalism generates, towards both maintaining the woman's role as domestic labourer and bringing women under the direct domination of capital as wage labourers. It is thus unable to provide any strategy for transforming the position of women which is rooted in the contradictions which capitalism generates, other than the assertion that women must join with the working class in revolutionary transformation.

29. I am aware that I have probably overemphasised the ways in which capitalism generates tendencies towards bringing women as wage labourers under the direct domination of capital, and have underemphasised the continuing role of domestic labour which is maintained within the family within capitalism. This stems in part from an attempt to provide a counter to the emphasis among Marxist Feminists upon domestic labour, and in part from the fact that I have not adequately managed to build the analysis of contradiction into my own account. This therefore tends towards the functionalist form of explanation.

assume more of the functions of reproduction, which stem from the fact that:

> since individual capitalists are concerned with production only for their own profit, they are not individually concerned with the processes through which the system as a whole is made to continue; they are not concerned with reproduction. This is where the State must step in to represent the interests of the capitalist class as a whole. [Mackintosh, Himmelweit and Taylor, p. 3]

However, as the writers of this paper point out, the State, while providing certain services, has never come close to removing the burden of the woman's work in the home. This is particularly true in the field of childcare, as the recent RCG paper 'Women's Oppression under Capitalism' points out.

The tendency to draw married women into wage labour under the direct domination of capital has also given rise to the tendency for capital to produce more labour-saving devices for use in the home, and to produce some of the use values which were previously produced in the home within the system of capitalist commodity production (e.g. take out meals, launderettes). Mandel points out in *Late Capitalism* that it is frequently small capitals which move into these areas of production. These frequently utilise women as wage labourers to produce those use values capitalistically which they had previously produced in the home as domestic labourers (and, indeed, often continue to produce for their families in their role as domestic labourers). The movement of women into wage labour under the direct domination of capital therefore creates the possibility for some use values to be produced capitalistically, and to a lesser extent to the tendency for the State to assume some of the functions of reproduction.[30]

These tendencies coexist with another tendency, however, emphasised by all the writers on domestic labour, towards the maintenance of the family as a unit for the reproduction of labour power, and of the woman's role as domestic labourer within it. The

---

30. However, this tendency does not *necessarily* entail the breakdown of the family, since the increasing capitalistic production of domestic use values could equally reinforce the family by making it possible for women to continue to perform a domestic role when they have been drawn into wage labour. In the same way, the tendency towards maintaining the woman's domestic labour in the family does not necessarily entail her removal from wage labour. These tendencies must therefore not be seen as determining tendencies, each with its own necessary outcome, but as tendencies which structure the boundaries within which struggle takes place.

woman's domestic labour within the family functions to lower the value of male labour power by producing use values which are necessary for the production and reproduction of labour power as a commodity, both on a day-to-day and a generational basis, without remuneration. The interest of capital in keeping down the value of labour power by maintaining the woman's domestic labour within the home thus creates a tendency towards the maintenance of the nuclear family, which is reflected in and reproduced through a host of social welfare policies.

Since the Second World War these contradictory tendencies have been embodied in a number of ways of organising the labour process – the creation of flexible shifts, part-time work, etc. – which have enabled women to perform both forms of labour, domestic labour and wage labour. Whether she labours as domestic labour outside the direct domination of capital, or as wage labourer under the direct domination of capital, the woman is vitally involved in capital's attempts to extract a high rate of surplus value, and to generate countertendencies to the tendency for the rate of profit to fall. This situation is bound to give rise to new contradictions, however, which Marxist Feminists must begin to analyse.

One new form of contradiction which is arising from this situation is, I suggest, the phenomenon which is known in popular discourse as the dissolution of the family, which can perhaps be more adequately described as the transformation of the family[31] (reflected in soaring divorce rates, rapid decline in the manual working class birth rate, increased incidence of physical and mental illness among women, etc.). Could it be that, just as the attempts to increase Absolute Surplus Value in the nineteenth century by inordinately extending the working day foundered upon the physical condition of the working class, so the tendencies both to bring women under the direct domination of capital as wage labourers and also to maintain them in the family as domestic labourers in order to extract a high rate of surplus value is beginning to founder on the impossibility of maintaining the family in its present form, and of combining within the woman two vital forms of labour for the capitalist mode of production?

31. I am aware that this phenomenon is usually seized upon by conservatives and anti-feminists, and that statistics referring to changes in the family are frequently invoked as arguments against the employment of women. I am also uncertain of the correctness of the argument which I am proposing here – I am certain, however, that it is essential to move towards analysing new contradictions, in order to avoid providing a functionalist explanation which renders the position of women impervious to change, and which renders useless the attempt to develop a Socialist Feminist strategy within capitalism.

Right-wing critics and anti-feminists argue that the so-called decline of the family results from the woman working and the independence to which this gives rise, and claim, as did the opponents of women working in the mills in the nineteenth century, that a woman's place *is* and *should be* in the home. They thus attempt to resolve the contradiction between the two forms of women's labour by preserving domesticity for women. Engels, in contrast, presumed that when women entered into social production, the monogamous family would disappear, and with it the oppression of women. He thus argued for resolving the contradiction between the two forms of female labour by advocating the entry of women into social production, without adequately analysing the contradiction between the two forms of female labour, in production and the family. The Women's Liberation Movement, with its demands for nurseries and for free abortion and contraception to relieve women from unwanted pregnancies, has demanded that the State should assume more of the functions of the reproduction of labour power, thus calling upon the State to resolve the contradiction between the woman's domestic and wage labour. Since the resolution of the contradiction between the two forms of female labour is ultimately determined by the processes of feminist and class struggle within the limits of capital accumulation, it is important that Marxist Feminist theory demonstrate the ways in which the subordination of women in each of its aspects is rooted in the contradictions which capitalism generates in the process of accumulation, and develop a socialist feminist strategy which is based upon this analysis.

Bibliography

Alexander, Sally, 'Women's Work in Nineteenth-century London: a Study of the Years 1820-1850', in Juliet Mitchell and Ann Oakley, eds., *The Rights and Wrongs of Women* (Penguin, 1976).

Andrews, Irene Osgood and Hobbs, Margaret A., *Economic Effects of the War upon Women and Children in Great Britain* (OUP, 1921).

Braverman, Harry, *Labor and Monopoly Capital* (Monthly Review, 1974).

Brennan, Irene, *Engels' Origin of the Family, Private Property and the State; Discussion Series on the Women's Movement no. 1* (Polytechnic of Central London, Cultural and Community Studies Unit, n.d.).

Brighton Labour Process Group, 'The Capitalist Labour Process', *Capital and Class*, no. 1, 1977, and second part of this paper (unpublished, CSE 1976 Conference paper).

Cole, G. D. H., *Trade Unionism and Munitions* (Clarendon Press, 1923).

Coulson, Margaret, Magas, Branca and Wainwright, Hilary, 'The Housewife and her Labour under Capitalism: a Critique', *New Left Review*, 89, Jan.-Feb. 1975.

Deere, Carmen Diana, 'Rural Women's Subsistence Production in the Capitalist Periphery', *Review of Radical Political Economics*, vol. 8, no. 1, 1976.

Delmar, Rosalind, 'Looking Again at Engels' "Origins of the Family, Private Property and the State"', in Juliet Mitchell and Ann Oakley, eds., *The Rights and Wrongs of Women* (Penguin, 1976).

Drake, Barbara, *Women in the Engineering Trades* (Labour Research Dept. and Allen and Unwin, 1918).

Engels, Frederick, 'The Origin of the Family, Private Property and the State', in Marx and Engels, *Selected Works* (1 vol., Lawrence and Wishart, 1968).

Finer Report on One-parent Families, Cmnd 5629, HMSO, 1974.

Gardiner, Jean, 'Women's Domestic Labour', *New Left Review*, 89, Jan.-Feb. 1975.

Gardiner, Jean, 'Women and Unemployment', *Red Rag*, no. 10, Winter 1975-6.

Ginsburg, Norman, 'Poor Relief: the Development of State Policy in the Context of Class Struggle and the Struggle for Accumulation' (unpublished, CSE Conference paper, 1977).

Gough, Kathleen, *The Origin of the Family* (New Hogtown Press pamphlet, 1973).

Hinton, James, *The First Shop Stewards Movement* (Allen and Unwin, 1973).

Hunt, Judith and Alan, 'Marxism and the Family', *Marxism Today*, Feb. 1974.

Legassick, Martin, 'The Analysis of Racism: the Case of the Mining Economy' (unpublished, 1976).

Legassick, Martin and Wolpe, Harold, 'The Bantustans and Capital Accumulation in South Africa', *Review of African Political Economy*, no. 7, 1977.

Mackintosh, Maureen, Himmelweit, Sue and Taylor, Barbara, 'Women and Unemployment, a Discussion Paper for London Women's Liberation and Socialist Conference', March 1977.

Mandel, Ernest, *Late Capitalism* (New Left Books, 1975).

Marwick, Arthur, *Women at War, 1914-1918* (Croom Helm, 1977).

Marx, Karl, *Capital*, vol. 1 (International Publishers, 1970).

Marx, Karl, *The Grundrisse* (Penguin, 1973).

Middleton, Chris, 'Sexual Inequality and Stratification Theory', in Frank Parkin, ed., *The Social Analysis of Class Structure* (Tavistock, 1974).

Milkman, Ruth, 'Women's Work and the Economic Crisis: Some Lessons of the Great Depression', *Review of Radical Political Economics*, vol. 8, no. 1, Spring 1976.

Mitchell, Juliet, *Woman's Estate* (Penguin, 1971).

Obregon, Anibal Quijano, 'The Marginal Pole of the Economy and the Marginalised Labour Force', *Economy and Society*, 3, 1974.

Palloix, Christian, 'The Labour Process: From Fordism to Neo-Fordism', in *The Labour Process and Class Strategies* (CSE Pamphlet no. 1, Stage 1, 1976).

Political Economy of Women Group, 'Women's Domestic Labour', in *On the Political Economy of Women* (CSE Pamphlet no. 2, Stage 1, 1976).

Revolutionary Communist Group, 'Women's Oppression under Capitalism', in *Revolutionary Communist*, no. 5, November 1976.

Sacks, Karen, 'Engels Revisited: Women, the Organisation of Production and Private Property', in Michelle Rosaldo and Louise Lamphere, eds., *Woman, Culture and Society* (Stanford, 1974).

Sivanandan, A., *Race, Class and the State: the Black Experience in Britain* (Race and Class Pamphlet no. 1, 1976).

Wolpe, Harold, 'Capitalism and Cheap Labour Power: from Segregation to Apartheid', *Economy and Society*, 14 November 1972.

Women and Labour Process Group, 'Women, the Family and Industrialisation in Britain' (unpublished, n.d.).

Young, Kate and Harris, Olivia, 'The Subordination of Women in Cross-cultural Perspective', in *Papers on the Patriarchy Conference* (Women's Publishing Collective, Dec. 1976).

Irene Bruegel

Women as a Reserve Army of Labour: a Note on Recent British Experience

In *Feminist Review*, no. 3, London, 1979, pp. 12-23

The idea that women workers are particularly useful to capital as a reserve army of labour – to be brought in and thrown out of wage labour as the interests of capital dictate – has a wide currency amongst marxists and feminists (Bland *et al.*, 1978; Beechey, 1978; Counter Information Services, 1976; Adamson *et al.*, 1976). Such a theory clearly has important implications: it places the specificity of female labour within a general marxist model of capital accumulation and so provides some material basis for the differentiation of male and female wage labour, and it also shows up the similarities between the situation of women as wage labourers and that of other groups of workers such as immigrants.

The theory has, however, been challenged. While no one disputes that women have provided a reservoir of labour to be tapped in times of boom and labour shortage, some marxist-feminists have questioned the assumption that female labour is particularly 'disposable' in times of economic crisis. This note examines the argument in the light of the experiences of women workers in Britain in the years 1974-8. It concludes that, taken as a whole, women's employment opportunities have been protected from the worst effects of the crisis by the continued expansion of service work in the period. Nevertheless, individually, women have been more susceptible to redundancy when compared to men in similar circumstances. Thus the reserve army of labour model holds, but the simple version needs qualification.

MARX AND THE INDUSTRIAL RESERVE ARMY

Marx (1867) saw the expansion of a reserve army of labour as an inevitable outcome of the process of capital accumulation (*Capital*, vol. I). As capital accumulated, it threw certain workers out of employment into a reserve army; conversely, in order to accumulate, capital needed a reserve army of labour. Without such a reserve, capital accumulation would cause wages to rise, and the process of accumulation would itself be threatened as surplus value was squeezed. While Marx did note that certain workers – the pauperized lumpen-proletariat – might bear the brunt of unemployment, he was concerned to show how the expansion of capitalism inevitably drew more and more people into a labour reserve of potential, marginal and transitory employment, rather than to identify any group of workers as particularly vulnerable. Marx did not consider women as a group in his reserve army of labour model. Nevertheless, the extension of women's involvement in wage labour in all Western economies clearly fits the picture of the continued expansion of the reserve army drawn by Marx.

Braverman (1974) and Kolko (1978) both argue this in relation to the United States. In Britain the net expansion of 2.5 million workers achieved between 1951 and 1971 was made up almost entirely (2.2 million) of women coming into wage labour. This expansion meant, as Marx argued it would, that wages, particularly those in industries where women predominate, have been kept down. The process becomes self-fuelling. Increasingly, the maintenance of family living standards has come to depend on two or more wage packets,[1] and all adult female labour has become potential wage labour – as many as a quarter of mothers of pre-school children are now employed (Office of Population Census and Surveys, 1978).

In the sense of providing a labour *reserve*, women's labour power has clearly become an important part of what Marx saw as the industrial reserve army.

THE HYPOTHESIS OF GREATER 'DISPOSABILITY'

This isn't really at issue. What is in dispute is whether or not women bear, to a disproportionate extent, the burden of unemployment in time of crisis, whether they are *more* 'disposable'. This is what the notion of women as a reserve army of labour has come to mean, notwithstanding Marx's use of the term.

1. This point comes out very clearly in the Royal Commission on the Distribution of Income and Wealth (Research Report 6, 1978). When wives do not go out to work, the chances of a family in Britain today being in poverty are almost one in three; where wives work, the chances are nearer one in fourteen.

There are a number of grounds on which one would indeed expect that women's labour power would be more readily dispensed with in times of redundancy (Barron and Norris, 1976). MacKay et al. (1971) concluded in their study of the engineering industry that 'there was a greater propensity to dismiss females in preference to males in a redundancy situation'.[2] They point to the fact that redundancy procedures often stipulated that, after people over the age of retirement, part-time and married women workers should be picked out for the sack. The seniority principle of last in, first out would also tend to discriminate against women, even if there was no explicit discrimination (Jenness et al., 1975).[3] Daniel and Stilgoe (1978) found that half of the firms in their recent survey of 300 companies operated the seniority principle in making redundancies. A Department of Employment Survey of redundancies in 1975-6 (Department of Employment, 1978) does confirm the vulnerability of shorter service workers, despite the bias in the Redundancy Payments Act which tends to increase the vulnerability of older (and hence more long-serving) workers. Significantly, the survey doesn't distinguish between male and female workers.

The fact that women tend to work in smaller, less unionized workplaces may also make them more vulnerable to redundancy. However, the poor record of many unions in fighting redundancies, particularly amongst part-time women workers (Counter Information Services, 1976), suggests that lower levels of unionization may not be a particularly important handicap as such.

MacKay et al. (1971) also saw the higher rates of redundancy amongst women as a reflection of their lower levels of skill;

2. MacKay et al., p. 375, give the following figures for redundancies in Birmingham and Glasgow over the 1959-66 period:

	Average quarterly redundancy rate	
	Birmingham	Glasgow
skilled men	.1	.6
all men	.2	.5
all women	.9	.6

3. The degree to which 'last in, first out' (LIFO) loads redundancy on to women depends on how the procedure is applied. If it was adopted company or plant wide, then women would indeed be particularly vulnerable. It seems in practice that unless the whole plant is closed, redundancies tend to be brought in shop by shop. Given the high level of job segregation within a workplace, this means that the LIFO procedure would tend to be applied separately to groups of men and women and would not necessarily lead to a higher rate of redundancy amongst women. As Jenness et al. (1975) point out, where women have broken through into male dominated jobs, as in the United States steelworks, the LIFO procedure will work against them.

employers are likely to keep on skilled men or put them on short time when work is slack because their skills are not easily replaced and, on dismissal, they may move elsewhere.[4] Women, on the other hand, can be more easily replaced or re-engaged when trade picks up, so there is much less of a deterrent to giving them the sack. The dependency of working wives, which forces them to live where their husbands work, contributes to this pattern. Twilight shifts in particular are closed down and started up again on the basis of a captive, relatively immobile workforce of married women. In the United States, where there is in any case more job mobility, the lesser mobility of married women is seen to contribute to higher levels of unemployment amongst women (Ferber and Lowry, 1976; Niemi, 1976).

The current pattern of limiting redundancies by freezing appointments (Daniel and Stilgoe, 1978) may also increase the relative vulnerability of women workers. This is because family responsibilities often force women to leave work; for a period as a result, at any given point in time, women workers are more likely to be looking for work than men.[5]

Moreover, ideology in the form of the notion that a woman's place is in the home may well contribute to a greater vulnerability of women to unemployment. The onslaught on married women working – blaming them, in effect, for the level of unemployment amongst men – is perhaps not as strong as it was in the 1930s,[6] nevertheless, it is still evident,[7] with youth unemployment in particular being 'explained' by the tendency of married women to work. Unemployment amongst women is never considered the personal and social problem which male unemployment

4. British statistics on short-time working do not distinguish between men and women. Däubler-Gmelin's research in Germany shows that men are far more likely to be put on short time than women but far less likely to be made redundant.

5. This is reflected in turnover figures. These show that over industry as a whole, for every one hundred women in work, nearly forty are taken on in a year, compared to thirty men; at the same time, nearly forty leave, compared to thirty men (*Department of Employment Gazette*, November 1978).

6. Rowbotham, 1973, Milkman, 1976, Humphries, 1976 all present evidence of hostility to married women workers in Britain and the United States in the 1930s. In both countries various bars were put on married women working; nevertheless, the long-term expansion in women's wage labour was not halted.

7. Occasional calls are made even today to sack married women. In 1977 the *Daily Mail* ran a campaign, 'Weed out the Working Wives', but no major party has explicitly questioned the right of married women to work.

is.[8] As a result, women's confidence in their right to work is weaker than men's, and may well contribute to a higher 'voluntary' redundancy rate as well as fuelling discriminatory practices by managements and unions.

These arguments, taken together, suggest that, other things being equal, one could expect women to be more vulnerable to unemployment than men. However, Gardiner (1976) and Milkman (1976) suggest different ways in which everything is not equal, in which female labour is quite distinct from male labour. Gardiner argues that the cheapness of female labour would lead capital to substitute women for men, rather than sack women in preference to men. This is indeed Marx's argument, and such a fear certainly underlay attempts by organized workers to exclude women from large areas of employment. Such a fear indeed led the Trades Union Congress into endorsing the provisions which forced unemployed women into domestic service before the war (Lewenhak, 1977). In this way women could be prevented from competing for men's jobs. However, it is not at all clear that such substitution (of women for men) would be especially common in periods of slump; the returns on, and the possibilities of, substituting women for men are greater when the economy is expanding.[9]

Gardiner's argument also conflicts with the point Milkman makes; namely that the sexual division of wage labour is so rigid as to preclude both the substitution of male by female labour (as in Gardiner's account) and the effective substitution of female by male labour (as in the 'women as a dispensable labour force' account). What Milkman is arguing is that the segregation of women into women's work is of such ideological importance that it cannot be breached, even where it would yield capital cheaper

8. None of the major studies of the impact of unemployment in Britain consider unemployed women. Government figures for unemployment amongst women are seriously inadequate and, even more disturbing, the various job creation schemes show a distinct bias towards male workers; in 1976 84 per cent of the young people on the Job Creation Scheme were boys, despite the fact that unemployment levels for girls are equally bad. One of the ill-fated Manpower Services Commission's posters did feature a girl, but the problem of youth unemployment is seen as a problem of boys out on the streets, of potential disruption to the social order; hence the emphasis in the Youth Opportunities Programme on training and integrating boys into work roles.

9. The process of substitution is rarely one where a woman takes on a job that was previously held by a man. More often substitution takes place in the context of capital restructuring, of bringing in new machinery which transforms a skilled job into a semi-skilled or unskilled one, or of moving jobs around the country. In either case the substitution of female for male labour, while bringing in long-term savings in wage costs, requires capital investment. Such investments are unlikely to be made where output is stagnant and wage rises are restricted.

labour.[10] Hence for Milkman the pattern of women's employment and unemployment over the cycle of booms and slumps simply reflects the fortunes of 'women's' industries and occupations. While the degree of segregation is great (Hakim, 1978), Milkman's argument cannot be sustained. As is shown below, the effect of a slump in any given industry is different for women than for men. Secondly, the pattern of segregation of women's work and men's work is not naturally determined, nor easily explained by 'ideology'. It reflects, in part, economic factors, and follows, in some degree, the dual labour market division (Barron and Norris, 1976). This means that women tend to be recruited to less stable areas of employment (Baudouin *et al.*, 1978); a job is 'women's work' partly *because* it doesn't offer stable and continuous employment.[11] Catering work in schools and colleges is a prime example of the use of female labour for 'unstable and seasonal work'.

UNEMPLOYMENT AMONGST WOMEN

If one looks at figures for women's unemployment over recent years, both in Britain and elsewhere, there seems to be little basis for either Gardiner's or Milkman's objections to the reserve army model. Between 1974 and 1978 in Britain the official rate of unemployment amongst women increased more than three times as fast as that of men. In Holland, Italy, Spain and Belgium (OECD, 1976; Wernecke, 1978) the rate of increase in unemployment was also greater amongst women than men. In other countries the level of unemployment amongst women is higher, although the rate of increase is on a par.[12] However, there are always severe problems in using the official statistics of unemployment as a measure of the effects of crisis on women's employment. In Britain, only women registered at the labour exchange are counted

10. Milkman maintains that it is 'ideologically' important to retain the image of women as dependent and passive, despite the drive to exploit their labour power. Milkman sees this contradiction only being resolved by segregating women into 'women's work'.

11. This is not to say that all areas of unstable employment are filled by women. Immigrant men fulfil a similar role in the economy; the construction industry, with very large fluctuations in demand for labour, is almost wholly dependent on male immigrant labour (Baudouin, 1978). Nor are all areas of women's work highly unstable, but in general women's work is characterized by a greater degree of instability in employment.

12. The OECD gives the following figures of relative unemployment rates (1975):

	Australia	France	Germany	Italy	Belgium	USA
male	3.2	3.5	4.5	2.9	4.4	8.0
female	5.0	7.9	5.2	4.9	9.9	9.2

as unemployed.[13] Given this narrow definition, something like half the women who say they are looking for work are not counted as unemployed (General Household Survey, 1976; Dex, 1978). This complicates the assessments of changes over time (quite apart from hiding the real extent of unemployment amongst women), because it is likely that the proportion of unemployed women who do register does vary over time (General Household Survey, 1974, 1976). Given a shift in unemployment towards younger people and hence towards single women, the proportion of women registering has probably risen (Moore, Rhodes et al., 1978). To some extent, then, the fast rise in official unemployment amongst women overestimates the real rise.

Nevertheless, from what evidence there is, it would seem that 'real' unemployment amongst women has risen faster than amongst men, the rise being particularly fast among single women.[14] Moore, Rhodes et al.'s estimates of the real unemployment level suggest that women have been disproportionately affected; while women are only 41 per cent of the labour force, they accounted for 53 per cent of the net rise in real unemployment. Thus the unemployment figures, even allowing for changes in registration, do not substantiate Gardiner's argument. Neither, however, can they be said to prove the disposability model, because it is single women who appear to have been particularly badly affected, while the hypotheses outlined above tend to emphasize the particular vulnerability of married women workers (Beechey, 1978), rather than women workers as a whole. However, even figures derived from surveys pose problems for measuring unemployment amongst 'housewives', and the survey figures could well underestimate the impact of a crisis on married women's employment. This is because unemployed housewives who would otherwise work may not consider themselves to be looking for work in a climate of restricted employment, childcare facilities,

13. This is justified on the grounds that: 'Many married women who state they are seeking work may be expressing a future intention rather than a current activity. In practice they are more inclined to attach conditions to the work they are prepared to take – working hours, ease of travel, availability of nursery schools and so on – and they can only be described as unemployed in a restricted sense.' (Cmnd 5157 Unemployment Statistics: Report of the Interdepartmental Working Party, 1972.)

14. Calculating from the General Household Survey data, 1974 and 1976:

	1974-6
change in total male unemployment (registered and unregistered)	+10%
change in total female unemployment (registered and unregistered)	+28%
change in single female unemployment (registered and unregistered)	+42%

transport provisions and so on, and so wouldn't therefore be counted as unemployed by a survey such as that undertaken by the General Household Survey. Because of the difficulties with any of the measures of unemployment, in this note employment figures rather than unemployment figures will be used to analyse the impact of the crisis on women's employment opportunities.

TRENDS OF WOMEN'S EMPLOYMENT

In attempting to evaluate a 'disposability' model, it is important to clarify exactly what the model proposes. On the one hand, the idea that women might cushion men from the full impact of recession could be taken to imply that women's employment opportunities, taken as a whole, deteriorate relative to men's in times of recession. On the other hand, it can be taken to mean that any individual woman is more susceptible to redundancy and unemployment than a man in an equivalent situation would be. This distinction is important.

At first glance the first form of the model appears to have little validity. In the years 1974-8 female employment *rose* by 145,000 jobs, while the number of men at work fell by 361,000, a pattern repeated in a number of countries. However, this pattern is simply a reflection of the long-term trend towards an increasingly female labour force. In 1951 only 32 per cent of the labour force were women; by 1977 over 40 per cent were. Had there been no recession and past trends had continued, then the rise in women's employment between 1974 and 1978 would have been greater than the 145,000 jobs created. This point is illustrated in figure 1, which shows how in each recession since the war the rate of growth of female employment slowed down relative to periods of expansion. If one takes into account the increasing need and desire for women to seek paid work, then it is far from clear that the rise in female employment over the last few years really signals a lesser deterioration in women's employment prospects relative to men's. The number of women seeking work between 1974 and 1977 increased faster, at 4 per cent, than the number of jobs created (1.5 per cent). Moore, Rhodes *et al.* (1978) calculated the shortfall in male jobs relative to male workers between 1973 and 1977 to be

615,000; for the smaller female labour force the shortfall is some 680,000.

Turning to the second form of the 'disposability' model, figure 2 makes it clear that in every industry[15] employing a substantial number of women and where employment declined between 1974 and 1977, the rate of employment decline was greater for women than for men. Of the major industries, only construction, public and miscellaneous services and the public administration sector, where reclassification has distorted the picture,[16] do not conform to this trend. In manufacturing as a whole, women lost nearly 9 per cent of their jobs, in a period when male manufacturing jobs fell by less than 5 per cent. The losses were particularly great in the new growth sectors such as electronics. Similar trends are found throughout Western manufacturing (OECD, 1976; Baudouin *et al.*, 1978). What kept women's employment buoyant as a whole was the continued expansion of parts of the service sector (figure 3); for example, professional and scientific and miscellaneous services. The growth of these matched the falls in employment elsewhere, despite public sector cuts.[17] To a degree, then, Ruth Milkman is right; the particular pattern of women's employment, the concentration in a limited range of the expanding service sector, has limited the impact of the recession on women's opportunities as a whole. If women had not been concentrated in 'women's work' – catering, nursing, teaching, cleaning – but had been distributed amongst industries in the same way as men, then the impact of the 1974-7 crisis would have been far greater – a decline of jobs of almost half a million, compared to an actual increase in the period

15. The data used are the Department of Employment annual census (June) of employment by industry, analysed at the 27-industry Standard Industrial Classification level. Unfortunately, data on occupational groups are not available on an annual basis. Such information would have been helpful for the analysis because the jobs (occupations) women do within an industry tend to be very different from those of men. In theory, the higher rate of job loss for women within each industry could be due to the particular vulnerability of the *jobs* that women do, rather than the vulnerability of women in any particular area of work. This point has been checked as far as possible with the published statistics for the electrical engineering industry. When the broadly defined industry is disaggregated into its nine constituent industries, the pattern of higher job loss for women in each of the declining industries remains; similarly, when each occupation within electrical engineering is analysed from the annual returns, there is still a tendency for women to suffer a higher rate of job loss in each of the declining occupations.

16. Some sixty to seventy thousand workers in public administration were reclassified into other services in the period under review.

17. Despite the public sector cuts, net employment in the public services has continued to grow, albeit at a much slower rate than previously. In the year 1977-8 the growth in female employment has been so slow that it has barely matched the declines elsewhere. See Hughes (1978) for a further discussion.

FIGURE 1. Annual changes in female employment, 1950-78 (June-June), Great Britain

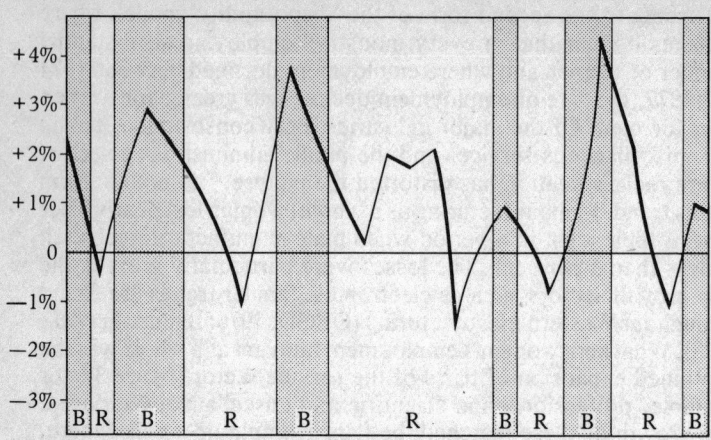

R — Recession years when unemployment as a whole was rising
B — Boom years when unemployment as a whole was stagnant or falling

FIGURE 2. Changes in employment by industry, 1974-7 (percentage change for each group), Great Britain

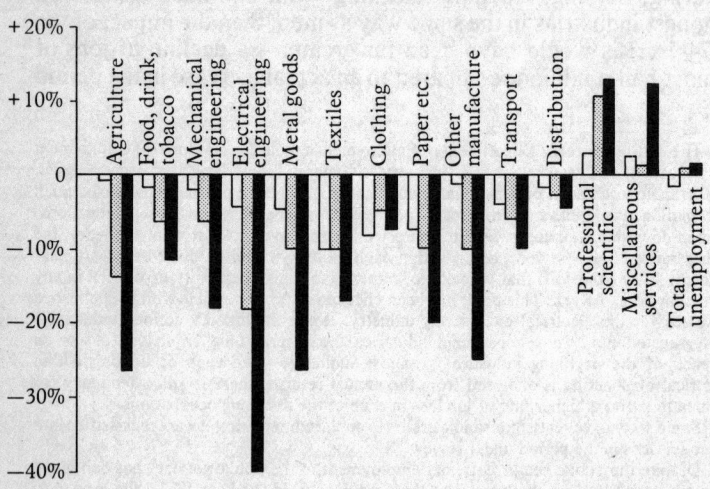

FIGURE 3. Components of change in women's employment, 1974-7, Great Britain. Change by industry

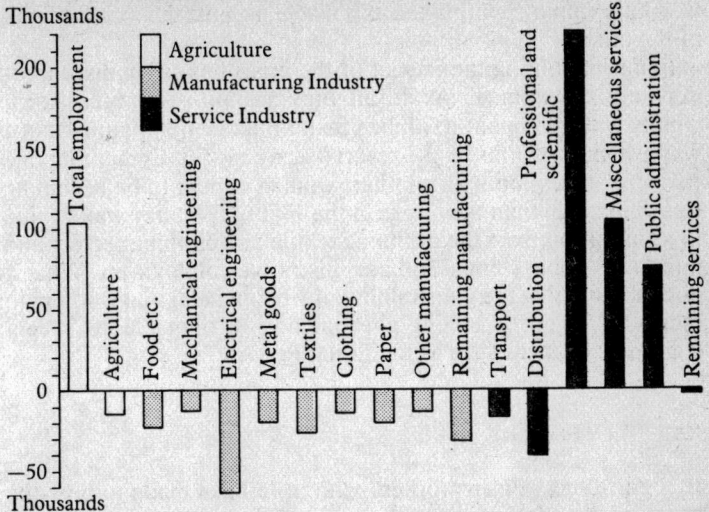

FIGURE 4. Annual change in manufacturing employment, male and female, 1950-78, Great Britain

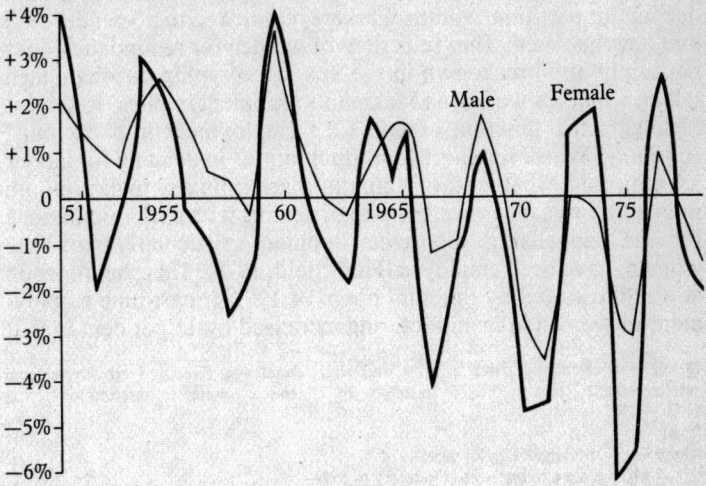

Source for figures: Department of Employment

of 140,000.[18] Thus, as in the United States (OECD, 1976), the 'favourable' industrial distribution of women has cushioned women's employment, *taken as a whole*, against the worst effects of the crisis.

In manufacturing the impact of the crisis has fallen disproportionately on women. As in all previous post-war recessions, women's employment has fallen faster than men's (figure 4), in a way which conforms to the reserve army model. Comparing one period of recession with another, women appear to be becoming less vulnerable than they were in the 1950s. This may well be due to a shift away from the declining textile and clothing sectors and into more stable clerical and administrative employment. What it does show is that the vulnerability of women industrial workers to recession is not a recent phenomenon attributable to recent legislative changes such as the Equal Pay Act.

PART-TIME WORK

It is part-time women workers who have been made to bear the brunt of the decline in employment. The pattern in electrical engineering shows this up particularly well. Between 1974 and 1977 38,000 unskilled and semi-skilled jobs were lost; 18,000 of these were part-time jobs done by women. This represents a 40 per cent decline for part-time women workers, compared to a 5 per cent job loss amongst men. The 'selection' of women for redundancy does not imply any breakdown in the sex stereotyping of jobs – men taking women's work – as Milkman's argument implies. Rather, it highlights the function of part-time employment in a capitalist economy. Wherever short-term fluctuations in demand for labour are expected, whether the fluctuations are from day to day, month to month, or year to year, the cost of dealing with such fluctuations for the capitalist is less when women, particularly part-time women, have been employed (Hurstfield, 1978). This phenomenon is well illustrated by the mini boom of 1973-4; part-time employment of women in manufacturing increased by 15 per cent in that

18. This is calculated using a 'shift and share' analysis. Expected growth in total employment on the basis of the male distribution is
$$\sum_i \frac{M_i . F}{M} . R_{fi}$$
where M = total male employment 1974
M_i = male employment in industry in 1974
F = total female employment 1974
R_{fi} = rate of change of female employment in industry in 1974-7

year, to fall subsequently by 10 per cent in 1974-5 and 8 per cent in 1975-6. In every industry where employment declined between 1974 and 1977, the rate of decline for part-time women exceeded that of men and full-time women (figure 2). It is part-time women workers, who form an increasing proportion of women workers (40 per cent are now part-time), who conform most closely to the model of women as a disposable reserve army. Nevertheless, in certain areas of work, their numbers are still increasing rapidly.

CONCLUSION

Over the last few years there have been two conflicting processes at work affecting women's employment. On the one hand, within any given industry or job, women, particularly part-time women workers, have suffered from greater rates of job loss than men. This has come about partly, no doubt, through explicit or barely veiled discriminatory policies, but more important, probably, has been the exploitation of the weaknesses of married women's labour market position, weaknesses which derive in one way or another from a primary definition of women as housewives and mothers. On the other hand, the continued expansion of parts of the service sector on the basis of the availability of cheap female labour has mitigated the effects of the crisis on women's employment opportunities. It is important to recognize that the 'protection' that women's jobs have had through the expansion of the service sector is a protection based on the cheapness of female labour. The low pay offered to women in the expanding service sectors virtually precludes any wholesale takeover by men, even when unemployment is high. Given certain technological constraints which have until now made the service sectors highly labour intensive (Braverman, 1974; Harris and Taylor, 1978), the service sector did require a 'reserve army' of cheap labour to draw on to expand its output. As a result, in virtually all capitalist countries the expansion of service industry went hand in hand with the expansion of women's paid employment in the post-war years. Since services were less vulnerable to recession than other sectors of employment, they have afforded women a certain protection from unemployment in times of recession. However, with the development of microprocessors this 'protection' is likely to wear thin, since the advantages women offer to capital – cheap and relatively docile labour – become less and less relevant (Counter Information Services, 1979; Downing and Barker, 1979). Moreover, the type of work women do – low level, repetitive and boring

– is probably more susceptible to rationalization, whether it is manufacturing or service work, than ever before. In Germany, where rationalization of office work has gone further than in Britain (Cooley, 1979), service work no longer protects women's employment as a whole from the impact of crisis (Däubler-Gmelin, 1977); the degree of protection in the United States is also significantly less than in Britain (OECD, 1976). Thus the analysis in this note must be seen in its historical perspective.

While it is probably true for all periods that the marginal position of married women in the labour force has made them, individual for individual, more vulnerable to redundancy than male workers, the particular form of capitalist expansion and restructuring over the last thirty years – the expansion of labour intensive public and private services and administrative occupations – greatly extended the employment opportunities of women. The result was that women's employment continued to expand even when men's jobs were being cut back fast.

The long-term shift towards women in the workforce cushioned women's employment against the shorter-term (cyclical) recessions. The signs are that this particular phase of capital restructuring may be over; that one of the bases of the long-term expansion of female employment – the cheapness of female employment – may be declining in relative significance, given new technological developments. Hence many groups of women who have traditionally regarded their jobs as secure will find themselves threatened with rationalization on a scale comparable to the wholesale elimination of jobs in the traditional male strongholds – mining, railways, docks. The implications of this analysis are not that the solution lies in attempting to equalize the incidence of increasing unemployment between men and women. Rather, it is that the fight for jobs will increasingly be a fight for women's jobs. Thus if the labour movement is to be able effectively to resist unemployment, now more than ever before it urgently needs to devise more effective strategies of defending women's jobs and the right of women to work.

References

Adamson, O., Brown, C., Harrison, J. and Price, J. (1976), 'Women's Oppression under Capitalism', *Revolutionary Communist*, no. 5.
Barron, R. D. and Norris, G. M. (1976), 'Sexual Divisions and the Dual Labour Market', in Barker, D. and Allen, S. (eds.), *Dependence and Exploitation in Work and Marriage*, London: Longman.

Baudouin, T., Collin, M. and Guillerm, D. (1978), 'Women and Immigrants: Marginal Workers', in Crouch, C. and Pizzorno, A. (eds.), *The Resurgence of Class Conflict*, vol. 2, London: Macmillan.

Beechey, V. (1978), 'Women and Production', in Kuhn, A. and Wolpe, A. M. (eds.), *Feminism and Materialism*, London: Routledge and Kegan Paul.

Bland, L., Brunsdon, C., Hobson, D. and Winship, J. (1978), 'Women Inside and Outside the Relations of Production', in Women's Studies Group, *Women Take Issue*, London: Hutchinson.

Braverman, H. (1974), *Labor and Monopoly Capital*, New York: Monthly Review.

Cooley, M. (1979), 'Computers, Politics and Unemployment', *European Computing Review*.

Counter Information Services (1976), *Women Under Attack*, London.

Counter Information Services (1979), *The New Technology*, London.

Daniel, W. and Stilgoe, E. (1978), *The Effects of the Employment Protection Act*, London: Policy Studies Institute.

Däubler-Gmelin, H. (1977), *Frauenarbeitslosigkeit*, Hamburg: Rowolt.

Department of Employment (1978), 'Age and Redundancy', *Employment Gazette*, September.

Dex, S. (1978), 'Measuring Women's Unemployment', *Social and Economic Administration*, Summer.

Downing, H. and Barker, J. (1979), 'Office Automation, Word Processing and the Transformation of Patriarchal Relations', Paper to CSE Microprocessors Group, January (mimeo), *Capital and Class* (forthcoming).

Ferber, M. and Lowry, H. (1976), 'Women, the New Reserve Army', in Blaxall, M. and Reagan, B. (eds.), *Women and the Workplace*, Chicago: University of Chicago Press.

Gardiner, J. (1976), 'Women and Unemployment', *Red Rag*, no. 10.

Hakim, C. (1978), 'Sexual Divisions in the Labour Force', *Employment Gazette*, November.

Harris, D. F. and Taylor, F. J. (1978), *The Service Sector*, London: Centre for Environmental Studies, Research Series no. 25.

Hughes, J. (1978), 'A Rakes Progress', in Barrett Brown, M. and Hughes, J. (eds.), *Full Employment – Priority*, Nottingham: Spokesman Books.

Humphries, J. (1976), 'Women as Scapegoats and Safety Valves', *Review of Radical Political Economy*.

Hurstfield, J. (1978), *The Part Time Trap*, London: Low Pay Unit.

Jenness, L., Hill, H., Reid, N. M., Lovell, F. and Davenport, S. E. (1975), *Last Hired, First Fired*, New York: Pathfinder.

Kolko, G. (1978), 'Working Wives, Their Effect on the Structure of the Working Class', *Science and Society*, Fall.

Lewenhak, S. (1977), *Women and Trade Unions*, London: Benn.

MacKay, D. I., Boddy, D., Brack, J., Diack, J. A. and Jones, N. (1971), *Labour Markets under Different Employment Conditions*, London: George Allen and Unwin.

Marx, K. (1867), *Capital* vol. I, ch. 25.

Milkman, R. (1976), 'Women's Work and the Economic Crisis', *Review of Radical Political Economy*.

Moore, B., Rhodes, J., Tarling, F. and Wilkinson, F. (1978), *Economic Policy Review*, University of Cambridge, Department of Applied Economics.

Niemi, B. (1976), 'Geographical Immobility and Labor Force Mobility: a Study of Female Unemployment', in Lloyd, C. B. (ed.), *Sex Discrimination and the Division of Labor*, New York: Columbia University Press.

Office of Population Census and Surveys, *General Household Survey*, 1974, 1976.

Office of Population Census and Surveys (1978), 'The Changing Circumstances of Women', *Population Trends*.

Organization for Economic Cooperation and Development (1976), *The 1974-5 Recession and the Employment of Women*, Paris.

Rowbotham, S. (1973), *Hidden From History*, London: Pluto Press.

Royal Commission on the Distribution of Income and Wealth (1978), Report no. 6, *Lower Incomes*, Cmnd 7175, London: HMSO.

Unemployment Statistics (1972), Report of an Interdepartmental Working Party, Cmnd 5157, London: HMSO.

Werneke, D. (1978), 'The Economic Slowdown and Women's Employment', *International Labour Review*, January-February.

Hilary Land

The Family Wage

In *New Statesman*, London, 18 December
1981, pp. 16-18

What are wages for? There are several answers to this question but
in one important respect at least the answer is likely to be different
for men and women. It is assumed implicitly that men's wages
should be sufficient to support a family whereas women's wages
are supplementary to others or at most need be sufficient to
support one adult. Men earn 'a family wage' and women earn 'pin
money'. If jobs are in short supply men should have prior claim to
them.

These assumptions do not accord with reality. The wages system
does not and *cannot* ensure that the needs of a worker's family are
met at all times as they vary over the family life cycle. Moreover,
not all men have dependants and conversely many women do.
Nevertheless the concept of the family wage has been a powerful
one for over a century and challenging it raises fundamental
questions about the basis of male trade unions bargaining strategies, what determines the level of wages and the extent and nature
of the State's responsibilities for meeting the costs of children.
These are controversial issues which, as the agendas of this year's
conferences show, are now surfacing again within the trade union
movement and the Labour Party as well as being debated among
feminist groups and pressure groups like CPAG. They were
thoroughly debated during the twenties and although then, as now,
there was little consensus on the answers it is worth looking at the
arguments put forward then because they were based on concerns
which are current today.

The concept of the family wage is based on assumptions about
the respective responsibilities of men and women in the labour
market and the home. These were established during the nineteenth century when the home and the workplace became separate
for the majority of men and the unit of labour changed from the
family to the individual. In many parts of the country in general
married women were no longer expected to make an economic
contribution to the household and if they did (as many had to) it
was not perceived to be either 'productive' or important. Men had
priority in the allocation of wages and jobs in the formal labour

market and were assumed to earn a 'family wage' (although many did not). At the same time a distribution of resources and services in the home was maintained which was to their benefit, for the breadwinner's 'needs' came first. The view that a man participated in the labour market in order to support himself *and* his family also helped to sustain male work incentives. Conversely the emphasis on a woman's responsibilities being primarily in the home put her at a disadvantage in the labour market and weakened her *right* to paid employment which was very useful in times of high male unemployment. Even if she did work outside the home pressure was on her to continue to give priority to her domestic responsibilities. Opposition to those who wished to abandon the concept therefore stemmed from concern not only about the effect this might have on men's pay, opportunities and incentives in the labour market but also that women would have less opportunity and incentive to provide domestic services in the home – for their husbands as well as their children. These concerns still exist.

Initially the discussion of the relationship between family needs and wages took place mainly in socialist and feminist circles. It broadened in the 1920s when the campaign for family allowances got underway. Eleanor Rathbone was one of the campaign's leading spokeswomen. Instead of the family wage she proposed a minimum wage sufficient for a single person plus allowances for each child together with an allowance paid to the mother in recognition both of her need for maintenance and of the job she was doing. Later she dropped the allowance for the mother and advocated a minimum wage sufficient to meet the needs of two people on the grounds that 'neither men nor women, married or unmarried should be expected to do their own housework while giving full-time service in the labour market.' Women would be given increased legal rights to claim maintenance from their husbands. At no stage did she want family allowances paid only to mothers who were prepared to stay at home.

Both the TUC and the Labour Party were directly confronted with the issue when in 1927 the Independent Labour Party adopted a living wage policy, i.e., a minimum wage sufficient for two adults plus family allowances. The joint committee set up to consider this policy failed to agree. Their minority report, in favour of developing social services before family allowances, was supported by the TUC and finally adopted at conference in 1930.

One set of arguments centred on the impact family allowances would have on wage levels and productivity. Views differed and much depended on where the analysis was focused and on what model of the economy was being used. In a market economy wages perform a variety of functions. At the micro level of analysis it is argued that the level of wages is based on the worker's productivity tempered by his or her bargaining power: wages serve as a reward for effort, experience and skill, which are not directly related to size of family. At the macro level of analysis, in the absence of other sources of income, wages must be sufficient to meet the costs of reproducing labour power and the next generation of workers – paid *and* unpaid. Minimum wages are determined by the subsistence cost of the worker (which varies over time and is a subjective measure). This *is* dependent on the size of the family and the number of wage earners in that family. Would family allowances reconcile the conflict between these different determinants of the wage and if so, at whose expense would the reconciliation occur – the worker or the employer?

The opinions of the trade unions, standing as they do at the interface between the family and the workplace and concerned with both these aspects of the wage, were divided. This was partly due to different perceptions of the appropriate functions and strategies of a trade union movement. The exchanges between representatives of the ILP and leading members of the TUC show that some of the latter's hostility to family allowances stemmed from the fact that it was part of the ILP's radical economic package of policies involving a very different relationship between the trade unions and the Labour Party. Their proposals and the analysis on which they were based also implied that the orthodox role of trade unions in Britain with its emphasis on collective bargaining over money wages had achieved, and could *only* achieve limited real improvements for the working class as a whole. Powerful trade unionists such as Bevin, Milne-Bailey and Citrine, took exception to this and it is difficult to conclude that this did not colour their attitude towards family allowances *per se.*

To the ILP, the living wage policy was part of a strategy involving reorganisation of industry, including the nationalisation of key services notably credit, transport, power and the import of essential raw materials and foodstuffs. They proposed family allowances as a way of increasing and maintaining the purchasing power of workers and so creating additional demand for goods leading to an increased and sustained demand for labour, thus reducing unemployment. Second, family allowances could be seen as one of the steps towards putting socialist principles into practice: to each according to his (*sic*) need. The middle classes already had tax rebates for children so the working classes, very few of whom were income tax payers, should have an analogous system. Third, if paid for out of taxation (the only scheme acceptable to trade unionists) resources would be redistributed from the rich to the poor. Others in favour of family allowances believed they would strengthen a trade union's bargaining position. For example, Dalton had calculated that had miners been receiving 12½p family allowance for each child then £125,000 a week would have been going into miners' homes:

> ... imagine the effect which the possession of this steady income would have had both upon the men's power to resist the employers' demands and upon the attitude of the employers themselves.[1]

Those against cash family allowances, however, argued that such a scheme would *reduce* the family man's will to bargain and would divide his interests from those of the single man. As a result workers' bargaining power would be reduced and wages would fall. To Bevin, who was always strongly opposed to family allowances, a living wage policy meant 'wages will be the subject of political conflict ... the problem must be dealt with by the Unions themselves.' While this might be tolerable under a Labour government over which they had some control, it would be disastrous with a Conservative government in power.

Another argument against family allowances was that if part of the subsistence cost of the family was met by the State then wages must fall because as Citrine believed 'people have some idea of a standard of decency and of what is right for the workers, of what is reasonable and fair', so, knowing that family needs were being met outside the wages system, employers would be able to pay less.

Others argued that social services should be developed first. These were more in keeping with the principle of collectivism and co-operation and as long as social conditions were so unequal money was far better spent on improving standards of housing, education, health services etc. Moreover, these would have less impact on money wage levels than family allowances, which, if financed by employers, were likely to be passed on in the form of increased prices, thus reducing real wages and harming the competitiveness of British exports.

The opponents of family allowances had some cause to be wary of their possible impact on wage levels. First, in 1926, the Samuel Commission on the Mining Industry had recommended a system

1. Hugh Dalton, *Memorandum of Evidence to the Joint Committee on the Living Wage*, London: HMSO, 1928.

of family allowance for miners, but hinted that it might be associated with a cut in wages. Beveridge, a member of the Commission, believed, like many economists of the time, that the rigidity of wages was one of the causes of the recession. If mining employers introduced family allowances wages could be cut during periods of depression without penalising those in greatest need. Production costs would fall, cheapening British coal in world markets and employers would need to lay off fewer workers. The earnings of the single and childless would be reduced but they were most guilty of absenteeism and could make up their wages by working longer hours.

Second, in France where employer-based schemes had been developing throughout the twenties, it was clear that they had been introduced in order to reduce demands for wage increases. Pronatalist motives came to the fore later. Also it was claimed that the payment of allowances had prevented trade unions from making use of family men for helping in their revolutionary aims. It was the French experience which later helped win the support of some Conservatives for family allowances.

However, behind some of the male trade unionists' arguments against family allowances it is hard not to conclude that there lurked a suspicion that their masculinity – as well as their wages and privileges – was under attack. As a leading member of the General and Municipal Workers Union said in 1930 in opposition to the proposal for family allowances:

> Let the men in industry take the mantle of manhood and come into the unions and fight to establish a standard of comfort that will enable them to make provision so long as work is open and they perform their service to the State through it.[2]

Feminists within the Labour movement also had mixed feelings towards family allowances. While many criticised the family wage because it failed to recognise the needs of *women* with dependants and was a barrier to equal pay, they too were concerned about the impact of family allowances on their bargaining power and were afraid working women might be pushed back into the home. Opposing family allowances, Ada Neild Chew, a radical suffragist, wrote:

> More than all should women discourage the fostering of the ideal of the domestic tabby cat as that to which all womanhood should

2. TUC General Council, *Report of the Annual Congress*, 1930.

aspire ... The children must be cared for, and women must care for them. But not by paying poor women to be mothers. Women must be financially independent of men. But not by paying poor women to be wives. Marriage and motherhood should not be for sale. They should be disassociated from what is for sale – domestic drudgery.[3]

In reply Mrs Arnot Robertson, a member of the Women's Labour League, argued for an allowance to cover a child's maintenance provided that:

children and not motherhood should be endowed ... If the mother determined to become the nurse and trainer of her children the money would be paid to her. She might, if she chose, become a nurse to the children of other women, who, although mothers did not feel themselves specially fitted to develop the best that was in their children and who therefore continued to work outside the home after marriage and motherhood.[4]

By enabling women to choose whether or not to take paid employment their bargaining position in the labour market would be substantially improved. They would then be able to fight not only for equal pay but also for improving housing standards and collective services – day nurseries, laundries, kitchens which provided cheap meals – thus reducing 'the brutal, unnecessary labour, which drains the vitality and strength of many women'.

However, other women in the trade union movement and the Fabian Society believed family allowances, while improving children's welfare, had nothing to do with women's independence or equality. Some even feared that by weakening the marriage relationship women's interests would be harmed. Anna Martin, an active trade unionist, was not prepared to abandon the concept of the family wage because:

Women with good cause dread anything which weakens the link between the breadwinner and his home ... each of them knows perfectly well that the strength of her position in the home lies in the physical dependence of husband and children upon her.[5]

3. Jill Liddington and J. Norris, *One Hand Tied Behind Us*, London: Virago, 1978, p. 259.
4. Mrs Arnot Robertson, in *Common Cause*, no. 20, March 1914.
5. A. Martin, 'The Married Working Woman: a Study II', *The Nineteenth Century*, January 1911, p. 109.

She was therefore opposed to family allowances and free school meals. Some economists, notably Alexander Gray, who believed family allowances would have disastrous effects on male work incentives, shared this concern but from the point of view of the man. To him, family allowances 'would eliminate the husband'.

Another constellation of arguments centred round the impact family allowances would have on the relationship between the State, parents and children, and in particular on a woman's opportunities and incentives to be a wife and a mother. Public discussion about family allowances had arisen before the First World War in the context of a growing eugenics movement as well as against the background of concern that women were undercutting male wages, or worse, taking jobs away from men. Eleanor Rathbone accepted that family allowances would put the State's hand 'on the tiller of maternity' and thought it right that the quality and quantity of the population should be controlled. Working-class feminists were suspicious of these views for they were not confident that the State would act in their interests unless women had considerably more political power. The Co-operative Women's Guild believed that the development of adequate maternity cash benefits covering the first year or two of the child's life followed by extensive day nursery provision and improved health and welfare services for women and children, had higher priority than family allowances. They were convinced that the point of view of 'the independent working woman was more important than "ladies" sitting on charity committees', and that she 'must be given a voice in the shaping of the policy to be pursued and deciding the ideals to be instilled otherwise there might be danger of scientific eugenic and official views of the work overruling individual and family right.'[6]

In the event it was not until 1941 that the majority accepted that the payment of family allowances would not 'materially handicap the unions in their present fight to maintain and improve standards'. The scheme introduced in 1946 was so modest it hardly constituted a threat to the concept of the family wage.

The evidence that the wages system cannot provide adequate support for all families is as strong now as ever it was. Indeed now that the tax and social security systems overlap even reasonable wage increases cannot help the low paid with children because of the poverty trap. As the Tobacco Workers Union told last year's TUC Congress: a radical rethink is needed. Should the State

6. Co-operative Women's Guild, *Memorandum on the National Care of Maternity*, 1917.

provide more support for children? Those who say yes must recognise and deal with the dangers of giving more power to the State to control the incomes and lives of families unless State policies become more responsive to the needs and wishes of women and working-class men. With this in mind are cash benefits the best form of child support? On the other hand those who cling to the ideal of the family wage, and there will be many because the assumptions upon which the family wage is based have greater currency at times of high male unemployment, must recognise that they are acting against the interests of women and children. It is encouraging that these questions are once again being discussed and it is to be hoped that whatever the outcome of the debate the needs of women and children will be accorded higher priority than they have been in the past.

Women and the State

In *The Origin of the Family, Private Property and the State*, Engels argued that the origins of the subordination of women lay in the transformation of a system of communally, or tribally, owned property into one of the private, individual ownership of property. As individual families came to own property, so a class of property-owners emerged, which was to organise itself into a centralised state, primarily designed to maintain the existing arrangements of the ownership of property. Capitalist society, whether industrial or not, had thereby created a formal arrangement for safeguarding the basic division within it: between those who owned property and those who did not. But within capitalism there was also another fundamental division, as Engels pointed out. Just as the proletariat was subordinate to the bourgeoisie, so was the wife to the husband, the female to the male. Whereas in pre-capitalist societies all work, whether performed by men or by women, had been regarded as of equal social value, work in capitalist societies was divided into production for exchange, which was performed by men, and production for use, which was performed by women. Through producing for exchange, men were able to accumulate wealth, and hence social power. Women, on the other hand, who produced only what was immediately consumed within the household, had no opportunity to acquire the means by which they might exercise social power. Women's labour was a necessary but socially subordinate part of producing an exchangeable surplus.

Engels' arguments have now been widely discussed by a number of critics, including many feminists. Many of his critics point out that aspects of Engels' anthropology are faulty and that the causal connections which he makes between changes in modes of production and the development of private property relationships cannot be substantiated by examination of a number of particular cases.[1] However, for feminists, Engels makes one contribution

1. See, for example, Karen Sacks, 'Engels Revisited: Women, the Organisation of Production and Private Property', in M. Rosaldo and L. Lamphere, eds., *Woman, Culture and Society*, Stanford: Stanford University Press, 1974; Peter Aaby, 'Engels and Women', *Critique of Anthropology*, vol. 3, nos. 9 and 10, 1977; and Rosalind Delmar, 'Looking Again at Engels', in A. Oakley and J. Mitchell, eds., *The Rights and Wrongs of Women*, Harmondsworth: Penguin, 1976.

that is of exceptional importance: the relationship that he suggests exists between the interests of the capitalist state and those of the patriarchal family. In both cases, the institution in question is essentially concerned with maintaining male interests, and in particular the ownership of private property by men. Women play a part in this process through bearing heirs to property and even, on occasion, owning property of their own, but it is largely a secondary and subordinate role, and one that is reflected in the institutional arrangements of the state. As far as the operation of social and political power is concerned, women's participation is minimal.

Since women's relationship to property in capitalist societies is largely a tangential one, which is chiefly concerned with maintaining and reproducing the social relationships through which property is owned and transferred, it is scarcely surprising that women's relationship to the state is also much less direct than that of men. As Mary McIntosh has pointed out in a seminal paper[2] on the subject, 'The relation of women to state agents is much more often indirect than that of men.' In a number of contexts, she continues, the state intervenes less in the lives of women than it does in those of men. Indeed, in some ways it could be argued that the state, because of its perception of women as generally passive and dependent creatures, is very unwilling to extend its formal authority over the lives of women.[3] A tacit assumption of individual male control over their female relatives and dependants can be detected in this *laissez-faire* attitude. The relationship of women to the state can best be illustrated by reference to two particular institutional contexts: the state's definition and control of various forms of deviant behaviour and the policies of almost all industrial capitalist states to the family.

All societies have definitions of what constitutes deviant behaviour, and in Western industrial societies an overall consensus can be detected about what is deemed as appropriate or inappropriate behaviour for both sexes. Both men and women are expected to conform to the law and to comply with a variety of formal rules about the possible limits of accepted social behaviour. But in

2. Mary McIntosh, 'The State and the Oppression of Women', in Ann Marie Wolpe and Annette Kuhn, eds., *Feminism and Materialism*, London: Routledge and Kegan Paul, 1978. On the relations between women and public power see Margaret Stacey and Marion Price, *Women, Power and Politics*, London: Tavistock, 1981.
3. The contradictions between the state's official ideology about the need to 'protect' women and its need for female labour are explored in Jane Humphries, 'Protective Legislation, the Capitalist State, and Working-class Men: the Case of the 1842 Mines Regulation Act', *Feminist Review*, no. 7, 1981.

addition to these formal and legal requirements, men and women are also expected to act in ways which meet social expectations of how men and women should behave. Thus, for example, it is assumed that it is 'normal' for youths and men to be noisy and physically active, while women are expected to be rather quieter and more docile. Men are expected to make sexual overtures to women, while modest, 'good' women do not act in ways which are sexually flamboyant. This latter expectation is borne out in the letter and expectation of the law: women are protected against male sexual harassment, but that protection is very rapidly withdrawn should it be demonstrated that a woman has violated social conventions about female modesty. The most striking examples of this condition of the legal protection of women can be seen in cases of rape and prostitution. In the former case, a prosecution of a man for rape will only be successful if it is demonstrated that the woman did not, in any way, encourage male attentions.[4] In the case of prostitution, the law deems that it is women who are 'guilty' of prostitution and not their male clients; women who exchange their physical favours for money place themselves so far outside general expectations about women that far from protecting them, the law prosecutes them.

Western law on all questions of sexual morality assumes, then, that a 'good' woman must be protected against predatory males, and against 'bad' women by the stigmatisation of the latter. This assumption, based as it is on accepted notions of female behaviour, very often works against the interests of women involved in cases where the law and sexual morality meet. Yet in cases where social, rather than sexual, morality is involved, the taken-for-granted view of female dependence and passivity often works to the advantage of women, in that if they break the law it is assumed that they do so because of malevolent male influence. 'She Did it All for Love', the title of the paper by Marcia Millman which is reproduced here, sums up a general attitude: women are only bad if men corrupt them. In their natural state, it would appear that women are docile, home-loving creatures.[5]

The assumption of the 'natural' domestic role of women underlies a second area where the state has an institutionalised view of women: namely, that of its welfare policies. In the majority

4. The searching cross-examination of the sexual histories of rape victims is documented in Zsuzsanna Adler's 'How the Rape Law really works', *The Times*, 10 February 1982.
5. A possible change in the legal processing of female deviants – namely that a less lenient view is being taken of female deviance – is discussed in S. Box and C. Hale, 'Liberation and Female Criminality in England and Wales Revisited', *British Journal of Criminology*, forthcoming, 1982.

of Western societies, the economic dependence of women that accompanies marriage and the birth of children is enshrined in law: men have a legal duty to maintain their wives and children. The law supposes (quite falsely, as Hilary Land points out) that all breadwinners are male, and that in any permanent sexual relationship between a man and a woman the man acquires an automatic duty to maintain the woman.[6] Feminists have campaigned long and hard against the 'cohabitation' rule that is a part of the welfare policies of Britain and the United States, arguing that sexual relationships between men and women should not be presumed to carry with them the expectation of female economic dependence. But at the same time feminists themselves point out that women, in marriage and heterosexual relationships in general, provide 'free' domestic services for men. Thus feminists have also campaigned for wages for housework, for financial settlements for women on divorce or separation and for the recognition of women's economic contribution (in the form of paid or unpaid labour) to the household. These arguments would seem to suggest that feminists see heterosexual relationships as inevitably involving the exchange of unpaid domestic services for economic support – a position that is not entirely incompatible with those justifications produced in favour of the cohabitation rule.[7]

It becomes evident, on even a cursory examination of women's relationship to the state, that the state sees women as inextricably bound to domestic life, and that those institutional arrangements maintained by the state that affect women are designed to continue and reinforce that association.[8] When women cease acting as dependent beings, the state is at present faced with problems that are too complex for its institutions to encompass adequately. Yet it is becoming increasingly apparent that women's social role is becoming far more various than the lifelong domestic role envisaged by the state, and that adaptations to this new role are long overdue.

But the adaptations that are required are not just to be located within laws or formal bureaucratic procedures. Indeed, many feminists in Britain have questioned the effectiveness of changes in the law in bringing about improvements in the status and position

6. Hilary Land, 'The Myth of the Male Breadwinner', *New Society*, 9 October 1975.

7. See Zoe Fairbairns, 'The Cohabitation Rule: Why it Makes Sense', *Spare Rib*, no. 104, March 1981.

8. See the article by O'Donovan reproduced here and L. Weitzman, 'Legal Regulation of Marriage', *California Law Review*, vol. 62, 1974.

of women.[9] It is the informal practices of the state, enacted every day by its personnel in schools, hospitals and a variety of other institutions, that have become the target of feminist attack and deemed as long overdue for change. Two examples will suffice to indicate how inadequate and anachronistic are state practices and assumptions in relationship to the contemporary position of women. The first concerns the education system, the second that of the organisation of health care.

The education systems of both Britain and the United States (and the majority of industrial capitalist societies) are such that they do little other than reproduce existing educational and social inequalities. Black children in the United States, and white working-class children in both countries, have consistently achieved less well in educational systems that are designed largely to cater for middle-class interests and ambitions. However, if children of both sexes from underprivileged social and racial groups gain little from schooling it is among girls that employment related educational achievement is most strikingly absent. Although girls and boys in Britain now take – and pass – approximately equal numbers of Ordinary and Advanced level examinations, it is still boys who predominate in professional and vocational training and in those subjects in higher education which have a scientific and technological association. Despite the increase in the number of women entering British universities, the impact of this change on the numbers of women entering managerial and professional employment remains minimal. Feminists thus argue that the hidden curriculum of the schools and higher education, which discriminates so heavily in favour of middle-class assumptions and habits, discriminates equally heavily in favour of boys and men, who are generally more likely to receive encouragement and assistance than girls.[10] Schools, as Jenny Shaw suggests in her paper, see themselves as preparing girls for marriage as much as the labour market, and are little inclined to exert extra effort to counteract the romantic inclinations of female teenage sub-cultures. Indeed, many feminists are now pointing out that the very curriculum and content of education (be they in higher or secondary education) serve to articulate and legitimate male interests and the sexual division of labour.[11]

The fact that women will both choose, and be forced, to enter

9. See Mandy Snell, 'The Equal Pay and Sex Discrimination Acts: Their Impact in the Workplace', Feminist Review, no. 1, 1979.
10. See Dale Spender, Invisible Women, London: The Women's Press, 1982.
11. See Mary Evans, 'In Praise of Theory: the Case for Women's Studies', Feminist Review, no. 10, 1982.

the labour market is apparently as of little interest to the health and welfare services of the state as it is to the education system. For example, many aspects of the organisation of the health service depend upon the belief that married women do not undertake paid work. Two instances illustrate this: the first is the now widely attacked presupposition of those organising maternity services that pregnant women, and mothers, unlike doctors and nurses, do not have jobs and can therefore spend long hours waiting for medical ministrations.[12] The second, and more serious, assumption is the belief that women will automatically undertake a great deal of home nursing and caring: for husbands, elderly relatives and children. This hidden subsidy of female care and nurturance provides the health and welfare services of all societies with an enormous amount of free labour.[13] It is thus perhaps more than coincidental that the state does little to challenge the domestic role of women and the social construction of appropriate female behaviour.

12. See the documentation in Ann Oakley's *Women Confined*, Oxford: Martin Robertson, 1980, and, by the same author, *Becoming a Mother*, Oxford: Martin Robertson, 1979.
13. This issue is discussed in Elizabeth Wilson, *Women and the Welfare State*, London: Tavistock, 1977; and Hilary Land, 'Who Cares for the Family?', *Journal of Social Policy*, vol. 7, no. 3, 1978.

Mary McIntosh

The State and the Oppression of Women

In A. Kuhn and A. Wolpe, eds., *Feminism and Materialism*, London: Routledge and Kegan Paul, 1978, pp. 255-89

Women have been subordinated to men and oppressed by them in many different sorts of society.[1] In the most general terms, the oppression of women is not unique to capitalism. But the relations between the sexes nevertheless take different forms in different social formations and even at different periods of development in capitalist societies. One of the features of capitalist societies, especially in the more advanced stages of capitalism, is the important part played by the state in the economy and in the society at large. It is not surprising, therefore, to find that the state plays a part in the oppression of women.

In this paper it will be argued that the state does this not directly but through its support for a specific form of household: the family household dependent largely upon a male wage and upon female domestic servicing. This household system is in turn related to capitalist production in that it serves (though inadequately) for the reproduction of the working class and for the maintenance of women as a reserve army of labour, low-paid when they are in jobs and often unemployed. This two-pronged relationship involves contradictions and, furthermore, the family household system has its own history and roots in pre-capitalist society, so that state effort cannot achieve a perfect fit between the household and the various needs of capitalism. State policy is thus constantly juggling to keep several balls in the air at once.

I

The way in which the state is commonly understood is in terms of

1. My thanks to the following friends who have kindly given me comments on an earlier version of this paper: Michèle Barrett, Veronica Beechey, Helen Crowley, Norman Ginsburg, Annette Kuhn, Maxine Molyneux, Kerry Schott, Harold Wolpe. They are not, however, to be held responsible for the outcome.

the relations between the 'state' and the 'citizen'. The state is seen as an alien body interfering in private lives. Radicals of both right and left deplore state intervention as limiting the spontaneity and freedom of individuals. People could run their businesses and bring up their children (according to the right) or run their local communities, solve their personal problems and educate themselves (according to the left) much better without central government meddling in their affairs.

This kind of perspective has informed some strands of thought in the women's liberation movement. The state is seen as denying us freedom to choose abortion, say, or to decide whether to do wage work or housework; as a purveyor of oppressively sexist ideologies in education, social services and medicine; as practising economic and legal discrimination against women in relation to Supplementary Benefit, social security and taxation, and in relation to rape, domestic violence and prostitution. All of this is true of course, and such analyses are indeed immediately useful given the exigencies of day-to-day struggles for improvements and resistance to threats to worsen our already bad situation.

It is none the less surprising that women have borrowed the idea of the state as a directly repressive mechanism from the libertarian and radical left. For, if intervention is conceived as a relationship between the citizen and agents of the state, one of the striking features of the situation is that the state 'intervenes' less conspicuously in the lives of women than of men, and when it does so it appears to be done more benevolently. It is not mere casuistry to point out that the notorious 'cohabitation rule', and the equally iniquitous rule from which it derives whereby a married woman, or a cohabiting one, cannot claim Supplementary Benefit for herself or her children, are rules *preventing* the government department's officers from intervening in a woman's life. They enter, albeit in the most intrusive manner, only if she attempts to claim the benefit. What this indicates is that we cannot expect to understand the impact of the state on the position of women in this sphere if we see the conflict between claimant and government officer as the observable form of that impact. Much more important is the non-claimant status of so many women. We must look at the whole structure of benefits, the part they play in the economy as a whole and the patterns of social relations that they establish and sustain.

The relation of women to state agents is much more often indirect than that of men. The state frequently defines a space, the family, in which its agents will not interfere but in which control is left to the man. In relation to the control of children, this is obvious and explicit. Fathers are held responsible for sending their children to school and providing minimum support and care. But how they do this, short of cruelty or neglect, is left largely to them and social workers are extremely reluctant to intervene by removing children from the parental home. Women are now full citizens in most purely legal respects; they have the right to vote, to own and dispose of property, to make contracts, to go to law, to hold passports. In many ways, however, the state relates to married women through their husbands, especially in income tax and the social security system, which will be examined more fully later.

The general pattern of non-interference and relative benevolence comes out most clearly in the exercise of the criminal law. Most laws apply to men and women alike and those that do not (like 'living on immoral earnings' and the 'age of consent') are designed to protect women against predatory man. Yet far more men are convicted of crimes than women, and far more men are sent to prison and other forms of harsh institution, and for far longer terms. The analysis of criminal statistics is a complex matter, but the differences are so gross that there can be no doubt that the main reason is that there are more laws against the kinds of thing that men and boys do than against the kinds of thing that women and girls do. Either women do not 'deviate' (whatever that may mean) so much, or their deviations are not counted as criminal but are subject to other forms of control. Furthermore, though this is less easy to demonstrate, it seems that even when women do commit crimes that are detected by the police they are more likely to be treated leniently by police and by courts; and the regime in prison, if they ever get that far, is more comfortable and less authoritarian. The prevailing ideology that women are not voluntarily criminal, that they must have been led astray, unbalanced by emotional or hormonal disturbances or else mentally sick, seems to inform the treatment of women criminals at every stage. They are let off with a caution, given a conditional discharge, or put on probation much more readily. Except for a tiny handful, the 'worst' prison cases are sent to the new Holloway prison which is vaunted as a place of treatment rather than of punishment.

Feminist criminologists are hard put to it to find a point of attack. Commonly they turn instead upon the invidious nature of the kind of explanations that are offered for female criminality and the kinds of stereotypical motivations that are attributed to women by agents of social control and by criminologists. Recently, however, the apparently benevolent non-interference of the state towards women has been examined more critically and it has been seen that the social controls outside the criminal law – the family, social work and ultimately psychiatry – are every bit as coercive and even more intrusive (Smart, 1976; Snäre and Steng-Dahl, 1978; Fox, 1977).

The situations in which the state's non-interference with women is most obviously less benevolent are those in which women are denied the adequate protection of the law: in rape and in domestic violence. Here the assumption that women's contexts are too private and personal to be subject to criminal sanction leaves women exposed to violence and abuse. In both cases the behaviour is seen as an extension of normal male-female relations, the boundary is too obscure for a jury to decide reliably and the whole issue is cast in an ambiguous light by the attribution of ambivalent motivations to the women victims. It is said that women often say 'no' to sex when they don't really mean it; or wives continue to live with husbands who beat them and though they may complain to the police at night, they refuse to press charges in the morning. The supposed irrationality of women places these in the category of 'victim-precipitated crimes' which cannot be solved satisfactorily by the supposed rationality of the law.

The study of such specific injustices is important for immediate political campaigns. But it can tell us little about the part played by the state in the oppression of women. Here the overall pattern of non-interference, of the family and personal relationships as mediators of social control, of the siting of women in the private rather than the public sphere are of much greater importance.

The level of analysis that is needed is one on which we ask not simply 'How does the state oppress women?', but 'What part does the state play in establishing and sustaining systems in which women are oppressed and subordinated to men?'

At this stage it can be stated simply that in capitalism the two systems in question are the family household and wage labour.[2] In the first, women and men are defined *with respect to each other* and located in asymmetrical relations of production, distribution and authority. In the second, women occupy relatively disadvantaged positions as compared to male wage workers, and usually also submit to supervisors who are men. The two systems are both

2. It is common to make the central question of women's oppression, 'How do women become different from and subordinated to men?' The position taken here is that these processes of socialization, and the institutions such as education in which they take place, can only be understood in relation to these two key systems. Ideology, sexuality, personality are all important elements in women's oppression, but they remain without an historical dynamic unless we relate them, through these two systems, to the capitalistic mode of production.

closely interdependent and contradictory; some of the links will be discussed in a later section. As Margaret Coulson put it: 'The position of women is structured by the *contradictory* tendencies which derive from the relationship between the private sphere of the family and the public sphere of general production' (1974, p. 2). But although these are systems in which women are oppressed by men, this oppression, as such, is neither their defining characteristic nor their *raison d'être*.

The part played by the state in these institutions is a complex one; and the state, like society, cannot be analysed simply in terms of 'patriarchy'. Capitalist society is one in which men as men dominate women; yet it is not this but class domination that is fundamental to the society. It is a society in which the dominant class is composed mainly of men; yet it is not as men but as capitalists that they are dominant.

Some writers, notably Christine Delphy (1970), have conceptualized a relation between capitalism and patriarchy in terms of a 'family mode of production', with its own patriarchal relations of appropriation, existing within the same social formation as the capitalist mode of production. This may well be a useful approach, but to conclude, as Delphy does, that this patriarchal system of production can be overthrown by 'seizing the political power over ourselves at present held by others', if this means 'over women by men', is mistaken. The state must be seen as a capitalist one, or at least as one that is to be understood primarily in relation to the capitalist mode of production.

Furthermore, the state cannot be conceived as external to the dominant mode of production, as is sometimes implied by a mechanical separation of the economic, the political and the ideological in which the state is located in the political sphere. The idea of contrasting an interventionist with a non-interventionist state – *laissez-faire* versus state control – is a mistaken one, since even *laissez-faire* capitalism depends, for the conditions of its existence, upon the bourgeois state. Capital itself, with its mode of extracting surplus value, is a specific form of property established by a complex set of laws administered (with an ultimate sanction of coercion) through specific institutions. The 'free exchange' of commodities requires quite different laws from those of, say, feudal production as well as new forms of regulated money and credit. Thus although we may speak of state monopoly capitalism as a relatively late stage in the development of the capitalist mode of production in order to indicate the increasing scale of the state institutions and their direct involvement in capitalist enterprise, we must not suppose that the part played by the state was any less essential in the earlier 'competitive' stage.

This paper will adopt the idea of 'capitalist reproduction' to conceptualize this relation: the capitalist state plays a part in producing and reproducing the conditions for capital accumulation at any given stage. It must be frankly admitted, however, that this formulation leads to an analysis that is functionalist in character. Some ways of mitigating this are suggested at the end of the paper, but they do not alter the fundamental functionalism of the approach.

II

In general terms, no mode of production can persist over time unless its conditions of existence are continually reproduced. If the labour process is analysed in terms of two distinct levels, the relations of production and the forces of production, then each of these must be reproduced. In capitalism, both are reproduced first and foremost within production itself. Some production is of commodities like machinery, raw materials and so forth, which are purchased and transformed into constant capital for the production of articles of consumption. In the production of commodities workers are paid a wage that is sufficient to reproduce their labour power, so that they can arrive at work each day in the same condition as the day before and provide for their children who will grow up to replace them;[3] capital, however (since commodity

3. The question of the size of the wage, which in marxist theory tends to be equivalent to the value of labour power, is a complex one. The aspect that has been most discussed recently is the effect that women's domestic labour has on the value of their husbands' labour power. Less discussed has been the question of whether the reproduction of the housewife and of the next generation is included in the value of the wage earner's labour power. Himmelweit and Mohun (1977) suggest that:

The value of labour power should be seen as the mediating link with which to analyse changes in women's role in production. It is determined partly by the extent of domestic labour and, relatedly, by the number of wage-labourers in the family. In turn, the value of labour power determines the extent to which women must work, both in wage-labour and at home, in order to provide an acceptable standard of living for their families.

It is important to note that not only are the amount and combination of housework and commodities required to reproduce and socialize an individual historically determined by class struggle (rather than being biologically fixed), but also the number of people dependent on each wage for their reproduction is an historical and not a theoretical question (see, for instance, Humphries [1977]). This paper will bypass these issues by taking up, in the next section, the more general question of the reproduction of the working class as a *whole*, which is obviously less amenable to quantitative analysis in terms of the value of labour power.

production is also production of surplus value), is each day expanded by the process of production. Marx explains how the wage regulation reproduces both itself as a relation of production and labour power as a productive force:

> The money which the labourer receives is spent by him in order to preserve his labour-power, or – viewing the capitalist class and the working-class in their totality – in order to preserve for the capitalist the instrument by means of which alone he can remain a capitalist. Thus the continuous purchase and sale of labour-power perpetuates on the one hand labour-power as an element of capital, by virtue of which the latter appears as the creator of commodities, articles of use having value, by virtue of which, furthermore, that portion of capital which buys labour-power is continually restored by labour-power's own production, and consequently the labourer himself constantly creates the fund of capital out of which he himself is paid. On the other hand, the constant sale of labour-power becomes the source, ever renewing itself, of the maintenance of the labourer and hence his labour-power appears as that faculty through which he secures the revenue by which he lives. [Marx, 1972, p. 385]

In this conception, then, consumption appears as a phase in the great 'circuit of capital' and as necessary to the self-expansion of capital. The usual 'social welfare' approach, which sees the central problem of consumption as one of unequal distribution, is thus displaced by one that focuses instead on the part played by consumption in the expanded reproduction of capital.

Although capitalist reproduction takes place first and foremost within production, politics and ideology have also played an essential part. The state has undertaken important tasks of reproduction. Even the reproduction of machines and raw materials, for instance, cannot always be undertaken by capital itself. Certainly a single firm cannot be self-sustaining, but even a multiplicity of firms cannot always provide all the raw materials and essential services that they need. Some items such as fuels, communications and transport systems require large capital investment, but 'without any immediate prospect of profit' (Engels, 1975, p. 147) and tend to be either established as legal monopolies or state enterprises, held on behalf, as it were, of all the individual capitals.

Similarly the reproduction of labour power takes place outside capitalist production itself. A central argument of this paper will relate to the part played by the state in this process. For the wage serves with certainty for the reproduction only of the workers themselves and although to a large extent the mediation of the wage for the reproduction of the class as a whole is provided through the institution of the family, this institution has required state support and, even when supported, has not been adequate to the task.[4]

In the nineteenth century it was a matter of great concern to the bourgeoisie that industry was working its labourers so hard and paying them so little that it exhausted them before the next generation was produced. No individual firm would benefit from stopping this; but the state, under pressure from the 'Ten Hours' movement, as well as from elements of the bourgeoisie, was able to restrict hours of work, especially for women and children, and to insist on somewhat improved conditions. In the twentieth century, the state has become massively involved in the education, housing, health and income maintenance of working people.

As far as the relations of production are concerned, Marx tended to concentrate on questions such as the property relation, the wage relation; so much so that in *Capital*, ideology appears in the rarefied form of 'commodity fetishism'. Recent writers have looked at a wide range of aspects of ideological reproduction in a reaction against the 'economism' of the previous period of marxist thought. They have pointed to the fact that although state coercion is sometimes used to establish capitalist relations, for the most part these are assured by ideological reproduction. Althusser (1971) has even gone so far as to identify a series of institutions (religious, educational, family, legal, political, trade union, communications and cultural) as ideological state apparatuses, since these perform what for him and for Poulantzas were state functions – the state being the 'cement' in the social formation and the 'factor of social cohesion'. The impact of Althusser's idea has been immense. It has enabled sociologists studying education, politics, medicine, socialization, culture and the media, industrial relations, social policy – indeed almost all the traditional fields of sociology – to relate their work to marxism, since they are able to show how the institutions they are concerned with function as ideological state apparatuses. The danger is that their work may still be fundamentally sociological rather than marxist in the problems it poses.[5]

4. To write of the 'adequacy' or 'inadequacy' of the family as an institution for serving certain 'needs of capital' highlights some of the problems inherent in the functionalist approach. It can, however, be understood as a necessary preliminary to an analysis of class struggle. Thus, to specify the requirements for the reproduction of capital is to specify the material basis on which ruling-class policies will be formed; though it may tell us little about the particular shape that these will take in the political class struggle.

5. For a full critique of the idea of ideological reproduction, see Hirst (1976).

There has been a tendency, however, to concentrate on ideological reproduction and to ignore the ways in which other aspects of the capital-labour relation are reproduced. Thus, matters such as the developing nature of labour law, company law and the determinations of the value of labour power have not been analysed sufficiently. The state has played a considerable part in the establishment of labour power as a commodity, that is, in the creation of a proletariat forced to sell its labour power in order to subsist. Historically in Britain this meant the virtual abolition of self-subsistence through such measures as the Enclosures, and the shrinking of the lumpenproletariat of the casual poor. By now (unless they have wealth, or engage in crime or prostitution, or join the for-ever-swallowed-and-recreated *petite bourgeoisie* of small business people) there are only four ways in which most of the population subsist: wage labour, dependence on state support, dependence on relatives, private pensions and savings. Given the relative inflexibility of the last two, the state is able, through the social security system, to define the size and structure of the workforce to a considerable extent (as well as to push down the price of labour power by keeping the state subsistence minimum as low as possible [Ginsburg, 1977]). In the case of women, the social security system has worked in a curious way, on the one hand to establish married women as dependent upon their husbands (and therefore as not entirely reliant upon wage labour) but on the other hand by restricting their direct eligibility for social security benefits, to make them more vulnerable to use as cheap labour power when they do have to engage in wage labour.

The notion of capitalist reproduction thus enables us to identify two distinct functions of the state, relating to the two major systems in which women are oppressed. On the one hand, for the reproduction of labour power the state sustains a family household system in which a number of people are dependent for financial support on the wages of a few adult members, primarily of a male breadwinner, and in which they are all dependent for cleaning, food preparation and so forth on the unpaid work done chiefly by a woman. At the same time, the state itself carries out some of these functions of financial support and of servicing; yet it usually does so under such ideological conditions that it is seen as 'taking over' functions properly belonging to the family or as 'substituting' for work that 'should' be done by a housewife.

On the other hand, for the reproduction of relations of production (specifically the nature of labour power as a commodity), the state has played an important part in establishing married women as a latent reserve army of labour, again by sustaining the family household system and particularly by assuring the financial dependence of unemployed wives on their husbands so that married women are not fully proletarianized even during a period when they are increasingly drawn into wage labour.

Marx wrote: 'The maintenance and reproduction of the working-class is, and must ever be, a necessary condition to the reproduction of capital. But the capitalist may safely leave its fulfilment to the labourer's instincts of self-preservation and of propagation' (Marx, 1970, p. 572). Unfortunately, matters are not quite as simple as Marx suggests. If the maintenance and reproduction of the working class is seen as involving at least the housing, feeding and clothing of all the members of the class, then it includes provision for children, the sick and disabled, the retired, the unemployed and those who do the domestic work, as well as provision for today's workers themselves. To a large extent, as stated earlier, this is provided from the worker's wage through the institution of the family. Yet it will be argued, first, that the specific form that the family takes is not simply an effect of 'the labourer's instinct of self-preservation and of propagation' but is a result in part of state policies, and, second, that the family is not adequate on its own to distribute support and maintenance through the class.

It may well be the case that the (male) labourer's 'instinct for self-preservation' would lead him to form a relationship something like that of marriage. For he might well wish to arrange a situation in which, in exchange for financial support, he would gain the domestic, sexual and emotional services of a woman on a long-term basis. Marriage is indeed such a relationship. But it is more than that, for marriage has never been a completely private affair, nor even a contract between the two parties. It has always involved the state or the church or some form of public regulation. One of the reasons that the state or, earlier, the church have sought to control weddings and provide for the formal solemnizing and recording of marriages has been that they could not conduct their jurisdiction over property and inheritance unless they could establish who was and who was not married.

Some writers, following Christine Delphy's interpretation of marriage as a unique form of labour contract (Delphy, 1970 and 1976), argue that the basis of the state's involvement is to guarantee, on behalf of men in general, a relationship in which men exploit women. Diana Leonard Barker writes:

The usual reasons advanced to justify legal regulation of, support for, and intervention into marriage and the family, are: the protection of women and children (assuring support obligation and assigning responsibility for child care), ensuring family stability (for the psychic good of all its members, and hence the stability and well-being of the polity), and the promotion of public morality. I suggest that a more important reason for the regulation of marriage – indeed *the* most important reason – is that in supporting marriage the (male) state supports a particular, exploitative relationship between men and women: whereby the wife provides unpaid domestic and sexual services, childbearing and rearing, and wage-earning and contribution to household income when convenient (i.e. her labour for life – with limited rights to quit, and herself as an instrument of production) in exchange for protection, assured upkeep and some rights to children. [Barker, 1978, p. 239 – italics and parentheses in original]

This position is a great advance upon much of what is written on family policy in that it recognizes the family as the prime location of the oppression of women, as the place where the relations of men and women *vis-à-vis* one another are defined. 'Family policy' purports to bolster the family in the interests of women. It is indeed true that marriage can provide certain protective rights for women; but these are best seen as secondary gains in a situation where women are at an overall disadvantage. Thus while in the short run desertion by a husband or widowhood may be a catastrophe, in the long run women as a whole would be better off without the institution of marriage as it stands.

The weakness of this position, however, is that it sees domestic production in marriage relations as a separate form; it does not enable us to raise questions about historical variations in this form as the dominant mode of production changes. The state is seen as a 'male' state, rather than as also, at one time, a feudal state and, at another, a capitalist state; its intervention is therefore in the (presumably unchanging) interests of men.

Nevertheless, writers in this vein have been right to emphasize the important part played by the state in sustaining the family. Hilary Land has done an immense amount of valuable work in exploring both the assumptions behind British family policy and the consequences of it (Land, 1976; Land, 1977; Land and Parker, 1978). She has also argued that the income maintenance system, in particular, assumes that married women will be financially dependent on their husbands. In fact, in 1974, there were in Britain over half a million married couples where the wife was the sole or primary earner, and out of eleven million couples with the husband under sixty-five, there were seven million working wives contributing an average of 25 per cent of the family budget (Hamill, 1976). Yet the massive weight of the official assumption of the economic dependence of wives and cohabiting women must surely play a part in keeping these numbers down: the ineligibility of the wife for many benefits makes it unwise for a couple to rely too heavily on her income (Lister and Wilson, 1976) and makes her more likely to take low-paid work; such provisions as the widow's pension (under both social security and occupational schemes) make it less necessary for a wife to be able to support herself alone.

It is clear, then, that the family household as we know it is not merely the social expression of an instinct but is importantly structured and constrained by state policies. The question is, what function does the state serve in its family policies? Barker, in the passage quoted earlier, says that 'the state supports a particular, exploitative relationship between men and women'. Land and Parker have pointed out that in studying the 'hidden dimensions' of family policies it is

> important to examine and understand the needs and obligations which are presumed to arise from marriage quite separately from those which are presumed to arise from parenthood. If not, the nature of marriage will too often be equated with that of parenthood. [1978, pp. 3-4]

They offer evidence that there are many presumptions that support a specific dependant-breadwinner form of marriage, regardless of whether there are any dependent children or not. A glaring instance is the 'married man's tax allowance', which he receives regardless of whether his wife works or not and regardless of whether there are children or other people in need of care in the household. Unlike Barker, though, they emphasize that:

> At the same time as preserving an unequal marriage relationship social policies which impinge on the family have not been allowed to interfere with work incentives for men. Indeed, we would argue that by assuming an unequal economic relationship between men and women, the man's duty to participate in the labour market is reinforced and although the wife may take paid employment too, her first duty is in caring for her husband, children and sick or elderly relatives. [p. 17]

They thus see a link between the family household and men's wage work in social production and see state policies as being concerned with establishing the link as well as with confirming men's dominant position in the family.

The family household of contemporary capitalist society is very different from that of, say, peasant society, where the family depends for its subsistence directly upon the productive work of its members, rather than upon a wage or wages to purchase needed commodities. The history of the Poor Laws and other 'income maintenance' policies, and the history of the protective legislation (see, for instance, Smelser, 1959) which limited the hours and conditions of women's and children's work in factories during the nineteenth century, are witness to the impact of the wage system, especially in its industrial form, upon the family. They represent the establishment of definitions of mutual financial dependence and of a social separation of 'work' from 'home' which are needed only under a wage system. Though such policies have often been seen by their proponents as attempts to support and defend a timeless family form, rooted in human nature and morality, in fact the end result has been a family form that is specific to capitalism and that changes, too, as capitalism develops.

One important feature of this family household, and the concomitant of the woman's dependence within it, is the woman's work as housewife. Housework, as the production, from commodities purchased with the wages, of use values for private consumption within the household, develops as the almost exclusive province of the wife and as the only productive activity within the household. It becomes rationalized and involves an increasing proportion of commodities (Davidoff, 1976; Ehrenreich and English, 1975). There has been a considerable debate about the analysis of the part played by this domestic labour in the daily reproduction of the husband's labour power. Much of this has revolved around the question of whether domestic labour is productive or unproductive for capital and the implications for the class location of housewives. Undoubtedly the existence of this domestic labour reduces the amount of commodities needed to reproduce the husband's labour power. At any given time, therefore, it reduces the value of these commodities. For instance, men whose jobs take them away from home are usually paid a great deal extra in wages or expenses. Domestic labour therefore helps to keep down the value of labour power, and so keep down wages. But the daily reproduction of the husband's labour power is only one aspect of the relation of the family household to capitalism.

It is, however, striking that, from the point of view of the reproduction of the working class as a whole in capitalism, the family household system is an extremely inadequate one; it may be this that explains both state efforts to force the family into a particular mould and the fact that the state itself undertakes some of these tasks of reproduction.

Even the biological reproduction of future members of the class cannot always be safely left to individuals. In Britain, where very little in the way of explicit population policy has been needed by the state, we are inclined to forget that in many countries the problem of 'underpopulation' or 'overpopulation' has been experienced as acute. Here pronatalist propaganda has been thought sufficient, despite the recommendation of the Royal Commission on Population (1949) that nurseries and maternity leave and benefits would make motherhood more attractive. Yet, writing in France, where policies to combat underpopulation have been given priority, Patrice Grevet (1976, pp. 430 ff.) has argued that there is a law of population specific to the capitalist wage system which tends to produce difficulties in the renewal of generations. The reason, he says, is that the material needs of the child (even for the average family size for renewal) are not recognized in the wage.[6] In certain circumstances, especially as needs and the awareness of needs develop in the monopoly stage of capitalism, this non-recognition results in a low birth rate. Grevet sees this problem of the renewal of generations as an important factor in the interwar crisis of the maintenance system in France, whose solution was to be the beginnings of a comprehensive social security system. Grevet's 'law of population' has, of course, to be seen as a countertendency to the one that Marx wrote of in *Capital*, vol. I, when he pointed out that the working population make some of their own number redundant by producing so much that future production involves more machines and fewer workers:

> The labouring population therefore produces, along with the accumulation of capital produced by it, the means by which itself is made relatively superfluous, is turned into a relative surplus-population; and it does this to an always increasing extent. This is a law of population peculiar to the capitalist mode of production; and in fact every special historic mode of production

6. There is not space here to elaborate Grevet's concept of 'needs'. It is not a biological one, but involves both an objective and a subjective moment, the former resulting from external exigencies connected with the forces of production and social relations, the latter being the conscious reflection of the objective moment. In capitalist society, 'even the limited covering of needs comes through the struggle for wages and other forms of resources for the people, a struggle whch itself presupposes a consciousness of the needs to be satisfied' (Grevet, 1976, p. 65).

has its own special laws of population, historically valid within its limits alone. [Marx, 1970, pp. 631-2]

Immigration, too, may help to solve the problem of the non-renewal of generations. Yet neither the growth of a relative surplus-population (which is in any case valuable to capital in keeping wages down), nor immigration, can explain why Britain has not had the absolute decline in birth rate that France experienced. The state support for an ideology of family and parenthood, especially motherhood, of which Elizabeth Wilson (1977) has written, may well have played a part in making a more explicit population policy and financial subsidies for parenthood unnecessary.

Grevet's idea of the non-recognition of certain needs in the capitalist wage system draws our attention to other ways in which the family is inadequate to the task of making the wage pay for the reproduction of the working class. It would be possible to imagine this task of reproduction being carried out in a world where every member of the class (children, trainees, the sick and disabled, the retired and people engaged in caring for all of these) lived in a household where there was at least one breadwinner permanently in work and where every household had the same ratio of earners to dependants so that a uniform wage could be fixed at such a level as to provide adequate maintenance for all. In practice, however, since not all wage earners have dependants, unless the working class resists, wages can be pushed down to such a level that they will not support them, the wage being just enough to maintain the workers themselves.

Furthermore, there are many would-be breadwinners who are out of work at any given time. These are the 'relative surplus population' of which Marx wrote (1970, p. 640 ff.). Some (the 'floating') may be able to survive because they are unemployed only briefly; others (the 'latent') because they have some source of support, say in agriculture, to which they can return; but others (the 'stagnant') 'dwell in the sphere of pauperism', that is to say they depend upon state support through the provisions of the nineteenth-century Poor Laws or parts of the twentieth-century social security.

Finally, and most importantly, in practice the *family* system of forming households results in a much less tidy pattern than can easily be supported through a wage system. Variations in numbers of children, and the chances of disablement, sickness, longevity and death produce households with very varying needs, in no way related to variations in the wages coming in to them. To a large extent the effects of these variations are simply absorbed by the families concerned. Households with many wage earners and few dependants live fairly well and households with large numbers of children are known to be in the greatest poverty (Child Poverty Action Group, 1976). Within these poor households it is women in particular who suffer since they normally sacrifice more than their share of consumption and have to work harder in order to convert a smaller amount of commodities into as high a standard of living as possible; in addition, they usually have to go out to work, or take in 'out work', in order to raise the household income. There are some social security provisions that serve to iron out some of the differences between family households, though they do not do so very effectively. Among these are child benefits, family income supplements (which, however, only apply where the male in the household is the full-time wage earner), disablement benefits, invalid care allowances, temporary sickness and unemployment benefits. In so far as these are effective at all on a wide scale, they serve to bolster the family household system by dealing with the instances where the needs of the reproduction of the working class are not met by the wage system. In doing so, as has been said earlier, they bolster a specific family household system in which the wife is assumed to be dependent and in which she is assumed to provide household services for all the other members.

The current concern about the 'one-parent family' has focused attention on many of the problems that arise from the attempt to rely on the 'normal' family. The solutions proposed all involve helping this odd family to approximate to the normal one in its effectiveness – to assist the one parent to play the part of two – without making the breaking-up of two-parent families or unmarried motherhood too attractive. The concern is in part a very old one, which flourished in the nineteenth century, about how to provide adequately for all children without encouraging immorality. To say that the emphasis on morality helped to establish a form of household that was as convenient to the capitalist wage system as any family-based household could be is not to deny the morality of female chastity its own dynamic, which could at times go far beyond the call of its duty to capitalism. Similarly today many of the anxieties about provisions for single parents are rooted only in morality; but many, like Sir Keith Joseph's (1972), are genuinely related to the needs of capital. The fear that unmarried women and women who have many children will bring them up less well-suited to modern wage labour is probably well-founded. They become involved in what Joseph called a 'cycle of deprivation'. On the whole, then, the policy will tend to be one of seeking a way to give support to the one-parent family that did not choose it or the 'genuine case of involuntary role-reversal'.[7] It will give minimal support to any who may have chosen to reject the normal pattern. But, above all, it will not encourage alternatives such as public responsibility for children or the disabled.

The extension and intensification of children's dependence upon their parents is a marked feature of the past hundred years. Universal elementary, and later primary and secondary education, made it impossible for children to earn wages or work in any way to support themselves. As long as they continue their education (up to the age of twenty-five or marriage) they are counted as dependants. The means test in grants for students in higher education, for instance, is applied to the parents' income, and unemployed school leavers living with their parents get smaller supplementary benefits than those living away. Children cannot easily be sent to live in another household. They are not company or help to the elderly, they do not care for younger children, they do not work in the home or in anything productive, they cannot be apprenticed until they are sixteen, nor can they be servants. The most usual ways for them to live apart from at least one parent are formalized fostering and adoption, where they are assimilated completely as children of the household. In 1851, in contrast, a large proportion of households contained children who were living with relatives other than their own parents. This pattern was a common one, probably in situations where the mother was unmarried, or had remarried, or where she was dead (Anderson, 1971, p. 84 ff.). A major reason why single motherhood is such a burden is the total dependence of children in the present period. The non-recognition of their needs by the state is premised on an assumption that in 'normal' cases there will be two parents to shoulder this dependence – the one financially, the other practically – and that this is viable.

Old age and the disablement of men are the two situations where the state has to some extent recognized needs unmet by the wage system and allowed the principle of individual dependence on the state regardless of household circumstances. In the case of old age, this has in part been made necessary by the fact that the practice of supporting old parents, of sharing a household with them if they had nothing to contribute, has never been a universal one in Britain (Anderson, 1971). Nevertheless the state pensions for the retired

7. This phrase is used in a letter from Brian O'Malley, Minister of State at the Department of Health and Social Security, to the Women's Liberation Campaign for Legal and Financial Independence, 14 May 1975.

and disabled have always been barely adequate for financial support. In practice, an enormous amount of care and domestic servicing is provided for the old and disabled by the women in their families, especially their daughters and their daughters-in-law (Land and Parker, 1978; Cartwright *et al.*, 1973; Moroney, 1976). About a quarter of old people are now in the same household as their children (Central Statistical Office, 1975, p. 78). The state provision for these needs takes the form only of institutions which appear to be planned as places of last resort.

Unemployment benefits and supplementary benefits represent, among other things, a partial state recognition of the needs, unrecognized in the wage system, arising from Marx's 'floating' and 'stagnant' reserve army of labour. But these benefits are not merely substitute wages for those who cannot find work. Women living with their husbands or lovers and school leavers living with their parents do not have the same benefit rights as men. A woman in such a situation cannot claim supplementary benefit at all; she can only claim unemployment benefit if she has paid full contributions rather than take the 'married women's option' (now being phased out, but formerly very common) to pay a tiny amount, and her benefit even then covers only herself and not her husband or her children. The benefits are thus largely geared to the needs of the *male* members of the industrial reserve army and their dependants, rather than to the needs of any workers who are not employed.

In various and piecemeal ways, then, state policy has sought, sometimes unsuccessfully, to remedy the fact that the family household system is inadequate for mediating the wage and the reproduction of the working class. It has always done so in such a way as to sustain that family system of a male breadwinner, dependent children and a dependent wife responsible for domestic and childrearing work. Where this would be seriously threatened, the needs have remained unmet.

Grevet does not introduce the notion of needs unrecognized by the wage system in order to examine family policy. He himself is concerned with a much wider problem: that of the growing need for collective forms of consumption, as, with the development of technology and the division of labour, people's needs become more diversified, more subject to risk and longer in phase, so that things like education, housing, health protection and transportation of people cannot be provided through a wage system in which labour power is purchased for only a brief period (Grevet, 1976, p. 120). He argues that in the stage of state monopoly capitalism, not only has state financing of the military and of research grown, along with state financing of production:

> But another public financing of consumption has played a growing role, under pressure from the people. This is the public financing of personal consumption: *education, health, housing, social security,* etc. This financing temporarily resolves the contradiction between the character of labour power as a commodity and the growth of needs that take more and more socialized forms. It intervenes directly in establishing new conditions of the productivity, the demand and the maintenance of labour power. [p. 324, my translation]

What Grevet refers to as 'collective consumption' has also had a very particular relation to the family. Its introduction is frequently accomplished with an ideology that retains a definition of the need as one that, in some sense, *should* be served by the family – and especially by the wife-mother. This idea that the family is the proper location of these needs can often be found in linguistic usage. One has only to think, in the commercial sphere, of the name 'Mother's Pride' for white, sliced, factory-baked bread or, in the sphere of the state, of the French *école maternelle* for a nursery school. Functionalist sociology reflects this ideology with its picture of a pre-industrial family of a multi-functional type and a complex internal structure transformed in the course of industrialization into a simpler structure with an irreducible minimum of functions: 'stable satisfaction of sex need, production and rearing of children, and provision of a home', according to MacIver and Page (1950, p. 264). In this picture, the functions remain the same – they are the requisites of all societies – but, with the advent of industrialization and the general evolutionary tendency towards the increasing complexity of overall structure and the increasing structural simplicity and functional specificity of parts, they are 'taken over' from the family by various specialized institutions, frequently ones that are related in the state. (For a full critique of these theories, see Morgan [1975].) The image of functions that once belonged to the family being taken over by the state is a very powerful one. The different functions vary in the degree to which their removal from the family is seen as being legitimate. Land and Parker (1978) have pointed out that the removal of education of small children is legitimate, whereas the removal of care is not, so that the state provision for the under-fives is largely in the form of nursery schools, whereas other forms of day care (nurseries and child minders) are largely private.

Child care (both preschool and during times when the schools are closed or the child is unwell) is indeed an example of the nature of state involvement with the family. In the period since the Second World War there has been a reaction against the policy of placing children from broken or incompetent homes in institutions, and immense efforts have been made by the new breed of social workers, caseworkers, using watered-down psychoanalytic theory, to enable these children to live in their mothers' homes and to persuade mothers to take responsibility for them in the officially approved manner (Wilson, 1977, p. 84 ff.). 'Shared care' – the care of children and other dependants shared between social agencies and the family – is a concept that has been discussed in social policy circles recently but that has little relation to practice. '... the state (both centrally and locally) has hitherto tended *either* to assume responsibility for child care *or* to leave the family to cope as best it can until crisis or tragedy occur' (Land and Parker, 1977; italics in original).

The health services, on the other hand, represent a more thoroughgoing 'takeover' by state institutions. Tasks that were carried out at home by women have been replaced by professional activities in clinics and hospitals. Most babies are born in hospital; the home confinement attended by a midwife is a declining practice. Ante-natal and post-natal care, and regular check-ups in schools, have made health a matter of professional expertise from an early age. Many senile people are looked after in hospitals, subject to geriatric care for a medical or psychiatric condition rather than in suitably organized old people's homes. Yet even this extensive change still wears the ideological garb of a 'takeover'. The recent cutbacks in public spending have revealed that when the money is not available for state provision, the responsibility for many fringe forms of care 'reverts' to women relatives (Counter Information Services, 1976, p. 27; Moroney, 1976). When homes for the old or the handicapped are not provided, or when schools work half days because they do not have enough teachers, these people who need supervision and care are sent 'home' and women have to give up wage work or work odd hours in order to be with them. The policy of 'community care' for the mentally ill, as embodied in the Mental Health Act of 1959, was a longer-term policy that reduced state expenditure (as well as the evil effects of institutionalization) by keeping hospital stays as short as possible and getting relatives – again mainly women – to provide care, with social work support, during periods when the patient's symptoms were controlled by drugs.

Thus, given the ideology that these forms of care belong in the family, the ultimate possibility of these aspects of reproduction being organized through the family household remains. The family is ever ready to provide care for dependants: the men to spread their wage a little further (though pensions often help to make this less necessary), the women to take on an extra burden of emotional and practical servicing.[8]

III

It is not necessary to argue here that women's – and above all married women's – place in wage labour is that of a reserve army. As far as the state is concerned, there are two aspects of this analysis that need to be developed: state participation in determining the conditions of employment and state participation in maintaining a situation in which married women are only semi-proletarianized.

The question of the conditions of employment raises a number of analytical problems that are not yet resolved. On the one hand the Sex Discrimination Act (1975), in breaking down occupational segregation, appears to make women more readily substitutable for men and therefore to enhance their usefulness as a reserve army, by locating throughout the occupational structure those workers who can both help in keeping the general level of wages down and be more easily laid off. Some problems of occupational segregation and the reserve army have been discussed by Milkman (1976). On the other hand we know that an Act geared to equality of opportunity for individuals and with almost no enforcement procedure other than an inadequate one of individual complaints is likely to have very little effect on occupational segregation. Or again, on the one hand the Employment Protection Act (1976), under which the jobs of some women have to be kept open for them when they have babies, appears to make women less easily disposed of by employers. On the other hand, the provisions only apply where the worker has been employed for two years or more, a condition that probably one half of women workers can satisfy, precisely because of their 'reserve army' character. These contradictory implications of recent state policies affecting women wage workers suggest that the state does not play a significant role in establishing the conditions of employment that permit or inhibit the

8. David (1978) has a much more sophisticated discussion of the complexities of the relations of family to education system.

use of married women as a reserve army of labour. Much more important are the various endeavours of trade unions and employers and the changes in the labour process discussed by Beechey (1977).

The other aspect of women's position in the labour market relates again to the family household system examined in the last section. For as well as being a system through which women's work contributes to the reproduction of the working class as a whole, it is also one of mutual financial dependence, which means that married women are not dependent on their own wage for the costs of the reproduction of their labour power. This enables them to be paid wages that are below the value of their labour power (Beechey, 1977) and it also enables them to 'disappear almost without trace back into the family' when they are redundant to waged employed.

In this last respect they provide an interesting parallel and contrast with Marx's example (an agricultural labouring population) of his concept of 'a constant latent surplus-population' (Marx, 1970, p. 642). For Marx saw these wage labourers as no longer needed with the increasing mechanization of agriculture and 'therefore constantly on the point of passing over into an urban or manufacturing proletariat'. The extent of the surplus population, he said, 'becomes evident only when its channels of outlet open to exceptional width'. So, too, do many married women remain only latent proletarians, not entering the statistics of the 'economically active' until there are job openings available to them. But in Marx's example, the process of primitive accumulation in agriculture as well as of the self-reproduction of capital in manufacturing play a part in the constitution of this element of the surplus population. The first provides a source that is 'constantly flowing'; the second results in both attraction and repulsion as effects of the expansion of capital and of its rising organic composition. In the case of married women, the attraction and repulsion of workers by modern capitalism (and, by repercussion, non-capitalist employment) is still relevant. The attraction-repulsion produces varied needs for labour power at different times and places and this is one of the reasons why a reserve army of labour is needed, as well as how it is produced. However, married women are not a source that is constantly flowing or awaiting transformation from a latent situation to a proletarian one. Rather they are constantly flowing to and fro, sometimes latently at home or semi-employed, sometimes fully employed, but never fully proletarian in the sense of being entirely dependent on wage labour for their livelihood. For, unlike agricultural labourers in Marx's day, they are not less

and less needed in their sphere of latency, for there are no overall
.changes in the family household system but those originating in the
capitalist sphere or indirectly in response to changes there.

The question of the role of the state is thus a particularly
significant one, because the state can initiate or guide changes in
the family household system in relation to capital's need for the
labour power of married women as well as in relation to the
reproduction of the class in general.[9] The immensely expanded
welfare services during the Second World War are an example of
this (Titmuss, 1950; Wilson, 1977, ch. 7). In part, improved
provisions for diet, health, mother-and-baby clinics and so forth
were a response to a new recognition of the unfitness of many
working-class people revealed by military service and evacuation;
in part provisions like residential nurseries were an attempt to deal
with the problems of family break-up which evacuation and
military service brought about; but to a large extent, day nurseries,
canteens and better maternity services were the price that had to
be paid to draw married women into war work. The state provided
these alternatives and aids to women's work in the household not
just because of changed needs in the reproduction of the working
class, but also because these women were needed for waged
labour. There is dispute as to the extent to which the social policy
introduced in wartime initiated permanent changes in welfare
provisions. It is certain, though, that the taking over of practical
servicing was largely reversed in the postwar period. While the
financial support provided by the social security system may have
been consolidated as a result of wartime experience, women's
household work was re-established in the late 1940s and 1950s,
often with considerable effort by state agencies as well as by
ideologues like John Bowlby.

Women's dependence on their husbands makes them very
suitable as a latent reserve of labour. But apart from such massive
upheavals as those of wartime, this dependence is not open to
short-term manipulation by the state. On its own it would sustain
a latent reserve that could respond simply to openings in the labour
market. However, it has been shown earlier that in practice many
women do not have husbands who can be depended on. For these
women, as for any people who have no one to depend on, the state
provides if they are not employed. For these women the conditions
of state provision establish their relation to the labour market: a

9. A comparable analysis of the reserve army of African labour in South Africa has been
made by Legassick and Wolpe (1977). They see the state policy of creating Bantustans in
much the same way as the state policy of supporting families is described here.

generous and unconditioned provision could keep them out of employment altogether; a meagre provision could force them to seek employment at whatever wages; a provision conditional on, say, having household responsibility could force some to look for work and enable others to stay at home. This area of welfare policy is therefore potentially a fairly flexible instrument keeping women more or less in reserve for wage labour.

Norman Ginsburg (1977) sees one of the main functions of poor relief and social insurance expenditures and administrations as being 'reconstructing labour and reproducing the front-line of the industrial reserve army of labour'. The Poor Law Amendment Act of 1834 played an important part in the creation of a proletariat dependent on wages for its livelihood, for it sought to eliminate any poor relief at levels higher than local wages or under conditions as attractive as those of the free wage labourer. At various periods women have been differentiated into categories and differentiated from men. Those defined as 'undeserving' or those for whom it was thought a 'liable relative' should be responsible could be subjected either to the 'workhouse test' or to the test of their willingness to seek work (Thane, 1977). Such people would presumably constitute the front line of the reserve army, or what Marx called the 'floating' element. Others, like the widowed mothers of young children, have nearly always qualified for outdoor (unconditional) relief, and only the inadequacy of the payments would make them want to take paid work at all. A more detailed historical analysis, relating changes in the organization of welfare payments to women to changes in the labour requirements of capital, needs to be done; the materials are there (see, for instance, Webb and Webb, 1910; Finer and McGregor, 1974; Thane, 1977) but they have not yet been analysed in this way.

It is possible to summarize the present situation as one in which:

(1) Women living with husbands or male sexual partners are assumed by the state to be dependent upon them (and so either *are* dependent on them or are forced to work at, possibly, very disadvantageous rates of pay).

(2) Women living with their children and without a man, and some other older widows, are supposed to be allowed to depend on state payments without being expected to seek work. In practice, however, they are often under pressure to accept jobs (Marsden, 1973).

(3) Most other women are required to seek work or prove

disablement, as (almost) all men are, before they can get either contributory or supplementary benefits.

When unemployed, the first two categories may be said to constitute a 'latent' reserve army and the third a 'floating' one.

IV

Up till now in this paper, the different ways in which the state contributes to sustaining systems of family household and wage labour in which women are oppressed have been described as functional for capital – as providing part of the social conditions for the accumulation of capital. There are certain dangers in this kind of 'marxist functionalism', as indeed in any form of functionalism, and so it is necessary to point out how the analysis here avoids these dangers. The great weakness of functionalism is that it presents a picture of society as an integrated whole in which any disturbances are met by equilibrating and adaptive mechanisms, so that the general tendency is towards equilibrium rather than disequilibrium. By contrast, in marxist theory, the social formation (particularly in its capitalist form), whilst conceived as an integrated whole, none the less contains internal contradictions of ever-increasing severity. These ultimately result in the destruction of the formation and its transformation into something new.

However, since the fundamental contradictions in society are found in the mode of production and since the tenets of materialism require that analysis ultimately relates all elements of the social formation to the economic level (even if the relation is conceived as one of relative autonomy), marxist statements on particular social developments often run the risk of taking a non-dialectical form, explaining them simply as serving certain 'needs of capital'. Paul Corrigan has pointed out that such forms of marxist functionalism in the study of the 'welfare state' have curious political implications:

> if we accept that welfare is controlled by capital and acts against the welfare of working people, then why should we fight the cuts? We should welcome them ... as a direct cut in the power of the ruling class over the working class. [Corrigan, 1977, p. 88]

The corresponding political positions are 'always negative and utopian', since, under capitalism, welfare can only serve the needs of the ruling class.

There are two common ways of introducing a dialectical element into the analysis. One is to reassert the fundamental contradictions of the mode of production – to point out, for instance, that the accumulation of capital intensifies the contradiction between the social character of production and the private character of appropriation. But this does not really help in making a more politically useful analysis, since it still provides no space for welfare politics, or education politics, or women's politics within capitalism. The other common way is to counterpose working-class struggle to ruling-class efforts to satisfy the 'needs of capital' and to see social policies as ways of guaranteeing the social conditions for the reproduction of capital whose specific forms are the outcome of class struggle. To some extent working-class struggle is the other side of the medal of functionalism. For if school dinners or a national health service help keep the working class healthy, they fulfil aspirations of the class as well as merely help to reproduce it; or, if welfare payments are used to damp down the fires of working-class protests, they can be seen as an achievement of that protest. The value of introducing the idea of class struggle can only be seen in concrete analyses of specific situations. Corrigan argues that Marx's discussion of the Factory Acts in *Capital*, vol. I, is a detailed analysis that unravels the various results (in the *form* that the legislation took) of a complex class struggle at a specific stage in the development of capitalist production.

Another problem that needs to be approached in this way is that of the historical determination of the value of labour power. Indeed, one of the questions that is central to the theme of this paper but has not yet been adequately analysed is whether the value of labour power includes the cost of reproducing the worker alone or the entire family of the worker. This is not a theoretical question but an historical one, since the value of labour power is socially determined by the class struggle and is different at different times. Jane Humphries (1977, pp. 247 ff.) argues that the 'family wage' for the married man, and his wife and children staying at home, was a goal and to some extent an achievement of working-class struggle during the nineteenth century.

The analysis in this paper points to further contradictions of a different sort: those between the sphere of the family and the sphere of capitalist production. Thus, it has been argued here that a specific form of family household (in which there is joint consumption based on the income from a limited number of wage earners and the domestic labour of a wife and in which the wife is, or can be, a dependant) functions broadly both with respect to the reproduction of the working class and with respect to maintaining married women as a latent reserve army of labour. It has been further argued that the state plays a vital part in sustaining this form of family household or in providing substitute support that approximates to it in its effects. Yet at any given conjuncture there may well be contradiction between the state policies needed for the reproduction of the class and those needed for reproducing the relation of women as a reserve army.

For example, pronatalist policies, or policies geared to combating child poverty may suggest child benefits and large-family benefits at such a level that mothers – and sometimes even fathers – of large families do not find it worthwhile to go out to work at the available low wages. Another example: when the expansion of production calls for an increase in the size of the labour force, wages may increase; but this means that in each family the man's wages have gone up and it may be less necessary for the woman to go out to work; in this case the reserve army, instead of advancing to the front, goes into retreat.

The key problem is the relative inflexibility of the family, as a social institution structured by ideologies of human nature, tradition, religion and so on, as well as by state policy. A pure functionalist analysis might lead to the conclusion that 'if the basis for the present family household form had not existed when capitalism emerged, it would have had to be invented'. The implication of the argument presented here, on the other hand, is that it would be possible to imagine systems for the reproduction of the working class and systems for sustaining reserve armies of labour that would function more effectively for capitalism. This is not to suggest, however, that there is any tendency to move from the present position towards any such imaginable systems.

A problem that has preoccupied feminist thought is whether there is any tendency within capitalism towards the socialization of domestic labour. The question may be interpreted in a number of different ways and the analysis presented here should help to clarify some of the issues. In one interpretation the question is a spurious one: in so far as this labour is domestic it is private and cannot be social.[10] In another, it is a belated one: the increasing use of commodities, both as raw materials and as instruments of

10. This seems to be the position of Adamson *et al.* (1976) who offer a very interesting discussion of the debate on domestic labour and women's oppression, but ultimately simply *assert* that domestic labour cannot be socialized under capitalism.

production, in the home testifies to the increasing component of 'dead' social labour in domestic production. Yet, as the demands made on them rise, women continue to spend long hours in domestic labour. In a third interpretation, the 'taking over' of certain functions by the state from the family constitutes a form of socialization. Yet this 'taking over' is either provisional in nature or else involves newly developed kinds of activity like specialized education or advanced medical care in hospitals.

At some periods, such as wartime, the state may take over more activities from women in the household, in order to free them for wage labour. At other periods there may be a shortage of labour in social production and if women's wages are sufficiently high, they may be able to afford more 'convenience goods' and 'labour saving devices' produced as commodities by capitalist enterprise (often, indeed, by the wage labour of the same women). In general, however, unpaid domestic labour reduces the value of labour power, so that maintaining the system in which it is performed benefits capital.

As well as the various contradictory tendencies found in the two systems that relate to the oppression of women, there are other more general contradictions such as those relating to the 'welfare state' in general, which affect these two systems. In this paper it has been assumed that the state simply steps in to maintain the social conditions of reproduction. Yet in doing so it is undertaking expenditure and thus performing an economic function.[11] From a feminist point of view, it is not merely the size but also the consequences of such state expenditure for sexual divisions that become objects of struggle.

If this paper can contribute anything towards guiding such struggle, it is in showing the ambiguities involved in the state support of a system of family households which can be dependent on a male wage and in which women carry out domestic production and servicing. This household system mediates the individual worker's wage for the reproduction of the working class as a whole; as such it is supported by the state. Yet since, for historical and ideological reasons, it is formed on a kinship basis, it is always inadequate to performing this function fully; the state then provides substitutes for the wage where this is missing. At the same

11. There is, at present, dispute between neo-Richardians (Gough, 1977) and marxists (e.g., Fine and Harris, 1977) about the analysis of the 'social wage'. Gough sees this as similar to the ordinary wage and equally an object of class struggle. Fine and Harris argue a similar position to that of this paper: that the 'social wage' is not a wage at all, in the sense of being an exchange for equivalent labour power, but, unlike the wage, is primarily the outcome of political struggle.

time, the fact that married women can often fall back on dependence on a man's wage keeps them semi-proletarianized, enabling them to serve as a very flexible latent reserve army of wage labour. Yet the varying need for women in wage labour is unlikely to coincide with the rather less varying need for them in the domestic labour of reproducing the working class. Such contradictions mean that there are always a number of conflicting principles articulated in state policy, so that there is always room for change.

References

Adamson, O., Brown, C., Harrison, J., and Price, J. (1976), 'Women's Oppression under Capitalism', *Revolutionary Communist*, no. 5, pp. 2-48.

Althusser, L. (1971), 'Ideology and Ideological State Apparatuses', in *Lenin and Philosophy and Other Essays*, New Left Books, London.

Anderson, M. (1971), 'Family, Housework and the Industrial Revolution', in *Sociology of the Family*, Penguin, Harmondsworth.

Anderson, M. (1972), *Family Structure in Nineteenth Century England*, Cambridge University Press.

Barker, D. L. (1978), 'The Regulation of Marriage: Repressive Benevolence', in Littlejohn *et al.* (1978).

Beechey, V. (1977), 'Female Wage Labour in Capitalist Production', *Capital and Class*, no. 3, pp. 45-66.

Cartwright, A., Hockey, L. and Anderson, J. L. (1978), *Life Before Death*, Routledge and Kegan Paul, London.

Central Statistical Office (1975), *Social Trends*, no. 6, HMSO, London.

Child Poverty Action Group (1976), *Child Benefit Now*, CPAG, London.

Corrigan, P. (1977), 'The Welfare State as an Arena of Class Struggle', *Marxism Today*, vol. 21, pp. 87-93.

Coulson, Margaret (1974), 'The Family and the Sexual Division of Labour in Capitalism', paper presented at the British Sociological Association annual conference.

Counter Information Services (1976), *Crisis: Women Under Attack*, CIS, London.

David, M. E. (1978), 'The State, Education and the Family', in Littlejohn *et al.* (1978).

Davidoff, L. (1976), 'The Rationalisation of Housework', in D. L. Barker and S. Allen, *Dependence and Exploitation in Work and Marriage*, Longman, London.

Delphy, C. (1970), 'L'ennemi principal', *Partisans*, no. 54-5; translated as 'The Main Enemy', in *The Main Enemy: a Materialist Analysis of Women's Oppression*, Women's Research and Resources Centre, London, 1977.

Delphy, C. (1976), 'Continuities and Discontinuities in Marriage and Divorce', in D. L. Barker and S. Allen, *Sexual Divisions and Society*, Tavistock, London.

Ehrenreich, B. and English, D. (1975), 'The Manufacture of Housework', *Socialist Revolution*, no. 26, pp. 5-40.

Engels, F. (1975), *Selected Works of Marx and Engels*, Progress Publishers, Moscow.

Fine, B. and Harris, L. (1977), 'State Expenditure in Advanced Capitalism: a Critique', *New Left Review*, no. 98, pp. 97-112.

Finer, M. and McGregor, O. R. (1974), 'The History of the Obligation to Maintain', in *Report of the Committee on One-parent Families*, vol. 2, HMSO, London.

Fox, G. (1977), 'Nice Girl: Social Control of Women through a Value Construct', *Signs: Journal of Women in Culture and Society*, vol. 2, pp. 805-17.

Ginsburg, N. (1977), 'Poor Relief: the Development of State Policy in the Context of Class Struggle and Struggle for Accumulation', paper presented at the Conference of Socialist Economists, July.

Gough, I. (1976), 'State Expenditure in Advanced Capitalism', *New Left Review*, no. 92, pp. 53-92.

Grevet, P. (1976), *Besoins populaires et financement publique*, Éditions Sociales, Paris.

Hamill, L. (1976), 'Wives as Sole and Joint Breadwinners', paper presented at the SSRC Social Security Research Workshop.

Himmelweit, S. and Mohun, S. (1977), 'Domestic Labour and Capital', *Cambridge Journal of Economics*, vol. 1, pp. 15-31.

Hirst, P. Q. (1976), 'Althusser's Theory of Ideology', *Economy and Society*, vol. 5, pp. 385-412.

Humphries, J. (1977), 'Class Struggle and the Persistence of the Working-class Family', *Cambridge Journal of Economics*, vol. 1, pp. 241-58.

Joseph, Sir K. (1972), speech to the Pre-school Playgroups Association, 29 June.

Land, H. (1976), 'Women: Supporters or Supported?', in D. L. Barker and S. Allen, *Sexual Divisions and Society: Process and Change*, Tavistock, London.

Land, H. (1977), 'Social Security and the Division of Unpaid Work in the Home and Paid Employment in the Labour Market', in Department of Health and Social Security, *Social Security Research Seminar*, HMSO, London.

Land, H. and Parker, R. (1978), 'Family Policies in Britain: the Hidden Dimensions', in J. Kahn and S. B. Kammerman, *Family Policy*, Columbia University Press, New York.

Legassick, M. and Wolpe, H. (1977), 'The Bantustans and Capital Accumulation in South africa', *Review of African Political Economy*, no. 7, pp. 87-107.

Lister, R. and Wilson, L. (1976), *The Unequal Breadwinner*, National Council for Civil Liberties, London.

Littlejohn, G., Wakeford, J., Smart, B. and Yuval-Davis, N. (1978), *Power and the State*, Croom Helm, London.

MacIver, R. M., and Page, C. H. (1950), *Society: an Introductory Analysis*, Macmillan, London.

Marsden, D. (1973), *Mothers Alone*, Penguin, Harmondsworth.

Marx, K. (1970), *Capital*, vol. I, Lawrence and Wishart, London.

Marx, K. (1972), *Capital*, vol. II, Lawrence and Wishart, London.

Milkman, R. (1976), 'Women's Work and the Economic Crisis: Some Lessons of the Great Depression', *Review of Radical Political Economy*, vol. 8, pp. 73-97.

Morgan, D. H. J. (1975), *Social Theory and the Family*, Routledge and Kegan Paul, London.

Moroney, R. M. (1976), *The Family and the State: Considerations for Social Policy*, Longman, London.

Royal Commission on Population (1949), *Report*, HMSO, London.

Smart, C. (1976), *Women, Crime and Criminology*, Routledge and Kegan Paul, London.

Smelser, N. J. (1959), *Social Change in the Industrial Revolution*, Routledge and Kegan Paul, London.

Snäre, A. and Steng-Dahl, T. (1978), 'The Coercion of Privacy', in C. Smart and B. Smart, *Women, Sex and Social Control*, Routledge and Kegan Paul, London.

Thane, P. (1977), 'Women and State "Welfare" in Victorian and Edwardian England', paper presented at the SSRC Social Security Research Workshop.

Titmuss, R. M. (1975), *Problems of Social Policy, U.K. History of the Second World War*, HMSO, London.

Webb, B. and Webb, S. (1910), *English Poor Law Policy*, Longman, London.

Wilson, E. (1977), *Women and the Welfare State*, Tavistock, London.

Marcia Millman

Images of Deviant Men and Women

From Marcia Millman, 'She Did it All for Love: a Feminist View of the Sociology of Deviance', in M. Millman and R. Kanter, eds., *Another Voice: Feminist Perspectives on Social Life and Social Science*, New York: Doubleday, 1975, pp. 255-79

Daniel Bell's essay 'Crime as an American Way of Life' (1960) is one of the best-known functionalist explanations of deviance (in functionalist theory the existence and persistence of deviant activity is analyzed in terms of its contribution to the ongoing social order). Bell argued convincingly that organized crime in America served several 'useful' purposes: for example, it provided Italian immigrants and their children a ladder of social and political mobility (otherwise closed to them) that would bring them into respectable middle-class life styles. One of the striking aspects of Bell's essay is that he portrays the racketeers and leaders of organized crime as not only loyal and helpful to their ethnic group, but also as brilliant, witty, and personally appealing characters. For example, he points out how one innovative gambling figure was more effective than the entire American military system:

> The racing-wire news service got started in the twenties through the genius of the late Moe Annenberg, who had made a fearful reputation for himself as Hearst's circulation manager in the rough-and-tough Chicago newspaper wars. Annenberg conceived of the idea of a telegraphic news service which would gather information from tracks and shoot it immediately to scratch sheets, horse parlors, and bookie joints. In some instances, track owners gave Annenberg the rights to send news from tracks; more often, the news was simply 'stolen' by crews operating inside or near the tracks. So efficient did this news distribution system become, that in 1942, when a plane knocked out a vital telegraph circuit which served an Air Force field as well as the gamblers, the Continental Press managed to get its racing wire service for gamblers resumed in fifteen minutes, while it took the Fourth Army, which was responsible for the defense of the entire West Coast, something like three hours. [1960, p. 134]

And finally, in addition to genius, sophistication, and loyalty to their ethnic group, Bell lets us know how funny and charming these crime figures could be. He tells of one gambler's answer to the Kefauver investigating committee that was trying to prove there was a national crime syndicate: 'As the loquacious late Willie Moretti of New Jersey said, in explaining how he had met the late Al Capone at a race track, "Listen, well-charactered people you don't need introductions to; you just meet automatically."' (1960, p. 140)

We should keep in mind the appealing portraits that Bell drew of his deviant characters when we later contrast it with another functionalist explanation of deviance, namely, Kingsley Davis's essay on prostitution.

Another example of how sociologists may identify with their deviant subjects[1] (and highlight the subjects' attractive features) can be drawn from Howard Becker's study *Outsiders* (1963), of marijuana smokers and jazz musicians; Becker's study is considered to be one of the most important works emerging from the currently popular 'labeling' school of deviance. (The labeling school, or 'interactionist' perspective, argues that deviance is not in any intrinsic qualities of actors or behavior, but rather occurs when an action gets labeled as deviant; consequently, sociologists of this persuasion study the interactions surrounding the labeling of deviance and the official caretakers and caretaking institutions: police, judges, psychiatrists and prisons, courts and mental hospitals.) No special perceptiveness is required to recognize the identification between Becker and his subjects, for Becker tells us that he did his research while working as a jazz musician himself. Just as Trilling described the modern literary hero as beyond the moral imperatives of ordinary persons because of his unusual talent or sensitivity, so does Becker tell us (sympathetically) that jazz musicians consider themselves to be more sensitive, gifted, and even sexier than ordinary men: 'The musician thus sees himself as a creative artist who should be free from outside control, a person different from and better than those outsiders he calls squares....' (1963, p. 91). Becker describes how the wives of jazz musicians try to force their husbands to give up the work they love in favor of conventional jobs. Becker quotes one of his subjects:

Man, my wife's a great chick, but there's no way for us to stay together, not as long as I'm in the music business. No way, no

1. For a more critical treatment of Becker's identification with 'underdogs', see Alvin Gouldner's essay (1963).

way at all. When we first got married it was great, I was working in town, making good gold, everybody was happy. But when that job was through, I didn't have anything. Then I got an offer to go on the road. Well, hell, I needed the money, I took it. Sally said, 'No, I want you here in town, with me.' She'd sooner have me go to work in a factory! Well, that's a bunch of crap. So I just left with the band. Hell, I like the business too much, I'm not gonna put it down for her or any woman. [1963, p. 117]

But some of Becker's musicians capitulate to their wives and compromise their talents and values; they go commercial:

If you want to keep on working, you have to put up with some crap once in a while.... I don't care. I've got a wife and I want to keep working. If some square comes up and asks me to play the 'Beer Barrel Polka' I just smile and play it. [1963, p. 118]

I don't wish to say that sociologists should be criticized for their identifications and sympathies with their subjects (although these tend to create problems of omission, as I shall show later). On the contrary, studies like Bell's and Becker's are excellent partly because they do succeed in presenting an interior view of their subjects' lives. My point is rather that it is only male deviants who have been studied with such empathy and appreciation. We might also note that the underworlds and subcultures that Becker and Bell describe apparently consist of men only, and women appear in these worlds, and hence in these studies, only in degraded and unpleasant positions.

Since there haven't been many sociologists who take note of women as deviants, women have largely been ignored in the literature or else abandoned to a few deviant categories (mental illness, prostitution, shoplifting) hard to glamorize (with the potential exception of prostitution) the way male deviant occupations are glamorized. It is difficult to imagine mentally ill women running together in gangs and having a lot of fun (though some might disagree), but, then again, in real life, juvenile delinquents probably don't have all that much fun either. A glance through any textbook or collection of articles demonstrates that in many areas of deviance that might just as logically talk about women as about men (for example, alcoholism or drug addiction), the writer has usually either studied only men or spoken as if his subjects were all male. Since prostitution is the only 'female' recognized area of deviance that has the potential for presenting portraits of its subjects as exciting and fascinating as most 'male' deviant occupations, we may usefully look at important or representative examples of sociological studies of prostitution, bearing in mind the male counterparts we have just reviewed.[2]

Perhaps the best-known sociological analysis of prostitution is Kingsley Davis's functionalist argument (1966) that prostitution is allowed to endure because it actually protects conventional institutions such as marriage. As Matza observed (1969), one of the contributions of functionalist theory to the study of deviance was the insight that there is much surprising 'overlap' between deviant and conventional behavior (for example, in his essay that we considered earlier, Daniel Bell compared organized crime to organized business in America). Since prostitution is an occupation, the most obvious point of 'overlap' with conventional life should have been on the basis of similarities with conventional occupations. But the tendency for sexual stereotyping was so strong that sociologists like Davis showed the overlap of prostitution with conventional life not through occupational similarities but only through sexual behavior. Davis (1966, p. 349) pointed out that conventional wives, like prostitutes, traded sexual favors for economic support, and Edwin Lemert (1951, p. 238) later extended the comparison to other conventional women whom he claimed used sexuality for economic purposes: the 'shopgirls who have sex relations in return for a dinner and a show from their dates obviously are employing sex as a means to certain material goals'. It was not until much later that a male sociologist[3] discovered that the 'overlap' between prostitution and conventionality could be drawn to include the professions; in this insight David Matza added to Lemert's analysis:

... If one omits the reference to the sexual act – the special province of prostitution – the elements of Lemert's conception suggest a similarity not limited to feminine activity. The rendering of a service for fee, the absence of discrimination in the choice of clientele (universalism), and a dissociation of deeper feelings from the service rendered (affective neutrality), are among the key elements of what is mainly a masculine activity – profession. There should be nothing surprising about

2. Of course, the other major area of 'female' designated deviance is mental illness. I have chosen to skip the literature on this subject since it is too vast to treat here and because there are several feminist critiques of the literature on women and mental illness. See Pauline Bart (1970, 1971, 1974) and Phyllis Chesler (1973).

3. Matza's statement is the strongest, but actually in an earlier article another sociologist, Travis Hirschi (1962), also made the point that the frequent comparison to marriage obscures the similarity of prostitution with other occupations.

this similarity: Prostitution is among the oldest of professions; and professionals always fear prostituting themselves. [1969, p. 84]

Since Bell's and Davis's essays are among the best known of functionalist studies of deviance, it is interesting to compare their respective portraits of the deviant subjects. We observed earlier that Bell presents his 'criminals' as likable, brilliant, interesting men. This is partly due to the fact that Bell selects some of the more colorful and outstanding characters of the underworld and quotes from their own words about their activities. In contrast, Davis never singles out specific prostitutes (although undoubtedly in the history of prostitution there must have been many interesting and appealing characters) in his analysis, and he certainly never quotes any prostitutes. His essay is only about prostitution (and not prostitutes), while Bell manages to interest us in the racketeer and gambler as well as in organized crime. Female deviants cannot appear as interesting, complicated, or even comprehensible when they are merely assigned to anonymous and passive membership in a category.

But how have prostitutes fared in more contemporary studies? There is no study of prostitution from the 'labeling' tradition of equal importance to Becker's study of jazz musicians. But some attention has been paid to prostitutes by sociologists with this orientation. One of the aspects of deviance that has been focused upon by labeling theorists is the world of the deviant subculture. The attention to subculture is related to an effort to return to the old Chicago school's commitment to present the subject's own view of the world and to demonstrate that deviants are not isolated figures but have friends, associates, and social worlds with their rules and regulations like anyone else. It is all the more noteworthy that even when a male sociologist from this persuasion sets out to study prostitute subcultures, the sexual stereotype of women as competitive and unable to create group culture and solidarity apparently outweighs the investigator's ability to discover group life. One recent study of apprenticeship and ideology among prostitutes, for example (Bryan, 1973), claims that prostitutes' relationships and feelings about one another are characterized by competitiveness, exploitation, distrust, disloyalty, suspiciousness, and lack of group culture. Prostitutes are described as trusting their pimps more than one another. While other (male) deviant subcultures are seen to have strong group solidarity, the world of prostitutes has always been portrayed in the contrary manner (Lemert, 1951, p. 275; Reckless, 1950). But if we consider certain realities about their situation – that they live and work together and depend upon one another to a great extent – we may suspect that it is the stereotype of women as mutually competitive and unable to recognize group interests that renders the male sociologist blind to what must be a complex, integrated female culture among prostitutes. It is probably more difficult for men to notice and understand female group culture when they see it than it is for women to observe male group life. Subordinate groups are generally better practiced in knowing and studying those in power than the other way round. But for whatever reason, it is a curious fact that unlike studies of male deviance, with their emphasis on fraternal bonding and high group commitment, sociologists tend to overlook subcultures of women, deviant or conventional.

Finally, we should note that whereas women appear only in the nagging, unpleasant edges of Becker's world of jazz musicians, in Bryan's study of prostitutes, the pimps not only get considerable attention, but also a large share of the quotations (almost as many as the prostitutes themselves). Indeed, Bryan regards the pimp as an authority on prostitution and uses the pimp's quotations as evidence rather than further material to consider; so in a supposedly empathetic study of prostitutes, the pimps are treated as more intelligent, observant, and trustworthy than the subjects of the study themselves! Howard Becker certainly never asked the wives of jazz musicians what *they* thought about their husbands' occupations, much less quoted them as authorities on the subject.

One major sociological study of prostitution does manage to avoid many of the mistakes of others, precisely because the author depended upon autobiographcal accounts from his subjects. Because of his effort to present an interior view of the subject's life, W. I. Thomas's study (1923) was in many ways much less sexually stereotyped than more contemporary works. One of its most impressive achievements was Thomas's ability (missing in many later generations of sociologists, as I shall argue) to describe the pain and suffering that accompanied the lot of the prostitute while simultaneously portraying his subjects as resourceful, intelligent women who coped with the difficulties of their lives as best they could. Like subsequent generations of sociologists, he was aware of the fact that there were many similarities between these 'unadjusted' women and conventional women, and he came to this insight some forty years before the labeling theorists made it one of their fundamental principles. For example, Thomas noted that it is difficult to draw a line on the basis of sexual behavior alone between those women one would call prostitutes and those one wouldn't. He also observed that prostitution is not usually a fixed status but rather a transitory activity, which most girls relinquish upon getting married (1923, p. 120), another kind of observation that contemporary sociologists like to make.

Just as Bell and Becker frequently quote their subjects (which allows us to become involved with and respectful of the subjects), so Thomas includes numerous remarkable autobiographical documents, such as the following letter written by a young woman to the Jewish newspaper the *Forward* on 7 June 1906, in which she describes how she was misled into trusting a man:

I am a girl from Galicia. I am neither old nor young. I am working in a shop like other girls. I have saved up several hundred dollars. Naturally, a young man began to court me and it is indeed this that we girls are seeking. I became acquainted with him through a Russian (Jewish) matchmaker who for a short while boarded with a countryman of mine. He is really handsome and, as the girls call it, 'appetizing'. But he is poor and this is no disgrace. He became dearer to me every day. One day he told me he was in want owing to a strike, so I helped him out. I was never stingy with him and besides money also bought him a suit of clothes and an overcoat. . . . Who else did I work for if not for him? In short we became happily engaged.

Some time after, we hired a hall in Clinton Street and we were on our way to the bank to draw some money for the wedding expenses and also to enter the savings in both our names. On the way we passed some of his countrymen who were musicians, and we needed music, so we stepped in. He introduced me as his bride, I offered to have them play at our wedding. Incidentally, I inquired about my fiancé and they gave good opinions of him. Only a musician's boy pitifully gazed at me and remarked, when my fiancé was not near us: 'Are there not enough people from the old country to ask for their opinion?' I understood the hint and asked him for an address, which he gave me. Meanwhile, we were late for the bank, and fortunately too. I could hardly wait for the evening when I rushed over to his counrymen and inquired about him. They were surprised at my questions and told me he had a wife and three children in – Street. . . . I then advertised in a Jewish newspaper, warning my sisters against such a 'fortune' as befell me. I was not ashamed and told of my misfortune wherever I came and gave warnings. The East Side has become full of such 'grooms', 'matchmakers', 'mistresses', 'sisters', and 'brothers'. Inquire of their countrymen. There are plenty of their kind. [1923, pp. 148-9]

Thomas's work can be credited as the major study of prostitution that not only presents a complex and respectful portrait of its subjects but also recognizes the subjects' awareness of group interests and loyalty to one another.

Thus far we have looked at the way that prostitution was examined by the three major orientations in the 'naturalistic' study of deviance (using David Matza's [1969] distinction between the early Chicago school, the functionalists, and what we call the 'labeling' theorists[4]). For the remainder of this section we should also briefly consider the sort of study that emerged from the traditional approach of demographic or statistical analysis. Most studies that rely on the 'official' statistics of law-enforcement or other governmental agencies tend to describe their subjects in much the same way as these same agencies would, and large sample studies of prostitution are no different in this regard. Perhaps the most famous study of this type was the report *Five Hundred Delinquent Women* written by Sheldon and Eleanor Glueck (1954), which is based on the official case records of 500 women in a state reformatory. The general disposition of this study can be described best by considering a few representative quotations from the Gluecks' summary of major findings:

> The women are themselves on the whole a sorry lot. Burdened with feeblemindedness, psychopathic personality, and marked emotional instability, a large proportion of them found it difficult to survive by legitimate means.
>
> This swarm of defective, diseased, antisocial misfits, then, comprises the human material which a reformatory and a parole system are required by society to transform into wholesome, decent, law-abiding citizens! [1954, pp. 299-303]

Apart from the Gluecks' inventory there has been historically little attention paid to female criminality. In a traditional textbook on crime widely used in the fifties, Walter Reckless (1950) devoted a special chapter to 'The Criminality of Women' in which he argued that the criminality of women must never be considered 'in the same order of phenomena as crime in general' (male being general). In an explanation oddly reminiscent of the old disclaimers for omitting discussions of female sexuality, Reckless claimed that 'although crime as a behavior problem or a social problem is

4. I regret that I was unable to obtain a copy of Marion Goldman's recent work on prostitutes in a Nevada frontier town in time for this review, but the little I have seen of the work (1972) suggests to me that her work does portray a solidarity and recognition of group interests among frontier prostitutes.

complicated and not easily understood or controlled, the criminality of women is even more complicated and less understood and not subject to easy control' (1950, p. 116). But Reckless does attempt to deal with the problem, and his analysis is so loaded with stereotypes about women, some tired and familiar and others so unusual and entertaining, that a few of them merit our attention:

> ... it appears that practically all the observers agree that women offenders, much more than men offenders, use deceit and indirection in the commission of their offenses. [1950, p. 122]
>
> Observers unanimously agree that poisoning is the principal method of killing used by women and that the outstanding form of poison is arsenic, with cyanide and bichloride of mercury coming next. As a shopper and housewife, a woman can readily purchase insecticides and rat poisons. And in her roles as preparer of food and nurse to the sick, it is easy for her to administer poison. [1950, p. 121]
>
> ... With regard to the offense of aggravated assault, one particular specific female pattern has been the throwing of sulphuric acid into the face of the victim, who was most usually the unfaithful lover. [1950, p. 122]
>
> ... A woman is also prone to make false accusations of a sexual nature. She either fantasies that she has been attacked or claims that she has been attacked when she has really cooperated. [1950, p. 123]

In reviewing how a male-biased orientation has shaped the sociological study of deviance, then, it is easy to demonstrate that women have either been largely overlooked in the literature (partly because of a general belief that women are very conventional) or else regarded as deviant in only sex-stereotyped (and less appealing than male counterpart) ways. The stereotypes have limited both the *forms* of female deviance that have been recognized (those related to sex or emotion, as in prostitution and mental illness) and the way that sociologists have characterized female deviant behavioral *styles* (being passive, uncritical, unlikely to recognize group interests or have solidarity with other deviant women). But there is an even more serious problem that follows from a male-biased view of deviance, and this is a problem of omission. Certain aspects of social reality involving deviance and conformity are systematically ignored: these have to do with ordinary, chronic, everyday suffering and with the extent to which conventional lives are continually and closely governed by interpersonal regulations about right and wrong. The importance of these subjects becomes more obvious in a feminist perspective and it is to these questions that we should now turn our attention.

References

Bart, Pauline (1970), 'Portnoy's Mother's Complaint', *Trans-Action*, 7 (13).

—(1971), 'Sexism and Social Science: from the Gilded Cage to the Iron Cage, or, The Perils of Pauline', *Journal of Marriage and the Family*, 33 (4), pp. 734-45.

—(1974), 'Although We Are Angry We Are No Longer Mad; a Review of *Women and Madness', Society* (forthcoming).

Becker, Howard S. (1963), *Outsiders*, New York: The Free Press.

Bell, Daniel (1960), 'Crime as an American Way of Life: a Queer Ladder of Social Mobility', *The End of Ideology*, Daniel Bell, New York: The Free Press.

Bryan, J. (1973), 'Occupational Ideologies of Call Girls', in E. Rubington and M. Weinberg, eds., *Deviants: the Interactionist Perspective*, London: Macmillan.

Chesler, Phyllis (1973), *Women and Madness*, Garden City, N.Y.: Doubleday.

Davis, Kingsley (1966), 'Sexual Behavior', *Contemporary Social Problems*, Robert K. Merton and Robert Nisbet, eds., New York: Harcourt, Brace and World.

Glueck, Sheldon and Glueck, Eleanor T. (1934), *Five Hundred Delinquent Women*, New York: Alfred A. Knopf.

Goldman, Marion (1972), 'Prostitution and Virtue in Nevada', *Society*, Nov./Dec., pp. 32-28.

Gouldner, Alvin W. (1973), 'The Sociologist as Partisan: Sociology and the Welfare State', *For Sociology*, New York: Basic Books.

Hirschi, Travis (1962), 'The Professional Prostitute', *Berkeley Journal of Sociology*, 7, Spring.

Lemert, Edwin (1951), *Social Pathology*, New York: McGraw-Hill.

Matza, David (1968), 'Review of Thomas J. Scheff, Being Mentally Ill', *Journal of Health and Social Behavior*, 9 (3).

—(1969), *Becoming Deviant*, Engelwood Cliffs, N.J.: Prentice-Hall.

Reckless, Walter C. (1950), *The Crime Problem*, New York: Appleton-Century-Crofts.

Thomas, William I. (1923), *The Unadjusted Girl*, Boston: Little, Brown.

Trilling, Diana (1964), 'The Image of Women in Contemporary Literature', *The Woman in America*, Robert Jay Lifton, ed., Boston: Beacon Press, pp. 52-71.

Katherine O'Donovan

The Male Appendage: Legal Definitions of Women

In Sandra Burman, ed., *Fit Work for Women*, London:
Croom Helm, 1979, pp. 134-52

ROLE ALLOCATION BY LAW

'You ought to help her because, after all, she is your mother.'[1] 'You ought to send your child to school.' 'You ought to work hard to support your family.' 'You ought to iron his shirts because he is your husband.' As can be seen, these statements are based on expectations of behaviour from incumbents of social roles in their relations with others. A way of acting is suggested as appropriate conduct from one in a specific relationship with another. However, the ought statement, whilst founded on the fact of a social relationship, varies according to a notion of conduct appropriate to a role. In the example 'You ought to help her because, after all, she is your mother', as Dorothy Emmet makes clear, the obligation to help follows not only from the fact of parenthood but also from a social relationship in which people occupy roles *vis-à-vis* each other. The obligation is moral not legal, and if there is a sanction it will be social.

The legal obligation in the statement 'You ought to send your child to school' does not preclude a moral judgement, but here failure to fulfil the expectations of the role of parent will probably result in legal intervention, as would failure to support one's family. The legal sanction may even be deprivation of the opportunity to play that particular role in that relationship. There may be disagreement among the actors as to suitable behaviour for a role, but where the relationship of the actors has been recognised by the law there will be specified rules to which the community will expect conformity. Such rules are usually referred to as the rights and duties of parents or the obligations of spouses. They may also be termed the minimum requirements for the role, that is, the rules to which all performers of the role must conform. Non-conformity with rules that comprise the minimum role requirement will result in legal sanction. Failure to provide for one's family may lead to

1. D. Emmet, *Rules, Roles and Relations* (London, Macmillan, 1966), p. 37.

imprisonment. A mother who cannot conform to the legal rules of motherhood may find herself deprived of the opportunity to play this role at all, if her child is taken into care. Thus the law gives its view of parenthood and, in so doing, helps to define the parent/child relationship and what a parent is. For a particular incumbent of a social role a personal definition will be based on norms worked out in the relationship with others, and in particular relationships the norms agreed may be unique to those involved. Nevertheless the legal definition is important because it specifies the minimum role requirement and reflects and informs expectations of how an individual incumbent of a role will behave.

The imposition of roles on the basis of anatomical and physiological differences between people is done by society, with reliance on legal institutions in many instances. Justifications for different treatment of men and women by law are various. They may rest on sex differences but usually it is gender role differences that are invoked. Yet it is the law itself which helps to construct the gender role differences, as is shown below. A distinction must be made between sex differences and gender. Sex differences are the natural anatomical and physiological differences between women and men: for instance, the ability to menstruate, gestate and breast-feed. Gender is the social classification of a person as feminine or masculine. Gender role is the social role allocated on the basis of gender, but which extends much further than mere biological disparity.[2] Legal institutions support the ordering of society on a gender role basis. That an individual has no choice of sex is clear, but society is free to choose the social consequences, if any, to be attached to sex – that is, the gender role to which the individual must conform. At present the law defines and reinforces gender roles for individuals which do not necessarily have an inevitable connection with sex differences. In so doing the law is inhibiting change and causing hardship to those who do not adjust their personal lives to the gender stereotyped expectations of legal institutions.

Relationships recognised by law are structured and defined by that recognition. Legal rules may constitute the relationship by defining its creation, its consequences and its termination. Other rules may specify behaviour, through the allocation of rights and duties according to role. In marriage the rules, both constitutive and behavioural, are based on gender and their sum constitutes the role of husband or wife.

Having espoused a role, the performers may hope to modify it

2. A. Oakley, *Sex, Gender and Society* (London, Temple Smith, 1972), p. 158.

in practice, but legal rules cannot be changed by personal redefinition. So the legal minimum role requirement will remain. Since marriage is central to the experience of most women, I propose to explore gender role allocation by law in marriage. In 1973, 88.4 per cent of women in the age group 33-44 were married, a further 3.1 per cent were divorced and 1.7 per cent were widowed: a total of 93.2 per cent with marriage experience. Of the age group 25-34, 89.1 per cent had experience of marriage.[3] Despite the fact that 49 per cent of married women were economically active in 1976,[4] married women are not treated as autonomous individuals by law and social policy. Instead, they are defined in terms of marriage, a unit headed by the husband with the wife as dependant.

THE TRADITIONAL LEGAL VIEW OF THE MARRIED WOMAN

The traditional view of the legal status of married women is to be found in the *Commentaries* of William Blackstone published in 1765. The *Commentaries*, considered today as 'an excellent primer of English law',[5] were one of the first compilations of the laws of England, both written and unwritten. In a legal system which looked to court precedent – earlier cases decided in court – for guidance in dispute resolution, Blackstone's writing was enormously influential because for many decades it was considered the most reliable statement of what the law then was. Blackstone laid down the effect of marriage on a woman as follows:

> By marriage, the husband and wife are one person in law: that is, the very being or legal existence of the woman is suspended during the marriage, or at least is incorporated and consolidated into that of the husband: under whose wing, protection, and cover, she performs everything.[6]

The legal consequences of the absorption of the wife's legal person

3. Central Statistical Office, *Social Trends No. 6* (London, HMSO, 1975), table 1.12.
4. Central Statistical Office, *Social Trends No. 7* (London, HMSO, 1976), table 5.3.
5. G. Jones, 'Introduction: The Sovereignty of the Law', *Selections from Blackstone's Commentaries on the Laws of England* (London, Macmillan, 1973), p. xlvii.
6. W. Blackstone, *Commentaries on the Laws of England*, 7th ed. (Oxford, Clarendon Press, 1775), bk. 1, p. 442.

into that of her husband have been documented elsewhere;[7] the principal effect was to deny the married woman access to property, to the courts, or to any form of legal action, without the concurrence of her husband.

Legislation has been passed, from the Married Women's Property Acts, 1870-82, to the Guardianship of Minors Act, 1971, in attempts to undo the state of the law as described by Blackstone. This process is usually described as putting 'a married woman in the same legal position as her unmarried sister'[8] and has not been altogether successful in changing the law, since it has not been formulated in terms of putting the married woman on the same footing as the married man. Consequently, for many legal and administrative purposes, husband and wife continue to be treated as a unit headed by the husband. This will be discussed in detail later; but here I wish to raise the question – less irrelevant than it at first appears to be for our understanding of modern marriage laws – of whether Blackstone was correct in his description, which he ended as follows: 'We may observe, that even the disabilities, which the wife lies under, are for the most part intended for her protection and benefit. So great a favourite is the female sex of the laws of England.'[9] No explanation was given by Blackstone for the principle that husband and wife are one person in law, yet his statement was highly influential on subsequent generations of judges and legislators, who used it as a justification for refusing to consider women as persons in their own right.[10] But there is evidence to suggest that, whatever the practice of the courts prior to Blackstone's publication of his *Commentaries*, married women in the seventeenth century were able to take an active part in the economic life of the community. Alice Clark gives details of married women who were accepted members of the business community and of guilds, able to trade as single women and be sued for their debts.[11] Similar evidence was found by Mary Beard, who said of Blackstone's principle of the unity of husband and wife that it 'contains a great deal of misleading verbalism, and . . . in upshot

7. M. Finer and O. R. McGregor, 'The History of the Obligation to Maintain', in *Report of the Committee on One-parent Families* (Finer Report), Cmnd 5629, vol. 2 (London, HMSO, 1974).
8. P. M. Bromley, *Family Law*, 5th ed. (London, Butterworths, 1976), p. 108.
9. Blackstone, *Commentaries*, bk. 1, p. 445.
10. A. Sachs, 'The Myth of Judicial Neutrality: the Male Monopoly Cases', in P. Carlen (ed.), *The Sociology of Law*, Sociological Review Monograph 23 (University of Keele, Wood and Mitchell, 1976).
11. A. Clark, *Working Life of Women in the Seventeenth Century* (London, Routledge, 1919).

it is false'.[12] She accused Blackstone of being a rhetorician who misled subsequent generations into citing his statement as evidence of women's subjection.

If the statement of the law in the *Commentaries* is correct, it is indeed surprising to find married women in the seventeenth century – who in legal theory were unable to contract or sue – engaging in commerce, and acting independently of their husbands. Their activities cannot be explained by a subsequent change in the law. The common law then and when Blackstone was writing was, so far as we know, based on the same principles. Indeed the earliest English legal textbook devoted exclusively to women's legal position confirms Blackstone's words. *The Lawes Resolution of Womens Rights*, printed in London in 1632[13] but which seems to have been written in the last years of Elizabeth I by an unknown lawyer, is addressed to women. The work is largely concerned with property rights and rules relating to dower, wife's estates, marriage and widowhood. Many examples are given of the principle that husband and wife are one person:

> a women is Covert Baron as soone as she is overshadowed with her husbands protection and supereminency. [Book 3; Sec. I]

> When a small brooke or little river incorporateth with Rhodanus, Humber or the Thames, the poore Rivolet loseth her name, it is carried and recarried with the main associate, it beareth no sway, it possesseth nothing during coverture. [Sec. III]

> The Wife must take the name of her Husband [Sec. V]; That which the Wife hath is the Husbands [Sec. IX]; her husband is her sterne, her primus motor, without whom she cannot doe much at home and lesse abroad. [Sec. XLII]

The text makes clear that 'here wanteth equality in the law, women goe downe stile, and many graines allowance will not make the ballance hang even'. The sympathetic author advises: 'Have

12. M. Beard, *Women as Force in History* (New York, Macmillan, 1946), p. 82.
13. This book, of which there are two copies in the British Museum, was printed in 1632. The preface is initialled by I.L. and there is a section entitled 'To The Reader' by T.E. T.E. did not know by whom the discourse had been composed, but implied that the author was already dead in 1632. From T.E.'s description of his decision to have the work printed, we can conclude that he (T.E.) was a lawyer, because he mentioned the Lent vacation as the time when he added 'many reasons, opinions, Cases and resolutions of Cases to the Authors store'.

patience (my Schollars) take not your opportunities of revenge, rather move for redresse by Parliament . . .' (Sec. XIV).

So although it may be considered that Blackstone was complacent and condescending about the legal status of married women, we cannot say he was wrong, since the earlier book of 1632 confirms his pronouncement. Yet there does seem to have been a dichotomy between legal theory and the lives led by some married women. One explanation for this may be drawn from the use of the world 'Schollars' in addressing readers of the *Lawes Resolution of Womens Rights*. The book was intended for literate women of the propertied class, just as the *Commentaries* were intended for lawyers. That is why both works are so concerned with property rights on, during and after marriage. English family law draws its character from laws concerned with the concentration and transmission of wealth in the families of the landed classes.

The married women in the seventeenth century found by Clark and Beard to be active in business and in guilds were, in some cases, treated as single women. Borough customs and the special laws of the City of London enabled married women to trade as single women.[14] There seems to have been a divergence between the common law – the law administered in the Royal courts – and 'the law of the smaller folk' which 'lives on only in some of the borough customs'.[15] The latter courts appear to have been more willing to indulge in legal fictions to circumvent the legal consequences of marriage. We may surmise that the classification of a woman as married or single was all-important to the Royal courts because on such matters of status depended the legitimacy of children and, therefore, inheritance, the right of a widow to dower, and questions of property generally. For those with little or no property, there are indications that the legal formalities of marriage may have been less material. Lord Hardwicke's Act, requiring solemnisation of marriage in the Church of England, was passed in 1753 and was the first serious attempt by English law to regulate marriage. Until then formal proof of marriage may sometimes have been difficult. Until 1753 there were three forms of marriage, the most lax of which required the parties merely to declare that they took each other as husband and wife (*per verba de praesenti* or *per verba de futuro* followed by consummation).[16] Marriage records will certainly have been kept in the Church of

14. M. Bateson, 'Introduction', *Borough Customs*, vol. II (London, Selden Society, vol. XXI, 1906), p. cxiii.
15. W. S. Holdsworth, *A History of English Law* (London, Methuen, 1923), vol. 3, p. 535.
16. Bromley, *Family Law*, p. 33.

England from 1753 because the Act required marriage in church and registration of marriage, and indeed parish records were kept prior to then, but in order to be married it was not necessary to go to church until 1753, and it was only in 1836 that the present system of registration was introduced.[17]

Proof of marriage is important today in law, as a comparison of the rights of co-habitees with those of the married will show. Its importance lies partly in the fact that 'upon it may depend rights and obligations owed by or to the State in relation, for example, to tax, social security, and allegiance'.[18] And in establishing claims to children and property on the ending of a marital or quasi-marital relationship, the first legal question is whether the couple were married. However, as has been suggested above, current notions of state-regulated marriage are fairly recent. As Laslett said of the pre-1753 relationships: 'Neighbours decided whether any particular association could be called a marriage.'[19] The modern state, in eliminating local court autonomy, eliminated recognised legal fictions which allowed exceptions to the legal concept of unity of husband and wife. This concept was also taken over in the state's regulation of the citizen through administrative machinery, yet originally the unity of husband and wife served quite different purposes and may have applied only to a small number of relationships in the past.

THE TREATMENT OF THE MARRIED COUPLE AS A SINGLE UNIT

For certain purposes – for instance, the administration of Supplementary Benefit – the household is the unit taken into account, and if there is a man present in a marital or cohabitation relationship he is assumed to be the head and it is he who gets the benefit, if any. There is a scale for householders which is considerably higher than that for dependants. The woman in the relationship will always be classified as a dependant, even if she is working and the man is not. Similarly, for National Insurance purposes, if the husband is present, he is assumed to be the head of the nuclear

17. For advice on this matter, I am grateful to Belinda Meteyard, whose M.Phil. dissertation entitled 'Legal and Administrative Provisions as a Factor in the Maintenance of the Marriage Rate' deals with Lord Hardwicke's Act of 1753.
18. Law Commission, *Report on Solemnisation of Marriage in England and Wales*, no. 53, 1973, para. 104.
19. P. Laslett, *Family Life and Illicit Love in Earlier Generations* (Cambridge, CUP, 1977), p. 108.

family – the relevant unit for this purpose – and a woman is expected to look to him for support of their children and, usually, of herself.

Hilary Land has explained the assumptions underpinning the treatment of married women as their husbands' dependants in the social security system. Beveridge's belief that 'during marriage most women will not be gainfully employed' determined the structure of the system.[20] Despite participation of married women in work outside the home, they cannot provide benefits for their husbands and children unless the husband is incapable of work; they are treated as single persons, which is an improvement of their position at the time when Land was writing, but continues the stereotype that a married woman does not support a family. Demands have been made in the United States for the benefits a wife receives as a single person to be added to those she receives as a dependent spouse. The argument is that the family is making double contributions for little gain.[21] However, it is unlikely that such a demand would have support in Britain, since recent developments in social security law have been away from the treatment of the wage-earning married woman as her husband's dependant. This trend has been, in part, a response to legal requirements of the European Economic Community. But the proposed *Directive* on equality of treatment in social security does not envisage provision of equal benefits for spouses and for parents regardless of sex.[22]

Symbolic of the man's headship of the household is the surname. English law does not require a woman to take her husband's name on marriage; but the ability to do so is seen as a 'right' in family law textbooks,[23] possibly a survival from the time when the wife – being unable to contract or own property – had the power to pledge her husband's credit for the necessities of life. The question of name is an emotive one, as evidenced by a number of court cases

20. H. Land, 'Women: Supporters or Supported?', in D. L. Barker and S. Allen (eds.), *Sexual Divisions and Society: Process and Change* (London, Tavistock, 1976), p. 110.

21. 'The social security system also places a double burden on the married woman who works outside the home. She is forced to pay a full social security tax, but the benefits she receives an an independent worker are not added to those she would be entitled to as a spouse. The family thus pays a double tax when she works, but she collects for only a single worker.' L. J. Weitzman, 'Legal Regulation of Marriage: Tradition and Change', 62 *Calif. L. Rev.*, vol. 62, 1974, p. 1191. In 1973 a bill was introduced in Congress (H.R. 11999, 93rd Cong., 1st Sess.) to enable working women to collect their own pension plus any pension as husband's dependant.

22. *Official Journal of the European Communities*, 11.2.77, No. C34/4, 'Proposal for a directive concerning the progressive implementation of the principle of equality of treatment for men and women in matters of social security'.

23. Bromley, *Family Law*, p. 112.

questioning a mother's right to change her children's surname to that which she has assumed. The courts have ruled that a change of name requires the consent of both parents.[24] This seems reasonable; but the judiciary bring to this issue the assumption that the child's (first) surname will be that of the father. So, in 1977, where a mother changed her name when pregnant and gave that surname to her child on its subsequent birth, she was considered to have changed the child's name without the father's consent. The court ruled that: 'The child's name is that of his father.'[25]

The Board of Inland Revenue persists in treating the married couple as a unit, and in assuming that the husband is head and breadwinner. From 1799, when income tax was introduced, husband and wife have been taxed as a unit represented by the husband. The husband was and is responsible for the payment of tax for the couple and therefore all correspondence and rebates are addressed to him. Since 1972, it has been possible for the wife, with her husband's agreement, to elect to be separately taxed on her earned income. She is then dealt with as a single person, but only as regards her earned income.[26]

THE OBLIGATION TO MAINTAIN

As a result of the doctrine of unity of the married couple, the traditional rule required the husband to maintain his wife and children, since the law did not recognise any capacity in the wife

24. See *R (BM) v. R (DN) (child: surname)* [1978] 2 All E.R. 33; *Practice Direction* 24 May 1976 [1978] 3 All E.R. 451; *Re W.G.* (1976) 6 Fam. Law 210.

25. In *D v. B (otherwise D) (child: surname)*, [1977] 3 All E.R. 751, the mother had left the father of the child she was expecting, and to whom she was married, before the birth. She registered the child's name as that which she had assumed by deed poll before the birth, and which was the surname of the man with whom she went to live. In the Family Division of the High Court, Lane J. considered the law on the matter and stated: 'Applying those authorities to this case, I hold that the mother was incompetent to change the child's surname, by deed poll or by registration of birth, without either the father's consent or an order of the court. The child's surname is that of his father.' The judge did not say what would happen in the case of a married couple with different surnames who had maintained these throughout marriage. The judge, in discussing the issue, used language like 'he should bear his father's name' – a phrase redolent of property rights. Since this paper was written the Court of Appeal has reversed the decision of Lane J. and held that a mother is competent to give her surname to her child. See *Times Law Report*, 25 May 1978. It is noticeable that *The Times* published this under the heading 'Child permitted to take name of mother's lover', suggesting that a woman does not have a surname of her own; it is either her husband's or her lover's.

26. Equal Opportunities Commission, *Income Tax and Sex Discrimination* (Manchester, EOC Pamphlet, 1977), p. 11. Since this paper was written the Finance Act 1978, S.22 has been passed to enable a wife who is paying taxes on a pay-as-you-earn basis to receive her own rebates.

to maintain herself. The wife's obligation to support her husband and children arose only when the husband was incapable of work. The refusal of National Insurance benefits for her husband and children to a wife whose husband is considered capable of work is officially explained on these grounds. A wife is classified as a dependant, even if she is a wage-earner. The rule that the husband must always support the family is based on a legal rather than a social role,[27] but it inhibits choice of activity within the family. The maintenance obligation of the husband is used to justify other legal rules defining wives as dependants, particularly in social security law. The denial of the invalid care allowance to married women is an example of this: unlike the husband, she is not considered to work outside the home (even if she in fact does) and therefore is held not to require a paid assistant to care for the invalid. However, the Domestic Proceedings and Magistrates Courts Act, 1978,[28] will impose equal maintenance obligations on spouses, thus removing a major rationale for institutional arrangements that treat spouses according to ascribed gender roles.

The husband's maintenance obligation is the explanation offered for refusal of financial benefits to the wife in a number of situations, yet in legal practice that obligation means very little. During marriage it is virtually impossible for a wife living with her husband to enforce maintenance. This is because the courts are traditionally unwilling to interfere in a marital relationship as just an 'ordinary domestic arrangement'. Behind this lurks the idea that, since husband and wife are a unit, their domestic life is a private world in which the law must not intervene. This was explained by a former Master of the Rolls, Lord Evershed, as follows:

> It was in the year 1604, not far removed from the date when Shakespeare wrote the lines from The Taming of the Shrew
>> [She is my goods, my chattels; she is my house
>> My household stuff, my field, my barn
>> My horse, my ox, my ass, my anything.]
> ... that, according to Coke's report of the judgement in

27. R. Lister and L. Wilson, *The Unequal Breadwinner* (London, National Council for Civil Liberties pamphlet, 1976).
28. This Act, which has just received the Royal Assent, provides: 'Either party to a marriage may apply to a magistrates' court for an order under section 2 of this Act on the ground that the other party to the marriage – (a) has failed to provide reasonable maintenance for the applicant; or (b) has failed to provide or make a proper contribution towards reasonable maintenance for any child of the family.' The Act also proposes that similar provisions apply in applications to the higher courts.

Semayne's Case, it was judicially laid down that the house of everyone is to him as his castle and fortress. More than three centuries later Atkin L.J., in a famous judgement, said: 'The parties themselves are advocates, judges, courts, sheriff's officer and reporter. In respect of these promises (of maintenance in marriage) each house is a domain into which the King's writ does not seek to run, and to which its officers do not seek to be admitted.'[29]

An indication of the law's traditional reluctance to enter this private domain was that little legal remedy was provided for domestic violence until the passing of the Domestic Violence and Matrimonial Proceedings Act, 1976.[30]

Although legal provisions contain a view of marriage in which the husband is breadwinner and the wife dependant, the law does little to protect the dependant-wife during marriage. The conditions of domestic production are unregulated and, as we have seen, there is no enforcement of payment for it. The only legal provision on housekeeping is the Married Women's Property Act of 1964, which provides that where savings are made 'from any allowance made by the husband for the expenses of the matrimonial home or for similar purposes ... the money ... shall ... be treated as belonging to the husband and wife in equal shares'. The gender role assumptions here are obvious, but even more interesting is the fact that the law does not intervene to enforce payment, but only to ensure that the husband retains a half interest in any savings made by a prudent wife.

Family lawyers explain this as an indication that the law is only directed to pathological situations, to family breakdown.

The normal behaviour of husband and wife or parents and children towards each other is beyond the law – as long as the family is 'healthy'. The law comes in when things go wrong. More than that, the mere hint of anyone concerned that the law may come in is the surest sign that things are or will soon be going wrong.[31]

However, should the family breakdown be indicated by the wife

29. Lord Evershed, 'Foreword' to R. H. Graveson and F. R. Crane, *A Century of Family Law* (London, Sweet and Maxwell, 1957), p. xv.
30. Select Committee on Violence in Marriage, *Report*, House of Commons, Session 1974-5, vol. 1, paras. 42-53.
31. O. Kahn-Freund and K. W. Wedderburn, 'Editorial Foreword' to J. Eckclaar, *Family Security and Family Breakdown* (Harmondsworth, Penguin, 1971), p. 7.

deserting or committing adultery, the courts have ruled that she cannot look to her husband for support while they remain married.[32]

On divorce a husband's responsibility for maintenance continues, especially where there are children, and a wife too acquires the duty of supporting the children. Thus the sexes would appear to have identical legal roles. However, the judicial attitude becomes apparent from the leading case on the subject, where the provision of future maintenance, known as periodical payment, was the justification for cutting the wife's share of property acquired during marriage from a half to a third.

> If we were only concerned with the capital assets of the family, and particularly with the matrimonial home, it would be tempting to divide them half and half ... That would be fair enough if the wife afterwards went her own way, making no further demands on her husband ... Most wives want their former husbands to make periodical payments as well to support them; because after the divorce he will be earning far more than she; and she can only keep up her standard of living with his help. He also has to make payments for the children out of his earnings, even if they are with her.[33]

So because of her calls on her husband's future income, a wife does not get an equal share of family assets. But the wife's future dependence, if it exists, is because of her child-care responsibilities; and one of the reasons why she will probably be a low-wage earner after divorce may be because she has foregone training and experience because of marriage.

Judicial imperviousness to women's lot was further evidenced by the following explanation for the award of the lion's share to husbands.

> When a marriage breaks up, there will thenceforth be two households instead of one. The husband will have to go out to work all day and must get some woman to look after the house – either a wife if he remarries or a housekeeper if he does not. He will also have to provide maintenance for the children. The wife will not usually have so much expense. She may go out to work herself, but she will not usually employ a housekeeper. She will do most of the housework herself, perhaps with some help.

32. *Gray v. Gray* [1976] Fam. 324.
33. *Watchel v. Watchel* [1973] Fam. 72 at 94, per Lord Denning.

Or she may marry, in which case her new husband will provide for her.[34]

Clearly the assumptions behind this statement are based on beliefs about the sexes and their roles. One method of testing the neutrality of the judiciary in the interpretation of legal provisions is to try to imagine how the above paragraph would sound if the gender roles were reversed. In the case quoted above, Lord Denning was interpreting the gender neutral language of the current divorce law. That gender neutral provisions can be interpreted in a biased manner is clear from Albie Sachs's work on the male monopoly cases from 1869 to 1929, where the neutral word 'person' was interpreted by the judiciary to mean men only.[35]

Another example of gender bias can be found in a recent study of divorce court registrars whose function it is to deal with issues of maintenance, property, and custody of and access to children. Registrars have wide discretion in the exercise of their powers and, consciously or unconsciously, they use it to favour the party in a conflict with whom they identify, or of whom they approve.

My own view is that I think some weight should go in favour of the good wife and I would be likely to order a bad wife less. The local community, which still retains strong traces of its religious upbringing, would respect this view.[36]

Must one treat all wives in the same way unless they are nymphomaniac or of the worst order – are they to be treated like a faithful wife of 20 years standing who has been nastily and shabbily treated by her husband?[37]

Although guidance from the higher courts indicates that the wife should be awarded (at least) one third of matrimonial assets, the report suggests that many registrars do not give her even this.

It might be argued that, in order to avoid the stigma of dependence, a wife should forego any claim to future maintenance.

---

34. *Idem*, at 95.
35. Sachs, 'Myth of Judicial Neutrality'; A. Sachs, 'The Myth of Male Protectiveness and the Legal Subordination of Women', in C. Smart and B. Smart (eds.), *Women, Sexuality and Social Control* (London, Routledge and Kegan Paul, 1978).
36. W. Barrington Baker, J. Eckclaar, C. Gibson and S. Raikes, *The Matrimonial Jurisdiction of Registrars* (Oxford, Centre for Socio-Legal Studies, 1977), para. 2.21, quoting an anonymous registrar.
37. *Ibid.*, para. 2.23.

But this overlooks two points. First, the courts take the view that a man ought to support his dependants, especially if they are otherwise likely to be supported by the state, and this view is shared by the Supplementary Benefits Commission. Second, domestic production, although unpaid, is treated as being of value by legal institutions where an accident has eliminated the producer of it, or increased the labour involved. This is not the place to go into the details of the domestic labour debate. It suffices to point out that within the terms of legal analysis the courts currently value housework and child care at about thirty pounds a week in actions relating to a wife's desertion or death.[38] So, for a woman to be paid by her ex-husband for such services would appear to be merely just.

Recently judges have adopted the attitude that marriage is not a 'bread ticket for life',[39] recognising that a woman without children may be able to support herself. But the woman with small children has little alternative to accepting maintenance from her former spouse or from the state. If maintenance is ordered by a court, current statistics show that it will be regularly complied with in only 45 per cent of cases[40] and that enforcement is difficult. Beveridge proposed that a wife should be paid an 'end of marriage benefit' which would consist of a temporary separation benefit, similar to widow's benefit, and guardian and training benefit where appropriate. This would have enabled the divorced woman to undertake training for employment, but the idea was rejected by the government in 1944.[41] Of course, in an ideal world where roles were chosen, a woman would not automatically take on the caring role in relation to the children on breakdown of marriage; but, as we shall see, women and men tend to specialise in activities considered appropriate to their gender roles.

ACTIVITY SPECIALISATION

There is no direct legal obligation on the wife to specialise in household matters, although by family law and policy it is assumed

38. In *Regan v. Williamson* [1976] 2 All E.R. 241, where the High Court considered compensation for the loss of a 'good wife and mother' in an accident, £21.50 per week was awarded after £10 had been deducted for the cost of previously keeping the deceased.
39. In *Brady v. Brady* [1973] 3 Fam. Law 78, Sir George Baker reduced an order for £3 a week to 10p where the marriage lasted only five months, saying: 'In these days of "woman's lib" there is no reason why a wife whose marriage has not lasted long, and who has no child, should have a bread ticket for life.'
40. Finer, *Report*, vol. 1, p. 100.
41. *Ibid.*, p. 147.

that she will. The most sensible arrangement in a marriage would be for the low-wage partner to specialise in household production, while the high-wage partner specialises in the market. In addition to the disincentive to wives joining a market which pays low wages for many types of 'women's work', families choosing to maximise their income in response to market forces will find that although there are no legal rules requiring the wife to undertake housework and child care, a myriad of structures with legal bases provide disincentives for the husband to do so. These disincentives reflect and reinforce assumptions about women's social role in contexts in which the assumptions may no longer be valid, or at least might not be valid if the legal structures were neutral. That the great majority of married women accept the tasks of housework and child care is undeniable, but so is women's increasing participation in the work force. If legal structures were neutral in role allocation, issues relating to the imposition of domestic production on women might be clarified. It is not intended here to suggest that legal changes would bring about material changes in society, but at least some of the complexities surrounding the question of sex roles and gender roles would be dissipated.

The assumption that a wife or 'some female person' should care for a man's children and do his housework underlies income tax and social security provisions. In the tax system this takes the form of giving additional personal allowances to married men with incapacitated wives and to single parents, but denying it to married women with incapacitated husbands. The allowance reflects the assumption that it is a married woman's unpaid job to care for children and that if she cannot do so, her husband is entitled to financial assistance for someone else to perform the job. In contrast, a woman on her own, even if working, is not considered by the courts as in need of an allowance for a substitute child-minder. Similarly, other financial provisions are so constructed that they provide incentives for women, where available, rather than men, to undertake a domestic role. The housekeeper tax allowance is paid only where a woman is employed, so a male housekeeper is not recognised for tax purposes. And the daughter's service allowance cannot be claimed for sons.[42] In social security legal provisions there are a number of examples of gender bias. The invalid care allowance is not paid to married women – presumably because they are expected to do such work unpaid.

42. Equal Opportunities Commission, *Income Tax and Sex Discrimination*, p. 15. The Finance Act, 1978, S. 19 has removed the gentler distinctions in the housekeeper allowance and has also amended the daughter's service allowance to cover 'son or daughter'.

Where additions for adult dependants are given to those who get the allowance, these are limited to a wife or to 'some female person ... who ... has the care of a child or children of the beneficiary's family'[43] – so a male dependant with care of children is excluded. The disabled married woman is ineligible for the non-contributory invalidity pension 'except where she is incapable of performing normal household duties'.[44] The additions for dependants are as shown above.

The award of custody of children in divorce and other matrimonial cases reflects the allocation of the role of child-caretaker to women. A recent study showed that in 81 per cent of divorce court cases and 94 per cent of magistrates' cases custody was given to the mother. Where there was a contest by the father, however, the outcome was not so predictable.[45] It is clear that women demand custody and men expect them to have it, accepting, not challenging, traditional assumptions.[46] While this is a fairly recent development in legal administration – until 1886 the law did not recognise any custody or guardianship rights of the mother – since it is combined with other assumptions in the law, it leaves the wife at a financial disadvantage. In order to perform child-care tasks, the divorced woman may need economic support. As has already been stated, she is at a disadvantage in the job market and the maintenance she needs will be used as an argument against her when divorce financial arrangements are made. Yet the maintenance is necessary for child care. Recently, a man forced to care for his two children (because of his wife's desertion after an accident befell him), was awarded twenty pounds a week to hire a substitute – this being the court's estimate of the value of his wife's services less her consumption.[47] This case indicates that maintenance of a child-caring wife is not full recompense for her work.

43. Social Security Act, 1975, S. 37 (3) and Statutory Instruments 1976/409, S. 13 (1).
44. Social Security Act, 1975, S. 36 (2).
45. S. Maidment, 'A Study in Child Custody', Family Law, vol. 6, no. 7., 1976, pp. 195-200; vol. 6, no. 8, 1976, pp. 236-41.
46. J. Eckclaar, E. Clive, K. Clarke and S. Raikes, Custody After Divorce (Oxford, Centre for Socio-Legal Studies, 1977). The authors found that in 73.3 per cent of their cases of breakdown of marriage the children were living with the wife; in the great majority of cases the court confirmed the status quo. The study indicates that 'wives are more tenacious than husbands in their attempts to obtain possession of the children' (p. 9); that husbands in most cases are content to leave to the wife the task of raising the children; but that where the children were already with the husband the court was unlikely to move them. This suggests that the courts do not necessarily assume that a father is unfit for childrearing.
47. In Oakley v. Walker [1977] 121 Sol. Jo. 619, where, because of his accident, a wife deserted her husband, leaving him with two small children to care for, he received compensation of £20 a week to enable him to employ a substitute.

In drawing up the pleadings for divorce, the legal profession uses clichés such as that the wife was a 'loyal, faithful and good wife',[48] or that she did not fulfil her 'wifely duties'. The 'loving and unselfish wife' is entitled to recognition of her good behaviour by the court in awarding maintenance.[49]

These phrases and the legal provisions discussed above suggest that, despite the judicial view that the law should not interfere in the marriage relationship, there is a definite legal notion of how a woman should act and what being a 'good wife' entails. In other words, the law does not intervene in the unequal economic relationship found in marriage, but maintains – through its provisions, assumptions, judicial and other official attitudes – an ideology of gender roles which ensures that individuals who deviate from these roles are penalised.

NEUTRALISING SEX-BASED LEGAL ROLES

Differentiation between men and women by law and custom appears to be a feature of all known societies and figures even in Engels's theory of the family, although not as sexual stratification in the early stages of his assumed pattern of evolution.[50] A society in which there was no official recognition of physiological sex differences between persons would be new to us and we cannot say what it would look like. Sexual integrationists have argued that an individual's sex is an entirely physiological characteristic and is no barrier to sexual integration. This is not to ignore the current form of reproduction which temporarily incapacitates mothers, although some feminists consider this an obstacle to be overcome by extra-uterine reproduction.[51] Any special provision for maternity can be justified as necessary to the infant's well-being rather than being seen as a peculiar right based on gender.[52]

There seems to be no reason why the law, which has espoused an ideology of equality as evidenced in recent legislation, should continue to reinforce roles by gender-based legal rules and incentives. It would be a fairly simple matter to phrase legislation

48. 'The wife put in an answer, some part of which is in what has become the standard form of cliché in these cases, alleging that she was a "loyal, faithful and good wife". Just why these three adjectives have crept into the standard form of pleading, I do not know.' Ormrod L.J. in *Le Marchant v. Le Marchant* [1977] 3 All E.R. 610 at 612.
49. *Duchesne v. Duchesne* [1950] 2 All E.R. 784 at 791 (Pearce J.).
50. F. Engels, *The Origin of the Family, Private Property and the State* (London, Lawrence and Wishart, 1972).
51. S. Firestone, *The Dialectic of Sex* (London, Jonathan Cape, 1971), p. 233.
52. A. Jaggar, 'On Sexual Equality', *Ethics*, vol. 84, July 1974, p. 285.

in gender-neutral terms, thus denying legal recognition to gender roles. The roles of breadwinner, homemaker, and child-caretaker would not necessarily subsequently disappear. It is arguable that social roles are part of the institutions of society. However, these social roles should be based on choice, not on sex. Gender roles are not chosen but imposed on individuals, and that such major social consequences should follow on the slight physiological differences between women and men is increasingly a surprise to scholars.[53] The abolition of legal allocation of roles based on gender would increase the areas of autonomy and freedom for people. This argument is not an objection to role-based law but to gender-based law. Indeed, it is clear that a person who provides unpaid services in the home and foregoes a cash income needs the protection and recognition of the law, and that such a person should receive direct any income, allowances and benefits (such as child benefit) that are intended for the support of domestic production. No doubt there would be problems of proof between couples as to who was performing the home role in the relationship. But these are not insuperable if the emphasis is placed on social function rather than on gender.

To accomplish such a change in legal institutions would require study of those different types of laws. In the area of law relating to current roles in marriage or quasi-marriage, whilst the roles of breadwinner and homemaker might be retained for administrative purposes, these would not be gender-based. Neutral words such as spouse or partner could be substituted for wife and husband. It would be a matter of personal choice for a family to decide its arrangements (although job market constraints would, of course, continue to limit choice). This would not resolve the complex problems of whether the family or the individual should be treated as the unit of account for matters of taxation and welfare, but it would help to expose issues masked by current sexual ideologies. The Supplementary Benefits Commission is actively considering adopting a neutral social security system 'leaving people as free as possible to make their own arrangements in whatever way suits them best'.[54]

Where laws are based on physiological differences between the sexes, I suggest that examination would reveal that the necessity for these laws is more apparent than real. The criminal law protects persons from rape and sexual assault but there is no reason why

53. E. Goffman, 'The Arrangement between the Sexes', *Theory and Society*, vol. 4, no. 3, Fall 1977, p. 302.
54. Supplementary Benefits Commission, *Annual Report 1976*, Cmnd 6910 (London, HMSO, 1977), 1.7.

this should be linked to sex. The South Australian legislature has amended its legislation on sexual offences to encompass male and female aggressors and victims. This has been done by the use of the words 'person' and 'his or her'. Where the criminal law has given special recognition to post-natal depression, this can be subsumed under general rules relating to diminished responsibility.

Legislation that protects women at work from adverse conditions considered suitable for men has been justified by both gender role differences and physiological differences. Its retention is supported by feminists as part of a general strategy for improving working conditions. Research would indicate whether the rationale for protective legislation was based on role or on physiology. If it is role-based, then it would seem logical that all those persons assuming a particular role in society – for instance, the care of small children – should benefit from protective legislation. If the rationale is physiological, then all persons with similar physiological needs must also be protected.

The third category is gender-neutral or androgynous laws. Where such laws already exist, study would reveal the extent to which, in the course of interpretation, judges and officials bring to their work conventional ideas and assumptions concerning women. As we have seen in the administration of the divorce laws, neutral wording of legal language is not good enough; it may mask deeply ingrained attitudes and prejudices on the part of the interpreter. It is debatable whether the veil of impartiality is more easily pierced when it covers blatantly discriminatory legislation or when legal provisions are ostensibly neutral. In my opinion, non-gender-specific legislation would clarify issues which at present are so often explained as 'that's the law'.

This plea for an end to official ascription of role based on sex is not intended to suggest that legal changes would bring about social revolution or even true economic equality between the sexes. Far more fundamental measures are required for that. However, gender-neutral legislation is a necessary, if far from sufficient, condition for justice to individuals in society.

Jenny Shaw

Finishing School: Some Implications of Sex-segregated Education

In D. Barker and S. Allen, eds., *Sexual Divisions and Society: Process and Change*, London: Tavistock, 1976, pp. 133-49

A proposition familiar to most sociologists is the claim that in the process of industrialization schools annexed some of the 'functions' of the family, thereby impoverishing the family and creating, amongst other things, conditions of conflict or problematic discontinuities between the home and the school. The nub of this argument lies in the view that specialization in technology and social relations was both increasing and inevitable, and that schools were simply part of the process. However, specialization, like upward mobility, has only ever been the destiny of a minority of those who pass through schools, and only recently has recognition and interest in the experiences of the majority led to a redefinition of the part educational institutions play in industrial societies.

De-schoolers are not alone in doubting the claim that schools uniquely provide children with either necessary or sufficient preparation for living in such societies. The duplication of content between what is learnt at home and at school reinforces the view that much of what is taught in schools could equally well be learnt away from them. Furthermore, looked at from the standpoint of girls, the educational objective of many schools might well be described as insurance *against* specialization.

This paper will examine educational institutions from the point of view of their effects on girls and, whilst this cannot be defended just because it is not the normal approach, it may help us at this moment in time to revise some of our assumptions about the central features of our society. The recognition that many of the models and ideas currently in use in sociology (as elsewhere) have been formulated explicitly or implicitly to account for male behaviour and that they are often inapplicable or misleading when applied to women is proceeding. This is most noticeable in fields such as deviance, occupational sociology and, most importantly, the analysis and measurement of social class but has yet to be accepted, and revised models systematically applied, in the sociology of education.

The choice of whether to stress the social control features of education or its potential for individual growth and mobility has depended largely on whether the life-chances of boys or of both sexes were being considered. The view that schools are opportunity structures for the able is not so strongly adhered to as it once was, but possibly it would never have had much appeal if the fortunes of girls had been considered as thoroughly as those of boys. However, most of the standard literature in the field has been based on studies of boys' schools, which has produced a 'bias', the dimensions of which we are only beginning to discover.[1] In considering some of the implications of the sex typing principle which is still embodied in our educational system – i.e. that the sex of a child should be a determinant of the education he or she receives – I must therefore stress the tentativeness of my thinking and that I rely upon material from scattered sources, having at present limited data of my own that directly bears on the subject.[2]

SCHOOLS AND THE DIVISION OF LABOUR IN SOCIETY

This paper has two related themes. Both concern the contribution that schools make to the division of labour. It is difficult to demonstrate that educational institutions are simply 'responsive' to or 'reflective' of the occupational structure, although such a view is intuitively attractive – as is the view of schools as major agencies for maintaining the dominant (and sexist) culture. But one central phenomenon does have to be explained: how is it that girls, who begin their school career with what appears to be a flying start over boys, being as much as two years ahead in reading and in physical and psychological maturity, come to leave school with far fewer qualifications (Douglas, 1968)? The other side of all selective educational systems is systematic discouragement, but the paradox of the British model is that by its own criteria of success its

1. Popular and important books in the sociology of education like Jackson and Marsden (1962), Lacey (1970), Banks (1955), Banks and Finlayson (1973), and Hargreaves (1967) are all based on data from boys' schools.
2. In some exploratory work I have made into the social context of truancy and non-attendance, the most striking variable was in fact that of sex. In one area, the lowest rate was for the boys' school, the highest for the girls', and the mixed school fell between the two.

most promising pupils persistently under-achieve. From a difference between the sexes in the girls' favour there follows an extraordinary reversal of fortune.

The argument of the first half of the paper rests on the assumption that divisions of knowledge, in their institutionalized form of curricula, correspond more or less directly to divisions of labour. We can see in the range of choice offered to boys and girls both the means and the expression of economic and social control. The second part of the paper deals with the accommodation made by schools to the demands of our present economy, which requires a minority of skilled specialists and a majority of less skilled, less specialized workers. One means of preparing children to enter the labour force (on terms set by the prevailing economic structure) has been to rely on skill-labels or educational certificates as a condition of entry to jobs, and to allow educational institutions a near monopoly of issuing them.

STREAMING BY SEX

Although this paper bears a title referring to the consequences of sex-segregated education, it is not intended to present the issue as one of mixed versus single sex schooling, despite the growing volume of work addressed to that subject. In part this is because I am not entirely happy with the available material, for, although Dale (1969, 1971, 1974) has dedicated his professional career to championing the cause of co-education and especially to showing that mixed schools are superior to single sex ones on social grounds, the evidence is far from consistent, and in fact the differences in performance between the two sexes show greater disparities than the differences between the two types of school.[3] Over the country as a whole there is one single sex school for every two mixed (Benn and Simon, 1972) but an individual's chances of attending a single sex or mixed school vary regionally and to some

3. The data on whether mixed or single sex schools are better for boys or girls in terms of academic achievement is not conclusive. Some of the differences in rates of achievement for either type of school may be a function of other characteristics associated with the school, for example mixed schools tend to be larger than single sex ones, are more likely to be rural, and to have lower proportions of children from middle-class backgrounds. Douglas (1968) lists these and other differences in his Supplementary Tables. To some extent Douglas's and Dale's findings differ but from the recent publication of Dale's final volume (1974) the evidence points more strongly to there being a distinct improvement in boys' performances, especially as measured by certificates gained (a finding earlier reported by Sutherland in N. Ireland [1961, pp. 158-69]) in mixed schools, whilst girls seem to do better in single sex schools.

extent reflect parental aspirations, for middle-class children are slightly more likely to go to a single sex school, which may be a real or 'disguised' grammar school (as Benn and Simon [1972] call some of the comprehensives). In rural areas the possibility of going to a mixed school is less, as there are fewer such schools, and in some urban areas (like London) the class variable is less noticeable, as 60 per cent of all secondary schools in the ILEA are single sex.

The question of sex segregation in education is not, however, simply a matter of physical location – of whether there be one or two sexes in the particular building; it is essentially one of curricula differences. Both single sex and mixed schools restrict certain subjects to children of each sex. The use of sex as a salient criterion in the provision of learning facilities occurs almost wholly amongst the directly vocational subjects, which can represent a considerable proportion of school time; and less formally as between science and the humanities, where boys take the former and girls the latter. Benn and Simon (1972) were obviously surprised when they asked the 587 mixed schools in their survey if any subjects were closed to pupils on the grounds of sex and discovered that 50 per cent restricted some subjects to boys and 49 per cent of schools did the same for girls. In Scotland the figures were even higher, with 70 per cent limiting some subjects to boys and 68 per cent to girls. The commonest reason for this was that the teachers of boys' subjects refused to include girls in their classes. The subjects frequently proscribed for girls included: engineering, gardening, woodwork, metalwork, technical drawing, building, navigation, physics with chemistry, rural science, pottery, and surveying. For boys, catering, needlework, clothes design, dancing, human biology, jewelry, and mothercraft were amongst the forbidden subjects. Occasionally it was said that a pupil of the 'wrong sex' was admitted on demand and some schools pointed out that the options were open in theory but that in practice no one ever took them.

The use of sex as an organizational principle is close in effect, if not design, to the institution of streaming, with all its sociological concomitants. Streaming, however, it is known, invariably implies differences in course content and is likely to have an attendant ideology in the form of the 'psychology' of cognitive differences, or administrative ease, which, as Simon (1971) shows, is itself an effect of curriculum differences. The manner in which differences in performance accommodate to levels of provision and expectations and are then reinforced as grounds for discrimination is well documented (Rosenthal and Jacobson, 1968). Lacey (1970) has indeed suggested that under-achievement is the product of streaming and the sub-culture of opposition or commitment that accompany it. His material, however, relates only to a boys' grammar school and there are grounds for thinking the same conditions would not apply in girls' schools. In a replication of Hargreaves's study, conducted in a girls' school, one of the striking differences was that the lower streams were actually *more* committed to the school norms than the higher streams and had less of a non-academic 'counter-culture', as expressed in distinctive forms of dress and values (Brown, 1972). In the replication study's school it is quite likely that criteria other than intelligence had been used as a basis for streaming, which may account for the differences, but if this is the case, the chances are that such practices are quite common in girls' schools. In the Lacey and Hargreaves studies of boys' schools, ability and commitment to school norms went together, as did sexual precocity, trendiness, opposition, and low performance; while in the girls' school and in Douglas's study, early maturity, extreme fashion consciousness, and high ability were associated.[4] In girls' schools the absence of the inverse polarization that has been noted in studies of boys' schools supports the view of female communities as being both less differentiated and less concerned with academic success.[5] A woman no longer has to repudiate her sex and enter a convent to get an education at all, but in so far as educational institutions are themselves seen as prizes for competing groups and ideologies, they will inevitably reinforce the values of whichever groups have gained control.

It is hardly surprising that mixed schools are actually more like boys' schools rather than being somewhere midway between all-male and all-female schools. The chances of the head of a mixed school being a woman are much smaller than of its being a man. Dale has gone to great lengths to promote co-education and he concludes that, despite the deterioration in girls' performance in mixed schools as compared to girls in single sex schools, 'the question of comparative progress in academic work should never again be raised as an obstacle to a policy of co-education' (Dale, 1974). But his grounds for supporting co-education rest entirely on

4. While protective anti-school sub-cultures are not formed by low-stream girls in the same manner as by boys, this does not mean that girls do not participate in some form of 'youth culture'. Rather, as Murdock and Phelps (1973) suggest, youth culture can be differentiated into 'street' and 'pop' culture, the former being more open to boys and the latter equally available but more subscribed to by girls.

5. There is an interesting parallel to this argument in the finding that the spread of girls' measured abilities is narrower than that of boys (Davie, 1973).

the substantial improvement in *boys'* performance and the overall greater happiness, maturity, and adjustment of pupils of both sexes in mixed schools, which he considers to be a result of some mutually moderating process.

Boys and girls educated together certainly do have an effect upon each other, but whether, under our prevailing culture, it is one of *mutual* benefit is questionable. Despite the possibility that mixed schools may offer a wider range of subjects than a single sex one, and that in this respect they compare favourably with girls' schools which often have poorer facilities for science and mathematics, the social structure of mixed schools may drive children to make even more sex-stereotyped subject choices, precisely because of the constant presence of the other sex and the pressure to maintain boundaries, distinctiveness, and identity. In all-girls' schools, being both clever and attractive is a compatible, but not necessary, combination. Such a combination may be less viable in a mixed school where, in a climate of overall anxiety about appropriate sex behaviour, dichotomies are present and choices have to be made. Little protection from, or alternatives to, failure (or success) in romantic competition are afforded. In some areas, such as sport and games, a double-bind situation may arise, whereby success in physical terms means failure in social ones (Willis and Critcher, 1974).

In a discussion of different types of streaming, Young and Brandis (1967) consider that, under certain conditions, one of the functions of a system based on a combination of ability and moral qualities would be to create tension between the streams and to use the threat of possible descent into the lower stream as a lever to keep the higher stream at work. Young and Brandis were concerned that where low IQ and moral evaluation were confounded in a comprehensive school, working-class children would lose the chance of a coherent and occupationally relevant course, albeit second class, and the chance of belonging to a fee-saving sub-culture. Further, they would suffer downward mobility more often than upward in those schools where movement between streams took place.

A version of this process may be becoming established via the sex-based subject boundaries and may describe the relations between the sexes in co-educational schools. From the little evidence that we have, girls' schools would seem to approach their second type of comprehensive, where children of mixed ability find themselves in the same stream; but there is one important difference: failure is not so 'personalized'. The sharpness of these processes described by Young may be modified in the girls' schools as occupational selection is regarded as less critical.

THE SOCIAL CONSTRUCTION OF GIRLS' FAILURE

The use of sex as a basis for organizational and curricular decisions is irrational in educational terms, for children usually have had no prior experience of the subject to which they are assigned. It makes 'sense' only in the wider perspective of schools as agencies maintaining and reproducing accepted social divisions. The effect of these decisions amount to what Goode (1967) calls 'the protection of the inept', as lower overall levels of skill may be produced both among those insulated from competition and those whose competition is feared. Furthermore, by using ascribed characteristics such as sex to 'legitimize' either the boundaries within education or between primary and secondary labour sectors, the chances of economically based forms of identification and solidarity are weakened.

Turner (1964), who addressed himself to the problem of women's ambition, thought, rather traditionally, that girls were more concerned with status than class and that they pursued their ambitions (especially material ones) indirectly through their menfolk. The reason he gave for the different meanings that his measures of ambition produced for the two sexes was, exactly, that educational and occupational aspirations were related to material ends for men but not for women, whose overall ambition was both 'lower' and more 'differentiated'. This really amounts, yet again, to the 'over-socialized conception of woman'. Implicitly this account is based on a version of the 'achievement motivation' thesis, for we are told that the values that distinguish ambitious from non-ambitious men also distinguished men from women. Only secondary importance was given to the constraints placed on the *direction* of ambition and, therefore, of motivation too. Turner found that his sample of women chose to add the role of career to that of traditional home-maker rather than choose between them (so much for cognitive dissonance) and certainly recent British material bears this out (Young and Willmott, 1973).

But the puzzle remains and for me is two-fold. First, do girls really believe that marriage and a family are going to provide a life-long activity when, even as long ago as 1950, the average age of first marriage was twenty-two and women's age at the time of the birth of their last child was twenty-six? With 42 per cent of all married women working, and more in the working class, is it likely that girls are totally unaware of this, especially if they take their own mothers as models? Or is it more likely that marriage and the expectations that accompany it function to interrupt girls' views of their future and to discourage long-term planning? Unqualified women and other low-paid workers probably get skilled at marginal analysis pretty quickly, so that the difference between working or not is a rational assessment of the situation, possibly learnt long before leaving school. A comment made to me by a thirteen-year-old pupil of an all-girls comprehensive on the relevance of compulsory subjects illustrates this: 'I can see the point of English as I might have to write to the Council or Social Services, but Art, I can't give my husband a painting for his dinner can I?'

One thing that is certain is that the distinctions that are embodied in school timetables are persistent. As long ago as 1923 the Consultative Committee of the Board of Education recommended that specialization of the curriculum by sex be discouraged. But the messages about the right and proper distribution of knowledge are also messages about power. This is illustrated by the study of Nailsea comprehensive (Richardson, 1973), for here, when concessions were made and each sex was allowed to take the subject traditionally reserved for the other, they could do so only by being organized into single sex groups in an otherwise mixed school. Further, although some loosening of the boundaries does seem to be taking place, it tends (as in the occupational structure at large) to be more in the direction of boys taking up girls' subjects, such as cookery, rather than the other way round. When boys take girls' subjects, the meanings swiftly change; thus cookery becomes a prelude to a career in catering for boys, whilst as taught to girls it is still intended as a general domestic skill, and not primarily a saleable one.

Bernstein (1973) has introduced the categories of classification to refer to the strength and degree of boundary maintenance between the contents of a curriculum, and framing to describe the context or relationship within which teaching and learning takes place. From these concepts he derives two basic types of curricula: a collection one, where subjects may be quite disparate but have very strong boundaries around them (consider the 'timetabling' restrictions that permit certain combinations of subjects and not others); and an integrated one, where few such prohibitions occur and subjects (or knowledge) are seen essentially as part of a piece. He argues that socialization into existing social structures is aided by a collection code which usually displays clear principles both in terms of what is taught and how it is taught (classification and frame).

In discussing the overt and covert ideological bases of the different types of curricula, Bernstein makes use of Durkheim's concepts of mechanical and organic solidarity. He suggests that the underlying structure of collection codes is one of mechanical solidarity, although it produces specialists who contribute to organic solidarity. Such a view corresponds well both with the style of girls' schools and their more rigid social structures (i.e., described as more centralized, rulebound, and bureaucratized than boys' schools) and with their pupils' probable occupational futures as members of a sector of the labour market which functions in the economy by providing a supply of necessary, low-cost labour. Whilst we cannot conclude that boys' education has necessarily adopted the 'integrated' type of curriculum, it becomes clear that the strongly hierarchical and sexist social structure in which we live has favoured the collection model for girls' education, with all its consequences. For example, if girls stay on to take 'A' levels they are more likely to follow a collection type curriculum; if they take a science subject at all it is likely they will take only one and not three, and this is obviously inevitable in schools where biology is the only science available.

There are of course other areas marginal to the curriculum, where sex is treated as pertinent, such as games and welfare. A physical education teacher explained to me that he did not know any of the girls in his form as he had never taught them. The reasons given for this were that the risk of misinterpretation or of accusations of improper behaviour were too great. Despite the virtual impossibility of guaranteed privacy in schools, this belief is widespread and male post-graduate certificate in education students are warned on entering schools never to be left alone with a girl pupil. Welfare is frequently seen as something women are innately well equipped to do because they are innately equipped to be mothers; so the job is often thrust upon women teachers. Moreover, the idea that there are specifically 'girls' problems' leads to further institutionalization of dual standards.

At present we can only speculate on the meanings of these boundaries. Quite why it is possible to have boys and girls doing the same subjects on different occasions but not both together, or what the deeper meanings are of the allocation to male and female of physical space such as playgrounds and places in assemblies, we are not yet in a position to say. But their survival indicates an importance attached to these boundaries, especially in a society where the public rhetoric has for so long supported co-education.

SEX-BASED EDUCATIONAL DIFFERENCES AND THE LABOUR MARKET

This part of the paper returns to the question of the steady and uninterrupted falling off of girls' attainments throughout secondary education which all the longitudinal studies document, and suggests that this can be linked to the construction of a differentiated work force. Girls' eventual over-representation in the part-time and unskilled sectors is due in part to having lower and fewer qualifications; which in turn has to be understood as a product of their schooling. The practice of segregating education, whether within schools by curricula means, or between schools physically, makes a unique contribution to the maintenance of separate labour forces.

The fact that the social structure maintains a low level of differentiation for women is expressed in one way by the lower levels of skill that they are expected to, and do, attain. But there are other expressions – for instance, in the organization of the schools themselves. Female organizations, including girls' schools, have been described as tending towards centralization, bureaucratization, and 'petty' rulefulness. One explanation of this has been offered in terms of their having either a weak 'knowledge base', or their being staffed by semi-professionals (Simpson and Simpson, 1969). With the possible exception of mathematics and science teaching, this view cannot be substantiated, because girls' schools are not notably less professionally staffed than boys' schools – although in the past there was a grain of truth in this judgement, especially for ex-secondary modern schools. An alternative view might be that women, like other subordinated groups deprived of adequate representation in positions of power and authority, are bound by social relationships of mechanical solidarity which imply both less differentiation and a greater reliance on rules and external control (Durkheim, 1947). Authority relations in girls' schools may be more bureaucratic, petty, and rule-bound precisely because of the difficulty women face in occupying positions of authority in a culture that associates masculinity with such positions, and with the consequent lack of female models, other than maternal ones.[6] Certainly the position of a senior woman teacher is a lonely one, especially in a mixed school, and it is a state that is perpetuated by the Burnham

6. A careful analysis of this situation can be found in Richardson (1973) which might be compared with a much older study by Milner (1938) on a girls' school and with Holmes's (1965) discussion of the difficulties inherent in establishing authority relations under initial conditions of mechanical solidarity.

Committee's insistence that if, in a mixed school, the deputy head is a man, then a woman on the staff must be made 'senior' mistress (and vice versa if the deputy head is a woman). The consequence of this is not only to reinforce marriage but its implied division of labour as a model of cross-sex relations, but for women in particular it often has the effect of blocking career routes because one is not of the 'right' sex for the job.

Whilst on the subject of role and sex segregation, the possible links with what has come to be called conjugal segregation can be considered. The 'density' of kinship networks as a condition for great conjugal segregation may be questioned, but the question of what leads to various divisions of labour remains (Bott, 1971). As Bott's critics have argued, a sharp division of labour in the marital home is a function of the values of the community; it is likely to occur if the community supports such arrangements. We might note though, that where schools treat sex as a basis for educational organization, they do nothing to counteract the marked tendency towards role-segregation based on sex in the home and elsewhere.

In the recent and otherwise comprehensive survey of the available material on inequality by Jencks (1973) there is little mention of inequality as applied to women (although there is an interesting footnote referring to the greater difficulties that upper middle-class families face in trying to ensure a good marriage for their daughters as compared to their attempts to secure a decent education [Jencks, 1973, p. 216]). While Jencks's preference for explanation in terms of initial class position and a measure of luck as determinants of the eventual distribution of income, may be acceptable, it is harder to agree with his view that the educational process is only marginal in establishing inequalities of opportunity, particularly when considering groups like women. For women, whatever their class origins and educational level, are likely to receive less pay than men of equivalent class position. As his critics have pointed out, inequality is not confined only to the rewards attached to certain jobs, but concerns how people are recruited into these, or any, jobs. Inequalities based on class position may reinforce those based on sex or vice versa, but neither can be clearly explained in terms of the other. The common tendency to treat a woman's class as derived from her husband if she is married and from her father if she is not, may have been reasonable when large numbers of women were not permanent members of the labour force (an anomalous situation of the inter-war years; see Parkin, 1971). Unfortunately, however, it has encouraged sociologists to locate women socially in terms of status, to discount housework as work, and to ignore its place amongst the forces of production, or to confine their economic understanding of women to hived-off consumption activities. These are, of course, not unimportant, but they only make sense when understood as part of a woman's total market situation. We have to look at her position within the whole mesh of relations of production and not just at whether she owns the means of production or sells her labour. Galbraith (1974) has recently indicated the complexity of the problem by suggesting the different functions that women play as 'consumer specialists' in an economy dominated by planning or in one governed by the market.

Although we know rather little about the processes of occupational choice, we do know that there is an extraordinary adjustment of ambition and aspiration to socio-economic realities and that as children pass through school they tailor and trim their expectations (Williams, 1974). Quite how they manage this is more of a mystery for, as Hill (1962) points out, it is precisely at the juncture of leaving school that children are given minimal formal assistance and direction, least of all by teachers. Their direct exposure to the dictates of the market is significant not only because of the schools' effective abdication, but because it suggests that if there is a correspondence between the organizational principles and values of the school and those of the labour market, it is a structural one unmediated by professional guidance 'experts'. I think there are some striking similarities between the patterns of education and those of the work force such that the two systems are mutually determining and release us from the search for theories of decision-making and choice, be they conscious or unconscious.

SEX DIFFERENCES AND SKILL-LABELLING

Sex must not be ignored as a critical variable in education for, as one of the authors of the National Child Development Survey shows (Davie, 1973), it accounts for an even bigger difference in measured ability than those other well tried indicators, class and overcrowding. Possibly the clearest difference of all is that girls leave school less well qualified than boys, although nowadays they do not leave all that much sooner. In 1971-2, 33.5 per cent of boys left school aged fifteen compared to 33.7 per cent of girls. But it is worth noting that, unlike boys, a larger proportion of the girls remaining at school after the official leaving age do not prepare for examinations – which might indicate the different values that sex confers on education. In 1971-2 girls got slightly more 'O' levels

(23 per cent had more than five subjects) than boys (22.5 per cent), but at 'A' level there was a considerable reversal, with 9.1 per cent of boys getting three or more but only 6.6 per cent of girls managing to do so; an outcome that is only partially explained by differential aims and relative length of schooling. When we look at curricular differences, the pupil who takes science is likely to remain longer in full-time education at every stage than is the arts student, who is more likely to be a girl (Phillips, 1969). Overall, the numbers of school leavers who go on to full-time higher education is pitifully small for both sexes. In 1970 only 7.6 per cent of boys and 4.4 per cent of girls went on to university (Department of Education and Science, 1974). Among the under-eighteens entitled to be released from employment to take part-time courses during working hours, only 10.1 per cent of the girls as compared with 38.8 per cent of the boys did so.

One may doubt the importance of all this if, like Leibenstein (1969), one believes that it is rare for the labels thus acquired really to indicate the degree of skill held, especially given the wide range of skill possessed by those bearing similar labels. But, as he has succinctly argued, although the sort of education that one receives is only marginally related to the type of work that individuals eventually do, the labels that they bear are much more important. One of the consequences of not being suitably labelled is that in so far as the 'higher standards' lobby is successful, the chances of occupational mobility once in the labour market are shortened and the barriers between job classifications consolidated, and not only at the professional level. This near impossibility of movement between jobs is part of the trap that the lower-paid workers suffer and it may be precisely as 'skill-labelling' institutions that schools feed into what has recently been called the dual labour market (Doeringer and Bosanquet, 1973; Barron and Norris, 1975). This formulation holds that there are two relatively autonomous sectors in the labour market, one characterized by high earnings, high skill levels, low staff turnover, career structures, and/or prospects for on-the-job training, and the other displaying the reverse features of low pay, high turnover rates, low skill levels, and no training on the job, nor career prospects. In analysing the labour market it is noted that women and coloured workers are grossly over-represented in the second sector. Further, the above characteristics really belong to the *sectors* and not to those working in them, although the attribution is often transferred.

Firms appear to have a choice of whether to be high or low wage employers as wide differences in pay have been shown to co-exist within the same job category, industry and region (MacKay *et al.*,

1971). This suggests that something other than the market is determining wage rates and firms' ability to act in this fashion. Most probably this is the cumulative result of their own discriminatory practices and of the acquired and rational responses of employees forced to remain in the unrewarding sector. But it is also a function of the use of educational qualifications to prevent mobility between jobs. Writers on the dual labour market have noted the near impossibility of moving out of the secondary sector once within it and that this amounts to an almost irreversible handicap for older, immigrant, or female workers – all the groups who left school early and without qualifications. Unfortunately it is a characteristic of low-paid jobs and of skill-labelling that workers' positions are not redeemed by value being placed on experience or by the chances of being upgraded. Sponsored mobility offers a slim chance in view of the fact that in the UK apprenticeship is preferred to upgrading the semi-skilled, but not for girls. At this point we must note that whilst nearly 39 per cent of boys leaving school in 1972 entered apprenticeships or their equivalent leading to skilled occupations, less than 8 per cent of the girls did so (a rate of 1.5 [Department of Employment, 1973]). Most of the girls who did were destined for hairdressing. Furthermore, in the electrical engineering industry, where women made up half the labour force in 1970, there were only fifty girl apprentices compared with 4,466 boys. If it were possible to obtain regional data on employment opportunities and first placements by sex, it might provide a way of testing whether there are sharper and more rigid curricula divisions in schools in areas where there is both high overall unemployment and distinct sectors within the labour market.

In the most general sense all schools are obviously mediators of the opportunity structure for both sexes, but it may be that schools, especially those in poorer areas, take a rather broad view of those 'opportunities' for their girl pupils and implicitly see themselves as preparing girls for the marriage market as well as for the labour market. The prospect of marriage as an alternative 'success' may account for the lower levels of ambition and the disaffection that girls display, though this should not necessarily be seen as a device for 'cooling out' the less able girls in particular. What schools may rather opportunistically be concerned with is the convenient distraction that the girls' romantic hopes provide, which reduce the schools' responsibility for their future (i.e., they can attribute the lack of scholastic success to the girls themselves). Certainly, by failing to present girls with futures in terms of careers, schools create the possibilities of later 'role-conflict', which may further 'qualify' women as especially suitable for the secondary labour market; for here, if anything is prized, it is precisely such dispensability or willingness to be separated from their jobs.

CONCLUSION

In this paper I have concentrated on secondary education because I consider it no accident that sex is most evident and debated as an organizing principle within this part of the education system, for this is the sector most responsive to the demands of the labour market. Sexual division has virtually disappeared as an issue in primary education where 'job choice' is five to ten years away. In higher education, however, there are other, still unresolved, divisions by sex.

The argument has centred on the mutual interdependence between certain features of the labour market and those aspects of education, especially curricular ones, that distinguish the sexes. The issuing of certificates and labels by schools makes a central contribution to that process and to the significant differences in educational outcome that the sexes achieve. The meanings and consequences of sexual divisions in our society are translated into educational terms so that the different sub-cultures of boys' and girls' schools are but specialized versions of a wider culture, in which female futures are still defined in essentially domestic terms – a stereotyping which our educational system does little to undermine.

References

Banks, O. (1955), *Parity and Prestige in English Secondary Education*, London: Routledge.

Banks, O. and Finlayson, D. (1973), *Success and Failure in the Secondary School*, London: Methuen.

Barron, R. and Norris, G. (1976), 'Sexual Divisions and the Dual Labour Market', in D. Leonard Barker and S. Allen (eds.), *Dependence and Exploitation in Work and Marriage*, Harlow: Longman.

Benn, C. and Simon, B. (1972), *Half-way There*, Harmondsworth: Penguin.

Bernstein, B. (1973), *Class, Codes and Control*, London: Routledge and Kegan Paul.

Bott, E. (1971), *Family and Social Network*, London: Tavistock.

Brown, V. (1972), *Social Relations in a Girls Secondary School*, Dissertation for B.Ed. Birmingham (unpublished).

Dale, R. (1969), Mixed or Single Sex School, vol. I, London: Routledge and Kegan Paul.

—(1971), Mixed or Single Sex School, vol. II, London: Routledge and Kegan Paul.

—(1974), Mixed or Single Sex School, vol. III, London: Routledge and Kegan Paul.

Davie, R. (1973), 'Eleven Years of Childhood', Statistical News, no. 22, August 1973.

Department of Education and Science (1974), Statistics of Education, vol. 2, London: HMSO.

Department of Employment (1973), Gazette, London: HMSO.

Doeringer, P. B. and Bosanquet, N. (1973), 'Is There a Dual Labour Market in Great Britain?', Economic Journal, June.

Douglas, J. W. B., Ross, J. M. and Simpson, S. R. (1968), All Our Future, London: Davies.

Durkheim, E. (1947), On the Division of Labour in Society, Glencoe, Illinois: Free Press.

Galbraith, J. K. (1974), Economics and the Public Purpose, London: Deutsch.

Goode, W. (1967), 'The Protection of the Inept', American Sociological Review, February.

Hargreaves, D. (1967), Social Relations in a Secondary School, London: Routledge.

Hill, J. M. (1962), From School to Work, London: Tavistock.

Holmes, R. (1965), 'Freud, Piaget and Democratic Leadership', British Journal of Sociology, 16 (2), pp. 123-39.

Jackson, B. and Marsden, D. (1962), Education and the Working Class, London: Routledge and Kegan Paul.

Jencks, C. (1973), Inequality, London: Allen Lane.

Lacey, C. (1970), Hightown Grammar, Manchester: Manchester UP.

Leibenstein, H. (1969), 'The Economics of Skill-Labelling', in J. A. Lawreys and D. G. Scanlon (eds.), World Year Book of Education, London: Evans.

MacKay, D. I., Boddy, D., Brack, J., Diack, J. A. and Jones, N. (1971), Labour Markets under Different Employment Conditions, London: Allen and Unwin.

Milner, M. (1938), The Human Problem in Schools, London: Methuen.

Murdock, G. and Phelps, G. (1973), Mass Media and the Secondary School, London: Macmillan.

Parkin, F. (1971), Class, Inequality and Political Order, London: MacGibbon and Kee.

Phillips, C. (1969), Changes in Subject Choice at School and University, London: Weidenfeld.

Richardson, E. (1973), The Teacher, the School and the Task of Management, London: Heinemann.

Rosenthal, R. and Jacobson, L. (1968), Pygmalion in the Classroom: Teacher Expectations and Pupils' Intellectual Development, New York: Holt, Rinehart and Winston.

Simon, B. (1971), Intelligence, Psychology and Education, London: Lawrence and Wishart.

Simpson, R. L. and Simpson, I. H. (1969), 'Women in Bureaucracy', in A.

Etzioni (ed.), *The Semi-Professions and their Organisation*, New York: Free Press.

Sutherland, M. (1961), 'Coeducation and School Attainment', *British Journal of Educational Psychology*, 31, pp. 158-69.

Turner, R. (1964), 'Some Aspects of Women's Ambition', *American Journal of Sociology*.

Williams, W. M. (1974), *Occupation Choices*, London: George Allen and Unwin.

Willis, P. and Critcher, C. (1974), 'Women in Sport', in *Cultural Studies*, 5, Birmingham: Centre for Contemporary Cultural Studies.

Young, D. A. and Brandis, W. (1967), 'Two Types of Streaming', *University of London Institute of Education Bulletin*.

Young, M. and Willmott, P. (1973), *The Symmetrical Family*, London: Routledge.

Culture and Ideology

Although many of feminism's battles have been concerned with the conditions in which women exist in the material world, a major concern of many feminists has also been to define and demonstrate the part which ideology and culture play in the reproduction of female subordination. Hence, the mass media, literature, the visual arts and the taken-for-granted cultural assumptions of everyday life have all become objects of feminist scrutiny. Few feminists would argue that cultural and ideological products are in themselves solely responsible for the subordination of women; but there is a general consensus that those social processes and structures which oppress women are reinforced by sexist and patriarchal assumptions in the media, culture and language.

Feminist attacks on patriarchal and sexist ideology were at first concentrated on the mass media, whose use of gross sexual stereotypes was an obvious target for attack. As a number of feminist critics pointed out, women were presented in two ways by the media: as glamorous objects for male sexual pleasure and gratification or as tender-hearted earth mothers, ready to comfort and nurture children and men. Yet even as these accusations were generally endorsed, it was also clear to many feminists that the general ideological and cultural representation of women was more complicated than some studies of the mass media suggested. Although the picture of women in the mass media was essentially a simple, uncomplicated one, much of what is sometimes described as 'high culture' presents a view of women which is frequently subtle and complicated.

The area of 'high culture' which has received the greatest attention from feminists is that of literature, and one of the most widely influential books of the revival of feminism in the late 1960s and early 1970s was Kate Millett's *Sexual Politics*, a study of sexism in the novels of D. H. Lawrence, Norman Mailer and Henry Miller. A number of books published at about the same time drew on literature in much the same way as Millett, in order to demonstrate both the existence of sexism and its integration into the central values of Western culture. Yet this use of literature, essentially as evidence to support a particular theory, contains numerous difficulties, not the least of which is the danger of extracting from a text only one aspect of a complex set of relationships between individuals and social processes. As Cora Kaplan, in the piece reprinted here, has argued in the case of Millett's work, there is a danger that feminist discussions of literature, in identifying sexism and relations between the sexes as the critical issues in human affairs, overlook other significant relationships. For example, a feminist reading of *Anna Karenina* might well see the fate of Anna as a result of a single factor: the subordination of women in Czarist Russia. Certainly, pre-Revolutionary Russia was hardly progressive in its attitudes to women, but the account ignores many of the complex relationships suggested by Tolstoy between the psychological characteristics of the central characters and their social situation.

However, the numerous feminist readings of classic Western literature which have now been published do not, on the whole, isolate sexual relationships to the exclusion of all others. What has been achieved by studies such as Ellen Moers' *Literary Women* and Elaine Showalter's *A Literature of Their Own* is a demonstration of the way in which generations of male authors and literary critics have misunderstood the meaning attached to female sexuality and women's social and sexual role by women themselves. Thus, however perceptively a man might write about women and their relations with men, the emphasis placed on certain factors in these relationships may differ with the sex of the author. A debate now exists about whether or not this is necessarily the case: one side arguing that the sexes will write essentially different accounts of the social and sexual world, the other asserting that great literature is sex-less, in the sense that an author of genius is capable of transcending the limits of his or her own sexual identity. The argument, in the case of the classic works of Western literature, is unlikely to be conclusive since the nature and complexity of the texts diminishes the possibility of definitive conclusions of any kind.

While it is likely that arguments will continue to rage about the treatment and discussion of women and female concerns in 'great' literature, the interpretation of the mass media and popular literature offers fewer problems as individuals and individual problems are presented more simply and with little suggestion of the possible complications of human existence. Yet because the view of women presented by the mass media is generally simple, this should not be taken to imply that the stereotypes that they produce – of sex goddesses and earth mothers – are not extremely influential and potent symbols, although there is very little academic evidence about the effects of the media's picture of women on the population as a whole. Nevertheless, we know from other sources that the media can have a significant reinforcement effect on existing social attitudes and predilections. Halloran's work on the media's presentation of the campaign against United States intervention in Vietnam suggested that people are affected by the vision of the world presented to them on television or in the press.[1] If that view is biased, or one-sided, then the bias is incorporated into an individual's understanding or interpretation of particular events and situations.

That a bias exists in the presentation of women in the media is now a taken-for-granted assumption of media studies. No study exists which gives the kind of detailed account of bias in the media provided by Glasgow University's Media Group in *Bad News* and *More Bad News*,[2] but numerous essays on popular literature, film, television and radio indicate a consistent trivialisation of women and a marked reluctance on the part of writers and directors to depart from stereotypical presentations of women. For example, Dorothy Hobson's essay on 'Housewives and the Mass Media' in *Culture, Media, Language* demonstrates the persistent tone of condescension and patronage with which male disc jockeys address their female audience.[3] As she points out, those same disc jockeys who could at times be heard praising 'sexy' female singers were equally likely to be voicing laudatory comments about traditional, home-making wives and mothers.

While the majority of feminist studies on women and culture have been of the content of cultural works, a number have also drawn attention to the difficulties which prevent women from taking as effective a part in the production of culture as men. From Virginia Woolf's *A Room of One's Own* to Germaine Greer's *The Obstacle Race* feminists have argued that women's under-representation in cultural life (particularly in the fine arts and music) is due not to women's lack of talent, but their lack of training and patronage. For generations, boys rather than girls were apprenticed to artists and sculptors; it was boys who received musical education and, more recently, men who control, or who had access to, the capital necessary to make films or produce plays. That is not to say that women never become great artists or musicians or singers, some did, and some do, but the numbers are significantly

---

1. See *Demonstrations and Communication: a Case Study* by J. D. Halloran, P. Elliott and G. Murdock, Harmondsworth: Penguin, 1970.
2. *Bad News* and *More Bad News* by the Glasgow University Media Group, London: Routledge and Kegan Paul, 1978 and 1980 respectively.
3. Dorothy Hobson, 'Housewives and the Mass Media', in S. Hall, D. Hobson, A. Lowe and P. Willis, eds., *Culture, Media, Language*, London: Hutchinson, 1980, pp. 105-14.

less than in the case of men. Only in literature where, as Virginia Woolf pointed out, what was necessary was literacy, leisure and determination, rather than formal training, have women made a contribution which is both qualitatively and quantitatively as great as that of men.

Yet Virginia Woolf's discussion of women and literature, like that of many other feminists, contains two assumptions which some contemporary feminists would challenge. The first is the distinction between great and popular art, and the second the objective nature of the basis of literature – that is, language. Today, some feminists would argue that the distinctions traditionally made between popular and great art and literature are frequently a reflection of male interests and activity. Thus they ask, for example, why landscape painting should be regarded as significant art, while patchwork and embroidery are seen as little more than domestic skills. Hence an extremely radical argument is proposed about the Western concept of art and culture: an argument whch challenges the age-old distinctions between high and popular culture. Not only, therefore, have feminists asked important questions about the content of art and the conditions of its production, they have challenged prevailing orthodoxy about its very nature.

A second assumption of traditional feminist writing on literature, that language is sexually neutral, has now also been found wanting by some contemporary women. Dale Spender, Susan Sontag and many others have argued that language contains numerous implicit prejudices – prejudices in favour of men and against women.[4] These prejudices go beyond such features of a language as titles of address (for example, the much vaunted case of men's marital status not being expressed in a particular form of address) and are, Ms Key and others argue, an important part of the reason why women cannot adequately express their feelings and desires. The world is constantly seen through someone else's glasses and consequently reality is always slightly blurred, if not actually obscured. For this reason, the attraction of non-verbal forms of communication for some feminists is considerable, and the visual

4. See Dale Spender, Man Made Language, London: Routledge and Kegan Paul, 1980; and Susan Sontag, 'The Third World of Women', Partisan Review, 40, no. 2, 1973. See also Mary Ritchie Key, Male/Female Language, Metuchen, New Jersey: Scarecrow Press, 1975; Robin Lakoff, Language and Woman's Place, New York: Harper and Row, 1975; Barrie Thorne and Nancy Henley, eds., Languages and Sex: Difference and Dominance, Rowley, Massachusetts: Newbury House, 1975; and Cheris Kramer, Barrie Thorne and Nancy Henley, 'Perspectives on Language and Communication', in Signs, vol. 3, no. 3, Spring 1978, pp. 638-51.

arts are seen to offer a more flexible means of the expression of women's experience. Yet in feminist art, just as much as in feminist literature, problems arise about interpretation and subjectivity. Although a bias against women is detectable in much of art and literature, the problem still remains unresolved about whether or not a specific feminist aesthetic judgment can, or even should, exist.

Cora Kaplan

Radical Feminism and Literature: Rethinking Millett's *Sexual Politics*

In *Red Letters*, no. 9, London, 1979, pp. 4-16

With the publication of Kate Millett's *Sexual Politics* (1970) radical Feminist theory can be said to have 'come out', costumed, not surprisingly, in something old – refurbished bits and pieces of sixties New Left radicalism – as well as something new – 'a systematic overview of patriarchy as a political institution'.[1] Millett's reworking of 'patriarchy' is conceptually co-ordinated with the left-libertarian policies that underwrote the civil rights, anti-imperialist and counter-culture movements. From this tendency *Sexual Politics* retained a violent hostility to the 'functionalist' bias of the academy coupled with a mildly receptive if somewhat duff ear for Marx and Engels, the latter modified by a firm rejection of Stalinist old-left politics. Patriarchy was defined as 'a political institution' rather than an economic or social relation, and political institutions were in their turn conceived as hierarchical power relations. Institutions were conceptualised as expressing oppression in homologous or analogous ways, so that the State, the Family, the University, the Mental Hospital or the Army, instead of having differentiated structures and a complex articulation, were, instead, metaphors for each other, emphasising through their similarities the dominance relations of the society as a whole, which were characterised by racism, sexism and capitalism. This type of analysis, which owed a great deal to the functionalism it refused, provided a theoretical justification for struggle on all possible sites in the sixties. The campus thus became as valid a place to fight as Mississippi. While it is unfair to ridicule or denigrate the resistance of the decade, it it crucial for us now to understand where this analysis, so simple, and often so simply wrong, was instrumental in the creation of radical Feminist theory.

Millett's influential book is especially useful if one asks why so

1. Kate Millett, *Sexual Politics*, London, 1972, p. xi. All references are to the Abacus paperback edition. *Sexual Politics* was first published in Great Britain in 1971 by Rupert Hart-Davis. A new edition (1978) is available from Virago.

disproportionate a number of declared Feminists have chosen literature as the particular object of their analysis of female subordination. For even given the relatively large numbers of academic women who read arts subjects rather than economics, politics or labour relations, and taking into account the primacy which 'ideology' holds in Feminist theories of all political complexions, the attention given to literature as a source of patriarchal ideology or Feminist liberation is peculiar, and surely requires some explanation and political justification. *Sexual Politics*, one of the most readable and innovative texts of the modern women's movement, helps to make sense of this tendency. Almost half the book is devoted to the theoretical and historical development of patriarchy; the third section examines 'The Literary Reflection' as revealed in the work of four male authors, D. H. Lawrence, Henry Miller, Norman Mailer and Jean Genet. In this final section Millett has made a lasting intervention in literary criticism. Since *Sexual Politics* it has been difficult for critics to ignore the wider social and political implications of the representation of sexual practice in fiction. In taking issue with Millett's interpretations, critics, myself included, have been forced on to her ground, made to admit that the depiction of sex in literature is an ideological issue for author, reader and critic. Once you have read Millett, an 'innocent' enjoyment of the sexual in literature is almost sure to be lost. This breaking-up of an unthinking 'broad-minded', liberal consensus about sexual representation has been a major achievement. *Sexual Politics* sets another excellent precedent, not generally acknowledged. Unlike most recent Feminist books on literature, even including Ellen Moers' brilliant, eclectic study of *Literary Women* (1975),[2] *Sexual Politics* sets literary analysis against a specific theory of women's subordination, in relation to ideologies of gender difference inscribed in other contemporary discourses and practices. The book provides the material for its own critique.

Rereading the first half of *Sexual Politics* is still rewarding. Millett had researched very widely; she touched most of the issues which Feminists have developed in the seventies. The historical section marks off the period 1830-1930 as a time of 'Sexual Revolution' and the period of 1930-60 as 'The Counter-revolution'. Even this periodisation, indicating radical putsch and inevitable backlash, harks back to a very sixties left description of the ebb and flow of radical movements. In the course of her historical exposition there are valuable discussions of Mill and Engels, and

2. *Literary Women* is available in the UK in paperback, The Women's Press, 1978.

a more central if wildly uneven account of the sinister patriarchal implications in the development of psychoanalytic and social theory.

Millett's prose is often denser than her arguments, but even so the first half of the book is so full of matter that it is sometimes difficult to keep track of the logic of her analysis. She is centrally concerned to show how patriarchal ideology has kept pace with profound changes in attitudes towards sexuality, which in Millett's broad definition generally means social, economic and political relations between men and women, but occasionally means sexuality alone. It would require a much longer piece to deal fully with Millett's concept of the workings of patriarchy; for the purposes of this essay I want to concentrate on two theoretical issues which have far-reaching implications for Millett's literary analysis: the first is her understanding of 'ideology' within her larger definition of patriarchy, and the second, related to the first but narrower in scope, is her critique of Freud. Once Millett's position on these subjects has been located it becomes much easier to see why she has tackled literature through male writers almost exclusively, and why Lawrence, Miller, Mailer and Genet have been chosen instead of an alternative group composed say, of James, Fitzgerald, Updike and Baldwin, novelists equally obsessed with the social and political implications of sexuality. We can see why literature, such an important area of concern for radical Feminism, remains, even in the hands of a skilful and academically trained critic like Millett, virtually untheorised.

RADICAL FEMINISM AND IDEOLOGY

Under the sixties' slogan 'the personal is political' a space was made for Feminists to include the psychological effects of female socialisation as one of the principal oppressions suffered by women in male-dominated societies. Franz Fanon and Kenneth Clark (the Black sociologist) had offered prior analyses of the internalised effects of racism in colonial countries and in the United States. It was easy to see that if racial stereotyping could induce feelings of inferiority and difference, gender distinctions, even more widely held by human societies, could be instilled at a deep level. Successful struggle by Africans and American Blacks against racism showed that its effects were damaging but not permanent. At the same time as Fanon, Clark and others were exploring the psychological implications of racist and imperialist ideologies, the radical right were heralding the end of ideology –

by which they meant the political and social theories held by the left. In choosing a working definition of ideology, Feminists did not hesitate to choose a loosely Marxist conception in which ideology was a world seen upside-down, alienated, mystified – a false representation which reflected the alienating conditions in which people lived. This definition is largely drawn from early Marxist texts which liberal academics in the sixties were pulling out of the dying fires to which they had been consigned by zealous book-burning McCarthyites a few years earlier. However in Marx early or late, ideologies are formed by material conditions of existence related to historically specific modes of production. One may go quite far in insisting on the relative autonomy of ideology, and still call oneself a Marxist, but one can never see ideology as taking a form which does not have a necessary dialectical relation with a given mode of production. However much the American New Left in the sixties concentrated on the political at the expense of the economic, however much it confused consciousness with struggle, it never quite forgot about capitalism, nor did it generally abandon the Marxist concept of the determination of the base, i.e. the economy, in the last instance, even if the last instance seemed as far off as the last trump. However a sea change occurs in the development of radical Feminist theory, which insists on the primacy of gender difference over all other determinations. In Marxist theory ideologies of the bourgeoisie and the proletariat were seen as class specific ideologies dictated by class divisions created by capitalism with bourgeois ideology dominant. 'Ideology' in Marxist shorthand means bourgeois ideology. In radical Feminist theory the notion of dominant ideology of a ruling group as distinct, say, from a 'national' ideology is retained, as is the concept of ideology as a false representation. However now *only* patriarchal ideology ruled, an ideology which ignored and/or transcended class division. Radical Feminism is by no means a theoretical unity, any more than Marxism, or Marxist-Feminism. Within radical Feminism the origin of women's subordination is variously described, yet it is always at pains to point out that the transhistorical, transcultural, transclass character of women's oppression proves that patriarchy is much more fundamental in the determination of women's condition of existence that the effects of any given mode of production. The original conditions under which men seized power over women, or maintained it at subsequent historical moments, hardly matters. What does matter is that power is maintained by men through ideologies of gender inequality. Just as Marx characterises capital as having as its raison d'etre the extraction of surplus value (unpaid labour) from the worker, so patriarchy's reason-for-being in this unmediated definition is to ensure the domination of men over women. It is easy to see how patriarchy becomes, given this emphasis, primarily a power relation, and patriarchal ideology its energy source.

Millett on Freud has become so familiar a part of anti-patriarchal rhetoric that there is some danger when looking again at Millett's anti-Freud passages[3] of watching mesmerised as the knife blade makes a telling stroke here and there at Viennese phallocentrism, and assuming the rest of the argument, as it has been taken up by Shulamith Firestone and others.[4] A more dutiful rereading is interesting. Millett's technique is to isolate elements of Freudian theory drawn from different periods and kinds of writing in order to emphasise the gross chauvinism of certain passages on women – as well as to ridicule the methodology together with the conclusions. She sees Freud's work on women as giving pseudo-scientific imprimatur to biological determinism, and, further, to be motivated centrally by Freud's distaste for 'feminist insurgence'. Penis envy, Millett's particular bete, noir or blanc, was 'in fact a superbly timed accusation, enabling masculine sentiment to take the offensive again as it had not since the disappearance of overt misogyny when the pose of chivalry became fashionable'.[5] As Millett herself points out later, in a rather more acute and milder discussion of Erik Erikson on women, chivalry is simply a polite form of misogyny. In any case her dating of the disappearance of overt misogyny is fuzzy. Did it ever disappear? Or does it simply recede in Millett's account so that she can place Freud in the foreground as the arch-enemy of Feminism? Here is an unhappily typical example of Millett's polemic, which itself commits the errors which she lays at Freud's door:

> Freud's circular method in formulating penis envy begins by reporting children's distorted impressions, gradually comes to accept them as the correct reaction, goes on to present its own irresponsible version of the socio-sexual context, and then, through a nearly imperceptible series of transitions, slides from description to a form of prescription which insures the continuance of the patriarchal status quo, under the guise of health and normality. Apart from ridicule, the counter-revolutionary period never employed a more withering or destructive weapon

3. Millett, p. 176-203.
4. Shulamith Firestone, The Dialectic of Sex, London, 1972. Until quite recently most American Feminists have been firmly anti-Freudian.
5. Millett, p. 189.

against feminist insurgence than the Freudian accusation of penis envy.[6]

Note the ambiguous use of 'children's distorted impressions' and the substitution of 'irresponsible' for incorrect. Millett concentrates on Freud's ascription of penis envy, narcissism and masochism to women. She does not concern herself very much *here* with oedipalisation and its consequences, or the concept of the unconscious, nor nearly enough with Freud's general point that our social identity is constructed through our taking on the position of one sex or another at an early age. Millett even feels that Freud's promisingly liberated theory that all humans are basically bisexual is vitiated because he still wishes to see healthy adults as normal at widely differentiated points in the spectrum of socialised gender difference. She insists that Freud's theories on women are an example of biological determinism, with women locked into their natural role of mothers. But even here she is convinced that Freud manages to denigrate women, denying them autonomy in this inferior role, by posing babies as penis substitutes. Freud's point is indirectly made but it seems pretty clearly to be about the unfair social overdetermination of the value of maleness in society. Millett opts for a deliberate misreading for the sake of a cheap flash: 'It somehow becomes the male prerogative even to give birth, as babies are but surrogate penises ... were she to deliver an entire orphanage of progeny, they would only be so many dildoes.'[7]

Millett's comments on Freud's deeply contradictory writings on women are frequently illuminating, but the whole attack is conducted with so much blinding vitriol, and is so determined not to salvage even a castrated version of Freudian theory that she weakens her case. Freud did not, after all, invent patriarchy; his chauvinism is of a very old-fashioned kind. It is hard to believe that 'penis envy', crude as its application has been, has smashed more female ambitions than its older common-sense cousin which merely sneered that women who entered 'male' occupations were imitation men. Marxist-Feminists, starting with Juliet Mitchell in *Psychoanalysis and Feminism* (1974), feel that Freud and some modern members of his school have done more to enable understanding of gender construction in spite of the phallocentric bias of their work than other psychoanalytic theorists seemingly more sympathetic to women. These Feminists are now concerned

6. *Ibid.*
7. Millett, p. 185.

with revision and reinterpretation of Freud's work, and an exploration of its uses for materialist theories of ideology. Millett, however, had to reject the unconscious, the pivotal concept in Freud, and something common to human subjects of both sexes, because she is committed to a view that patriarchal ideology is a conscious conspiratorial set of attitudes operated by men against all empirical evidence of women's equal status, in order to support patriarchal power in office. It must be imposed on an essential, but already social, female subject who is not tainted with femininity, i.e. passivity, penis envy, narcissism, etc. Freud's understanding of the internalisation of femininity is indeed conservative, even pessimistic from certain Feminist perspectives, and Millett is out to prove that, though the conspirators are formidable, the struggle is easier than we think. To this end she is not even afraid to misquote that most famous of Freud's pronouncements on women which comes at the end of his essay on 'Femininity' where he warns his readers that he has discussed women 'only insofar as their nature is determined by their sexual function'.[8] (This reservation, of course, governs most of his discussions of men, as well.) Millett naughtily clips this sentence so that 'Freud warns that "their nature is determined by their sexual function"'.[9] Freud's destiny at Millett's hands is determined less by his anatomy than the 'cheap and chippy chopping' of his words.

Juliet Mitchell in *Psychoanalysis and Feminism* (1974) refuses the simple homologies of Millett's analysis, and rehabilitates for English-speaking readers Freudian theory and its modern articulation, both as part of an analysis of femininity and as a way of introducing a more complex and comprehensible theory of ideology into Marxist-Feminist thought. Her contribution is invaluable and has been widely influential in providing a powerful critique of Millett. But the integration of Marx and Freud, by Mitchell and others, has not proved easy. Mitchell, following Louis Althusser's use of Freud and Lacan, makes the unconscious central to the workings of ideology. She lays a heavy emphasis on the importance of oedipalisation in the development of femininity. Ideology is endowed with a material existence and given a 'relative autonomy' from other determinations, thus avoiding a crudely economistic analysis of female subordination, but separating ideology from the mode of production so that their interrelation is hard to specify. For 'if the kinship system that defines matriarchy'

8. Sigmund Freud, *New Introductory Lectures on Psychoanalysis*, vol. 2, 'Femininity', London, 1973, p. 169.
9. Millett, p. 202.

(now redundant) is 'forced into the straightjacket of the nuclear family' (capitalist family) (Mitchell, p. 412) – how can it be forced out again? The functionalist formulation of these problems may help to define the problem but it also tends towards the production of dualistic analyses of the economy and female socialisation as they articulate women's subordination in modern industrial societies. Freudian theory, with its emphasis on repetition and reproduction of ideological positions, emphasises, perhaps too heavily, the unalterable distance between gender positions so that they remain rather like Marvell's 'Definition of Love' stuck at distant poles, 'begotten by Despair/Upon Impossibility'.

Moreover there is a peculiar congruence between Millett and Mitchell which stems from their common preoccupation with 'ideology'. Millett's already constituted 'free' female subject, who has only to throw off her ideological bondage, boards in the same house where Mitchell's internally bound 'lady' lives her ideological imprisonment in material ideology. Neither of them really works for a living, or at least not in the sense in which women who are considered more fully in terms of class *and* gender work. For this establishment whether it goes under the name of Relative Autonomy or Idealism is marked by its transhistorical and transclass character, and houses only the oldest profession: its inmates are women who trade exclusively in their sexuality.

The tendency both of Mitchell's Marxist-Feminist structuralism and Millett's radical Feminist idealism is to displace the complex if mundane questions of women's subordination through the sexual division of labour under different modes of production. Mitchell poses the contradiction between patriarchy and capitalism as a loophole through which Feminism can view the creation of the feminine unconscious, but like big Alice with her eye to the keyhole there's not much she can do about it. Patriarchy creates and recreates the psychic conditions for women's subordination which are not the thin voile of false consciousness, but rather the very flesh and blood of female subjectivity. It must be hoped, given this analysis, that struggle can take place where patriarchal ideology and capitalist ideology and interests clash. This is certainly an argument worth having, and one which certain Marxist-Feminists are taking up. Mitchell's own explorations of the problem run into difficulty where she continues to use a very formalist description of 'levels' in which women's work is the most remote and sketchy, and her psychic processes the most prominent and solid. In Millett, on the other hand, capitalism is disappeared except as an effect of patriarchy. Ideology is the universal penile club which men of all classes use to beat women with. Women *do not* beat themselves, the unconscious, both its formation and its effects, are denied and 'penis envy' has only to be exposed for the pathetic support to patriarchal power that it is for women, the real woman hidden under male propaganda to be free in her individual consciousness if not yet *en masse*. As a consequence of this optimistic view very few women speak for themselves in the pages of *Sexual Politics*, maybe because a real woman is hard to find. Millett lets her male chauvinist social scientists and authors speak about them; even Feminist fellow travellers like Mill and Engels are more prominent than nineteenth century Feminist voices. Gender renegades, such as Mill and Engels, are allowed to espouse contradictions, but Feminism itself must be positivistic, fully conscious, morally and politically correct. It must know what it wants, and since what many women wanted was full of contradictions and confusions, still entangled in what patriarchy wanted them to be or wanted for them, Millett does not let them reveal too much of their 'weakness'.

IDEOLOGY AND LITERATURE

In Millett's world weakness and masochism are male projections of women's character. She believes that Freud's theories and Lawrence's fictions are discourses of essentially the same order and type, except that one provides the scientific rationale for the other. Hardest to accept in Millett's literary analysis is the unproblematic identification of author, protagonist and point of view, and the unspoken assumption that literature is always a conscious rendering of an authorial ideology. Although this assumption slips now and then, it is always shoved back stage centre. For if the unconscious were allowed expression then the writer would be, like the dreamer, or the children with 'distorted' ideas about sexuality, off the hook. If he were, slyly, to disengage somewhat from his most monstrous creations then he would be like Freud, lying in the name of objectivity. Millett loves Lawrence, Mailer, Miller and Genet because they seem to be so autobiographically centred in their work.

Consequently Millett has more respect for MCP novelists than for their brother psychoanalysts or social scientists, for although literature is a 'reflection' of the reality of patriarchal ideology it at least admits to being an imaginary tale of male potency. It accepts, in part, its status as a fiction. Moreover it takes the place of the revelations of psychoanalysts in that it discloses the relationship between sexuality and sociality without reference to objective knowledge of their real relationship, that is without the intervention of social science 'proofs'. Lawrence, Miller and Mailer are analyst and patient rolled into one, the onlie begetter of male fantasies which they themselves interpret. And since, in Millett's words, literature affords large insights 'into the life it describes, or interprets, or even distorts',[10] the critic can make 'a radical investigation which can demonstrate why Lawrence's analysis of a situation is inadequate, or biased, or his influence pernicious, without ever needing to imply that he is less than a great and original artist, and in many respects a man of distinguished moral and intellectual integrity'.[11] One does not have to quarrel with this judgement of Lawrence to wonder why it cannot be applied equally to Freud, why in the midst of this radical reordering of values that Feminism entails only great art, of all the patriarchal discourses, survives the dust heap or the pyre. It would be easy, too easy, to call Millett's preference for the true art of lying, bourgeois humanism, to see its conversion in the too uncritical praise of other Feminist critics for women's art, cultural Feminism, and to criticise both attitudes as 'elitist' or sentimental. There is another more disturbing element in Millett's stay of execution. Phallocratic novelists can survive in Millett's brave new world because they have performed exactly as patriarchal ideologists are supposed to. Caught in the missionary position, in the act of 'describing, interpreting and distorting life simultaneously', the male novelist can only plead guilty to creating women consciously to do his bidding and fulfil his desires. Literature emerges, in this view, as having a formal homology with the working of patriarchy, except in literature the male writer can, presumably, have it all his own way. Millett reads *Sons and Lovers, Tropic of Cancer* or 'The Time of Her Time' as models of patriarchal power in action, sadistic, depersonalised sexuality and the subordination of women in full swing. But since the writing is fiction the author can be represented as telling the truth about his desires and gross falsehoods about cultural reality. Millett's contempt for Freud is based on her belief that he is doing the same thing behind the mask of science. Writers are confessed criminals, or better still, criminal informers; they have integrity because they admit to their lack of it. Ironically, this is also why Millett prefers her phallocratic authors to be reliable narrators who identify wholly with their protagonists, although she recognises uncomfortably that even these unregenerate chauvinists can occasionally act as double agents and project into their

10. Millett, p. xii.
11. *Ibid.*

women characters. To fit her case they must be immersed, without contradiction, in their ideology of gender polarity and male dominance, so that their frictions become the ideal empirical verification of patriarchy's desired practice.

The consequence of this position is that Millett interrogates text and author simultaneously, using a popularised version of Freudian theory as it relates to male psychology as the major tool in her analysis. Discrete points are often sharp and revealing but since three different objects, author, text and social relations not to mention 'politics' have been collapsed into a single object the conclusions she draws from her readings are inevitably muddled. One can only look at a few examples of this process in action.

Millett has especial trouble in making *Lady Chatterley's Lover* fit her schema. She acknowledges that it is Lawrence's most sympathetic book about women, his 'attempt to make his peace with the female',[12] that it contains little of the sexual violence so prominent in Miller and Mailer, and even offers 'a program for social as well as sexual redemption'.[13] Generously, she reminds us that Lawrence's working title for the novel was 'Tenderness'.[14] Then she launches her attack on the book, using the crudest form of Freudian literary interpretation which reduces the author's work to his early familial relationships. As with penis envy, but with less justification, Millett assumes that the Oedipus complex is inevitably a pathological diagnosis instead of an essential process in human development which can under certain circumstances produce adult neurosis or pathology. She intimates somehow that Freud has invented it because he suffers from it, calling him 'another Oedipal son', like Lawrence.[15] As Millett deals with the relationship between author and character, the latter becomes transformed into a real historical figure.

We are frequently told that Lawrence made restitution to his father and the men of his father's condition in creating Mellors and others like him. Such, alas, is not the case. Mellors is as one critic observes 'really a sort of gentleman in disguise', and if the portrait of the broken drunkard in *Sons and Lovers* is cruel, and it is undeniably, it is less cruel than converting the victim of industrial brutality into a blasé sexual superman who is too much of a snob to belong to either the working or the middle classes. The late Lawrentian hero is clearly Lawrence's own fantasy of

12. Millett, p. 238.
13. Millett, p. 242.
14. Millett, p. 238.
15. Millett, p. 248.

the father he might have preferred. In the same way, Lady Chatterley is a smartened-up version of his mother herself. Like his own wife Frieda von Richthofen, she is a real lady, not that disappointed little woman of the mining village with chapped red hands who fears her clothes are too shabby to be seen in Lincoln cathedral. Yet Mrs Morel is a brave, even a great woman, though waitresses in teahouses snub her when she can only order custard, too poor to pay for a full meal. *Sons and Lovers* gives us Lawrence's parents without the glamor with which his snobbishness later invested them. All the romances of his later fiction are a reworking of his parents' marriage, and of his own too, modeled on theirs, but a notable advance in social mobility. For Lawrence saw his course, saw it with a Calvinistic sense of election, as a vocation to rise and surpass his origins.[16]

Millett doesn't expand upon what could or ought to constitute literary 'restitution' to one's father. *Pace* Graham Hough, the most superficial reading of *Lady Chatterley* will show that Mellors is not drawn as a 'gentleman in disguise', but as a type still extant in British life, an embittered, educated man of working-class origins, unwilling quite to become a class renegade, but cut off from class identity.[17] He is not drawn as a blasé sexual superman, but rather as someone whose sexual experience has been bad enough to make him temporarily continent. Connie may owe something to Frieda, but the only thing that she has in common with Mrs Morel is her gender, though Millett is free to prefer the latter character. They are quite distinct portraits of two different women with different class backgrounds, psychology and experience. Millett's claim that writing about the aristocracy if you are not yourself of it is an attempt at class mobility makes a snob of everyone from Shakespeare – no, wait a minute, Chaucer – on upwards. If you're black and write about whites, or female and write about men or Irish and write about the English . . . ?

These are all minor cavils however. What is worst about this passage is not its ad hominem attack on Lawrence's supposed regressive, snobbish and false use of his personal history, but Millett's wish to eat her Freud and castrate him too. She does not seem to see that you can't demolish and denounce a psychic schema of development for one sex and accept its linked application to the other without a much more elaborate and careful

16. *Ibid.*
17. Graham Hough, *The Dark Sun, a Study of D. H. Lawrence*, London, 1956, 1968, p. 31.

critique than she has presented. Thus she accepts Freud's assessment of masculinity – aggressive, sadistic, Oedipally bound, terrified of castration, fetishistic, etc., but rejects the sexual bipolarity implied by identifying real men (admitted homosexuals excepted) with these attributes.

The whole of *Sexual Politics* is permeated by a coercive sexual morality, meant to replace those mores inscribed in patriarchy. Typical of the early years of the modern women's movement, it borrows from the sexual libertarianism of the sixties alternative ideologies, which in turn reacted against the macho poses of the post-war fifties. It is marked, among other things, by an extreme distaste for the recrudescent sado-mas elements of sexuality, however 'playfully' practiced. Surprisingly it has very rigid notions of sexual health. Thus in spite of Millett's sympathy towards overt homosexuality she is clinically severe towards authors who seem to identify with their heroines. Tennyson is a case in point and she puts this tendency in his work down to his 'problems of sexual identity', unconsciously lining herself up with the very normative views she ascribes to Freud, Lawrence, Miller, Mailer.[18] Now that it has become less fashionable to promote a 'correct' Feminist sexuality, so that it is no longer so important to be clitoral and/or gay as opposed to vaginal and straight, most of this moralising comes over as specious and naive, especially in regard to literature. Millett comes close, but never close enough, to understanding that literature is the place where bisexuality is spoken even by the most consciously phallocratic authors.

A less positivistic but equally 'Feminist' literary criticism would read not only *Lady Chatterley* but many of Millett's chosen texts quite differently. Mailer's 'The Time of Her Time', for instance, need not be read as a serious account of how Mailer-the-cocksman triumphs again, but rather as a Feiffer-like send up of the Greenwich Village macho scene, where Mailer's fake Irish bullfighter goads and gores his way through elaborate sexual games, in a parody of machismo and Hemingway. Mailer encourages such a reading by giving the girl the last word, allowing her to undermine with language the 'manhood' that had just been physically vindicated. Mailer is hard to interpret because his writing about America identifies and criticises fascism and imperialism with male fantasies about power and sexuality. These are fantasies that Mailer shares: at certain points they seem to take over his work, as in *The American Dream*, a tendency which suggests the instability of the metaphor between sexuality and

18. Millett, pp. 76-7.

politics. Perhaps what these writers ought to have suggested to Millett is that the sociology of sex, particularly sexuality as expressed in literature, is not the key to or the symbol of power politics. (She does seem to lean towards this view somewhat in her treatment of Genet.) If there is a central conviction in Mailer it is his unshaken belief that the personal is political and vice-versa. He keeps snapping away at the same view from every possible angle. In this belief Mailer and Millett are united and equally stubborn. *Flying*, Millett's Feminist rewrite of Mailer, gets no closer to the relationship between sex, gender and politics than Mailer's work, though it contains as much coupling and campaigning.

Millett may take her authors seriously, but it is hard for her, given her rejection of formalist or structuralist methodologies of literary criticism, to stay with a single text long enough to let the contradictory elements in its ideological inscription play themselves out in her analysis. She tends to note them in passing as detours from the general coherence of her readings, but since these readings must support such literature as the vanguard of an ideological counterrevolution with a well-planned, coherent, fully conscious attack on women it would be counterproductive of her to foreground conflict and sabotage, even fragging,[19] within the ranks. She looks for, and in most cases finds, a concrete reading, ties it to the text and heaves it over the side.

This method adds nothing to the development of a Marxist-Feminist literary criticism, which must look more carefully at the complex interrelation of class and gender ideologies in literature by men and women, which must attempt to theorise imaginative writing as something more specific, strange and fragmented than a 'reflection' of either patriarchal ideology or real social relations, and which may wish to cut loose, finally, from Feminism's overemphasis in the last decade on high culture as a leading influence, benign or vicious, on women's subordination or struggle. Millett's radical Feminism is quite clear about culture's central place in the sexual revolution: given the errors in her definition of patriarchy and the function of patriarchal ideology we should, as Marxists and Feminists, be wary of placing too many of our hopes and fears in the revision of culture. In her postscript, Millett concludes:

> The enormous social change involved in a sexual revolution is basically a matter of altered consciousness, the exposure and

---

19. 'fragging', a word coined in the Vietnam war for attacks on US officers by their own men.

elimination of social and psychological realities underlining political and cultural structures. We are speaking then, of a cultural revolution, which, while it must necessarily involve the political and economic reorganisation traditionally implied by the term revolution, must go far beyond this as well. And here it would seem that the most profound changes implied are ones accomplished by human growth and true re-education, rather than those arrived at through the theatrics of armed struggle – even should the latter become inevitable.[20]

Much of this statement is politically impeccable, but its emphasis, written as it was in the midst of the Vietnam war, is a little worrying; the theatrics of armed struggle seem more of a distant fiction than the realities of altered consciousness and human growth.

20. Millett, pp. 362-3.

Barbara Bellow Watson

On Power and the Literary Text

In *Signs*, vol. 1, no. 1, Chicago, Autumn
1975, pp. 111-18

For about 200 years, all discussions of women and power have had
to deal with the old and unsavory notion that the proper exercise
of power for women was through the use of their sexual attractions
to influence men. Now that this idea is no longer a matter for
serious discussion, the debate about women and power stands at
an interesting juncture. Issues concerning real power are now
before us, and women are facing their own potential for power,
paradoxically, at a time when the values surrounding power
structures in general are in question. One result has been a battle
of abstractions. On the one hand, there are those who believe that
women should acquire every power base they can and recognize
the reality pointed out by John Stuart Mill 100 years ago in the
classic essay, 'The Subjection of Women', that power is never
relinquished by its holders but must be wrested away by superior
force.[1] On the other hand, there are those who believe that for
women to move into the power structure is a capitulation to
masculine values and one that involves us in complicity with the
destructive social order the patriarchy has made. Stated so
crudely, and stated as polarized alternatives, these positions seem
difficult to relate to literature or to the sense of life enhanced by
literature. Yet I believe it is precisely the incompatibility of these
two ways of approaching the question that makes any fresh insight
to be gained through literature so helpful. Literature has always
been a way of saying, not so much, 'There *is* another world' as,
'Another world can be imagined.' When we turn from the political
statements about power to the literary works that may bear upon
them, we turn from the abstract to the imagined specific, and not
just to specific characters in specific circumstances but to the
deeper specification of meanings through language, imagery, and
structure. Because feminist criticism as a movement began as part
of the second wave of political feminism in the 1960s, its
judgmental and polemical functions have been more noticed than

1. John Stuart Mill and Harriet Taylor Mill, *Essays on Sex Equality*, ed. Alice S. Rossi,
Chicago: University of Chicago Press, 1970, p. 134.

its descriptive and analytic functions, its attentiveness to specific elements of the text. Yet feminist criticism can by such means provide a method of reading with a new consciousness, not narrower than the old but broader.

One experience many of us share as women is that some interpretations and some value judgments by eminent critics have always made us a little uncomfortable. We have tended to distrust our own judgment rather than theirs in explaining the fact that we could not really validate these interpretations out of our own perceptions. Certain critical dicta were false not just to our personal experience but to our literary experience. Coming back to the same books some years later, we have been able to find the reasons for our uneasiness. It is no longer so difficult to justify, so 'subjective'. At least, if we are subjective, they are subjective too. The *ad feminam* and the *ad hominem* arguments cancel each other out. We are then left facing the work itself. In the light of a new consciousness, previously obscure themes and tensions may stand revealed. In the novels of D. H. Lawrence, for example, the passages of painful stylistic inadequacy are often those passages in which a masculinist doctrine is being forced on the materials in a way that is actually at war with the artistic integrity of the novel. In the 'Excurse' chapter of *Women in Love*, descriptions, both turgid and obscure, of thighs, loins, dark floods, darkest fires, intolerable accessions, marvelous fullnesses, mystic sources, ineffable darkness, and ineffable richness are set down in the midst of brilliant simplicities of narrative description. Even in *Lady Chatterley's Lover*, where the excuse of fear of censorship does not apply, similar passages intrude. There is something to be learned from such lapses. Shaw practiced feminist criticism in this sense when he advised Ellen Terry on cutting *Cymbeline* '... so as to leave the paragon out and the woman in ...'[2] In 1896 this was not intended as feminist criticism, but Shaw understood that the falsification, however partial, of the woman's role must detract from the effectiveness of the drama, no matter how traditional the role itself. In effect, this is feminist criticism. It picks up the discord between the vitality of existence and the rigidity of social myth.

The way of reading I contemplate is an escape from the dilemma of two polarized abstractions by means of a literary restatement of the realities of power, a method analogous to Elaine Showalter's delineation of three stages in the development of women's

2. *Ellen Terry and Bernard Shaw: a Correspondence*, ed. Christopher St. John, New York: Theater Art Books, 1931, p. 26.

literature: the first, imitation; the second, protest; the third, exploring the female experience.[3] Nothing Hegelian here. Merely a change of approach. The first two stages are obviously governed by an outside force, the intractable presence of a literary world dominated by men. The third shifts the focus from method to matter, turning to concrete reality to describe what *is*, distracted as little as possible by either anger or apology. If the two positions on women and power mentioned earlier correspond to Showalter's first two phases – imitation of masculine power succeeded by protest and rejection of masculine power and power structures – the contribution of literature to the quarrel between the two might correspond to Showalter's third category: exploring the female experience and moving debate into a realm that is real to the imagination.

What *has* been the experience of women in regard to power? Literature has more to say about this subject than might at first appear. Women, like other groups with minority status, adopt various forms of accommodation to protect themselves. The most essential form of accommodation for the weak is to conceal what power they do have and to avoid anything that looks like threat or competition. Therefore we must not expect either the literature written by women or that written by men based on their observations of women to tell us much about so sensitive a topic in the form of declarations, manifestos, plot summaries, or even the broad outlines of characterization. We begin instead to look at such techniques as ambiguity, equivocation, and expressive symbolic structure.

On questions like these, feminism, far from blunting the critical instruments, sharpens them further. The meanings naively called 'hidden meanings', those not asserted in declarative form, are where we must look in literature for a certain realism about women's experience of power. In doing so, I believe we will find that the experience of women helps to clarify the definitions of power and the distinctions between them. The definition of power as dominance covers one range of uses. The definition of power as ability, competence, and the closely related definition of power as energy, cover another, much wider and more interesting cluster of meanings. The quarrel over the concept of power in the women's movement clearly refers to the first meaning, the political meaning. The complex relations between the kind of power that involves dominance, with its requisite, submission, and the kind of power

3. Elaine Showalter, 'Is There a Female Aesthetic?', *Woman: Advocate and Scholar. Proceedings of the Conference at Montclair State College*, 17 May 1974.

that involves competence and energy have never had enough explicit consideration. Literature suggests that for women the two are likely to be in conflict but also suggests that the two kinds of power are more separable in practice than they have been so far in argument. Setting aside the characters who enter the masculine power struggle with feminine weapons, characters like Christina Pontifex in *The Way of All Flesh* and Lady Macbeth, there may be some profit in reading the language of characters who have abilities and energies without having or even seeking dominance over other people. These characters are not always recognized as exemplars of power.

Besides the intellectual barrier to perceiving the issues raised by characters of this kind, there is an emotional barrier. A sense of hopelessness is engendered by the parade of female characters seduced and abandoned in new worlds and old, victimized by psychotherapy, by marriage, by the whole spectrum of social forces. The woman as victim is an enervating spectacle with an ambiguous message. Is it, as we originally assumed it would be, 'Rebel!' or is it instead, 'Give up! The odds are hopeless'? What, then, is to be done? This reality of oppression is all too real. Perhaps, instead of looking for success and failure in the outer events of story, in fiction or historical fact, we should look for the meanings of success and failure, the meanings of power.

The term 'sex object' may be a clue. Sex and power have been closely joined in the masculine mystique. The protest against the portrayal of women exclusively as sex objects is familiar enough. (I am not confounding the showing of woman as sex object by an author with the showing *that* woman is viewed as sex object by one or more characters.) The first period of women's studies in literature focused on images of women and found dominant among them the sex object (with her horrid converse, the killer-woman of misogynist imagination). Even now that field is still rich in unmined social and aesthetic perceptions. This representation of women simply as sex objects has an exact parallel in the representation of women as powerless victims. A sex object lives by someone else's sexuality, not her own; a victim, a 'power object', lives by somebody else's power. The shift that needs to be made certainly cannot be to the portrayal of women as 'triomphatrices', as one critic dubbed the women protagonists of Shaw's plays,[4] triumphant as only comedy, and only the most genial of comedy, can make them.

4. Augustin Hamon, *Le Molière du XX siècle: Bernard Shaw*, Paris: E. Figuere, 1913, p. 224.

Shaw's powerful women and his brilliantly simple method of imagining them are a clue to another approach. To explain his knowledge of women Shaw said, 'I always assumed that a woman was a person exactly like myself, and that is how the trick is done.'[5] This suggests a shift from the woman as object to the woman as subject, from woman imagined as a phenomenon of the outside world – in Simone de Beauvoir's terminology, 'the other'[6] – to woman as a sentient being. It is odd to think that the debate over whether women have souls is closed in Christian theology but not, practically speaking, in literature. We need to observe women in literature as acting and perceiving, not only as acted upon and perceived. It may be only this distinction between subject and object that can counter without dishonesty the personal sense of hopelessness engendered by the facts of history and the facts of fiction. We cannot change the history, even the current history, of our many defeats, including most painfully the defeats we are led to visit on ourselves; we can only treat literature, and perhaps distinguish between literatures, on the basis of their ability to imagine *all* characters as subjects. We must observe women as agents – even when secret agents – as agonists though not always protagonists.

The material is there, mainly in books written by women but also in books written by men who are *not* prisoners of sex – in Shaw, in Ibsen, in Meredith, in Gissing. But the most powerful may not be the most obvious. Let me mention a few instances, remembering that none will justify euphoria: these are not visions of woman triumphant but of woman militant, the agonist who is active and perceptive and, if she loses, defeated by circumstances and overpowering forces not by masochism or passivity.

Because Mrs Ramsay in *To the Lighthouse* is a domestic, nurturing woman, her figure may not be immediately recognized as the powerful feminist statement it is. In fact the entire structure of the novel conveys a division of powers that is far from being a credit to the male, whose power is sterile and negative. Mrs Ramsay's power is liberating and fertile. It is not by having many children that Mrs Ramsay fulfills herself and others; her numerous children are but an element in the iconography of her generative power – she is the begetter of many things in others around her. As Annis Pratt has shown,[7] the imagery is distinctly phallic, not

5. 'As Bernard Shaw Sees Woman', *New York Times Magazine*, 19 June 1927, p. 2.

6. Simone de Beauvoir, *The Second Sex*, New York: Alfred A. Knopf, 1952, pp. xvi-xviii, 129-32.

7. Annis Pratt, 'Sexual Imagery in *To the Lighthouse:* a New Feminist Approach', *Modern Fiction Studies*, 18, no. 3, Autumn 1972, pp. 417-31.

yonic: 'Mrs Ramsay, who had been sitting loosely, folding her son in her arm, braced herself, and, half turning, seemed to raise herself with an effort, and at once to pour into the air a rain of energy, a column of spray, looking at the same time animated and alive as if all her energies were being fused into force, burning and illuminating. . . . And into this delicious fecundity, this fountain of life, the fatal sterility of the male plunged itself, like a beak of brass, barren and bare.'[8] James is 'standing between her knees, very stiff',[9] and this stiffness is not only an audacious image of an erection but simultaneously the harbinger of another emotional note. He is stiff with resentment at his parasitical father. We are told that Mrs Ramsay, in a graphically imaged detumescence, feels first rapture, then fatigue after these occasions, tinged with 'some faintly disagreeable sensation with another origin'. This sensation has to do with 'their relation' and with 'not being able to tell him the truth'. That truth is her active power and his feeding at it in passive need. Though Mrs Ramsay has fertilized her husband with this powerful jet of energy, just as she has filled all the rooms of the house with life, she must not expect him to recognize this force or to call it power. He must be allowed to go away thinking of this power as mere comfort and of that fierce activity as passivity. The dishonesty of this fiction, the denial of her energies, produces in Mrs Ramsay the 'disagreeable sensation'. Like Torvald in *A Doll's House* and James Morell in *Candida*, the husband must play the role of strong oak and she the clinging vine – her power cramped and unacknowledged but real and conscious. The message is neither simple nor optimistic. The different resolutions of this strikingly similar conflict in Ibsen, Shaw, and Woolf are in themselves most revealing, but in all three the woman is a subject, controlling her own destiny and the destinies of others and perceiving reality in her own terms.

In *The Awakening*, Kate Chopin tells the story of a quest for autonomy, and the symbolic emphasis is on power, again associated with sexuality. Her suicide may seem to negate Edna Pontellier as a feminist character. If, like the suicides of Emma Bovary and Anna Karenina, this act expressed the despair of a complete loss of control (as distinct from loss of hope), that might be true, but the meaning of the act is determined by the whole context. Around this woman lies one great image of power and fertility: the sea. At her awakening, in fact a resurrection, she has mastered, along with the essence of art and the essence of

8. Virginia Woolf, *To the Lighthouse*, New York: Harcourt Brace and Co., 1937, p. 58.
9. *Ibid.*, p. 59.

sexuality, the power of being able, for the first time in her life, to swim. Her death is neither a passive nor a desperate act. It is a conscious choice that rejects the power of others over her and refuses even the necessity of choosing among the possibilities to which she is limited by society. Her awakening has involved learning to swim. Her death by water involves action, nakedness, night, solitude, and the sea as a solvent for the infinite. The hero, who begins by quarreling with her husband over his petty exercises of power, ends by quarreling with the whole world over its particular domination of a woman's life. The power that wins battles is out of reach for this hero. The power that judges and acts, the power of one who cannot be reduced to an object, is hers.

The horror of power is a pervasive theme in *The Golden Notebook*: executions, repressions, conquests, the power of white Africans over black Africans, of husbands over wives, of governments over subjects, of revolutionary leaders over revolutionary followers, and above all, of rigid systems of belief over the minds of people desperate to make sense of painful experience. Even the presumably benevolent process of psychoanalysis is tainted with coercion. The games of each system must be played according to the rules. Each of the notebooks shows the paralysis caused by the rules of one system. The 'free women', ironically so called, are differentiated from the conventional women and from the almost universally self-deceived men by their clear subjectivity in regard to these systems, and the protagonist struggles within each system to use its power in liberating rather than exploitative ways. That the monoliths defeat her is only a partial truth. She does lose battles, she does connive at her own exploitation, but with a consciousness of what is happening and even with some sense of choosing her mistakes and keeping various escape routes open. Here, as so often, the surest escape seems to be out of the self and into the making of art – transcendence, in fact. This kind of power, of control, limited as it is, still is outside the dualism of ordinary life, in which dumb submissiveness is the lot of most women and many men, and is opposed only by the idea of gathering power oneself and becoming one of the exploiters. The long times of observing, waiting, pasting up clippings, chatting, and dreaming, provide such a woman with a profusion of imaginative alternatives waiting only for the power to effect them. To the extent that knowledge is power, the clearsightedness of the 'free woman' is her avenue of power.

But that is probably not the most significant lesson of power in *The Golden Notebook*. There is, at least arguably, a lesson in the structure. The novel is heavily loaded with political and speculative material, heavily enough to sink it, or so I thought when I first read the book.

Now it seems to me that the weight of the political sections in this novel, their adumbration in such full detail, expresses an essential meaning. If the four notebooks are imagined as transparencies, each one read with the outlines of the others perceptible, the emerging pattern shows that art is political, that psychology is political, and that sexual politics, marital politics, maternal politics, exhibit the same features as apartheid, the Rosenberg trial, party discipline, and bomb testing. The *Miss Lonelyhearts* atmosphere surrounding the British housewife going quietly mad is not essentially different from that surrounding the rank-and-file Communist writing fictions that can be read either as pure irony or total naivete.[10] The book is a network of these correspondences, raising by its very structure the question of how we could have failed for so long to see power as the thread that runs through the fabric of existence, public and private, with an instructive sameness.

In saying that the relation of women to power can best be read in literature by moving inside the expressive elements of the text I am, of course, only saying what has always been known about any critical approach. Read in this way, literature teaches that power is relative and confused; that power is everywhere in a variety of forms and degrees; that all our formulations about power are too simple.

If we learn to read ourselves as well as we read books, we may recognize women's experience of power, our suitability to it, and the skills we have already developed. This recognition may be the first step to taking a share of power. If many women have like Mrs Ramsay exercised positive power called by other names, and many more have like Edna Pontellier exercised negative power – the power to refuse – a recognition of that fact, our previous experience of power, should by no means be taken to imply that women should rest content with what we have had. We would be like musicians practicing on a silent piano, which may have strengthened our fingers more than we have realized, but we cannot play our concerts on a silent piano.

The possibility raised by considering the experience of women as conveyed in literature, from Chaucer's Wife of Bath to Gail Godwin's *The Odd Woman*, is that women, having experienced power dissociated from its most famous gratifications and having learned their need for power as a practical thing, a means to an end,

10. Doris Lessing, *The Golden Notebook*, London: Michael Joseph, 1972, p. 259.

might be able to exercise power without necessarily forgetting the lessons of the outsider. Separating conceptually the power that depends primarily on personal domination of others from the power that depends on civil rights, educated skills, and the management of energies, some women in some positions of power may be able to reject megalomania without allowing themselves to be shunted into illusory or second-hand or peripheral forms of power. If women cultivate through literature and through introspection their dearly bought insights into the abuse of power, its subtleties as well as its horrors, it may be possible to make some progress toward detaching the ego from power and experimenting with more humane and liberating uses of power. Women have never been able to afford the luxury of illusions on this subject. Acting without the illusions that have tempted and destroyed so many men, we may sometimes be able to approach power without capitulating to a patriarchal system that, like most forms of absolutism, has never known more than a part of any story – and often not the most interesting part.

Janice Winship

Sexuality for Sale

In S. Hall, D. Hobson, A. Lowe and P. Willis, eds.,
Culture, Media, Language, London: Hutchinson, 1980,
pp. 217-23

Despite its glorifying display of commodities, advertising repre-sents a *moment of suspension* in their production and circulation: production – the sweat and exploitation of work – is over and hidden in its verbal and visual persuasion: the consumption of someone else's (or your own) objectified labour, to which you, the as-yet-passive spectator, are invited, has not begun. Yet in monopoly capitalism advertising has become integral to these circuits of production and circulation: it sustains the movement of commodities, from their social production to their *individual* but socially repeated consumption, which eventually ensures the reproduction not only of the individual but of capital too.

> The individual produces an object and, by consuming it, returns to himself, but returns as a productive and self-reproducing individual. Consumption thus appears as a moment of produc-tion.[1]

By concealing the production process, advertising similarly covers up class distinctions between people, through a form of fetishism: 'the definite social relation between men ... assumes here, for them, the fantastic form of a relation between things'.[2] It replaces them with the distinctions achieved through the consumption of particular goods. As Judith Williamson points out: 'Instead of being identified by what they produce, people are made to identify themselves with what they consume.'[3] However, in order to cement identification with consumption, ads move away from capital's terrain proper; we individually consume *outside* the production process:

I would like to acknowledge my debt to Judith Williamson, whose own analysis has elaborated many of the ideas I have taken up here.
1. Karl Marx, *Grundrisse* (Penguin, 1973), p. 94.
2. Karl Marx, *Capital*, vol. 1 (Penguin, 1976), p. 165.
3. Judith Williamson, *Decoding Advertisements* (Boyars, 1978), p. 13.

In consumption, the product steps outside this social movement [of production and distribution] and becomes a direct object and servant of individual need, and satisfies it in being consumed.[4]

In confirmation of consumption outside economics, ads rarely exhort us to *buy* the commodities, but merely to *use* them, hence glossing over the capitalist moment of exchange – the purchase with money. Further, they never simply sell us the use values of commodities; they sell them as 'exchange values'[5] for qualities in our private relationships with people that are unattainable through the capitalist production process. For example, a commodity cannot 'buy' you love (with a man), but ads give just such an illusion of capital's ubiquitous power: 'Your face is your fortune: look after it with Outdoor Girl.'

Addressing us in our private personae, ads sell us, as women, not just commodities but also our personal relationships in which we are *feminine*: how we are/should be/can be a certain feminine woman, whose attributes in relation to men and the family derive from the use of these commodities. Femininity is recuperated by the capitalist form: the exchange between the commodity and 'woman' in the ad establishes her as a commodity too. In ads addressing women this process is insidious: it is the modes of femininity themselves which are achieved through commodities and are *replaced* by commodities. A woman is nothing more than the commodities she wears: the lipstick, the tights, the clothes and so on are 'woman'. Here the ads not only conceal the labour which produces the commodity; they also, contradictorily, omit the *work* of femininity which women carry out as they use commodities, yet always sell commodities for that purpose. This is in striking contrast to ads directed at men, in which the terrain of activity which is appealed to is that of *leisure* – leisure defined in relation to *completed* work for *capital*. Women, on the other hand, are sold commodities for their work: the *patriarchal* work of domesticity and child care; the work of beautification and 'catching a

4. Marx, *Grundrisse*, p. 89.
5. Judith Williamson takes the concept of 'exchange values' from Marx's use of it as an economic definition: the value of commodities in terms of the embodiment of one identical social substance – human labour – which allows them to be exchanged with each other, irrespective of their use value, their individual bodily forms (Marx, *Capital*, vol. 1, ch. 1). But Williamson shifts its use to an ideological level (cf. Mauss's and Lévi-Strauss's 'symbolic exchange'). Thus it is used analogously rather than identically but always retains its relation to the commodity form: 'The ad translates these "thing" statements/use values to us as human statements; they are given a humanly symbolic "exchange value" ' (*Decoding Advertisements*, p.12).

man'.[6] This work, like that of social production, is collapsed in the ad into mere consumption of commodities by us as individual women. To consume the commodity (even just to consume the ad itself) is already to have accomplished the tasks of femininity until, at its extreme, it appears almost as if the commodity can replace femininity, can take on femininity without female intervention.

We can conceptualize ads therefore as representing a particular articulation of capitalist production and consumption. But in that articulation they also particularly, if not exclusively, operate through ideological representations of femininity. This *ideological work* relies on, but also constructs, an ideology of femininity which is completed through our *collusion* as we read and consume the ads. We are never just spectators who gaze at 'images' of women as though they were set apart, differentiated from the 'real' us. Within the ads are inscribed the images and subject positions of 'mother', 'housewife', 'sexually attractive woman' and so on, which, as we work to understand the ad, embroil us in the process of signification that we complete. Yet we do not come 'naked' to the ads or to any ideological representation and simply take on those representations. We already have both a knowledge of images of women from other discourses and an acquaintance with 'real' women in our everyday lives. The signification of an ad only has meaning in relation to this 'outside' knowledge of the ideology of femininity. Even when it appears that ads are producing a *new* representation (for example, 'Dress to kill'), not merely reproducing an idea of femininity found elsewhere, the signification is not completely autonomous but anchored by the patriarchal and capitalist relations in which we as individuals already have a history and which we already know about.

The signifier 'woman' always signifies woman: we recognize ourselves in *any* representation of woman, however 'original', because we are always already defined by our gender. Having recognized ourselves in the ad, we are then 'freshly' positioned as specific feminine subjects in an identification achieved through a misrecognition of ourselves – the signifier 'woman' can never in fact represent us as individual women. It is through this process

6. For more on this work of beautification in women's and girls' magazines, see A. McRobbie, 'Working-class Girls and the Culture of Femininity' (unpublished MA thesis, University of Birmingham, 1977); J. Winship, 'A Woman's World: *Woman* – an Ideology of Femininity', in Women's Studies Group, *Women Take Issue* (CCCS/Hutchinson, 1978), and 'Woman Becomes an "Individual": Femininity and Consumption in Women's Magazines 1954-69', in *Sociological Review* monograph (1979). For more on the work of domesticity, see A. Oakley, *The Sociology of Housework* (Martin Robertson, 1974), and A. Oakley, *Housewife* (Allen Lane, 1974).

of misrecognition that ads are effective in producing and reproducing the particular ideological modes in which we live.

The discourse of ads contradictorily places us both in relation to other discourses and, more particularly, in relation to those economic and political positions which, through feminist struggle, begin to challenge patriarchal relations. If we are to sustain and further those material gains, we have also to recognize ideological fields as a terrain for women's struggle. As Coward argues, 'The struggle for power within discourses becomes an issue of political importance for the Women's Movement.'[7] To be able to engage politically at that level we need first to understand the processes of signification which are at work.

In ads, as elsewhere, femininity is contradictorily constructed. Ideologies of 'motherhood', 'domesticity', 'beauty', 'sexuality' and 'feminine independence', as they are cut across by an ideology of the 'free' individual, are all separately and sometimes jointly mobilized and constructed anew. In this extract, however, I want only to consider some elements of an ideology of sexuality.

To make yourself passively attractive is, by the mid-1960s, to make yourself specifically *sexually* attractive and *available*: as if, it is represented, the act of beautifying yourself is *already* to engage in sexual relations – it is not just the promise of it. This is always implicit: 'Girls are coming back warm lipped,' says Yardley. 'So come out of the cold and into the warm. Be lit up. Alive. All girl.' Or: 'Lips are too sensitive to withstand the sensation of harsh lipstick contact and much too important to expose to experimentation. Super Jewelfast 22 Special is a *new experience itself* . . . Soft and gentle and kindness itself . . .' (my emphasis). Or you are perhaps prepared for sex: 'Your lips have never looked this wet before'; 'You're getting warmer . . . three new bronzed lip-polishes wetter than wet. The warmest colours you ever saw. Each one spiced with excitement.'

This ideology of sexuality in the ad context admits both to a *passive*, virginal and innocent sexuality – waiting for men, typified by the image of a young woman in long white robes and flowing blonde hair ('A Clairol Summer Blonde') – and to an *active* experience of sexuality. However, the active experience of sexuality only takes place in a fetishistic mode (in the Freudian sense of fetish). Women are invited by the ads to respond to themselves through the imagined fetishes of men – the tights/legs, the lipstick/lips which fragments or distortion of them stand for all

7. Rosalind Coward, 'Sexual Liberation and the Family', in *M/F*, no. 1 (1978).

of their womanness.[8] Yet since men are absent, there is an ambiguity: is it a sexual experience with men that is inferred, or are women 'masturbating' with 'phallic substitutes' or through masculine fantasies? 'Your lips have never looked this wet before': we see just a woman's red lips, open, a lipstick resting against them, alongside an army of big, shiny, erect and partially encased lipsticks.

This ambiguity extends to the more obviously narcissistic representations in which pleasure is self-induced rather than being reliant on men. 'Imagine the clinging soft caress of stockings' – a girl, nude, gently holds her ankles almost suggestively, caressing herself and looking out at us (or at men?); or 'A Touch of Fenjal Silky' (see below). As John Berger discusses and Ros Coward takes up, the naked woman is always a *nude* woman, 'framed in the beautiful photograph', a representation comparable with soft-porn photos, potentially to be gazed at by men even if it is women who look at it.[9] Thus women not only *see* themselves as men see them but are encouraged in these ads to enjoy their sexuality through the eyes of men. It is a narcissism which, at the moment of self-masturbation and scopophilia (looking, in this instance, at one's *own* body), is also exhibitionist, inviting voyeurism from men.[10]

There is a further narcissism which affirms women's self-indulgence and involvement but plays down the sexually exhibitionist elements. 'Only drink it if you never bathe before noon. Freezomint Crème de Menthe. Green, cool and slightly wicked.' It is an independence of sensual pleasure, however, which we can translate into more heterosexual terms through the visuals of the ad: the virginal white of the woman's dress; the abundant *fertile*, as well as fresh, green of the plants.

This ideology of sexuality is therefore disparate and contradictory for women, though nevertheless contained within patriarchal relations: active/passive; heterosexual/narcissistic; dependent on men/independent of men; fetishistic, masturbatory. And it is set firmly apart from 'motherhood' and 'domesticity', which admit to no sexuality even though premised on reproductive sexuality.

The three examples described below have been chosen to illustrate

8. Sigmund Freud, 'Fetishism', in *On Sexuality* (Penguin, 1977).
9. John Berger, *Ways of Seeing* (Penguin, 1972); H. Butcher, R. Coward *et al.*, 'Images in the Media', CCCS Stencilled Paper, no. 31 (1974).
10. For Freud's discussion, in psychoanalytic terms, of scopophilia and exhibitionism, see 'Instincts and Their Vicissitudes' (1915), in *Complete Psychological Works* (Standard Edition, Hogarth), vol. 14.

(a) the construction of an 'original' femininity which we did not know about until we read the ad,

(b) its containment within patriarchal relations,

(c) the 'penetration' of femininity by masculinity – the 'masculinization' of femininity by the commodity form to create a dependence both on men and commodities,

(d) the contradictory modes in which we, as readers, are inescapably ensnared in the signification processes and in those modes of femininity.

PITTARD'S GLOVES (*19*, March 1968, p. 1 – colour)

The caption, 'Dress to kill', draws on two opposing ideological referent systems,[11] 'femininity' concerned with 'dress' and a form of 'masculinity' concerned with 'aggression', which are brought together. Visually, the condensed signifier also embraces this contradiction: a woman, partly shown, her one eye looking at us, has her arms round a man whose back is towards us. She is 'killing' her man – but with her 'dress' (in fact, her gloves) and not with the gun which the gloved hand holds: she is 'killing' him in order – we know 'outside' the ad – to catch him. The power of the gun has slipped over into the *red* gloved hand. That colour is a signifier in a discourse organized around blood, killing and danger, but is also associated with a chain of meaning organized around the danger of *sexuality*. Simultaneously, the gloves are both tough, 'killing', almost masculine weapons and feminine – 'soft' and 'supple' and daringly sexy.

She is in control of the situation, has power over the man who, vulnerably, has his back towards us (imagine us with that gun/those gloves). She looks at us, almost winking, woman to woman, knowing about men and how to catch them. She controls him as if he were just another rather dangerous *object*: 'Don't be caught barehanded. Whether you're dealing with a man or a Mauser.' However, she does not have this power independently: she needs the gloves, not to be '*bare*handed' (my emphasis). Paradoxically, 'dressing' herself she becomes *more* sexual: she has 'the Pittard swing ticket'. Ostensibly the 'swing ticket is your guarantee of washability' but in the underlying sexual discourse it guarantees you a man: Pittard's gloves 'buy' you a man.

11. Williamson defines a 'referent system' as a 'hollowed-out system of meaning' (*Decoding Advertisements*, p. 168), which refers to a reality but is 'lifted from the materiality of our lives' (*ibid.*, p. 74).

The reciprocal emptying and exchange of meaning between the signs 'dress' and 'kill' create a new sign which conflates into a new referent – an 'aggressive femininity'. Even though such a masculinization of femininity exists 'outside' the ad, the means of signification permissible in the ad allows a *heightened* signification (the gun as signifier) not possible in the 'real' relations between a woman and a man: it is, in this sense, an 'original' construction. Nevertheless, the ad must be seen as participating in those relations by 'voicing', making explicit and setting the terms within which 'femininity' operates. 'Masculinity' retains its dominance, even while being subverted – woman is 'aggressive' precisely for the feminine aims of catching a man.

FENJAL BATH OIL (*Cosmo*, May 1974, p. 146 – colour)

Narcissism, here, is very private; almost without men, but with a public edge, directed at men. On the one hand, it is a representation of woman that is typical of soft porn: there is a movement in the ad from the 'natural' petals of the pink carnation at her breast, to the caption, down to the carnation's reappearance with the product and finally to 'A touch of Fenjal Silky' – a reference by this time both to the product and to the woman's sexuality, signified by her pubic area, her hair, which hides the site/sight of her female genitalia, her 'petals', the 'heart' of her sexuality within patriarchal relations.

Thus the text and visuals can be read as suggesting that you bathe in Fenjal to await a *man's* touch. But we also have to recognize that the ad is directed to women and we can therefore read a contrary meaning: she is touching herself in the photo, privately, behind the mistiness; eyes directed at herself, she is self-sufficient, though dependent on the commodity: 'As you lie in a Fenjal bath you can feel the gently cleansing action beautifying your skin and when you step out one touch tells you how effective the Fenjal moisturizer has been. A touch of Fenjal Silky.' Even though that kind of pose is a sign in a patriarchal discourse – and since we still live within patriarchal relations, its meaning must over-determine and carry over into any oppositional signification – we should not refuse to recognize it also, contradictorily, establishing a *difference* from that patriarchal representation. We must, however, be wary of our assessment of it. As Griselda Pollock, writing of feminist attempts to create 'an alternative imagery outside ideological forms', relevantly argues:

The attempt to decolonize the *nude* female body, a tendency which walks a tightrope between subversion and reappropriation, often serves rather to consolidate the potency of the signification rather than actually rupture it.[12]

It is finally as a 'reappropriation' of feminine sexual independence with patriarchal and capitalist relations that we must understand this ad.

GUINNESS (*Honey*, November 1974, p. 99 – colour)

Concisely and illustratively, this ad not only brings together many of the tendencies in the representation of 'femininity' in ads but also poses the limits to such a representation. It constructs and works through fetishistic relations in both Freudian and Marxist forms.

The ad is surreal, its surrealism constructed by the camera: a close-up shot obscures the shape and dimensions of the face, merging it into the foam of the Guinness, so that the vivid, glossy, red lips stand out above the flattened, labelled glass of dark Guinness. It is a condensation involving *absence* and *contradiction* which 'Ladylike – Guinness' *denies* but also demands that we necessarily decipher. When we set in play the signifying chain we move from the 'inside' to the 'outside' of the ad; we 'fill' the absences and recognize the contradictions. The absences concern 'femininity' and 'masculinity' which *we already know about*, which the ad presupposes and which are in contradiction with each other. The one bit of woman, the vivid red lips, signifies the whole of 'femininity' (woman) through a metonymic relation – in that sense the 'lips' are 'ladylike'. But metaphorically their colour and texture and shape signify daring, excitement, sexuality, in contradiction to the sober connotations of 'ladylike'; 'masculinity', in its difference from these red lips, is signified by the dark drink. We participate in a 'joke': the red lips are *not* 'ladylike', although it says they are; Guinness is not ladylike either, but the ad dares the *impossible* and declares that it is. Unlike the Benson and Hedges ads, for example, which rely on a similar joke that is fantastical because there is no way in which the ad can bring about what it signifies (that is, a Benson and Hedges packet can never be a pyramid, a fountain pen nib, and so on), Guinness *can* be 'ladylike';

12. Griselda Pollock, 'What's Wrong with Images of Women?', *Screen Education*, no. 24 (Autumn 1977), p. 29.

the ad may generate 'Ladylike – Guinness' because women will drink it. Benson and Hedges remains at the level of a joke, at the level of signs; Guinness, on the other hand, potentially *intervenes* in the reality to which initially it only refers – 'femininity'.

Reading the ad as women, we are constantly caught in its contradictions, oscillating between 'ladylike'/'not ladylike' (masculine), and not drinking Guinness/drinking Guinness, but are finally ensnared within its imaginary unity: not either/or but *both* – the dare of 'ladylike' and drinking Guinness which empties 'ladylike' of its referred meaning and fills it with the product, Guinness. However, that engagement with the meanings of the ad involves *submitting* ourselves to the means of signification – to fetishistic relations. First, the 'human' element of face, to which the lips belong, has been obliterated; yet we understand those lips as representing *women's* lips, even if they are only a thing – painted lips, a sign of women, like a lipstick. It is another 'thing', the commodity Guinness, which is the sign for masculinity. The relation between 'femininity' and 'masculinity', in its particularity of the gender-organized social conventions of drinking, is set up for us to see as 'the fantastic relation between things':[13] a pair of lips and a glass of Guinness, which appear 'naturally' to have the characteristics of 'femininity' and 'masculinity'. Marx writes:

> The mysterious character of the commodity-form consists therefore simply in the fact that the commodity reflects the social characteristics of men's own labour as objective characteristics of the products of labour themselves, as the socio-natural properties of these things.[14]

But here both capitalist commodity production and patriarchal ideological construction are hidden.

Furthermore, we have to engage with the representations of a fetishistic sexual relation structured in masculine dominance. The (closed) lips represent a displacement from the genital area of the lips of the vagina, a displacement which does not bring to light the absence of a penis and women's castration. According to Freud,[15] the fetish is substitute for the penis which the little boy believes his mother has and the absence of which he refuses to take cognizance of when he observes her lack. However, he both retains the belief and gives it up: he affirms and disavows

13. Marx, *Capital*, vol. 1, p. 165.
14. *Ibid.*, pp. 164-5.
15. Freud, 'Fetishism'.

castration of women by appointing a *substitute*, which takes over his sexual interest, while avoiding the site/sight of female genitalia for which he has an aversion. In the ad the fetish is obviously not a literal one in the sense Freud meant it; nevertheless, the signification of the ad works in a mode very similar to the operation of these fetishistic relations for men. The ad depends on our knowledge that women do not usually drink Guinness – they are 'ladylike' (and castrated): it depends on the *difference* between women's 'lack' and men's plenitude – the full glass of Guinness. However, that difference is *disavowed* in the condensation of 'Ladylike – Guinness': women can and do drink Guinness but remain 'ladylike'. But the future pouring of the commodity Guinness between the as-yet-closed lips – the as-yet-'ladylike' lips – is also a metaphor for the sexual act: man's penetration of the lips, the vagina, which provides affirmation of women's 'castration'. We are dared to drink Guinness, but our daring, after the grounds of 'femininity' have slightly shifted, continues to place us firmly within the conventional bounds of patriarchal relations.

Wendy Martyna

Beyond the 'He/Man' Approach: the Case for Nonsexist Language

In *Signs*, vol. 5, no. 3, Chicago, Spring
1980, pp. 482-93

Time calls it 'Ms-guided',[1] a syndicated columnist 'linguistic lunacy'.[2] *TV Guide* wonders what the 'women's lib redhots' with 'the nutty pronouns' are doing.[3] A clear understanding of the sexist language issue continues to elude the popular press. The medium is not alone in its misunderstanding. This discussion separates the strands of argument often tangled in current approaches to the issue, whether these approaches appear in the popular media, academic journals, or feminist publications. The arguments against sexist language have been mistranslated more often than not. Those mistranslations have then been responded to by opponents of language change. Clarifying these, and synthesizing the case against sexist language, can help to offset the continuing, annoying trivialization of this issue, which has constituted a major roadblock on the path toward a language that speaks clearly and fairly of both sexes.

The 'he/man' approach to language involves the use of male terms to refer both specifically to males and generically to human beings (*A Man for All Seasons* is specific; 'No man is an island' is generic). The he/man approach has received most attention in current debates on sexist language, not only because of its ubiquity but also because of its status as one of the least subtle of sexist forms. In linguistic terms, some have characterized the male as an

This work is dedicated to the memory of Kate De Pierri, who was a contemporary in spirit, energy, and commitment, despite the fifty years between us. Early encouragement, much appreciated, came from Catharine Stimpson, Barrie Thorne, Nancy Henley, Cheris Kramer, and Adrienne Rich. Valuable resources were provided by Mary Ritchie Key, Virginia Valian, Simon Klevansky, Patti Leasure, LeeAnn Slinkard, and the many generous people who are part of the 'women-and-language grapevine'. I am particularly grateful for the critical readings of earlier drafts by Len Erickson, Herb Clark, Sandra Bem, Leigh Star, and Terri Daly.
1. Stefan Kanfer, 'Sispeak: A Ms-guided Attempt to Change Herstory', *Time*, 100, 23 October 1972, p. 79.
2. Harriet Van Horne, 'Women's Movement Foolishly Assaults the English Language', *Rocky Mountain News*, 19 February 1976, p. 51.
3. 'As We See It', *TV Guide*, 19, 17 July 1971, p. 1.

unmarked, the female as a marked, category. The unmarked category represents both maleness and femaleness, while the marked represents femaleness only.[4] Thus the male in Lionel Tiger's *Men in Groups* excludes the female in Phyllis Chesler's *Women and Madness*, while the male in Thomas Paine's *Rights of Man* is supposed to encompass the female of Mary Wollstone-craft's *Vindication of the Rights of Women*.

The outlines of the he/man debate are evident in an exchange of letters in the *Harvard Crimson* in 1971. The linguistics faculty of Harvard criticized an attempt by a theology class to eliminate sexist language from its discussions: 'The fact that the masculine is the unmarked gender in English ... is simply a feature of grammar. It is unlikely to be an impediment to change in the patterns of the sexual division of labor towards which our society may wish to evolve. There is really no cause for anxiety or pronoun-envy on the part of those seeking such changes.'[5]

Virginia Valian, a psychologist, and Jerrold Katz, a linguist, countered by posing this hypothetical situation: 'In culture R the language is such that the pronouns are different according to the color of the people involved, rather than their sex ... the unmarked pronoun just happens to be the one used for white people. In addition, the colored people just happen to constitute an oppressed group. Now imagine that this oppressed group begins complaining about the use of the "white" pronoun to refer to all people. Our linguists presumably then say, "Now, now, there is really no cause for anxiety or pronoun-envy." It isn't a question of linguistics, but of how the people involved feel.'[6] The students' claim: the generic masculine is both ambiguous and discriminatory. The linguists' claim: it is simply a feature of grammar, unrelated to the issue of sex discrimination. The students' counterresponse: it is more than a feature of grammar, but a factor which both reflects and maintains societal sexism. This 1971 scenario has been enacted many times in the years since: the cast varies, but the plot and dialogue remain familiar. William James noted three stages a new idea moves through: it is first attacked as absurd; then admitted to be true, but seen as obvious and insignificant; and finally, seen as so important that its adversaries claim they discovered it. If James is correct, then the controversy over sexist language now sits somewhere between stages one and two.

4. Herbert H. Clark and Eve V. Clark, *Psychology and Language: an Introduction to Psycholinguistics*, New York: Harcourt Brace Jovanovich, Inc., 1977, p. 524.
5. Harvard Linguistics Faculty, 'Pronoun Envy', *Harvard Crimson*, 16 November 1971.
6. Virginia Valian and Jerrold Katz, 'The Right to Say "He"', *Harvard Crimson*, 24 November 1971.

RESISTANCE TO CHANGE

Comments on the he/man issue vary in their subtlety. Among the most blatant are personal attacks on those who attack the generic masculine. One columnist describes the editor who had altered his sexist prose as 'an ardent Amazonian'. He later bursts out: 'Women are irrational, all women: when some women threaten to disembowel me unless I say "personhole-cover", I am surer even than I was that all women are irrational.'[7] Trivializations of the movement for nonsexist language appear in a wide range of locations, from *Time*'s article on 'sispeak' to a nationally syndicated columnist's critique of the 'libspeak tantrum'.[8] This reaction to sexist language appears more striking when contrasted to the popular response to racist language. The US secretary of agriculture, Earl Butz, left office following public outcry over his racist remarks (which the media refused to repeat, 'even in this liberated age').[9] Butz's remarks were equally sexist, but he apologized only to the black male members of Congress, not the females; and it was his racism, not his sexism, which caused his censure. Public reaction to Billy Carter's 'witticisms', often as racist and sexist as Butz's remarks, illustrate this same contrast. Sexist language is popularly treated as a source of humor more often than outrage. Pauli Murray has called this ridicule of women 'the psychic counterpart of violence against blacks',[10] and Naomi Weisstein speaks of this humor as 'a weapon in the social arsenal constructed to maintain ... sex inequalities, ... showing that women can't be taken seriously'.[11] If pronouns are as amusingly insignificant as some consider them to be, we should expect no outcry were the situation reversed, and the female pronoun became the generic. Yet when the female pronoun has been used to refer to both sexes, as in the teaching profession, males have lobbied for use of the male pronoun. They argue that use of 'she' is responsible, in part, for their poor public image and low salaries.[12]

7. Milton Mayer, 'On the Siblinghood of Persons', *Progressive*, September 1975, pp. 20-1.
8. Kanfer.
9. David Felton, 'Butz Is Just a 4-Letter Word', *Rolling Stone*, 18 November 1976.
10. Pauli Murray, testimony, US Congress, House, Special Subcommittee on Education of the Committee on Education and Welfare, *Discrimination against Women*, 91st Cong., 2d sess., 1970, on section 805 of HR 16098.
11. Naomi Weisstein, 'Why We Aren't Laughing – Anymore', *Ms*, 2, no. 5, November 1973, p. 49.
12. M. S. Fenner, 'After All: Proposal for Unisex Pronoun', *Today's Education*, 63, Summer 1974, p. 110 ('ne').

Resistance to language change has also involved more sophisticated lines of argument. The first centers on the meaning of 'he'.
The generic masculine does not need replacement, argue some, for
'he' can include 'she' (or 'man' can embrace 'woman', as grammar
teachers are fond of saying). Frank M. argues this position in a
letter to 'Dear Abby': 'I'm tired of the ignorance of those who insist
that the word "man" applies only to males. My dictionary has
several definitions, of which the first two are: (1) human being,
person. . . (2) the human race. So why don't we stop all this asinine
changing of words?'[13] Jacques Barzun similarly explains: 'No one
until recently ever saw in the phrase [Madame Chairman] any
paradox, incongruity, or oppugnancy between terms. It is consistent with common sense and perfect equity; the "man" in it denotes
either sex.'[14]

Others argue that the generic masculine includes both sexes
because they intend it to. Anthony Burgess, for example, says that
his use of 'he' and 'man' is neutral, and that it is women who 'force
chauvinistic sex on to the word'.[15]

Yet the question of what 'he' and 'man' really mean is fully
answered neither by turning to dictionary definitions nor by
consulting the intentions of their users. Good intentions are not
enough, unfortunately, to guarantee that generic meaning will be
conveyed. And guided tours through Latin and Old English are not
enough to guarantee that the generic masculine is used clearly and
fairly today. Further, the denotations found in dictionaries do not
always reveal the connotations that 'he' and 'man' can carry.

Others who resist language change deny neither that sexist
language can serve as a symbol of sexist society nor that sexist
society needs to be changed. What they do disclaim is that the one
has much to do with the other. The need, they say, is to change the
sources, rather than the symbols, of sexism in society. Nina
Yablok puts forth in rhyme: 'If I had my choice, if I had my
druthers/I'd take equal rights. Leave equal words to the others.'[16]
To Stefan Kanfer, the hope for a nonsexist language reveals 'a
touching, almost mystical trust in words'.[17]

Another group, which also tends to support social change,
wonders about the very possibility of language change. Robin

13. 'Dear Abby', *Los Angeles Times*, 17 August 1976.
14. Jacques Barzun, 'A Few Words on a Few Words', *Columbia Forum*, Summer 1974, pp. 17-19.
15. Anthony Burgess, 'Dirty Words', *New York Times Magazine*, 8 August 1976.
16. Nina Yablok, 'A Woperchild Joins the Arguthing', *New York Times*, 30 March 1977.
17. Kanfer.

Lakoff, whose work has encouraged a greater awareness of sexist language, has nevertheless argued that pronouns are 'too common, too thoroughly mixed throughout the language, for the speaker to be aware each time he uses them. It is realistic only to hope to change those linguistic uses of which speakers themselves can be made aware, as they use them.'[18] Others are deterred by the difficulty, rather than the impossibility, of language change. One writer, referring to 'the ugly and awkward "he or she" forms', says, 'They may be only a passing fad, but they offend the traditional eye.'[19] Eye trouble is not the only complaint. To William Buckley, the 'distortions ring in the ear'.[20] This pessimism about language change is at least partly due to a misrepresentation of the causes for optimism. A common view seems to be that feminists have failed to take into account the complexities of language change, viewing it as a relatively quick and easy process. In fact, those who advocate nonsexist language do not pretend that change will be quick, easy, or unopposed.

Much resistance to change arises from a confusion over *what* will be changed, as well as *why* there should be change. The widespread worry is that both specific and generic forms of 'he' and 'man' will be eliminated, should language change go according to feminist plan. Some writers manifest a mania for manipulating each 'man' in our language into a 'person', and then mentioning the menace such manipulations pose. Russell Baker, for example, would have substituted 'person' for 'each "man"'' in the previous sentence, as he did in his satire of 'Nopersonclature'.[21] Despite the many suggestions to the contrary, we do not have to begin language change by renaming NOW the National Organization for Wo-people. The many fears of retitling such works as *Four Horsemen of the Apocalypse* and *A Man for All Seasons* are similarly unfounded: the term 'man' as used here is specific, not generic. Sexism, not *sex*, is under attack.

The fear of losing all sex-specific terms in the language has led to the characterization of a nonsexist language as 'sexually obscure', 'a unisex tongue ... a dull tongue and a false one', and 'a spaying of the language'.[22] One member of the California State

18. Robin Lakoff, *Language and Woman's Place*, New York: Harper & Row, 1975.
19. Edward Devol, 'The He-She Dilemma Built into the Tongue', *San Francisco Chronicle*, 13 February 1977.
20. William J. Buckley, Jr, 'Unsex Me Now', *National Review*, 28 May 1976, p. 583.
21. Russell Baker, 'Nopersonclature', *New York Times*, 4 March 1973.
22. Israel Shenker, 'Is It Possible for a Woman to Manhandle the King's English?', *New York Times*, 29 August 1971; E. B. White, as quoted in Blake Green, 'A New English: Unbiased or Unsexed?', *San Francisco Chronicle*, 11 October 1974; and Charles McCabe, 'Spaying the Language', *San Francisco Chronicle*, 25 May 1977.

Assembly opposed a move to replace 'assemblyman' with 'assembly member'. 'That takes the masculinity out of it!' he declared.[23] Not only a 'sexless' language, but also an ungrammatical one, is dreaded. William Buckley, Jr, is among those refusing to substitute singular 'they' for generic 'he'. Those who issue guidelines for nonsexist language, he says, 'want us to validate improper usage'. Anyone who uses a singular 'they', in Buckley's view, 'should not be hired as a professional writer'.[24]

ARGUMENTS FOR CHANGE

Those who oppose the generic masculine are concerned with both equal rights *and* equal words. Nonsexist language would not only reflect a move toward a nonsexist ideology; it would also functon in itself as one form of social equality. Eliminating the ambiguity and sex exclusiveness of the he/man approach would enable us to communicate more clearly and fairly about the sexes.

The New York State Supreme Court housed a confrontation in 1976 between those who differ on this question of equity. Ellen Cooperman's petition to change her name to 'Cooperperson' was denied by the court, on grounds it would set a precedent for other 'ludicrous changes (Mannings becoming Peoplings)' and expose the women's movement to ridicule. However, she considered her petition as personally and politically important, arguing that 'Cooperman' reflects 'the pervasiveness of linguistic male predominance' and is among those factors complicating women's efforts to achieve self-identity.[25] Her view is shared by many others who testify to the importance of the he/man issue. For example, Susan Sontag sees language as 'the most intense and stubborn fortress of sexist assumptions', one which 'crudely enshrines the ancient bias against women'.[26]

The damage the generic masculine has done is itself a strong argument for change. Research has begun to suggest the behavioral implications of sexist language. Sandra Bem and Daryl Bem, for instance, have assessed the impact of sex-biased job advertisements, finding that sex-unbiased advertisements encourage more

23. 'Assembly Moves to Desex Its Titles', *Los Angeles Times*, 14 January 1977.
24. Buckley.
25. 'Fighting for Her Cooperpersonhood', *Los Angeles Times*, 24 October 1976; and Ellen Cooperson, 'What's in a Name? Sexism', *New York Times*, 21 November 1976.
26. Susan Sontag, 'The Third World of Women', *Partisan Review*, 40, no. 2, 1973, p. 186.

high school females to apply for male-related jobs.[27] Most of such studies have focused on the psychological impact of broad gender cues. While there are ample data to suggest that manipulating such cues has psychological impact, we have not yet assessed the particular contribution the generic masculine makes in creating these cues. The data on the way the generic 'he' encourages a male rather than neutral interpretation, however, suggest that that role is considerable.

Cognitive confusion is another consequence of the generic masculine, one particularly relevant for the academic disciplines.[28] Joan Huber, for example, has characterized the use of 'he' and 'man' as 'an exercise in doublethink that muddles sociological discourse'. She cites the recent sociology text which proclaims: 'The more education an individual attains, the better his occupation is likely to be, and the more money he is likely to earn.' The statement is accurate only if the individual is male.[29] The American Anthropological Association is among many scholarly associations to caution its members that use of the generic masculine is 'conceptually confusing'.[30] Ambiguity results when generic and specific meanings are not easily separable; exclusion results when context prohibits a generic interpretation. Watch what context does to the supposedly generic 'he' used by Paul Meehl to describe this hypothetical researcher: 'He' produces a long list of publications but little contribution to the enduring body of knowledge, and 'his true position is that of a potent-but-sterile intellectual rake, who leaves in his merry wake a long train of ravished maidens, but no viable scientific offspring.'[31]

Context, many say, should be sufficient to decide whether a specific or generic meaning of 'he' and 'man' is intended. Yet my empirical explorations demonstrate that, even in a clearly generic context (e.g., 'When someone is near a hospital, he should be quiet'), 'he' is ambiguous, allowing both specific and generic

---

27. Sandra Bem and Daryl Bem, 'Does Sex-biased Job Advertising "Aid and Abet" Sex Discrimination?', *Journal of Applied Social Psychology*, 3, no. 1, 1973, pp. 6-18.

28. Mary Beard observed in 1946, 'For hundreds of years the use of the word "man" has troubled critical scholars, careful translators, and lawyers. Difficulties occur whenever and wherever it is important for truth-seeking purposes to know what is being talked about and the context gives no intimation of [what] "man" means' (Mary Beard, *Woman as Force in History*, New York: Macmillan Publishing Co., 1946, p. 59).

29. Joan Huber, 'On the Generic Use of Male Pronouns', *American Sociologist*, 11, May 1976, p. 89.

30. American Anthropological Association, *Newsletter*, January 1974, p. 12.

31. Paul Meehl, 'Theory Testing in Physics: a Methodological Paradox', *Philosophy of Science*, 34, 1967, pp. 103-15.

interpretations to be drawn.[32] My research does not argue that 'he' *cannot* function generically, but that it allows both specific and generic interpretation, even in a context which should force a generic inference. Moreover, our encounters with 'he' rarely take place in clearly generic contexts. In educational materials, for instance, the sex-specific 'he' appears five to ten times for every single generic 'he'.[33] The generic masculine thus appears amidst a profusion of references to specific males. Based on this predominantly sex-specific usage, our best guess when encountering a 'he' is that it will not contain an implicit 'she'.

Startled laughter often greets such sentences as 'Menstrual pain accounts for an enormous loss of manpower hours,' or 'Man, being a mammal, breast-feeds his young.' We do a double take when hearing of the gynecologist who was awarded a medical award for 'service to his fellowman'. C. S. Lewis captures the importance of these reactions: 'In ordinary language the sense of a word ... normally excludes all others from the mind. ... The proof of this is that the sudden intrusion of any irrelevant sense is funny. It is funny because it is unexpected. There is a semantic explosion because the two meanings rush together from a great distance; one of them was not in our consciousness at all till that moment. If it had been, there would be no detonation.'[34] To avoid this 'semantic explosion', we are cautioned by writers' manuals to avoid a generic 'he' when the issue of sex 'is present and pointed', as in 'The pool is open to both men and women, but everyone must bring his or her own towel.'[35] Similarly, we avoid a generic 'he' when the female meaning is predominant. An investigation of psychology textbooks found that hypothetical professors, physicians, and psychologists were referred to as 'he', while hypothetical nurses, teachers, and librarians were 'she'.[36] If 'he' includes 'she' – if 'man' embraces 'woman' – why these shifts to the female pronoun?

Empirical explorations of how we comprehend the generic masculine also indicate its sex exclusiveness. My studies of

32. Wendy Martyna, 'Using and Understanding the Generic Masculine: a Social-psychological Approach' (Ph.D. diss., Stanford University, 1978).

33. Carol Tittle, Karen McCarthy, and Jane Steckler, *Women and Educational Testing*, Princeton, N.J.: Educational Testing Service, 1974; and Alma Graham, 'The Making of a Nonsexist Dictionary', *Ms*, 2, December 1973, pp. 12-16.

34. C. S. Lewis, *Studies in Words*, Cambridge: Cambridge University Press, 1960, p. 11.

35. Theodore Bernstein, *The Careful Writer: a Modern Guide to English Usage*, New York: Atheneum Publishers, 1965, p. 351.

36. American Psychological Association Task Force on Issues of Sexual Bias in Graduate Education, 'Guidelines for Nonsexist Use of Language', *American Psychologist*, 30, no. 6, June 1975, pp. 682-4.

pronoun usage show striking sex differences in both the use and understanding of the generic masculine. Females use 'he' less often than do males, and turn more frequently to alternatives such as 'he or she' and 'they'. Males have an easier time imagining themselves as members of the category referenced by generic 'he'. Seven times as many males as females say they see themselves in response to sex-neutral sentences referring to a 'person' or 'human being'. In general, males appear to be using and understanding 'he' in its specific more often than in its generic sense. Females both avoid the use of 'he' and respond to its use with a more generic than specific interpretation. For females to do otherwise would be to encourage self-exclusion.[37]

The confusion and exclusion caused by the generic masculine have striking social implications. Although one legal scholar notes the 'useful function' ambiguity can perform, 'by virtue of its lack of precision',[38] the ambiguity of 'he' and 'man' is far from useful for those who are included by reference only. A member of the Canadian Parliament, Simma Holt, challenged the equity of the Federal Interpretation Act, which reads: 'Words importing male persons include female persons and corporations.' Holt was reassured that the act creates no injustice, for females are explicitly included within the definition of the generic masculine. Doubting that assurance, Marguerite Richie surveyed some 200 years of Canadian law and discovered that the ambiguity of the generic masculine has allowed judges to include or exclude women, depending on the climate of the times and their own personal biases. As she concludes: 'Wherever any statute or regulation is drafted in terms of the male, a woman has no guarantee that it confers on her any rights at all.'[39] Legal controversy over the generic masculine has arisen in the United States as well, involving, for example:

Administration of a scholarship fund set up for 'worthy and ambitious young men';[40]

37. Wendy Martyna, 'What Does 'He' Mean – Use of the Generic Masculine', *Journal of Communication*, 28, no. 1, Winter 1978, pp. 131-8; and Wendy Martyna, 'Using and Understanding the Generic Masculine' (paper presented at the Ninth World Congress of Sociology, Uppsala, Sweden, August 1978).

38. Ovid Lewis, 'Law, Language and Communication', *Case Western Reserve Law Review*, 23, 1972, p. 316.

39. Marguerite Richie, 'Alice through the Statutes', *McGill Law Journal*, 21, Winter 1975, p. 702.

40. Frederick Cusick, 'Law Students Win Their Case – against a Will', *Daily Hampshire (Northampton, Mass.) Gazette*, 1 March 1975.

dispute over a Kiwanis Club admission of women, despite bylaws specifying 'men' as members;[41]

the appeal of a murder conviction in which the self-defense intructions to the jury were phrased in the generic masculine, thus 'leaving the jury with the impression that the objective standard to be applied is that applicable to an altercation between two men';[42] and

sex-biased application of the legal notion of 'a reasonable man'.[43]

PROSPECTS FOR LANGUAGE CHANGE

Language change may be difficult, but it is not impossible. Some prominent individuals, for example, have made striking changes in their language use. Millions were listening when Harry Reasoner apologized for referring, on a previous broadcast, to the 'men' of the Judiciary Committee. In response to the many objections he had received, he not only apologized but also asked indulgence for future language offenses he might inadvertently commit.[44] A variety of government agencies, feminist groups, professional associations, religious organizations, educational institutions, publishing firms, and media institutions have also endorsed language change, issuing guidelines or passing regulations concerning sexist language.[45] Initial empirical studies suggest considerable language changes among university faculty and politicians.[46]

The strongest argument for the possibility of language change is that substantial numbers of language users have already managed

41. B. W. O'Hearn, 'N.Y. Kiwanis Club Admits First Woman', *Middletown Connecticut Press*, 23 January 1974.

42. State of Washington v. Yvonne Wanrow, Supreme Court of Washington 559 Pacific Report, 2d ser., 1977, pp. 548-9.

43. Ronald K. L. Collins, 'Language, History, and the Legal Process: a Profile of the "Reasonable Man", *Camden Law Journal*, 8, no. 2, Winter 1977, pp. 312-23.

44. Jean Ward, 'Attacking the King's English: Implications for Journalism in the Feminist Critiques', *Journalism Quarterly*, 52, Winter 1975, pp. 699-705.

45. For example, American Psychological Association, 'Guidelines for Nonsexist Language in APA Journals', *Publication Manual Change Sheet 2*, Washington, D.C.: American Psychological Association, 1977; Scott, Foresman and Co., *Guidelines for Improving the Image of Women in Textbooks*, Glenview, Ill.: Scott, Foresman and Co., 1974; Macmillan Publishing Co., *Guidelines for Creating Positive Sexual and Racial Images in Educational Materials*, New York: Macmillan Publishing Co., 1975; and 'Assembly Panel Acts to Rid Laws of Sexism', *New York Times*, 19 February 1976.

46. Barbara Bate, 'Nonsexist Language Use in Transition', *Journal of Communication*, 28, no. 1, Winter 1978, pp. 139-49; and Sandra Purnell, 'Politically Speaking, Do Women Exist?', *Journal of Communication*, 28, no. 1, Winter 1978, pp. 150-6.

to construct detours around generic 'he' and 'man'. Ann Bodine[47] surveys instances of socially motivated language change in England, Sweden, and Russia; Paul Friedrich[48] investigates the Russian example in detail, exploring how pronominal change resulted from a growing concern for social equality.

Many guidelines for nonsexist language encourage either the replacement of the generic masculine with sex-inclusive or sex-neutral forms or rewriting to avoid the need for a single pronoun or noun.[49] 'They' has long been in use as an alternative to 'he'; Bodine claims that 'despite almost two centuries of vigorous attempts to analyze and regulate it out of existence, singular "they" is alive and well'.[50] Research on pronoun use confirms Bodine's observation.[51] Maija Blaubergs and Barbara Bate have both categorized the many proposed alternatives to sexist language forms.[52] The two main ones are sex-inclusive forms (such as 'he or she' and 'women and men') and sex-neutral terms (such as 'chairperson' and 'humanity'). Since 1970, several new pronouns, including 'tey', 'co', 'na', and 'E', have been suggested.[53] The difficulty of changing the language must also be contrasted with the difficulty of *not* changing. The awkwardness that may result from the 'he or she' construction may be less troublesome than the ambiguity and sex exclusiveness of the he/man approach, and even that awkwardness will eventually decline.

Why the persistent misrepresentation and misunderstanding of the sexist language issue?[54] The simplest explanation is antifeminism, yet this by itself is not enough. Why should this issue remain

47. Ann Bodine, 'Androcentrism in Prescriptive Grammar: Singular "They", Sex-indefinite "He" and "He or She"', *Language in Society*, 4, August 1975, pp. 129-46.
48. Paul Friedrich, 'Social Context and Semantic Feature: the Russian Pronominal Usage', in *Directions in Sociolinguistics*, ed. J. Gumperz and D. Hymes, New York: Holt, Rinehart and Winston, 1972.
49. An example of such guidelines: McGraw-Hill Book Co., *Guidelines for Equal Treatment of the Sexes*, New York: McGraw-Hill Book Co., 1974.
50. Bodine, pp. 129-46.
51. Martyna, 'What Does "He" Mean – Use of the Generic Masculine'; and D. Terence Langendoen, *Essentials of English Grammar*, New York: Holt, Rinehart and Winston, 1970.
52. Maija Blaubergs, 'Changing the Sexist Language: the Theory behind the Practice', *Psychology of Women Quarterly*, 2, no. 3, Spring 1978, pp. 244-61; and Bate.
53. Casey Miller and Kate Swift, 'De-Sexing the English Language', *Ms*, 1, Spring 1972, p. 7 ('tey'); Mary Orovan, 'Humanizing English', mimeographed, Hackensack, N.J.: Mary Orovan, 1971 ('co'); June Arnold, *The Cook and the Carpenter*, Houston, Tex.: Daughters Publishing Co., 1975 ('na'); Fenner ('ne'); and Donald F. MacKay, 'Birth of a Word', manuscript, Department of Psychology, University of California at Los Angeles ('E').
54. Nonsexist language change has also been ridiculed. See, e.g., 'Of Men and Wopersons', *New York Times*, 12 April 1975; 'Dr Spock Treats His Gender Problem', *San Francisco Chronicle*, 5 April 1976; and 'Dr Spock Tells Why He No Longer Sings in Praise of Hims', *New York Times*, 13 October 1973.

a source of ridicule when other feminist claims have come to be treated seriously? Why do some feminists, both female and male, consider the fight for 'equal words' to be a misdirection of energy? There seems to be a general cultural reluctance to acknowledge the power of language in our lives, an insistence that language is of symbolic rather than actual importance. We chant in childhood, 'Sticks and stones can break my bones, but words can never hurt me,' yet we carry the psychological scars from words long after the bruises and scrapes have healed. We may still be in the midst of a cultural reaction against early preoccupation with the magical power of words.

The importance of this kind of 'magic' was suggested by the Sapir/Whorf hypothesis, which states that language can determine our thought and behavior patterns and that different languages can shape different world views.[55] It is usually assumed that feminist argument is grounded in the Sapir/Whorf hypothesis. Michael Schneider and Karen Foss worry that 'feminists inadvertently have helped to perpetuate and diffuse an outdated, oversimplified, and basically inaccurate view of the relationship between thought and language'.[56] In its strongly stated form, this hypothesis has seen little empirical support and strong theoretical criticism since its formulation in the 1920s and 1930s. Yet it has come to be generally accepted in its moderate version: that language may influence, rather than determine, thought and behavior patterns. The moderate version of the Sapir/Whorf hypothesis is reflected in the feminist move for nonsexist language. The issue is not what *can* be said about the sexes, but what can be *most easily* and *most clearly* said, given the constraints of the he/man approach and other forms of sexist language.

What can be done to resolve the controversy over sexist language? A dual strategy, involving both research and action, can be most effective in accelerating the language changes already in progress. The many research projects, articles, and course offerings described in *Women and Language News*, a national newsletter, reflect the increasing interdisciplinary and international interest in language and sexism.[57] These theoretical and empirical approaches contribute to our understanding of the nature

55. Benjamin Whorf, *Language, Thought and Reality: Essays of Benjamin Whorf*, ed. J. B. Carrol, Cambridge, Mass.: MIT Press, 1956.

56. Michael Schneider and Karen Foss, 'Thought, Sex, and Language: the Sapir-Whorf Hypothesis in the American Women's Movement', *Bulletin: Women's Studies in Communication*, 1, no. 1, 1977, p. 3.

57. *Women and Language News*, Stanford, Calif.: Stanford University, Department of Linguistics, various issues, 1976-8.

and consequences of sexist language and lend a credibility to feminist claims. Such approaches need to be translated into other persuasive forms. Pressure on government agencies and the media, for example, can involve letter-writing campaigns, public advertisements, popularization of research results, workshops for those with power to effect language change, and organized demands for guidelines and regulations encouraging nonsexist language use.

Despite the misinterpretation of the sexist language controversy, the movement toward nonsexist language has begun. That movement has been slowed by confusion. Increased clarity can help us be more effective in crafting future changes. Edward Sapir was aware of the psychological implications of language. 'All in all,' he claimed, 'it is not too much to say that one of the really important functions of language is to be constantly declaring to society the psychological place held by all of its members.'[58] The goal of those of us who argue for language change is to revise the character of that declaration, so that our language comes to suggest the equal humanity of *all* its users.

58. Edward Sapir, *Selected Writings of Edward Sapir in Language, Culture, and Personality*, ed. David Mandelbaum, Berkeley: University of California Press, 1963.

Tillie Olsen

Silences: When Writers Don't Write

In Susan Koppelman Cornillon, ed., *Images of Women in Fiction: Feminist Perspectives*, Ohio: Bowling Green University Popular Press, 1972, pp. 97-112 (first published in 1965)

Literary history and the present are dark with silences: some the silences for years by our acknowledged great; some silences hidden; some the ceasing to publish after one work appears; some the never coming to book form at all.

What is it that happens with the creator, to the creative process in that time? What *are* creation's needs for full functioning? Without intention of or pretension to literary scholarship, I have had special need to learn all I could of this over the years, myself so nearly remaining mute and having let writing die over and over again in me.

These are not *natural* silences, what Keats called *agonie ennuyeuse* (the tedious agony), that necessary time for renewal, lying fallow, gestation, in the natural cycle of creation. The silences I speak of here are unnatural; the unnatural thwarting of what struggles to come into being, but cannot. In the old, the obvious parallels: when the seed strikes stone; the soil will not sustain; the spring is false; the time is drought or blight or infestation; the frost comes premature.

The very great have known such silences – Thomas Hardy, Melville, Rimbaud, Gerard Manley Hopkins. They tell us little as to why or how the creative working atrophied and died in them – if it ever did.

'Less and less shrink the visions then vast in me,' writes Thomas Hardy in his thirty-year ceasing from novels after the Victorian vileness to his *Jude the Obscure*. ('So ended his prose contributions to literature, his experiences having killed all his interest in this form' – the official explanation.) But the great poetry he wrote to the end of his life was not sufficient to hold, to develop, the vast visions which for twenty-five years had had scope in novel after novel. People, situations, interrelationships, landscape – they cry for this larger life in poem after poem.

It was not visions shrinking with Hopkins, but a different torment. For seven years he kept his religious vow to refrain from writing poetry, but the poet's eye he could not shut, nor win 'elected silence to beat upon [his] whorled ear'. 'I had *long* had haunting my ear the echo of a poem which now I realized on paper,' he writes of the first poem permitted to end the seven years' silence. But poetry ('to hoard unheard; be heard, unheeded') could be only the least and last of his heavy priestly responsibilities. Nineteen poems were all he could produce in his last nine years – fullness to us, but torment pitched past grief to him, who felt himself become 'time's eunuch, never to beget'.[1]

Silence surrounds Rimbaud's silence. Was there torment of the unwritten; haunting of rhythm, of visions; anguish at dying powers; the seventeen years after he abandoned the unendurable literary world? We know only that the need to write continued into his first years of vagabondage, and that on his deathbed he spoke again like a poet-visionary.

Melville's stages to his thirty-year prose silence are clearest. The presage is in his famous letter to Hawthorne, as he had to hurry *Moby Dick* to an end:

> I am so pulled hither and thither by circumstances. The calm, the coolness, the silent grass growing mood in which a man ought always to compose, that can seldom be mine. Dollars damn me. What I feel most moved to write, that is banned, it will not pay. Yet altogether, write the other way I cannot. So the result is a final hash.

Reiterated in *Pierre* (Melville himself), writing 'that book whose unfathomable cravings drink his blood'. . .

> when at last the idea obtruded that the wiser and profounder he should grow, the more he lessened his chances for bread.

To have to try final hash; to have one's work met by 'drear ignoring'; to be damned by dollars into a Customs House job; to have only occasional weary evenings and Sundays left for writing –

> How bitterly did unreplying Pierre feel in his heart that to most of the great works of humanity, their authors had given not weeks and months, not years and years, but their wholly surrendered and dedicated lives.

1. A letter to Bridges, four years before he wrote the poem.

Is it not understandable why Melville began to burn work, then refused to write it, 'immolating' it, 'sealing in a fate subdued'? Instead he turned to sporadic poetry, manageable in a time sense, 'to nurse through night the ethereal spark' where once had been 'flame on flame'. A thirty-year night. He was nearly seventy before he could quit the Customs dock and again have full time for writing, start back to prose. 'Age, dull tranquilizer', and devastation of 'arid years that filed before' to work through before he could restore the creative process. Three years of tryings before he felt capable of beginning *Billy Budd* (the kernel waiting half a century); three years more, the slow, painful, never satisfied writing and rewriting of it.

Kin to these years-long silences are the *hidden* silences; work aborted, deferred, denied – hidden by the work which does come to fruition. Hopkins' last years rightfully belong here, as does Kafka's whole writing life, that of Mallarmé, Olive Schreiner, probably Katherine Anne Porter, and many other contemporary writers.

Censorship silences. Deletions, omissions, abandonment of the medium (as with Thomas Hardy). Self-censorship, like Mark Twain's. Publishers' censorship, refusing subject matter or treatment. Religious, political censorship – sometimes spurring inventiveness – most often (read Dostoevski's letters) a wearing attrition.

The extreme of this: those writers physically silenced by governments. Isaac Babel, the years of imprisonment, what took place in him with what wanted to be written? Or in Oscar Wilde, who was not permitted even a pencil until the last months of his imprisonment?

Other silences. The truly memorable poem, story, or book, then the writer never heard from again. Was one work all the writer had in him, and he respected literature too much to repeat himself? Was there the kind of paralysis psychiatry might have helped? Were the conditions not present for establishing the habits of creativity (a young Colette who lacked a Willy to lock her in her room each day? or other claims, other responsibilities so writing could not be first)? It is an eloquent commentary that this one-book silence is true of most Negro writers; only eleven, these last hundred years, have published more than twice.

There is a prevalent silence I pass by quickly, the absence of creativity where it once had been; the ceasing to create literature, though the books keep coming out, year after year. That suicide of the creative process Hemingway describes so accurately in *The Snows of Kilimanjaro*:

He had destroyed his talent himself – by not using it, by betrayals of himself and what he believed in, by drinking so much that he blunted the edge of his perceptions, by laziness, by sloth, by snobbery, by hook and by crook; selling vitality, trading it for security, for comfort.

No, not Scott Fitzgerald. His not a death of creativity, not silence, but what happens when (his words) there is 'the sacrifice of talent, in pieces, to preserve its essential value'.

Almost unnoted are the foreground silences, *before* the achievement. (Remember when Emerson hailed Whitman's genius, he guessed correctly, 'which yet must have had a long *foreground* for such a start'.) George Eliot, Joseph Conrad, Isak Dinesen, Sherwood Anderson, Elizabeth Madox Roberts, A. E. Coppard, Kate Chopin, Angus Wilson, Joyce Cary – all close to, or in their forties before they became writers; Lampedusa, Maria Dermout (*The Ten Thousand Things*), Laura Ingalls Wilder, the 'children's writer', in their sixties. Their capacities evident early in the 'being one on whom nothing is lost'. Not all struggling and anguished, like Anderson, the foreground years; some needing the immobilization of long illness or loss, or the sudden lifting of responsibility to make writing necessary, make writing possible; others waiting circumstances and encouragement (George Eliot, her Henry Lewes; Laura Wilder, a daughter's insistence that she transmute her storytelling gift onto paper).

UNMINED GENIUS

Very close to this last grouping are the silences where the lives never came to writing. Among these, the mute inglorious Miltons: those whose waking hours are all struggle for existence; the barely educated; the illiterate; women. Their silence the silence of centuries as to how life was, is, for most of humanity. Traces of their making, of course, in folk song, lullaby, tales, language itself, jokes, maxims, superstitions, but we know nothing of the creators or how it was with them. In the fantasy of Shakespeare born in deepest Africa (as at least one Shakespeare must have been), was the ritual, the oral storytelling a fulfillment? Or was there restlessness, indefinable yearning, a sense of restriction? Was it as Virginia Woolf in *A Room of One's Own* guesses – about women?

Genius of a sort must have existed among them, as it existed among the working classes, but certainly it never got itself onto paper. When, however, one reads of a woman possessed by the devils, of a wise woman selling herbs, or even a remarkable man who had a remarkable mother, then I think we are on the track of a lost novelist, a suppressed poet, or some Emily Brontë who dashed her brains out on the moor, crazed with the torture her gift had put her to.

Rebecca Harding Davis whose work sleeps in the forgotten (herself as a woman of a century ago so close to remaining mute)[2] also guessed about the silent in that time of the twelve-hour-a-day, six-day work week. She writes of the illiterate iron worker in 'Life in the Iron Mills' who sculptured great shapes in the slag, 'his fierce thirst for beauty, to know it, to create it, to *be* something other than he is – a passion of pain', *Margaret Howth* in the textile mill:

> There were things in the world, that like herself, were marred, did not understand, were hungry to know. . . . Her eyes quicker to see than ours, delicate or grand lines in the homeliest things. . . . Everything she saw or touched, nearer, more human than to you or me. These sights and sounds did not come to her common; she never got used to living as other people do.

She never got used to living as other people do. Was that one of the ways it was?

So some of the silences, incomplete listing of the incomplete, where the need and capacity to create were of a high order.

THE FRIGHTFUL TASK

Now, what *is* the work of creation and the circumstances it demands for full functioning – as told in the journals and notes of the practitioners themselves: Harry James, Katherine Mansfield, Gide, Virginia Woolf; the letters of Flaubert, Rilke, Conrad; Thomas Wolfe's *Story of a Novel*, Valéry's *Course in Poetics*. What do they explain of the silences?

'Constant toil is the law of art, as it is of life,' says (and demonstrated) Balzac:

> To pass from conception to execution, to produce, to bring the

2. See my afterword on Rebecca Harding Davis in the Feminist Press reprint of her *Life in the Iron Mills* (1973).

idea to birth, to raise the child laboriously from infancy, to put it nightly to sleep surfeited, to kiss it in the mornings with the hungry heart of a mother, to clean it, to clothe it fifty times over in new garments which it tears and casts away, and yet not revolt against the trials of this agitated life – this unwearying maternal love, this habit of creation – this is execution and its toils.

'Without duties, almost without external communication,' Rilke specifies, 'unconfined solitude which takes every day like a life, a spaciousness which puts no limit to vision and in the midst of which infinities surround.'

Unconfined solitude as Joseph Conrad experienced it:

For twenty months I wrestled with the Lord for my creation . . . mind and will and conscience engaged to the full, hour after hour, day after day . . . a lonely struggle in a great isolation from the world. I suppose I slept and ate the food put before me and talked connectedly on suitable occasions, but I was never aware of the even flow of daily life, made easy and noiseless for me by a silent, watchful, tireless affection.

So there is a homely underpinning for it all, the even flow of daily life made easy and noiseless.

'The terrible law of the artist' – says Henry James – 'the law of fructification, of fertilization. The old, old lesson of the art of meditation. To woo combinations and inspirations into being by a depth and continuity of attention and meditation.'

'That load, that weight, that gnawing conscience,' writes Thomas Mann –

That sea which to drink up, that frightful task. . . . The will, the discipline and self-control to shape a sentence or follow out a hard train of thought. From the first rhythmical urge of the inward creative force towards the material, towards casting in shape and form, from that to the thought, the image, the word, the line, what a struggle, what Gethsemane.

Does it become very clear what Melville's Pierre so bitterly remarked on, and what literary history bears out, why most of the great works of humanity have come from wholly surrendered and dedicated lives? How else sustain the constant toil, the frightful task, the terrible law, the continuity? Full self, this means, full time for the work. (That time for which Emily Dickinson withdrew from the world.)

But what if there is not that fullness of time, let alone totality of self? What if the writer, as in some of these silences, must work regularly at something besides his own work – as do nearly all in the arts in the United States today?

I know the theory (kin to starving in the garret makes great art) that it is this very circumstance which feeds creativity. I know, too, that for the beginning young, for some who have such need, the job can be valuable access to life they would not otherwise know. A few (I think of the doctors, Chekhov and William Carlos Williams) for special reasons sometimes manage both. But the actuality testifies: substantial creative work demands time, and with rare exceptions only full-time workers have created it. Where the claims of creation cannot be primary, the results are atrophy; unfinished work; minor effort and accomplishment; silences. (Desperation which accounts for the mountains of applications to the foundations for grants – undivided time – in the strange breadline system we have worked out for our artists.)

Twenty years went by on the writing of *Ship of Fools*, while Katherine Anne Porter, who needed only two years, was 'trying to get to that table, to that typewriter, away from my jobs of teaching and trooping this country and of keeping house'. 'Your subconscious needed that time to grow the layers of pearl,' she was told. Perhaps, perhaps, but I doubt it. Subterranean forces can make you wait, but they are very finicky about the kind of waiting it has to be. Before they will feed the creator back, they must be fed, passionately fed, what needs to be worked on. 'We hold up our desire as one places a magnet over a composite dust from which the particle of iron will suddenly jump up,' says Paul Valéry. A receptive waiting, that means, not demands which prevent 'an undistracted center of being'. And when the response comes, availability to work must be immediate. If not used at once, all may vanish as a dream; worse, future creation be endangered, for only the removal and development of the material frees the forces for further work.

There is a life in which all this is documented: Franz Kafka's. For every one entry from his diaries here, there are fifty others which testify as unbearably to the driven stratagems for time, the work lost (to us), the damage to the creative powers (and the body) of having to deny, interrupt, postpone, put aside, let work die.

'I cannot devote myself completely to my writing,' Kafka explains (in 1911). 'I could not live by literature, if only, to begin with, because of the slow maturing of my work and its special character.' So he worked as an official in a state insurance agency, and wrote when he could.

These two can never be reconciled.... If I have written something one evening, I am afire the next day in the office and can bring nothing to completion. Outwardly I fulfill my office duties satisfactorily, not my inner duties however, and every unfulfilled inner duty becomes a misfortune that never leaves. What strength it will necessarily drain me of.

[1911] No matter how little the time or how badly I write, I feel approaching the imminent possibility of great moments which could make me capable of anything. But my being does not have sufficient strength to hold this to the next writing time. During the day the visible world helps me; during the night it cuts me to pieces unhindered.... Calling forth such powers which are then not permitted to function.

Which are then not permitted to function.

[1912] When I begin to write after such a long interval, I draw the words as if out of the empty air. If I capture one, then I have just this one alone, and all the toil must begin anew.

[1914] Yesterday for the first time in months, an indisputable ability to do good work. And yet wrote only the first page. Again I realize that everything written down bit by bit rather than all at once in the course of the larger part is inferior, and that the circumstances of my life condemn me to this inferiority.

[1915] My constant attempt by sleeping before dinner to make it possible to continue working [writing] late into the night, senseless. Then at one o'clock can no longer fall asleep at all, the next day at work insupportable, and so I destroy myself.

[1917] Distractedness, weak memory, stupidity.... Always this one principal anguish – if I had gone away in 1911 in full possession of all my powers. Not eaten by the strain of keeping down living forces.

Eaten into tuberculosis. By the time he won through to himself and time for writing, his body could live no more. He was forty-one.

I think of Rilke who said: 'If I have any responsibility, I mean and desire it to be responsibility for the deepest and innermost essence of the loved reality [writing] to which I am inseparably bound'; and who also said: 'Anything alive, that makes demands, arouses in me an infinite capacity to give it its due, the consequences of which completely use me up.' These were true with Kafka, too, yet how different their lives. When Rilke wrote that about responsibility, he is explaining why he will not take a job to support his wife and baby, nor live with them (years later will not come to his daughter's wedding nor permit a two-hour honeymoon visit lest it break his solitude where he awaits poetry). The 'infinite capacity' is his explanation as to why he cannot even bear to have a dog. Extreme – and justified. He protected his creative powers.

WHAT'S SPECIAL ABOUT WOMEN

Kafka's, Rilke's 'infinite capacity' and all else that has been said here of the needs of creation, illuminate women's silence of centuries. I will not repeat what is in Virginia Woolf's *A Room of One's Own*, but talk of this last century and a half in which women have begun to have voice in literature. (It has been less than that time in Eastern Europe, and not yet, in many parts of the world.)

In the last century, of the women whose achievements endure for us in one way or another, nearly all never married (Jane Austen, Emily Brontë, Christina Rossetti, Emily Dickinson, Louisa May Alcott, Sarah Orne Jewett) or married late in their thirties (George Eliot, Elizabeth Barrett Browning, Charlotte Brontë, Olive Schreiner). I can think of only four (George Sand, Harriet Beecher Stowe, Helen Hunt Jackson, and Kate Chopin) who married and had children as young women. All had servants. All but Sand were foreground silences.

In our century, until very recently, it has not been so different. Most did not marry (Lagerlöf, Cather, Glasgow, Gertrude Stein, Sitwell, Gabriela Mistral, Elizabeth Madox Roberts, Charlotte Mew, Welty, Marianne Moore) or, if married, have been childless (Undset, Wharton, Woolf, Katherine Mansfield, H. H. Richardson, Bowen, Dinesen, Porter, Hellman, Dorothy Parker). Colette had one child. If I include Kay Boyle, Pearl Buck, Dorothy Canfield Fisher, that will make a small group who had more than one child. Nearly all had household help.

Am I resaying the moldy theory that women have no need, some say no capacity, to create art, because they can create babies? And the additional proof is precisely that the few women who have created it are nearly all childless? No.

The power and the need to create, over and beyond reproduction, is native in both men and women. Where the gifted among women (*and men*) have remained mute, or have never attained full capacity, it is because of circumstances, inner or outer, which oppose the needs of creation.

Wholly surrendered and dedicated lives; time as needed for the work; totality of self. But women are traditionally trained to place others' needs first, to feel these needs as their own (the 'infinite capacity'); their sphere, their satisfaction to be in making it possible for others to use their abilities. This is what Virginia Woolf meant when, already a writer of achievement, she wrote in her diary:

> Father's birthday. He would have been 96, 96 yes, today; and could have been 96, like other people one has known; but mercifully was not. His life would have entirely ended mine. What would have happened? No writing, no books; – inconceivable.

It took family deaths to free more than one woman writer into her own development.[3] Emily Dickinson freed herself, denying all the duties expected of a woman of her social position except the closest family ones, and she was fortunate to have a sister, and servants, to share those. How much is revealed of what happened to their own talents in the diaries of those sisters of great men, Dorothy Wordsworth, Alice James.

And where there is no servant or relation to assume the responsibilities of daily living? Listen to Katherine Mansfield in the early days of her relationship with John Middleton Murry, when they both dreamed of becoming great writers:

> The house seems to take up so much time. . . . I mean when I have to clean up twice over or wash up extra unnecessary things. I get frightfully impatient and want to be working [writing]. So often this week you and Gordon have been talking while I washed dishes. Well someone's got to wash dishes and get food. Otherwise 'there's nothing in the house but eggs to eat.' And after you have gone I walk about with a mind full of ghosts of saucepans and primus stoves and 'will there be enough to go around?' And you calling, whatever I am doing, writing, 'Tig, isn't there going to be tea? It's five o'clock.'

> I loathe myself today. This woman who superintends you and rushes about slamming doors and slopping water and shouts 'You might at least empty the pail and wash out the tea leaves.'

3. Kate Chopin, George Eliot, Helen Hunt Jackson, Elizabeth Gaskell.

O Jack, I wish that you would take me in your arms and kiss my hands and my face and every bit of me and say, 'It's all right, you darling thing, I understand.'

A long way from Conrad's favorable circumstance for creation: the flow of daily life made easy and noiseless.

And, if in addition to the infinite capacity, to the daily responsibilities, there are children?

Balzac, you remember, described creation in terms of motherhood. Yes, in intelligent passionate motherhood there are similarities, and in more than the toil and patience. The calling upon total capacities; the re-living and new using of the past; the comprehensions; the fascination, absorption, intensity. All almost certain death to creation.

Not because the capacities to create no longer exist, or the need (though for a while, as in any fullness of life, the need may be obscured) but because the circumstances for sustained creation are almost impossible. The need cannot be first. It can have at best, only part self, part time. (Unless someone else does the nurturing. Read Dorothy Fisher's 'Babushka Farnham' in *Fables for Parents*.) More than in any human relationship, overwhelmingly more, motherhood means being instantly interruptible, responsive, responsible. Children need one *now* (and remember, in our society, the family must often be the center for love and health the outside world is not). The very fact that these are needs of love, not duty, that one feels them as one's self; that there is no one else to be responsible for these needs, gives them primacy. It is distraction, not meditation, that becomes habitual; interruption, not continuity; spasmodic, not constant toil. The rest has been said here. Work interrupted, deferred, postponed, makes blockage – at best, lesser accomplishment. Unused capacities atrophy, cease to be.

When H. H. Richardson, who wrote the Australian classic *Ultima Thule*, was asked why she – whose children, like all her people, were so profoundly written – did not herself have children, she answered: 'There are enough women to do the childbearing and childrearing. I know of none who can write my books.' I remember thinking rebelliously, yes, and I know of none who can bear and rear my children either. But literary history is on her side. Almost no mothers – as almost no part-time, part-self persons – have created enduring literature – so far.

A PRIVATE JOURNEY

If I talk now quickly of my own silences – almost presumptuous after what has been told here – it is that the individual experience may add.

In the twenty years I bore and reared my children, usually had to work on a job as well, the simplest circumstances for creation did not exist. Nevertheless writing, the hope of it, was 'the air I breathed, so long as I shall breathe at all'. In that hope, there was conscious storing, snatched reading, beginnings of writing, and always 'the secret rootlets of reconnaissance'.

When the youngest of our four was in school, the beginnings struggled toward endings. This was a time, in Kafka's words, 'like a squirrel in a cage: bliss of movement, desperation about constriction, craziness of endurance'.

Bliss of movement. A full extended family life; the world of my job (transcriber in a dairy-equipment company); and the writing, which I was somehow able to carry around within me through work, through home. Time on the bus, even when I had to stand, was enough; the stolen moments at work, enough; the deep night hours for as long as I could stay awake, after the kids were in bed, after the household tasks were done, sometimes during. It is no accident that the first work I considered publishable began: 'I stand here ironing, and what you asked me moves tormented back and forth with the iron.'

In such snatches of time I wrote what I did in those years, but there came a time when this triple life was no longer possible. The fifteen hours of daily realities became too much distraction for the writing. I lost craziness of endurance. What might have been, I don't know, but I asked for, and received, eight months' writing time. There was still full family life, all the household responsibilities, but I did not have to go out on a job. I had continuity, three full days, sometimes more, and it was in those months I made the mysterious turn and became a writing writer.

Then had to return to the world of work, someone else's work, nine hours, five days a week.

This was the time of festering and congestion. For a few months I was able to shield the writing with which I was so full against the demands of jobs on which I had to be competent, through the joys and responsibilities of family. For a few months. Always roused by the writing, always denied. 'I could not go to write it down. It convulsed and died in me. I will pay.' My work died. What demanded to be written, did not; it seethed, bubbled, clamored, peopled me. At last moved into the hours meant for sleeping. I worked now full time on temporary jobs, a Kelly, a Western Agency girl (girl!), wandering from office to office, always hoping we could manage two, three writing months ahead. Eventually there was time.

I had said: always roused by the writing, always denied. Now, like a woman made frigid, I had to learn response, to trust this possibility for fruition that had not been before. Any interruption dazed and silenced me. It took a long while of surrendering to what I was trying to write, of invoking Henry James's 'passion, piety, patience', before I was able to reestablish work.

When again I had to leave the writing, I lost consciousness. A time of anesthesia. There was still an automatic noting that did not stop, but it was as if writing had never been. No fever, no congestion, no festering. I ceased being peopled, slept well and dreamlessly, took a 'permanent' job. The few pieces which had been published seemed to have vanished like the not-yet-written. I wrote someone, unsent: 'So long they fed each other – my life, the writing; the writing or hope of it, my life – and now they destroy each other.' I knew, but did not feel the destruction.

A Ford grant in literature, awarded me on nomination by others, came almost too late. Time granted does not necessarily coincide with time that can be most fully used, as the congested time of fullness would have been. Still, it was two years.

TO GIVE ONE'S ALL

Drowning is not so pitiful as the attempt to rise, says Emily Dickinson. I do not agree, but I know of what she speaks. For a long time I was that emaciated survivor trembling on the beach, unable to rise and walk. Said differently, I could manage only the feeblest, shallowest growth on that devastated soil. Weeds, to be burnt like weeds, or used as compost. When the habits of creation were at last rewon, one book went to the publisher, and I dared to begin my present work. It became my center, engraved on it: 'Evil is whatever distracts.' (By now, had begun a cost to our family life, to my own participation in life as a human being.) I shall not tell the 'rest, residue, and remainder' of what I was 'leased, demised, and let unto' when once again I had to leave work at the flood to return to the Time Master, to business-ese and legalese. This most harmful of all my silences has ended, but I am not yet recovered, may still be a one-book instead of a hidden and foreground silence.

Cross-cultural Studies

A fundamental organising principle of all societies is the sexual division of labour, even though there are enormous differences between societies in the ways in which this division is implemented. Yet feminist anthropologists have observed, in the words of Michelle Rosaldo, that 'women may be important, powerful and influential, but it seems that, relative to men of their age and social status, women everywhere lack generally recognised and culturally valued authority'.[1] The question raised by this observation is inevitably that of why women should be so universally subordinate, particularly in social and symbolic power, to men. The first, and by far the most influential, answer to this question was suggested by Engels in *The Origin of the Family, Private Property and the State*, when he argued that the key to the subordination of women was the transition from communally owned property to privately owned property, and with it the rise of class society. In pre-class societies, he maintained, there was a sexual division of labour, but no system of sexual stratification. Men and women contributed to the maintenance of the household, and neither sex had a monopoly of social or sexual power. Unfortunately for women, this system of 'primitive communism' came to an end when technological improvements in the work of men made possible the systematic accumulation of property. Goods which had once been owned collectively by a clan or a household became the property of individual men whose interests involved a continuity of ownership over the fruits of their labours. In order to achieve a clear right of succession to property a nuclear, rather than an extended, family developed through which inheritance could pass in a clearly defined line from father to legitimate son. Women, from being equal partners in social production, became the means by which male property was transmitted and controlled. Even in matrilineal societies, where property passes not from the father of a child, but from the mother's brother, only the means of transferring male power is different: women remain essential, but second-class, persons.

1. Michelle Rosaldo, 'Woman, Culture and Society: a Theoretical Overview', in Michelle Rosaldo and Louise Lamphere, eds., *Woman, Culture and Society*, Stanford: Stanford University Press, 1974, p. 17.

The development of private property – 'the world historical defeat of the female sex', as Engels described it – involved the emergence of class societies. Within these societies, sexual stratification has been complicated by class stratification, making it difficult for feminist anthropologists or sociologists to speak with confidence of a single social position of women. To quote Michelle Rosaldo again: 'Male dominance, though apparently universal, does not in actual behavioural terms assume a universal content or a universal shape.' But as she goes on to say:

> Men's dominance is evidenced, I believe, when we observe that women almost everywhere have daily responsibilities to feed and care for children, spouse and kin, while men's economic obligations tend to be less regular and more bound up with extra familial ties ... the formal initiation and arrangement of permanent heterosexual bonds is something organised by men. Women may have ritual powers of considerable significance to themselves as well as men, but women never dominate in rites requiring the participation of the community as a whole.... Finally, women often form organisations of real and recognised political and economic strength; at times they rule as queens, acquire followings of men, beat husbands who prefer strange women to their wives, or perhaps enjoy a sacred status in their role as mothers. But again, I know of no political system in which women individually or as a group are expected to hold more offices or have more political clout than their male counterparts.[2]

Yet these universal facts about the subordination of women can easily lead to the search for inclusive generalisations about the position of women which can obscure significant differences both between societies and between the roles of men and women within societies. Thus, for example, an assertion of the universal subordination of women would ignore the very real distinctions between the position of women in some Islamic societies, where sexual divisions and distinct social worlds for the two sexes are very much apparent, and other societies, such as that of the !Kung, where sexual divisions in all areas of social life are minimal.[3] Indeed, to equate these two forms of social formation simply on

2. Michelle Rosaldo, 'The Use and Abuse of Anthropology: Reflections on Feminism and Cross-Cultural Understanding', *Signs*, vol. 5, no. 3, Spring 1980, pp. 389-417.
3. See the article by Patricia Draper, '!Kung Women: Contrasts in Sexual Egalitarianism in Foraging and Sedentary Contexts', in Rayna Reiter, ed., *Toward an Anthropology of Women*, London and New York: Monthly Review Press, 1975, pp. 77-109.

the grounds that in both cases women have less symbolic or political power, obscures a number of crucial differences between the societies, the majority of which inevitably affect the position of individual women within those societies.

It is thus apparent that for feminists to assume that the universal subordination of women takes a universal form is both quite incorrect and utterly misleading. However, the temptation to make sweeping judgments about the global situation of women is one that on the whole feminist anthropologists (unlike some feminist polemicists) have ignored. In part this reluctance to generalise arises out of the traditional form of training and recruitment into anthropology – that of fieldwork and the collection of detailed ethnographic data about one particular society. Although there are obvious similarities between all societies, in that all societies must produce their means of material subsistence and reproduce labour power and social relations, it is one of the first premises of anthropology that the form which these activities takes differs widely from society to society. Hence feminist anthropologists have pointed out the wide variations between societies in the sexual division of labour and have acknowledged that there is no universal concept or understanding of what constitutes 'male' or 'female' work. While it is generally true that women have a prime responsibility for the care of young infants, it is not generally true that the socialisation of the young is solely and exclusively a female task.

All the evidence from anthropology suggests that a search for universals in the behaviour of men and women is doomed to failure. Yet male anthropologists, just as much as some feminists, have been attracted by the appeal of a universal theory and have suggested theories about the social roles of men and women that are essentially universalistic. Perhaps best known of such theories is that of Claude Lévi-Strauss, who argues, in *The Elementary Structures of Kinship*, that the exchange of women in marriage is the means by which all societies establish social relations – relations that are independent of a single family or kin group. The establishment of these extra-familial ties produces social, rather than biological relations, and makes it possible for people to extend their activities, and in some cases their authority and power, beyond the limits of the nuclear family. An important part of Lévi-Strauss' argument is his assertion that it is one of the essential needs of human societies to establish clearly the differences between the sexes. Thus societies will develop gender differences: differences in the social roles and expectations of the sexes which are not necessarily related to their biology. As Lévi-Strauss writes:

> The very fact that the sexual division of labour varies endlessly according to the society selected for consideration shows that ... it is the mere fact of its existence which is mysteriously required, the form under which it comes to exist being utterly irrelevant, at least from the point of view of any natural necessity ... the sexual division of labour is nothing else than a device to institute a reciprocal state of dependency between the sexes.[4]

Gender differences are therefore produced, according to Lévi-Strauss, so that social beings called 'men' and 'women' can be recognised, individuals who must seek a partner of the opposite sex in order to achieve wholeness. Implicit in this theory is the idea that regardless of an individual's natural inclinations or rational choice the fact of his or her biology must be developed in socially acceptable ways. There is no escaping heterosexuality or assuming the kind of behaviour which is conventionally expected of men and women. In many ways the argument of *The Elementary Structures of Kinship* is appealing, since it does suggest why societies should be so anxious to institutionalise the behaviour of each sex and why sexual deviance (however defined) should be so universally condemned and perceived as threatening to the social order.

But Lévi-Strauss' theory, like all general theories, poses as many problems as it contains illuminations. Many of the problems are discussed by Gayle Rubin in an article entitled 'The Traffic in Women: Notes on the Political Economy of Sex',[5] but one in particular is worth mentioning here. It is that the social construction of sexuality is more varied than Lévi-Strauss assumes. In both anthropological and socio-historical literature, there are numerous examples of societies which institutionalise heterosexual marriage and yet also allow homosexuality. Sexual identity is not therefore the single, unambiguous, identity which Lévi-Strauss suggests is the case.

Evidence from numerous societies suggests therefore that the varieties of sexual division and sexual expression are numerous. Even within our own society it is difficult to speak with absolute authority of any single concept of a man or a woman. Yet this self-conscious reluctance to generalise has not always been shared

4. Claude Lévi-Strauss, 'The Family', in H. Shapiro, ed., *Man, Culture and Society*, Oxford: Oxford University Press, 1971, pp. 347-8.
5. Gayle Rubin, 'The Traffic in Women: Notes on the Political Economy of Sex', in R. Reiter, ed., *op. cit.*, pp. 157-210.

by anthropologists, and both feminists and Marxists have pointed out that many anthropological (and indeed historical) studies have been guilty of the most gross ethnocentrism or androcentrism. In two widely influential papers Sally Slocum and Elizabeth Fee have argued[6] that some aspects of many anthropological studies are of questionable accuracy because the male anthropologists conducting the research either ignored women, or – in the case of cultures with strict segregation of the sexes – could not obtain access to them. While Marxists have also pointed out the ethnocentrism of many Western accounts of non-industrial and technologically simple societies, Marxist feminists have also suggested that although Marxist anthropologists may be more sensitive to issues such as colonialism than some traditional anthropologists, this does not make them any less androcentric. For example, in her review of Emmanuel Terray's *Marxism and Primitive Societies* Maxine Molyneux shows how a Marxist assumed a state of primitive communism and lack of exploitation in a society (in this case the Gouro of the Ivory Coast) by completely overlooking the exploitative relationships that existed within that society between men and women.[7]

What emerges from a study of cultures and societies other than our own is the grave danger of making any kind of general statement about the situation of women or men. Moreover, for feminists, as much as for any social scientist, there exists the fundamental problem of determining the meaning of other people's actions or interpretations of events. A social practice which may appear normal to one society is savage to another. Yet while recognising that truth can be different on the different sides of the Pyrenees, we must also recognise that there are some social practices concerning women which do constitute an assault on the health and chances of physical survival of women. The most notorious examples of legitimate physical violence towards women are foot-binding and clitoridectomy. These practices highlight particularly vividly the dangers of describing something called the 'universal subordination' of women, since in those societies where these practices existed (or exist) the chances of women's survival in any social role were much decreased. Where those practices do not exist, women may be subject to the same appalling conditions

6. See Sally Slocum, 'Woman the Gatherer: Male Bias in Anthropology', reprinted here, and Elizabeth Fee, 'The Sexual Politics of Victorian Social Anthropology', *Feminist Studies*, vol. 1, 1973.
7. Maxine Molyneux, 'Androcentrism in Marxist Anthropology', *Critique of Anthropology*, vol. 3, nos. 9 and 10, 1977, pp. 55-81.

of life as men, but they are not so obviously penalised by the mere fact of their biology.

In all, it would appear that the search for the single explanation for the universal subordination of women is doomed to failure. The wide variations in the social role of women, in the social construction of sexuality and sexual relations, the problems of the accuracy of some anthropological and historical data about women and, finally, although by no means least, the difficulties inherent in the universal application of the concept of subordination, should caution any feminist intent on general theories about the position of women and relations between the sexes.

Kate Young and *Olivia Harris*

The Subordination of Women in Cross-cultural Perspective

In *Papers on Patriarchy*, Lewes: Women's Publishing Collective, 1976, pp. 38-52

Our work starts from the premise that women are subordinate in all societies known to anthropology and history. This immediately raises the question why this should be so, and, as a corollary, that of whether this must always be so. As anthropologists we attempt to answer these questions not in terms of psychological or biological characteristics, but in terms of social constructs. These we relate to the structuring of relationships between different categories of people within society in response to ecological, demographic and economic constraints which interact and come into contradiction with the level of development of the productive forces and the relations of production. By the level of development of the productive forces we refer to the Marxist concept expressing the extent to which nature has been harnessed by man and technology is developed. And by relations of production we mean at its simplest the relationship between the people involved in the productive process.

We make the suggestion that with the increasing development of the productive forces, both biological and social, the control over women's capacities as producers and reproducers becomes increasingly crucial for specific categories of males and for the reproduction of the conditions of production.

We also suggest that the dominant mechanism whereby women are controlled and their subordination is ensured changes with the level of development of the productive forces and the degree to which women have the potential for autonomy.

Our approach in this whole paper is very general because we think that at first it is a useful exercise to discuss the general tendencies that appear before later trying to develop a more comprehensive theory. We base the discussion on different types of societies which can be crudely assimilated to an evolutionary schema of social development, but in doing so we do not wish to imply that we discern any simple linear process. Also, while we restrict the discussion to two main aspects of the subordination of women, we do not wish to imply necessarily that these are the only important ones. We feel that the subordination of women cannot be understood by appeal to any single or reductionist principle, but that it is as complex as society itself.

Clearly, in starting from this premise, we are not saying that individual women do not have the power of choice, the means of influencing political decision, the possibility of achieving high status, etc.; nor are we arguing that women are passive objects/receivers of male domination. Nonetheless we are saying that in the societies that we know of women as a category are always subordinate to some category of men: in some societies they are subordinate to men as a group, in others to older males.

On the question we initially asked, whether this must always be so, we would argue that capitalism provides the conditions for the liberation of women from the social fetters placed upon them by demographic, ecological and economic constraints which are used to subordinate them in societies in which the level of development of the productive forces is much lower. Nonetheless capitalism has developed its own mechanisms for the subordination of women within a class system. It is probably not necessary to repeat the suggestion made by Marxist feminists that the liberation of women will come only within the context of the overthrow of capitalism itself. However the ideas outlined in this paper should make it clear that we do not believe that the demise of capitalism is a sufficient premise for the end of sexual asymmetry.

The structure of the paper is as follows: firstly we discuss two categories of analysis that we have isolated as being crucial for an understanding of women's subordination in pre-capitalist societies:

1. the exchange of women and the creation of alliances between groups;
2. the sexual division of labour and the creation of dependence between the sexes.

Following on from this, we discuss some of the difficulties and the benefits of using Marxist categories of analysis. Finally we pick out three key mechanisms by which women's acquiescence in their own subordination is ensured, namely the institutionalised use of physical violence, ideological constructs, and economic institutions, and we try to link this up with the notion of patriarchy.

I. THE EXCHANGE OF WOMEN, AND MARRIAGE

The purpose of starting our discussion with the nature of marriage is to stress its central importance in the ordering of human society in a way that is not necessarily obvious under advanced capitalism. That is to say that marriage is not only the institution that determines socially the distribution of the sexes for the purposes of biological reproduction, but is also the basis for a whole series of necessary economic and social tasks as well.

It has moreover been the subject of an important general theory on the position of women in society, namely that of the French anthropologist Lévi-Strauss (hereafter LS), whose ideas have been incorporated by various feminist writers, such as Simone de Beauvoir and Juliet Mitchell, both of whom make close connections between LS's theory and that of Freud. It will only be possible to give here a very summary outline of his position and our criticisms of it. (See booklist.)

Structuralist anthropology and the notion of society as communication, of which LS is a prime exponent, is based on linguistic theory: it is interested primarily in understanding the deep structures of the human mind. Language is used as a paradigm in analysis not only because it forms a relatively self-contained system, but also because it is one of the few uniquely human institutions, and thus particularly symptomatic of the human condition. The structures of the human psyche that can be deduced from its language-forming and language-learning capacities, and the fact that language is an essentially social phenomenon, both in its origin and in its practice, has made it a particularly useful paradigm for all sorts of other social activities.

The practice of language is the exchange of words between social subjects, and exchange has been posited as the fundamental social act: humans live in groups not in an abstract sense but because there is continual exchange between the individuals that go to form a group on all sorts of levels. Not only words and symbols, stories and ideas are exchanged continuously but also material goods and services. This is the basis of the anthropological notion of reciprocity: items are exchanged not haphazardly and chaotically, but by means of a socially-instituted regularity.

Under capitalism kinship has been reduced to a relatively residual role, and thus it is important to realise that in many pre-capitalist societies kinship appears as the fundamental ordering principle. Groups and their members are defined in terms of it, relations of production, the allocation of resources and most social roles are based on it. Because of its 'natural' basis in biological ties it is tempting to see kinship as somehow prior to the particular functions it may play. A quick look at the multifarious ways in which kinship links are organised and defined in different societies suggests that it is more related to the particular conjuncture of ecological, demographic, technological and superstructural conditions that go to shape a particular society at a given historical period.

As such, it is a highly sophisticated adaptive device for instituting relationships between groups in the language of permanent bonds. The peculiar feature of kinship ties is that they are in some cases immutable, and in all cases of a long-term nature. Kinship is thus not only rooted in biological fact, but provides a flexible language for expressing a far wider range of ties than can actually be demonstrated genealogically. It is thus perhaps comparable to the phenomenon of totemism as theorised by LS, whereby species from the natural world are used by societies to conceptualise the culturally instituted differences between human groups. Kinship relations are similarly used to conceptualise social relations, leading to the widespread phenomenon noted by anthropologists in simple societies whereby all members of the society stand apparently in kinship relations to each other.

Putney original

In LS's theory, exchange is the definitive social act and women are 'the archetype of exchange' because they are the 'valuables par excellence from both the biological and the social points of view, without which life is impossible, or, at best, is reduced to the worst forms of abjection'. It depends ultimately on the universality of the incest taboo, which guarantees that human life does not reproduce itself within the nuclear family, but presupposes a wider unit. If people cannot mate with their parents, siblings or children, then they must enter into relationships with others who do not fall into these categories. LS draws attention to the important social implications of the incest taboo, whereas others have constructed theories about it on the basis of psychological or biological/genetic ideas.

LS sees the incest taboo as the negative corollary of a positive rule – that of *exogamy* – namely that people must marry outside their own nuclear family, or as he puts it, that women must be exchanged between men. As he, and many primitive peoples put it: if one does not marry out one is killed out. For him the precondition of society is the kinship ties created by marrying out, and the bonds of reciprocal exchange thereby created. He sees the fundamental bonds as being those between men, or groups of men, by means of women. For him it is a 'basic fact that men exchange women and not vice versa. . . . The total relationship of exchange which constitutes marriage is not established between a man and a woman where each owes and receives something, but between groups of men, and the woman figures only as one of the objects in the exchange, not as one of the partners between whom the exchange takes place.'

Such, very briefly, is LS's theory, and it seems to us that he fails to make explicit its basis. He merely makes appeal to the 'facts', and the way it is empirically documented for pre-capitalist societies that many women have little or no say in the choice of a spouse, let alone whether they wish to be married. If it is indeed the case that society is constituted by the exchange of sexual partners, why is it women that are exchanged, and if so, are they part of 'society' or not? Even more problematic is his suggestion that the exchange of women is located in the conceptualising capacity of the human psyche, by analogy with the deep structures of language.

LS does not pose these problems for himself, and the reason seems to be that he implicitly appeals to Freudian theory and the predominance of the phallus. Thus he cannot be used to explicate Freudian theory, but only to illustrate it. His conceptualisation of society leaves us in an impasse, in which we are presented with a fundamental social act – that of the exchange of women – without any idea of the necessity for society, of why groups rather than individuals.

We must begin by positing the necessity of groups to furnish the material needs of human beings. If we look at the objective value of co-operation between individuals we can see the incest taboo, and the positive, if minimal rule of exogamy that it entails, as a hugely significant evolutionary step. On this basis, individuals potentially gain access to a whole range of new goods and services. By starting from a materialist position we can also avoid falling into the trap of separating analytically a hypothetical 'human nature' from the material conditions of its existence. Thus it seems methodologically wrong to separate the erotic value of women from their economic value. (LS is characteristically ambiguous on this point.) On the same materialist lines we can posit the superior physical strength of the male as an important adaptive device, without seeing it in some way as prior to its realisation and use in particular historical circumstances.

At a basic level, the incest taboo in our own society merely insists that the individual must not have sexual intercourse with members of the nuclear family. But in many pre-capitalist societies there are a whole series of positive rules about whom one may have intercourse with, whom one must marry, which represent a far more total ordering of society than that presented by the negative incest taboo. A distinction is often made between those whom one may not have any sexual liaison with on pain of the direst punishment (i.e., the incest taboo) and those whom one may have casual sexual relationships with but may not marry. Thus in empirical terms it is clear that there is a distinction to be made between sexual access and marital relationship.

Furthermore even though the incest taboo is universal, its particular form differs considerably from one society to another. The basic parent-child and sibling taboos seem to be universal, but some societies include a wider range of kin under the category of strictly prohibited. Such variation should make us wary of positing innate structures of the human psyche to explain it, but perhaps it can be more fruitfully seen as the way a particular kinship structure reproduces itself at the level of the individual.

Are we then to see the incest taboo in a general sense as necessarily entailing the exchange of women? Is the exchange of women axiomatic to human society, or is it a historically specific phenomenon? The exchange of women is more plausibly seen as related in a complex way to a positive structuring of society in terms of kinship by positive rules of exogamy. The argument might run something like this: at the earliest stages of human development when the material conditions of existence depended entirely on an unmediated appropriation from nature, there can have been little accumulation of material goods, both because such goods were freely available to all and because the necessary mobility of the group would make accumulation impracticable. On the other hand there would be distinct adaptive advantages in having access to a wide range of territories since nature is unpredictable, and thus groups which were able to institute wide-ranging bonds would have an adaptive advantage. The particular nature of kinship makes it a unique means of forming long-term bonds. There are however good demographic reasons for trying to gain access to women of other groups. It has been suggested (cf. C. Meillasoux, booklist) that the smallest viable demographic group consists of c. 150 people. If this group has access to potential child-bearers from another group its possibilities of survival are much greater. Clearly forcible capturing of women is a possibility, but peaceful exchange of them is more adaptive in the long run. The important consideration at this stage is that it is lateral – i.e., affinal links within this generation – rather than vertical links – i.e., of descent from a common ancestor – which are of importance.

An example of this, in which the exchange of women is an explicit construct of the participants, is provided by the Australian aborigines. They lived at a very simple level of appropriation from nature. Nonetheless they had a highly complicated system of marriage rules, in which the divisions of the group into various exogamic sections meant that there was a constant interlocking between the sections as they exchanged women between them. Moreover this system is not restricted to a single tribe, but by a process of transformations of rules a man away from his own group can readily discover those to whom he is 'related' and with whom he thus has an automatic series of rights and obligations. In this way the 'kinship' system has been shown to extend over huge areas, straddling different ecological zones, and providing a framework of risk-spreading which in an environment as harsh as that of central Australia, where man's control over nature was minimal, was obviously highly adaptive. And the exchange of women was certainly part of this mechanism. However it must also be borne in mind that such a mechanism can in no sense be seen as primitive or primeval: it has been evolved over the millennia. The Australian aborigines who seemingly developed it to coun-terbalance the effects of their harsh environment do not provide a counter-example to our general supposition that the exchange of women is found more typically in societies of a high level of development of the productive forces.

Hundreds of examples of this type, showing how complicated marriage structures form an integral part of a whole socio-economic system, could be quoted, but in this paper we can only draw out the general conclusions, i.e., that marriage is a political and economic institution as well as one to ensure the biological reproduction of the society. The exchange of people between groups creates bonds of a more enduring nature than the exchange of material goods and services, however strict the rules of reciprocity, because the fact that they result in children who in some degree belong to both groups materialises the bond over time. The way marriages have been used in political alliance are too well known to need documenting, but certain economic features of marriage may be less obvious. By this we refer not so much to the way transfers of property are made through the medium of marriage, but to the crucial role of women in production and transformation activities. This will be discussed in more detail later in the paper, but here one can point out, for example, that the institution of polygamy, which we often associate with rich sultans whose harems exist purely for their sensual enjoyment, is much more typically an institution whereby a man, usually an elder, can gain access to the labour of women, and via them to the labour of their children, and consolidate and extend his wealth and power.

The economic importance of women is obviously not restricted to polygamous societies: many people must be familiar with the widespread pattern in 'peasant' economies whereby a wife is picked not for her attractiveness so much as her strength and capacity for hard work. It is no accident that in most societies with a simple division of labour, a man only becomes an adult on marriage (on the grounds, one might suggest, that he cannot fulfil his social obligations in a satisfactory manner until he is in a position to exploit a woman's labour). The mature bachelor is derided in such societies in a way that spinsters are not. A spinster can be incorporated in the household and perform the normal tasks of a woman with her status only impaired by not having children, whereas a bachelor in many such societies simply does not have a social role.

Does the exchange of women play a crucial role in all societies? It seems that there is a case for saying that an advanced social division of labour in some sense replaces the function of the exchange of women as a mechanism for creating bonds between groups, and women become a means of integrating the group internally. (By 'group' we understand a relative and socially defined unit, and not an absolute category in any sense.)

A clear example of this process is the Indian caste system, where groups or castes are defined by their role in the social division of labour, which makes them all interdependent – e.g., washers, tanners, sweepers, smiths, landlords, warriors. Significantly, the caste system is also a classic example of endogamy – the opposite principle to exogamy and one which requires that women be married *within* the group, in this case the subcaste.

Perhaps a parallel can be drawn between the caste system and our own society, in which the exogamic rule is the minimal one provided by the incest taboos. Except in the case of high-level financial or political empires, women are rarely used to cement ties between groups, but the high statistical rate of marriage *within* one's class or cultural group seems to be of roughly the same dimensions as the caste system; that is to say, under capitalism the social division of labour is advanced to the degree that the cohesion of society is determined in its economic organisation, and the traffic in women becomes a significantly less important mechanism in bonding groups, but still forms an important bond of solidarity within the groups.

To recapitulate: the theory that the exchange of women is an irreducible axiom of human society contains certain crucial ambiguities, particularly with regard to the exact status of the theory. For LS society is premised on the exchange of women between men, but since his main interests are in the universals of human nature and the human mind, he systematically fails to locate society within its productive base. That is to say, he appeals to hypothetical fundamental structures of the human mind, and its capacity to conceptualise, in his theory of the exchange of women, without exposing the patriarchal bases of such a theory, and the reasons *why men* are defined as superior, as the constitutive elements of human society.

We would argue that in tracing very general features of human evolution, there are very clear material reasons why women should have been exploited by men, but that this is essentially a historical question, and not one of human nature. The apparently universal subordination of women is of widely differing degrees and forms and the suggestion that women are in some sense always controlled by men does not of itself necessarily entail that they are universally exchanged.

II. THE SEXUAL DIVISION OF LABOUR

The allocation of tasks by gender is one of the commonest features of societies with a low level of development of productive forces and it is easy to be uncritical about the demonstrable biological bases of differences between the sexes – the more powerful physique of men as compared to that of women, and women's reproductive capacities. However that it is a social rather than a biological construct is clearly demonstrated by the great diversity of ways in which roles are allocated by sex. As Lévi-Strauss writes: 'the very fact that it [sexual division of labour] varies endlessly according to the society selected for consideration shows that . . . it is the mere fact of its existence that is mysteriously required, the form under which it comes to exist being utterly irrelevant, at least from the point of view of any natural necessity.' Lévi-Strauss goes on to suggest that the 'mysterious requirement' is nothing less than the need to institute a *reciprocal state of dependency between the sexes*. Leaving aside the question of why there should be an apparently universal need for such a state of dependency at all, I would argue that available evidence shows that the dependence it creates is often asymmetrical.

At its most rudimentary the sexual division of labour may derive from the biological facts of pregnancy, birth and lactation but the importance of any constraints arising from these biological facts varies considerably from society to society, not only because of the effect of cultural factors (such as the norm that mothers should breastfeed on demand) but also economic factors.

In societies where the development of productive forces is very low, where the land is not an object of labour but rather where nature, as Marx says, acts as a primitive larder and a toolhouse of the means of labour, the ability of the social group to reproduce itself may not only be dependent on women's fecundity but also their ability to provide the sole source of their children's nourishment for anything up to four or five years. This is the case for example in societies where the basic source of nourishment is meat (Eskimos) or indigestible roots and tubers (Kung Bushmen of the Kalahari Desert). In these societies (commonly called hunting and gathering societies) women have to invest a considerable proportion of their energies in breastfeeding in addition to their other activities (gathering, fetching water, cooking, making clothes, etc.). We don't really have enough demographic data to work on but it seems probable that the restrictions against women undertaking hunting of large game, or participating institutionally in warfare (hunting of men) may well be related to factors such as the nature of the food supply, the level of fertility, rates of mortality, length of lactation, life expectancy and so on. The loss of a few women in child-bearing years may put a group (especially in the case of hunting and gathering bands which tend to be small) at risk of extinction, while the loss of all but a few males will not biologically speaking.

Ecological constraints (including the vagaries of natural production) make it important that bands have a command over the resources of differing ecological niches (or merely of different areas) so as to insure against food-resource failure. Thus children are not monopolised either by their parents or the band, and geographic mobility of all or some members of the social group may be a crucial feature for its survival. The importance given to lateral links (already mentioned above) derives from these constraints. The degree of specificity of the sexual division of labour on the other hand does depend to some extent on the nature of the food resource – where animal protein provides the bulk of the food there is a strict control on the number of females permitted to survive and population ratios are maintained by the practice of infanticide (and geronticide) with girls being more often killed than boys. One might assume that in the temperate regions (where Gale has calculated that males provide 67 per cent of subsistence in hunting and gathering societies) and in the tropics (where they provide 48 per cent) that male infanticide might be more common, but we have no data on this. In the temperate zone and the tropics (where 50 per cent of extant hunting and gathering societies are found) the sexual division of labour may be relatively unspecific and not create a great degree of dependency between the sexes or even the generations; nonetheless hunting is given higher status than gathering.

It is clear that our argument as to the constraints imposed by biology and ecology does not give us a reason for sexual asymmetry, only difference. Why is this difference made the basis of order/rank?

The importance given to hunting may be partly derived from the fact that meat, even in cases where it provides a low percentage of the bulk of food, often provides a high percentage of the caloric needs as well as a welcome change from the bland taste of roots and tubers. Clearly this is not a sufficient explanation, but neither is recourse to hypothetical mental structures. It is evident, however, that hunting is often the idiom by which women are relegated to a subordinate position. They are often excluded from some or all of the hunting rituals; menstruating women (and their consorts in some cases) are considered to be polluting and dangerous to hunters, likely to cause the animals to flee, etc. In many cases women who accidentally see/overhear part of the hunting ritual are gang raped by the men as a formal punishment – this punishment may also be meted out under other circumstances when a woman is supposedly in breach of social rules.

Physical violence is not the only way in which women are controlled, however. If we look at the amount of social labour invested, women contribute more over the year than men. Women's responsibility for their children, and the nature of the food they gather, often means that they have a daily commitment to collecting foodstuffs, water and firewood. On the other hand it is quite common to read that hunting is sporadic, that individual men may be poor hunters (either coming back empty-handed or not taking part at all). Women are rarely permitted the luxury of not being good gatherers or of not doing their share of gathering. Their constant, repetitive and often monotonous work constitutes in itself a mechanism of control by men, we would argue.

Despite the very great differences between societies or a low development of productive forces, and between the degree of subordination and control exercised over women in them, in a very general way it would appear that the sexual division of labour does not necessarily create a reciprocal state of dependence, rather it may be the basis for sexual asymmetry.

In societies categorised as horticultural (i.e., where tubers, roots, etc., found in the wild state are cultivated in forest clearings, often supplemented by hunting and gathering) certain significant differences appear. Their increased productivity is often accompanied by an increase in fertility rates, a decrease in the need for prolonged lactation, and an increase in the amount of time spent on acquiring the means of livelihood. The rate of mobility drops, groups appear to be more stable in composition over time, there may be extensive exchanges of goods and services between groups (including warfare, exchange of women, etc.).

The greater degree of command over nature may make lateral linkages of less importance. More labour is usually invested in such activities as cutting trees, preparing the ground, etc.; the productive unit becomes more consolidated, often exercising exclusive rights over temporary plots. Control over the allocation of marriage partners thus becomes important and the socialisation of the out-marrying child to accept this fate stressed. Women's share of the total labour-time expended on cultivation and other forms of getting subsistence, in addition to child-care, cooking, making clothing, etc., may be equivalent to that of men, but usually it is in excess. They may also have to spend relatively large amounts of time on transformation activities, such as grinding grains, pounding roots, rendering poisonous manioc edible. Their ability to share these tasks with other women is a key to the degree to which the sexual division of labour is more or less oppressive. Children are often incorporated into productive activities from an early age, and girls take over a large share of child-care.

Men's labour on the other hand is increasingly invested in what we call the social reproduction of nature – that is there is often a proliferation of rituals to insure that nature fulfils her task, e.g., the garden magic of the New Guinea area or milpa magic in Mexico. Women are often excluded from these rites, or they may be obliged to have a ritual intercourse with the men of the group. Women may have their own series of rituals, but these are rarely concerned with the reproduction of the society as a whole, but rather with the wellbeing of the particular social unit to which they are deemed to belong.

In many of these societies not only are men believed to be performing the important productive tasks, they may also ideologically control the fertility of females through their communication with the spirit world. Thus children are 'given' to women by the ancestors thanks to the mediation of men. In other words, athough women undertake the bulk of the productive, transformation and reproductive activities, through ideological mechanisms the actual relations of production are inverted. At the same time, as far as rights over land are concerned, they often have no control over the distribution of these rights nor of the products of their labour; thus the ideological constructs reflect their real exclusion from effective control over production.

Once again, it appears that the sexual division of labour in many of these societies does, superficially at least, emphasise some aspects of reciprocal dependency but the dependency is markedly asymmetrical.

A third type of society is that in which, with the further development of the productive forces, sedentarisation plays an important role in social organisation and long-term labour inputs may be undertaken (permanent clearing of forest, irrigation, terracing, a balanced agricultural/livestock mix). The flexibility of the systems mentioned earlier is replaced by more rigidly structured systems, often hierarchical; the sexual division of labour may be more elaborate with tasks assigned not only by the criteria of age and sex but also to specialists (often hereditary). Women may provide the bulk of agricultural labour while young men are allocated to preparation for warfare, or may work with them under the direction of older males. Societies based on lineage-organisation come under this group.

Ecological constraints are less important and the emphasis is on control of labour now and in the future, thus there may be an elaboration of rules regarding preferred or prescribed marriage partners, allocation of children, allocation of rights over women's labour, etc. Emphasis is also given to the organisation of production, control over the surplus, and reproduction of the conditions of production.

Often demographic balance is socially maintained. It is common to find taboos on intercourse after childbirth, or childbirth after a certain age, on multiple births and so on; in other words social regulation of the number, spacing and sex ratios of children. The degree to which this represents women's control over their own fertility is questionable since, for example, taboos on intercourse after childbirth (often lasting up to two or three years) apply only to women – men may have other wives to whom they can turn for sexual services. The question that arises is to what extent these taboos enable women to bear children with as little loss of productive capacity as possible. Successful men (i.e., those who can insure the production of a surplus and thus appropriate larger numbers of women) accumulate benefits both in terms of larger numbers of children and sons- and brothers-in-law. It is also interesting to ask whether these taboos act to regulate the supply of female labour via the spacing of births. The extension of life expectancy may also be a factor in the increased importance given to elders and in turn they may use the surplus generated by the labour of women and young men plus access to their female children to maintain the young men's dependence on (and political allegiance to) them.

We have already noted that women may be exchanged by men in order to create links between groups, to spread risks in situations of great dependence on the vagaries of nature. Here we are arguing that the result of giving the main productive tasks to women (a point overlooked by Engels) creates a situation in which men are more dependent on women for survival than vice versa, so that women's dependence on men must be socially created by other means. At the same time control over women may be used to insure the dependence of young men upon the old, since elders can keep women to themselves and prevent young men from marrying (i.e., becoming social adults, having access to land, or the labour to work the land, etc.). This as a corollary insures that men in their old age have young people who will maintain them.

Where women are the main producers, their objective potential for independence, as contrasted to the real dependence of men upon them, seems to result in their being even more strictly under the control of men, whether husband, father or lineage elders. Their subordination is expressed both in material terms (in the high proportion of socially necessary labour they provide and their lack of control of the surplus they generate) as well as in ritual terms, e.g., food taboos, pollution taboos, their exclusion from sacrifices, etc., and from political decision making.

The point we have tried to make here is that the subordination of women cannot be related only to their participation in social production but also to social reproduction. We are suggesting that there is no direct correlation between women's status and the amount of their participation in production, but there may be between it and women's ability to control labour in the production process. Women's exclusion from the political sphere may in fact be a direct consequence of their participation in social production. If women have to spend the major part of their time and energies on exhausting tasks of cultivation, firewood collection, carrying water, childbirth, lactation and child-care, their ability to participate in other spheres of activity is greatly diminished.

Denying importance to women's work helps to maintain women's subordinate position, but there is an inbuilt logical contradiction. The more men become economically (and politically) dependent on women the more the contradiction becomes untenable. Taboos, myths, etc., are, it is argued, means of mediating contradictions, but in this case they present an inversion of the actual (objective) conditions of production and reproduction. Nonetheless enforcing their practice insures that women themselves live out the representations of their own inferiority and inhibits their potential for conscious rejection of, or rebellion against, male dominance and perhaps creates structures of subordination (false consciousness) which only conscious knowledge, and practice based on it, can prevail against.

So far we've been talking about how the sexual division of labour can allocate more or fewer tasks to women, but the degree to which any specific sexual division of labour bears upon the individual woman must be related to the possibilities for communalising her work; in other words, woman's ability to form solidary groups sharing the burden of production, transformation and child-care. This in turn is clearly affected by rules of residence on marriage, and the patterning of residence itself. An infinite variety of residential arrangements are found in non-capitalist societies. In addition to the particular form of spatial layout which may separate the sexes, or emphasise the solidary unit of one sex and the individuation of the other, there are also residential rules which may or may not work in favour of women forming solidary groups.

On marriage a woman may have to live in her husband's father's house (i.e., virilocal marriage): she may remain there for the rest of her married life, or she may gain residential independence (but within her husband's village) after she has established her family of procreation. A man on the other hand may have to go to live with his wife's family and remain there until he becomes residentially independent – he may then return to his father's village, remain in his wife's village or even go to that of his mother's brother.

Generally speaking, a woman benefits from the presence of close kinswomen with whom she has grown up and groups of women may co-operate in these situations in production and transformation activities and child-care. Co-operation between the women mitigates the effects of male dominance – they may help each other in organising love affairs, concealing illegitimate births, helping with abortions, etc. The degree to which co-operation is instituted seems to vary with other institutional arrangements, particularly with the degree of emphasis on the household as the unit of consumption and production and the nature of access to land and factors of production.

We would suggest that the household is a key ideological construct used to divide women, to help mask their essential common interests. Where resources are restricted (not necessarily because of absolute scarcity – surplus appropriation by men of the group or by a dominant class, etc., could account for the scarcity) the pressure on the individual woman to put the needs of her children/household above all others (*vide* peasant societies) and to minimise her co-operative links with others is considerable. In societies where women depend on their children – especially their sons – for their maintenance in the future (i.e., where they possess no rights to land, livestock or other means of production) women may be pitted against each other for command over sufficient resources for the maintenance of their children. Witchcraft accusation, often couched in terms of quarrels between women over men's services, or attempts to injure a child, etc., may be common.

III. METHODOLOGY

From what we have been discussing it will already be clear that we owe a lot of our concepts and methodology to Marxism. At this point it is perhaps worth summarising where we feel ourselves to have departed from a strict Marxist interpretation.

Firstly it will be evident that we disagree with the theory of Engels in *The Origin of the Family, Private Property and the State*. He makes a close connection between the development of private property (first in animals, then in land) and the subjugation of women. Thus for him the stage of savagery, roughly what we call hunting and gathering societies, is one characterised by promiscuity and mother-right in which women are the equals of men, because the means of subsistence are directly appropriated from nature. We on the other hand have tried to stress that the evidence suggests that in primitive societies no such direct correlation can be made. In addition the incidence of matrilineal societies, which Engels, following Morgan and Bachofen, tries to use as proof of an earlier stage of mother-right, on the available evidence cannot be used in this way since matriliny is the system by which inheritance goes from a man to his sister's son, *not* from mother to daughter. Present day matrilineal societies incidentally tend to be correlated with horticulture as a means of appropriation from nature. We have already mentioned that Engels was wrong in supposing that women in the latter type of society (categorised by him as barbarism) do not take part in social production and therefore his correlation of low status and little involvement in social production is incorrect. We would suggest that a materialist analysis of women's position in pre-capitalist societies must proceed via a far more complex mapping of the interrelations of different variables such as we have outlined in the previous sections.

Similarly we find it impossible to base an analysis on the abstract construction of modes of production, partly because the theorisation of pre-capitalist modes is still relatively unelaborated and partly because they tend to be of a generality which excludes consideration of the sorts of factors which we feel are essential to the understanding of women's subordination. Thus, while we use a very general schema of societal evolution based on the notion of the development of the productive forces, we do not find it useful to posit a direct correlation between stages of evolution and the position of women.

Any discussion of societal evolution is made difficult both through the quality of data and the absence of theoretical tools. In the former, part of the problem is the difficulty of generalising from present day hunting and gathering or horticultural societies to those that existed millennia ago. It is completely inaccurate to suppose that today's primitive societies are somehow stopped in their evolutionary tracks and got 'frozen' in the stone age. Moreover the quality of the data of the ethnographies or reports on primitive peoples of the last few centuries is highly questionable. Most of it was written by Western European men, with their special prejudices, and primarily based on the reports of the male members of the societies they visited. The male bias in many ethnographies is perhaps most clearly shown by comparing the work of Jane Goodale with Hart and Pilling on the Tiwi (both mentioned in the booklist).

With regard to the absence of adequate theoretical tools, the problem is as acute within Marxist discourse as outside it. As Marxists we must ask how far can categories evolved in the study of capitalism be useful in the understanding of pre-capitalist modes of production and particularly in understanding the position of women. Concepts such as *socially necessary labour time* are general enough to be useful but those of *productive* and *unproductive* labour, *exploitation* and *surplus value* are all highly problematic in the analysis of societies not characterised by fully developed commodity production. The debate on the nature of domestic labour under capitalism also suggests that women's role in social reproduction cannot in any case be easily subsumed under the existing categories either. In other words it is impossible to deduce the nature of women's subordination under capitalism from a specification of the relations of production and their articulation with a determinate level of forces of production and the superstructure.

IV. PATRIARCHY

Throughout our discussion we have principally considered social forms variously described in Marxist texts as primitive communism, lineage mode of production, savagery or barbarism. In a recent book entitled *Pre-capitalist Modes of Production*, Hindess and Hirst describe the primitive mode of production as being characterised by a collective appropriation of surplus labour and without classes, state or politics. Yet as we have demonstrated in this paper there are considerable differences in the position and status of women within the so-called primitive communism mode of production.

Since there does not appear to be a very clear or direct way in which the type and level of subordination of women is related to particular modes of production (and we have already mentioned some of the problems involved in the use of this concept), we narrowed our investigation to the analysis of the mechanisms of subordination and their associated rationales. The ever greater elaboration of the mechanisms by which women are controlled warns against any sort of reductionism, and makes it hard to discern more general historical processes. We would however like to suggest a tentative pattern.

We found the notion that there might well be a dominant mode of subordination associated in some way with the level of the development of the productive forces (but not derived solely from it) a useful way of approaching the problem. In societies of a low level of development of the productive forces (of simple appropriation from nature), the mechanism appears to be that of unmediated physical violence. By this we mean the institutionalised use of force rather than a more casual coercion of individual women by individual men. Gang rape is the example of this institutional use of force par excellence: here representatives of the dominant group (i.e., men) collectively punish individual women who are held to have violated the social rules. At a more abstract level we would say that in these sorts of societies the dominant mechanism of control is political.

A greater degree of control over nature seems to be correlated with the dominance of ideological mechanisms. One finds a proliferation of lived, repressive institutions (which may also repress certain categories of men as well) such as menstrual and food taboos, alienation from the process of reproduction, exclusion from ritual, as well as myths which justify the subordination of women in terms of their past failure. Although the ideological dominates, the use of physical violence may not diminish, but becomes restricted to individual violence of one man against one woman.

We would suggest that predominance moves to the economic sphere when there is a degree of control over nature which permits relative geographic stability. Women are denied access to the means of production, have no access to labour, do not control the distribution of the products of their labour (including the allocation of their children as marriage partners). Ideological control weakens, but by no means disappears. Institutionalised violence is further masked, as individual men become responsible for the good conduct of their 'own' women.

These mechanisms may or may not coincide in intensity to effect the degree of subordination of women in any one society; they may even be in contradiction with each other, in which case the subordination of women will be correspondingly contradictory, mediated by opposing tendencies in social practice, and therefore incomplete. On the other hand, we would suggest that societies in which all these mechanisms are given equal weight can most usefully be described as patriarchal. So we would not indiscriminately call all societies patriarchal, but restrict this term to cases such as the ancient Hebrews, the ancient Romans, pre-revolutionary China, and most European peasantry. This usage of the term also accords with its use within the social sciences.

This is not to argue that only in such societies is sexual asymmetry such that women are considered to be inferior to men in physical, mental and creative capacities. Rather, we would maintain that in societies such as ours in which the dominant mechanism of women's subordination is the economic, there is a good case to be made for women concentrating their efforts on unmasking the ideological mechanisms – not just the ideas of women's inferiority, but also the institutions which reinforce their dependence on males. This precisely because ideology is not the dominant mechanism, and there is a degree of contradiction between women's necessary economic roles and their ideological subordination. By concentrating on unmasking the ideological basis of women's oppression we therefore help to deny the possibility of ideology in the future being used against us.

Booklist

de Beauvoir, Simone, *The Second Sex* (Penguin).
Engels, Frederick, *The Origin of the Family, Private Property and the State*, ed. E. Leacock (Lawrence and Wishart).

Gale, Fay (ed.), *Woman's Role in Aboriginal Society* (Australian Institute of Aboriginal Studies).

Goodale, Jane, *Tiwi Wives* (University of Washington Press).

Hart, C. W. M. and Arnold Pilling, *The Tiwi of North Australia* (New York: Holt, Rinehart and Winston).

Hindess, Barry and Paul Hirst, *Pre-capitalist Modes of Production* (Routledge and Keegan Paul).

Lévi-Strauss, Claude, *Elementary Structures of Kinship* (Eyre and Spottis-woode); *Structural Anthropology* (Penguin).

Meillasoux, Claude, *Femmes, Greniers et Capitaux* (Paris: Maspero).

Mitchell, Juliet, *Psychoanalysis and Feminism* (Penguin).

Rubin, Gayle, 'The Traffic in Women', in ed. Rayna Reiter, *Toward an Anthropology of Women* (Monthly Review Press).

Sally Slocum

Woman the Gatherer: Male Bias in Anthropology

In Rayna Reiter, ed., *Toward an Anthropology of Women*, London and New York: Monthly Review Press, 1975, pp. 36-50 (first published in 1971)

Little systematic attention has been given in our discipline to an 'anthropology of knowledge'. While some anthropologists have concerned themselves with knowledge in general, as seen through the varieties of human cultures, few have examined anthropological knowledge itself. An anthropology of knowledge would have several parts. First is what Peter Berger (1967, pp. 1-18) has called 'philosophical anthropology': a study of the nature of the human species. This has always been a legitimate concern of anthropology, but too often we become so concerned with minute differences that we forget we are studying a single species. Second is how we 'know' anything – what is accepted as 'proof', what is reality, what are the grounds for rationality (Garfinkel, 1960), what modes are used in gathering knowledge, what are the effects of differences in culture and world view on what we 'know'. Third is a close examination of the questions asked in anthropology, for questions always determine and limit answers.

It is the third point, the nature of anthropological questions, to which I wish to speak in this paper. We are human beings studying other human beings, and we cannot leave ourselves out of the equation. We choose to ask certain questions, *and not others*. Our choice grows out of the cultural context in which anthropology and anthropologists exist. Anthropology, as an academic discipline, has been developed primarily by white Western males, during a specific period in history. Our questions are shaped by the particulars of our historical situation, and by unconscious cultural assumptions.

Given the cultural and ethnic background of the majority of anthropologists, it is not surprising that the discipline has been

Many of the ideas were developed during conversations with Jane Kephart and Joan Roos over a period of several months. Since it was the interaction which produced the ideas, it is difficult to credit any particular idea to any one person. Suffice it to say that without their help and encouragement this paper would not have been written.

biased. There are signs, however, that this selective blindness is beginning to come under scrutiny. For example, in the exchange in the journal *Current Anthropology* (1968), anthropologists like Kathleen Gough and Gerald Berreman point out the unconscious effects of American political and economic assumptions on our selection of problems and populations to be studied. Restive minority groups in this country are pointing to the bias inherent in anthropological studies of themselves through books such as Vine Deloria's *Custer Died for Your Sins*. We have always encouraged members of American minority groups, and other 'foreigners', to take up anthropology because of the perspective on the world that they can supply. The invitation is increasingly being accepted. As we had both hoped and feared, repercussions from this new participation are being felt in theory, method, interpretation, and problem choice, shaking anthropology to the roots.

The perspective of women is, in many ways, equally foreign to an anthropology that has been developed and pursued primarily by males. There is a strong male bias in the questions asked, and the interpretations given. This bias has hindered the full development of our discipline as 'the study of the human animal' (I don't want to call it 'the study of man' for reasons that will become evident). I am going to demonstrate that Western male bias by reexamining the matter of evolution of Homo sapiens from our nonhuman primate ancestors. In particular, the concept of 'Man the Hunter' as developed by Sherwood Washburn and C. Lancaster (1968) and others is my focus. This critique is offered in hopes of transcending the male bias that limits our knowledge by limiting the questions we ask.

Though male bias could be shown in other areas, hominid evolution is particularly convenient for my purpose because it involves speculations and inferences from a rather small amount of data. In such a case, hidden assumptions and premises that lie behind the speculations and inferences are more easily demonstrated. Male bias exists not only in the ways in which the scanty data are interpreted, but in the very language used. All too often the word 'man' is used in such an ambiguous fashion that it is impossible to decide whether it refers to males or to the human species in general, including both males and females. In fact, one frequently is led to suspect that in the minds of many anthropologists, 'man', supposedly meaning the human species, is actually exactly synonymous with 'males'.

This ambiguous use of language is particularly evident in the writing that surrounds the concept of Man the Hunter. Washburn and Lancaster make it clear that it is specifically males who hunt, that hunting is much more than simply an economic activity, and that most of the characteristics which we think of as specifically human can be causally related to hunting. They tell us that hunting is a whole pattern of activity and way of life: 'The biology, psychology, and customs that separate us from the apes – all these we owe to the hunters of time past' (1968, p. 303). If this line of reasoning is followed to its logical conclusion, one must agree with Jane Kephart when she says:

> Since only males hunt, and the psychology of the species was set by hunting, we are forced to conclude that females are scarcely human, that is, do not have built-in the basic psychology of the species: to kill and hunt and ultimately to kill others of the same species. The argument implies built-in aggression in human males, as well as the assumed passivity of human females and their exclusion from the mainstream of human development. [1970, p. 5]

To support their argument that hunting is important to human males, Washburn and Lancaster point to the fact that many modern males still hunt, though it is no longer economically necessary. I could point out that many modern males play golf, play the violin, or tend gardens: these, as well as hunting, are things their culture teaches them. Using a 'survival' as evidence to demonstrate an important fact of cultural evolution can be accorded no more validity when proposed by a modern anthropologist than when proposed by Tylor.

Regardless of its status as a survival, hunting, by implication as well as direct statement, is pictured as a male activity to the exclusion of females. This activity, on which we are told depends the psychology, biology, and customs of our species, is strictly male. A theory that leaves out half the human species is unbalanced. The theory of Man the Hunter is not only unbalanced; it leads to the conclusion that the basic human adaptation was the desire of males to hunt and kill. This not only gives too much importance to aggression, which is after all only one factor of human life, but it derives culture from killing. I am going to suggest a less biased reading of the evidence, which gives a more valid and logical picture of human evolution, and at the same time a more hopeful one. First I will note the evidence, discuss the more traditional reading of it, and then offer an alternative reconstruction.

The data we have to work from are a combination of fossil and archeological materials, knowledge of living nonhuman primates, and knowledge of living humans. Since we assume that the protohominid ancestors of Homo sapiens developed in a continuous fashion from a base of characteristics similar to those of living nonhuman primates, the most important facts seem to be the ways in which humans differ from nonhuman primates, and the ways in which we are similar. The differences are as follows: longer gestation period; more difficult birth; neoteny, in that human infants are less well developed at birth; long period of infant dependency; absence of body hair; year-round sexual receptivity of females, resulting in the possibility of bearing a second infant while the first is still at the breast or still dependent; erect bipedalism; possession of a large and complex brain that makes possible the creation of elaborate symbolic systems, languages, and cultures, and also results in most behavior being under cortical control; food sharing; and finally, living in families. (For the purposes of this paper I define families as follows: a situation where each individual has defined responsibilities and obligations to a specific set of others of both sexes and various ages. I use this definition because, among humans, the family is a *social* unit, regardless of any biological or genetic relationship which may or may not exist among its members.)

In addition to the many well-known close physiological resemblances, we share with nonhuman primates the following characteristics: living in social groups; close mother-infant bonds; affectional relationships; a large capacity for learning and a related paucity of innate behaviors; ability to take part in dominance hierarchies; a rather complex nonsymbolic communication system which can handle with considerable subtlety such information as the mood and emotional state of the individual, and the attitude and status of each individual toward the other members of the social group.

The fossil and archeological evidence consists of various bones labeled Ramapithecus, Australopithecus, Homo habilis, Homo erectus, etc.; and artifacts such as stone tools representing various cultural traditions, evidence of use of fire, etc. From this evidence we can make reasonable inferences about diet, posture and locomotion, and changes in the brain as shown by increased cranial capacity, ability to make tools, and other evidences of cultural creation. Since we assume that complexity of material culture requires language, we infer the beginnings of language somewhere between Australopithecus and Homo erectus.

Given this data, the speculative reconstruction begins. As I was taught anthropology, the story goes something like this. Obscure selection pressures pushed the protohominid in the direction of erect bipedalism – perhaps the advantages of freeing the hands for food carrying or for tool use. Freeing the hands allowed more manipulation of the environment in the direction of tools for gathering and hunting food. Through a hand-eye-brain feedback process, coordination, efficiency, and skill were increased. The new behavior was adaptive, and selection pressure pushed the protohominid further along the same lines of development. Diet changed as the increase in skill allowed the addition of more animal protein. Larger brains were selected for, making possible transmission of information concerning tool making, and organizing cooperative hunting. It is assumed that as increased brain size was selected for, so also was neoteny – immaturity of infants at birth with a corresponding increase in their period of dependency, allowing more time for learning at the same time as this learning became necessary through the further reduction of instinctual behaviors and their replacement by symbolically invented ones.

Here is where one may discover a large logical gap. From the difficult-to-explain beginning trends toward neoteny and increased brain size, the story jumps to Man the Hunter. The statement is made that the females were more burdened with dependent infants and could not follow the rigorous hunt. Therefore they stayed at a 'home base', gathering what food they could, while the males developed cooperative hunting techniques, increased their communicative and organizational skills through hunting, and brought the meat back to the dependent females and young. Incest prohibitions, marriage, and the family (so the story goes) grew out of the need to eliminate competition between males for females. A pattern developed of a male hunter becoming the main support of 'his' dependent females and young (in other words, the development of the nuclear family for no apparent reason). Thus the peculiarly human social and emotional bonds can be traced to the hunter bringing back the food to share. Hunting, according to Washburn and Lancaster, involved 'cooperation among males, planning, knowledge of many species and large areas, and technical skill' (1968, p. 296). They even profess to discover the beginnings of art in the weapons of the hunter. They point out that the symmetrical Acheulian biface tools are the earliest beautiful man-made objects. Though we don't know what these tools were used for, they argue somewhat tautologically that the symmetry indicates they may have been swung, because symmetry only makes a difference when irregularities might lead to deviations in the line of flight. 'It may well be that it was the attempt to produce efficient high-speed weapons that first produced beautiful, symmetrical objects' (1968, p. 298).

So, while the males were out hunting, developing all their skills, learning to cooperate, inventing language, inventing art, creating tools and weapons, the poor dependent females were sitting back at the home base having one child after another (many of them dying in the process), and waiting for the males to bring home the bacon. While this reconstruction is certainly ingenious, it gives one the decided impression that only half the species – the male half – did any evolving. In addition to containing a number of logical gaps, the argument becomes somewhat doubtful in the light of modern knowledge of genetics and primate behavior.

The skills usually spoken of as being necessary to, or developed through, hunting are things like coordination, endurance, good vision, and the ability to plan, communicate, and cooperate. I have heard of no evidence to indicate that these skills are either carried on the Y chromosome, or are triggered into existence by the influence of the Y chromosome. In fact, on just about any test we can design (psychological, aptitude, intelligence, etc.) males and females score just about the same. The variation is on an individual, not a sex, basis.

Every human individual gets half its genes from a male and half from a female; genes sort randomly. It is possible for a female to end up with all her genes from male ancestors, and for a male to end up with all his genes from female ancestors. The logic of the hunting argument would have us believe that all the selection pressure was on the males, leaving the females simply as drags on the species. The rapid increase in brain size and complexity was thus due entirely to half the species; the main function of the female half was to suffer and die in the attempt to give birth to their large-brained male infants. An unbiased reading of the evidence indicates there was selection pressure on both sexes, and that hunting was not in fact the basic adaptation of the species from which flowed all the traits we think of as specifically human. Hunting does not deserve the primary place it has been given in the reconstruction of human evolution, as I will demonstrate by offering the following alternate version.

Picture the primate band: each individual gathers its own food, and the major enduring relationship is the mother-infant bond. It is in similar circumstances that we imagine the evolving protohominids. We don't know what started them in the direction of neoteny and increased brain size, but once begun the trends would prove adaptive. To explain the shift from the primate individual gathering to human food sharing, we cannot simply jump to hunting. Hunting cannot explain its own origin. It is much more logical to assume that as the period of infant dependency began to lengthen, *the mothers would begin to increase the scope of their gathering to provide food for their still-dependent infants.* The already strong primate mother-infant bond would begin to extend over a longer time period, increasing the depth and scope of social relationships, and giving rise to the first sharing of food.

It is an example of male bias to picture these females with young as totally or even mainly dependent on males for food. Among modern hunter-gatherers, even in the marginal environments where most live, the females can usually gather enough to support themselves and their families. In these groups gathering provides the major portion of the diet, and there is no reason to assume that this was not also the case in the Pliocene or early Pleistocene. In the modern groups women and children both gather and hunt small animals, though they usually do not go on the longer hunts. So, we can assume a group of evolving protohominids, gathering and perhaps beginning to hunt small animals, with the mothers gathering quite efficiently both for themselves and for their offspring.

It is equally biased, and quite unreasonable, to assume an early or rapid development of a pattern in which one male was responsible for 'his' female(s) and young. In most primate groups when a female comes into estrus she initiates coitus or signals her readiness by presenting. The idea that a male would have much voice in 'choosing' a female, or maintain any sort of individual, long-term control over her or her offspring, is surely a modern invention which could have had no place in early hominid life. (Sexual control over females through rape or the threat of rape seems to be a modern human invention. Primate females are not raped because they are willing throughout estrus, and primate males appear not to attempt coitus at other times, regardless of phsyiological ability.) In fact, there seems to me no reason for suggesting the development of male-female adult pair-bonding until much later. Long-term monogamy is a fairly rare pattern even among modern humans – I think it is a peculiarly Western male bias to suppose its existence in protohuman society. An argument has been made (by Morris, 1967, and others) that traces the development of male-female pair-bonding to the shift of sexual characteristics to the front of the body, the importance of the face in communication, and the development of face-to-face coitus. This argument is insufficient in the first place because of the assumption that face-to-face coitus is the 'normal', 'natural', or even the most common position among humans (historical evidence casts grave doubt on this assumption). It is much more probable that the coitus position was invented *after* pair-bonding had developed for other reasons.

Rather than adult male-female sexual pairs, a temporary consort-type relationship is much more logical in hominid evolution. It is even a more accurate description of the modern human pattern: the most dominant males (chief, headman, brave warrior, good hunter, etc.) mate with the most dominant females (in estrus, young and beautiful, fertile, rich, etc.), for varying periods of time. Changing sexual partners is frequent and common. We have no way of knowing when females began to be fertile year-round, but this change is not a necessary condition for the development of families. We need not bring in any notion of paternity, or the development of male-female pairs, or any sort of marriage in order to account for either families or food sharing.

The lengthening period of infant dependency would have strengthened and deepened the mother-infant bond; the earliest families would have consisted of *females and their children*. In such groups, over time, the sibling bond would have increased in importance also. The most universal, and persumably oldest, form of incest prohibition is between mother and son. There are indications of such avoidance even among modern monkeys. It could develop logically from the mother-children family: as the period of infant dependency lengthened, and the age of sexual maturity advanced, a mother might no longer be capable of childbearing when her son reached maturity. Another factor which may have operated is the situation found in many primates today where only the most dominant males have access to fertile females. Thus a young son, even after reaching sexual maturity, would still have to spend time working his way up the male hierarchy before gaining access to females. The length of time it would take him increases the possibility that his mother would no longer be fertile.

Food sharing and the family developed from the mother-infant bond. The techniques of hunting large animals were probably much later developments, after the mother-children family pattern was established. When hunting did begin, and the adult males brought back food to share, the most likely recipients would be first their mothers, and second their siblings. In other words, a hunter would share food *not* with a wife or sexual partner, but with those who had shared food with him: his mother and siblings.

It is frequently suggested or implied that the first tools were, in fact, the weapons of the hunters. Modern humans have become so accustomed to the thought of tools and weapons that it is easy for us to imagine the first manlike creature who picked up a stone or club. However, since we don't really know what the early stone tools such as hand-axes were used for, it is equally probable that they were not weapons at all, but rather *aids in gathering*. We know that gathering was important long before much animal protein was added to the diet, and continued to be important. Bones, sticks, and hand-axes could be used for digging up tubers or roots, or to pulverize tough vegetable matter for easier eating. If, however, instead of thinking in terms of tools and weapons, we think in terms of *cultural inventions*, a new aspect is presented. I suggest that two of the *earliest and most important* cultural inventions were containers to hold the products of gathering, and some sort of sling or net to carry babies. The latter in particular must have been extremely important with the loss of body hair and the increasing immaturity of neonates, who could not cling and had less and less to cling to. Plenty of material was available – vines, hides, human hair. If the infant could be securely fastened to the mother's body, she could go about her tasks much more efficiently. Once a technique for carrying babies was developed, it could be extended to the idea of carrying food, and eventually to other sorts of cultural inventions – choppers and grinders for food preparation, and even weapons. Among modern hunter-gatherers, regardless of the poverty of their material culture, food carriers and baby carriers are always important items in their equipment.

A major point in the Man the Hunter argument is that cooperative hunting among males demanded more skill in social organization and communication, and thus provided selection pressure for increased brain size. I suggest that longer periods of infant dependency, more difficult births, and longer gestation periods also demanded more skills in social organization and communication – creating selective pressure for increased brain size without looking to hunting as an explanation. The need to organize for feeding after weaning, learning to handle the more complex social-emotional bonds that were developing, the new skills and cultural inventions surrounding more extensive gathering – all would demand larger brains. Too much attention has been given to the skills required by hunting, and too little to the skills required for gathering and the raising of dependent young. The techniques required for efficient gathering include location and identification of plant varieties, seasonal and geographical knowledge, containers for carrying the food, and tools for its preparation. Among modern hunting-gathering groups this knowledge is an extremely complex, well-developed, and important part of their cultural equipment. Caring for a curious, energetic, but still dependent human infant is difficult and demanding. Not only must the infant be watched, it must be taught the customs, dangers, and knowledge of its group. For the early hominids, as their cultural equipment and symbolic communication increased, the job of training the young would demand more skill. Selection pressure for better brains came from many directions.

Much has been made of the argument that cooperation among males demanded by hunting acted as a force to reduce competition for females. I suggest that competition for females has been greatly exaggerated. It could easily have been handled in the usual way for primates – according to male status relationships already worked out – and need not be pictured as particularly violent or extreme. The seeds of male cooperation already exist in primates when they act to protect the band from predators. Such dangers may well have increased with a shift to savannah living, and the longer dependency of infants. If biological roots are sought to explain the greater aggressiveness of males, it would be more fruitful to look toward their function as protectors, rather than any supposedly basic hunting adaptation. The only division of labor that regularly exists in primate groups is the females caring for infants and the males protecting the group from predators. The possibilities for both cooperation and aggression in males lie in this protective function.

The emphasis on hunting as a prime moving factor in hominid evolution distorts the data. It is simply too big a jump to go from the primate individual gathering pattern to a hominid cooperative hunting-sharing pattern without some intervening changes. Cooperative hunting of big-game animals could only have developed *after* the trends toward neoteny and increased brain size had begun. Big-game hunting becomes a more logical development when it is viewed as growing out of a complex of changes which included sharing the products of gathering among mothers and children, deepening social bonds over time, increase in brain size, and the beginnings of cultural invention for purposes such as baby carrying, food carrying, and food preparation. Such hunting not only needed the prior development of some skills in social organization and communication; it probably also had to await the development of the 'home base'. It is difficult to imagine that most or all of the adult primate males in a group would go off on a hunting expedition, leaving the females and young exposed to the danger of predators, without some way of communicating to arrange for their defense, or at least a way of saying, 'Don't worry, we'll be back in two days.' Until that degree of communicative skill developed, we must assume either that the whole band traveled *and hunted* together, or that the males simply did not go off on large cooperative hunts.

The development of cooperative hunting requires, as a prior condition, an increase in brain size. Once such a trend is established, hunting skills would take part in a feedback process of selection for better brains just as would other cultural inventions and developments such as gathering skills. By itself, hunting fails to explain any part of human evolution and fails to explain itself.

Anthropology has always rested on the assumption that the mark of our species is our ability to *symbol*, to bring into existence forms of behavior and interaction, and material tools with which to adjust and control the environment. To explain human nature as evolving from the desire of males to hunt and kill is to negate most of anthropology. Our species survived and adapted through the invention of *culture*, of which hunting is simply a part. It is often stated that hunting *must* be viewed as the 'natural' species' adaptation because it lasted as long as it did, nine-tenths of all human history. However:

> Man the Hunter lasted as long as 'he' did from no natural propensity toward hunting any more than toward computer programming or violin playing or nuclear warfare, but because that was what the historical circumstances allowed. We ignore the first premise of our science if we fail to admit that 'man' is no more natural a hunter than 'he' is naturally a golfer, for after symboling became possible our species left forever the ecological niche of the necessity of any one adaptation, and made all adaptations possible for ourselves. [Kephart, 1970, p. 23]

That the concept of Man the Hunter influenced anthropology for as long as it did is a reflection of male bias in the discipline. This bias can be seen in the tendency to equate 'man', 'human', and 'male'; to look at culture almost entirely from a male point of view; to search for examples of the behavior of males and assume that this is sufficient for explanation, ignoring almost totally the female half of the species; and to filter this male bias through the 'ideal' modern Western pattern of one male supporting a dependent wife and minor children.

The basis of any discipline is not the answers it gets, but the questions it asks. As an exercise in the anthropology of knowledge, this paper stems from asking a simple question: what were the females doing while the males were out hunting? It was only possible for me to ask this question after I had become politically conscious of myself as a woman. Such is the prestige of males in our society that a woman, in anthropology or any other profession, can only gain respect or be attended to if she deals with questions deemed important by men. Though there have been women anthropologists for years, it is rare to be able to discern any difference between their work and that of male anthropologists. Learning to be an anthropologist has involved learning to think from a male perspective, so it should not be surprising that women have asked the same kinds of questions as men. But political consciousness, whether among women, blacks, American Indians, or any other group, leads to reexamination and reevaluation for taken-for-granted assumptions. It is a difficult process, challenging the conventional wisdom, and this paper is simply a beginning. The male bias in anthropology that I have illustrated here is just as real as the white bias, the middle-class bias, and the academic bias that exist in the discipline. It is our task, as anthropologists, to create a 'study of the human species' in spite of, or perhaps because of, or maybe even by means of, our individual biases and unique perspectives.

References

Berger, Peter and Luckmann, Thomas (1967), *The Social Construction of Reality*, Garden City, New York: Doubleday Anchor.

Current Anthropology (1968), *Social Responsibilities Symposium*, 1968.

Deloria, Vine Jr (1969), *Custer Died for Your Sins: An Indian Manifesto*, New York: Macmillan.

Garfinkel, Harold (1960), 'The Rational Properties of Scientific and Common Sense Activities', *Behavioural Science*, vol. 5, no. 1

Kephart, Jane (1970), 'Primitive Woman as Nigger, or, The Origin of the Human Family as Viewed Through the Role of Women', M.A. Dissertation, University of Maryland.

Washburn, S. and Lancaster, C. (1968), 'The Evolution of Hunting', in R. B. Lee and Irven De Vore, eds., *Man the Hunter*, Chicago: Aldine.

Sherry B. Ortner

Is Female to Male
as Nature Is to Culture?

In *Feminist Studies*, vol. 1, no. 2, Maryland, Fall
1972, pp. 5-31

Much of the creativity of anthropology derives from the tension
between two sets of demands: that we explain human universals,
and that we explain cultural particulars. By this canon, woman
provides us with one of the more challenging problems to be dealt
with. The secondary status of woman in society is one of the true
universals, a pan-cultural fact. Yet within that universal fact, the
specific cultural conceptions and symbolizations of woman are
extraordinarily diverse and even mutually contradictory. Further,
the actual treatment of women and their relative power and
contribution vary enormously from culture to culture, and over
different periods in the history of particular cultural traditions.
Both of these points – the universal fact and the cultural variation
– constitute problems to be explained.

My interest in the problem is of course more than academic: I
wish to see genuine change come about, the emergence of a social
and cultural order in which as much of the range of human potential
is open to women as is open to men. The universality of female
subordination, the fact that it exists within every type of social and
economic arrangement and in societies of every degree of
complexity, indicates to me that we are up against something very
profound, very stubborn, something we cannot rout out simply by
rearranging a few tasks and roles in the social system, or even by
reordering the whole economic structure. In this paper I try to
expose the underlying logic of cultural thinking that assumes the

The first version of this paper was presented in October 1972 as a lecture in the course
'Women: Myth and Reality' at Sarah Lawrence College. I received helpful comments from
the students and from my co-teachers in the course: Joan Kelly Gadol, Eva Kollisch, and
Gerda Lerner. A short account was delivered at the American Anthropological Association
meetings in Toronto, November 1972. Meanwhile, I received excellent critical comments
from Karen Blu, Robert Paul, Michelle Rosaldo, David Schneider, and Terence Turner,
and the present version of the paper, in which the thrust of the argument has been rather
significantly changed, was written in response to those comments. I, of course, retain
responsibility for its final form. The paper is dedicated to Simone de Beauvoir, whose book
The Second Sex (1953), first published in French in 1949, remains in my opinion the best
single comprehensive understanding of 'the woman problem'.

inferiority of women; I try to show the highly persuasive nature of the logic, for if it were not so persuasive, people would not keep subscribing to it. But I also try to show the social and cultural sources of that logic, to indicate wherein lies the potential for change.

It is important to sort out the levels of the problem. The confusion can be staggering. For example, depending on which aspect of Chinese culture we look at, we might extrapolate any of several entirely different guesses concerning the status of women in China. In the ideology of Taoism, *yin*, the female principle, and *yang*, the male principle, are given equal weight; 'the opposition, alternation, and interaction of these two forces give rise to all phenomena in the universe' (Siu, 1968, p. 2). Hence we might guess that maleness and femaleness are equally valued in the general ideology of Chinese culture.[1] Looking at the social structure, however, we see the strongly emphasized patrilineal descent principle, the importance of sons, and the absolute authority of the father in the family. Thus we might conclude that China is the archetypal patriarchal society. Next, looking at the actual roles played, power and influence wielded, and material contributions made by women in Chinese society – all of which are, upon observation, quite substantial – we would have to say that women are allotted a great deal of (unspoken) status in the system. Or again, we might focus on the fact that a goddess, Kuan Yin, is the central (most worshiped, most depicted) deity in Chinese Buddhism, and we might be tempted to say, as many have tried to say about goddess-worshiping cultures in prehistoric and early historical societies, that China is actually a sort of matriarchy. In short, we must be absolutely clear about *what* we are trying to explain before explaining it.

We may differentiate three levels of the problem:

1. The universal fact of culturally attributed second-class status of woman in every society. Two questions are important here. First, what do we mean by this; what is our evidence that this is a universal fact? And second, how are we to explain this fact, once having established it?

2. Specific ideologies, symbolizations, and socio-structural arrangements pertaining to women that vary widely from culture to culture. The problem at this level is to account for any particular

1. It is true of course that *yin*, the female principle, has a negative valence. Nonetheless, there is an absolute complementarity of *yin* and *yang* in Taoism, a recognition that the world requires the equal operation and interaction of both principles for its survival.

cultural complex in terms of factors specific to that group – the standard level of anthropological analysis.

3. Observable on-the-ground details of women's activities, contributions, powers, influence, etc., often at variance with cultural ideology (although always constrained within the assumption that women may never be officially preeminent in the total system). This the level of direct observation, often adopted now by feminist-oriented anthropologists.

This paper is primarily concerned with the first of these levels, the problem of the universal devaluation of women. The analysis thus depends not upon specific cultural data but rather upon an analysis of 'culture' taken generically as a special sort of process in the world. A discussion of the second level, the problem of cross-cultural variation in conceptions and relative valuations of women, will entail a great deal of cross-cultural research and must be postponed to another time. As for the third level, it will be obvious from my approach that I would consider it a misguided endeavor to focus only upon women's actual though culturally unrecognized and unvalued powers in any given society, without first understanding the overarching ideology and deeper assumptions of the culture that render such powers trivial.

THE UNIVERSALITY OF FEMALE SUBORDINATION

What do I mean when I say that everywhere, in every known culture, women are considered in some degree inferior to men? First of all, I must stress that I am talking about *cultural* evaluations; I am saying that each culture, in its own way and on its own terms, makes this evaluation. But what would constitute evidence that a particular culture considers women inferior?

Three types of data would suffice: (1) elements of cultural ideology and informants' statements that *explicitly* devalue women, according them, their roles, their tasks, their products, and their social milieux less prestige than are accorded men and the male correlates; (2) symbolic devices, such as the attribution of defilement, 'which may be interpreted as *implicitly* making a statement of inferior valuation; and (3) social-structural arrangements that exclude women from participation in or contact with some realm in which the highest powers of the society are felt to reside.[2] These three types of data may all of course be interrelated in any particular system, though they need not necessarily be. Further, any one of them will usually be sufficient to make the point of female inferiority in a given culture. Certainly, female exclusion from the most sacred rite or the highest political council is sufficient evidence. Certainly, explicit cultural ideology devaluing women (and their tasks, roles, products, etc.) is sufficient evidence. Symbolic indicators such as defilement are usually sufficient, although in a few cases in which, say, men and women are equally polluting to one another, a further indicator is required – and is, as far as my investigations have ascertained, always available.

On any or all of these counts, then, I would flatly assert that we find women subordinated to men in every known society. The search for a genuinely egalitarian, let alone matriarchal, culture has proved fruitless. An example from one society that has traditionally been on the credit side of this ledger will suffice. Among the matrilineal Crow, as Lowie (1956) points out, 'Women ... had highly honorific offices in the Sun Dance; they could become directors of the Tobacco Ceremony and played, if anything, a more conspicuous part in it than the men; they sometimes played the hostess in the Cooked Meat Festival; they were not debarred from sweating or doctoring or from seeking a vision' (p. 61). Nonetheless, 'Women [during menstruation] formerly rode inferior horses and evidently this loomed as a source of contamination, for they were not allowed to approach either a wounded man or men starting on a war party. A taboo still lingers against their coming near sacred objects at these times' (p. 44). Further, just before enumerating women's rights of participation in the various rituals noted above, Lowie mentions one particular Sun Dance Doll bundle that was not supposed to be unwrapped by a woman (p. 60). Pursuing this trail we find: 'According to all Lodge Grass informants and most others, the doll owned by Wrinkled-face took precedence not only of other dolls but of all other Crow medicines whatsoever.... This particular doll was not supposed to be handled by a woman' (p. 229).[3]

2. Some anthropologists might consider this type of evidence (social-structural arrangements that exclude women, explicitly or de facto, from certain groups, roles, or statuses) to be a subtype of the second type of evidence (symbolic formulations of inferiority). I would not disagree with this view, although most social anthropologists would probably separate the two types.
3. While we are on the subject of injustices of various kinds, we might note that Lowie secretly bought this doll, the most sacred object in the tribal repertoire, from its custodian, the widow of Wrinkled-face. She asked $400 for it, but this price was 'far beyond [Lowie's] means', and he finally got it for $80 (p. 300).

In sum, the Crow are probably a fairly typical case. Yes, women have certain powers and rights, in this case some that place them in fairly high positions. Yet ultimately the line is drawn: menstruation is a threat to warfare, one of the most valued institutions of the tribe, one that is central to their self-definition; and the most sacred object of the tribe is taboo to the direct sight and touch of women.

Similar examples could be multiplied ad infinitum, but I think the onus is no longer upon us to demonstrate that female subordination is a cultural universal; it is up to those who would argue against the point to bring forth counterexamples. I shall take the universal secondary status of women as a given, and proceed from there.

NATURE AND CULTURE[4]

How are we to explain the universal devaluation of women? We could of course rest the case on biological determinism. There is something genetically inherent in the male of the species, so the biological determinists would argue, that makes them the naturally dominant sex; that 'something' is lacking in females, and as a result women are not only naturally subordinate but in general quite satisfied with their position, since it affords them protection and the opportunity to maximize maternal pleasures, which to them are the most satisfying experiences of life. Without going into a detailed refutation of this position, I think it is fair to say that it has failed to be established to the satisfaction of almost anyone in academic anthropology. This is to say, not that biological facts are irrelevant, or that men and women are not different, but that these facts and differences only take on significance of superior/inferior within the framework of culturally defined value systems.

If we are unwilling to rest the case on genetic determinism, it seems to me that we have only one way to proceed. We must attempt to interpret female subordination in light of other universals, factors built into the structure of the most generalized situation in which all human beings, in whatever culture, find themselves. For example, every human being has a physical body and a sense of nonphysical mind, is part of a society of other individuals and an inheritor of a cultural tradition, and must engage in some relationship, however mediated, with 'nature', or the nonhuman realm, in order to survive. Every human being is born (to a mother) and ultimately dies, all are assumed to have an

4. With all due respect to Lévi Strauss (1969a, b, and *passim*).

interest in personal survival, and society/culture has its own interest in (or at least momentum toward) continuity and survival, which transcends the lives and deaths of particular individuals. And so forth. It is in the realm of such universals of the human condition that we must seek an explanation for the universal fact of female devaluation.

I translate the problem, in other words, into the following simple question. What could there be in the generalized structure and conditions of existence, common to every culture, that would lead every culture to place a lower value upon women? Specifically, my thesis is that woman is being identified with – or, if you will, seems to be a symbol of – something that every culture devalues, something that every culture defines as being of a lower order of existence than itself. Now it seems that there is only one thing that would fit that description, and that is 'nature' in the most generalized sense. Every culture, or, generically, 'culture', is engaged in the process of generating and sustaining systems of meaningful forms (symbols, artifacts, etc.) by means of which humanity transcends the givens of natural existence, bends them to its purposes, controls them in its interest. We may thus broadly equate culture with the notion of human consciousness, or with the products of human consciousness (i.e., systems of thought and technology), by means of which humanity attempts to assert control over nature.

Now the categories of 'nature' and 'culture' are of course conceptual categories – one can find no boundary out in the actual world between the two states or realms of being. And there is no question that some cultures articulate a much stronger opposition between the two categories than others – it has even been argued that primitive peoples (some or all) do not see or intuit any distinction between the human cultural state and the state of nature at all. Yet I would maintain that the universality of ritual betokens an assertion in all human cultures of the specifically human ability to act upon and regulate, rather than passively move with and be moved by, the givens of natural existence. In ritual, the purposive manipulation of given forms toward regulating and sustaining order, every culture asserts that proper relations between human existence and natural forces depend upon culture's employing its special powers to regulate the overall processes of the world and life.

One realm of cultural thought in which these points are often articulated is that of concepts of purity and pollution. Virtually every culture has some such beliefs, which seem in large part (though not, of course, entirely) to be concerned with the relationship between culture and nature (see Ortner, 1973, n.d.). A well-known aspect of purity/pollution beliefs cross-culturally is that of the natural 'contagion' of pollution; left to its own devices, pollution (for these purposes grossly equated with the unregulated operation of natural energies) spreads and overpowers all that it comes in contact with. Thus a puzzle – if pollution is so strong, how can anything be purified? Why is the purifying agent not itself polluted? The answer, in keeping with the present line of argument, is that purification is effected in a ritual context; purification ritual, as a purposive activity that pits self-conscious (symbolic) action against natural energies, is more powerful than those energies.

In any case, my point is simply that every culture implicitly recognizes and asserts a distinction between the operation of nature and the operation of culture (human consciousness and its products); and further, that the distinctiveness of culture rests precisely on the fact that it can under most circumstances transcend natural conditions and turn them to its purposes. Thus culture (i.e. every culture) at some level of awareness asserts itself to be not only distinct from but superior to nature, and that sense of distinctiveness and superiority rests precisely on the ability to transform – to 'socialize' and 'culturalize' – nature.

Returning now to the issue of women, their pan-cultural second-class status could be accounted for, quite simply, by postulating that women are being identified or symbolically associated with nature, as opposed to men, who are identified with culture. Since it is always culture's project to subsume and transcend nature, if women were considered part of nature, then culture would find it 'natural' to subordinate, not to say oppress, them. Yet although this argument can be shown to have considerable force, it seems to oversimplify the case. The formulation I would like to defend and elaborate on in the following section, then, is that women are seen 'merely' as being *closer* to nature than men. That is, culture (still equated relatively unambiguously with men) recognizes that women are active participants in its special processes, but at the same time sees them as being more rooted in, or having more direct affinity with, nature.

The revision may seem minor or even trivial, but I think it is a more accurate rendering of cultural assumptions. Further, the argument cast in these terms has several analytic advantages over the simpler formulation; I shall discuss these later. It might simply be stressed here that the revised argument would still account for the pan-cultural devaluation of women, for even if women are not equated with nature, they are nonetheless seen as representing a lower order of being, as being less transcendental of nature than men are. The next task of the paper, then, is to consider why they might be viewed in that way.

WHY IS WOMAN SEEN AS CLOSER TO NATURE?

It all begins of course with the body and the natural procreative functions specific to women alone. We can sort out for discussion three levels at which this absolute physiological fact has significance: (1) woman's *body and its functions*, more involved more of the time with 'species life', seem to place her closer to nature, in contrast to man's physiology, which frees him more completely to take up the projects of culture; (2) woman's body and its functions place her in *social roles* that in turn are considered to be at a lower order of the cultural process than man's; and (3) woman's traditional social roles, imposed because of her body and its functions, in turn give her a different *psychic structure*, which, like her physiological nature and her social roles, is seen as being closer to nature. I shall discuss each of these points in turn, showing first how in each instance certain factors strongly tend to align woman with nature, then indicating other factors that demonstrate her full alignment with culture, the combined factors thus placing her in a problematic intermediate position. It will become clear in the course of the discussion why men seem by contrast less intermediate, more purely 'cultural' than women. And I reiterate that I am dealing only at the level of cultural and human universals. These arguments are intended to apply to generalized humanity; they grow out of the human condition, as humanity has experienced and confronted it up to the present day.

1. Woman's physiology seen as closer to nature. This part of my argument has been anticipated, with subtlety, cogency, and a great deal of hard data, by de Beauvoir (1953). De Beauvoir reviews the physiological structure, development, and functions of the human female and concludes that 'the female, to a greater extent than the male, is the prey of the species' (p. 60). She points out that many major areas and processes of the woman's body serve no apparent function for the health and stability of the individual; on the contrary, as they perform their specific organic functions, they are often sources of discomfort, pain, and danger. The breasts are irrelevant to personal health; they may be excised at any time of a woman's life. 'Many of the ovarian secretions function for the benefit of the egg, promoting its maturation and adapting the uterus to its requirements; in respect to the organism as a whole, they make for disequilibrium rather than for regulation – the woman is adapted to the needs of the egg rather than to her own requirements' (p. 24). Menstruation is often uncomfortable, sometimes painful; it frequently has negative emotional correlates and in any case involves bothersome tasks of cleansing and waste disposal; and – a point that de Beauvoir does not mention – in many cultures it interrupts a woman's routine, putting her in a stigmatized state involving various restrictions on her activities and social contacts. In pregnancy many of the woman's vitamin and mineral resources are channeled into nourishing the fetus, depleting her own strength and energies. And finally, childbirth itself is painful and dangerous (pp. 24-7 *passim*). In sum, de Beauvoir concludes that the female 'is more enslaved to the species than the male, her animality is more manifest' (p. 239).

While de Beauvoir's book is ideological, her survey of woman's physiological situation seems fair and accurate. It is simply a fact that proportionately more of woman's body space, for a greater percentage of her lifetime, and at some – sometimes great – cost to her personal health, strength, and general stability, is taken up with the natural processes surrounding the reproduction of the species.

De Beauvoir goes on to discuss the negative implications of woman's 'enslavement to the species' in relation to the projects in which humans engage, projects through which culture is generated and defined. She arrives thus at the crux of her argument (pp. 58-9):

Here we have the key to the whole mystery. On the biological level a species is maintained only by creating itself anew; but this creation results only in repeating the same Life in more individuals. But man assures the repetition of Life while transcending Life through Existence [i.e. goal-oriented, meaningful action]; by this transcendence he creates values that deprive pure repetition of all value. In the animal, the freedom and variety of male activities are vain because no project is involved. Except for his services to the species, what he does is immaterial. Whereas in serving the species, the human male also remodels the face of the earth, he creates new instruments, he invents, he shapes the future.

In other words, woman's body seems to doom her to mere reproduction of life; the male, in contrast, lacking natural creative functions, must (or has the opportunity to) assert his creativity externally, 'artificially', through the medium of technology and

· symbols. In so doing, he creates relatively lasting, eternal, transcendent objects, while the woman creates only perishables – human beings.

This formulation opens up a number of important insights. It speaks, for example, to the great puzzle of why male activities involving the destruction of life (hunting and warfare) are often given more prestige than the female's ability to give birth, to create life. Within de Beauvoir's framework, we realize it is not the killing that is the relevant and valued aspect of hunting and warfare; rather, it is the transcendental (social, cultural) nature of these activities, as opposed to the naturalness of the process of birth: 'For it is not in giving life but in risking life that man is raised above the animal; that is why superiority has been accorded in humanity not to the sex that brings forth but to that which kills' (*ibid.*).

Thus if male is, as I am suggesting, everywhere (unconsciously) associated with culture and female seems closer to nature, the rationale for these associations is not very difficult to grasp, merely from considering the implications of the physiological contrast between male and female. At the same time, however, woman cannot be consigned fully to the category of nature, for it is perfectly obvious that she is a full-fledged human being endowed with human consciousness just as man is; she is half of the human race, without whose cooperation the whole enterprise would collapse. She may seem more in the possession of nature than man, but having consciousness, she thinks and speaks; she generates, communicates, and manipulates symbols, categories, and values. She participates in human dialogues not only with other women but also with men. As Lévi-Strauss says, 'Woman could never become just a sign and nothing more, since even in a man's world she is still a person, and since insofar as she is defined as a sign she must [still] be recognized as a generator of signs' (1969a, p. 496).

Indeed, the fact of woman's full human consciousness, her full involvement in and commitment to culture's project of transcendence over nature, may ironically explain another of the great puzzles of 'the woman problem' – woman's nearly universal unquestioning acceptance of her own devaluation. For it would seem that, as a conscious human and member of culture, she has followed out the logic of culture's arguments and has reached culture's conclusions along with the men. As de Beauvoir puts it (p. 59):

For she, too, is an existent, she feels the urge to surpass, and her project is not mere repetition but transcendence towards a different future – in her heart of hearts she finds confirmation of the masculine pretensions. She joins the men in the festivals that celebrate the successes and victories of the males. Her misfortune is to have been biologically destined for the repetition of Life, when even in her own view Life does not carry within itself its reasons for being, reasons that are more important than life itself.

In other words, woman's consciousness – her membership, as it were, in culture – is evidenced in part by the very fact that she accepts her own devaluation and takes culture's point of view.

I have tried here to show one part of the logic of that view, the part that grows directly from the physiological differences between men and women. Because of woman's greater bodily involvement with the natural functions surrounding reproduction, she is seen as more a part of nature than man is. Yet in part because of her consciousness and participation in human social dialogue, she is recognized as a participant in culture. Thus she appears as something intermediate between culture and nature, lower on the scale of transcendence than man.

2. *Woman's social role seen as closer to nature.* Woman's physiological functions, I have just argued, may tend in themselves to motivate[5] a view of woman as closer to nature, a view she herself, as an observer of herself and the world, would tend to agree with. Woman creates naturally from within her own being, whereas man is free to, or forced to, create artificially, that is, through cultural means, and in such a way as to sustain culture. In addition, I now wish to show how woman's physiological functions have tended universally to limit her social movement, and to confine her universally to certain social contexts which *in turn* are seen as closer to nature. That is, not only her bodily processes but the social situation in which her bodily processes locate her may carry this significance. And insofar as she is permanently associated (in the eyes of culture) with these social milieux, they add weight (perhaps the decisive part of the burden) to the view of woman as closer to nature. I refer here of course to woman's confinement to the domestic family context, a confinement motivated, no doubt, by her lactation processes.

5. Semantic theory uses the concept of motivation of meaning, which encompasses various ways in which a meaning may be assigned to a symbol because of certain objective properties of that symbol, rather than by arbitrary association. In a sense, this entire paper is an inquiry into the motivation of the meaning of woman as a symbol, asking why woman may be unconsciously assigned the significance of being closer to nature. For a concise statement on the various types of motivation of meaning, see Ullman (1963).

Woman's body, like that of all female mammals, generates milk during and after pregnancy for the feeding of the newborn baby. The baby cannot survive without breast milk or some similar formula at this stage of life. Since the mother's body goes through its lactation processes in direct relation to a pregnancy with a particular child, the relationship of nursing between mother and child is seen as a natural bond, other feeding arrangements being seen in most cases as unnatural and makeshift. Mothers and their children, according to cultural reasoning, belong together. Further, children beyond infancy are not strong enough to engage in major work, yet are mobile and unruly and not capable of understanding various dangers; they thus require supervision and constant care. Mother is the obvious person for this task, as an extension of her natural nursing bond with the children, or because she has a new infant and is already involved with child-oriented activities. Her own activities are thus circumscribed by the limitations and low levels of her children's strengths and skills:[6] she is confined to the domestic family group; 'woman's place is in the home.'

Woman's association with the domestic circle would contribute to the view of her as closer to nature in several ways. In the first place, the sheer fact of constant association with children plays a role in the issue; one can easily see how infants and children might themselves be considered part of nature. Infants are barely human and utterly unsocialized; like animals they are unable to walk upright, they excrete without control, they do not speak. Even slightly older children are clearly not yet fully under the sway of culture. They do not yet understand social duties, responsibilities, and morals; their vocabulary and their range of learned skills are small. One finds implicit recognition of an association between children and nature in many cultural practices. For example, most cultures have initiation rites for adolescents (primarily for boys; I shall return to this point below), the point of which is to move the child ritually from a less than fully human state into full participation in society and culture; many cultures do not hold funeral rites for children who die at early ages, explicitly because they are not yet fully social beings. Thus children are likely to be categorized with nature, and woman's close association with children may compound her potential for being seen as closer to nature herself. It is ironic that the rationale for boys' initiation rites in many cultures is that the boys must be purged of the defilement accrued from being around mother and other women so much of

6. A situation that often serves to make her more childlike herself.

the time, when in fact much of the woman's defilement may derive from her being around children so much of the time.

The second major problematic implication of women's close association with the domestic context derives from certain structural conflicts between the family and society at large in any social system. The implications of the 'domestic/public opposition' in relation to the position of women have been cogently developed by Rosaldo (in Rosaldo and Lamphere, eds., *Woman, Culture and Society*), and I simply wish to show its relevance to the present argument. The notion that the domestic unit – the biological family charged with reproducing and socializing new members of the society – is opposed to the public entity – the superimposed network of alliances and relationships that *is* the society – is also the basis of Lévi-Strauss's argument in the *Elementary Structures of Kinship* (1969a). Lévi-Strauss argues not only that this opposition is present in every social system, but further that it has the significance of the opposition between nature and culture. The universal incest prohibition[7] and its ally, the rule of exogamy (marriage outside the group), ensure that 'the risk of seeing a biological family become established as a closed system is definitely eliminated; the biological group can no longer stand apart, and the bond of alliance with another family ensures the dominance of the social over the biological, and of the cultural over the natural' (p. 479). And although not every culture articulates a radical opposition between the domestic and the public as such, it is hardly contestable that the domestic is always subsumed by the public; domestic units are allied with one another through the enactment of rules that are logically at a higher level than the units themselves; this creates an emergent unit – society – that is logically at a higher level than the domestic units of which it is composed.

Now, since women are associated with, and indeed are more or less confined to, the domestic context, they are identified with this lower order of social/cultural organization. What are the implications of this for the way they are viewed? First, if the specifically biological (reproductive) function of the family is stressed, as in Lévi-Strauss's formulation, then the family (and hence woman) is identified with nature pure and simple, as opposed to culture. But this is obviously too simple; the point seems more adequately formulated as follows: the family (and hence woman) represents

---

7. David M. Schneider (personal communication) is prepared to argue that the incest taboo is not universal, on the basis of material from Oceania. Let us say at this point, then, that it is virtually universal.

lower-level, socially fragmenting, particularistic sorts of concerns, as opposed to interfamilial relations representing higher-level, integrative, universalistic sorts of concerns. Since men lack a 'natural' basis (nursing, generalized to child care) for a familial orientation, their sphere of activity is defined at the level of interfamilial relations. And hence, so the cultural reasoning seems to go, men are the 'natural' proprietors of religion, ritual, politics, and other realms of cultural thought and action in which universalistic statements of spiritual and social synthesis are made. Thus men are identified not only with culture, in the sense of all human creativity, as opposed to nature; they are identified in particular with culture in the old-fashioned sense of the finer and higher aspects of human thought – art, religion, law, etc.

Here again, the logic of cultural reasoning aligning woman with a lower order of culture than man is clear and, on the surface, quite compelling. At the same time, woman cannot be fully consigned to nature, for there are aspects of her situation, even within the domestic context, that undeniably demonstrate her participation in the cultural process. It goes without saying, of course, that except for nursing newborn infants (and artificial nursing devices can cut even this biological tie), there is no reason why it has to be mother – as opposed to father, or anyone else – who remains identified with child care. But even assuming that other practical and emotional reasons conspire to keep woman in this sphere, it is possible to show that her activities in the domestic context could as logically put her squarely in the category of culture.

In the first place, one must point out that woman not only feeds and cleans up after children in a simple caretaker operation; she in fact is the primary agent of their early socialization. It is she who transforms newborn infants from mere organisms into cultured humans, teaching them manners and the proper ways to behave in order to become full-fledged members of the culture. On the basis of her socializing functions alone, she could not be more a representative of culture. Yet in virtually every society there is a point at which the socialization of boys is transferred to the hands of men. The boys are considered, in one set of terms or another, not yet 'really' socialized; their entrée into the realm of fully human (social, cultural) status can be accomplished only by men. We still see this in our own schools, where there is a gradual inversion in the proportion of female to male teachers up through the grades:

most kindergarten teachers are female; most university professors are male.[8]

Or again, take cooking. In the overwhelming majority of societies cooking is the woman's work. No doubt this stems from practical considerations – since the woman has to stay home with the baby, it is convenient for her to perform the chores centered in the home. But if it is true, as Lévi-Strauss has argued (1969b), that transforming the raw into the cooked may represent, in many systems of thought, the transition from nature to culture, then here we have woman aligned with this important culturalizing process, which could easily place her in the category of culture, triumphing over nature. Yet it is also interesting to note that when a culture (e.g. France or China) develops a tradition of *haute cuisine* – 'real' cooking, as opposed to trivial ordinary domestic cooking – the high chefs are almost always men. Thus the pattern replicates that in the area of socialization – women perform lower-level conversions from nature to culture, but when the culture distinguishes a higher level of the same functions, the higher level is restricted to men.

In short, we see once again some sources of woman's appearing more intermediate than man with respect to the nature/culture dichotomy. Her 'natural' association with the domestic context (motivated by her natural lactation functions) tends to compound her potential for being viewed as closer to nature, because of the animal-like nature of children, and because of the infrasocial connotation of the domestic group as against the rest of society. Yet at the same time her socializing and cooking functions within the domestic context show her to be a powerful agent of the cultural process, constantly transforming raw natural resources into cultural products. Belonging to culture, yet appearing to have stronger and more direct connections with nature, she is once again seen as situated between the two realms.

3. Woman's psyche seen as closer to nature. The suggestion that woman has not only a different body and a different social locus from a man but also a different psychic structure is most controversial. I will argue that she probably *does* have a different psychic structure, but I will draw heavily on Chodorow's paper (in Rosaldo and Lamphere, eds.) to establish first that her psychic structure need not be assumed to be innate; it can be accounted for, as Chodorow convincingly shows, by the facts of the probably universal female socialization experience. Nonetheless, if we grant

8. I remember having my first male teacher in the fifth grade, and I remember being excited about that – it was somehow more grown-up.

the empirical near universality of a 'feminine psyche' with certain specific characteristics, these characteristics would add weight to the cultural view of woman as closer to nature.

It is important to specify what we see as the dominant and universal aspects of the feminine psyche. If we postulate emotionality or irrationality, we are confronted with those traditions in various parts of the world in which women functionally are, and are seen as, more practical, pragmatic, and this-worldly than men. One relevant dimension that does seem pan-culturally applicable is that of relative concreteness vs. relative abstractness: the feminine personality tends to be involved with concrete feelings, things, and people, rather than with abstract entities; it tends toward personalism and particularism. A second, closely related, dimension seems to be that of relative subjectivity vs. relative objectivity: Chodorow cites Carlson's study (1971), which concludes that 'males represent experiences of self, others, space, and time in individualistic, objective, and distant ways, while females represent experiences in relatively interpersonal, subjective, immediate ways' (p. 270). Although this and other studies were done in Western societies, Chodorow sees their findings on the differences between male and female personality – roughly, that men are more objective and inclined to relate in terms of relatively abstract categories, women more subjective and inclined to relate in terms of relatively concrete phenomena – as 'general and nearly universal differences' (Rosaldo and Lamphere, eds., p. 43).

But the thrust of Chodorow's elegantly argued paper is that these differences are not innate or genetically programed; they arise from nearly universal features of family structure, namely that 'women, universally, are largely responsible for early child care and for (at least) later female socialization' (p. 43) and that 'the structural situation of child rearing, reinforced by female and male role training, produces these differences, which are replicated and reproduced in the sexual sociology of adult life' (p. 44). Chodorow argues that, because mother is the early socializer of both boys and girls, both develop 'personal identification' with her, i.e. diffuse identification with her general personality, behavior traits, values, and attitudes (p. 51). A son, however, must ultimately shift to a masculine role identity, which involves building an identification with the father. Since father is almost always more remote than mother (he is rarely involved in child care, and perhaps works away from home much of the day), building an identification with father involves a 'positional identification', i.e. identification with father's male role as a collection of abstract elements, rather than a personal identification with father as a real individual (p. 49).

Further, as the boy enters the larger social world, he finds it in fact organized around more abstract and universalistic criteria (see Rosaldo, in Rosaldo and Lamphere, pp. 28-9; Chodorow, p. 58), as I have indicated in the previous section; thus his earlier socialization prepares him for, and is reinforced by, the type of adult social experience he will have.

For a young girl, in contrast, the personal identification with mother, which was created in early infancy, can persist into the process of learning female role identity. Because mother is immediate and present when the daughter is learning role identity, learning to be a woman involves the continuity and development of a girl's relationship to her mother, and sustains the identification with her as an individual; it does not involve the learning of externally defined role characteristics (Chodorow, p. 51). This pattern prepares the girl for, and is fully reinforced by, her social situation in later life; she will become involved in the world of women, which is characterized by few formal role differences (Rosaldo, p. 29), and which involves again, in motherhood, 'personal identification' with *her* children. And so the cycle begins anew.

Chodorow demonstrates to my satisfaction at least that the feminine personality, characterized by personalism and particularism, can be explained as having been generated by social-structural arrangements rather than by innate biological factors. The point need not be belabored further. But insofar as the 'feminine personality' has been a nearly universal fact, it can be argued that its characteristics may have contributed further to the view of women as being somehow less cultural than men. That is, women would tend to enter into relationships with the world that culture might see as being more 'like nature' – immanent and embedded in things as given – than 'like culture' – transcending and transforming things through the superimposition of abstract categories and transpersonal values. Woman's relationships tend to be, like nature, relatively unmediated, more direct, whereas man not only tends to relate in a more mediated way, but in fact ultimately often relates more consistently and stongly to the mediating categories and forms than to the persons or objects themselves.

It is thus not difficult to see how the feminine personality would lend weight to a view of women as being 'closer to nature'. Yet at the same time, the modes of relating characteristic of women undeniably play a powerful and important role in the cultural process. For just as relatively unmediated relating is in some sense at the lower end of the spectrum of human spiritual functions, embedded and particularizing rather than transcending and synthesizing, yet that mode of relating also stands at the upper end of that spectrum. Consider the mother-child relationship. Mothers tend to be committed to their children as individuals, regardless of sex, age, beauty, clan affiliation, or other categories in which the child might participate. Now any relationship with this quality – not just mother and child but any sort of highly personal, relatively unmediated commitment – may be seen as a challenge to culture and society 'from below', insofar as it represents the fragmentary potential of individual loyalties vis-à-vis the solidarity of the group. But it may also be seen as embodying the synthesizing agent for culture and society 'from above', in that it represents generalized human values above and beyond loyalties to particular social categories that transcend personal loyalties, but every society must also generate a sense of ultimate moral unity for all its members above and beyond those social categories. Thus that psychic mode seemingly typical of women, which tends to disregard categories and to seek 'communion' (Chodorow, p. 55, following Bakan, 1966) directly and personally with others, although it may appear infracultural from one point of view, is at the same time associated with the highest levels of the cultural process.

THE IMPLICATIONS OF INTERMEDIACY

My primary purpose in this paper has been to attempt to explain the universal secondary status of women. Intellectually and personally, I felt strongly challenged by this problem; I felt compelled to deal with it before undertaking an analysis of woman's position in any particular society. Local variables of economy, ecology, history, political and social structure, values, and world view – these could explain variations within this universal, but they could not explain the universal itself. And if we were not to accept the ideology of biological determinism, then explanation, it seemed to me, could only proceed by reference to other universals of the human cultural situation. Thus the general outlines of the approach – although not of course the particular solution offered – were determined by the problem itself, and not by any predilection on my part for global abstract structural analysis.

I argued that the universal devaluation of women could be explained by postulating that women are seen as closer to nature than men, men being seen as more unequivocally occupying the high ground of culture. The culture/nature distinction is itself a product of culture, culture being minimally defined as the transcendence, by means of systems of thought and technology, of the natural givens of existence. This of course is an analytic definition, but I argued that at some level every culture incorporates this notion in one form or other, if only through the performance of ritual as an assertion of the human ability to manipulate those givens. In any case, the core of the paper was concerned with showing why women might tend to be assumed, over and over, in the most diverse sorts of world views and in cultures of every degree of complexity, to be closer to nature than men. Woman's physiology, more involved more of the time with 'species of life'; woman's association with the structurally subordinate domestic context, charged with the crucial function of transforming animal-like infants into cultured beings; 'woman's psyche', appropriately molded to mothering functions by her own socialization and tending toward greater personalism and less mediated modes of relating – all these factors make woman appear to be rooted more directly and deeply in nature. At the same time, however, her 'membership' and fully necessary participation in culture are recognized by culture and cannot be denied. Thus she is seen to occupy an intermediate position between culture and nature.

This intermediacy has several implications for analysis, depending upon how it is interpreted. First, of course, it answers my primary question of why woman is everywhere seen as lower than man, for even if she is not seen as nature pure and simple, she is still seen as achieving less transcendence of nature than man. Here intermediate simply means 'middle status' on a hierarchy of being from culture to nature.

Second, intermediate may have the significance of 'mediating', i.e. performing some sort of synthesizing or converting function between nature and culture, here seen (by culture) not as two ends of a continuum but as two radically different sorts of processes in the world. The domestic unit – and hence woman, who in virtually every case appears as its primary representative – is one of culture's crucial agencies for the conversion of nature into culture, especially with reference to the socialization of children. Any culture's continued viability depends upon properly socialized individuals who will see the world in that culture's terms and adhere more or less unquestioningly to its moral precepts. The functions of the domestic unit must be closely controlled in order to ensure this outcome; the stability of the domestic unit as an institution must be placed as far as possible beyond question. (We see some aspects of the protection of the integrity and stability of the domestic group in the powerful taboos against incest, matricide, patricide, and fratricide.[9]) Insofar as woman is universally the primary agent of early socialization and is seen as virtually the embodiment of the functions of the domestic group, she will tend to come under the heavier restrictions and circumscriptions surrounding that unit. Her (culturally defined) intermediate position between nature and culture, her having the significance of her *mediation* (i.e. performing conversion functions) between nature and culture, would thus account not only for her lower status but for the greater restrictions placed upon her activities. In virtually every culture her permissible sexual activities are more closely circumscribed than man's, she is offered a much smaller range of role choices, and she is afforded direct access to a far more limited range of its social institutions. Further, she is almost universally socialized to have a narrower and generally more conservative set of attitudes and views than man, and the limited social contexts of her adult life reinforce this situation. This socially engendered conservatism and traditionalism of woman's thinking is another – perhaps the worst, certainly the most insidious – mode of social restriction, and would clearly be related to her traditional function of producing well-socialized members of the group.

Finally, woman's intermediate position may have the implication of greater symbolic ambiguity. Shifting our image of the culture/nature relationship once again, we may envision culture in this case as a small clearing within the forest of the larger natural system. From this point of view, that which is intermediate between culture and nature is located on the continuous periphery of culture's clearing; and though it may thus appear to stand both above and below (and beside) culture, it is simply outside and around it. We can begin to understand then how a single system of cultural thought can often assign to woman completely polarized and apparently contradictory meanings, since extremes, as we say, meet. That she often represents both life and death is only the simplest example one could mention.

For another perspective on the same point, it will be recalled that the psychic mode associated with women seems to stand at both the bottom and the top of the scale of human modes of relating. The tendency in that mode is to get involved more directly with people as individuals and not as representatives of one social category or another; this mode can be seen as either 'ignoring' (and thus subverting) or 'transcending' (and thus achieving a higher synthesis of) those social categories, depending upon the cultural

9. Nobody seems to care much about sororicide – a point that ought to be investigated.

view for any given purpose. Thus we can account easily for both the subversive feminine symbols (witches, evil eye, menstrual pollution, castrating mothers) and the feminine symbols of transcendence (mother goddesses, merciful dispensers of salvation, female symbols of justice, and the strong presence of feminine symbolism in the realms of art, religion, ritual, and law). Feminine symbolism, far more often than masculine symbolism, manifests this propensity toward polarized ambiguity – sometimes utterly exalted, sometimes utterly debased, rarely within the normal range of human possibilities.

If woman's (culturally viewed) intermediacy between culture and nature has this implication of generalized ambiguity of meaning characteristic of marginal phenomena, then we are also in a better position to account for those cultural and historical 'inversions' in which women are in some way or other symbolically aligned with culture and men with nature. A number of cases come to mind: the Sirionó of Brazil, among whom, according to Ingham (1971, p. 1098), 'nature, the raw, and maleness' are opposed to 'culture, the cooked, and femaleness';[10] Nazi Germany, in which women were said to be the guardians of culture and morals; European courtly love, in which man considered himself the beast and woman the pristine exalted object – a pattern of thinking that persists, for example, among modern Spanish peasants (see Pitt-Rivers, 1961; Rosaldo, in Rosaldo and Lamphere). And there are no doubt other cases of this sort, including some aspects of our own culture's view of women. Each such instance of an alignment of women with culture rather than nature requires detailed analysis of specific historical and ethnographic data. But in indicating how nature in general, and the feminine mode of interpersonal relations in particular, can appear from certain points of view to stand both under and over (but really simply outside of) the sphere of culture's hegemony, we have at least laid the groundwork for such analyses.

In short, the postulate that woman is viewed as closer to nature than man has several implications for further analysis, and can be interpreted in several different ways. If it is viewed simply as a *middle* position on a scale from culture down to nature, then it is still seen as lower than culture and thus accounts for the pan-cultural assumption that woman is lower than man in the order

10. Ingham's discussion is rather ambiguous itself, since women are also associated with animals: 'The contrasts man/animal and man/woman are evidently similar ... hunting is the means of acquiring women as well as animals' (p. 1095). A careful reading of the data suggests that both women and animals are mediators between nature and culture in this tradition.

of things. If it is read as a *mediating* element in the culture-nature relationship, then it may account in part for the cultural tendency not merely to devalue woman but to circumscribe and restrict her functions, since culture must maintain control over its (pragmatic and symbolic) mechanisms for the conversion of nature into culture. And if it is read as an *ambiguous* status between culture and nature, it may help account for the fact that, in specific cultural ideologies and symbolizations, woman can occasionally be aligned with culture, and in any event is often assigned polarized and contradictory meanings within a single symbolic system. Middle status, mediating functions, ambiguous meaning – all are different readings, for different contextual purposes, of woman's being seen as intermediate between nature and culture.

CONCLUSIONS

Ultimately, it must be stressed again that the whole scheme is a construct of culture rather than a fact of nature. Woman is not 'in reality' any closer to (or further from) nature than man – both have consciousness, both are mortal. But there are certainly reasons why she appears that way, which is what I have tried to show in this paper. The result is a (sadly) efficient feedback system: various aspects of woman's situation (physical, social, psychological) contribute to her being seen as closer to nature, while the view of her as closer to nature is in turn embodied in institutional forms that reproduce her situation. The implications for social change are similarly circular: a different cultural view can only grow out of a different social actuality; a different social actuality can only grow out of a different cultural view.

It is clear, then, that the situation must be attacked from both sides. Efforts directed solely at changing the social institutions – through setting quotas on hiring, for example, or through passing equal-pay-for-equal-work laws – cannot have far-reaching effects if cultural language and imagery continue to purvey a relatively devalued view of women. But at the same time efforts directed solely at changing cultural assumptions – through male and female consciousness-raising groups, for example, or through revision of educational materials and mass-media imagery – cannot be successful unless the institutional base of the society is changed to support and reinforce the changed cultural view. Ultimately, both men and women can and must be equally involved in projects of creativity and transcendence. Only then will women be seen as aligned with culture, in culture's ongoing dialectic with nature.

References

Bakan, David (1966), *The Duality of Human Existence*, Boston.

Carlson, Rae (1971), 'Sex Differences in Ego Functioning: Exploratory Studies of Agency and Communion', *Journal of Consulting and Clinical Psychology*, 37, pp. 267-77.

de Beauvoir, Simone (1953), *The Second Sex*, New York; originally published in French in 1949.

Ingham, John M. (1971), 'Are the Sirionó Raw or Cooked?', *American Anthropologist*, 73, pp. 1092-9.

Lévi-Strauss, Claude (1969a), *The Elementary Structures of Kinship*, tr. J. H. Bell and J. R. von Sturmer; ed. R. Needham, Boston.

— (1969b), *The Raw and the Cooked*, tr. J. and D. Weightman, New York.

Lowie, Robert (1956), *The Crow Indians*, New York; originally published in 1935.

Ortner, Sherry B. (1973), 'Sherpa Purity', *American Anthropologist*, 75, pp. 49-63.

— (n.d.), 'Purification Beliefs and Practices', *Encyclopaedia Britannica*; forthcoming.

Pitt-Rivers, Julian (1961), *People of the Sierra*, Chicago.

Rosalda, M. and Lamphere, L., eds. (1974), *Woman, Culture and Society*, Stanford University Press.

Siu, R. G. H. (1968), *The Man of Many Qualities*, Cambridge, Mass.

Ullman, Stephen (1963), 'Semantic Universals', in Joseph H. Greenberg, ed., *Universals of Language*, Cambridge, Mass.

Ernestine Friedl

The Position of Women: Appearance and Reality

In *Anthropological Quarterly*, vol. 40,
Washington, DC, 1967, pp. 97-108

The purpose of this paper[1] is to describe the ways in which the appearances of prestige can obscure the realities of power. More specifically, the substance of this discussion is an analysis of the position of women in the social structure of a Greek village community. As the first sentence indicates, I believe the elements of Greek culture and society that lead most observers to consider it strongly male-centered do, indeed, exist but that they may mislead the observer into a polarized view of the relative power of men and women in Greek society. The problem is not unique to Greece. It is possible to argue that male activities have more prestige than those of females in all societies, and if this is true, the discovery of the relative social power of men and women may require more careful investigation in each case than is usually given to the question.

One of the factors of this investigation which, so far as I know, has been generally neglected, is the distinction between the public and the private sector as far as the actual importance of each in the power-structure of the community is concerned. From the standpoint of the ceremonial mores of the community, there may be many cultures in which male activity is accorded pre-eminence in the public sector. But if a careful analysis of the life of the community shows that, pragmatically the family is the most significant social unit, then the private, and not the public sector, is the sphere in which the relative attribution of power to males and females is of the greatest real importance. If, as I hope to show, the women in a Greek village hold a position of real power in the life of the family, and, as I have shown earlier, the life of the family is the most significant structural and cultural element of the Greek

---

1. This paper was read at the December 1966 conference held in Athens, Greece, by the Social Sciences Centre of Athens under the direction of Professor John Peristiany.

village,[2] then there is unmistakable need for a reassessment of the role of the Greek woman in village life.

For the Greek village of Vasilika, I shall begin with those appearances which express high male prestige. Most conspicuous in this regard is the segregation of men and women in the public space of the village, and the ritual deference accorded men by women in public situations. Stress on the distinction between public and private contexts is essential for the understanding of much of Greek social life; it is a binary classification especially important for analyzing the roles of men and women.

The most conspicuous public space in the village of Vasilika is the agora; that portion of the main road where the two stores and coffee houses face each other. The area is a thoroughfare for the various kinds of traffic moving through the village as well as a convenient stopping place for visitors and vendors. In its function as a thoroughfare, it is not closed to women; they walk through it on their way to and from the fields, or on their way to church, or to the main bus stop located on the asphalt road about a quarter of a mile away. Women may even wait briefly at the agora to board the bus that stops there to pick up passengers twice a day. But no female over the age of fourteen, in the ordinary course of events, goes to the agora as a final destination. They do not sit in the coffee houses; they do not even go to the store connected with the coffee houses to make purchases. Nor will they buy from itinerant vendors when these vendors are in the agora. On ordinary days, then, the agora, as a public place, is a male place. Little girls and young boys may run errands to the stores and may be sent to fetch their fathers, but with other evidence this fact indicates the immunity of children from many types of sex role expectations.

There are a few exceptional occasions when the women do go to the agora and its establishments. The most traditional of these are the festival days at Christmas, Easter, and the village patron saint's day when the coffee houses' owners provide musicians and dance space and sell beer to their customers. Accompanied by their male relatives, women sit at tables listening to the music, sipping beer very slowly, and watching the dancing. Sometimes the men will underwrite a dance for them and the girls and women dance alone or along with some of the men.

In the last year or two a movie truck has come to the village on some Sundays and movies are shown in one of the coffee houses. I do not know what the pattern of attendance at the movie is; the

2. Ernestine Friedl, Vasilika, a Village in Modern Greece, New York: Holt, Rinehart and Winston, 1962, chapters 2-4.

one time I went the audience consisted largely of children, but a few older men and women were there as well. Movies apparently are being assimilated into the special occasion festival pattern rather than into the patterns of daily routine.

The village churches are, of course, also public places. Inside the church, the condition of femaleness results in social segregation on certain occasions throughout a woman's lifetime. No female may go behind the altar screen, female infants, in contrast to males, are not carried there as part of the baptismal ceremonies, and women and girls stand in the rear of the church throughout the services, while men and boys stand in the front. Like the situation in the agora, however, there are certain occasions when the spatial separation of men and women in the main part of the church is not maintained; at baptisms when all gather round the baptismal font and at weddings when the guests crowd in a semi-circle around the bride and groom.

Still another public place in Vasilika is the school and here there is no spatial segregation. Boys and girls sit together according to grade level and not according to sex, but of course these are children.

That the pattern of public adult male and female segregation I have just described constitutes an expression of higher male prestige is obvious.

Differential right of access to space is a common cultural form for expressing superiority and inferiority in social position. The daily prohibitions on adult women may be presumed through sheer frequency of occurrence to have a greater impact than the exceptions for children at all times and for women on special occasions.

Public situations in Vasilika are not limited to activities in public space. On certain occasions, the homes of the villagers take on the aspect of public places in a festival setting. The most conspicuous of these is the celebration of the Saint's Day of the head of the household, when the family is 'at home' to visitors. As Gearing has indicated, all villagers are entitled to come, even enemies.

On Saint's Days more men than women actually visit the celebrants. Inside the house male guests are seated nearest the fire, if it is winter, and they are traditionally offered refreshments before the female guests even though these arrived at the same time or slightly earlier. If there are not enough chairs to go around, the women of the household, not the men, remain standing. Although daughters or wives serve the guests, it is perfectly clear that the celebrating father is the host. He prompts his women when he thinks they are too slow at serving, he and not his wife slices the bread and distributes it to the guests; he and not his wife picks out the choice morsels for direct presentation on a fork to a male guest; and he is the one who urges his guests to eat. A man is a host on these occasions but his womenfolk are not hostesses. They serve his and his household's honor by their good cooking and by the proper presentation of enough food, but they do not create honor by being in charge of the festivities.

In this connection, I remember my surprise at a lecture on table manners given at the King's Institute to village policemen and village secretaries when the men not only showed considerable interest in the subject, but also asked many detailed questions about what the correct sequence was in serving food and drink to visitors. In the villages, they consider the solution of these questions a part of their responsibility, and a proof of their culture, and not something to be learned from the womenfolk in the family.

What is of interest to my thesis also is the discovery that festival and therefore extraordinary public occasions are accompanied by a change in the permitted movements and activities of women. And, indeed, I should like to suggest that this change may be their most distinctive feature. Men listen to radio music and even occasionally dance in the coffee house: they do regularly sit around sipping coffee or soft drinks and occasionally ouzo, wine and beer. They can pay calls on each other at home during negotiations of contracts and receive some sweet and drink as a part of the hospitality of the house. On Saint's Days and holidays the food and drink are more abundant and of higher quality and the entertainment more intense and concentrated. But for men, what is most extraordinary about festivals is that women who are not relatives are around in large numbers as audience and participants. The song 'Ime andras' exemplifies the spirit of this unusual circumstance. The lyrics imply that a man is defying the female audience which he sees as trying to curb his exuberance and enjoyment of the events.

A reversal of roles, particularly among role sets in which one is recognized as superior and the other inferior, as a concomitant of celebrations is common enough in human societies. The Greek village pattern I have described does not constitute a reversal of roles for both men and women, but it does involve a change of role for women, and for the period of the holiday, entitles them to privileges similar to if not entirely equal to those of men.

In Vasilika, there are two occasions on which there is an actual reversal of roles; the celebration of the carnival, and the skits performed for the national holiday on the 25th of March.

At carnival, some unmarried men and women become transvestites; they wear the clothes of the opposite sex and march around exaggerating the gestures and mien of the sex they are imitating. One of the playlets put on the 25th of March by the unmarried young men of the village involved a boy who played the part of a woman. He wore women's clothes and much of the amusement of the audience derived from his deliberate awkwardness in the role. The license afforded by this situation did not extend to girls playing men's parts.

Too much need not be made of this transvestism. My point is that the decrease in the physical and symbolic separateness of women from men permitted on holidays underlines the significance of such separateness in the course of routine existence in the village.

To return to our main theme, the deference accorded men in public situations is paralleled by public comments about the relative merits of men and women. The birth of a son is reason for rejoicing and happy congratulations to the father in the coffee house, that of a daughter, reason for some teasing and behind the scenes amusement on the part of the villagers. Both men and women warn their sons about the dangers of associating with loose women who can ruin a man's life; in cases of marital discord, if there is any possible way of blaming the women, the villagers do so. They tell tales about how the wife runs around with other men, neglects her children and her household. They say these things often on the flimsiest evidence or on none at all. Clearly in her role as potential sex partner, a woman is assumed to be a danger to men. The laments about the economic burdens of raising daughters add to the chorus of verbal expressions of irritation with women.

Let us shift from symbolism and attitudinal expressions of higher male prestige to the differences in the activities available to each sex and to the prestige evaluation of these activities. The only prestige-bearing public professional activities available to women in the village are school teaching and other civil service posts. Vasilika has no resident female school teacher, but one of the village girls is now a civil servant in Athens. At the lower end of the scale of public professions, girls who accompany the musicians and sing with them at village festivals are classed as somewhat shameless. In between are girls who sew for others, or who work as agricultural extension agents, and the like.

There are two significant types of public official statuses in the village from which women are barred. One is the higher religious offices and the other the village political posts. Women may not be priests or cantors, nor do they get elected to the village council. The latter is based on custom rather than law, but even though the women have the vote, there is no indication that any one of them will be elected to office in the near future. With respect to religious offices, women may perform service functions as sextons, but they do not get elected to the council of laymen who help the priest to run the affairs of the church. Nor are there any women doctors around Vasilika.

In sum, with the putative exception of school teaching, the public female roles with which the villagers have experience do not include persons with public power. Higher echelon provincial or national government officials who visit the village are always men, religious officials are men, and their own village officers are men. For the moment our interest is in the fact that regardless of the reason, there are more prestigious public roles open to men than to women and by a wide margin.

When we turn to analyzing differences in prestige with respect to the standard division of labor within the household's economy, the matter is considerably more difficult. Certainly, there are household tasks carried out by men and others usually handled by women, and still others taken care of indifferently by either or both. A listing is not complicated.

For the most part men do work outside the house itself, in the fields and barns and storehouses. The field jobs include pruning grape vines, deep hoeing the vineyards, plowing with horses or tractors, cultivating grain fields, planting wheat and cotton, running irrigation pumps and clearing irrigation ditches. Young men also collect the brush used for firing ovens. Within the house compound, men store cotton, press and store tobacco bales, and make and store the household's supply of wine. They take care of any horses or donkeys owned by the household, and generally look after carts and any farm machinery belonging to them. Men do not work inside the house at cooking, baking, cleaning, washing clothes, sweeping, or the like. They do, however, regularly purchase household supplies like rice, pasta, olive oil, kerosene, canned goods, and other staples, as well as meat and fresh vegetables brought by vendors. In the States when men started pushing supermarket carts and collecting groceries from a list, the fact was cited as evidence for the proposition that men were taking on more women's household tasks. In Vasilika, the purchase of supplies for cash requires leaving the home and negotiating with outsiders in a public context – activities the villagers consider improper for women.

The activities I have listed so far are carried out almost exclusively by men; but there are some in which they assist women in tasks more typically done by women. In the fields, men help the women hoe cotton, they help pick the cotton and they can join the women in transplanting and picking tobacco. Men even pick wild greens for food and collect wild plant fodder for the sheep and goats if the need arises. When a mother is ill and there are no daughters in the household, a husband and sons may even take on the cooking and washing.

Women's tasks inside the house have been mentioned. To these, caring for infants and children, sewing, mending, weaving, embroidering and similar trousseau preparations, and caring for the household religious shrine can be added. Women also supply the church with the necessary sacred breads and memorial wheat when it is the household's turn to do so. Within the house compound, women feed and care for the chickens and look after new lambs and kids. They tend to care for small vegetable gardens now planted near the house because water is piped into the house yards, and they also have responsibility for the household's decorative plants and flowers. Women also are expected to keep the house compound tidy.

The jobs connected with the agricultural cycle that can be done near the houses rather than out in the fields also tend to be female tasks. Women plant tobacco seedlings, string the tobacco, and put the poles on drying racks. They also pick cotton from the pod when, in wet weather, they have been unable to make the separation at the original picking. Their field tasks have already been mentioned as those with which, when necessary, men will assist.

The sexual division of labor in Vasilika is part of the private realm of life. It concerns the economic welfare of the household, of the family consisting of a husband and wife and their unmarried or resident married children and an occasional elderly parent or in-law. A kind of continuum of tasks may be observed under three headings. (1) Those inside the house, linked with women, (2) those in the house compound, linked with both men and women, and (3) those in the fields, linked preponderantly with men. The division of these familial tasks is complementary; there appears to be no noticeable conception among the villagers that either the men's or the women's jobs have the greater prestige. If anything, they share a common attribution of distaste.

Unlike the situation among the shepherds of Epirus, Vasilika's men are not called upon to exhibit heroic feats of endurance, strength, and skill simply to be able to maintain themselves and their families. Men's and women's tasks require similar expenditures both of energy and skill; kneading dough for ten large loaves of bread and washing clothes thoroughly clean in a wooden trough are comparable in their calls upon skill and strength with plowing or cultivating. If there is any deficit in energy expenditure in any single woman's task, it is made up for by the longer duration of her jobs and their repetitive quality. In Vasilika, both men and women dislike physical labor and especially that which is dirty and messy. From the latter standpoint, the men have an edge on unpleasantness, because nothing women do covers them with mud the way channeling irrigation water does men. It appears to be no more disgraceful or ignominious for a man to take over a woman's job like cooking and washing up if an emergency requires it, than it is for a woman to take over the man's job of deep hoeing if there is no other way of getting it done.

These are the shared physical tasks imposed by the household economy. Its public managerial roles, however, are assumed by men when the household must be represented to the outside world. The men do the job. They talk to government officials, merchants, the school teacher, and any strangers who may come to the village. The husband in a household in which his wife takes over these public functions is ridiculed and despised by all. Of these public functions the most significant in relation to women is the set of marriage negotiations undertaken by a father in his daughter's behalf. In the discussions preliminary to the agreement in a dowry contract, the men of the bride's household speak to the go-between and represent her interests. The groom may represent himself or may have his father with him. In any case, it is the men who formally and overtly oversee the establishment of the marriage connections between households.

To summarize, the evidence that male prestige is higher than that of females in Vasilika lies in the nature of routine segregation in contrast with what is permitted at celebrations, in the esteem accorded public and extra-household occupational and political roles held by men, and in the man's representation of the household to the outside when he functions as host, entrepreneur, and marriage negotiator.

So much for appearances, that is for prestige and esteem. Let us now turn to the realities of power which may be discovered as operating behind the external patterns we have discussed. We shall begin with the social power of women within the economic structure of the households. In Vasilika, land still constitutes the most significant investment. It produces income by virtue of the subsistence and cash crops that can be raised on it. The economic power of women lies in their ability to bring land into the household as part of their dowry, and to maintain control of that land, which cannot be alienated by their husbands without their consent or, in some cases, without the consent of their fathers, brothers, or guardians. The trousseau and the household goods a woman brings with her add to the prestige of the new household but only indirectly to its ability to produce income. In the traditional structure of the village, a man is expected to find a wife who would bring in the equivalent of the land he would inherit upon the division of the patrimony of his own family. Therefore, although his wife had no more control over the household property than he did, she had at least as much. That the husband's symbolic prestige as a male did not entirely override the wife's position as a substantial contributor to the new household is proved negatively by the position of the *soghambros*, the in-marrying son-in-law. Man or no man, his prestige and the esteem accorded him is seriously impaired by the fact that it is his wife who provides the land from which he derives his and his children's livelihood. It is assumed that he makes fewer decisions in his household than a man is expected to make. No in-marrying son-in-law of the village has been elected to the village council or to the church council, although at least two of them are strong personalities interested in politics. This is an index of lack of public prestige. Within the household, since the processes of decision-making are not easily observed, and because I conducted no systematic investigation of the question in the soghambros households, my evidence for the superior decision-making power of the women in this situation rests on impressions, and the clear evidence that the children of the soghambros households established connections with their mother's relatives outside the village and not with those of their fathers. Moreover, my recent studies in Athens indicate that the choice of career of the sons of one of the soghambros families was determined by the advice of the mother's sister; a particular kind of kin affiliation that is rarely influential in this regard in the village as a whole.

Within the ordinary land owning household, the power of the women over their dowry properties is reflected, I believe, in the degree of give and take in the private discussions leading to entrepreneurial decisions as to how to utilize the property. In the households, where I could observe the process, women participated vigorously in decisions concerning what and how much to plant, how many laborers to bring in, whether to sell crops or to hold them for higher prices, what credit to accept and what sums to pay back, and the like. All this is hidden behind the facade of public male dominance.

The same control over property gave the concern of women over the future of their daughters a base in something more than affection and sentiment. The dowry of the girls consisted partly of property their mothers had contributed, and their mothers felt quite free to engage in the discussions about a future son-in-law. This was partly in terms of his potential as a conserver of the mother's original property. Mothers of sons were eager to have daughters-in-law who would not squander their grandchildren's patrimony.

The suggestion that the power of women over household economic decisions and over the marriages of their children is dependent on property control should be tested by research in the contemporary village situation. If Vasilika is typical, the urban marriages of rural girls with substantial dowries have left for the rural men only girls with poor dowries. A village farmer, we're told, can no longer expect to marry a girl who will bring in land equivalent to the value of his, but may have to take girls with smaller properties because they are the only ones left who will consent to live in the rural villages and to do farm work. For a poor rural girl, marrying a man who brings to the marriage more land than she herself can contribute as a dowry is a form of hypergamy from her point of view just as is the marriage of a farm girl to an urban husband. The current gossip in the village suggests that there is less respect for the poorer new brides and an examination of decision-making within their households would be instructive.

My hypothesis can also be tested in urban centers where the substantial dowries of the village girls who marry low salaried husbands would be expected to give them an excess of power in their households. I do not believe they do. The reason may be that the husband's educational qualifications and his urban sophistication (both greater than those of his rural wife) added to what is after all a steady low income combine to become the equivalent of his wife's seemingly disproportionately large dowry. For the urban family, a job and the knowledge of how to get along in the city is just as important for the continued welfare of the family as the husband's contribution of land is in the farming communities. Education and access to employment are not quite as easily and directly transmitted to a new generation as land is. Neither is an urban woman's property consisting of a house and its furnishings. If the erstwhile farm girl is to continue to influence the marriages of her children, her influence may have to rest on a power base other than that of property. A study of these matters is among my present interests.

To return to the farm households to which husbands and wives have contributed about equally. It must be clearly understood that formal authority even about household and farm management rests with the husband and father. It is in the informal organization of the household that the very real power of the women is felt.

But to say that women have informal power over household economic decisions and over the economic and marital future of their sons and daughters is not a trivial statement. To repeat what I said at the outset, the family is the significant unit of social and economic structure in the Greek village community, and therefore power within that unit must have important consequences for power distribution in Greek society as a whole.

There is another sense, a negative sense, in which women have power in Vasilika. This does not operate in affecting decisions or actions affirmatively. It is a check upon the power of men through women's ability to disrupt orderly relationships in the men's world. Insofar as men's honor depends on the behavior of their women-folk, these women exercise a real measure of control over them. It is the women's willingness to behave chastely, modestly, and becomingly that is a prime necessity for the maintenance of men's self-esteem.

But it is not only by the implied threat of misbehavior that a wife or daughter influences her husband or father. This indeed is probably always latent rather than expressed. What is expressed by the women to the men in the privacy of the household is a constant reminder of the lengths to which the women go in the toil and the trouble which they take in the performance of those household tasks which enable the men of the family to preserve their public honor. The effect of these complaints, which are culturally sanctioned, is to keep the men aware of their dependence on their womenfolk, of how they must in their turn and in their own way uphold the honor of the family by reciprocating all the women do for them. For the weaker partner in a social structure, the ability to create and maintain such a sense of obligation in the stronger is a real exercise of power, and one in which Greek village women are past masters.

Frederick Engels

Private Property and the World Historic Defeat of the Female Sex

From Frederick Engels, *The Origin of the Family,
Private Property and the State*, Moscow: Foreign
Language Publishing House, 1969, pp. 86-94 (first
published in 1884)

We now leave America, the classical soil of the pairing family.
There is no evidence to enable us to conclude that a higher form
of the family developed there, or that strict monogamy existed in
any part of it at any time before its discovery and conquest. It was
otherwise in the Old World.

Here the domestication of animals and the breeding of herds had
developed a hitherto unsuspected source of wealth and created
entirely new social relationships. Until the lower stage of barbarism, fixed wealth consisted almost entirely of the house, clothing,
crude ornaments and the implements for procuring and preparing
food: boats, weapons and household utensils of the simplest kind.
Food had to be won anew day by day. Now, with herds of horses,
camels, donkeys, oxen, sheep, goats and pigs, the advancing
pastoral peoples – the Aryans in the Indian land of the five rivers
and the Ganges area, as well as in the then much more richly
watered steppes of the Oxus and the Jaxartes, and the Semites on
the Euphrates and the Tigris – acquired possessions demanding
merely supervision and most elementary care in order to propagate
in ever-increasing numbers and to yield the richest nutriment in
milk and meat. All previous means of procuring food now sank into
the background. Hunting, once a necessity, now became a
luxury.

But to whom did this new wealth belong? Originally, undoubtedly, to the gens. But private property in herds must have
developed at a very early stage. It is hard to say whether Father
Abraham appeared to the author of the so-called First Book of
Moses as the owner of his herds and flocks in his own right as head
of a family community or by virtue of his status as actual hereditary
chief of a gens. One thing, however, is certain, and that is that we
must not regard him as a property owner in the modern sense of
the term. Equally certain is it that on the threshold of authenticated

history we find that everywhere the herds are already the separate property of the family chiefs, in exactly the same way as were the artistic products of barbarism, metal utensils, articles of luxury and, finally, human cattle – the slaves.

For now slavery also was invented. The slave was useless to the barbarian of the lower stage. It was for this reason that the American Indians treated their vanquished foes quite differently from the way they were treated in the upper stage. The men were either killed or adopted as brothers by the tribe of the victors. The women were either taken in marriage or likewise just adopted along with their surviving children. Human labour power at this stage yielded no noticeable surplus as yet over the cost of its maintenance. With the introduction of cattle breeding, of the working up of metals, of weaving and, finally, of field cultivation, this changed. Just as the once so easily obtainable wives had now acquired an exchange value and were bought, so it happened with labour power, especially after the herds had finally been converted into family possessions. The family did not increase as rapidly as the cattle. More people were required to tend them; the captives taken in war were useful for just this purpose, and, furthermore, they could be bred like the cattle itself.

Such riches, once they had passed into the private possession of families and there rapidly multiplied, struck a powerful blow at a society founded on pairing marriage and mother-right gens. Pairing marriage had introduced a new element into the family. By the side of the natural mother it had placed the authenticated natural father – who was probably better authenticated than many a 'father' of the present day. According to the division of labour then prevailing in the family, the procuring of food and the implements necessary thereto, and therefore, also, the ownership of the latter, fell to the man; he took them with him in case of separation, just as the woman retained the household goods. Thus, according to the custom of society at that time, the man was also the owner of the new sources of food stuffs – the cattle – and later, of the new instrument of labour – the slaves. According to the custom of the same society, however, his children could not inherit from him, for the position in this respect was as follows:

According to mother right, that is, as long as descent was reckoned solely through the female line, and according to the original custom of inheritance in the gens, it was the gentile relatives that at first inherited from a deceased member of the gens. The property had to remain within the gens. At first, in view of the insignificance of the chattels in question, it may, in practice, have passed to the nearest gentile relatives – that is, to the blood relatives on the mother's side. The children of the deceased, however, belonged not to his gens, but to that of their mother. In the beginning, they inherited from their mother, along with the rest of their mother's blood relatives, and later, perhaps, had first claim upon her property; but they could not inherit from their father, because they did not belong to his gens, and his property had to remain in the latter. On the death of the herd owner, therefore, his herds passed, first of all, to his brothers and sisters and to his sisters' children or to the descendants of his mother's sisters. His own children, however, were disinherited.

Thus as wealth increased, it, on the one hand, gave the man a more important status in the family than the woman, and, on the other hand, created a stimulus to utilize this strengthened position in order to overthrow the traditional order of inheritance in favour of his children. But this was impossible as long as descent according to mother right prevailed. This had, therefore, to be overthrown, and it was overthrown; and it was not so difficult to do this as it appears to us now. For this revolution – one of the most decisive ever experienced by mankind – need not have disturbed one single living member of a gens. All the members could remain what they were previously. The simple decision sufficed that in future the descendants of the male members should remain in the gens, but that those of the females were to be excluded from the gens and transferred to that of their father. The reckoning of descent through the female line and the right of inheritance through the mother were hereby overthrown and male lineage and right of inheritance from the father instituted. As to how and when this revolution was effected among the civilized peoples we know nothing. It falls entirely within prehistoric times. That it was actually effected is more than proved by the abundant traces of mother right which have been collected, especially by Bachofen. How easily it is accomplished can be seen from a whole number of Indian tribes, among whom it has only recently taken place and is still proceeding, partly under the influence of increasing wealth and changed methods of life (transplantation from the forests to the prairies), and partly under the moral influence of civilization and the missionaries. Of eight Missouri tribes, six have male and two still retain the female lineage and female inheritance line. Among the Shawnees, Miamis and Delawares it has become the custom to transfer the children to the father's gens by giving them one of the gentile names obtaining therein, in order that they may inherit from him. 'Innate human casuistry to seek to change things by changing their names! And to find loopholes for breaking through tradition within tradition itself, wherever a direct interest provided a sufficient motive!' (Marx) As a consequence, hopeless confusion arose; and matters could only be straightened out, and partly were straightened out, by the transition to father right. 'This appears altogether to be the most natural transition.' (Marx) As for what the experts on comparative law have to tell us regarding the ways and means by which this transition was effected among the civilized peoples of the Old World – almost mere hypotheses, of course – see M. Kovalevsky, *Outline of the Origin and Evolution of the Family and Property*, Stockholm 1890.[1]

The overthrow of mother right was the *world-historic defeat of the female sex*. The man seized the reins in the house also, the woman was degraded, enthralled, the slave of the man's lust, a mere instrument for breeding children. This lowered position of women, especially manifest among the Greeks of the Heroic and still more of the Classical Age, has become gradually embellished and dissembled and, in part, clothed in a milder form, but by no means abolished.

The first effect of the sole rule of the men that was now established is shown in the intermediate form of the family which now emerges, the patriarchal family. Its chief attribute is not polygamy – of which more anon – but 'the organization of a number of persons, bond and free, into a family, under the paternal power of the head of the family. In the Semitic form, this family chief lives in polygamy, the bondsman has a wife and children, and the purpose of the whole organization is the care of flocks and herds over a limited area.' The essential features are the incorporation of bondsmen and the paternal power; the Roman family, accordingly, constitutes the perfected type of this form of the family. The word *familia* did not originally signify the ideal of our modern philistine, which is a compound of sentimentality and domestic discord. Among the Romans, in the beginning, it did not even refer to the married couple and their children, but to the slaves alone. *Famulus* means a household slave and *familia* signifies the totality of slaves belonging to one individual. Even in the time of Gaius the *familia, id est patrimonium* (that is, the inheritance) was bequeathed by will. The expression was invented by the Romans to describe a new social organism, the head of which had under him wife and children and a number of slaves, under Roman paternal power, with power of life and death over them all. 'The term, therefore, is no older than the ironclad family system of the Latin tribes, which came in after field agriculture and after legalized

1. Maxim Kovalevsky, *Tableau des origines et de l'évolution de la famille et de la propriété*, Stockholm 1890.

servitude, as well as after the separation of the Greeks and (Aryan) Latins.' To which Marx adds: 'The modern family contains in embryo not only slavery (*servitus*) but serfdom also, since from the very beginning it is connected with agricultural services. It contains within itself in *miniature* all the antagonisms which later develop on a wide scale within society and its state.'

Such a form of the family shows the transition of the pairing family to monogamy. In order to guarantee the fidelity of the wife, that is, the paternity of the children, the woman is placed in the man's absolute power; if he kills her, he is but exercising his right.

With the patriarchal family we enter the field of written history and, therewith, a field in which the science of comparative law can render us important assistance. And in fact it has here procured us considerable progress. We are indebted to Maxim Kovalevsky (*Outline of the Origin and Evolution of the Family and Property*, Stockholm 1890, pp. 60-100) for the proof that the patriarchal household community (*Hausgenossenschaft*), such as we still find it today among the Serbs and the Bulgars under the designations of *Zadruga* (meaning something like fraternity) or *Bratstvo* (brotherhood), and among the Oriental peoples in a modified form, constituted the transition stage between the mother-right family which evolved out of group marriage and the individual family known to the modern world. This appears to be proved at least as far as the civilized peoples of the Old World, the Aryans and Semites, are concerned.

Bibliography

Parveen Adams, 'A Note on Sexual Division and Sexual Difference', *M/F*, no. 3, 1979

O. Adamson, C. Brown, J. Harrison and J. Price, 'Women's Oppression under Capitalism', *Revolutionary Communist*, no. 5, November 1976

Sally Alexander, 'Women's Work in Nineteenth-century London', in A. Oakley and J. Mitchell, eds., *The Rights and Wrongs of Women*, Harmondsworth: Penguin, 1976

Sally Alexander and Barbara Taylor, 'In Defence of "Patriarchy"', in Ralph Samuel, ed., *People's History and Socialist Theory*, London: Routledge and Kegan Paul, 1981

Jean Baker Miller, *Toward a New Psychology of Women*, Harmondsworth: Penguin, 1979

Diana Leonard Barker and Sheila Allen, *Sexual Divisions and Society: Process and Change*, London: Tavistock, 1976; and *Dependence and Exploitation in Work and Marriage*, Harlow: Longman, 1976

Michèle Barrett, *Women's Oppression Today*, London: Virago, 1980

Michèle Barrett and Mary McIntosh, 'Christine Delphy: Towards a Materialist Feminism?', *Feminist Review*, no. 1, 1979

Michèle Barrett and Mary McIntosh, 'The Family Wage: Some Problems for Socialists and Feminists', *Capital and Class*, no. 11, 1980

R. D. Barron and G. Norris, 'Sexual Divisions and the Dual Labour Market', in D. Barker and S. Allen, eds., *Dependence and Exploitation in Work and Marriage*, Harlow: Longman, 1976

Simone de Beauvoir, *The Second Sex*, Harmondsworth: Penguin, 1978

Veronica Beechey, 'Some Notes on Female Wage Labour in Capitalist Production', *Capital and Class*, no. 3, 1977

Veronica Beechey, 'On Patriarchy', *Feminist Review*, no. 3, 1979

Colin Bell and Howard Newby, 'Husbands and Wives: the Dynamic of the Deferential Dialectic', in D. Barker and S. Allen, eds., *Dependence and Exploitation in Work and Marriage*, Harlow: Longman, 1976

Barbara Bellow Watson, 'On Power and the Literary Text', *Signs*, vol. I, no. I, 1975

Margaret Benston, 'The Political Economy of Women's Liberation', *Monthly Review*, vol. 21, no. 4, 1969

Jessie Bernard, *The Future of Marriage*, Harmondsworth: Penguin, 1976

Boston Women's Health Book Collective, *Our Bodies, Ourselves*, New York: Simon and Schuster, 1973; English edition edited by Angela Phillips and Jill Rakusen, Harmondsworth: Penguin, 1978

George Brown and Tirrel Harris, *The Social Origins of Depression: a Study of Psychiatric Disorder in Women*, London: Tavistock, 1978

Irene Bruegel, 'Women as a Reserve Army of Labour', *Feminist Review*, no. 3, 1979.

Bea Campbell, 'Feminist Sexual Politics', *Feminist Review*, no. 5, 1980

Gail Chester, 'I Call Myself a Radical Feminist', in *Feminist Practice: Notes from the Tenth Year*, London: In Theory Press, 1979

Nancy Chodorow, *The Reproduction of Mothering: Psycho-analysis and the Sociology of Gender*, Berkeley: University of California Press, 1978

Margaret Coulson, Branka Magas and Hilary Wainwright, 'The Housewife and her Labour under Capitalism', *New Left Review*, no. 89, 1975

Rosalind Coward, 'Sexual Liberation and the Family', *M/F*, no. 1, 1978

Rosalind Coward, 'Are Women's Novels Feminist Novels?', *Feminist Review*, no. 5, 1980

Elizabeth Cowie, 'Woman as Sign', *M/F*, vol. 1, no. 1, 1978

Critique of Anthropology, *Women's Issue*, vol. 3, nos. 9 and 10, 1977

Mary Daly, *Gyn/Ecology*, Boston: Beacon Press, 1978

Rosemary Deem, *Women and Schooling*, London: Routledge and Kegan Paul, 1978

Christine Delphy, *The Main Enemy: a Materialist Analysis of Women's Oppression*, London: Women's Research and Resources Centre, Explorations in Feminism, 1977

Felicity Edholm, Olivia Harris and Kate Young, 'Conceptualising Women', *Critique of Anthropology*, vol. 3, nos. 9 and 10, 1977

Barbara Ehrenreich and Deidre English, *Witches, Midwives and Nurses: a History of Women Healers*, London, Writers and Readers Publishing Co-operative, 1973

Barbara Ehrenreich and Deidre English, *For Her Own Good: 150 Years of The Expert's Advice to Women*, London: Pluto, 1979

Sarah Elbert and Marion Glastonbury, *Inspiration and Drudgery: Notes on Literature and Domestic Labour in the Nineteenth Century*, London: Women's Research and Resources Centre, 1978

F. Engels, *The Origin of the Family, Private Property and the State*, Moscow: Progress Publishers, 1964

Zoe Fairbairns, 'The Cohabitation Rule: Why it Makes Sense', *Spare Rib*, no. 104, March 1981

Shulamith Firestone, *The Dialectic of Sex*, New York: Morrow, 1970

Betty Friedan, *The Feminine Mystique*, New York: Norton, 1963

Ernestine Friedl, 'The Position of Women', *Anthropological Quarterly*, vol. 40, no. 3, 1967

Jean Gardiner, 'Women's Domestic Labour', *New Left Review*, no. 89, 1975

Charlotte Gilman, *Women and Economics*, New York: Harper and Row, 1966

Linda Gordon, *Woman's Body, Woman's Right: a Social History of Birth Control in America*, New York, Grossmann Publishers, 1976

Roberta Hamilton, *The Liberation of Women*, London: Allen and Unwin, 1978

Heidi Hartmann, 'The Unhappy Marriage of Marxism and Feminism: Towards a More Progressive Union', *Capital and Class*, no. 8, 1979

Molly Haskell, *From Reverence to Rape: the Treatment of Women in the Movies*, New York: Holt, Rinehart and Winston, 1974

Dorothy Hobson, 'Housewives and the Mass Media', in S. Hall, D. Hobson, A. Lowe and P. Willis, eds., *Culture, Media, Language*, London: Hutchinson, 1980

Jane Humphries, 'Protective Legislation, the Capitalist State and Working Class Men: the Case of the 1842 Mines Act', *Feminist Review*, no. 7, 1981

Stevi Jackson, *On the Social Construction of Female Sexuality*, London: Women's Research and Resources Centre, 1978

Jill Johnston, *Lesbian Nation*, New York: Simon and Schuster, 1973

Cora Kaplan, 'Radical Feminism and Literature', *Red Letters*, no. 9, 1979

Mary Ritchie Key, *Male/Female Language*, Metuchen, New Jersey: Scarecrow Press, 1975

Mirra Komarovsky, *Blue-collar Marriage*, New York: Vintage, 1967

Annette Kuhn and Ann Marie Wolpe, *Feminism and Materialism*, London: Routledge and Kegan Paul, 1978

Robin Lakoff, *Language and Woman's Place*, New York: Harper and Row, 1975

Hilary Land, 'The Myth of the Male Breadwinner', *New Society*, 9 October 1975

Hilary Land, 'The Family Wage', *New Statesman*, 18 December 1981

Laura Lederer, *Take Back the Night*, New York: Morrow, 1980

J. Leeson and J. Gray, *Women and Medicine*, London: Tavistock, 1979

Eleanor Maccoby, ed., *The Development of Sex Differences*, Stanford: Stanford University Press, 1966

E. Maccoby and C. Jacklin, *The Psychology of Sex Differences*, Stanford: Stanford University Press, 1974

Wendy Martyna, 'Beyond the "He/Man" Approach: the Case for Nonsexist Language', *Signs*, vol. 5, no. 3, Spring 1980

O. R. McGregor, 'The Social Position of Women in England, 1850-1914: a Bibliography', *British Journal of Sociology*, vol. 6, 1955

Mary McIntosh, 'Who Needs Prostitutes? The Ideology of Male Sexual Needs', in Carol Smart and Barry Smart, eds., *Women, Sexuality and Social Control*, London: Routledge and Kegan Paul, 1978

Mary McIntosh, 'The State and the Oppression of Women', in A. Kuhn and A. Wolpe, eds., *Feminism and Materialism*, London: Routledge and Kegan Paul, 1978

Chris Middleton, 'Sexual Inequality and Stratification Theory', in F. Parkin, ed., *The Social Analysis of Class Structure*, London: Tavistock, 1974

John Stuart Mill, *On the Subjection of Women*, London: Dent, 1970

Kate Millett, *Sexual Politics*, New York: Equinox Books, 1969

Marcia Millman, 'She Did it All for Love: a Feminist View of the Sociology of Deviance', in M. Millman and R. Kanter, eds., *Another Voice: Feminist Perspectives on Social Life and Social Science*, New York: Anchor Books, 1975

Juliet Mitchell, *Psychoanalysis and Feminism*, Harmondsworth: Penguin, 1975

Ellen Moers, *Literary Women*, New York: Doubleday, 1976

Maxine Molyneux, 'Beyond the Domestic Labour Debate', *New Left Review*, no. 116, 1980

Ann Oakley, *Becoming a Mother*, Oxford: Martin Robertson, 1979

Ann Oakley, *Women Confined*, Oxford: Martin Robertson, 1980

Ann Oakley, *Subject Women*, Oxford: Martin Robertson, 1981

Ann Oakley and Juliet Mitchell, eds., *The Rights and Wrongs of Women*, Harmondsworth: Penguin, 1976

Katherine O'Donovan, 'The Male Appendage: Legal Definitions of Women', in S. Burman, ed., *Fit Work for Women*, London: Croom Helm, 1979

Tillie Olsen, 'Silences: When Women Don't Write', in Susan Cornillon, ed., *Images of Women in Fiction*, Bowling Green, Ohio: Bowling Green Popular Press, 1972

William O'Neill, *Everyone was Brave: the Rise and Fall of Feminism in America*, Chicago: Quadrangle Books, 1979

Sherry Ortner, 'Is Male to Female as Nature is to Culture?', in M. Rosaldo and L. Lamphere, eds., *Woman, Culture and Society*, Stanford: Stanford University Press, 1974

Jan Pahl, 'Patterns of Money Management in Marriage', *Journal of Social Policy*, vol. 9, no. 3, 1980

Rayna Reiter, ed., *Toward an Anthropology of Women*, New York: Monthly Review Press, 1975

Adrienne Rich, *Of Woman Born: Motherhood as Experience and Institution*, London: Virago, 1976

Adrienne Rich, 'Compulsory Heterosexuality and Lesbian Experience', *Signs*, vol. 5, no. 4, 1980

Eric Richards, 'Women in the British Economy since 1700: an Interpretation', *History*, vol. 59, no. 197, 1974

Susan Rogers, 'Woman's Place: a Critical Review of Anthropological Theory', *Comparative Studies in Society and History*, vol. 20, no. 1, January 1978

Michelle Rosaldo and Louise Lamphere, eds., *Woman, Culture and Society*, Stanford: Stanford University Press, 1974

Ellen Ross, 'The Love Crisis: Couples Advice Books of the Late 1970s', *Signs*, vol. 6, no. 1, 1980

Sheila Rowbotham, *Hidden from History*, London: Pluto, 1973

Sheila Rowbotham, Lynne Segal and Hilary Wainwright, *Beyond the Fragments*, London: The Merlin Press, 1979

Sheila Rowbotham, 'The Trouble with "Patriarchy"', in R. Samuel, ed., *People's History and Socialist Theory*, London: Routledge and Kegan Paul, 1981

Janet Sayers, 'Anatomy is Destiny: Variations on a Theme', *Women's Studies International Quarterly*, vol. 2, 1979

Janet Sayers, *Biological Politics*, London: Tavistock, 1982

Richard Scase and Robert Goffee, 'Home Life in a Small Business', *New Society*, 30 October 1980

Betty Scharf, 'Sexual Stratification and Social Stratification', *British Journal of Sociology*, vol. 28, no. 4, 1977

Joan Scott and Louise Tilly, 'Women's Work and Family in Nineteenth Century Europe', *Comparative Studies in Society and History*, January 1975

Wally Secombe, 'The Housewife and her Labour under Capitalism', *New Left Review*, no. 83, 1973

Jenny Shaw, 'Finishing School: Some Implications of Sex-segregated Education', in D. Barker and S. Allen, eds., *Sexual Divisions and Society: Process and Change*, London: Tavistock, 1976

Carol Smart, *Women, Crime and Criminology*, London: Routledge and Kegan Paul, 1976

Carol Smart and Barry Smart, *Women, Sexuality and Social Control*, London: Routledge and Kegan Paul, 1978

Dale Spender and Elizabeth Sarah, *Learning to Lose: Sexism and Education*, London: The Women's Press, 1980

Dale Spender, *Man Made Language*, London: Routledge and Kegan Paul, 1980

Dale Spender, *Invisible Women*, London: The Women's Press, 1982

Margery Spring Rice, *Working-class Wives*, London: Virago, 1981

Margaret Stacey and Marion Price, 'Women and Power', *Feminist Review*, no. 5, 1980

Margaret Stacey and Marion Price, *Women and Power*, London: Tavistock, 1981

A. Szymanski, 'The Socialisation of Women's Oppression: a Marxist Theory of the Changing Position of Women in Advanced Capitalist Society', *Insurgent Sociologist*, vol. VI, no. 2, 1976

Barbara Taylor, 'The Men are as Bad as their Masters: Socialism, Feminism and Sexual Antagonism in the London Tailoring Trade in the early 1830s', *Feminist Studies*, vol. 5, no. 1, 1975

Barbara Taylor and Anne Phillips, 'Sex and Skill: Notes Towards a Feminist Economics', *Feminist Review*, no. 6, 1980

Judith Walkowitz, *Prostitution and Victorian Society: Women, Class and the State*, Cambridge: Cambridge University Press, 1980

Elizabeth Wilson, *Women and the Welfare State*, London: Tavistock, 1977

Janice Winship, 'Sexuality for Sale', in S. Hall, D. Hobson, A. Lowe and P. Willis, eds., *Culture, Media, Language*, London: Hutchinson, 1980

Ann Marie Wolpe, *Some Processes in Sexist Education*, London: Women's Research and Resources Centre, 1976

Kate Young and Olivia Harris, 'The Subordination of Women in Cross-cultural Perspective', in *Papers on Patriarchy*, Lewes: Women's Publishing Collective, 1976

Copyright Acknowledgments

For permission to reprint copyright material I am grateful to the authors and publishers mentioned below. (Further details of sources are noted in the text.)

Lawrence Stone, from *The Family, Sex and Marriage in England 1500-1800*: George Weidenfeld and Nicolson Ltd. Sheila Rowbotham, from *Hidden from History*: copyright © Pluto Press 1974. Simone de Beauvoir, from *The Second Sex*: Jonathan Cape Ltd. 'I Call Myself a Radical Feminist', copyright © Gail Chester 1979 (*Feminist Practice, Notes from the Tenth Year* is available from 33 Clissold Crescent, London N.16). Leeds Revolutionary Feminist Group, 'Political Lesbianism: the Case against Heterosexuality' and 'Afterward'. Sheila Rowbotham, 'The Trouble with "Patriachy"': *New Statesman*. Sally Alexander and Barbara Taylor, 'In Defence of "Patriarchy"': *New Statesman*. Sheila Rowbotham, Lynne Segal and Hilary Wainwright, from *Beyond the Fragments*: The Merlin Press Ltd. Ann Oakley, from *Subject Women*: Martin Robertson Ltd. From *Toward a New Psychology of Women*, copyright © Jean Baker Miller 1976: reprinted by permission of Penguin Books Ltd. Jessie Bernard, from *The Future of Marriage*: World Publishing Co. Inc. Beatrix Campbell, 'A Feminist Sexual Politics: Now You See It, Now You Don't'. Stevi Jackson, from *On the Social Construction of Female Sexuality*. Adrienne Rich, from *Of Woman Born: Motherhood as Experience and Institution*: Virago Press, Ely House, 37 Dover Street, London W1X 4HS. Margery Spring Rice, from *Working-class Wives*: Virago Press, 37 Dover Street, London W1X 4HS. Mirra Komarovsky, from *Blue-collar Marriage*: copyright © 1967 by Random House Inc.; reprinted by permission of Random House Inc. Margaret Benston, 'The Political Economy of Women's Liberation': copyright © 1969 by Monthly Review Inc.; reprinted by permission of Monthly Review Press. Richard Scase and Robert Goffee, 'Home Life in a Small Business'. Eric Richards, 'Women in the British Economy since about 1700: an Interpretation': K. G. Robbins, editor of *History*. Veronica Beechey, 'Some Notes on Female Wage Labour in Capitalist Production': copyright © 1977 Conference of Socialist Economists. Irene Bruegel, 'Women as a Reserve Army of Labour: a Note on Recent British Experience'. Hilary Land, 'The

Index

Index

Aborigines, of Australia 458-9
Alexander, Sally 28, 80-3, 251
Althusser, Louis 138, 310, 392
Anna Karenina 382, 406
Armstrong, W.A. 230
Awakening, The 406-7
Anthropology, assumptions of re women 450-1, 469-70, 473-84
Arapesh 122

Bachofen 468, 521
Bad News 383
Baker Miller, Jean 95-106
Balzac, Honore de 44, 437-8, 443
Banks, J. and O. 238
Barker, J. 285
Barrett, Michèle 169, 217
Barron, R.D. 215, 275, 278, 375
Barzun, Jacques 423
Bate, Barbara 430
Baudouin, T. 278, 281
Beam, L. 129
Beard, Mary 347-8, 349
de Beauvoir, Simone 27, 43-9, 121, 128, 130, 141, 146-53, 157, 405, 455, 492-5
Becker, Howard 335-6, 339, 340
Beechey, Veronica 246-72, 279, 324
Bell, Daniel 334-5, 337, 340
Bellow Watson, Barbara 401-9
Benn, C. 365-6
Benston, Margaret 192-202
Berger, John 414
Berger, Peter 473

Bernard, Jessie 92-3, 107-19
Berreman, Gerald 474
Best, G. 236
Beveridge, William 293, 351, 357
Bevin, Ernest 291, 292
Blackstone, William 346-9
Blauberg, Maija 430
Blue-collar Marriage 89, 167, 187ff
Bodine, Ann 430
Bosanquet, N. 375
Boserup, E. 245
Bott, E. 373
Boyson, Rhodes 227
Brandis, W. 368
Braverman, Harry 254, 263, 274
Bruegel, Irene 217, 273-88
Brovermann, I.K. 117
Brown, V. 367
Bryan, J. 338-9
Buckley, William 425
Butler, Josephine 122
Butz, Earl 422

Campbell, Bea 125-45
Candida 406
Capital 60, 250, 252, 254, 256-7, 260-1, 263, 273-4, 310, 316, 328, 418
Captive Wife, The 167
Carlson, Rae 500
Caste system 460
Citrine, Walter 291
Chesser, Eustace 130, 132, 134
Chester, Gail 28, 58-62

Chew, Ada Neild 293
Chicago School 338
Childbirth 27-8, 54-6, 164-6, 322
China, position of women in 486
Chodorow, Nancy 89-90, 499-502
Chopin, Kate 406-7, 436, 441
Christianity 56, 169, 405
Civil War (in England) 29-30
Clark, Alice 226, 347, 349
Clitoridectomy 451
Clitoris 52, 54, 130-4, 156, 158
Cohabitation 300, 304, 350
Cole, W. 233
Colette 151, 435, 441
Commentaries on the Laws of England 346-50
Conrad, Joseph 437, 438, 443
Consciousness-raising 18, 60-1, 138, 139, 167
Contraception 23, 48, 64, 78, 129
Cooley, M. 286
Cooperman, Ellen 425
Corrigan, Paul 327-8
Costa, Mariarosa Dalla 168
Coulson, Margaret 267, 307
Coward, Rosalind 25, 413, 444
Critcher, C. 368
Crow Indians 488-9
Culture, Media, Language 383
Cymbeline 402

Dale, R. 365, 367
Dalton, Hugh 292
Daly, Mary 124
Deronda, Daniel 17
Daniel, W. 275-6
Daubler, G.H. 276, 286
Davie, R. 374
Davis, Kingsley 337-8
Davis, Rebecca Harding 437

Deane, P. 233
Delmar, Rosalind 80, 248
Deloria, Vine 474
Delphy, Christine 168-9, 307, 312
Denning, Lord 356
Dialectic of Sex, The 28, 83
Dickinson, Emily 438, 441, 442, 445
Dickinson, R. 129
Divorce, financial arrangements upon 352-7
Doll's House, A 406
Doeringer, P. 375
Domestic violence 170, 306
Domestic Violence and Matrimonial Proceedings Act, 1976 354
Downing, H. 285
Douglas, J.W.B. 364, 367
Durkheim, E. 371, 372

Elementary Structures of Kinship, The 449-50, 497
Eliot, George 17, 436, 441
Ellis, Havelock 131
Emmet, Dorothy 344
Employment Protection Act 323
Engels, F. 196, 200, 218-19, 228, 247-50, 297-8, 309, 360, 386, 387, 394, 447, 466, 468, 519-23
Equal Pay Act 284, 301

Fairbairns, Z. 300
Family, Sex and Marriage in England 1500-1800, The 26, 29ff
Family wage 289-96, 328
Fanning, D.M. 111-12
Fanon, F. 388
Fee, Elizabeth 451

Feminine Mystique, The 17-18
Feminism 25-8, 78-9, 125ff
Feminism, Radical 58-62, 139ff, 251, 286ff
Ferber, M. 276
Firestone, Shulamith 28, 83, 390
Fisher, Dorothy 443
Fitzgerald, Scott 388, 436
Five Hundred Delinquent Women 341
Foote, Nelson 110
Foss, Karen 431
Freud, Sigmund 19, 53-4, 82-3, 87-8, 148, 154-60, 161-3, 388, 390-8, 418-19, 457
Friedan, Betty 16, 17-18
Friedl, E. 508-18
Friedrich, Paul 430
Fridgidity 128-37

Gagnon, J. 154-6, 159-60, 161-2
Galbraith, J.K. 374
Gale, Fay 462
Gardiner, Jean 168, 263, 277-8
Garfinkel, Harold 473
Gavron, Hannah 167
Gilman, Charlotte Perkins 171-5
Glueck, S. and E. 341
Godwin, Gail 408
Goffee, Robert 169, 203-11
Golden Notebook, The 407-8
Goodale, Jane 469
Gough, Kathleen 474
Grevet, Patrice 316-17, 320-1

Hakim, C. 278
Halloran, James 383
Hardy, Thomas 434, 435
Hargreaves, D. 366, 367
Harris, D. 285
Harris, O. 453-72

Hart, C. 469
Hartmann, Heidi 83, 217
Hartwell, R.M. 227, 234
Harvard Crimson 421
Heterosexuality 26-7, 64-5, 123, 125, 137, 140-3
Hill, J. 374
Hindess, B. 470
Hirschfeld, Magnus 129-30
Hirst, P. 470
Hobsbawm, E.J. 230, 232
Hobson, Dorothy 383
Holt, Simma 428
Hopkins, Gerard Manley 433-4
Housewife 167
Huber, Joan 426
Humphries, Jane 217, 308, 328
Hurstfield, J. 284
Hutt, Corinne 88

Ibsen, H. 405, 406
ILP 290-2
Income Tax (provisions for husbands and wives) 352, 358-9
Industrial Revolution 167, 197, 213, 218, 220-38
Ingham, John 505

Jacklin, C. 21, 88
Jackson, Stevi 154-63
Jacobson, L. 366
James, Henry 388, 437, 438
James, William 421
Jencks, C. 373
Jenkin, Patrick 13
Jenness, L. 275
Johnson, V. 53-5, 64, 126, 133-6, 137, 158, 164
Johnston, Jill 27, 50-7
Joseph, Sir Keith 318

Kafka, Franz 435, 439-41, 444
Kanfer, Stefan 423
Kaplan, Cora 382, 386-400
Katz, Jerrold 421
Kephart, Jane 475, 483
Kierkegaard 44
Kinsey, Alfred 107, 126, 132, 133, 134, 135, 136
Kolko, G. 274
Komarovsky, Mirra 89, 167, 187-91
!Kung 448, 462

Labour Party 289, 290-1
Lacey, C. 367
Lady Chatterley's Lover 396-8, 402
Lakoff, Robin 423-4
Lamphere, Louise 497, 499, 500, 501, 505
Lancaster, C. 474-5, 477
Land, Hilary 289-96
Late Capitalism 268
Laslett, Peter 223, 350
Lawrence, D.H. 147, 381, 387, 388, 394-8, 402
Leeds Revolutionary Feminist Group 63-72, 142
Lemert, Edwin 337-8
Leonard, Diana 312-13, 314
Lesbianism 51, 63-72, 123, 125, 140
Lewenhak, S. 277
Levi-Strauss, Claude, 449-50, 455-60, 461, 494, 497, 499
Lewis, C.S. 427
Literary Women 382, 387
Literature of their Own, A 382
Lowie, R. 488
Lowry, H. 276

Maccoby, Eleanor 21, 88
MacIver, R.M. 321
Magas, B. 267
Mailer, Norman 381, 387, 388, 394-6, 398-9
Males and Females 88
Mandel, Ernest 193-4, 263, 266, 268
Mann, Thomas 438
Mansfield, Katherine 437, 441, 442-3
Marcuse, Herbert 56, 138
Margaret Howth 437
Marriage:
  breakdown of (see divorce)
  economic relations in 169-70, 352-7
  lack of communication in 187-91
  legal relations of 343-62
Married Women's Property Act (1882) 240, 347
Married Women's Property Act (1964) 354
Martin, Anna 294-5
Martyna, Wendy 420-32
Marx, Karl 60, 74-5, 228, 234, 247, 250, 252-70, 273-4, 309, 310, 312, 316, 317, 324, 328, 386, 389, 392, 462, 521-2
Marxism and Primitive Societies 451
Masochism 149-51
Mass Media 382-3
Masters, W. 53-5, 64, 126, 135-6, 137, 158, 164
Matza, David 337-8, 341
McIntosh, Mary 169, 298, 303-33
Mead, Margaret 114, 222
Meehl, Paul 426
Meillasoux, Claude 458

Melville, H. 433-5, 438
Milkman, Ruth 217, 263, 277-8, 281, 284, 323
Mill, John Stuart 14, 16, 27, 36-7, 41, 387, 394, 401
Miller, Henry 381, 387, 388, 394-8, 398
Miller, Hugh 225-6
Millett, Kate 83, 381-2, 386-400
Millman, Marcia 299, 334-43
Mitchell, Juliet 81, 83, 87, 158, 195-6, 250, 391-4, 455
Moers, Ellen 382, 387
Molyneux, Maxine 168, 451
Moore, B. 279, 280
Monogamy 15, 89
More Bad News 383
Morgan, D.H.J. 321
Mothering 89-94, 443, 496
  and ideology of 321, 413
Murray, Pauli 422
Myth of the Vaginal Orgasm, The 134

Niemi, B. 276
Norris, G.M. 215, 275, 278, 375

Oakley, Ann 91-4, 167, 302
Obstacle Race, The 383
O'Donovan, Katherine 344-62
Odd Woman, The 408
Olsen, Tillie 433-45
Orgasm, female 50-7, 125, 128-37, 146-7, 158
Origin of the Family, Private Property and the State, The 218, 247, 297, 447, 468
Ortner, Sherry 485-507

Page, C.H. 321
Pahl, Jan 170

Pankhurst, Mrs E. 41-2
Parkin, F. 373
Patriarchy 73-83, 307, 393, 470-1
Petchesky, Rosalind 76
Phillips, Anne 216
Pilling, A. 469
Pinchbeck, Ivy 214, 221, 224-5, 227-8, 231, 233
Pitt-Rivers, J. 505
Pollard, S. 240, 242, 243
Pollock, Griselda 416-17
Pontellier, Edna 406
Pornography 124
Porter, Katherine Anne 439
Prostitution 299, 304, 336ff
Psychoanalysis 80-1, 103
Psychoanalysis and Feminism 81, 83, 87, 391-4

Rape 122, 299, 463, 470
Rathbone, Eleanor 290, 295
Reasoner, Harry 429
Reckless, W. 338, 341-2
Reproduction of Mothering, The 89
Rhodes, J. 279, 280
Rich, Adrienne 164-6
Richards, Eric 213-14, 220-45
Richardson, E. 370
Richardson, H.H. 443
Richie, Marguerite 428
Rilke, Rainer Maria 437, 438, 440-1
Ritchie Key, Mary 384
Robertson, Mrs Arnot 294
Rogers, Barbara 219
Room of One's Own, A 383, 436-7, 441
Rosaldo, Michelle 447-8, 497, 499, 500, 501, 505
Rosenthal, R. 366

Rossi, Alice 165
Routh, Guy 243-4
Rowbotham, Sheila 28, 38-42, 73-9, 84-5
Rubin, Gayle 450
Russell, Dora 129-30
Ruth 17

Sachs, Albie 356
Sapir, E. 431-2
Sayers, Janet 88
Scase, Richard 169, 203-11
Schneider, Michael 431
Scott, J. 213-14
Secombe, W. 168
Second Sex, The 141
Segal, Lynne 84-5
Sex Discrimination Act 301, 323
Sex Disqualification Act 241
Sexual Politics 83, 381, 386-400
Sexual harassment at work 219
Sexuality, female 26, 50-7, 121-4, 128-37, 146, 149, 298-9
    social construction of 154-63
Sexuality, male 26, 65-6, 122, 128-37, 146, 298-9
Shaw, G.B. 129, 402, 404-5, 406
Shaw, Jenny 301, 363-79
Ship of Fools 439
Shirley 39
Showalter, Elaine 382, 402-3
Simon, W. 154-6, 159-60, 161-2
Slater, Philip 56, 107, 109, 111
Slocum, Sally 451, 473-84
Smart, C. 306
Snows of Kilimanjaro 435-6
Sociology of Housework, The 167
Sontag, Susan 384, 425
Soviet Union 22, 48
Spender, Dale 216, 384

Spring Rice, Margery 167, 176-86
State socialist societies 21-3, 219
Silgoe, E. 275-6
Stone, Lawrence 26, 29-32
Stopes, Marie 129, 131
Subjection of Women, On the 36-7, 41, 401
Supplementary Benefit 304, 350-2
Supplementary Benefits Commission 350, 357, 361
Szymanski, A. 217

Taylor, A.J.P. 241
Taylor, B. 28, 80-3, 216, 268
Taylor, F. 285
Terray, Emmanuel 451
Tilly, L. 213-14
Time 420, 422
To the Lighthouse 405-6

Valian, Virginia 421
Vasilika 509-18
Velde, Van de 131-2
Victorian Britain 16-17, 38-42, 220, 234-9, 243-5

Wainwright, Hilary 28, 84-5, 267
Walkowitz, Judith 17
Washburn, S. 474-5, 477
Way of All Flesh, The 404
Whorf, Benjamin 431
Williams, W. 374
Williamson, Judith 410-11
Willis, P. 368
Willmott, Peter 369
Wilson, Elizabeth 317, 322
Winship, Janice 410-19
Wollstonecraft, Mary 16, 31, 33-5, 244, 421

Women:
  deviance of 299, 305-6, 334-43
  education of 14, 17, 35, 39,
    301, 363-77
  mental and physical health
    100-6, 112-13, 124, 180-3,
    190
  paid work 213-96
  relations with men *passim*
  representation of 383, 410-19
  unpaid work 13-14, 22-3,
    108-13, 167-70, 171-211
*Women in the Industrial
  Revolution* 221

Women's Co-operative Guild
  177, 295
Women's Liberation Movement
  15-16, 58-62, 84-5, 114, 126-7,
  137-9, 246
Woolf, Virginia 383-4, 406,
  436-7, 441, 442
Working-class Wives 167
Wright, Helena 132-3

Young, D. 368-9
Young, Kate 453-72
Young, Michael 369

SIMONE DE BEAUVOIR

She Came to Stay

The passionately eloquent and ironic novel she wrote as an act of revenge against the woman who so nearly destroyed her life with the philosopher Sartre. 'A writer whose tears for her characters freeze as they drop.' *Sunday Times*

Les Belles Images

Her totally absorbing story of upper-class Parisian life. 'A brilliant sortie into Jet Set France.' *Daily Mirror*. 'As compulsively readable as it is profound, serious and disturbing.' *Queen*

The Mandarins

'A magnificent satire by the author of *The Second Sex*. *The Mandarins* gives us a brilliant survey of the post-war French intellectual . . . a dazzling panorama.' *New Statesman*. 'A superb document . . . a remarkable novel.' *Sunday Times*

The Woman Destroyed

'Immensely intelligent, basically passionless stories about the decay of passion. Simone de Beauvoir shares, with other women novelists, the ability to write about emotion in terms of direct experience . . . The middle-aged women at the centre of the three stories in *The Woman Destroyed* all suffer agonisingly the pains of growing older and of being betrayed by husbands and children.' *Sunday Times*

FONTANA PAPERBACKS